P9-ELX-124

Fodor's

FLORENCE & TUSCANY

WELCOME TO FLORENCE AND TUSCANY

Florence and Tuscany conjure images of superb Renaissance art and landscapes famous for rolling hills, olive groves, and cypress trees. In Florence, ancient palaces and churches await exploration. You can choose between seeing masterpieces by Michelangelo or shopping for locally made goods. The many pleasures of Tuscany include tasting wine in Chianti and simply relaxing in the piazzas of medieval towns. Whatever you do, the combination of great art, sumptuous countryside, and memorable food and wine makes a trip to this enchanting part of Italy unforgettable.

TOP REASONS TO GO

★ **Renaissance Art:** Works by da Vinci and Michelangelo, the Uffizi's treasures, and more.

★ **Authentic Shops:** Leather goods, gold, and handmade paper delight discerning buyers.

★ **Iconic Churches:** Florence's Duomo and Arezzo's Basilica di San Francesco, to start.

★ **Charming Towns:** Lucca, Siena, Cortona, San Gimignano, and others are enthralling.

★ **Wineries:** At visitor-friendly vineyards, you can taste the wine and meet the makers.

★ **Traditional Cuisine:** Tuscany's earthy, farm-fresh seasonal fare is heaven for foodies.

Fodor's FLORENCE & TUSCANY

Publisher: Amanda D'Acierno, *Senior Vice President*

Editorial: Arabella Bowen, *Editor in Chief*; Linda Cabasin, *Editorial Director*

Design: Fabrizio La Rocca, *Vice President, Creative Director*; Tina Malaney, *Associate Art Director*; Chie Ushio, *Senior Designer*; Ann McBride, *Production Designer*

Photography: Melanie Marin, *Associate Director of Photography*; Jessica Parkhill and Jennifer Romains, *Researchers*

Maps: Rebecca Baer, *Senior Map Editor*; Mark Stroud and Henry Colomb (Moon Street Cartography), and David Lindroth, *Cartographers*

Production: Linda Schmidt, *Managing Editor*; Evangelos Vasilakis, *Associate Managing Editor*; Angela L. McLean, *Senior Production Manager*

Sales: Jacqueline Lebow, *Sales Director*

Marketing & Publicity: Heather Dalton, *Marketing Director*; Katherine Fleming, *Senior Publicist*

Business & Operations: Susan Livingston, *Vice President, Strategic Business Planning*; Sue Daulton, *Vice President, Operations*

Fodors.com: Megan Bell, *Executive Director, Revenue & Business Development*; Yasmin Marinaro, *Senior Director, Marketing & Partnerships*

Copyright © 2014 by Fodor's Travel, a division of Random House LLC

Writers: Peter Blackman, Patricia Rucidlo, Jonathan Willcocks

Editor: Kristan Schiller

Production Editor: Carolyn Roth

12th Edition

ISBN 978-0-8041-4211-3

ISSN 1533–1628

SPECIAL SALES

This book is available at special discounts for bulk purchases for sales promotions or premiums. For more information, e-mail specialmarkets@randomhouse.com

PRINTED IN COLOMBIA

10 9 8 7 6 5 4 3 2 1

CONTENTS

CONTENTS

MAPS

ABOUT THIS GUIDE

Fodor's Recommendations

Everything in this guide is worth doing—we don't cover what isn't—but exceptional sights, hotels, and restaurants are recognized with additional accolades. Fodor'sChoice★ indicates our top recommendations; and **Best Bets** call attention to notable hotels and restaurants in various categories. Care to nominate a new place? Visit Fodors.com/contact-us.

Trip Costs

We list prices wherever possible to help you budget well. Hotel and restaurant price categories from $ to $$$$ are noted alongside each recommendation. For hotels, we include the lowest cost of a standard double room in high season. For restaurants, we cite the average price of a main course at dinner or, if dinner isn't served, at lunch. For attractions, we always list adult admission fees; discounts are usually available for children, students, and senior citizens.

Hotels

Our local writers vet every hotel to recommend the best overnights in each price category, from budget to expensive. Unless otherwise specified, you can expect private bath, phone, and TV in your room. For expanded hotel reviews, facilities, and deals visit Fodors.com.

Restaurants

Unless we state otherwise, restaurants are open for lunch and dinner daily. We mention dress code only when there's a specific requirement and reservations only when they're essential or not accepted. To make restaurant reservations, visit Fodors.com.

Credit Cards

The hotels and restaurants in this guide typically accept credit cards. If not, we'll say so.

Top Picks
★ Fodor'sChoice

Listings
⊠ Address
⊠ Branch address
☎ Telephone
🖷 Fax
⊕ Website
✉ E-mail
🎫 Admission fee
🕐 Open/closed times
Ⓜ Subway
⊹ Directions or Map coordinates

Hotels & Restaurants
🏨 Hotel
🛏 Number of rooms
🍴 Meal plans
✕ Restaurant
🕯 Reservations
👔 Dress code
⊟ No credit cards
$ Price

Other
⇨ See also
☞ Take note
🏌 Golf facilities

EXPERIENCE FLORENCE & TUSCANY

FLORENCE AND TUSCANY TODAY

Taking it Sweet—and Slow

La dolce vita ("the sweet life") is perhaps the reason visitors flock to Florence. *La dolce vita* translates loosely as sitting back and smelling the roses—maybe with a glass of wine in hand while admiring the view.

Life in Florence remains largely what it was centuries ago. Old-city skylines still look as good as they used to, as do views of the surrounding hills. In Tuscany, silver-gray olive trees dot the landscape, which is divided by rows of tall, noble cypress.

The pace of life remains unchanged, too. When they are not in their cars or on their Vespa scooters, Florentians still prefer to move to a more leisurely drumbeat. It's not just that the population is aging; it's that they don't like to appear rushed. And so natives make a point of stopping to greet acquaintances, comment on the latest news, or catch up on gossip. Even the waiters take their time, and you should be grateful to them for it. After all, why rush a meal with food that's this good, wine this divine?

In Florence, when the going gets tough, the food gets *slower*. Keep an eye out for local food purveyors and restaurants displaying the Slow Food emblem, which is a most handsome snail. (You'll see the sticker prominently displayed in any Slow Food establishment.) These remain the standard-setters for regional and seasonal specialties at reasonable prices. The Slow Food movement was actually born in northern Italy and promotes seasonal cuisine that doesn't harm the environment, animal welfare, or consumers' health. The term is meant to stand in stark contrast to the notion of "fast food" and represents the joys of living a slow-paced lifestyle, beginning at the table. Not all Slow Food is organic, but the movement does promote the principles behind organic agriculture. And remember, whenever you are where food is sold in Florence, even in the larger supermarkets, you never go wrong by inquiring as to what local specialties or seasonal excellences might be available. Most shopkeepers will appreciate your interest in what they are proudest to sell.

Even McDonald's seems to be taking a cue from the Slow Food book: soon a McDonald's near you in Italy will be serving burgers and Big Macs made with prized DOP *Chianina* and *Piemontese* beef. (DOP means *Denominazione di origine protetta*, a trademark sanctioned by the European Union.) Italian kids and teens flock to McDonald's; perhaps their target audience is *nonne* (grandmothers). It remains to be seen.

And let's not forget the wine. In 2013, a new category of Chianti Classico wine was created called "Gran Selezione." Grapes can come only from the same estate, with a lengthy release date of nearly three years. It remains to be seen whether this will work; vintners are equally divided.

High hopes abound for a super vintage—some winemakers think this might be a most marvelous *vendemmia* (harvest) due to a rainy spring and a very hot and sunny September in 2013. Expectations run high: it could be one of the best vintages of the millennium, rivaling the glory years of 1997 (especially), 2001, and 2003.

A Shifting Cultural Landscape

In recent years (since the formation of the European Union), there has been a rapid growth of the immigrant populations in both Tuscany and Umbria—predominantly Romanians and Albanians

(roughly 20% each of the regions' immigrants), as well as Chinese, Moroccans, Ukrainians, Filipinos, Egyptians, and sub-Saharans.

In the 1950s, Italy's largely agrarian population began to move to the cities, abandoning farmhouses in Tuscany and Umbria. Many of these farmhouses have since been restored by English, Germans, and Americans, among others. Frances Mayes, in her 1996 *Under the Tuscan Sun*, gave just about everyone the romantic itch to restore a house in olive-tree dotted countryside. However, in deep pockets in the countryside, this peasant culture does survive—but not for much longer, as most of these hardy folk are in their late 80s and early 90s.

The New Uffizi

Since 2007, the Uffizi, arguably the world's greatest museum for Italian Renaissance art, has been steadily expanding with the ultimate goal of doubling its exhibition space. At press time, 24 rooms had been added, creating an additional 4,800 square feet of space.

The expansion has been gradual and ongoing. In 2011, Le Sale Blu (the Blue Rooms) opened. Also known as the Sale degli Stranieri (Foreigner's Rooms), these rooms house gems by Rembrandt, Rubens, Velasquez, and other Old World Masters. Space was further increased in 2012 with the introduction of Le Rosse del Cinquecento (16th-Century Red Rooms), dedicated to Italian masters of the 16th century.

The Vasari Corridor, an enclosed passageway connecting Palazzo Vecchio with Palazzo Pitti via the Uffizi Gallery, has also received considerable attention. In 2013, 127 additional artist self-portraits were added. Most are by 20th-century artists; Robert Rauschenberg's x-ray skeletal structure might be the most interesting. The collection of self-portraits was formed by Cardinal Leopoldo de'Medici, brother of Grand Duke Ferdinand II. The starter portraits were by Guercino and Pietro da Cortona, two baroque masters. But the earliest self-portrait dates from the early 14th century (it actually includes three members of the Gaddi family, all painters).

As of January 2014, a new entrance policy has been proposed: there will be 12 scheduled openings, for groups of no more than 25; reservations are a must, and the ticket (which includes an hour in the Uffizi) is €34.

Museum Admissions Deals and Steals

In autumn 2013, the Museo dell'Opera del Duomo shut its doors for a grand restructuring expected to last two years. Well, most of its doors: Ghiberti's stunning *Gates of Paradise* are still visitable, as are Michelangelo's mangled and moving *Pietà*. This museum houses objects (paintings, sculptures, liturgical objects, reliquaries, and parts of the original cathedral facade) from the Baptistery, Campanile (bell tower), and the cathedral itself.

In the meantime, a cumulative ticket has been created (called the Grand Museum of the Cathedral of Florence ticket), which allows access to the cathedral, the highly reduced Museo dell'Opera del Duomo, Brunelleschi's dome, Giotto's bell tower, the Baptistery of San Giovanni, and the crypt of Santa Reparata. It's a great deal: the ticket costs €10 and is valid for six days once it's activated. This means that you can climb both the cupola (463 steps) and the bell tower (414 steps) with a break in-between.

Serious museumgoers might want to invest €72 in the Firenze Card (⊕ *www.firenzecard.it*). This card grants entrance to most major museums (including the Uffizi and the Accademia) and allows you to skip the lines. In high season, this is only a good thing; Musei Statali (State Museums) have been overbooking many of their gems, which means that, even with a reservation, you don't sail in at the appointed time. A Firenze Card is good for 72 hours once it's activated, and also includes free bus and tram transportation.

Faster than a Speeding Bullet

High-speed train options—on the north–south Milan–Naples route as well as the east–west Venice–Bologna–Florence route—should continue to improve, thanks in part to the competition in this sector between state-owned railways and privately owned Italo trains. Keep your eyes out for round-trip travel specials resulting from ongoing price wars: there are real deals to be had, for the first time in eons. Riding the high-speed train line from Turin to Lyon and Paris, meanwhile, will probably have to wait for the next edition of this book as work on the Italian stretch is hotly contested by residents of the valleys through which the line would run.

Increased competition among high-speed train lines does not happen with local (regionali) commuter trains, because they are still a state-controlled monopoly. Expect delays, cancellations, and trains that need renovating. Patience is a virtue.

The Walking of the Green

Meanwhile, visitors to Florence should be able to enjoy longer leisurely strolls and window-shopping in the expanded pedestrian-only area in the center of town, now including Florence's fashion High Street, *via Tornabuoni*, and the bridge across the Arno river at the southern end of this street, *ponte Santa Trinita*.

In fact, at press time, rumors were swirling in Florence that plans were advancing to ban cars altogether on this beautiful 13th-century bridge, which was dynamited by the Germans in 1944 and painstakingly rebuilt after the war's end. The newly installed bike lane would remain, which is only good news for cyclists, as the lane is clearly marked and divided from pedestrians.

This green dream builds on the initiatives begun a few years ago by Mayor Matteo Renzi, a young left-leaning politician who aspires to higher political office. He created a pedestrian-only zone around Piazza del Duomo, artfully dodging a political bullet while doing so, as well as Palazzo Pitti. He has great designs for the remaking of his city.

FAQS

How likely am I to find English-speaking locals? English is widely spoken, especially in cities. Odds are if the person you want to speak to doesn't know English, there will be someone within earshot who can translate. Nonetheless, if you pick up a few common phrases in Italian, your effort will be appreciated.

Are Italian drivers as crazy as I've heard? Yes—at least many of them are. Italians have a phrase for the non-passing lane: *la corsia di vergogna* (the lane of shame). When you hit the road, don't be surprised to encounter tailgating, high-risk passing, and impatient drivers flashing their lights at you (which means they want you to get out of their way immediately). Your best response is to take the same safety-first approach you use at home; on the road is one place you don't want to be mistaken for a local. On the plus side, Italy's road are usually well maintained (though *strade regionali*—local roads—often are not.) Note that wearing a seat belt and having your lights on at all times are required by law. From November to April, law mandates that you must have chains in your car—even if it's a rental.

You do need to worry about ZTLs (zona limitato traffico). This means that only certain kinds of vehicles can access various parts of town during the day (taxis are exempt). Most historic centers ban vehicular traffic to everyone; even locals sometimes have to be careful about driving in and out. Surveillance cameras photograph each and every car entering the area. You might think you're off the hook, but you're not. Months after your wonderful vacation has come and gone, you'll receive in the mail sometimes astronomical fines. There's no getting around this, as rental companies have your credit card information on file.

Is it okay to drink cappuccino after 11 am? For most Italians, a frothy cappuccino is a morning thing: drinking milk later in the day is thought to be bad for the stomach. Some Italians, however, drink cappuccino late in the afternoon: there's no reason not to order whatever suits your fancy.

Is the Cinque Terre a viable day trip from Florence? Technically, it's doable, but we don't recommend it, unless you want to spend a great deal of the day getting there and coming back. It's about five hours on the train round-trip, or something close to that if you go by car. And if it's summer and you want to hike the trails (which most people do), you're better off getting started early in the morning so that you can beat the heat (which is rather intense). The Cinque Terre is a beautiful, one-of-a-kind destination, and it deserves an overnight—you'll have the little towns to yourself, as the daytrippers have come and gone. If you are determined to do a day trip, it's easier and quicker to start from either Pisa or Lucca.

Reservations Necessary? It is best to reserve museums and restaurants, particularly in high season (from Easter to mid-June, and from September to late October). July and August finds most major cities—Florence, especially—teeming with cruise ship folk and other large tour groups. State museums in Florence charge a €4 reservation fee, and it is well worth it for both the Uffizi and the Accademia, regardless of what time of year it is. It will save you at least an hour of waiting in line. In 2012, these museums decided to accept credit cards, which makes paying so much easier. The same holds for restaurants.

WHAT'S WHERE

Numbers refer to chapters.

2 **Florence.** In the 15th century Florence was at the center of the artistic revolution that would later be known as the Renaissance. Today, the Renaissance remains the main reason people come here—the abundance of art treasures is mind-boggling.

3 **Northwest Tuscany.** West of Florence the main attractions are **Pisa,** home of the Leaning Tower, and **Lucca,** a town with a charming historic center. Farther north and west are snowcapped peaks, thermal waters, and miles of Mediterranean coast, including, across the regional border in Liguria, the **Cinque Terre**—five fishing villages that have become a major destination.

4 **Central Tuscany.** The hills spreading south from Florence to Siena make up **Chianti,** a region of sublime wine and marvelous views. **Siena,** once Florence's main rival, remains one of Italy's most appealing medieval towns. To its northwest, little **San Gimignano** is famous for its 13th- and 14th-century towers. Farther west still is **Volterra,** a town dating back to the Etruscans.

5 **Eastern Tuscany. Arezzo,** Tuscany's third-largest city (after Florence and Pisa), has a car-free historic center and a basilica containing beautiful frescoes. **Cortona,** perched on a steep hill with sweeping views, exemplifies an alluringly old-fashioned way of life.

6 **Southern Tuscany.** In the **Val d'Orcia** the towns of **Montalcino** and **Montepulciano** are surrounded by some of Italy's finest vineyards, and **Pienza** is a unique example of Renaissance urban planning. Farther south is the **Maremma,** Tuscany's cattle-ranching country. Off the coast, the lush island of **Elba** is a popular resort destination.

7 **Umbria.** Like Tuscany, Umbria has beautiful rolling hills topped by attractive old towns. **Perugia** is Umbria's largest city, but it's far from overwhelming, and it has a well-preserved medieval core. In **Assisi,** birthplace of St. Francis, the grand basilica draws millions of pilgrims annually. **Spoleto** is a quiet, elegant hill town, but each summer it brims with activity during the Festival dei Due Mondi. To the east in the Marches region, **Urbino** is famed for its splendid Renaissance palace.

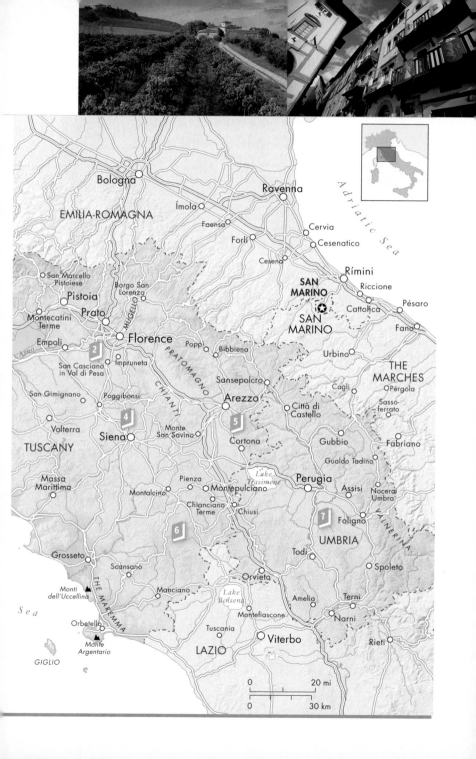

Bologna

Ímola

Faenza

Forlì

Cesena

Cesenatico

Cervia

Ravenna

EMILIA-ROMAGNA

Adriatic Sea

SAN
MARINO

Rímini

Riccione

Cattolica

Pésaro

Fano

SAN
MARINO

O San Marcello
Pistoiese

Pistoia

Prato

Montecatini
Terme

Empoli

Arno

Borgo San
Lorenzo

MUGELLO

Florence

2

San Casciano
in Val di Pesa

Imprunetà

Poppi

Bibbiena

PRATOMAGNO

Urbino

THE
MARCHES

Sansepolcro

Cagli

O Pérgola

Sasso-
ferrato

San Gimignano

Poggibonsi

CHIANTI

Arezzo

Città di
Castello

Volterra

Siena

4

Monte
San Savino

5

Cortona

Gubbio

Fabriano

TUSCANY

Massa
Marittima

Pienza

Montalcino

Montepulciano

Chianciano
Terme

Chiusi

Lake
Trasimene

Perugia

Assisi

Nocera
Umbra

7

Foligno

VALNERINA

6

UMBRIA

Grosseto

Scansano

Manciano

Lake
Bolsena

Orvieto

Todi

Amelia

Terni

Spoleto

Monti
dell'Uccellina

THE
MAREMMA

Sea

Orbetello

Monte
Argentario

GIGLIO

Tuscania

Montefiascone

Narni

Rieti

Viterbo

LAZIO

0   20 mi

0   30 km

FLORENCE AND TUSCANY PLANNER

Getting Here

Most flights to Tuscany originating in the United States stop either in Rome, London, Paris, or Frankfurt, and then connect to Florence's small Aeroporto Amerigo Vespucci (commonly called Peretola), or to Pisa's Aeroporto Galileo Galilei. The only exception at this writing is Delta's seasonal New York/JFK direct flight to Pisa. At press time, the Florence airport was clamoring to add a new, longer runway (enabling larger planes to land), which has caused great consternation in Pisa. It's unclear how the situation will resolve itself.

There are several other alternatives for getting to the region. If you want to start your trip in Umbria, it makes sense to fly into Rome's Aeroporto Leonardo da Vinci (commonly called Fiumicino) and rent a car or take the train from Rome's Termini station. The drive to the Umbrian hill town of Orvieto takes an hour and a half, and the train ride is an hour. Another option is to fly to Milan and pick up a connecting Alitalia flight to Pisa, Florence, or Perugia.

What to Pack

In summer, stick with light clothing, as things get steamy in June, July, and August, but throw in a sweater in case of cool evenings, especially if you're headed for the mountains and/or islands. Sunglasses, a hat, and sunblock are essential. In winter, bring a coat, gloves, hats, scarves, and boots. Winter weather used to be generally milder than in the northern and central United States, but things have changed. It snows here, and it can sometimes get quite cold. Take wools or flannel rather than sheer fabrics. Bring sturdy shoes for winter (boots would not be a bad idea) and comfortable walking shoes in any season.

As a rule, Italians are more particular about dress than Americans are. To their minds, shorts are for the beach or for hiking, not for urban settings. Men aren't required to wear ties or jackets in most places other than some of the grander hotel dining rooms and top-level restaurants, but they are expected to look reasonably sharp—and they do. Formal wear is the exception rather than the rule at the opera nowadays, though people in expensive seats usually do get dressed up.

Modesty of dress (no bare shoulders or knees) is expected of both men and women in all churches. For sightseeing, pack a pair of binoculars; they will help you get a good look at poorly lighted ceilings and domes. Best to bring your own soap if you plan to stay in budget hotels.

Restaurants: The Basics

A meal in Tuscany and Umbria (and elsewhere in Italy) has traditionally consisted of five courses, and every menu you encounter will still be organized along this five-course plan: First up is the *antipasto* (appetizer), usually *affettati misto* consisting of cured meats, cheese, and crostini. Next to appear is the *primo,* usually pasta or soup, and after that the *secondo,* a meat or fish course with, perhaps, a *contorno* (vegetable dish) on the side. A simple *dolce* (dessert) rounds out the meal.

This, you've probably noticed, is a lot of food. Italians have noticed this as well—a full, five-course meal is an indulgence usually reserved for special occasions. Instead, restaurant meals are a mix-and-match affair: you might order a primo and a secondo, or an antipasto and a primo, or a secondo and a contorno.

The crucial rule of restaurant dining is that you should **order at least two courses.** It's a common mistake for tourists to order only a secondo, thinking they're getting a "main course" complete with side dishes, known as *contorno.* What they usually wind up with is one lonely piece of meat. To round out the meal, order a contorno.

Hotels: The Basics

Hotels in these regions are usually well maintained (especially if they've earned our recommendation in this book), but in some respects they won't match what you find at comparably priced U.S. lodgings. Keep the following points in mind as you set your expectations, and you're likely to have a good experience:

■ First and foremost, rooms are usually smaller, particularly in cities. If you're truly cramped, ask for another room, but don't expect things to be spacious.

■ A "double bed" is usually two singles pushed together.

■ In the bathroom, tubs are not a given—request one if it's essential. In budget places, showers sometimes use a drain in the middle of the bathroom floor.

■ Most hotels have satellite TV, but there are fewer channels than in the United States, and only one or two will be in English.

■ Wall-to-wall carpet is uncommon. Terra-cotta or tiled floors are the norm.

How's the Weather?

Throughout Tuscany and Umbria the best times to visit are spring and fall. Days are warm, nights are cool, and though there are still tourists, the crowds are smaller. In the countryside the scenery is gorgeous, with abundant greenery and flowers in spring, and burnished leaves in autumn.

July and August are the most popular times to visit. Note, though, that the heat is often oppressive and mosquitoes are prevalent. Try to start your days early and visit major sights first to beat the crowds and the midday sun. For relief from the heat, head to the mountains of the Garfagnana, where hiking is spectacular, or hit the beach at resort towns such as Forte dei Marmi and Viareggio, along the Maremma coast, or the island of Elba.

November through March, you might wonder who invented the term "sunny Italy." The panoramas are still beautiful, even with overcast skies, frequent rain, and occasional snow. In winter, Florence benefits from shorter museum lines and less competition for restaurant tables. Outside the cities, though, many hotels and restaurants close for the season.

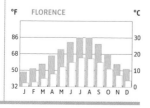

FLORENCE & TUSCANY TOP ATTRACTIONS

Galleria degli Uffizi, Florence

(A) Florence has many museums, but the Uffizi is king. Walking its halls is like stepping into an art-history textbook, except here you're looking at the genuine articles—masterpieces by Leonardo, Michelangelo, Raphael, Botticelli, Caravaggio, and dozens of other luminaries. When planning your visit, make a point to reserve a ticket in advance. (⇨ *Chapter 2*)

Duomo, Florence

(B) The Cathedral of Santa Maria del Fiore, Florence's Duomo, is the city's most distinctive landmark, sitting at the very heart of the city and towering over the neighboring rooftops. Its massive dome is one of the world's great engineering masterpieces. For an up-close look, you can climb the 463 steps to the top—then gaze out at the city beneath you. (⇨ *Chapter 2*)

Leaning Tower, Pisa

(C) This tower may be too famous for its own good (it's one of Italy's most popular tourist attractions), but there's something undeniably appealing about its perilous tilt, and climbing to the top is a kick. The square on which it sits, known as the Campo dei Miracoli, has a majestic beauty that no quantity of tourists can diminish. (⇨ *Chapter 3*)

Piazza del Campo, Siena

(D) The sloping, fan-shaped square in the heart of Siena is one of the best places in Italy to engage in the distinctly Italian activity of hanging out and people-watching. The flanking Palazzo Pubblico and Torre del Mangia are first-rate sights. (⇨ *Chapter 4*)

San Gimignano, Central Tuscany

(E) This classic Tuscan hill town has been dubbed a "medieval Manhattan" because of its numerous towers, built by noble families of the time, each striving

to outdo its neighbors. The streets fill with tour groups during the day, but if you stick around until sunset they all go away and you see the town at its most beautiful. (⇨ *Chapter 4*)

Abbazia di Sant'Antimo, Southern Tuscany

In a peaceful valley, surrounded by gently rolling hills, olive trees, and thick oak woods, Sant'Antimo is one of Italy's most beautifully situated abbeys—and a great "off the beaten path" destination. Stick around for Mass and you'll hear the halls resound with Gregorian chants. (⇨ *Chapter 6*)

Palazzo Ducale, Urbino, the Marches

(F) East of Umbria in the Marches region, Urbino is a university town in the Italian style—meaning its small but prestigious university dates to the 15th century. The highlight here is the Palazzo Ducale, a palace that exemplifies Renaissance ideals of grace and harmony. (⇨ *Chapter 7*)

Basilica di San Francesco, Assisi

(G) The basilica, built to honor Saint Francis, consists of two great churches—one Romanesque, fittingly solemn with its low ceilings and deep shadows; the other Gothic, with soaring arches and stained-glass windows (possibly the first in Italy). They're both filled with some of Europe's finest frescoes. (⇨ *Chapter 7*)

Duomo, Orvieto

(H) The facade of Orvieto's monumental Duomo contains a bas-relief masterpiece depicting the stories of the Creation and the Last Judgment (with the horrors of hell shown in striking detail). Inside, there's more glorious gore in the right transept, frescoed with Luca Signorelli's *The Preaching of the Antichrist* and *The Last Judgment*. (⇨ *Chapter 7*)

TOP EXPERIENCES

The View from Florence's Piazzale Michelangelo

One of the best ways to introduce yourself to Florence is by walking up to this square on the hill south of the Arno. From here you can take in the whole city, and much of the surrounding countryside, in one spectacular vista. To extend the experience, linger at one of the outdoor cafés, and for the finest view of all, time your visit to correspond with sunset.

Strolling the Ramparts of Lucca

Lucca, 80 km (50 miles) west of Florence, isn't situated on a hilltop in the way commonly associated with Tuscan towns, and it doesn't have quite the abundance of art treasures that you find in Siena or Pisa (to say nothing of Florence). Yet for many visitors, Lucca is a favorite Tuscan destination, and the source of its appeal has everything to do with its ramparts. These hulking barricades, built around the city between 1544 and 1645, were a source of security; now they are an elevated, oval park, complete with walkways, picnic areas, grass, and trees. The citizens of Lucca spend much of their spare time here, strolling, biking, and lounging.

Taking the Waters at a Tuscan Spa

Tuscany is dotted throughout with small *terme* (thermal baths), where hot water flows from natural springs deep beneath the earth's surface. It's been believed for millennia that these waters have the power to cure whatever ails you; although their medicinal power may be questionable, that doesn't keep a dip from being an extremely pleasant way to spend an afternoon. In northwest Tuscany you can take the waters at Montecatini Terme (made famous as a setting for Fellini's 8½ and seemingly little has changed since then) or Bagni di Lucca (which had its heyday in the era of the 19th-century Romantic poets). To the south, Saturnia is the biggest draw, along with the more humble Chianciano Terme and Bagno Vignoni.

Discovering the Cinque Terre

A short trip west across the Tuscan border, along the Ligurian coast, are five tiny, remote fishing villages known collectively as the Cinque Terre. Tourism here was once limited to backpackers, but the beauty of the landscape—with steep, vine-covered hills pushing smack-dab against an azure sea—and the charm of the villages have turned the area into one of Italy's top destinations. The number-one activity is hiking the trails that run between the villages—the views are once-in-a-lifetime gorgeous—but if hiking isn't your thing, you can still have fun lounging about in cafés, admiring the water, and perhaps sticking a toe in it.

Of late, this area has been been badly hit by awful weather, which has caused the sporadic closing of many trails, depending upon where the damage landed. In September 2013, violent rain storms caused a mini-landslide, and parts of the trail were closed. It's always best to check with the tourist information office a few days before setting out on a hike.

Wine-Tasting in Chianti

The gorgeous hills of the Chianti region, between Florence and Siena, produce exceptional wines, and they never taste better than when sampled on their home turf. Many Chianti vineyards are visitor-friendly, but the logistics of a visit are different from what you may have experienced in other wine regions. If you just drop in, you're likely to get a tasting, but for a tour you usually need to make an

appointment several days ahead of time. The upside is that your tour may end up being a half day of full immersion—including extended conversation with the winemakers and even a meal.

Passeggiata Along Corso Vanucci, Perugia

The *passeggiata*—the evening stroll—is a ritual practiced in towns throughout Italy. One of its most pleasant manifestations is along Perugia's Corso Vanucci, a wide, pedestrian-only boulevard through the heart of the city, lined with elegant palaces—and many bars where you can stop for a predinner *aperitivo* and watch the world go by.

Sampling Umbrian Truffles

The truffle (*tartufo* in Italian) is a peculiar delicacy; a gnarly clump of fungus that grows wild in the forest a few inches underground, is hunted down by specially trained truffle-sniffing dogs (or sometimes pigs), and can sell for a small fortune. The payoff is a powerful, aromatic flavor that makes food lovers swoon. Umbria is one of Italy's richest black truffle–hunting grounds, and in many of the region's restaurants you'll encounter truffle-infused dishes or be offered a shaving of truffle over your pasta. Indulge yourself at least once—it's an experience you won't forget.

Hiking in the Footsteps of Saint Francis

Umbria, which bills itself as "Italy's Green Heart," is fantastic hiking country. Among the many options are two with a Franciscan twist: from the town of Cannara, 16 km (10 miles) south of Assisi, an easy half-hour walk leads to the fields of Pian d'Arca, where Saint Francis delivered his sermon to the birds. For slightly more demanding walks, you can follow the saint's path from Assisi to the Ermeo delle Carceri (Hermitage of Prisons), where Francis and his followers went to "imprison" themselves in prayer, and from here continue along the trails that crisscross Monte Subasio.

Spoleto's Festival dei Due Mondi

For two weeks in late June–early July the Umbrian town of Spoleto is entirely given over to the Festival dei Due Mondi (Festival of Two Worlds), one of Europe's great performing-arts events. Classical music, opera, dance, and theater fill every conceivable venue with performances mixing old with new and tradition with innovation. In many cases it's the opportunity to see world-renowned talent in one-of-a-kind, intimate settings. Attending the festival takes planning months in advance—most events sell out, and hotel rooms are at a premium—but for a dedicated arts lover, it's an effort that's richly rewarded.

Il Dolce Far Niente

"The sweetness of doing nothing" has long been an art form in Italy. This is a country in which life's pleasures are warmly celebrated, not guiltily indulged. Of course, doing "nothing" doesn't really mean nothing. It means doing things differently. It means lingering over a glass of wine or two for the better part of an evening just to watch the sun slowly set. It means savoring a slow and flirtatious evening passeggiata along the main street of a little town, a procession with no destination other than the town and its streets. And it means making a commitment—however temporary—to thinking, feeling, and believing that there is nowhere that you have to be next, that there is no other time but the magical present.

QUINTESSENTIAL FLORENCE & TUSCANY

Il Caffé (Coffee)

The Italian day begins and ends with coffee, and more cups of coffee punctuate the time in between. To live like the Italians do, drink as they drink, standing at the counter or sitting at an outdoor table of the corner bar. (In Italy a "bar" is a place that mostly serves coffee, but also light snacks, wine, and mixed drinks.) A primer: *caffé* means coffee, and Italian standard issue is what Americans call espresso—short and strong. *Cappuccino* is a foamy half-and-half of espresso and steamed milk; cocoa powder *(cacao)* on top is acceptable, cinnamon is not—unless, of course, you want it. If you're thinking of having a cappuccino for dessert, you'll get it, but realize that most Italians drink only caffé or caffé *macchiato* (with a spot of steamed milk) after lunchtime. Confused? Homesick? Order caffé *americano* for a reasonable facsimile of good-old filtered joe.

Il Calcio (Soccer)

Imagine the most rabid American football fans—the ones who paint their faces on game day and sleep in pajamas emblazoned with the logo of their favorite team. Throw in a dose of melodrama along the lines of a sentimental Puccini opera. Ratchet up the intensity by a factor of 10, and you'll start to get a sense of how Italians feel about their national game, soccer—known in the mother tongue as *calcio* (meaning *"kick"*). On Sunday afternoons throughout the long September–May season, stadiums are packed throughout Italy. Those who don't get to games in person tend to congregate around television sets in restaurants and bars, rooting for the home team with a passion that feels like a last vestige of the days when the country was a series of warring medieval city-states. How calcio mania affects your stay in Italy depends on how eager you are to

If you want to get a sense of contemporary Italian culture and indulge in some of its pleasures, start by familiarizing yourself with the rituals of daily life. These are a few highlights—things you can take part in with relative ease.

get involved. At the very least, you may notice an eerie Sunday-afternoon silence on the city streets, or erratic restaurant service around the same time, accompanied by cheers and groans from a neighboring room. If you want a truly memorable Italian experience, go to *lo stadio* (the stadium). Availability of tickets may depend on the current fortunes of the team in the town where you're staying, but they often can be acquired with help from your hotel concierge.

Il Gelato (Ice Cream)
During warmer months *gelato*—the Italian equivalent of ice cream—is a national obsession. It's considered a snack more than a dessert, bought at stands and shops in piazzas and on street corners, and consumed on foot, usually at a leisurely stroll *(see La Passeggiata, following)*. Gelato is softer, less creamy, and more intensely flavored than its American counterpart. It comes in simple flavors

that capture the essence of the main ingredient. At most gelaterias choices include pistachio, *nocciola* (hazelnut), caffé, and numerous fruit varieties. Look for signs boasting *produzione propria* for gelato made in-house. Quality varies; the surest sign that you've hit on a good spot is a line at the counter.

La Passeggiata (Strolling)
A favorite Italian pastime is the passeggiata (literally, the promenade). In the late afternoon and early evening, especially on weekends, couples, families, and packs of teenagers stroll the main streets and piazzas of Italy's towns. It's a ritual of exchanged news and gossip, window-shopping, flirting, seeing and being seen, that adds up to a uniquely Italian experience. To join in, simply hit the streets for a bit of wandering. You may feel more like an observer than a participant, until you realize that observing is what la passeggiata is all about.

IF YOU LIKE

Renaissance Art

Travel veterans will tell you that the seemingly countless masterpieces of Italian art can cause first-time visitors—eyes glazed over from a heavy downpour of images, dates, and names—to lean, Tower of Pisa–like, on their companions for support. The secret is to take your sweet time.

Allow the splendors of the age to unfold slowly. Take in Michelangelo's *David* in Florence's Accademia, but don't miss his other gems in the Bargello and the Cappelle Medicee. Here's where to go when you're ready for an art feast:

Basilica di San Francesco, Arezzo, Eastern Tuscany. Piero della Francesa's *Legend of the True Cross* merits a pilgrimage to this Tuscan town.

Galleria degli Uffizi, Florence. Allow at least several hours to explore the world's greatest collection of Italian Renaissance art.

Galleria Nazionale dell Umbria, Perugia. At one of Italy's finest small museums the art is the star, but the first-class presentation adds to the appeal.

Palazzo Ducale, Urbino, the Marches. Head off the beaten path to visit a palace that perfectly displays the values of the Renaissance.

Monumental Churches

Few images are more identifiable with Italy than the country's great churches, stunning works of architecture that often took centuries to build.

The name *duomo* (derived from the Latin for "house," *domus*) is used to refer to the cathedral of a town or city. Generally speaking, the bigger the city, the more splendid its duomo. Still, some impressive churches inhabit surprisingly small locales.

Basilica di San Francesco, Assisi. This fresco illustrating the life of Saint Francis is a masterpiece of the Renaissance; the massive double basilica is a contrast of darkness and light.

Cripta, Siena, Central Tuscany. Siena's Duomo is large and lush with art, but the vivid frescoes in its crypt merit special mention.

Duomo, Florence. Brunelleschi's beautiful dome, the most recognizable in Italy, is an unequaled feat of 15th-century engineering.

Duomo, Orvieto, Southern Umbria. Here you'll find Italy's most perfect Gothic facade matched with Luca Signorelli's phenomenal frescoes in the Cappella di San Brizio.

Santa Croce, Florence. The resting place of Michelangelo, Galileo, and Machiavelli (among others) also contains the most important art of any church in Florence.

Charming Towns

Tuscany and **Umbria** are two gorgeous towns that ooze quiet charm.

Travel to **Carmignano,** and look at **Pontormo**'s stunning *Visitation* before heading off to a meal in **Artimino**, with a view of la Ferdinanda, a 17th-century Medici villa, as a backdrop.

If you have a car, visit **San Miniato al Monte;** of the two parts, *bassa* (lower) and *alta* (higher), it's the latter where you'll want to be. The town, with its Renaissance church, fine restaurants, and local truffle, makes a trip memorable. Visit in November, when the truffle festival is in full swing.

In summer, a visit to **Barga**, north of Lucca, is worthwhile. This little town, with its clean mountain air, hosts Barga Jazz, and music fills its streets.

In Chianti, foodophiles should not miss **Antica Macelleria Cecchini**, where Dario Cecchini, butcher extraordinaire, quotes Dante while serving up marvelous samples of his craft (including delicious sushi di Chianina—raw slices of best-quality beef lightly dressed with lemon juice and olive oil.)

If you're heading to **Siena**, detour to the glorious town of **Colle val d'Elsa**, a medieval town high on a hill with beautiful views and great restaurants and wine bars.

In southern Tuscany, **Pienza** not only charms but so, too, does nearby **Bagni Vignoni** (where Catherine of Siena took the waters), and **San Quirico val d'Orcia**, a jewel not often visited by tourists.

Umbria is ripe for exploration. **Gubbio**, where St. Francis tamed the wolf, has views that don't quit, and **Todi**, while it has been "discovered" by the cognoscenti, still retains its charm.

Shopping

"Made in Italy" is synonymous with quality and craftsmanship, whether it refers to high fashion or Maserati automobiles.

If you're in Florence and want to buy local, your best bets are leather, paper, and gold, for which the city has been famous for centuries. Do remember that you get what you pay for as you eye a leather jacket that seems incredibly expensive. Paper shops are dotted all over town; you can admire the gold shops on Ponte Vecchio, and perhaps buy elsewhere.

Siena is known for its lace, and its local culinary products, panforte (strong bread; it's a dense concoction of flour, nuts, and spices) and *ricciarelli*, almond paste cookies.

Wine lovers will want to make their way to just about any town in Tuscany, with stops in Chianti to sample the local juice. Farther south, there are the glories of Brunello di Montalcino, and Rosso di Montalcino (its younger cousin.) The same holds for Montepulciano, with its truly noble Nobile di Montepulciano. Most shops ship, which spares the agony of carting only two bottles home.

Chocolate lovers might want to stop in Perugia to sample the local wares which, in this case, is Perugina chocolate.

Serious ceramics have been crafted in Deruta for centuries. Combine a trip to the Museo Regionale della Ceramica before setting out for some serious acquisitioning.

And, almost every town in Tuscany and Umbria has its own candidate for Italy's best olive oil.

Enoteca Italia, Siena, Central Tuscany. Italy's only state-sponsored wineshop is like a library of wine (with a vast collection).

Via Tiberina Nord, Deruta, Northern Umbria. Deruta is the top spot for Umbrian ceramics.

Via Tornabuoni, Florence. Whether you're looking to splurge or just browse, Florence's chicest shopping street is the place to find Italian high style.

A GREAT ITINERARY

Day 1: Florence

If you're coming in on an international flight, you'll probably settle in Florence in time for an afternoon stroll or siesta (depending on your jet-lag strategy) before dinner.

Logistics: On your flight in, read through the restaurant listings in this guide and begin anticipating the first dinner of your trip. Look for a place near your hotel, and when you arrive, reserve a table (or have your concierge do it for you). Making a meal the focus of your first day is a great way to ease into Italian life.

Day 2: Florence

Begin your morning at the **Uffizi Gallery** (reserve your ticket in advance). The extensive collection will occupy much of your morning. Next, take in the neighboring **Piazza della Signoria,** one of Florence's impressive squares, then head a few blocks north to the **Duomo.** There, check out Ghiberti's famous bronze doors on the **Battistero** (they're high-quality copies; the originals are normally in the Museo dell'Opera del Duomo). Work up an appetite by climbing the 463 steps to the cupola of Brunelleschi's splendid cathedral dome, from which you'll experience a memorable view. Spend the afternoon relaxing, shopping, and wandering Florence's medieval streets; or, if you're up for a more involved journey, head out to **Fiesole** to experience the ancient amphitheater and beautiful views of the Tuscan countryside.

Day 3: Florence

Keep the energy level up for your second full day in Florence, sticking with art and architecture for the morning, trying to see most of the following: Michelangelo's *David* at the **Galleria dell'Accademia,** the **Medici Chapels,** the **Palazzo Pitti** and **Boboli Gardens,** and the churches of **Santa Maria Novella** and **Santa Croce.** If it's a clear day, spend the afternoon on a trip to **Piazzale Michelangelo,** high on a hill, for sweeping views of idyllic Florentine countryside. Given all the walking you've been doing, tonight would be a good night to recharge by trying the famed *bistecca alla fiorentina* (a grilled, very rare T-bone steak cooked one way only, and that's very, very rare.)

Logistics: You can get up to the Piazzale Michelangelo by taxi or by taking Bus 12 or 13 from the Lungarno. Otherwise, do your best to get around on foot; Florence is a brilliant city for walking.

Day 4: San Gimignano

Now that you've been appropriately introduced to the bewildering splendor of Renaissance Italy, it's time for a change of pace—and time for a rental car, which will enable you to see the back roads of Tuscany and Umbria. After breakfast, pick up your car, taking great care to attend to ZTLs (Zona Traffico Limitato—cross into one unwittingly, and you can expect huge fines to arrive at your doorstep many moons after your return), and head on out. On a good day the lazy drive from Florence to **San Gimignano,** past vineyards and typical Tuscan landscapes, is truly spectacular. The first thing that will hit you when you arrive at the hill town of San Gimignano will be its multiple towers. The medieval skyscrapers of Italy were public displays of wealth and family power. And they provided sanctuary and security during times of civic strife, which was often. After finding your way to a hotel in the old town, set out on foot and check out the city's turrets and alleyways, doing your best to get away from the trinket shops, and later enjoying a leisurely dinner with the light but delicious local white wine, Vernaccia di San Gimignano.

Logistics: Once you navigate your way out of Florence (no easy task), San Gimignano is only 57 km (35 miles) to the southwest, so it's an easy drive; you could even take a detour on the SS222 (Strada Chiantigiana), stop at one of the Chianti wine towns, and visit a winery along the way.

Day 5: Siena

In the morning, set out for nearby **Siena**, which is known worldwide for its Palio, a horse-race competition among the 17 *contrade* (medieval neighborhoods) of the city. Siena is one of Tuscany's most impressive sights; however many tourists you have to bump elbows with, it's hard not to be blown away by the city's precious medieval streets and memorable fan-shaped **Piazza del Campo.** Not to be missed while in town are the spectacular **Duomo,** the **Battistero,** and the **Spedale di Santa Maria della Scala,** an old hospital and hostel that now contains an underground archaeological museum.

Logistics: It's a short and pretty drive from San Gimignano to Siena, but once there, parking can be a challenge. Look for the *stadio* (soccer stadium), where there's a parking lot that often has space.

Day 6: Arezzo/Cortona

Get an early start, because there's a lot to see today. From Siena you'll first head to **Arezzo,** home to the **Basilica di San Francesco,** which contains important frescoes by Piero della Francesca. Check out the **Piazza Grande** along with its beautiful Romanesque church of **Pieve di Santa Maria.** Try to do all of this before lunch, after which you'll head straight to **Cortona.** If Arezzo didn't capture your imagination, Cortona, whose origins date to the 5th century BC, will. Olive trees and vineyards give way to a medieval hill town with views over idyllic Tuscan countryside and Lake Trasimeno. Cortona is a town for walking and relaxing, not sightseeing, so enjoy yourself, wandering through the **Piazza della Repubblica** and **Piazza Signorelli,** perhaps doing a bit of shopping.

Logistics: Siena to Arezzo is 63 km (39 miles) on the E78. From Arezzo to Cortona, it's just 30 km (18 miles)—take S71.

Day 7: Assisi

Today you'll cross over into Umbria, a region just as beautiful as Tuscany but still less trodden. Yet another impossibly beautiful hill town, **Assisi,** is the home of Saint Francis and host to the many religious pilgrims who come to celebrate his legacy. Visiting here is the most treasured

memory of many a traveler's visit to Italy. Upon arriving and checking into your lodging, head straight for the **Basilica di San Francesco,** which displays the tomb of Saint Francis and unbelievable frescoes. From here take Via San Francesco to **Piazza del Commune** and see the **Tempio di Minerva** before a break for lunch. After lunch, see **San Rufino,** the town cathedral, and then go back through the piazza to Corso Mazzini and see **Santa Chiara.** If you're a true fan of the Franciscans, you could instead devote the afternoon to heading out 16 km (10 miles) to **Cannara,** where Saint Francis delivered his sermon to the birds.

Logistics: From Cortona, take the S71 to the A1 autostrada toward Perugia. After about 40 km (24 miles), take the Assisi exit (E45), and it's another 14 km (8 miles) to Assisi.

Day 8: Spoleto

This morning will take you from a small Umbrian hill town to a slightly bigger one: **Spoleto,** a walled city that's home to a world-renowned arts festival each summer. But Spoleto needs no festival to be celebrated. Its **Duomo** is wonderful. Its fortress, **La Rocca,** is impressive. And the **Ponte delle Torri,** a 14th-century bridge that separates Spoleto from Monteluco, is a marvelous sight, traversing a gorge 260 feet below and built upon the foundations of a Roman aqueduct. See all these during the day, stopping for a light lunch of a *panino* (sandwich) or salad, saving your appetite for a serious last dinner in Italy: Umbrian cuisine is excellent everywhere, but Spoleto is a memorable culinary destination. Do your best to sample black truffles, a proud product of the region; they're delicious on pasta or meat.

AN ITINERARY TIP

Because of spotty train service to Tuscan hill towns, this itinerary is extremely difficult to complete without a car. Driving is easy and often (but not always) relaxing in the region, whose roads can be winding but are generally wide, well kept, well marked, and not too crowded. If you absolutely don't want to drive, buses are the best way to go, but you'll often have to change buses in hubs like Florence, and it would be best to cut out some of the smaller Tuscan hill towns and spend extra time in Siena and Spoleto.

Logistics: One school of thought would be to time your visit to Spoleto's world-renowned arts festival that runs from mid-June through mid-July. Another would be to do anything you can to avoid it. It all depends on your taste for big festivals and big crowds. The trip from Assisi to Spoleto is a pretty 47-km (29-mile) drive (S75 to the S3) that should take you less than an hour.

Day 9: Spoleto/Departure

It's a fair distance from Spoleto to the Florence airport, your point of departure. Depending on your comfort level with Italian driving, allow at least 2½ hours to reach Florence's airport.

Logistics: An alternative possibility would be to try to get a flight out of Perugia's tiny airport, which is a lot closer to Spoleto than Florence. It offers connections to Milan and Rome (Ciampino)—but not many. Otherwise, just get an early start and drive to Florence along the A1 autostrada.

WHO'S WHO IN RENAISSANCE ART

Michelangelo. Leonardo da Vinci. Raphael. This heady triumvirate of the Italian Renaissance is synonymous with artistic genius. Yet they are only three of the remarkable cast of characters whose work defines the Renaissance, that extraordinary flourishing of art and culture in Italy, especially in Florence, as the Middle Ages drew to a close. The artists were visionaries, who redefined painting, sculpture, architecture, and even what it means to be an artist.

THE PIONEER. In the mid-14th century, a few artists began to move away the flat, two-dimensional painting of the Middle Ages. **Giotto**, who painted seemingly three-dimensional figures who show emotion, had a major impact on the artists of the next century.

THE GROUNDBREAKERS. The generations of **Brunelleschi** and **Botticelli** took center stage in the 15th century. **Ghiberti, Masaccio, Donatello, Uccello, Fra Angelico**, and **Filippo Lippi** were other major players. Part of the Renaissance (or "re-birth") was a renewed interest in classical sources—the texts, monuments, and sculpture of Ancient Greece and Rome. Perspective and the illusion of three-dimensional space in painting was another discovery of this era, known as the Early Renaissance. Suddenly the art appearing on the walls looked real, or more realistic than it used to.

Roman ruins were not the only thing to inspire these artists. There was an incredible exchange of ideas going on. In Santa Maria del Carmine, Filippo Lippi was inspired by the work of Masaccio, who in turn was a friend of Brunelleschi. Young artists also learned from the masters via the apprentice system. Ghiberti's workshop (*bottega* in Italian) included, at one time or another, Donatello, Masaccio, and Uccello. Botticelli was apprenticed to Filippo Lippi.

THE BIG THREE. The mathematical rationality and precision of 15th-century art gave way to what is known as the High Renaissance. **Leonardo, Michelangelo**, and **Raphael** were much more concerned with portraying the body in all its glory and with achieving harmony and grandeur in their work. Oil paint, used infrequently up until this time, became more widely employed: as a result, Leonardo's colors are deeper, more sensual, more alive. For one brief period, all three were in Florence at the same time. Michelangelo and Leonardo surely knew one another, as they were simultaneously working on frescoes (never completed) inside Palazzo Vecchio.

When Michelangelo left Florence for Rome in 1508, he began the slow drain of artistic exodus from Florence, which never really recovered her previous glory.

A RENAISSANCE TIMELINE

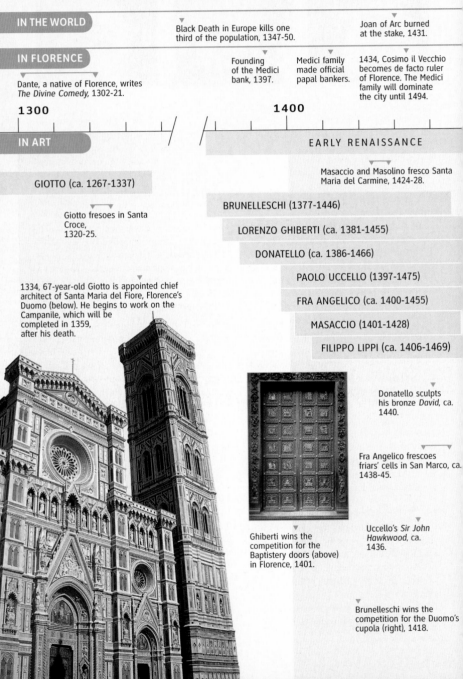

IN THE WORLD

Black Death in Europe kills one third of the population, 1347-50.

Joan of Arc burned at the stake, 1431.

IN FLORENCE

Dante, a native of Florence, writes *The Divine Comedy*, 1302-21.

Founding of the Medici bank, 1397.

Medici family made official papal bankers.

1434, Cosimo il Vecchio becomes de facto ruler of Florence. The Medici family will dominate the city until 1494.

1300

1400

IN ART

EARLY RENAISSANCE

Masaccio and Masolino fresco Santa Maria del Carmine, 1424-28.

GIOTTO (ca. 1267-1337)

Giotto fresoes in Santa Croce, 1320-25.

BRUNELLESCHI (1377-1446)

LORENZO GHIBERTI (ca. 1381-1455)

DONATELLO (ca. 1386-1466)

PAOLO UCCELLO (1397-1475)

FRA ANGELICO (ca. 1400-1455)

MASACCIO (1401-1428)

FILIPPO LIPPI (ca. 1406-1469)

1334, 67-year-old Giotto is appointed chief architect of Santa Maria del Fiore, Florence's Duomo (below). He begins to work on the Campanile, which will be completed in 1359, after his death.

Donatello sculpts his bronze *David*, ca. 1440.

Fra Angelico frescoes friars' cells in San Marco, ca. 1438-45.

Ghiberti wins the competition for the Baptistery doors (above) in Florence, 1401.

Uccello's *Sir John Hawkwood*, ca. 1436.

Brunelleschi wins the competition for the Duomo's cupola (right), 1418.

1

IN FOCUS WHO'S WHO IN RENAISSANCE ART

Gutenberg Bible
is printed, 1455.

Columbus discovers
America, 1492.

Martin Luther posts his 95 theses on
the door at Wittenberg, kicking off the
Protestant Reformation, 1517.

Constantinople falls
to the Turks, 1453.

Machiavelli's *Prince*
appears, 1513.

Copernicus proves that
the earth is not the center
of the universe, 1530-43.

Lorenzo "il Magnifico"
(right), the Medici
patron of the arts, rules
in Florence, 1449-92.

Two Medici popes Leo X
(1513-21) and Clement
VII (1523-34) in Rome.

Catherine de'Medici
becomes Queen of
France, 1547.

1450　　　　　　　　　**1500**　　　　　　　　　**1550**

HIGH RENAISSANCE　　　　　　MANNERISM

Fra Filippo Lippi's
*Madonna and
Child,* ca. 1452.

1508, Raphael begins
work on the chambers
in the Vatican, Rome.

Giorgio Vasari
publishes his first
edition of *Lives
of the Artists,*
1550.

1504, Michelangelo's
David is put on
display in Piazza
della Signoria,
where it remains
until 1873.

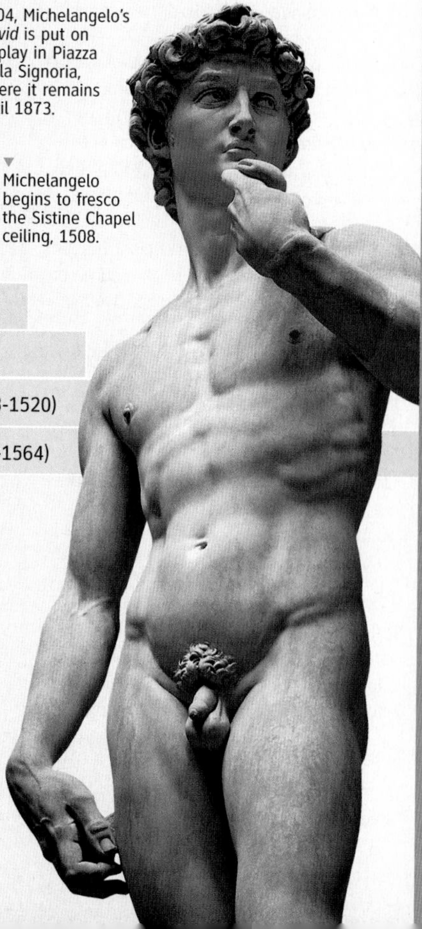

Botticelli paints the
Birth of Venus, ca.
1482.

Michelangelo
begins to fresco
the Sistine Chapel
ceiling, 1508.

BOTTICELLI (ca. 1444-1510)

LEONARDO DA VINCI (1452-1519)

RAPHAEL (1483-1520)

MICHELANGELO (1475-1564)

Leonardo paints *The Last Supper* in Milan,
1495-98.

Giotto's *Nativity*   Donatello's *St. John the Baptist*   Ghiberti's *Gates of Paradise*

GIOTTO (CA. 1267-1337)
Painter/architect from a small town north of Florence.

He unequivocally set Italian painting on the course that led to the triumphs of the Renaissance masters. Unlike the rather flat, two-dimensional forms found in then prevailing Byzantine art, Giotto's figures have a fresh, life-like quality. The people in his paintings have bulk, and they show emotion, which you can see on their faces and in their gestures. This was something new in the late Middle Ages. Without Giotto, there wouldn't have been a Raphael.

In Florence: **Santa Croce; Uffizi; Campanile; Santa Maria Novella**
Elsewhere in Italy: **Scrovegni Chapel, Padua; Vatican Museums, Rome**

FILIPPO BRUNELLESCHI (1377-1446)
Architect/engineer from Florence.

If Brunelleschi had beaten Ghiberti in the Baptistery doors competition in Florence, the city's Duomo most likely would not have the striking appearance and authority that it has today. After his loss, he sulked off to Rome, where he studied the ancient Roman structures first-hand. Brunelleschi figured out how to vault the Duomo's dome, a structure unprecedented in its colossal size and great height. His Ospedale degli Innocenti employs classical elements in the creation of a stunning, new architectural statement; it is the first truly Renaissance structure.

In Florence: **Duomo; Ospedale degli Innocenti; San Lorenzo; Santo Spirito; Baptistery Doors Competition Entry, Bargello; Santa Croce**

LORENZO GHIBERTI (CA. 1381-1455)
Sculptor from Florence.

Ghiberti won a competition—besting his chief rival, Brunelleschi—to cast the gilded bronze North Doors of the Baptistery in Florence. These doors, and the East Doors that he subsequently executed, took up the next 50 years of his life. He created intricately worked figures that are more true-to-life than any since antiquity, and he was one of the first Renaissance sculptors to work in bronze. Ghiberti taught the next generation of artists; Donatello, Uccello, and Masaccio all passed through his studio.

In Florence: **Door Copies, Baptistery; Original Doors, Museo dell'Opera del Duomo; Baptistry Door Competition Entry, Bargello; Orsanmichele**

DONATELLO (CA. 1386-1466)
Sculptor from Florence.

Donatello was an innovator who, like his good friend Brunelleschi, spent most of his long life in Florence. Consumed with the science of optics, he used light and shadow to create the effects of nearness and distance. He made an essentially flat slab look like a three-dimensional scene. His bronze *David* is probably the first free-standing male nude since antiquity. Not only technically brilliant, his work is also emotionally resonant; few sculptors are as expressive.

In Florence: ***David*, Bargello; *St. Mark*, Orsanmichele; Palazzo Vecchio; Museo dell'Opera del Duomo; San Lorenzo; Santa Croce**
Elsewhere in Italy: **Padua; Prato; Venice**

Fra Angelico's *The Deposition*

Masaccio's *Trinity*

Filippo Lippi's *Madonna and Child*

PAOLO UCCELLO (1397-1475)
Painter from Florence.
Renaissance chronicler Vasari once observed that had Uccello not been so obsessed with the mathematical problems posed by perspective, he would have been a very good painter. The struggle to master single-point perspective and to render motion in two dimensions is nowhere more apparent than in his battle scenes. His first major commission in Florence was the gargantuan fresco of the English mercenary Sir John Hawkwood (the Italians called him Giovanni Acuto) in Florence's Duomo.
In Florence: ***Sir John Hawkwood**, Duomo; **Battle of San Romano**, Uffizi; Santa Maria Novella*
Elsewhere in Italy: **Urbino, Prato**

FRA ANGELICO (CA. 1400-1455)
Painter from a small town north of Florence.
A Dominican friar, who eventually made his way to the convent of San Marco, Fra Angelico and his assistants painted frescoes for aid in prayer and meditation. He was known for his piety; Vasari wrote that Fra Angelico could never paint a crucifix without a tear running down his face. Perhaps no other painter so successfully translated the mysteries of faith and the sacred into painting. And yet his figures emote, his command of perspective is superb, and his use of color startles even today.
In Florence: **Museo di San Marco; Uffizi**
Elsewhere in Italy: **Vatican Museums, Rome; Fiesole; Cortona; Perugia; Orvieto**

MASACCIO (1401-1428)
Painter from San Giovanni Valdarno, southeast of Florence.
Masaccio and Masolino, a frequent collaborator, worked most famously together at Santa Maria del Carmine. Their frescoes of the life of St. Peter use light to mold figures in the painting by imitating the way light falls on figures in real life. Masaccio also pioneered the use of single-point perspective, masterfully rendered in his *Trinity*. His friend Brunelleschi probably introduced him to the technique, yet another step forward in rendering things the way the eye sees them. Masaccio died young and under mysterious circumstances.
In Florence: **Santa Maria del Carmine;** *Trinity*, **Santa Maria Novella**

FILIPPO LIPPI (CA. 1406-1469)
Painter from Prato.
At a young age, Filippo Lippi entered the friary of Santa Maria del Carmine, where he was highly influenced by Masaccio and Masolino's frescoes. His religious vows appear to have made less of an impact; his affair with a young nun produced a son, Filippino (Little Philip, who later apprenticed with Botticelli), and a daughter. His religious paintings often have a playful, humorous note; some of his angels are downright impish and look directly out at the viewer. Lippi links the earlier painters of the 15th century with those who follow; Botticelli apprenticed with him.
In Florence: **Uffizi; Palazzo Medici Riccardi; San Lorenzo; Palazzo Pitti**
Elsewhere in Italy: **Prato**

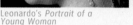

Botticelli's *Primavera*

Leonardo's *Portrait of a Young Woman*

Raphael's *Madonna on the Meadow*

BOTTICELLI (CA. 1444-1510)
Painter from Florence.
Botticelli's work is characterized by stunning, elongated blondes, cherubic angels (something he undoubtedly learned from his time with Filippo Lippi), and tender Christs. Though he did many religious paintings, he also painted monumental, nonreligious panels—his *Birth of Venus* and *Primavera* being the two most famous of these. A brief sojourn took him to Rome, where he and a number of other artists frescoed the Sistine Chapel walls.
In Florence: **Birth of Venus, Primavera, Uffizi; Palazzo Pitti**
Elsewhere in Italy: **Vatican Museums, Rome**

LEONARDO DA VINCI (1452-1519)
Painter/sculptor/engineer from Anchiano, a small town outside Vinci.
Leonardo never lingered long in any place; his restless nature and his international reputation led to commissions throughout Italy, and took him to Milan, Vigevano, Pavia, Rome, and, ultimately, France. Though he is most famous for his mysterious *Mona Lisa* (at the Louvre in Paris), he painted other penetrating, psychological portraits in addition to his scientific experiments: his design for a flying machine (never built) predates Kitty Hawk by nearly 500 years. The greatest collection of Leonardo's work in Italy can be seen on one wall in the Uffizi.
In Florence: **Adoration of the Magi, Uffizi**
Elsewhere in Italy: **Last Supper, Santa Maria delle Grazie, Milan**

RAPHAEL (1483-1520)
Painter/architect from Urbino.
Raphael spent only four highly productive years of his short life in Florence, where he turned out made-to-order panel paintings of the Madonna and Child for a hungry public; he also executed a number of portraits of Florentine aristocrats. Perhaps no other artist had such a fine command of line and color, and could render it, seemingly effortlessly, in paint. His painting acquired new authority after he came up against Michelangelo toiling away on the Sistine ceiling. Raphael worked nearly next door in the Vatican, where his figures take on an epic, Michelangelesque scale.
In Florence: **Uffizi; Palazzo Pitti**
Elsewhere in Italy: **Vatican Museums, Rome**

MICHELANGELO (1475-1564)
Painter/sculptor/architect from Caprese.
Although Florentine and proud of it (he famously signed his St. Peter's *Pietà* to avoid confusion about where he was from), he spent most of his 89 years outside his native city. He painted and sculpted the male body on an epic scale and glorified it while doing so. Though he complained throughout the proceedings that he was really a sculptor, Michelangelo's Sistine Chapel ceiling is arguably the greatest fresco cycle ever painted (and the massive figures owe no small debt to Giotto).
In Florence: **David, Galleria dell'Accademia; Uffizi; Casa Buonarroti; Bargello**
Elsewhere in Italy: **St. Peter's Basilica, Vatican Museums, and Piazza del Campidoglio in Rome**

FLORENCE

WELCOME TO FLORENCE

TOP REASONS TO GO

★ **Galleria degli Uffizi:** Italian Renaissance art doesn't get much better than this vast collection bequeathed to the city by the last Medici, Anna Maria Luisa.

★ **Brunelleschi's Dome:** His work of engineering genius is the city's undisputed centerpiece.

★ **Michelangelo's *David*:** One look and you'll know why this is one of the Western world's most famous sculptures.

★ **The view from Piazzale Michelangelo:** From this perch the city is laid out before you. The colors at sunset heighten the experience.

★ **Piazza Santa Croce:** After you've had your fill of Renaissance masterpieces, hang out here and watch the world go by.

1 Around the Duomo. You're in the heart of Florence here. Among the numerous highlights are the city's greatest museum (the Uffizi) and arguably its most impressive square (Piazza della Signoria).

2 San Lorenzo. The blocks from the basilica of San Lorenzo to the Galleria dell'Accademia bear the imprints of the Medici and of Michelangelo, culminating in the latter's masterful *David*. Just to the north, the former convent of San Marco is an oasis of artistic treasures decorated with ethereal frescoes.

3 Santa Maria Novella. This part of town includes the train station, 16th-century palaces, and the city's most swank shopping street, Via Tornabuoni.

4 Santa Croce. The district centers on its namesake basilica, which is filled with the tombs of Renaissance (and other) luminaries. The area is also known for its leather shops.

5 The Oltrarno. Across the Arno you encounter the massive Palazzo Pitti and the narrow streets of the Santo Spirito neighborhood, filled with artisans' workshops and antiques stores. A climb to Piazzale Michelangelo gives you a spectacular view of the city.

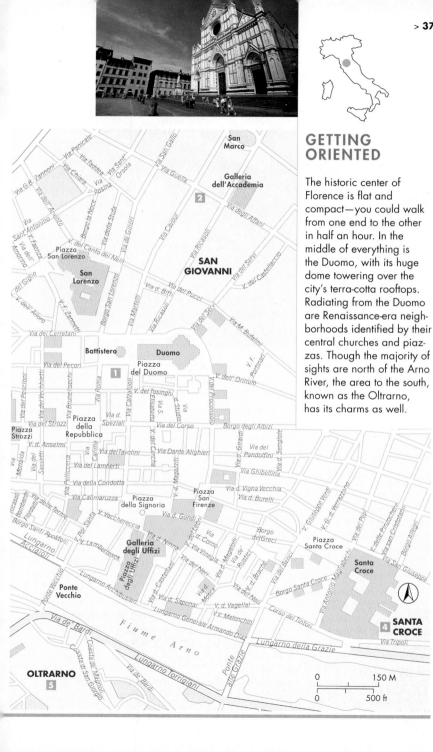

2

GETTING ORIENTED

The historic center of Florence is flat and compact—you could walk from one end to the other in half an hour. In the middle of everything is the Duomo, with its huge dome towering over the city's terra-cotta rooftops. Radiating from the Duomo are Renaissance-era neighborhoods identified by their central churches and piazzas. Though the majority of sights are north of the Arno River, the area to the south, known as the Oltrarno, has its charms as well.

EATING AND DRINKING WELL IN FLORENCE

In Florence simply prepared meats, grilled or roasted, are the culinary stars, usually paired with seasonal vegetables like artichokes or porcini. Bistecca's big here, but there's plenty more that tastes great on the grill, too.

Traditionalists go for their gustatory pleasures in trattorie and osterie, places where decor is unimportant and place mats are mere paper. Culinary innovation comes slowly in this town, though some cutting-edge restaurants have been appearing, usually with young chefs who've worked outside Italy. Some of these places lack charm, but their menus offer updated versions of Tuscan standards.

By American standards, Florentines eat late: 1:30 or 2 is typical for lunch and 9 for dinner is considered early. Consuming a primo, secondo, and dolce is largely a thing of the past. For lunch, many Florentines simply grab a panino and a glass of wine at a bar. Those opting for a simple trattoria lunch often order a plate of pasta and dessert.

STALE AND STELLAR

Florence lacks signature pasta and rice dishes, perhaps because it has raised frugality with bread to culinary craft. Stale bread is the basis for three classic Florentine primi: *pappa al pomodoro, ribollita,* and *panzanella.* "Pappa" is made with either fresh or canned tomatoes and that stale bread. Ribollita is a vegetable soup fortified with *cavolo nero* (called Tuscan kale in the United States), cannellini beans, and thickened with bread. Panzanella, a summertime dish, is reconstituted Tuscan bread combined with tomatoes, cucumber, and basil. They all are greatly enhanced with a generous application of fragrant Tuscan olive oil.

2

A CLASSIC ANTIPASTO: *CROSTINI DI FEGATINI*

This beloved dish consists of a chicken-liver spread, served warm or at room temperature, on toasted, garlic-rubbed bread. It can be served smooth, like a pâté, or in a chunkier, more rustic version. It's made by sautéing chicken livers with finely diced carrot and onion, enlivened with the addition of wine, broth, or Marsala reductions, and mashed anchovies and capers.

A CLASSIC SECONDO: *BISTECCA FIORENTINA*

The town's culinary pride and joy is a thick slab of beef, resembling a T-bone steak, from large white oxen called Chianina. The meat's slapped on the grill and served rare, sometimes with a pinch of salt.

It's always seared on both sides, and just barely cooked inside (experts say 5 minutes per side, and then 15 minutes with the bone sitting perpendicularly on the grill). To ask for it more well-done is to incur disdain; if you can't eat it this way, do please order something else.

A CLASSIC CONTORNO: *CANNELLINI BEANS*

Simply boiled, they provide the perfect accompaniment to bistecca. The small white beans are best when they go straight from the garden into the pot. They should be anointed with a generous dose of Tuscan olive oil; the

combination is oddly felicitous, and it goes a long way toward explaining why Tuscans are referred to as *mangiafagioli* (bean eaters) by other Italians.

A CLASSIC DOLCE: *BISCOTTI DI PRATO*

These are sometimes the only dessert on offer (if you find yourself in such a restaurant, you'll know you're in a really, truly Tuscan eatery) and are more or less an afterthought to the glories that have preceded them. "Biscotti" means twice-cooked (or, in this case, twice baked). They are hard almond cookies that soften considerably when dipped languidly into *vin santo* ("holy wine"), a sweet dessert wine, or into a simple *caffè*.

A CLASSIC WINE: *CHIANTI CLASSICO*

This blend from the region just south of Florence relies mainly on the local, hardy Sangiovese grape; it's aged for at least one year before hitting the market. (*Riserve*—reserves—are aged at least an additional six months.)

Chianti is usually the libation of choice for Florentines, and it pairs magnificently with grilled foods and seasonal vegetables. Traditionalists opt for the younger, fruitier (and usually less expensive) versions often served in straw flasks. You can sample Chianti *classico* all over town, and buy it in local *salumerie, enoteche,* and supermarkets.

Updated
by Patricia
Rucidlo

FLORENCE, THE CITY OF THE LILY, gave birth to the Renaissance and changed the way we see the world. For centuries it has captured the imaginations of travelers, who have come seeking rooms with views and phenomenal art. Florence's is a subtle beauty—its staid, unprepossessing palaces built in local stone are not showy, even though they are very large. They take on a certain magnificence when day breaks and when the sun sets; their muted colors glow in this light. A walk along the Arno offers views that don't quit and haven't much changed in 700 years; navigating Piazza della Signoria, always packed with tourists, requires patience. There's a reason why everyone seems to be here, however. It's the heart of the city, and home to the Uffizi—the world's finest repository of Italian Renaissance art.

Florence was "discovered" in the 1700s by upper-class visitors from everywhere making the grand tour. Today millions of us follow in their footsteps. When the sun sets over the Arno and, as Mark Twain described it, "overwhelms Florence with tides of color that make all the sharp lines dim and faint and turn the solid city to a city of dreams," it's hard not to fall under the city's spell.

PLANNING

MAKING THE MOST OF YOUR TIME

With some planning, you can see Florence's most famous sights in a couple of days. Start off at the city's most awe-inspiring architectural wonder, the **Duomo,** climbing to the top of the dome if you have the stamina (and are not claustrophobic: it gets a little tight going up and coming back down). On the same piazza, check out Ghiberti's bronze doors at the **Battistero.** (They're actually high-quality copies; the Museo dell'Opera del Duomo has the originals). Set aside the afternoon for the **Galleria degli Uffizi,** making sure to reserve tickets in advance.

On Day 2, visit Michelangelo's *David* in the **Galleria dell'Accademia**—reserve tickets here, too. Linger in **Piazza della Signoria,** Florence's central square, where a copy of *David* stands in the spot the original occupied for centuries, then head east a couple of blocks to **Santa Croce,** the city's most artistically rich church. Double back and walk across Florence's landmark bridge, the **Ponte Vecchio.**

Do all that, and you'll have seen some great art, but you've just scratched the surface. If you have more time, put the **Bargello,** the **Museo di San Marco,** and the **Cappelle Medicee** at the top of your list. When you're ready for an art break, stroll through the **Boboli Gardens** or explore Florence's lively shopping scene, from the food stalls of the **Mercato Centrale** to the chic boutiques of the **Via Tornabuoni.**

FLORENTINE HOURS

Florence's sights keep tricky hours. Some are closed Wednesday, some Monday, some every other Monday. Quite a few shut their doors each day (or on most days) by 2 in the afternoon. Things get even more confusing on weekends. Make it a general rule to check the hours closely for any place you're planning to visit; if it's someplace you have your heart set on seeing, it's worthwhile to call to confirm.

Here's a selection of major sights that might not be open when you'd expect *(consult the sight listings within this chapter for the full details)*. And be aware that, as always, hours can and do change.

The **Accademia** and the **Uffizi** are both closed Monday.

The **Battistero** is open from 11 until 7, Monday through Saturday, and Sunday from 8:30 to 2.

The **Bargello** closes at 1:50 pm, and is closed entirely on alternating Sundays and Mondays. However, it's often open much later during high season and when there's a special exhibition on.

The **Cappelle Medicee** are closed alternating Sundays and Mondays (those Sundays and Mondays when the Bargello is open).

The **Duomo** closes at 4 Thursday (as opposed to 5 other weekdays, 4:45 Saturday, and Sunday it's open only from 1:30 to 4:45). The dome of the Duomo is closed Sunday.

Museo di San Marco closes at 1:50 weekdays but stays open until 7 weekends—except for alternating Sundays and Mondays, when it's closed entirely.

Palazzo Medici-Riccardi is closed Wednesday.

UFFIZI RESERVATIONS

At most times of day you'll see a line of people snaking around the Uffizi. They're waiting to buy tickets, and you don't want to be one of them. Instead, call ahead for a reservation (☎ *055/294883*; reservationists speak English). You'll be given a reservation number and a time of admission—the sooner you call, the more time slots you'll have to choose from. Go to the museum's reservation door at the appointed hour, give the clerk your number, pick up your ticket, and go inside. You'll pay €4 for this privilege, but it's money well spent. You can also book tickets online through the website ⊕ *www.polomuseale.firenze.it*; the booking process takes some patience, but it works.

Use the same reservation service to book tickets for the Galleria dell'Accademia, where lines rival those of the Uffizi. (Reservations can also be made for the Palazzo Pitti, the Bargello, and several other sights, but they usually aren't needed—although, lately, in summer, lines can be long at Palazzo Pitti.) An alternative strategy is to check with your hotel—many will handle reservations.

PACING YOUR ART INTAKE

Even for the most dedicated art enthusiast, trying to take in Florence's abundance of masterpieces can turn into a headache—there's just too much to see. Especially if you don't count yourself as an art lover, remember to pace yourself. Allow time to wander and follow your whims, and ignore any pangs of guilt if you'd rather relax in a café and watch the world go by than trudge on sore feet through another breathtaking palace or church.

Florence isn't a city that can be "done." It's a place you can return to again and again, confident there will always be more treasures to discover.

GETTING HERE AND AROUND

AIR TRAVEL

Aeroporto A. Vespucci. Florence's small Aeroporto A. Vespucci, commonly called **Peretola**, is just outside of town, and receives flights from Milan, Rome, London, and Paris. ⊠ *10 km [6 miles] northwest of Florence* ☎ *055/30615* ⊕ *www.aeroporto.firenze.it.*

To get into the city center from the airport by car, take the autostrada A11. A SITA bus will take you directly from the airport to the center of town. Buy the tickets within the train station.

Aeroporto Galileo Galilei. Pisa's Aeroporto Galileo Galilei is the closest landing point with significant international service, including a few direct flights from New York each week on Delta. Sadly, the flight is seasonal and shuts down when it's cold outside. It's a straight shot down the SS67 to Florence. A train service, which used to connect Pisa's airport station with Santa Maria Novella, has as of press time been temporarily suspended. It's possible to take a bus to the train station at Pisa Centrale, and then go on to Florence Santa Maria Novella. ⊠ *12 km [7 miles] south of Pisa and 80 km [50 miles] west of Florence* ☎ *050/849300* ⊕ *www.pisa-airport.com.*

BIKE AND MOPED TRAVEL

Brave souls (cycling in Florence is difficult at best) may rent bicycles at easy-to-spot locations at Fortezza da Basso, the Stazione Centrale di Santa Maria Novella, and Piazza Pitti. Otherwise, try **Alinari** (⊠ *Via San Zanobi 38/r, San Marco* ☎ *055/280500* ⊕ *www.alinarirental. com*). You'll be up against hordes of tourists and those pesky *motorini* (mopeds). (For a safer ride, try Le Cascine, a former Medici hunting ground turned into a large public park with paved pathways.) The historic center can be circumnavigated via bike paths lining the *viali,* the ring road surrounding the area. If you want to go native and rent a noisy Vespa (Italian for "wasp") or other make of motorcycle or *motorino,* you may do so at **Massimo** (⊠ *Via Campo d'Arrigo 16/r* ☎ *055/573689*).

BUS TRAVEL

Florence's flat, compact city center is made for walking, but when your feet get weary you can use the efficient bus system, which includes small electric buses making the rounds in the center. Buses also climb to Piazzale Michelangelo and San Miniato south of the Arno.

Maps and timetables for local bus service are available for a small fee at the ATAF (Azienda Trasporti Area Fiorentina) booth next to the train station, or for free at visitor information offices. Tickets must be bought in advance from tobacco shops, newsstands, automatic ticket machines near main stops, or ATAF booths. The ticket must be canceled in the small validation machine immediately upon boarding.

You have several ticket options, all valid for one or more rides on all lines. A €1.20 ticket is good for one hour from the time it is first canceled. A multiple ticket—four tickets, each valid for 70 minutes—costs €4.50. A 24-hour tourist ticket costs €5. Two-, three-, and seven-day passes are also available.

Long-distance buses provide inexpensive service between Florence and other cities in Italy and Europe. **Lazzi Eurolines** (⊠ *Via Mercadante 2*

☎ *055/363041* ⊕ *www.lazzi.it*) and **SITA** (⊠ *Via Santa Caterina da Siena 17/r* ☎ *055/47821* ⊕ *www.sitabus.it*) are the major lines.

CAR TRAVEL

Florence is connected to the north and south of Italy by the Autostrada del Sole (A1). It takes about 1½ hours of driving on scenic roads to get to Bologna (although heavy truck traffic over the Apennines often makes for slower going), about 3 hours to Rome, and 3 to 3½ hours to Milan. The Tyrrhenian Coast is an hour west on the A11.

An automobile in Florence is a major liability. If your itinerary includes parts of Italy where you'll want a car (such as Tuscany), pick the vehicle up on your way out of town.

TAXI TRAVEL

Taxis usually wait at stands throughout the city (in front of the train station and in Piazza della Repubblica, for example), or you can call for one (☎ *055/4390 or 055/4242*). The meter starts at €3.30 from any taxi stand; if you call Radio Dispatch (that means that a taxi comes to pick you up wherever it is you are), it starts at €5.40. Extra charges apply at night, on Sunday, for radio dispatch, and for luggage. Women out on the town after midnight seeking taxis are entitled to a 10% discount on the fare; you must, however, request it.

TRAIN TRAVEL

Florence is on the principal Italian train route between most European capitals and Rome, and within Italy it is served frequently from Milan, Venice, and Rome by Intercity (IC) and nonstop Eurostar trains. Avoid trains that stop only at the Campo di Marte or Rifredi station, which are not convenient to the city center.

Stazione Centrale di Santa Maria Novella. Florence's main train station is in the center of town. ☎ *892021* ⊕ *www.trenitalia.com.*

VISITOR INFORMATION

The Florence tourist office, known as the APT (☎ *055/290832* ⊕ *www. firenzeturismo.it*), has branches next to the Palazzo Medici-Riccardi, across the street from Stazione di Santa Maria Novella (the main train station), and at the Bigallo, in Piazza del Duomo. The offices are generally open from 9 in the morning until 7 in the evening. The multilingual staff will give you directions and the latest on happenings in the city. It's particularly worth a stop if you're interested in finding out about performing-arts events. The APT website provides information in both Italian and English.

AROUND THE DUOMO

The heart of Florence, stretching from the Piazza del Duomo south to the Arno, is as dense with artistic treasures as any place in the world. Its churches, medieval towers, Renaissance palaces, and world-class museums and galleries contain some of the most outstanding achievements of Western art history.

Much of the *centro storico* (historic center) is closed to automobile traffic, but you still must dodge mopeds, cyclists, and masses of fellow tourists as you walk the narrow streets, especially in the area bounded by the Duomo, Piazza della Signoria, Galleria degli Uffizi, and Ponte Vecchio. Via dei Calzaiuoli, between Piazza del Duomo and Piazza della Signoria, is the city's favorite *passeggiata.*

TOP ATTRACTIONS

Bargello. This building started out as the headquarters for the *Capitano del Popolo* (captain of the people) during the Middle Ages, and was later used as a prison. The exterior served as a "most wanted" billboard: effigies of notorious criminals and Medici enemies were painted on its walls. Today it houses the **Museo Nazionale,** home to what is probably the finest collection of Renaissance sculpture in Italy. The concentration of masterworks by Michelangelo (1475–1564), Donatello (circa 1386–1466), and Benvenuto Cellini (1500–71) is remarkable; the works are distributed among an eclectic collection of arms, ceramics, and miniature bronzes, among other things. For Renaissance art lovers, the Bargello is to sculpture what the Uffizi is to painting.

In 1401 Filippo Brunelleschi (1377–1446) and Lorenzo Ghiberti (circa 1378–1455) competed to earn the most prestigious commission of the day: the decoration of the north doors of the Baptistery in Piazza del Duomo. For the contest, each designed a bronze bas-relief panel depicting the sacrifice of Isaac; the panels are displayed together in the room devoted to the sculpture of Donatello, on the upper floor. The judges chose Ghiberti for the commission; see if you agree with their choice. ✉ *Via del Proconsolo 4, Bargello* ☎ *055/294883* ⊕ *www.polomuseale. firenze.it* 🎫 *€4* ☉ *Daily 8:15–1:50; closed 2nd and 4th Mon. of month.*

Battistero (*Baptistery*). The octagonal Baptistery is one of the supreme monuments of the Italian Romanesque style and one of Florence's oldest structures. Local legend has it that it was once a Roman temple dedicated to Mars, and modern excavations suggest that its foundations date from the 1st century AD. The round Romanesque arches on the exterior date from the 11th century, and the interior dome mosaics from the beginning of the mid-13th century are justly renowned, but—glittering beauties though they are—they could never outshine the building's famed bronze Renaissance doors decorated with panels crafted by Lorenzo Ghiberti. These doors—or at least copies of them— on which Ghiberti worked most of his adult life (1403–52) are on the north and east sides of the Baptistery, and the Gothic panels on the south door were designed by Andrea Pisano (circa 1290–1348) in 1330. Ghiberti's original doors were removed to protect them from the effects of pollution and acid rain and have been beautifully restored; they are now on display in the Museo dell'Opera del Duomo. Ghiberti's north doors depict scenes from the life of Christ; his later east doors (dating from 1425–52), facing the Duomo facade, render scenes from the Old Testament. Both merit close examination, for they are very different in style and illustrate the artistic changes that marked the beginning of the Renaissance. Look at the far right panel of the middle row on the earlier (1403–24) north doors (*Jesus Calming the Waters*). Ghiberti here captured the chaos of a storm at sea with great skill and economy, but the artistic conventions he used are basically pre-Renaissance: Jesus is the most important figure, so he is the largest; the disciples are next in

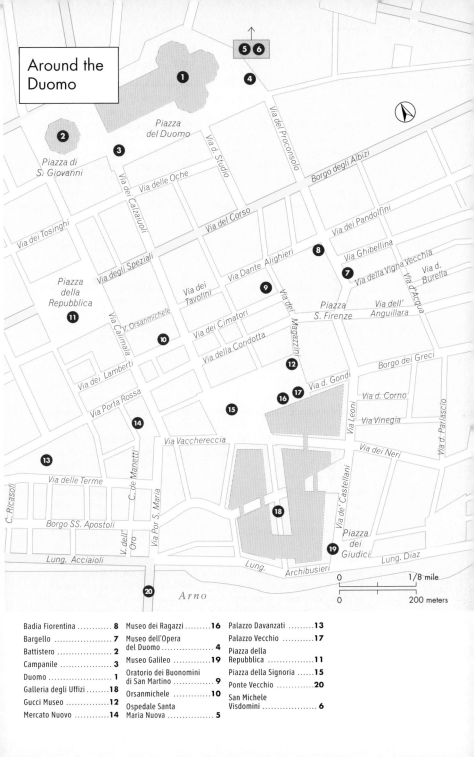

Around the Duomo

Piazza del Duomo

Piazza di S. Giovanni

0   1/8 mile

0   200 meters

FLORENCE THROUGH THE AGES

Guelph vs. Ghibelline. Though Florence can lay claim to a modest importance in the ancient world, it didn't come into its own until the Middle Ages. In the early 1200s the city, like most of the rest of Italy, was rent by civic unrest. Two factions, the Guelphs and the Ghibellines, competed for power. The Guelphs supported the papacy, and the Ghibellines supported the Holy Roman Empire. Bloody battles—most notably one at Montaperti in 1260—tore Florence and other Italian cities apart. By the end of the 13th century the Guelphs ruled securely, and the Ghibellines had been vanquished. This didn't end civic strife, however: the Guelphs split into the Whites and the Blacks for reasons still debated by historians. Dante, author of *The Divine Comedy*, was banished from Florence in 1301 because he was a White.

The Guilded Age. Local merchants had organized themselves into guilds by sometime beginning in the 12th century. In that year, they proclaimed themselves the *primo popolo* (literally, "first people"), making a landmark attempt at elective, republican rule. Though the episode lasted only 10 years, it constituted a breakthrough in Western history. Such a daring stance by the merchant class was a byproduct of Florence's emergence as an economic powerhouse. Florentines were papal bankers; they instituted the system of international letters of credit; and the gold florin became the international standard of currency. With this economic strength came a building boom. Sculptors such as Donatello and Ghiberti decorated them; painters such as Giotto and Botticelli frescoed their walls.

Mighty Medici. Though ostensibly a republic, Florence was blessed (or cursed) with one very powerful family, the Medici, who came to prominence in the 1430s and were initially the de facto rulers and then the absolute rulers of Florence for several hundred years. It was under patriarch Cosimo il Vecchio (1389–1464) that the Medici's position in Florence was securely established. Florence's golden age occurred during the reign of his grandson Lorenzo de' Medici (1449–92). Lorenzo was not only an astute politician but also a highly educated man and a great patron of the arts. Called "Il Magnifico" (the Magnificent), he gathered around him poets, artists, philosophers, architects, and musicians.

Lorenzo's son Piero (1471–1503) proved inept at handling the city's affairs. He was run out of town in 1494, and Florence briefly enjoyed its status as a republic while dominated by the Dominican friar Girolamo Savonarola (1452–98). After a decade of internal unrest, the republic fell and the Medici were recalled to power, but Florence never regained its former prestige. By the 1530s most of the major artistic talent had left the city—Michelangelo, for one, had settled in Rome. The now-ineffectual Medici, eventually attaining the title of grand dukes, remained nominally in power until the line died out in 1737, after which time Florence passed from the Austrians to the French and back again until the unification of Italy (1865–70), when it briefly became the capital under King Vittorio Emanuele II.

size, being next in importance; the ship on which they founder looks like a mere toy.

The exquisitely rendered panels on the east doors are larger, more expansive, more sweeping—and more convincing. The middle panel on the left-hand door tells the story of Jacob and Esau, and the various episodes of the story—the selling of the birthright, Isaac ordering Esau to go hunting, the blessing of Jacob,

and so forth—have been merged into a single beautifully realized street scene. Ghiberti's use of perspective suggests depth: the background architecture looks far more credible than on the north-door panels, the figures in the foreground are grouped realistically, and the naturalism and grace of the poses (look at Esau's left leg and the dog next to him) have nothing to do with the sacred message being conveyed. Although the religious content remains, the figures and their place in the natural world are given new prominence, and are portrayed with a realism not seen in art since the fall of the Roman Empire nearly a thousand years before.

As a footnote to Ghiberti's panels, one small detail of the east doors is worth a special look. To the lower left of the Jacob and Esau panel, Ghiberti placed a tiny self-portrait bust. From either side, the portrait is extremely appealing—Ghiberti looks like everyone's favorite uncle—but the bust is carefully placed so that you can make direct eye contact with the tiny head from a single spot. When that contact is made, the impression of intelligent life—of *modern* intelligent life—is astonishing. It's no wonder that these doors received one of the most famous compliments in the history of art from an artist known to be notoriously stingy with praise: Michelangelo declared them so beautiful that they could serve as the Gates of Paradise. ✉ *Piazza del Duomo* ☎ *055/2302885* ⊕ *www. operaduomo.firenze.it* ✉ *€10* ⊘ *Mon.–Sat. 11:15–7; Sun. 8:30–2, 1st Sat. of month 8:30–2.*

Fodor's Choice ★ **Galleria degli Uffizi.** The venerable Uffizi Gallery occupies two floors of the U-shaped **Palazzo degli Uffizi**, designed by Giorgio Vasari (1511–74) in 1560 to hold the *uffizi* (administrative offices) of the Medici grand duke Cosimo I (1519–74). Later, the Medici installed their art collections here, creating what was Europe's first modern museum, open to the public (at first only by request) since 1591.

Among the highlights are Paolo Uccello's *Battle of San Romano,* its brutal chaos of lances one of the finest visual metaphors for warfare ever captured in paint (returned from a glorious restoration in the summer of 2012); the *Madonna and Child with Two Angels,* by Fra Filippo Lippi (1406–69), in which the impudent eye contact established by the angel would have been unthinkable prior to the Renaissance; the *Birth of Venus* and *Primavera* by Sandro Botticelli (1445–1510), the goddess of the former seeming to float on air and the fairy-tale charm of the latter exhibiting the painter's idiosyncratic genius at its zenith; the

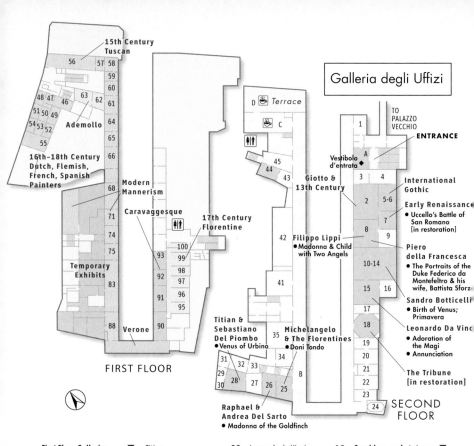

Galleria degli Uffizi

FIRST FLOOR

- 15th Century Tuscan — 56, 57, 58
- Ademollo — 48, 47, 46, 63, 62, 61, 51, 50, 49, 54, 53, 52, 55, 59, 60, 64, 65
- 16th–18th Century Dutch, Flemish, French, Spanish Painters — 66, 68
- Modern Mannerism — 68
- Caravaggesque — 71, 74, 75
- 17th Century Florentine — 100, 99, 98, 97, 96, 95
- Temporary Exhibits — 83, 93, 92, 91, 90
- Verone — 88, 90
- Titian & Sebastiano Del Piombo — Venus of Urbino — 31, 32, 33, 29, 28, 27, 26, 25, 30, 35, 34
- Michelangelo & The Florentines — Doni Tondo
- Raphael & Andrea Del Sarto — Madonna of the Goldfinch

SECOND FLOOR

- Terrace — D
- C
- Vestibolo d'entrata — A
- TO PALAZZO VECCHIO — ENTRANCE
- Giotto & 13th Century — 1, 3, 4, 2, 5-6
- International Gothic
- Early Renaissance — 7
  - Uccello's Battle of San Romano [in restoration]
- Filippo Lippi — 42, 8, 9
  - Madonna & Child with Two Angels
- Piero della Francesca — 10-14
  - The Portraits of the Duke Federico da Montefeltro & his wife, Battista Sforz
- Sandro Botticelli — 15, 16
  - Birth of Venus; Primavera
- Leonardo Da Vinci — 17, 18
  - Adoration of the Magi
  - Annunciation
- The Tribune [in restoration] — 19, 20, 21, 22, 23, 24, B, 41, 45, 44, 43

portraits of the Renaissance duke Federico da Montefeltro and his wife Battista Sforza, by Piero della Francesca (circa 1420–92); the *Madonna of the Goldfinch* by Raphael (1483–1520), which underwent a stunning years-long restoration, completed in 2009 (check out the brilliant blues that decorate the sky, as well as the eye contact between mother and child, both clearly anticipating the painful future; Michelangelo's *Doni Tondo*; the *Venus of Urbino* by Titian (circa 1488/90–1576); and the splendid *Bacchus* by Caravaggio (circa 1571/72–1610). In the last two works, the approaches to myth and sexuality are diametrically opposed (to put it mildly). Don't forget to see the Caravaggios, which you'll pass through during the exiting process. In the summer of 2012, many new rooms were opened (complementing the blue rooms housing non-Italian art which occurred the year before), which means that getting out of the museum takes even longer; don't think you've missed the Raphaels, which used to live in the room next door to Michelangelo's stunning panel painting. They are now practically the last thing you'll see before leaving, so remember to save some stamina in order to truly appreciate their splendor. And don't think you've missed the Michelangelo, as in winter 2013 it was moved from Sala 25 to Sala 35. At press time, and at last count, the Uffizi numbered 79 rooms, many of which were empty awaiting more recent, non-Italian Renaissance additions. In addition, a restaurant is forecast, which should be open sometime in 2014.

Late in the afternoon is the least crowded time to visit. For a €4 fee, advance tickets can be reserved by phone, online, or, once in Florence, at the Uffizi reservation booth (*advance tickets* ✉ *Consorzio ITA, Piazza Pitti 1* ☎ *055/294883)* at least one day in advance of your visit. Keep the confirmation number and take it with you to the door at the museum marked "Reservations." In the past, you were ushered in almost immediately. But overbooking (especially in high season) has led to long lines and long waits even with a reservation, but you may pay by credit card. When there's a special exhibit on, which is often, the base ticket price goes up to €11. ✉ *Piazzale degli Uffizi 6, Piazza della Signoria* ☎ *055/23885* ⊕ *www.uffizi.firenze.it* 🎫 *€11 during special exhibitions; reservation fee €4* ☉ *Tues.–Sun. 8:15–6:50.*

Piazza della Signoria. This is by far the most striking square in Florence. It was here, in 1497, that the famous "bonfire of the vanities" took place, when the fanatical friar Savonarola induced his followers to hurl their worldly goods into the flames; it was also here, a year later, that he was hanged as a heretic and, ironically, burned. A bronze plaque in the piazza pavement marks the exact spot of his execution.

The statues in the square and in the 14th-century **Loggia dei Lanzi** on the south side vary in quality. Cellini's famous bronze *Perseus* holding the severed head of Medusa is certainly the most important sculpture in the loggia. Other works here include *The Rape of the Sabine* and *Hercules and the Centaur,* both late-16th-century works by Giambologna (1529–1608), and in the back, a row of sober matrons dating from Roman times.

In the square, the Neptune Fountain, created between 1550 and 1575, takes something of a booby prize. It was created by Bartolomeo Ammannati, who considered it a failure himself. The Florentines call it

il Biancone, which may be translated as "the big white man" or "the big white lump." Giambologna's equestrian statue, to the left of the fountain, portrays Grand Duke Cosimo I. Occupying the steps of the Palazzo Vecchio are a copy of Donatello's proud heraldic lion of Florence, the *Marzocco* (the original is now in the Bargello); a copy of Donatello's *Judith and Holofernes* (the original is in the Palazzo Vecchio); a copy of Michelangelo's *David* (the original is in the Galleria dell'Accademia); and Baccio Bandinelli's *Hercules* (1534). The Marzocco, the Judith, and the David were symbols of Florentine civic pride—the latter two subjects had stood up to their oppressors. They provided apt metaphors for the republic-loving Florentines, who often chafed at Medici hegemony.

Ponte Vecchio (*Old Bridge*). This charmingly simple bridge was built in 1345 to replace an earlier bridge swept away by flood. Its shops first housed butchers, then grocers, blacksmiths, and other merchants. But in 1593 the Medici grand duke Ferdinand I (1549–1609), whose private corridor linking the Medici palace (Palazzo Pitti) with the Medici offices (the Uffizi) crossed the bridge atop the shops, decided that all this plebeian commerce under his feet was unseemly. So he threw out the butchers and blacksmiths and installed 41 goldsmiths and eight jewelers. The bridge has been devoted solely to these two trades ever since.

The **Corridoio Vasariano** (✉ *Piazzale degli Uffizi 6, Piazza della Signoria* ☎ *055/23885 or 055/294883*), the private Medici elevated passageway, was built by Vasari in 1565. Though the ostensible reason for its construction was one of security, it was more likely designed so that the Medici family wouldn't have to walk amid the commoners. The corridor is notoriously fickle with its operating hours; at this writing, it is temporarily open but only to groups. It can sometimes be visited by prior special arrangement. Call for the most up-to-date details. Take a moment to study the Ponte Santa Trinita, the next bridge downriver, from either the bridge or the corridor. It was designed by Bartolomeo Ammannati in 1567 (probably from sketches by Michelangelo), blown up by the retreating Germans during World War II, and painstakingly reconstructed after the war. The view from the Ponte Santa Trinita is beautiful, which might explain why so many young lovers seem to hang out there.

WORTH NOTING

Badia Fiorentina. Originally endowed by Willa, Marquess of Tuscany, in 978, this ancient church is an interesting mélange of 13th-century, Renaissance, baroque, and 18th-century architectural refurbishing. Its graceful bell tower, best seen from the interior courtyard, is beautiful for its unusual construction—a hexagonal tower built on a quadrangular base. The interior of the church (open Monday afternoon only) was halfheartedly remodeled in the baroque style during the 17th century. Three tombs by Mino da Fiesole (circa 1430–84) line the walls, including the *monumento funebre di Conte Ugo* (tomb sculpture of Count Ugo), widely regarded as Mino's masterpiece. Executed in 1469–81, it shows Mino at his most lyrical: the faces seem to be lit from within—no small feat in marble. The best-known work of art here is the delicate *Vision of St. Bernard,* by Filippino Lippi (circa 1457–1504), on the left as you enter. The painting—one of Filippino's finest—is in superb

Continued on page 57

THE DUOMO
FLORENCE'S BIGGEST MASTERPIECE

For all its monumental art and architecture, Florence has one undisputed centerpiece: the Cathedral of Santa Maria del Fiore, better known as the Duomo. Its cupola dominates the skyline, presiding over the city's rooftops like a red hen over her brood. Little wonder that when Florentines feel homesick, they say they have *"nostalgia del cupolone."*

The Duomo's construction began in 1296, following the design of Arnolfo da Cambio, Florence's greatest architect of the time. By modern standards, construction was slow and haphazard—it continued through the 14th and into the 15th century, with some dozen architects having a hand in the project.

In 1366 Neri di Fioravante created a model for the hugely ambitious cupola: it was to be the largest dome in the world, surpassing Rome's Pantheon. But when the time finally came to build the dome in 1418, no one was sure how—or even if—it could be done. Florence was faced with a 143-ft hole in the roof of its cathedral, and one of the greatest challenges in the history of architecture.

Fortunately, local genius Filippo Brunelleschi was just the man for the job. Brunelleschi won the 1418 competition to design the dome, and for the next 18 years he oversaw its construction. The enormity of his achievement can hardly be overstated. Working on such a large scale (the dome weighs 37,000 tons and uses 4 million bricks) required him to invent hoists and cranes that were engineering marvels. A "dome within a dome" design and a novel herringbone bricklaying pattern were just two of the innovations used to establish structural integrity. Perhaps most remarkably, he executed the construction without a supporting wooden framework, which had previously been thought indispensable.

Brunelleschi designed the lantern atop the dome, but he died soon after its first stone was laid in 1446; it wouldn't be completed until 1461. Another 400 years passed before the Duomo received its façade, a 19th-century neo-Gothic creation.

DUOMO TIMELINE

1296 Work begins, following design by Arnolfo di Cambio.

1302 Arnolfo dies; work continues, with sporadic interruptions.

1331 Management of construction taken over by the Wool Merchants guild.

1334 Giotto appointed project overseer, designs campanile.

1337 Giotto dies; Andrea Pisano takes leadership role.

1348 The Black Plague; all work ceases.

1366 Vaulting on nave completed; Neri di Fioravante makes model for dome.

1417 Drum for dome completed.

1418 Competition is held to design the dome.

1420 Brunelleschi begins work on the dome.

1436 Dome completed.

1446 Construction of lantern begins; Brunelleschi dies.

1461 Antonio Manetti, a student of Brunelleschi, completes lantern.

1469 Gilt copper ball and cross added by Verrocchio.

1587 Original façade is torn down by Medici court.

1871 Emilio de Fabris wins competition to design new façade.

1887 Façade completed.

WHAT TO LOOK FOR INSIDE THE DUOMO

The interior of the Duomo is a fine example of Florentine Gothic with a beautiful marble floor, but the space feels strangely barren—a result of its great size and the fact that some of the best art has been moved to the nearby **Museo dell'Opera del Duomo**.

Notable among the works that remain are two towering equestrian frescoes of famous mercenaries: *Niccolò da Tolentino* (1456), by Andrea del Castagno, and *Sir John Hawkwood* (1436), by Paolo Uccello. There's also fine terra-cotta work by Luca della Robbia. Ghiberti,

Brunelleschi's great rival, is responsible for much of the stained glass, as well as a reliquary urn with gorgeous reliefs. A vast fresco of the Last Judgment, painted by Vasari and Zuccari, covers the dome's interior. Brunelleschi had wanted mosaics to go there; it's a pity he didn't get his wish.

In the crypt beneath the cathedral, you can explore excavations of a Roman wall and mosaic fragments from the late sixth century; entry is near the first pier on the right. On the way down you pass Brunelleschi's modest tomb.

1. Entrance; stained glass by Ghiberti
2. Fresco of Niccolò da Tolentino by Andrea del Castagno
3. Fresco of John Hawkwood by Paolo Uccello
4. *Dante and the Divine Comedy* by Domenico di Michelino
5. Lunette: *Ascension* by Luca della Robbia
6. Above altar: two angels by Luca della Robbia. Below the altar: reliquary of St. Zenobius by Ghiberti.
7. Lunette: *Resurrection* by Luca della Robbia
8. Entrance to dome
9. Bust of Brunelleschi by Buggiano
10. Stairs to crypt
11. Campanile

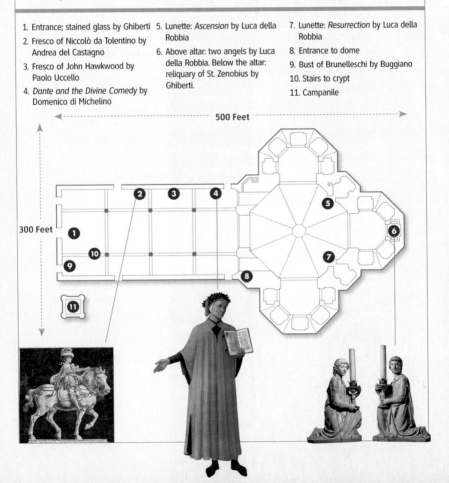

MAKING THE CLIMB

Climbing the 463 steps to the top of the dome is not for the faint of heart—or for the claustrophobic—but those who do it will be awarded a smashing view of Florence ❶. Keep in mind that the way up is also the way down, which means that while you're huffing and puffing in the ascent, people very close to you in a narrow staircase are making their way down ❷.

300 Feet

75 Feet

DUOMO BASICS

- Even first thing in the morning during high season (May through September), a line is likely to have formed to climb the dome. Expect an hour wait.

- For an alternative to the dome, consider climbing the less trafficked campanile, which gives you a view from on high of the dome itself.

- Dress code essentials: covered shoulders, no short shorts, and hats off upon entering.

✉ Piazza del Duomo
☎ 055/2302885
⊕ www.operaduomo.firenze.it
🎫 Free, crypt €3, cupola €8
🕐 Crypt: Mon.–Wed., Fri., Sun. 10–5; Thurs. 10–4:30; Sat. 10–5:45; first Sat. of month 10–3:30. Cupola: Weekdays 8:30–7, Sat. 8:30–5:40, 1st Sat. of month 8:30–4. Duomo: Mon.–Wed. and Fri. 10–5, Thurs. 10–4:30, Sat., 10–4:45, Sun 1:30–4:45, 1st Sat. of month 10–3:30.

BRUNELLESCHI vs. GHIBERTI
The Rivalry of Two Renaissance Geniuses

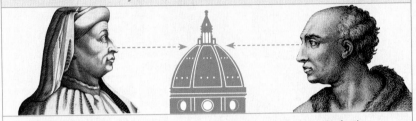

In Renaissance Florence, painters, sculptors, and architects competed for major commissions, with the winner earning the right to undertake a project that might occupy him (and keep him paid) for a decade or more. Stakes were high, and the resulting rivalries fierce—none more so than that between Filippo Brunelleschi and Lorenzo Ghiberti.

The two first clashed in 1401, for the commission to create the bronze doors of the Baptistery. When Ghiberti won, Brunelleschi took it hard, fleeing to Rome, where he would remain for 15 years. Their rematch came in 1418, over the design of the Duomo's cupola, with Brunelleschi triumphant. For the remainder of their lives, the two would miss no opportunity to belittle each other's work.

FILIPPO BRUNELLESCHI (1377–1446)

MASTERPIECE: The dome of Santa Maria del Fiore.

BEST FRIENDS: Donatello, whom he stayed with in Rome after losing the Baptistery doors competition; the Medici family, who rescued him from bankruptcy.

SIGNATURE TRAITS: Paranoid, secretive, bad tempered, practical joker, inept businessman.

SAVVIEST POLITICAL MOVE: Feigned sickness and left for Rome after his dome plans were publicly criticized by Ghiberti, who was second-in-command. The project proved too much for Ghiberti to manage on his own, and Brunelleschi returned triumphant.

MOST EMBARRASSING MOMENT: In 1434 he was imprisoned for two weeks for failure to pay a small guild fee. The humiliation might have been orchestrated by Ghiberti.

OTHER CAREER: Shipbuilder. He built a huge vessel, *Il Badalone*, to transport marble for the dome up the Arno. It sank on its first voyage.

INSPIRED: The dome of St. Peter's in Rome.

LORENZO GHIBERTI (1378–1455)

MASTERPIECE: *The Gates of Paradise,* the ten-paneled east doors of the Baptistery.

BEST FRIEND: Giovanni da Prato, an underling who wrote diatribes attacking the dome's design and Brunelleschi's character.

SIGNATURE TRAITS: Instigator, egoist, know-it-all, shrewd businessman.

SAVVIEST POLITICAL MOVE: During the Baptistery doors competition, he had an open studio and welcomed opinions on his work, while Brunelleschi labored behind closed doors.

OTHER CAREER: Collector of classical artifacts, historian.

INSPIRED: *The Gates of Hell* by Auguste Rodin.

The Gates of Paradise detail

condition; note the Virgin Mary's hands, perhaps the most beautifully rendered in the city. On the right side of the church, above the **cappella di San Mauro,** is a monumental organ dating from 1558. Constructed by Onofrio Zeffirini da Cortona (1510–86), it's largely intact but is missing its 16th-century keyboard. ⊠ *Via Dante Alighieri 1, Bargello* ☎ *055/264402* ⊗ *Mon. 3–6.*

Campanile. The Gothic bell tower designed by Giotto (circa 1266–1337) is a soaring structure of multicolor marble originally decorated

with sculptures by Donatello and reliefs by Giotto, Andrea Pisano, and others (which are now in the Museo dell'Opera del Duomo). A climb of 414 steps rewards you with a close-up of Brunelleschi's cupola on the Duomo next door and a sweeping view of the city. ⊠ *Piazza del Duomo* ☎ *055/2302885* ⊕ *www.operaduomo.firenze.it* ⊠ *€10* ⊗ *Daily 8:30–7:30.*

NEED A BREAK?

Gucci Caffè. It's got a view of a piazza that doesn't quit (Piazza della Signoria), indoor and outdoor seating, and a menu that caters to every whim. They offer fine pastas, as well as meat and fish dishes; sandwiches and other light fare are also on the menu. This is a perfect place to have a rest before charging on to the next sight. Order a glass of wine, and the little nibbles that accompany restore the soul. ⊠ *Piazza della Signoria 10* ☎ *055/75923827* ⊕ *www.gucci.com.*

Gucci Museo. Open since September 2011, this museum has all the class and elegance associated with the Gucci name. Tasteful displays of their famous luggage, shoes, and sporting goods (including snorkels and flippers) fill this 14th-century building called the Palazzo del Tribunale di Mercatanzia. Centuries ago, the place heard and tried cases by disgruntled guildsmen, and it's an odd juxtaposition to see an early 15th-century fresco of Christ crucified in a room filled with 20th-century jewelry. You can also see Hillary Swank's 2011 Academy Awards dress, as well as several others in a dramatically lit room. Also on hand are rooms for temporary exhibitions, a bookstore devoted mostly to things fashionista, and a café serving light lunches and other, more substantial fare. ⊠ *Piazza della Signoria 10* ☎ *055/75923300* ⊕ *www.gucci.com* ⊠ *€6* ⊗ *Museum: Daily 10–8. Café/Restaurant and Bookstore: Daily 10 am–11 pm.*

FAMILY **Mercato Nuovo** (*New Market*). The open-air loggia, built in 1551, teems with souvenir stands, but the real attraction is a copy of Pietro Tacca's bronze *Porcellino* (which translates as "little pig" despite the fact the animal is, in fact, a wild boar). The *Porcellino* is Florence's equivalent of the Trevi Fountain: put a coin in his mouth, and if it falls through the grate below (according to one interpretation), it means you'll return to Florence someday. What you're seeing is a copy of a copy: Tacca's original version, in the Museo Bardini, is actually a copy of an ancient Greek work. ⊠ *Corner of Via Por Santa Maria and Via Porta Rossa, Piazza della Repubblica* ⊘ *Market: Tues.–Sat. 8–7, Mon. 1–7.*

FAMILY **Museo dei Ragazzi.** Florence's "Children's Museum" may be the best-kept public access secret in Florence. A series of interactive tours includes "Encounters with History," during which participants meet and talk with Giorgio Vasari or Galileo Galilei and explore secret passageways. Events occur at different venues (Palazzo Vecchio, Museo Stibbert, Cappella Brancacci, and the Museo Galileo). Tours are in English and must be booked in advance. Though most of the tours are geared for the 3- to 8-year-old crowd, adults will find it lots of fun, too. ⊠ *Piazza della Signoria 1* ☎ *055/2768224* ⊕ *www.museoragazzi.it* ⊠ €6 ⊘ *By reservation only.*

Museo dell'Opera del Duomo (*Cathedral Museum*). At press time, the museum was undergoing some serious expansion, and the results will be splendid when work is completed in October 2015. In the meantime, you can still see two of the museum's greatest treasures, Lorenzo Ghiberti's newly and brilliantly restored *Doors of Paradise* and Michelangelo's *Pietà*, which are on temporary display. Michelangelo's heart-wrenching *Pietà* (not to be confused with his more famous *Pietà* in St. Peter's in Rome) was unfinished at his death; the female figure supporting the body of Christ on the left was added by Tiberio Calcagni (1532–65), and never has the difference between competence and genius been manifested so clearly. ⊠ *Piazza del Duomo 9* ☎ *055/2302885* ⊕ *www.operaduomo.firenze.it* ⊠ €10 ⊘ *Mon.–Sat. 9–7:30, Sun. 9–1:45.*

Museo Galileo. Although it tends to be obscured by the glamour of the neighboring Uffizi, this science museum has much to commend it: Galileo's own instruments, antique armillary spheres—some of them real works of art—and other reminders that the Renaissance made not only artistic but also scientific history. ⊠ *Piazza dei Giudici 1, Piazza della Signoria* ☎ *055/265311* ⊕ *www.museogalileo.it* ⊠ €9 ⊘ *Mon., Wed., and Fri.–Sat. 9:30–6, Tues. 9:30–1.*

Oratorio dei Buonomini di San Martino. Founded in 1441 by Antoninus, Bishop of Florence, to offer alms to the *poveri vergognosi* (the ashamed poor), this one-room oratory is decorated with 15th-century frescoes by the school of Ghirlandaio that vividly depict the confraternity's activities. More than 500 years later, the Compagnia dei Buonomini, or Confraternity of the Good Men, continues to perform charitable works, linking Renaissance notions of charity to the 21st century. ⊠ *Piazza San Martino, Bargello* ⊠ *Free* ⊘ *Mon.–Thurs. and Sat. 10–noon and 3–5, Fri. 10–noon.*

Orsanmichele. This multipurpose structure began as an 8th-century oratory and then in 1290 was turned into an open-air loggia for selling grain. Destroyed by fire in 1304, it was rebuilt as a loggia-market. Between 1367 and 1380 the arcades were closed and two stories were added above; finally, at century's end it was turned into a church. Inside is a beautifully detailed 14th-century Gothic tabernacle by Andrea Orcagna (1308–68). The exterior niches contain sculptures (all copies) dating from the early 1400s to the early 1600s by Donatello and

Verrocchio (1435–88), among others, which were paid for by the guilds. Although it is a copy, Verrocchio's *Doubting Thomas* (circa 1470) is particularly deserving of attention. Here you see Christ, like the building's other figures, entirely framed within the niche, and St. Thomas standing on its bottom

ledge, with his right foot outside the niche frame. This one detail, the positioning of a single foot, brings the whole composition to life. It's possible to see the original sculptures at the **Museo di Orsanmichele,** which is open Mondays only. ⊠ *Via dei Calzaiuoli, Piazza della Repubblica* ☎ *055/284944* ⊘ *Museum: Mon. 10–5.*

Ospedale Santa Maria Nuova. Folco Portinari, the father of Dante's Beatrice, founded this sprawling complex in 1288. It was originally a hostel for visiting pilgrims and travelers. During the Black Death of 1348 it served as a hospice for those afflicted. At another point it served as an office where money could be exchanged and deposited and letters could be received; Michelangelo did his banking here. It had been lavishly decorated by the top Florentine artists of the day, but most of the works, such as the frescoes by Domenico Veneziano and Piero della Francesca, have disappeared or been moved to the Uffizi for safekeeping. Today it functions as a hospital in the modern sense of the word, but you can visit the single-nave church of **Sant'Egidio,** in the middle of the complex, where the frescoes would have stood. Imagine, too, Hugo van der Goes's (1435–82) magnificent *Portinari Altarpiece,* which once crowned the high altar; it's now in the Uffizi. Commissioned by Tommaso Portinari, a descendent of Folco's, it arrived from Bruges in 1483 and created quite a stir. Bernardo Rossellino's immense marble tabernacle (1450), still in the church, is worth a look. ⊠ *Via Sant'Egidio and Piazza di Santa Maria Nuova, San Lorenzo.*

Palazzo Davanzati. The prestigious Davanzati family owned this 14th-century palace in one of Florence's swankiest medieval neighborhoods. The place is a delight, as you can wander through the surprisingly light-filled courtyard, and climb the steep stairs to the *piano nobile* (there's also an elevator), where the family did most of its living. The beautiful *Sala dei Pappagalli* (Parrot Room) is adorned with trompe-l'oeil tapestries and gaily painted birds. ⊠ *Piazza Davanzati 13, Piazza della Repubblica* ☎ *055/2388610* ⊕ *www.polomuseale.firenze.it* ✉ *€2* ⊘ *Daily 8:15–1:50. Closed 1st, 3rd, and 5th Sun. and 2nd and 4th Mon. of month.*

Palazzo Vecchio (*Old Palace*). Florence's forbidding, fortresslike city hall was begun in 1299, presumably designed by Arnolfo di Cambio, and its massive bulk and towering campanile dominate Piazza della Signoria. It was built as a meeting place for the guildsmen governing the city at the time; today it is still City Hall. The interior courtyard is a good deal less severe, having been remodeled by Michelozzo (1396–1472) in 1453; a copy of Verrocchio's bronze *puttino* (cherub), topping the central fountain, softens the space. (The original is upstairs.)

The main attraction is on the second floor: two adjoining rooms that supply one of the most startling contrasts in Florence. The first is the opulently vast **Sala dei Cinquecento** (Room of the Five Hundred), named for the 500-member Great Council, the people's assembly established after the death of Lorenzo the Magnificent, that met here. Giorgio Vasari and others decorated the room, around 1563–65, with gargantuan frescoes celebrating Florentine history; depictions of battles with nearby cities predominate. Continuing the martial theme, the room also contains Michelangelo's *Victory*, intended for the never-completed tomb of Pope Julius II (1443–1513), plus other sculptures of decidedly lesser quality.

In comparison, the little **Studiolo,** just off the Sala dei Cinquecento's entrance, was a private room meant for the duke and those whom he invited in. Here's where the melancholy Francesco I (1541–87), son of Cosimo I, stored his priceless treasures and conducted scientific experiments. Designed by Vasari, it was decorated by him, Giambologna, and many others. ✉ *Piazza della Signoria* ☎ *055/2768465* ⊕ *museicivicifiorentini.comune.fi.it* 🖥 *€6* ⊗ *Mon.–Wed. and Fri.–Sun. 9–7, Thurs. 9–2.*

Piazza della Repubblica. The square marks the site of the ancient forum that was the core of the original Roman settlement. While the street plan around the piazza still reflects the carefully plotted Roman military encampment, the Mercato Vecchio (Old Market), which had been here since the Middle Ages, was demolished and the current piazza was constructed between 1885 and 1895 as a neoclassical showpiece. The piazza is lined with outdoor cafés, affording an excellent opportunity for people-watching.

San Michele Visdomini. Aficionados of 16th-century mannerism should stop in this church, which has a *Sacra Conversazione* by Jacopo Pontormo (1494–1556). The early work, said by Vasari to have been executed on paper, is in dire need of a cleaning. Its palette is somewhat bereft of the lively colors typically associated with Pontormo. ✉ *Via dei Servi at Via Bufalini, Duomo* ⊗ *Daily 7–noon and 3–6.*

SAN LORENZO

A sculptor, painter, architect, and poet, Florentine native son Michelangelo was a consummate genius, and some of his finest creations remain in his hometown. The Biblioteca Medicea Laurenziana is perhaps his most fanciful work of architecture. A key to understanding Michelangelo's genius can be found in the magnificent Cappelle Medicee, where both his sculptural and architectural prowess can be clearly seen. Planned frescoes were never completed, sadly, for they would have shown in one space the artistic triple threat that he certainly was. The towering yet graceful *David,* perhaps his most famous work, resides in the Galleria dell'Accademia.

After visiting San Lorenzo, resist the temptation to explore the market that surrounds the church: the market is open until 7 pm, while the churches and museums you may want to visit are not. Come back to the market later, after other sites have closed. Note that the Museo di San Marco closes at 1:50 on weekdays.

2

TOP ATTRACTIONS

Cappelle Medicee (*Medici Chapels*). This magnificent complex includes the **Cappella dei Principi**, the Medici chapel and mausoleum that was begun in 1605 and kept marble workers busy for several hundred years, and the **Sagrestia Nuova** (New Sacristy), designed by Michelangelo and so called to distinguish it from Brunelleschi's Sagrestia Vecchia (Old Sacristy) in San Lorenzo.

Michelangelo received the commission for the New Sacristy in 1520 from Cardinal Giulio de' Medici (1478–1534), who later became Pope Clement VII. The cardinal wanted a new burial chapel for his cousins Giuliano, Duke of Nemours (1478–1534), and Lorenzo, Duke of Urbino (1492–1519), and he also wanted to honor his father, also named Giuliano, and his uncle, Lorenzo il Magnifico. The result was a tour de force of architecture and sculpture. Architecturally, Michelangelo was as original and inventive here as ever, but it is, quite properly, the powerfully sculpted tombs that dominate the room. The scheme is allegorical: on the tomb on the right are figures representing Day and Night, and on the tomb to the left are figures representing Dawn and Dusk; above them are idealized sculptures of the two men, usually interpreted to represent the active life and the contemplative life. But the allegorical meanings are secondary; what is most important is the intense presence of the sculptural figures and the force with which they hit the viewer. Ticket prices jump to €9 when special exhibitions are on—which is frequently. ⊠ *Piazza di Madonna degli Aldobrandini, San Lorenzo* ☎ *055/294883 reservations* 🎟 *€6; €9 during special exhibits* ⊙ *Daily 8:15–1:50. Closed 1st, 3rd, and 5th Mon. and 2nd and 4th Sun. of month.*

FAMILY **Galleria dell'Accademia** (*Accademia Gallery*). The collection of Florentine paintings, dating from the 13th to the 18th centuries, is largely unremarkable, but the sculptures by Michelangelo are worth the price of admission. The unfinished *Slaves*, fighting their way out of their marble prisons, were meant for the tomb of Michelangelo's overly demanding patron Pope Julius II (1443–1513). But the focal point is the original *David*, moved here from Piazza della Signoria in 1873. *David* was commissioned in 1501 by the Opera del Duomo (Cathedral Works Committee), which gave the 26-year-old sculptor a leftover block of marble that had been ruined forty years earlier by two other sculptors. Michelangelo's success with the block was so dramatic that the city showered him with honors, and the Opera del Duomo voted to build him a house and a studio in which to live and work.

Today *David* is beset not by Goliath but by tourists, and seeing the statue at all—much less really studying it—can be a trial. Save yourself a long wait in line by reserving tickets in advance. A Plexiglas barrier surrounds the sculpture, following a 1991 attack on it by a self-proclaimed hammer-wielding art anarchist who, luckily, inflicted only a few minor nicks on the toes. The statue is not quite what it seems. It is so poised and graceful and alert—so miraculously alive—that it is often considered the definitive sculptural embodiment of the High Renaissance perfection. But its true place in the history of art is a bit more complicated.

San Lorenzo

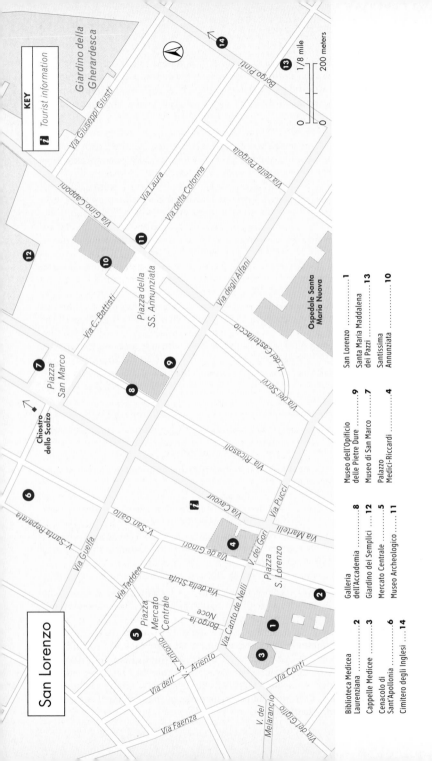

KEY

🚹 Tourist information

Giardino della Gherardesca

Chiostro dello Scalzo

Piazza San Marco

Piazza della SS. Annunziata

Ospedale Santa Maria Nuova

Piazza Mercato Centrale

Piazza S. Lorenzo

0   1/8 mile
0   200 meters

Biblioteca Medicea
Laurenziana **2**
Cappelle Medicee **3**
Cenacolo di
Sant'Apollonia **6**
Cimitero degli Inglesi **14**

Galleria
dell'Accademia **8**
Giardino dei Semplici **12**
Mercato Centrale **5**
Museo Archeologico **11**

Museo dell'Opificio
delle Pietre Dure **9**
Museo di San Marco **7**
Palazzo
Medici-Riccardi **4**

San Lorenzo **1**
Santa Maria Maddalena
dei Pazzi **13**
Santissima
Annunziata **10**

2

As Michelangelo well knew, the Renaissance painting and sculpture that preceded his work were deeply concerned with ideal form. Perfection of proportion was the ever-sought Holy Grail; during the Renaissance, ideal proportion was equated with ideal beauty, and ideal beauty was equated with spiritual perfection. But *David*, despite its supremely calm and dignified pose, departs from these ideals. Michelangelo didn't give the statue perfect proportions. The head is slightly too large for the body, the arms are too large for the torso, and the hands are dramatically large for the arms. The work was originally commissioned to adorn the exterior of the Duomo and was intended to be seen from a distance and on high. Michelangelo knew exactly what he was doing, calculating that the perspective of the viewer would be such that, in order for the statue to appear proportioned, the upper body, head, and arms would have to be bigger, as they are farther away from the viewer. But he also did it to express and embody, as powerfully as possible in a single figure, an entire biblical story. David's hands *are* big, but so was Goliath, and these are the hands that slew him. Music lovers might want to check out the Museo degli Instrumenti Musicali contained within the Accademia; its Stradivarius is the main attraction. ⊠ *Via Ricasoli 60, San Marco* ☎ *055/294883 reservations, 055/2388609 gallery* ⊕ *www.gallerieaccademia.org* ⊠ *€11, reservation fee €4* ☉ *Tues.– Sun. 8:15–6:50.*

Museo di San Marco. A Dominican convent adjacent to the church of San Marco now houses this museum, which contains many stunning works by Fra Angelico (circa 1400–55), the Dominican friar famous for his piety as well as for his painting. When the friars' cells were restructured between 1439 and 1444, he decorated many of them with frescoes meant to spur religious contemplation. His unostentatious and direct paintings exalt the simple beauties of the contemplative life. Fra Angelico's works are everywhere, from the friars' cells to the superb panel paintings on view in the museum. Don't miss the famous *Annunciation,* on the upper floor, and the works in the gallery off the cloister as you enter. Here you can see his beautiful *Last Judgment*; as usual, the tortures of the damned are far more inventive and interesting than the pleasures of the redeemed. ⊠ *Piazza San Marco 1* ☎ *055/2388608* ⊠ *€4* ☉ *Weekdays 8:15–1:15, Sat. 8:15–4:15. Closed 1st, 3rd, and 5th Sun., and 2nd and 4th Mon. of month.*

San Lorenzo. Filippo Brunelleschi designed this basilica, as well as that of Santo Spirito in the Oltrarno, in the 15th century. He never lived to see either finished. The two interiors are similar in design and effect. San Lorenzo, however, has a grid of dark, inlaid marble lines on the floor, which considerably heightens the dramatic effect. The grid makes the rigorous geometry of the interior immediately visible, and is an illuminating lesson on the laws of perspective. If you stand in the middle of the nave at the church entrance, on the line that stretches to the high altar, every element in the church—the grid, the nave columns, the side aisles, the coffered nave ceiling—seems to march inexorably toward a hypothetical vanishing point beyond the high altar, exactly as in a single-point-perspective painting. Brunelleschi's **Sagrestia Vecchia** (Old Sacristy) has stucco decorations by Donatello; it's at the end of the left

CLOSE UP

Florence's Trial by Fire

One of the most striking figures of Renaissance Florence was Girolamo Savonarola, a Dominican friar who, for a moment, captured the spiritual conscience of the city. In 1491 he became prior of the convent of San Marco, where he adopted a life of austerity and delivered sermons condemning Florence's excesses and the immorality of his fellow clergy. Following the death of Lorenzo de' Medici in 1492, Savonarola was instrumental in the re-formation of the republic of Florence, ruled by a representative council with Christ enthroned as monarch. In one of his most memorable acts he urged Florentines to toss worldly possessions—from sumptuous dresses to Botticelli paintings—onto a "bonfire of the vanities" in Piazza della Signoria. Savonarola's antagonism toward church hierarchy led to his undoing: he was excommunicated in 1497, and the following year was hanged and burned on charges of heresy. Today, at the Museo di San Marco, you can visit Savonarola's cell.

transept. ⊠ *Piazza San Lorenzo* 🕾 *055/2645144* 💶 *€4.50* 🕙 *Mon.–Sat. 10–5 year round; Mar.–Oct., Sun. 1:30–5. Closed Sun. Nov.–Feb.*

WORTH NOTING

Biblioteca Medicea Laurenziana (*Laurentian Library*). Michelangelo the architect was every bit as original as Michelangelo the sculptor. Unlike Brunelleschi (the architect of the Spedale degli Innocenti), however, he wasn't obsessed with proportion and perfect geometry. He was interested in experimentation and invention and in the expression of a personal vision that was at times highly idiosyncratic.

It was never more idiosyncratic than in the Laurentian Library, begun in 1524 and finished in 1568 by Bartolomeo Ammannati. Its famous **vestibolo,** a strangely shaped anteroom, has had scholars scratching their heads for centuries. In a space more than two stories high, why did Michelangelo limit his use of columns and pilasters to the upper two-thirds of the wall? Why didn't he rest them on strong pedestals instead of on huge, decorative curlicue scrolls, which rob them of all visual support? Why did he recess them into the wall, which makes them look weaker still? The architectural elements here do not stand firm and strong and tall, as inside San Lorenzo, next door; instead, they seem to be pressed into the wall as if into putty, giving the room a soft, rubbery look that is one of the strangest effects ever achieved by 16th-century architecture. It's almost as if Michelangelo intentionally flouted the conventions of the High Renaissance to see what kind of bizarre, mannered effect might result. His innovations were tremendously influential, and produced a period of architectural experimentation. As his contemporary Giorgio Vasari put it, "Artisans have been infinitely and perpetually indebted to him because he broke the bonds and chains of a way of working that had become habitual by common usage."

The anteroom's staircase (best viewed straight-on), which emerges from the library with the visual force of an unstoppable lava flow, has been exempted from the criticism, however. In its highly sculptural conception and execution, it is quite simply one of the most original and fluid staircases in the world. ✉ *Piazza San Lorenzo 9, entrance to left of San Lorenzo* ☎ *055/210760* ⊕ *www.bml.firenze.sbn.it* ✉ *Special exhibitions €3* ⊙ *Sun.–Fri. 9–1.*

Cenacolo di Sant'Apollonia. The frescoes of the refectory of a former Benedictine nunnery were painted in sinewy style by Andrea del Cast-

agno, a follower of Masaccio (1401–28). The *Last Supper* is a powerful version of this typical refectory theme. From the entrance, walk around the corner to Via San Gallo 25 and take a peek at the lovely 15th-century cloister that belonged to the same monastery but is now part of the University of Florence. ✉ *Via XXVII Aprile 1, San Marco* ☎ *055/2388607* ⊙ *Daily 8:15–1:50. Closed 1st, 3rd, and 5th Sun. of month, and 2nd and 4th Mon. of month.*

Giardino dei Semplici. Created by Cosimo I in 1550, this delightful garden was designed by favorite Medici architect Niccolò Tribolo. Many of the plants here have been grown since the 16th century. Springtime, especially May, is a particularly beautiful time to visit, as multitudes of azaleas create a riot of color. ✉ *Via Pier Micheli 3, San Marco* ☎ *055/2757402* ⊕ *www.unifi.it* ✉ *€6* ⊙ *Thurs.–Tues. 9–1.*

Fodor'sChoice ★ **Mercato Centrale.** Some of the food at this huge, two-story market hall is remarkably exotic. The ground floor contains meat and cheese stalls, as well as some very good bars that have *panini* (sandwiches), and the second floor teems with vegetable stands. At press time, the second floor was closed for renovations. ✉ *Piazza del Mercato Centrale, San Lorenzo* ⊙ *Mon.–Sat. 7–2.*

Museo Archeologico (*Archaeological Museum*). Of the Etruscan, Egyptian, and Greco-Roman antiquities here, the Etruscan collection is particularly notable—one of the most important in Italy (the other being in Turin). The famous bronze *Chimera* was discovered (without the tail, which is a 16th-century reconstruction by Cellini). If you're traveling with kids, they might particularly enjoy the small mummy collection. Those with a fondness for gardens should visit on Saturday morning, when the tiny but eminently pleasurable garden is open for tours. ✉ *Piazza Santissima Annunziata 9/b* ☎ *055/23575* ⊕ *www.archeotoscana. beniculturali.it* ✉ *€4* ⊙ *Tues.–Fri. 8:30–7, weekends 8:30–2.*

Museo dell'Opificio delle Pietre Dure. Adjacent to this fascinating small museum is an *opificio*, or workshop, that Ferdinand I established in 1588 to train craftsmen in the art of working with precious and semiprecious stones and marble (*pietre dure* means "hard stones"). Four hundred–plus years later, the workshop is renowned as a center for the restoration of mosaics and inlays in semiprecious stones. The museum is highly informative, and includes some magnificent late Renaissance examples of this highly specialized and beautiful craft. ✉ *Via degli Alfani 78, San Marco* ☎ *055/26511* ⊕ *www.firenzemusei.it* ✉ *€4* ⊙ *Mon.–Sat. 8:15–1:30.*

Museo di Casa Martelli. The wealthy Martelli family, long associated with the all-powerful Medici, lived, from the 16th century, in this palace on a quiet street near the basilica of San Lorenzo. The last Martelli died in 1986, and in October 2009 the casa-museo (house-museum) opened to the public. It's the only non-reconstructed example of such a house in all of Florence, and for that reason alone it's worth a visit. The family collected art, and while most of the stuff is B-list, a couple of gems by Beccafumi, Salvatore Rosa, and Piero di Cosimo adorn the walls. Reservations are essential, and you will be shown the glories of this place by well-informed, English-speaking guides. ⊠ *Via Zanetti 8, San Lorenzo* ☎ *055/294883* ⊕ *www.uffizi.firenze.it* ⊑*€3* ⊙ *Guided tours Thurs. 2, 3:30, and 5; Sat. 9, 10:30, and noon.*

Palazzo Medici-Riccardi. The main attraction of this palace, begun in 1444 by Michelozzo for Cosimo de' Medici, is the interior chapel, the so-called **Cappella dei Magi** on the piano nobile (second) floor. Painted on its walls is Benozzo Gozzoli's famous *Procession of the Magi,* finished in 1460 and celebrating both the birth of Christ and the greatness of the Medici family. Gozzoli wasn't a revolutionary painter, and today is considered by some not quite first-rate because of his technique, which was old-fashioned even for his day. Gozzoli's gift, however, was for entrancing the eye, not challenging the mind, and on those terms his success here is beyond question. Entering the chapel is like walking into the middle of a magnificently illustrated children's storybook, and this beauty makes it one of the most enjoyable rooms in the city. Do note that officially only eight visitors are allowed in at a time for a maximum of seven minutes; sometimes, however, there are lenient guards. ⊠ *Via Cavour 1, San Lorenzo* ☎ *055/2760340* ⊕ *www.palazzo-medici.it* ⊑*€7* ⊙ *Thurs.–Tues. 9–7.*

Santissima Annunziata. Dating from the mid-13th century, this church was restructured in 1447 by Michelozzo, who gave it an uncommon (and lovely) entrance cloister with frescoes by Andrea del Sarto (1486–1530), Pontormo (1494–1556), and Rosso Fiorentino (1494–1540). The interior is a rarity for Florence: an overwhelming example of the baroque. But it's not really a fair example, because it's merely 17th-century baroque decoration applied willy-nilly to an earlier structure—exactly the sort of violent remodeling exercise that has given the baroque a bad name. The **Cappella dell'Annunziata,** immediately inside the entrance to the left, illustrates the point. The lower half, with its stately Corinthian columns and carved frieze bearing the Medici arms, was commissioned by Piero de' Medici in 1447; the upper half, with its erupting curves and impish sculpted cherubs, was added 200 years later. Fifteenth-century-fresco enthusiasts should also note the very fine *Holy Trinity with St. Jerome* in the second chapel on the left. Done by Andrea del Castagno (circa 1421–57), it shows a wiry and emaciated St. Jerome with Paula and Eustochium, two of his closest followers. ⊠ *Piazza di Santissima Annunziata* ☎ *055/266186* ⊙ *Daily 7–12:30 and 4–6:30.*

OFF THE BEATEN PATH **Chiostro dello Scalzo.** Often overlooked, this small, peaceful 16th-century cloister was frescoed in grisaille by Andrea del Sarto (1486–1530) and Franciabigio with scenes from the life of St. John the Baptist, Florence's patron saint. ⊠ *Via Cavour 69, San Marco* ☎ *055/2388604* ⊙ *Mon., Thurs., and Sat. 8:30–1:50.*

SANTA MARIA NOVELLA

Piazza Santa Maria Novella, near the train station, suffered from a degree of squalor until a restoration several years in the making and completed in spring 2009, gave it a boost. It's now a gorgeous, pedestrian-only square, with grass (laced with roses) and plenty of places to sit and rest your feet. The streets in and around the piazza have their share of architectural treasures, including some of Florence's most tasteful palaces. Between Santa Maria Novella and the Arno is Via Tornabuoni, Florence's finest shopping street.

TOP ATTRACTIONS

Santa Maria Novella. The facade of this church looks distinctly clumsy by later Renaissance standards, and with good reason: it is an architectural hybrid. The lower half was completed mostly in the 14th century; its pointed-arch niches and decorative marble patterns reflect the Gothic style of the day. About 100 years later (around 1456), architect Leon Battista Alberti was called in to complete the job. The marble decoration of his upper story clearly defers to the already existing work below, but the architectural motifs he added evince an entirely different style. The central doorway, the four ground-floor half-columns with Corinthian capitals, the triangular pediment atop the second story, the inscribed frieze immediately below the pediment—these are borrowings from antiquity, and they reflect the new Renaissance style in architecture, born some 35 years earlier at the Spedale degli Innocenti. Alberti's most important addition—the S-curve scrolls (called volutes) surmounting the decorative circles on either side of the upper story—had no precedent whatsoever in antiquity. The problem was to soften the abrupt transition between wide ground floor and narrow upper story. Alberti's solution turned out to be definitive. Once you start to look for them, you will find scrolls such as these (or sculptural variations of them) on churches all over Italy, and every one of them derives from Alberti's example here.

The architecture of the interior is, like that of the Duomo, a dignified but somber example of Florentine Gothic. Exploration is essential, however, because the church's store of art treasures is remarkable. Highlights include the 14th-century stained-glass rose window depicting the *Coronation of the Virgin* (above the central entrance); the Cappella Filippo Strozzi (to the right of the altar), containing late-15th-century frescoes and stained glass by Filippino Lippi; the *cappella maggiore* (the area around the high altar), displaying frescoes by Ghirlandaio; and the Cappella Gondi (to the left of the altar), containing Filippo Brunelleschi's famous wood crucifix, carved around 1410 and said to have so stunned the great Donatello when he first saw it that he dropped a basket of eggs.

Of special interest for its great historical importance and beauty is Masaccio's *Trinity,* on the left-hand wall, almost halfway down the nave. Painted around 1426–27 (at the same time he was working on his frescoes in Santa Maria del Carmine), it unequivocally announced the arrival of the Renaissance. The realism of the figure of Christ was revolutionary in itself, but what was probably even more startling to

DID YOU KNOW?

Goldsmiths and jewelers have been selling their wares on the Ponte Vecchio since 1593.

contemporary Florentines was the barrel vault in the background. The mathematical rules for employing single-point perspective in painting had just been discovered (probably by Brunelleschi), and this was one of the first works of art to employ them with utterly convincing success.

In October 2012, the entire complex was opened to the public under a single ticket. The resulting visit is a revelation, as the space flows, easily and continuously, from the interior of the basilica, to the cloister outside, which leads directly to the Spanish Chapel, which in turn leads to other, previously closed-to-the-public space (including the marvelous Chiostro dei Morti).

In the the first cloister is a faded and damaged fresco cycle by Paolo Uccello depicting tales from Genesis, with a dramatic vision of the Deluge (at press time, in restoration). Earlier and better-preserved frescoes painted in 1348–55 by Andrea da Firenze are in the chapter house, or the **Cappellone degli Spagnoli** (Spanish Chapel), off the cloister. ✉ *Piazza Santa Maria Novella 19* ☎ *055/210113, 055/282187 museo* ⊕ *www.museicivicifiorentini.it* 🎫 *€5* 🕙 *Mon.–Thurs. 9–5:30, Fri. 11–5:30, Sat. 9–5, Sun. 12–5 (1–5 Oct.–June).*

Santa Trinita. Started in the 11th century by Vallombrosian monks and originally Romanesque in style, the church underwent a Gothic remodeling during the 14th century. (Remains of the Romanesque construction are visible on the interior front wall.) The major works are the fresco cycle and altarpiece in the Cappella Sassetti, the second to the high altar's right, painted by Ghirlandaio between 1480 and 1485. His work here possesses such graceful decorative appeal as well as a proud depiction of his native city (most of the cityscapes show 15th-century Florence in all her glory). The wall frescoes illustrate scenes from the life of St. Francis, and the altarpiece, depicting the *Adoration of the Shepherds*, veritably glows. ✉ *Piazza Santa Trinita, Santa Maria Novella* ☎ *055/216912* 🕙 *Mon.–Sat. 8–noon and 4–6.*

WORTH NOTING

Colonna della Giustizia. In the center of **Piazza Santa Trinita** is this column from Rome's Terme di Caracalla, given to the Medici grand duke Cosimo I by Pope Pius IV in 1560. Typical of Medici self-assurance, the name translates as the Column of Justice. The column was raised here by Cosimo in 1565 to mark the spot where he heard the news that Florentine ducal forces had prevailed over a ragtag army composed of Florentine republican exiles and their French allies at the 1554 battle of Marciano near Prato; the victory made his power in Florence all but absolute. ✉ *Piazza Santa Trinita, Santa Maria Novella.*

Croce al Trebbio. In 1338 the Dominican friars (the Dominican church of Santa Maria Novella is down the street) erected this little granite column near Piazza Santa Maria Novella to commemorate a famous local victory: it was here in 1244 that they defeated their avowed enemies, the Patarene heretics, in a bloody street brawl. ✉ *Via del Trebbio, Santa Maria Novella.*

Le Cascine. In the 16th century this vast park belonged to the Medici, who used it for hunting, one of their favorite pastimes. It was opened to the public in the 19th century. The park runs for nearly 3 km (2

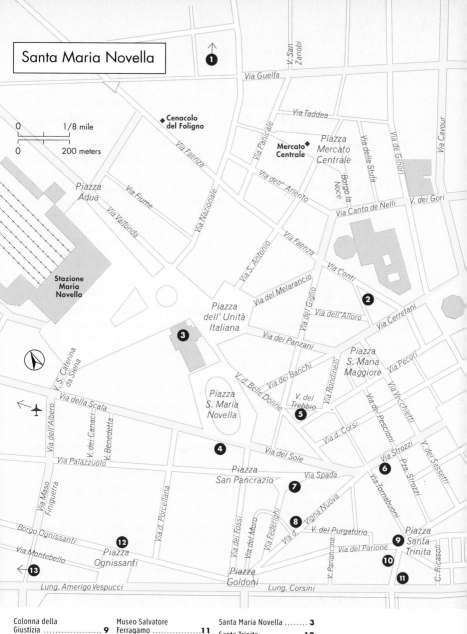

Santa Maria Novella

miles) along the Arno and has roughly 291 acres. It's ideal for strolling on sunny days, and there are paths for jogging, allées perfect for biking, grassy fields for picnicking, and lots of space for rollerblading (as well as a place to rent skates). At the northern tip of the park is the **Piazzaletto dell'Indiano,** an oddly moving monument dedicated to Rajaram Cuttraputti, Marajah of Kolepoor, who died in Florence in 1870. The park hosts sports enthusiasts, a weekly open-air market, and discotheques. But be warned: at night there's a booming sex-for-sale trade. ⊠ *Main entrance: Piazza Vittorio Veneto, Viale Fratelli Roselli (at Ponte della Vittoria).*

Museo Marino Marini. A 21-foot-tall bronze horse and rider, one of the major works by artist Marini (1901–80), dominates the space of the main gallery here. The museum itself is an eruption of contemporary space in a deconsecrated 9th-century church, designed with a series of open stairways, walkways, and balconies that allow you to peer at Marini's work from all angles. In addition to his Etruscanesque sculpture, the museum houses Marini's paintings, drawings, and engravings. ⊠ *Piazza San Pancrazio, Santa Maria Novella* ☏ *055/219432* ⊕ *www. museomarinomarini.it* ⌨ €6 ⊙ *Mon. and Wed.–Sat. 10–5.*

Museo Nazionale Alinari della Fotografia. Housed in part of what was once an ancient hospice across the piazza from the church of Santa Maria Novella, this museum hosts temporary photography exhibitions in its two largest rooms. The rest of the ground floor and the long narrow hall upstairs hold part of the museum's vast permanent collection devoted to the history of photography. There are many old cameras of all sizes dating as far back as 1820, and special niches dedicated to specific camera models. ⊠ *Piazza Santa Maria Novella 14/a* ☏ *055/216310* ⊕ *www. alinari.it* ⌨ €9 ⊙ *Thurs.–Tues. 10:30–7:30.*

Museo Salvatore Ferragamo. If there's such a thing as a temple for footwear, this is it. The shoes in this dramatically displayed collection were designed by Salvatore Ferragamo (1898–1960) beginning in the early 20th century. Born in southern Italy, the late master jump-started his career in Hollywood by creating shoes for the likes of Mary Pickford and Rudolph Valentino. He then returned to Florence and set up shop in the 13th-century Palazzo Spini Ferroni. The collection includes about 16,000 shoes, and those on exhibition are frequently rotated. Special exhibitions are also mounted here and are well worth visiting—past shows have been devoted to Audrey Hepburn, Greta Garbo, and Marilyn Monroe. ⊠ *Via dei Tornabuoni 2, Santa Maria Novella* ☏ *055/3561* ⌨ €6 ⊙ *Wed.–Mon. 10–6.*

Museo Stibbert. Federico Stibbert (1838–1906), born in Florence to an Italian mother and an English father, liked to collect things. Over a lifetime of doing so, he amassed some 50,000 objects. This museum, which was also his home, displays many of them. He had a fascination with medieval armor and also collected costumes, particularly Uzbek costumes, which are exhibited in a room called the Moresque Hall. These are mingled with an extensive collection of swords, guns, and other devices whose sole function was to kill people. The paintings, most of which date from the 15th century, are largely second-rate. The

CLOSE UP

Meet the Medici

The Medici were the dominant family of Renaissance Florence, wielding political power and financing some of the world's greatest art. You'll see their names at every turn around the city. These are some of the clan's more notable members:

Cosimo il Vecchio (1389–1464), incredibly wealthy banker to the popes, was the first in the family line to act as de facto ruler of Florence. He was a great patron of the arts and architecture; he was the moving force behind the family palace and the Dominican complex of San Marco.

Lorenzo il Magnifico (1449–92), grandson of Cosimo il Vecchio, presided over a Florence largely at peace with her neighbors. A collector of cameos, a writer of sonnets, and lover of ancient texts, he was the preeminent Renaissance man.

Leo X (1475–1521), also known as Giovanni de' Medici, became the first Medici pope, helping extend the family power base to include Rome and the Papal States. His reign was characterized by a host of problems, the biggest one being a former friar named Martin Luther.

Catherine de' Medici (1519–89) was married by her great uncle Pope Clement VII to Henry of Valois, who later became Henry II of France. Wife of one king and mother of three, she was the first Medici to marry into European royalty. Lorenzo il Magnifico, her great-grandfather, would have been thrilled.

Cosimo I (1537–74), the first grand duke of Tuscany, should not be confused with his ancestor Cosimo il Vecchio.

house itself is an interesting amalgam of neo-Gothic, Renaissance, and English eccentric. To get here, take Bus 4 (across the street from the station at Santa Maria Novella) and get off at the stop marked "Fabbroni 4." Then follow signs to the museum. ⊠ *Via Federico Stibbert 26* ☎ *055/475520* ⊕ *www.museostibbert.it* ⊠ *€8* ☉ *Mon.–Wed. 10–2, Fri.–Sun. 10–6. Tours every half hr.*

Ognissanti. The Umiliati owned this architectural hodgepodge of a church before the Franciscans took it over in the mid-16th century. (They were ousted in 2001, and replaced by the Benedictines, who moved out in 2003, only to be replaced, once again, by the Franciscans.) Beyond the fanciful baroque facade by Matteo Nigetti (1560–1649) are a couple of wonderful 15th-century gems. On the right in the nave is the *Madonna della Misericordia* by Ghirlandaio; a little farther down is Botticelli's *St. Augustine in His Study.* A companion piece, directly across the way, is Ghirlandaio's *St. Jerome.* Also check out the recently restored (as of 2011) wooden crucifix by Giotto: the colors dazzle. Pass through the rather dreadfully frescoed cloister to view Ghirlandaio's superb *Last Supper*—which proves definitively that Leonardo da Vinci was not the only Tuscan painter who could do them well. ⊠ *Piazza Ognissanti, Santa Maria Novella* ☎ *055/2398700* ⊠ *Free* ☉ *Church: daily 7–noon and 3–6; Last Supper: Mon., Tues., and Sat. 9–noon.*

Palazzo Rucellai. Architect Leon Battista Alberti (1404–72) designed perhaps the very first private residence inspired by antique models—which goes a step further than the Palazzo Strozzi. A comparison between the two is illuminating. Evident on the facade of the Palazzo Rucellai, dating between 1455 and 1470, is the ordered arrangement of windows and rusticated stonework seen on the Palazzo Strozzi, but Alberti's facade is far less forbidding. Alberti devoted a far larger proportion of his wall space to windows, which lighten the facade's appearance, and filled in the remainder with rigorously ordered classical elements borrowed from antiquity. The result, though still severe, is less fortress-like, and Alberti strove for this effect purposely (he is on record as saying that only tyrants need fortresses). Ironically, the Palazzo Rucellai was built some 30 years *before* the Palazzo Strozzi. Alberti's civilizing ideas here, it turned out, had little influence on the Florentine palazzi that followed. To Renaissance Florentines power—in architecture, as in life—was equally as impressive as beauty. While you are admiring the facade (the palazzo isn't open to the public), turn around and look at the Loggia dei Rucellai across the street. Built in 1463–66, it was the private "terrace" of the Rucellai family, in-laws to the Medici. Its soaring heights and grand arches are a firm testament to the family's status and wealth. ⊠ *Via della Vigna Nuova, Santa Maria Novella.*

Palazzo Strozzi. The Strozzi family built this imposing palazzo in an attempt to outshine the nearby Palazzo Medici. Based on a model by Giuliano da Sangallo (circa 1452–1516) dating from around 1489 and executed between 1489 and 1504 under il Cronaca (1457–1508) and Benedetto da Maiaino (1442–97), it was inspired by Michelozzo's earlier Palazzo Medici-Riccardi. The palazzo's exterior is simple, severe, and massive: it's a testament to the wealth of a patrician, 15th-century Florentine family. The interior courtyard, entered from the rear of the palazzo, is another matter altogether. It is here that the classical vocabulary—columns, capitals, pilasters, arches, and cornices—is given uninhibited and powerful expression. The palazzo frequently hosts blockbuster art shows. ⊠ *Via Tornabuoni, Piazza della Repubblica* ☎ *055/2776461* ⊕ *www.palazzostrozzi.org* 🏷 *Free, except during exhibitions* ⊙ *Daily 10–7.*

OFF THE BEATEN PATH

Cenacolo del Foligno. This delightful *Last Supper,* executed sometime in the 1470s, has been variously attributed to Perugino or to one of his followers. Its placement, at the end of a long room—the former refectory for a group of nuns—is simply breathtaking; because the white walls are otherwise unadorned, the fresco packs quite a visual punch. In the middle of the lunette in the upper center, Christ appears in the Garden of Gethsemane with the sleeping apostles. The delicate brush strokes of the leaves in the trees are exquisite. Judas, as is typical of so many representations of the Last Supper, is shown seated at the other side of the table, quite apart from the other 11 apostles. Note how the artist has carefully labeled each apostle except for Judas. The tondi surrounding the fresco show portraits of prominent Franciscans such as St. Anthony of Padua, Francis of Assisi, St. Bernardino of Siena, and St. Louis of Toulouse. ⊠ *Via Faenza 42, Santa Maria Novella* ☎ *055/286982* 🏷 *Free* ⊙ *Mon., Tues., and Sat. 9–noon.*

SANTA CROCE

2

The Santa Croce quarter, on the southeast fringe of the historic center, was built up in the Middle Ages outside the second set of medieval city walls. The centerpiece of the neighborhood was (and is) the basilica of Santa Croce, which could hold great numbers of worshipers; the vast piazza could accommodate any overflow and also served as a fairground and, allegedly since the middle of the 16th century, as a playing field for no-holds-barred soccer games. A center of leatherworking since the Middle Ages, the neighborhood is still packed with leatherworkers and leather shops.

TOP ATTRACTIONS

Piazza Santa Croce. Originally outside the city's 12th-century walls, this piazza grew with the Franciscans, who used the large square for public preaching. During the Renaissance it was used for *giostre* (jousts), including one sponsored by Lorenzo de' Medici. "Bonfires of the vanities" occurred here, as well as soccer matches in the 16th century. Lined with many palazzi dating from the 15th century, the square remains one of Florence's loveliest piazze and is a great place to people-watch.

Sinagoga. Jews were well settled in Florence by the end of the 14th century, but by 1570 they were required to live within the large "ghetto," at the north side of today's Piazza della Repubblica, by decree of Cosimo I, who had cut a deal with Pope Pius V (1504–72): in exchange for ghettoizing the Jews, he would receive the title Grand Duke of Tuscany.

Construction of the modern Moorish-style synagogue began in 1874 as a bequest of David Levi, who wished to endow a synagogue "worthy of the city." Falcini, Micheli, and Treves designed the building on a domed Greek cross plan with galleries in the transept and a roofline bearing three distinctive copper cupolas visible from all over Florence. The exterior has alternating bands of tan travertine and pink granite, reflecting an Islamic style repeated in Giovanni Panti's ornate interior. Of particular interest are the cast-iron gates by Pasquale Franci, the eternal light by Francesco Morini, and the Murano glass mosaics by Giacomo dal Medico. The gilded doors of the Moorish ark, which fronts the pulpit and is flanked by extravagant candelabra, are decorated with symbols of the ancient Temple of Jerusalem and bear bayonet marks from vandals. The synagogue was used as a garage by the Nazis, who failed to inflict much damage in spite of an attempt to blow up the place with dynamite. Only the columns on the left side were destroyed, and even then, the Women's Balcony above did not collapse. Note the Star of David in black and yellow marble inlay on the floor. The original capitals can be seen in the garden.

Some of the oldest and most beautiful Jewish ritual artifacts in all of Europe are displayed upstairs in the small **Museo Ebraico.** Exhibits document the Florentine Jewish community and the building of the synagogue. The donated objects all belonged to local families and date from as early as the late 16th century. Take special note of the exquisite needlework and silver pieces. A small but well-stocked gift shop is downstairs. ✉ *Via Farini 4, Santa Croce* ☎ *055/2346654* ⌨ *Synagogue* *and museum €6.50* ⊙ *Apr.–Sept., Sun.–Thurs. 10–6, Fri. 10–2; Oct.–Mar., Sun.–Thurs. 10–3, Fri. 10–2. English guided tours: 10, 11, noon, 1, 2 (no tour at 2 on Fri.).*

■ NEED A BREAK?

Ruth's. The only kosher–vegetarian restaurant in Tuscany (at this writing) is Ruth's, adjacent to Florence's synagogue. On the menu: inexpensive vegetarian and Mediterranean dishes and a large selection of kosher wines. It's closed for Friday dinner and Saturday lunch. ⊠ *Via Farini 2/a, Santa Croce* ☎ *055/2480888* ⊕ *www.kosheruth.com.*

WORTH NOTING

Casa Buonarroti. If you are really enjoying walking in the footsteps of the great genius, you may want to complete the picture by visiting the Buonarroti family home. Michelangelo lived here from 1516 to 1525, and later gave it to his nephew, whose son, called Michelangelo il Giovane (Michelangelo the Younger) turned it into a gallery dedicated to his great-uncle. The artist's descendants filled it with art treasures, some by Michelangelo himself. Two early marble works—the *Madonna of the Steps* and the *Battle of the Centaurs*—show the boy genius at work. ⊠ *Via Ghibellina 70, Santa Croce* ☎ *055/241752* ⊕ *www.casabuonarroti.it* ▭ *€6.50, cumulative ticket with the basilica of Santa Croce €8.59* ⊙ *Fri.–Wed. 9:30–2.*

Cimitero degli Inglesi. Familiarly known as the English Cemetery, this is the final resting place for some 1,400 souls. It was designed in 1828 by Carlo Reishammer and originally intended for the Swiss community in Florence. Just outside Florence's 14th-century walls (no longer visible), the cemetery grew to accommodate other foreigners living here, and thus earned another of its names, the Protestant Cemetery. Perhaps its most famous resident is Elizabeth Barrett Browning (1809–61), who spent the last 15 years of her life in the city. Other expats, including Arthur Clough, Walter Savage Landor, Frances Trollope (mother of Anthony), and the American preacher Theodore Parker are buried in this cemetery, which is also referred to as the "Island of the Dead." (Swiss painter Arnold Böcklin [1827–1901] used the cemetery as inspiration for his haunting painting of that name.) ⊠ *Piazzale Donatello 38, Santa Croce* ☎ *055/582608* ▭ *Free; suggested €3 per person for large groups* ⊙ *Mon. 9–12, Tues.–Fri. 2–5.*

Museo Horne. Englishman Herbert P. Horne (1864–1916), architect, art historian, and collector, spent much of his life in his 15th-century palazzo surrounded by carefully culled paintings, sculptures, and other decorative arts mostly from the 14th to 16th centuries. His home has since been turned into a museum, and the jewel of the collection is Giotto's *St. Stephen*. The rest of the collection is decidedly B-list (he owned plenty of minor works by major artists such as Masaccio and Bernini), but it's still worth a visit to see how a gentleman lived in the 19th century. Many of the furnishings, such as the 15th-century *lettuccio* (divan), are exemplary. ⊠ *Via dei Benci 6, Santa Croce* ☎ *055/244661* ⊕ *www.museohorne.it* ▭ *€6* ⊙ *Mon.–Sat. 9–1.*

Piazza dei Ciompi. Now the site of a daily flea market, this piazza was a working-class neighborhood of primarily wool- and silk-trade workers

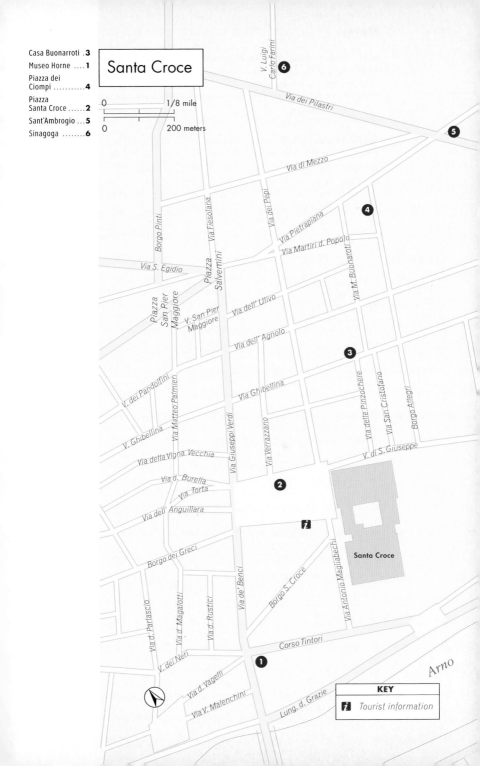

Santa Croce

0   1/8 mile

0   200 meters

V. Luigi Carlo Farini

Via dei Pilastri

Via di Mezzo

Borgo Pinti

Via Fiesolana

Via dei Pepi

Via Pietrapiana

Via Martiri d. Popolo

Via M. Buonarroti

Via S. Egidio

Piazza Salvemini

Piazza San Pier Maggiore

V. San Pier Maggiore

Via dell' Ulivo

Via dell' Agnolo

V. dei Pandolfini

Via Ghibellina

Via delle Pinzochere

Via San Cristofano

Borgo Allegri

V. Ghibellina

Via Matteo Palmieri

Via Giuseppi Verdi

Via Verrazzano

V. di S. Giuseppe

Via della Vigna Vecchia

Via d. Buretta

Via Torta

Via dell' Anguillara

Borgo dei Greci

Santa Croce

V. d. Parlascio

V. d. Magalotti

Via d. Rustici

Via de' Benci

Borgo S. Croce

Via Antonio Magliabechi

Corso Tintori

V. dei Neri

Via d. Vagelli

Via V. Malenchini

Lung. d. Grazie

Arno

KEY
🛈   *Tourist information*

in the 14th century. The disenfranchised wool workers, forbidden entry to the Arte della Lana (the Wool Guild, whose members included those who traded in wool), briefly seized control of the government. It was a short-lived exercise in rule by the nonrepresented and was eventually overpowered by the ruling upper class. The loggia, executed in 1567, is by Giorgio Vasari. ⊠ *Santa Croce.*

Sant'Ambrogio. Named for the Bishop of Milan, this 10th-century church once belonged to an order of Benedictine nuns. Just this side of austere, the church is one of the oldest in Florence. Though its facade is 19th-century, inside are 15th-century panel paintings and a lovely but rather damaged 1486 fresco by Cosimo Roselli, in the chapel to the left of the high altar. The tabernacle of the Blessed Sacrament was carved by Mino da Fiesole, who, like Verrocchio, il Cronaca, and Francesco Granacci (1469/77–1543), is buried here. ⊠ *Piazza Sant'Ambrogio, Santa Croce* ☎ *Free* ☉ *Daily 8–noon and 3–6.*

OFF THE BEATEN PATH

American Military Cemetery. About 8 km (5 miles) south of Florence on the road to Siena is one of two American cemeteries in Italy (the other is in Nettuno). It contains 4,402 bodies of Americans who died in Italy during World War II. Spread across a gently rolling hill, the simple crosses and Stars of David bearing only name, date of death, and state seem to stretch endlessly. At the top of the hill is a place for reflection and large mosaic maps depicting the Allied assault in 1943. The two fronts—called the Gothic Line and the Gustav Line—are vividly rendered. So, too, is the list containing 1,409 names of those missing in action. ⊠ *From Florence, take Via Cassia south to Località Scopeti* ☎ *055/2020020* ☎ *Free* ☉ *Daily 9–5.*

Museo del Cenacolo. This way-off-the-beaten-path museum (the name translates as the Museum of the Last Supper) has a stunning fresco by Andrea del Sarto. Begun sometime around 1511 and finished in 1526–27, the fresco depicts the moment when Christ announced that one of his apostles would betray him. Andrea has rendered the scene in subtle yet still brilliant colors. Also on display are a couple of lesser-known works by Pontormo and copies of other 16th-century works. (Down the street is the church of San Salvi, founded by John Gualbert and begun in 1048. Though it suffered damage during the siege of 1529–30, the interior has a modest but lovely *Madonna and Child* by Lorenzo di Bicci as well as a 16th-century wood cross on the altar.) To get here, take Bus 6 from Piazza San Marco and get off at the Lungo L'Affrico stop—it's the first stop after crossing the railroad tracks. ⊠ *Via San Salvi 16, Santa Croce* ☎ *055/2388603* ☎ *Free* ☉ *Tues.–Sun. 8:15–1:50.*

THE OLTRARNO

A walk through the Oltrarno (literally "the other side of the Arno") takes in two very different aspects of Florence: the splendor of the Medici, manifest in the riches of the mammoth Palazzo Pitti and the gracious Giardino di Boboli; and the charm of the Oltrarno, a slightly gentrified but still fiercely proud working-class neighborhood with artisans' and antiques shops.

Continued on page 82

SANTA CROCE

The Duomo may catch your eye first, but to discover Florence's most impressive tombs and finest church art, cross town to this Gothic masterpiece.

Construction of Santa Croce was initiated in 1294 by Florence's Franciscan friars, who were aiming to outdo Santa Maria Novella, the church of their Dominican rivals. In the centuries that followed, Santa Croce would fulfill this goal in ways the Franciscans never could have imagined: it became the resting place of Italian geniuses—a sort of Florentine Westminister Abbey—and the site of revolutionary frescoes that helped change the course of Western art.

Clockwise from left: Sacristy inside Santa Croce; detail from Michelangelo's tomb; exterior of Sante Croce; Dante Alighieri monument.

WHAT TO LOOK FOR INSIDE SANTA CROCE

THE ART WITHIN SANTA CROCE is the most impressive of any church in Florence. Historically, the most significant works are the Giotto frescoes. Time hasn't been kind to them; over the centuries, they've been whitewashed, plastered over, and clumsily restored. But you can still sense the realism and drama of Giotto's work—it may look primitive, but in the 14th century it sparked a revolution. Before Giotto, the role of painting was to symbolize the attributes of God; after him, it was to imitate life.

Giotto fresco, Capella Bardi

Donatello's Crucifixion

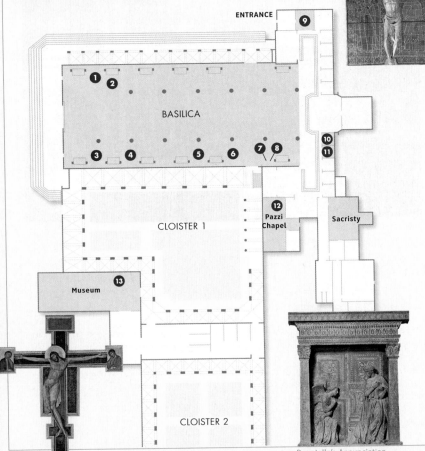

Cimabue's Triumphal Cross

Donatello's Annunciation

❻ Donatello's Annunciation (c. 1435) exquisitely renders the surprise of the Virgin as Gabriel announces that the Lord is with her.

❾ Donatello's Crucifixion (1425) annoyed his friend Brunelleschi, who complained that it made Christ look like a peasant. It's located in the Cappella Bardi di Vernio, the chapel at the end of the left transept.

❿ Giotto's Cappella Bardi frescoes (1320–25), in the first chapel to the right of the main altar, show scenes from the life of St. Francis.

⓫ Giotto's Cappella Peruzzi frescoes (1320–25), in the second chapel to the right of the main altar, depict scenes from the lives of John the Evangelist and Baptist.

⓬ Brunelleschi's Cappella Pazzi (begun 1429) shows the master architect in an intimate light; Brunelleschi did not live to see it completed.

⓭ Cimabue's Triumphal Cross (1287–88), in the attached Museo dell'Opera di Santa Croce, heartbreakingly shows what damage the flood of 1966 did to some very important works of art.

TOMBS & MONUMENTS OF GREAT MEN

❶ Galileo Galilei (1564–1642). Galileo's tomb wasn't given prominence until 100 years after his death, as his evidence that the earth was not the center of the universe was highly displeasing to the Church.

❷ Lorenzo Ghiberti (1378–1455). The tomb slab of sculptor Lorenzo Ghiberti, who created the Baptistery doors, is on the floor near Galileo's tomb.

❸ Michelangelo (1475–1564; tomb shown above). The great master supposedly picked this spot so he'd see Brunelleschi's dome on Judgment Day.

❹ Dante Alighieri (1265–1321). A memorial to Dante was built in 1829 to honor the poet, who was banished from Florence and buried in Ravenna.

❺ Niccolò Machiavelli (1469–1527). The Renaissance political theoretician has the quote *Tanto nomini nullum par elogium* ("For so great a name, no praise is adequate") on his tomb, built in 1787.

❼ Leonardo Bruni (1370–1444). Bernardo Rossellino's *Tomb of Leonardo Bruni* (1444–45), one of Santa Croce's finest works, depicts the humanist chancellor of Florence, the first *uomo illustre* (illustrious man) to be buried in the church.

❽ Gioacchino Rossini (1792–1868). The great Italian composer wrote more than 30 operas; his most famous was *Il barbiere di Siviglia* (The Barber of Seville).

Santa Croce Basics

Like the Duomo, Santa Croce is Gothic in design, and in all likelihood the two churches had the same initial architect, Arnolfo di Cambio. In the typical fashion of the Middle Ages, construction continued for decades—the church was finally consecrated by Pope Eugene IV in 1442. And, also like the Duomo, Santa Croce's neo-Gothic façade is a 19th-century addition.

✉ Piazza Santa Croce 16
☎ 055/2466105
🎫 €5 Basilica and museum (combined ticket)
🕐 Mon.–Sat. 9:30–5:30, Sun. 1–5:30.

Farther east across the Arno, a series of ramps and stairs climb to Piazzale Michelangelo, where the city lies before you in all its glory (skip this trip if it's a hazy day). More stairs (behind La Loggia restaurant) lead to the church of San Miniato al Monte. You can avoid the long walk by taking Bus 12 or 13 at the west end of Ponte alle Grazie and getting off at Piazzale Michelangelo; you still have to climb the monumental stairs to and from San Miniato, but you can then take the bus from Piazzale Michelangelo back to the center of town. If you decide to take a bus, remember to buy your ticket before you board.

TOP ATTRACTIONS

Giardino di Boboli (*Boboli Gardens*). The main entrance to these landscaped gardens is from the right side of the courtyard of **Palazzo Pitti**. The gardens began to take shape in 1549, when the Pitti family sold the palazzo to Eleanor of Toledo, wife of the Medici grand duke Cosimo I. Niccolò Tribolo (1500–50) laid out the first landscaping plans, and after his death, Ammannati, Giambologna, Bernardo Buontalenti (circa 1536–1608), and Giulio (1571–1635) and Alfonso Parigi (1606–56), among others, continued his work. Italian landscaping is less formal than French, but still full of sweeping drama. A copy of the famous *Morgante*, Cosimo I's favorite dwarf astride a particularly unhappy tortoise, is near the exit. Sculpted by Valerio Cioli (circa 1529–99), the work seems to illustrate the perils of culinary overindulgence. A visit here can be disappointing, because the gardens are somewhat underplanted and under-cared for, but it's still a great walk with some terrific views. ⊠ *Enter through Palazzo Pitti* ☎ *055/294883* ⊕ *www.polomuseale. firenze.it* ⊠ *€10, combined ticket with Museo degli Argenti, Museo delle Porcellane, Villa Bardini, and Giardino Bardini* ⊗ *Jan., Feb., Nov., and Dec., daily 8:15–4:30; Mar., daily 8:15–5:30; Apr., May, Sept., and Oct., daily 8:15–6:30; June–Aug., daily 8:15–7:30. Closed 1st and last Mon. of month.*

Palazzo Pitti. This enormous palace is one of Florence's largest architectural set pieces. The original palazzo, built for the Pitti family around 1460, comprised only the main entrance and the three windows on either side. In 1549 the property was sold to the Medici, and Bartolomeo Ammannati was called in to make substantial additions. Although he apparently operated on the principle that more is better, he succeeded only in producing proof that more is just that: more.

Today the palace houses several museums: The **Museo degli Argenti** displays a vast collection of Medici treasures, including exquisite antique vases belonging to Lorenzo the Magnificent. The **Galleria del Costume** showcases fashions from the past 300 years. The **Galleria d'Arte Moderna** holds a collection of 19th- and 20th-century paintings, mostly Tuscan. Most famous of the Pitti galleries is the **Galleria Palatina**, which contains a broad collection of paintings from the 15th to 17th centuries. The rooms of the Galleria Palatina remain much as the Lorena, the rulers who took over after the last Medici died in 1737, left them. Their floor-to-ceiling paintings are considered by some to be Italy's most egregious exercise in conspicuous consumption, aesthetic overkill, and trumpery. Still, the collection possesses high points, including a number of portraits by Titian and an unparalleled collection of paintings

A GOOD WALK: FLORENTINE PIAZZAS

You may come to Florence for the art, but once here you're likely to be won over by the vibrant, pedestrian-friendly street life played out on its numerous and wonderfully varied piazzas—which are often works of art themselves. This walk, designed for a beautiful day, takes you through many of them (but bypasses some of the most prominent ones you'll inevitably encounter while sightseeing).

Start off in **Piazza Santa Maria Novella,** by the train station; note the glorious facade by Leon Battista Alberti decorating the square's church. Take Via delle Belle Donne, a narrow little street running southeast from the piazza, and go left heading toward Via del Trebbio. Here you'll see a cross marking the site of a 13th-century street scuffle between Dominican friars and Patarene heretics. (The Dominicans won.) A right on Via Tornabuoni takes you to tiny **Piazza Antinori**; the 15th-century Antinori palace has been in the hands of its wine-producing namesake family for generations.

Continue south on Via Tornabuoni, stopping in **Piazza Strozzi** to admire the gargantuan Palazzo Strozzi, a 16th-century family palace designed specifically to dwarf the Palazzo Medici. Step into the courtyard, which is as graceful and delicate as the facade is not. Next stop on Via Tornabuoni is the lovely little **Piazza Santa Trinita.** Take a quick look into the church of Santa Trinita; in its Sassetti Chapel in the right transept, Ghirlandaio's 15th-century frescoes neatly depict the square in which you were just standing.

Continue south to the Arno and cross it via the Ponte Trinita. Go

south on Via Maggio, then make a right on Via Michelozzi, which leads to **Piazza Santo Spirito,** one of the loveliest—and liveliest—squares in Florence. Walking away from the piazza's church (heading south), make a left on Via Sant'Agostino, which quickly turns into Via Mazzetta. Stop briefly in **Piazza San Felice** and note No. 8, home of the English poets Elizabeth Barrett Browning and Robert Browning from 1849 to 1861.

From here Via Guicciardini takes you to the massive **Piazza dei Pitti.** Palazzo Pitti was intended to outstrip Palazzo Strozzi in size and ostentation, and it certainly succeeds. Behind the palazzo is the Giardino di Boboli. Walking the straight axis to its top, you'll pass man-made lakes, waterfalls, and grottoes. Head for the 18th-century Giardino dei Cavalieri; when you arrive, pause and admire the view. It's hard to believe the pastoral scene in front of you, complete with olive groves, is in the city center.

If you still have stamina, head back toward the Arno along Via Guicciardini. Just before the Ponte Vecchio, turn right onto Via de' Bardi. Stop for a moment in **Piazza Maria Sopr'Arno** and check out the eerie, yet highly arresting, 20th-century sculpture of John the Baptist, patron saint of Florence. Continue along Via de' Bardi until it becomes Via San Niccolò. Make a right on Via San Miniato, passing through the city walls at Porta San Niccolò. Head up, steeply, on Via Monte alle Croci, and veer left, taking the steps of Via di San Salvatore al Monte. At the top is **Piazzale Michelangelo,** where your effort is rewarded with a breathtaking view of Florence below.

The Oltrarno

1/4 mile
400 meters

by Raphael, notably the double portraits of Angelo Doni and his wife, the sullen Maddalena Strozzi. The price of admission to the Galleria Palatina also allows you to explore the former **Appartamenti Reali,** containing furnishings from a remodeling done in the 19th century. ✉ *Piazza Pitti* ☎ *055/210323* ✑ *Galleria Palatina and Galleria d'Arte Moderna, combined ticket €9.50; Galleria del Costume, Giardino Bardini, Giardino di Boboli, Museo degli Argenti, and Museo Porcelleane, combined ticket €10* ☉ *Tues.–Sun. 8:15–6:50.*

FAMILY **Piazzale Michelangelo.** From this lookout you have a marvelous view of Florence and the hills around it, rivaling the vista from the Forte di Belvedere. A copy of Michelangelo's *David* overlooks outdoor cafés packed with tourists during the day and with Florentines in the evening. In May the **Giardino dell'Iris** (Iris Garden) off the piazza is abloom with more than 2,500 varieties of the flower. The **Giardino delle Rose** (Rose Garden) on the terraces below the piazza is also in full bloom in May and June.

San Miniato al Monte. This church, like the Baptistery, is a fine example of Romanesque architecture and is one of the oldest churches in Florence, dating from the 11th century. A 12th-century mosaic topped by a gilt bronze eagle, emblem of San Miniato's sponsors, the Calimala (cloth merchants' guild) crowns the lovely green-and-white marble facade. Inside are a 13th-century inlaid-marble floor and an apse mosaic. Artist Spinello Aretino (1350–1410) covered the walls of the **Sagrestia** with frescoes depicting scenes from the life of St. Benedict. The **Cappella del Cardinale del Portogallo** (Chapel of the Portuguese Cardinal) is one of the richest 15th-century Renaissance works in Florence. It contains the tomb of a young Portuguese cardinal, Prince James of Lusitania, who died in Florence in 1459. Its glorious ceiling is by Luca della Robbia, and the sculpted tomb by Antonio Rossellino (1427–79). ✉ *Viale Galileo Galilei, Piazzale Michelangelo, Oltrarno* ☎ *055/2342731* ☉ *Daily 8–12:30 and 3–5:15.*

Santa Maria del Carmine. The **Cappella Brancacci,** at the end of the right transept of this church, houses a masterpiece of Renaissance painting: a fresco cycle that changed the course of Western art. Fire almost destroyed the church in the 18th century; miraculously, the Brancacci Chapel survived almost intact. The cycle is the work of three artists: Masaccio and Masolino (1383–circa 1447), who began it around 1424, and Filippino Lippi, who finished it some 50 years later, after a long interruption during which the sponsoring Brancacci family was exiled. It was Masaccio's work that opened a new frontier for painting, as he was among the first artists to employ single-point perspective; tragically, he died in 1428 at the age of 27, so he didn't live to experience the revolution his innovations caused.

Masaccio collaborated with Masolino on several of the frescoes, but his style predominates in the *Tribute Money,* on the upper-left wall; *St. Peter Baptizing,* on the upper altar wall; the *Distribution of Goods,* on the lower altar wall; and the *Expulsion of Adam and Eve,* on the chapel's upper-left entrance pier. If you look closely at the last painting and compare it with some of the chapel's other works, you should see a pronounced difference. The figures of Adam and Eve possess a startling presence primarily thanks to the dramatic way in which their bodies seem to reflect light. Masaccio here shaded his figures consistently, so as to suggest a single, strong source of light within the world of the painting but outside its frame. In so doing, he succeeded in imitating with paint the real-world effect of light on mass, and he thereby imparted to his figures a sculptural reality unprecedented in his day.

These matters have to do with technique, but with the *Expulsion of Adam and Eve* his skill went beyond mere technical innovation.

In the faces of Adam and Eve, you see more than finely modeled figures; you see terrible shame and suffering depicted with a humanity rarely achieved in art. Reservations to see the chapel are mandatory, but can be booked on the same day. Your time inside is limited to 15 minutes—a frustration that's only partly mitigated by a highly informative 40-minute DVD about the history of the chapel you can watch either before or after your visit. ⊠ *Piazza del Carmine, Santo Spirito* ☎ *055/2768224 reservations* 🎟 *€6* 🕑 *Mon. and Wed.–Sat. 10–5, Sun. 1–5.*

Santo Spirito. The plain, unfinished facade gives nothing away, but the interior, although it appears chilly compared with later churches, is one of the most important examples of Renaissance architecture in Italy.

The interior is one of a pair designed in Florence by Filippo Brunelleschi in the early decades of the 15th century (the other is San Lorenzo). It was here that Brunelleschi supplied definitive solutions to the two major problems of interior Renaissance church design: how to build a cross-shaped interior using classical architectural elements borrowed from antiquity and how to reflect in that interior the order and regularity that Renaissance scientists (among them Brunelleschi himself) were at the time discovering in the natural world around them.

Brunelleschi's solution to the first problem was brilliantly simple: turn a Greek temple inside out. While ancient Greek temples were walled buildings surrounded by classical colonnades, Brunelleschi's churches were classical arcades surrounded by walled buildings. This brilliant architectural idea overthrew the previous era's religious taboo against pagan architecture once and for all, triumphantly claiming that architecture for Christian use.

Brunelleschi's solution to the second problem—making the entire interior orderly and regular—was mathematically precise: he designed the ground plan of the church so that all its parts were proportionally related. The transepts and nave have exactly the same width; the side aisles are precisely half as wide as the nave; the little chapels off the side aisles are exactly half as deep as the side aisles; the chancel and transepts are exactly one-eighth the depth of the nave; and so on, with dizzying

2

exactitude. For Brunelleschi, such a design technique was a matter of passionate conviction. Like most theoreticians of his day, he believed that mathematical regularity and aesthetic beauty were flip sides of the same coin, that one was not possible without the other.

In the refectory, adjacent to the church, you can see Andrea Orcagna's highly damaged fresco of the Crucifixion. ⊠ *Piazza Santo Spirito* 🕾 *055/210030* 🕮 *Church free, refectory €3* ⊙ *Church, Mon.–Sat. 10–12:30 and 4–5:30, Sun. 4–5:30. Refectory, Sat.–Mon. 10–4.*

WORTH NOTING

Certosa. The incredible Carthusian complex was largely funded in 1342 by the wealthy Florentine banker Niccolò Acciaiuoli, whose guilt at having amassed so much money must have been at least temporarily assuaged with the creation of such a structure to honor God. In the grand cloister are stunning (but faded) frescoes of *Christ's Passion* by Pontormo. Though much of the paint is missing, their power is still unmistakable. Also of great interest are the monks' cells; the monks could spend most of their lives tending their own private gardens without dealing with any other monks. To get here, you must either take Bus 37 and get off at the stop marked "Certosa" or have a car. Tours, which are mandatory, are given only in Italian, but even if you can't understand what's being said, you can still take in the sights. ⊠ *From Florence, take Viale Petrarca to Via Senese and follow it for about 10 mins; the Certosa is on the right, Via di Colleramole 11, Galluzzo* 🕾 *055/2049226* 🕮 *Suggested €3–€4* ⊙ *Tues.–Sat. guided visits at 9, 10, 11, 3, 4, and 5; Sun. guided visits at 3, 4, and 5.*

Fodor's Choice ★ **Giardino Bardini.** Garden lovers, those who crave a view, and those who enjoy a nice hike should visit this lovely villa and garden, whose history spans centuries. The villa had a walled garden as early as the 14th century; the "Grand Stairs"—a zigzag ascent well worth scaling—has been around since the 16th. The garden is filled with irises, roses, and heirloom flowers, and includes a Japanese garden and statuary. A very pretty walk (all for the same admission ticket) takes you through the Giardino di Boboli and past the Forte Belvedere to the upper entrance to the giardino. ⊠ *Via de'Bardini, San Niccolò* 🕾 *005/294883* 🕮 *€10, combined ticket with Galleria Costume, Giardino di Boboli, Museo Argenti, Museo Porcellane* ⊙ *Jan., Feb., Nov., and Dec., daily 8:15–4:30; Mar., daily 8:15–5:30; Apr., May, Sept., and Oct., daily 8:15–6:30; June–Aug., daily 8:15–7:30. Closed 1st and last Mon. of month.*

Museo Bardini. The 19th-century collector and antiquarian Stefano Bardini turned his palace into his own private museum. Upon his death, the collection was turned over to the state and includes an interesting assortment of Etruscan pieces, sculpture, paintings, and furniture that dates mostly from the Renaissance and the Baroque. ⊠ *Piazza de' Mozzi 1, San Niccolò* 🕾 *055/2342427* ⊕ *museicivicifiorentini.comune. fi.it* 🕮 *€6* ⊙ *Thurs.–Mon. 11–5.*

Santa Felicita. This late-baroque church (its facade was remodeled between 1736 and 1739) contains the mannerist Jacopo Pontormo's *Deposition*, the centerpiece of the Cappella Capponi (executed 1525–28) and a masterpiece of 16th-century Florentine art. The remote figures, which transcend the realm of Renaissance classical form, are portrayed in tangled shapes and intense pastel colors (well preserved because of the low lights in the church), in a space and depth that defy reality. Note, too, the exquisitely frescoed *Annunciation*, also by Pontormo, at a right angle to the *Deposition*. The granite column in the piazza was erected in 1381 and marks a Christian cemetery. ⊠ *Piazza Santa Felicita, Via Guicciardini, Palazzo Pitti* ☾ *Mon.–Sat. 9–noon and 3–6, Sun. 9–1.*

WHERE TO EAT

Florence's popularity with tourists means that, unfortunately, there's a higher percentage of mediocre restaurants here than you'll find in most Italian towns (Venice, perhaps, might win the prize). Some restaurant owners cut corners and let standards slip, knowing that a customer today is unlikely to return tomorrow, regardless of the quality of the meal. So, if you're looking to eat well, it pays to do some research, starting with the recommendations here. Dining hours start at around 1 for lunch and 8 for dinner. Many of Florence's restaurants are small, so reservations are a must. You can sample such specialties as creamy *fegatini* (a chicken-liver spread) and *ribollita* (minestrone thickened with bread and beans and swirled with extra-virgin olive oil) in a bustling, convivial trattoria, where you share long wooden tables set with paper place mats, or in an upscale *ristorante* with linen tablecloths and napkins.

Those with a sense of culinary adventure should not miss the tripe sandwich, served from stands throughout town. This Florentine favorite comes with a fragrant *salsa verde* (green sauce) or a piquant red hot sauce—or both. Follow the Florentines' lead and take a break at an *enoteca* (wine bar) during the day and discover some excellent Chiantis and Super Tuscans from small producers who rarely export.

Eating ethnic in Florence is a hit-or-miss affair. Although numerous Asian restaurants have sprung up since the 1990s, most are nothing to write home about. Still, if you need a break from Italian, some relief is available.

Pizzas in Florence can't compete with their counterparts in Rome or Naples, but you can sample a few good approximations.

Cafés in Italy serve not only coffee concoctions and pastries but also sweets, drinks, and panini, and some have hot pasta and lunch dishes. They usually open from early in the morning to late at night, and are often closed Sunday.

AROUND THE DUOMO

$ ✕ **Birreria Centrale.** The feel here is more Munich beer hall than Floren-
ECLECTIC tine trattoria; indeed, although the menu lists plenty of Italian dishes, it also emphasizes sausages and sauerkraut. The *würstel rossi con crauti, speck, e patate alla tedesca* (a large and quite plump hot dog with sauerkraut, cured beef, potatoes, and pickles), for instance, comes with a dollop of spicy mustard. Heavy wooden tables are set closely together,

BEST BETS FOR FLORENCE DINING

With hundreds of restaurants to choose from, how will you decide where to eat? Fodor's writers and editors have selected their favorite restaurants by price, cuisine, and experience in the Best Bets lists below. In the first column, Fodor's Choice properties represent the "best of the best."

Fodor'sChoice ★

Cibrèo, $$$, p. 97
da Nerbone, $, p. 91
da Sergio, $, p. 91
Il Santini, $, p. 103
La Reggia degli Etruschi, $$, p. 123
Mario, $$, p. 94
Osteria de'Benci, $$, p. 100
Procacci, $$, p. 96
Rivoire, $$, p. 91
Taverna del Bronzino, $$$$, p. 94
Trattoria Sostanza, $$, p. 96

Best by Price

$

Cibrèo Trattoria, p. 97
da Nerbone, p. 91
da Rocco, p. 98
La Casalinga, p. 101
La Mescita, p. 94
Osteria Antica Mescita San Niccolò, p. 102

$$

Il Latini, p. 95
Il Santo Bevitore, p. 101
Mario, p. 94
Simon Boccanegra, p. 100

$$$

Buca Lapi, p. 95
Cibrèo, p. 97
La Giostra, p. 99

$$$$

Taverna del Bronzino, p. 94

Best Experiences

FOR KIDS

Il Latini, $$, p. 95

ROMANTIC

Enoteca Pinchiorri, $$$$, p. 99

CASALINGA (HOME COOKING)

La Casalinga, $, p. 101
Mario, $$, p. 94

LUNCH SPOTS

Antico Noe, $, p. 97
Cantinetta Antinori, $$, p. 95
Coquinarius, $, p. 90
da Nerbone, $, p. 91
da Sergio, $, p. 91

WINE LIST

Cantinetta Antinori, $, p. 95
Enoteca Pinchiorri, $$$$, p. 99
Fuori Porta, $, p. 101
La Giostra, $$$, p. 99
Taverna del Bronzino, $$$$, p. 94

BISTECCA FIORENTINA (TUSCAN STEAK)

Buca Lapi, $$$, p. 95
Il Latini, $$, p. 95
La Giostra, $$$, p. 99
Osteria de'Benci, $$, p. 100

OUTDOOR DINING

Fuori Porta, $, p. 101
Osteria de'Benci, $$, p. 100
Vincanto, $$, p. 97

WINE BARS

Casa del Vino, $, p. 103
Il Santino, $, p. 103
Le Volpi e l'Uva, $, p. 103

ALTA CUCINA (SOPHISTICATED CUISINE)

Cibrèo, $$$, p. 97
Enoteca Pinchiorri, $$$$, p. 99
Taverna del Bronzino, $$$$, p. 94

and copies of 19th-century paintings adorn the intensely yellow walls, along with two frescoed Michelangelesque nudes that cavort over a brick arch. There's outside seating in warm weather—a great place to enjoy a beer. $ *Average main: €13* ⊠ *Piazza Cimatori 1/r, Duomo* ☎ *055/211915* ⊘ *Closed Sun.* ✛ *F3.*

$
ITALIAN
✕ **Caffè delle Carrozze.** The convenient Caffè delle Carrozze, around the corner from the Uffizi and practically at the foot of the Ponte Vecchio, has many terrific flavors, especially the chocolate-chip laced coffee. $ *Average main: €3* ⊠ *Piazza del Pesce 3–5/r, Piazza della Signoria, Around the Duomo* ☎ *055/2396810* ▭ *No credit cards* ✛ *E4.*

$
ITALIAN
✕ **Coquinarius.** This rustically elegant space, which has served many purposes over the past 600 years, offers some of the tastiest food in town at great prices. It's the perfect place to come if you aren't sure what you're hungry for, as they offer a little bit of everything: salad-lovers will have a hard time choosing from the lengthy list (the Scozzese, with poached chicken, avocado, and bacon, is a winner); those with a yen for pasta will face agonizing choices (the ravioli with pecorino and pears is particularly good). A revolving list of *piatti unici* (single dishes that can be ordered on their own, usually served only at lunch) can also whet the whistle, as well as terrific cheese and cured meat plates. The well-culled wine list has lots of great wines by the glass, and even more by the bottle. $ *Average main: €10* ⊠ *Via delle Oche 15/r, Piazza della Signoria* ☎ *055/2302153* ⊕ *www.coquinarius.it* ⌕ *Reservations essential* ✛ *F3.*

$$$
TUSCAN
✕ **Frescobaldi Wine Bar.** The Frescobaldi family has run a vineyard for more than 700 years, and this swanky establishment offers tasty and sumptuous fare to accompany the seriously fine wines. Warm terracotta-color walls with trompe-l'oeil tapestries provide a soothing atmosphere. The menu is typically Tuscan, but turned up a notch or two: the *faraona in umido con l'uva* (stewed guinea fowl with grapes) comes with a side of feather-light mashed potatoes. Save room for dessert, as well as one of the dessert wines. A separate, lovely little wine bar called Frescobaldino has a shorter—but equally good—menu and a delightful, multilingual barman called Primo. $ *Average main: €35* ⊠ *Via de' Magazzini 2–4/r, Piazza della Signoria* ☎ *055/284724* ⊘ *Closed Sun. No lunch Mon.* ✛ *E4.*

$
TUSCAN
✕ **Le Mosacce.** Come to this tiny, cramped, and boisterous place for a quick bite to eat. The menu, written in three languages, includes hearty, stick-to-the-ribs Florentine food such as *ribollita*. Seating is communal, and fellow diners share the big, straw-covered flask of wine. Service is prompt and efficient; two nimble cooks with impeccable timing staff the small kitchen. $ *Average main: €7* ⊠ *Via del Proconsolo 55/r, Duomo* ☎ *055/294361* ⌕ *Reservations not accepted* ⊘ *Closed weekends* ✛ *F3.*

$$$$
MODERN ITALIAN
✕ **Ora d'Aria.** The name means "Hour of Air" and refers to the time of day when prisoners were let outside for fresh air—alluding to the fact that this gem was originally located across the street from what was once the old prison. In the kitchen, gifted young chef Marco Stabile turns out exquisite Tuscan classics as well as more fanciful dishes, which are as beautiful as they are delicious; intrepid diners will be vastly rewarded for ordering the tortellini *farciti con piccione* (stuffed with pigeon) if it's on the day's menu. Two tasting menus give Stabile even

2

greater opportunity to shine, and the carefully culled wine list has something to please every palate. Do not miss his tiramisu espresso—something halfway between a dessert and a coffee. In fact, if you're a serious gourmand, do not miss this place. (If the prices seem daunting, the lunch menu is significantly less expensive than the dinner.) $ *Average main: €76* ✉ *Via Georgofili 79/r, Piazza della Signoria* ☎ *055/2001699* 🍷 *Reservations essential* ☾ *Closed Sun.* ✛ *E4.*

$$ ✕ **Rivoire.** One of the best spots in Florence for people-watching offers
ITALIAN stellar service, light snacks, and terrific aperitivi. It's been around since
Fodor's Choice the 1860s, and has been famous for its hot and cold chocolate (with
★ or without cream) for more than a century. Though the food is mostly good (it's not a bad place for a light, but expensive, lunch), it's best to stick to drinks (both alcoholic and non-) and their terrific cakes, pies, and pastries. $ *Average main: €15* ✉ *Via Vaccereccia 4/r, Piazza della Signoria* ☎ *055/214412* ✛ *E4.*

SAN LORENZO

$ ✕ **Alfio e Beppe.** Watch chickens roast over high flames as you decide
ITALIAN which of the other delightful things you're going to eat with it. The beauty of this place is that it's closed Saturdays (when most things are open), and open on Sundays (when most things are not). $ *Average main: €9* ✉ *Via Cavour 118–120/r, San Marco* ☎ *055/214108* ▭ *No credit cards* ✛ *F1.*

$ ✕ **da Nerbone.** This *tavola calda* in the middle of the covered Mer-
TUSCAN cato Centrale has been serving up food to Florentines who like their
Fodor's Choice tripe since 1872. Tasty primi and secondi are available every day, but
★ cognoscenti come for the *panino con il lampredotto* (tripe sandwich). Less adventurous sorts might want to sample the *panino con il bollito* (boiled beef sandwich). Ask that the bread be *bagnato* (briefly dipped in the tripe cooking liquid), and have both the salsa verde and salsa *piccante* (a spicy cayenne sauce) slathered on top. $ *Average main: €13* ✉ *Mercato San Lorenzo* ☎ *055/219949* ▭ *No credit cards* ☾ *Closed Sun. No dinner* ✛ *D1.*

$ ✕ **da Sergio.** In 2015, this little eatery will celebrate its centenary, and
TUSCAN with good reason. It's been in the capable hands of the Gozzi family,
Fodor's Choice who have ensured continuity and stuck to Tuscan tradition. The food's
★ terrific, eminently affordable, and just across the way from the basilica of San Lorenzo, which means that you can imbibe well-prepared food while marveling at the Brunelleschi and Michelangelo you've just seen. The menu is short, and changes daily. Their *lombatina alla griglia* (a grilled veal T-bone steak) is almost always on, and meat eaters should not miss it. Pastas are equally terrific. Dessert, in true Florentine fashion, is usually limited to biscotti with *vin santo* (twice-cooked biscuits with sweet wine). $ *Average main: €9* ✉ *Piazza San Lorenzo 8/r* ☾ *Closed Sun. No dinner* ✛ *E2.*

$ ✕ **Dioniso.** Located in the midst of university buildings, Dioniso draws
GREEK a mostly student crowd that comes to enjoy kebab and other tasty, inexpensive Greek fare. $ *Average main: €7* ✉ *Via San Gallo 16/r* ☎ *055/217882* ✛ *E1.*

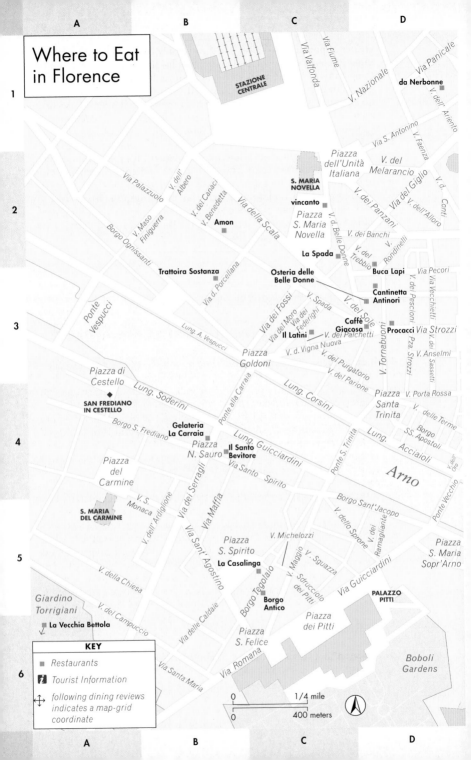

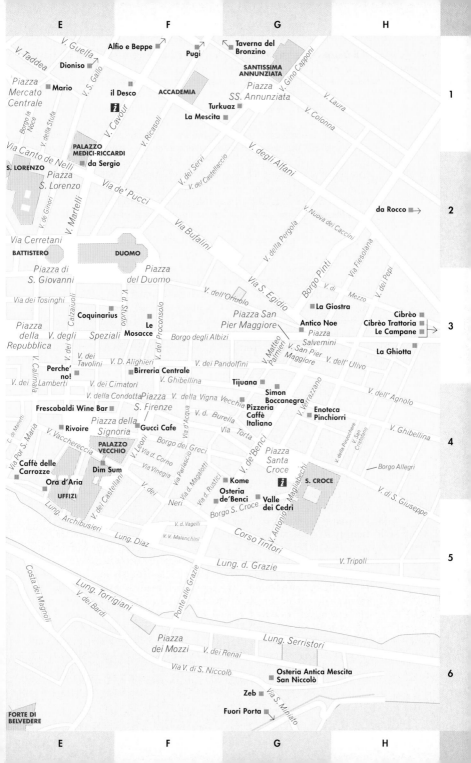

$ ✕ **il Desco.** This tiny boite, with a mere handful of tables, is an oasis
CONTEMPORARY   in an area that is pretty much a culinary wasteland. It's owned by the Bargiacchi family, who are proprietors of the lovely hotel Guelfo Bianco just next door. Their organic farm in the Tuscan countryside provides much of what is on the frequently changing menu. The menu plays to all tastes—classic Tuscan dishes such as *peposo* (a hearty, black pepper–filled beef stew) can be found, as well as vegetarian plates. Even vegans have options: the seitan in *salsa fredda di ceci ai capperi e rosmarino* (a room-temperature puréed chickpea sauce flavored with capers and rosemary) is a winner. The wine list is well thought out, and artisanal beer is also on the menu. $ *Average main: €13* ⊠ *via, Cavour 55/r, San Lorenzo* ☎ *055/288330* ⊕ *www.ildescofirenze.it* ✛ *F1.*

$ ✕ **La Mescita.** Come early (or late) to grab a seat at this tiny spot fre-
TUSCAN   quented by Florentine university students and businesspeople. You can get a sandwich to go or sit and enjoy the day's primi (such as a terrific lasagne) and follow it with their *polpettona* (meat loaf) and tomato sauce. Though seats are cramped and the wine is no great shakes, the service is friendly and the food hits the spot. Groups of 15 or more can reserve in the evening for special meals. $ *Average main: €7* ⊠ *Via degli Alfani 70/r* ⊟ *No credit cards* ⊗ *Closed Sun. No dinner* ✛ *G1.*

$$ ✕ **Mario.** Florentines flock to this narrow family-run trattoria near San
TUSCAN   Lorenzo to feast on Tuscan favorites served at simple tables under a
Fodor'sChoice   wooden ceiling dating from 1536. A distinct cafeteria feel and genuine
★   Florentine hospitality prevail: you'll be seated wherever there's room, which often means with strangers. Yes, there's a bit of extra oil in most dishes, which imparts calories as well as taste, but aren't you on vacation in Italy? Worth the splurge is *riso al ragù* (rice with ground beef and tomatoes). $ *Average main: €20* ⊠ *Via Rosina 2/r, corner of Piazza del Mercato Centrale, San Lorenzo* ☎ *055/218550* ⬦ *Reservations not accepted* ⊗ *Closed Sun. and Aug. No dinner* ✛ *E1.*

$ ✕ **Pugi.** Handily across the street from San Marco, Pugi sells the popular
PIZZA   pizza *a taglio* (by the slice); their *focaccie* and other breads are equally good. It's a great place to grab a quick lunch or snack. $ *Average main: €3* ⊠ *Piazza San Marco 9/b, San Marco* ☎ *055/280981* ⊟ *No credit cards* ⊗ *Closed Sun.* ✛ *F1.*

$$$$ ✕ **Taverna del Bronzino.** Want to have a sophisticated meal in a 16th-
TUSCAN   century Renaissance artist's studio? The former studio of Santi di Tito,
Fodor'sChoice   a student of Bronzino's, has a simple, formal decor, with white table-
★   cloths and place settings. The classic, elegantly presented Tuscan food is superb, and the solid, affordable wine list rounds out the menu—especially because Stefano, the sommelier, really knows his stuff. The service is outstanding. Reservations are advised, especially for eating at the wine cellar's only table. $ *Average main: €45* ⊠ *Via delle Ruote 25/r, San Marco* ☎ *055/495220* ⊗ *Closed Sun. and 3 wks in Aug.* ✛ *G1.*

$ ✕ **Turkuaz.** Döner kebabs at Turkuaz have a killer hot sauce; you can
TURKISH   order hot rice and meat dishes to eat in or take out. It's generally agreed by aficionados that this is the best kebab in town. $ *Average main: €5* ⊠ *Via de'Servi 65/r, Santissima Annunziata* ☎ *055/2399959* ✛ *G1.*

SANTA MARIA NOVELLA

$
MIDDLE EASTERN
✕**Amon.** This standing-only spot serves tasty Egyptian and other Middle Eastern fare at rock-bottom prices. Ⓢ *Average main: €6* ✉ *Via Palazzuolo 26/28r, Santa Maria Novella* ▭ *No credit cards* ✛ *B2.*

$$$
TUSCAN
✕**Buca Lapi.** The Antinori family started selling wine from their palace's basement in the 15th century. Six hundred years later, this *buca* (hole) is a lively, subterranean restaurant filled with Florentine aristocrats chowing down on what might be the best (and most expensive) bistecca fiorentina in town. The classical Tuscan menu has the usual suspects: *crostino di cavolo nero* (black cabbage on toasted garlic bread), along with *ribollita* and *pappa al pomodoro* (two bread-based soups). You might want to cut directly to the chase, however, and order the bistecca, an immense slab of Chianina beef impeccably grilled on the outside, just barely warmed on the inside. (If you're not into rare meat, order something else from the grill.) Roast potatoes and cannellini beans make perfect accompaniments. Ⓢ *Average main: €35* ✉ *Via del Trebbio 1, Santa Maria Novella* ☎ *055/213768* ⊕ *www.bucalapi.com* ✍ *Reservations essential* ✛ *D2.*

$$
ITALIAN
✕**Caffè Giacosa.** This café opens early in the morning for coffee, serves tasty light lunches, and makes excellent cocktails in the evening. Ⓢ *Average main: €15* ✉ *Via della Spada 10/r, Santa Maria Novella* ☎ *055/2776328* ⊕ *www.caffegiacosa.it* ✛ *D3.*

$$
TUSCAN
✕**Cantinetta Antinori.** After a morning of shopping on Via Tornabuoni, stop for lunch in this 15th-century palazzo in the company of Florentine ladies (and men) who come to see and be seen over lunch. The panache of the food matches its clientele: expect treats such as *tramezzino con pane di campagna al tartufo* (country pâté with truffles served on bread) and the *insalata di gamberoni e gamberetti con carciofi freschi* (crayfish and prawn salad with shaved raw artichokes). Ⓢ *Average main: €24* ✉ *Piazza Antinori 3, Santa Maria Novella* ☎ *055/292234* ⊘ *Closed weekends, 20 days in Aug., and Dec. 25–Jan. 6* ✛ *D3.*

$$
TUSCAN
✕**Il Latini.** It may be the noisiest, most crowded trattoria in Florence, but it's also one of the most fun. The genial host, Torello ("little bull") Latini, presides over his four big dining rooms, and somehow it feels as if you're dining in his home. Ample portions of *ribollita* prepare the palate for the hearty meat dishes that follow. Both Florentines and tourists alike tuck into the *agnello fritto* (fried lamb) with aplomb. There's almost always a wait, even with a reservation. Ⓢ *Average main: €15* ✉ *Via dei Palchetti 6/r, Santa Maria Novella* ☎ *055/210916* ⊘ *Closed Mon. and 15 days at Christmas* ✛ *C3.*

$
ITALIAN
✕**La Spada.** Near Santa Maria Novella is La Spada. Walk in and inhale the fragrant aromas of meats cooking in the wood-burning oven. You can either eat in, or take it away. Ⓢ *Average main: €10* ✉ *Via del Moro 66/r, Santa Maria Novella* ☎ *055/218757* ▭ *No credit cards* ✛ *C2.*

$
TUSCAN
✕**Osteria delle Belle Donne.** Down the street from the church of Santa Maria Novella, this gaily decorated spot, festooned with ropes of garlic and other vegetables, has an ever-changing menu and stellar service led by the irrepressible Giacinto who, after a brief sabbatical, has returned to oversee tasty-again food emerging from the kitchen. The menu offers Tuscan standards, but shakes things up with alternatives such as *sedani*

CLOSE UP

Sweets for the Sweet

Sweet-lovers have a bounty of gelato and pastry shops to choose from in Florence.

✕ **Dolci e Dolcezze.** The *pasticceria* (bakery) Dolci e Dolcezze, just off Borgo La Croce, has the tastiest cakes, sweets, and tarts in town. It's closed Monday. $ *Average main: €15* ⊠ *Piazza C. Beccaria 8/r, Sant'Ambrogio* ☎ *055/2345458* ▬ *No credit cards.*

✕ **Gelateria Carabe.** Specializing in things Sicilian, this shop is known for its tart and flavorful *granità* (granular flavored ices), made only in the summer. $ *Average main: €3* ⊠ *Via Ricasoli 60/r, San Marco* ☎ *055/289476* ⊕ *www.gelatocarabe.com* ▬ *No credit cards.*

✕ **Gelateria La Carraia.** Try the *limone ai biscotti* (a delicate lemon sorbet dotted with crumbled cookie) here and you won't be disappointed. $ *Average main: €3* ⊠ *Piazza, Nazario Sauro 25, Lungarno* ☎ *055/280695* ⊕ *www.lacarraiagroup.eu.*

Fodor'sChoice★ ✕ **Grom.** A stone's throw from the Duomo, this is one of the best gelaterias in town. Flavors change according to the season, so expect a fragrant gelato *di cannella* (cinnamon ice cream) in winter and lively fresh fruit flavors in summer. (The original Grom hails from Turin and there's a Grom in New York City.) $ *Average main: €5* ⊠ *Via del Campanile, Duomo* ☎ *055/216158* ⊕ *www.grom.it* ▬ *No credit cards.*

✕ **I Dolci di Patrizio Corsi.** Florentines with serious sweet tooths come to i Dolci di Patrizio Corsi, which has a deliciously bewildering selection of chocolate- and cream-filled pastries. $ *Average main: €10* ⊠ *Borgo Albizi 15/r, Santa Croce* ☎ *055/2480367* ☾ *Open daily; closed Sun. afternoon.*

✕ **Vestri.** This shop is devoted to chocolate in all its guises. The sublime selection of chocolate-based gelati includes one with hot peppers. $ *Average main: €3* ⊠ *Borgo Albizi 11/r, Santa Croce* ☎ *055/2340374* ⊕ *www.vestri.it* ▬ *No credit cards.*

---

con bacon, verza, e uova (thick noodles sauced with bacon, cabbage, and egg); when avocados are ripe, they're on the menu, too (either with cold boiled shrimp or expertly grilled chicken breast). If you want to eat alfresco, request a table outside when booking—and remember to save room for dessert. $ *Average main: €12* ⊠ *Via delle Belle Donne 16/r, Santa Maria Novella* ☎ *055/2382609* ✛ *D3.*

$$
ITALIAN
Fodor'sChoice
★

✕ **Procacci.** At this classy Florentine institution dating to 1885, try one of the panini tartufati and swish it down with a glass of Prosecco. It's closed Sunday. $ *Average main: €15* ⊠ *Via Tornabuoni 64/r, Santa Maria Novella* ☎ *055/211656* ✛ *D3.*

$$
TUSCAN
Fodor'sChoice
★

✕ **Trattoria Sostanza (il Troia).** Since opening its doors in 1869, this trattoria has been serving top-notch, unpretentious food to Florentines who like their *bistecca fiorentina* very large and very rare. A single room with white tiles on the wall and paper mats on the tables provides the setting for delicious meals. Along with fine Tuscan classics, they have two signature dishes: the *tortino di carciofi* (artichoke tart) and the *pollo al burro* (chicken with butter). The latter is an amazing surprise, a succulent chicken breast cooked very quickly and served as soon as it leaves the grill. Leave room for dessert, as their *torta alla Meringa* (a semi-frozen dessert flecked with chocolate and topped with meringue) is scrumptious. [$] *Average main: €15* ✉ *Via della Porcellana 25, Santa Maria Novella* ☎ *055/212691* ✍ *Reservations essential* 💳 *No credit cards* ✥ *B3.*

$$ ITALIAN 🍴 **vincanto.** It opens at 11 am and closes at midnight: this is a rarity in Florentine dining. They do a little bit of everything here, including fine pastas (don't miss the ignudi), salads, and pizze. The burgers shine here, however. And all of this can be enjoyed with a splendid view of Piazza Santa Maria Novella. [$] *Average main: €18* ✉ *Piazza Santa Maria Novella 23/r, Santa Maria Novella* ☎ *055/267–9300* 🌐 *www.ristorantevincanto.com* ✥ *C2.*

SANTA CROCE

$ TUSCAN 🍴 **Antico Noe.** If Florence had diners (it doesn't), this would be the best diner in town. The short menu at the one-room eatery relies heavily on seasonal ingredients picked up daily at the market. Though the secondi are good, it's the antipasti and primi that really shine. The menu comes alive particularly during truffle and artichoke season (don't miss the grilled artichokes if they're on the menu). Locals rave about the tagliatelle *ai porcini* (with mushrooms); the fried eggs liberally laced with truffle might be the greatest truffle bargain in town. Ask for the menu in Italian, as the English version is much more limited. The short wine list has some great bargains, and note that if you opt to order bistecca, you'll jump to a higher price category. [$] *Average main: €10* ✉ *Volta di San Piero 6/r, Santa Croce* ☎ *055/2340838* ⏲ *Closed Sun. and 2 wks in Aug.* ✥ *G3.*

$$$ TUSCAN Fodor's Choice ★ 🍴 **Cibrèo.** The food at this upscale trattoria is fantastic, from the creamy crostini *di fegatini* (a savory chicken-liver spread) to the melt-in-your-mouth desserts. Many Florentines hail this as the city's best restaurant, and Fodor's readers tend to agree—though some take issue with the prices and complain of long waits for a table (even with a reservation). If you thought you'd never try tripe—let alone like it—this is the place to lay any doubts to rest: the *trippa in insalata* (cold tripe salad) with parsley and garlic is an epiphany. The food is traditionally Tuscan, impeccably served by a staff that's multilingual—which is a good thing, because there are no written menus. [$] *Average main: €30* ✉ *Via A. del Verrocchio 8/r, Santa Croce* ☎ *055/2341100* ✍ *Reservations essential* ⏲ *Closed Sun. and Mon. and July 25–Sept. 5* ✥ *H3.*

$ TUSCAN 🍴 **Cibrèo Trattoria.** This intimate little trattoria, known to locals as Cibreino, shares its kitchen with the famed Florentine culinary institution from which it gets its name. They share the same menu, too, though

CLOSE UP

Salumerie

Salumerie, specialty food shops similar to delis, are strong on fine fresh ingredients such as meats and cheeses. They're great places to assemble a picnic lunch.

⚔ **Antico Salumificio Anzuini-Massi.** This salumeria shrink-wraps their own pork products, making it a snap to take home some *salame di cinghiale* (wild boar salami). $ *Average main: €10* ✉ *Via de' Neri 84/r, Santa Croce* ☎ *055/294901* 🟰 *No credit cards.*

⚔ **Baroni.** The cheese collection at Baroni may be the most comprehensive in Florence. They also have high-quality truffle products, vinegars, and other delicacies. $ *Average main: €10* ✉ *Mercato Central, enter at Via Signa, San Lorenzo* ☎ *055/289576* 🌐 *www. baronialimentari.it.*

Conti. Stop here for top-quality wines, olive oils, and dried fruits; they'll shrink-wrap the highest-quality dried porcini for traveling. Closed Sunday. For a very small fee, they'll also offer up a top-notch balsamic vinegar tasting. ✉ *Mercato Centrale, enter at Via Signa, San Lorenzo* ☎ *055/2398501* 🌐 *www. tuscanyflavours.com.*

Fodor'sChoice ★ ⚔ **'ino.** Serving arguably the best panini in town, proprietor Alessandro sources only the very best ingredients. Located right behind the Uffizi, 'ino is a perfect place to grab a tasty sandwich and glass of wine before forging on to the next museum. $ *Average main: €8* ✉ *Via dei Georgofili 3/r–7/r* ☎ *055/219208.*

⚔ **Pegna.** Looking for some cheddar cheese to pile in your panino? Pegna has been selling both Italian and non-Italian food since 1860. It's closed Saturday afternoon in July and August, Wednesday afternoon September through June, and Sunday year-round. $ *Average main: €25* ✉ *Via dello Studio 8, Duomo* ☎ *055/282701* 🌐 *www. pegnafirenze.com.*

⚔ **Perini.** It's possible to break the bank here, as this might be the best salumeria in Florence. Perini sells prosciutto, mixed meats, sauces for pasta, and a wide assortment of antipasti, and is closed Sunday. $ *Average main: €20* ✉ *Mercato Centrale, enter at Via dell'Aretino, San Lorenzo* ☎ *055/2398306.*

Cibreino's is much shorter. Start with *il gelatina di pomodoro* (tomato gelatin) liberally laced with basil, garlic, and a pinch of hot pepper, and then sample the justifiably renowned *passato in zucca gialla* (pureed yellow-pepper soup) before moving on to any of the succulent second courses. Save room for dessert, as the pastry chef has a deft hand with chocolate tarts. To avoid sometimes agonizingly long waits, come early (7 pm) or late (after 9:30). $ *Average main: €12* ✉ *Via dei Macci 118, Santa Croce* ☎ *055/2341100* 🍽 *Reservations not accepted* 🟰 *No credit cards* ⊗ *Closed Sun. and Mon. and July 25–Sept. 5* ✛ *H3.*

$

TUSCAN

⚔ **da Rocco.** At one of Florence's biggest markets you can grab lunch to go, or you could cram yourself into one of the booths and pour from the straw-cloaked flask (wine here is *da consumo,* which means they charge you for how much you drink). Food is abundant, Tuscan, and fast; locals pack in. The ample menu changes daily (nine secondi are the norm), and the prices are great. $ *Average main: €10* ✉ *In*

Mercato Sant'Ambrogio, Piazza Ghiberti, Santa Croce ✍ *Reservations not accepted* ▭ *No credit cards* ⏲ *Closed Sun. No dinner* ✥ *H2.*

$$ ASIAN FUSION 🍴 **Dim Sum.** Florence has long been in dire need of a top-notch Asian restaurant, and now it finally has one. The imported-from-Shandong (in eastern China) Chi Hu, who's worked in China, Italy, Japan, and France, has brought his considerable skills to the table. You can watch men make dumplings right before your very eyes. The vast range of dumplings includes the classics (steamed, pork-stuffed) as well as Tuscan variations (beef with *lardo di colonnata* or truffled beef). But the place isn't limited to just dumplings: various rolls—from spring to Saigon—provide a perfect starting point, as does the cold two-seaweed salad. Noodle dishes, with noodles made right in front of you, are also on offer. [$] *Average main: €20* ✉ *via, dei Neri, Santa Croce* ☎ *055/284 331* 🌐 *www.dimsumrestaurant.it* ✥ *E4.*

$$$$ ITALIAN 🍴 **Enoteca Pinchiorri.** A sumptuous Renaissance palace with high frescoed ceilings and bouquets in silver vases provides the backdrop for this restaurant, one of the most expensive in Italy. Some consider it one of the best, and others consider it a non-Italian rip-off, as the kitchen is presided over by a Frenchwoman with sophisticated, yet internationalist, leanings. Prices are high (think $100 for a plate of spaghetti) and portions are small; the vast holdings of the wine cellar (undoubtedly the best in Florence), as well as stellar service, dull the pain, however, when the bill is presented. [$] *Average main: €90* ✉ *Via Ghibellina 87, Santa Croce* ☎ *055/242777* 🌐 *www.enotecapinchiorri.com* ✍ *Reservations essential* 👔 *Jacket required* ⏲ *Closed Sun., Mon., and Aug. No lunch.* ✥ *G4.*

$$ JAPANESE 🍴 **Kome.** If you're looking for a break from the ubiquitous ribollita, stop in at this eatery, which may be the only Japanese restaurant in the world to be housed in a 15th-century Renaissance palazzo. High, vaulted arches frame the Kaiten sushi conveyor belt. It's Japanese food, cafeteria style: selections, priced according to the color of the plate, make their way around a bar, where diners pick whatever they find appealing. Those seeking a more substantial meal head to the second floor, where Japanese barbecue is prepared at your table. The minimalist basement provides a subtle but dramatic backdrop for a well-prepared cocktail. [$] *Average main: €20* ✉ *Via de' Benci 41/r, Santa Croce* ☎ *055/2008009* 🌐 *www.komefirenze.it* ✥ *G4.*

$ FAST FOOD 🍴 **La Ghiotta.** This shop sells whole and half chickens, grilled or roasted, among other things. You can assemble a perfect dinner, from soup to nuts, at this Florentine favorite. [$] *Average main: €8* ✉ *Via Pietrapiana 7/r, Santa Croce* ☎ *055/241237* ▭ *No credit cards* ⏲ *Closed Mon.* ✥ *H3.*

$$$ ITALIAN 🍴 **La Giostra.** This clubby spot, whose name means "carousel" in Italian, was created by the late Prince Dimitri Kunz d'Asburgo Lorena, and is now expertly run by his handsome twin sons. In perfect English they will describe favorite dishes, such as the *taglierini con tartufo bianco,* a decadently rich pasta with white truffles. The constantly changing menu has terrific vegetarian and vegan options, and any meal that does not include truffles is significantly less expensive than those that do. For dessert, this might be the only show in town with a sublime tiramisù *and* a wonderfully gooey Sacher torte. [$] *Average main: €30* ✉ *Borgo Pinti 12/r, Santa Croce* ☎ *055/241341* 🌐 *www.ristorantelagiostra.com* ✍ *Reservations essential* ⏲ *No lunch weekends.* ✥ *G3.*

$ ITALIAN 🍴 **Le Campane.** The *pizziauoli* (pizza-makers) successfully merge Roman (thin) crust with Neapolitan (thick) crust at Le Campane. [$] *Average main: €10* ✉ *Borgo La Croce 85–87/r, Santa Croce* ☎ *055/2341101* 🌐 *www.lecampane.it* 💳 *No credit cards* ✥ *H3.*

$$ ITALIAN Fodor's Choice ★ 🍴 **Osteria de'Benci.** A few minutes from Santa Croce, this charming osteria serves some of the most eclectic food in Florence. Try the spaghetti *degli eretici* (in tomato sauce with fresh herbs). The grilled meats are justifiably famous; the *carbonata* is a succulent piece of grilled beef served rare. Weekly specials complement what's happening in the market, and all of the food pairs beautifully with their wine list, which is heavy on things Tuscan. When it's warm, you can dine outside with a view of the 13th-century tower belonging to the prestigious Alberti family. [$] *Average main: €15* ✉ *Via de' Benci 11–13/r, Santa Croce* ☎ *055/2344923* ✍ *Reservations essential* 🕒 *Closed 2 wks in Aug.* ✥ *F5.*

$ 🍴 **Perché No.** They've been making ice cream at this much-loved-by-Florentines place since 1939. Such continuity might be the reason why this might be the best gelateria in the historic center. [$] *Average main: €3* ✉ *Santa Croce* ☎ *055/239–8969* 🌐 *www.percheno.firenze.it* 💳 *No credit cards* ✥ *E3.*

$ PIZZA 🍴 **Pizzeria Caffè Italiano.** This small pizzeria is favored by locals. Come early to grab one of the few tables, and don't mind the fact that service here is intentionally rushed: turning tables is paramount. [$] *Average main: €10* ✉ *Via Isole delle Stinche 11/r, Santa Croce* ☎ *055/289368* 💳 *No credit cards* ✥ *G4.*

$$ ITALIAN 🍴 **Simon Boccanegra.** Florentine epicures flock to this place named for a condottiere (mercenary) hero in a Verdi opera. Under high ceilings, candles on every table cast a rosy glow; the fine wine list and superb service make a meal here a true pleasure. The chef has a deft hand with fish dishes, as well as an inventiveness when it comes to reinterpreting such classics as risotto with chicken liver—he adds leek and saffron to give it a lift. A less expensive, less formal wine bar serving a basic Tuscan menu is also on the premises. [$] *Average main: €20* ✉ *Via Ghibellina 124/r, Santa Croce* ☎ *055/2001098* ✍ *Reservations essential* 🕒 *Closed Sun. No lunch* ✥ *G4.*

$ MEXICAN 🍴 **Tijuana.** Tijuana is frequented by young Florentines and U.S. junior year abroad students (and others) craving enchiladas, fajitas, and burgers with jalapeño peppers. [$] *Average main: €10* ✉ *Via Ghibellina 156–158/r, Santa Croce* ☎ *055/2341330* 🌐 *www.ristorantetijuana.it* 🕒 *No lunch Aug.* ✥ *G3.*

$$ LEBANESE 🍴 **Valle dei Cedri.** For delicious Lebanese fare at more than reasonable prices, head here. Florentines pack this place for both lunch and dinner; reservations are essential, especially at night. The kitchen stays open until midnight—a blessing in this town. [$] *Average main: €15* ✉ *Borgo Santa Croce 11/r, Santa Croce* ☎ *055/2346340* ✥ *G4.*

THE OLTRARNO

$ PIZZA 🍴 **Borgo Antico.** In the Oltrarno, try Borgo Antico, which serves fine pizza and other trattoria fare. [$] *Average main: €10* ✉ *Piazza Santo Spirito 6/r, Santo Spirito* ☎ *055/210437* ✥ *C5.*

What Tripe!

While in Florence, those with a sense of culinary adventure should seek out a tripe sandwich, which is just about as revered by local gourmands as the *bistecca alla fiorentina*. In this case, however, the treasure comes on the cheap—sandwiches are sold from small stands found in the city center, topped with a fragrant green sauce or a piquant red hot sauce, or both. *Bagnato* means that the hard, crusty roll is first dipped in the tripe's cooking liquid; it's advisable to say "*sì*" when asked if that's how you like it. Sandwiches are usually taken with a glass of red wine poured from the tripe seller's *fiasco* (flask). If you find the tripe to your liking, you might also enjoy *lampredotto*, another (some

say better) cut of stomach. For an exalted, high-end tripe treat, try Fabio Picchi's cold tripe salad, served gratis as an *amuse-bouche* at the restaurant Cibrèo. It could make a convert of even the staunchest "I'd never try *that*" kind of eater.

Tripe carts are lunchtime favorites of Florentine working men—it's uncommon, but not unheard of, to see a woman at a tripe stand. Aficionados will argue which sandwich purveyor is best; here are three that frequently get mentioned:

Il Trippaio ⊠ *Via de' Macci at Borgo La Croce, Santa Croce* ⊗ *Closed Sun..*

La Trippaia ⊠ *Via dell'Ariento, Santa Maria Novella* ⊗ *Closed Sun..*

$
WINE BAR
✕ **Fuori Porta.** One of the oldest and best wine bars in Florence, this place serves cured meats and cheeses, as well as daily specials such as the sublime spaghetti *al curry*. *Crostini* and *crostoni*—grilled breads topped with a mélange of cheeses and meats—are the house specialty; the *verdure sott'olio* (vegetables with oil) are divine. The lengthy wine list offers great wines by the glass, and terrific bottles from all over Italy and beyond. All this can be enjoyed at rustic wooden tables, and outdoors when weather allows. $ *Average main: €10* ⊠ *Via Monte alle Croci 10/r, San Niccolò* ☎ *055/2342483* ✛ *G6.*

$$
TUSCAN
✕ **Il Santo Bevitore.** Florentines and other lovers of good food flock to "The Holy Drinker" for tasty, well-priced dishes. Unpretentious white walls, dark wood furniture, and paper placemats provide the simple decor; start with the exceptional vegetables *sott'olio* (marinated in olive oil) or the *terrina di fegatini* (a creamy chicken-liver spread) before sampling any of the divine pastas, such as the fragrant spaghetti with shrimp sauce. Count yourself lucky if the extraordinary potato gratin, served in compact triangular wedges, is on the menu. The extensive wine list is well priced, and the well-informed staff is happy to explain it. $ *Average main: €16* ⊠ *Via Santo Spirito 64/66r, Santo Spirito* ☎ *055/211264* ⊗ *No lunch Sun.* ✛ *B4.*

$
TUSCAN
✕ **La Casalinga.** *Casalinga* means "housewife," and this place has the nostalgic charm of a 1950s kitchen with Tuscan comfort food to match. If you eat *ribollita* anywhere in Florence, eat it here—it couldn't be more authentic. Mediocre paintings clutter the semipaneled walls, tables are set close together, and the place is usually jammed. The menu is long, portions are plentiful, and service is prompt and friendly. For dessert,

the lemon sorbet perfectly caps off the meal. $ *Average main: €13* ✉ *Via Michelozzi 9/r, Santo Spirito* ☎ *055/218624* ☾ *Closed Sun., 1 wk at Christmas, and 3 wks in Aug.* ✛ *C5.*

$$$ ✕ **La Vecchia Bettola.** The name doesn't exactly mean "old dive," but
TUSCAN   it comes pretty close. This lively trattoria has been around only since 1979, but it feels as if it's been a whole lot longer. Tile floors and simple wood tables and chairs provide the interior decoration, such as it is. The recipes come from "wise grandmothers" and celebrate Tuscan food in its glorious simplicity. Here prosciutto is sliced with a knife, portions of grilled meat are tender and ample, service is friendly, and the wine list is well priced and good. This place is worth a taxi ride, even though it's just outside the centro storico. $ *Average main: €30* ✉ *Viale Vasco Pratolini, Oltrarno* ☎ *055/224158* ▭ *No credit cards* ✛ *A6.*

$ ✕ **Osteria Antica Mescita San Niccolò.** It's always crowded, always good,
TUSCAN   and always inexpensive. The osteria is next to the church of San Nic-colò, and if you sit in the lower part you'll find yourself in what was once a chapel dating from the 11th century. The subtle but dramatic background is a nice complement to the food, which is simple Tuscan at its best. The *pollo con limone* is tasty pieces of chicken in a lemon-scented broth. In winter, try the *spezzatino di cinghiale con aromi* (wild boar stew with herbs). Reservations are advised. $ *Average main: €7* ✉ *Via San Niccolò 60/r, San Niccolò* ☎ *055/2342836* ☾ *Closed Sun. and Aug.* ✛ *G6.*

$ ✕ **Zeb.** The food is incredibly tasty at this well-priced *alimentari* (deli-
TUSCAN   catessen). Zeb stands for *zuppa e bollito* (soup and boiled things), and nothing here disappoints. This is home-style Tuscan cuisine at its very best, served in unpretentious, intimate surroundings: there's only room for about 15 guests. In the kitchen is Giuseppina, who staunchly insists on cooking what's best that day; which means the menu changes daily, reflecting the season's best offerings. $ *Average main: €10* ✉ *Via San Miniato 2, Oltrarno* ☎ *055/2342864* ⊕ *www.zeb gastronomia.com* ✛ *G6.*

WHERE TO STAY

For expanded hotel reviews, visit Fodors.com.

Florence is equipped with hotels for all budgets; for instance, you can find both budget and luxury hotels in the *centro storico* (historic center) and along the Arno. Florence has so many famous landmarks that it's not hard to find lodging with a panoramic view. The equivalent of the genteel *pensioni* of yesteryear can still be found, though they are now officially classified as hotels. Generally small and intimate, they often have a quaint appeal that usually doesn't preclude modern plumbing.

Florence's importance not only as a tourist city but also as a convention center and the site of the Pitti fashion collections guarantees a variety of accommodations. The high demand also means that, except in winter, reservations are a must.

If you find yourself in Florence with no reservations, go to **Consorzio ITA** (✉ *Stazione Centrale, Santa Maria Novella* ☎ *055/282893*). You must go there in person to make a booking.

CLOSE UP

Florence's Wine Bars

Wine bars are found all over Florence, and most of them have light fare as well as lengthy wine lists—perfect places for lunch or dinner. Many are closed Sunday.

Casa del Vino. Come here for creative panini, such as *sgrombri e carciofini sott'olio* (mackerel and marinated baby artichokes), and an ever-changing list of significant wines by the glass. They also have a well-stocked collection of bottles to go, at more than fair prices. ⊠ *Via dell'Ariento 16/r, San Lorenzo* ☎ *055/215609.*

I Fratellini. A hop, skip, and a jump from Orsanmichele in the centro storico is I Fratellini, in existence since 1875. It sells wines by the glass and has a lengthy list of panini, including pecorino with sun-dried tomatoes and spicy wild-boar salami with goat cheese. There are no seats, so perch on the curb and make like a local. ⊠ *Via dei Cimatori 38/r, Piazza della*

Signoria ☎ *055/2396096* ⊕ *www. iduefratellini.com.*

FodorsChoice ★ **Il Santino.** Though it has only four tables and four small stools at an equally small bar, Il Santino is blessed with a big wine list and superior cheeses, cured meats, and other delicacies to match. ⊠ *Via Santo Spirito 60/r, Santo Spirito* ☎ *055/2302820.*

Le Volpi e l'Uva. Le Volpi e l'Uva, off Piazza Santa Trinita, is an oenophile's dream: the waiters pour significant wines by the glass and serve equally impressive cheeses and little sandwiches to go with them. ⊠ *Piazza de' Rossi 1, Palazzo Pitti* ☎ *055/2398132.*

Olio & Convivium. Here you'll find a great selection of cheeses and cured meats, wines by the glass, food products to take home (like powdered porcini mushrooms), daily specials, as well as some tasty food served in situ. ⊠ *Via Santo Spirito 4, Santo Spirito* ☎ *055/2658198.*

AROUND THE DUOMO

$
HOTEL
⌖ **Cristina.** A friendly and enthusiastic staff runs this tiny hotel one block from the Uffizi and the Bargello. **Pros:** great deal for families. **Cons:** steep flight of stairs; some rooms share bath. $ *Rooms from: €70* ⊠ *Via della Condotta 4, Duomo* ☎ *055/214484* ⊕ *www.hotelcristina-florence. com* ⊅ *9 rooms, 5 with bath* ⫶◯⫶ *No meals* ⊕ *F4.*

$$
HOTEL
⌖ **Hermitage.** All rooms here are decorated with lively wallpaper, and some have views of Palazzo Vecchio and others of the Arno. **Pros:** views; friendly, English-speaking staff; enviable position a stone's throw from the Ponte Vecchio. **Cons:** short flight of stairs to reach elevator. $ *Rooms from: €198* ⊠ *Vicolo Marzio 1, Piazza della Signoria* ☎ *055/287216* ⊕ *www.hermitagehotel.com* ⊅ *27 rooms, 1 suite* ⫶◯⫶ *Breakfast* ⊕ *E4.*

$$$
HOTEL
⌖ **Hotel Benivieni.** This tranquil, former 15th-century palace is one block from the Duomo. **Pros:** location. **Cons:** smallish bathrooms; some Fodor's readers detect street noise, despite triple-glazed windows. $ *Rooms from: €220* ⊠ *Via delle Oche 5, Duomo* ☎ *055/2382133* ⊕ *www.hotelbenivieni.it* ⊅ *15 rooms* ⫶◯⫶ *Breakfast* ⊕ *E3.*

$$ **Hotel degli Orafi.** A key scene
HOTEL in *A Room with a View* was shot
in this pensione, which is today a
luxury hotel adorned with chintz
and marble. **Pros:** stellar Arno
views, welcome drink upon arrival.
Cons: extra charge for Internet use.
$ *Rooms from: €175* ✉ *Lungarno
Archibusieri 4, Piazza della Signo-
ria* ☎ *055/26622* ⊕ *www.hoteldegli
orafi.it* ↻ *42 rooms* ⦿ *Breakfast*
♢ *E5.*

WORD OF MOUTH

"Two nights in Florence is just not
long enough—but anyone could
have told me this and did. It was
a choice between doing a little
of Florence, and a little of Venice,
or more of only one. I chose the
two and don't regret it, but if you
can stretch your holidays do more
than two nights." —drjem

$$$$ **Hotel Helvetia and Bristol.** From
HOTEL the cozy yet sophisticated lobby with its stone columns to the guest
Fodor'sChoice rooms decorated with prints, you might feel as if you're a guest in a
★ sophisticated manor house. **Pros:** central location; superb staff. **Cons:**
rooms facing the street get some noise. $ *Rooms from: €390* ✉ *Via
dei Pescioni 2, Piazza della Repubblica* ☎ *055/26651* ⊕ *www.hbf.
royaldemeure.com* ↻ *54 rooms, 13 suites* ⦿ *No meals* ♢ *D3.*

$$$ **In Piazza della Signoria.** A cozy feeling permeates these charming
B&B/INN rooms, all of which are uniquely decorated and lovingly furnished;
Fodor'sChoice some have damask curtains, others fanciful frescoes in the bathroom.
★ **Pros:** marvelous staff; tasty breakfast with a view of Piazza della Signo-
ria. **Cons:** short flight of stairs to reach elevator. $ *Rooms from: €250*
✉ *Via dei Magazzini 2, Near Piazza della Signoria* ☎ *055/2399546*
⊕ *www.inpiazzadellasignoria.com* ↻ *10 rooms, 3 apartments*
⦿ *Breakfast* ♢ *E4.*

$$ **Palazzo Niccolini al Duomo.** The graceful Marchesa Ginevra Nicco-
HOTEL lini di Camugliano has taken her husband's family's palazzo (acquired
by an ancestor in 1532) and turned it into a luxurious place that still
manages to evoke a cozy, yet highly sophisticated, home. **Pros:** steps
away from the Duomo. **Cons:** street noise sometimes a problem.
$ *Rooms from: €150* ✉ *Via dei Servi 2, Duomo* ☎ *055/282412* ⊕ *www.
niccolinidomepalace.com* ↻ *5 rooms, 5 suites* ♢ *F2.*

$$$$ **Palazzo Vecchietti.** If you're looking for a swank setting, and the pos-
HOTEL sibility of staying in for a meal (each room has a tiny kitchenette), look
no further than this hotel which, while thoroughly modern, dates to
the 15th century. $ *Rooms from: €379* ✉ *via, degli Strozzi 4, Piazza
della Republica, Duomo* ☎ *055/230–2802* ↻ *12 rooms, 2 apartments*
⊗ *www.palazzovecchietti.it* ⦿ *Breakfast* ♢ *D3.*

$ **Sani Tourist House.** Hosts Elizabeth and Remi have taken their former
B&B/INN no-frills accommodation and spruced it up a bit, adding such ameni-
ties as air-conditioning and the occasional private bath to make a stay
here more pleasant. **Pros:** good deals for single travelers; even lower
rates off-season. **Cons:** no reception. $ *Rooms from: €104* ✉ *Piazza dei
Giuochi 1, Duomo* ☎ *335/82244133* ⊕ *www.sanibnb.it* ↻ *6 rooms, 2
with shared bath* ⦿ *No meals* ♢ *F3.*

SAN LORENZO

$$
B&B/INN

🏨 **Antica Dimora Firenze.** Each simply furnished room in the intimate *residenza* is painted a different pastel color—peach, rose, powder-blue—while double-glazed windows ensure a peaceful night's sleep. **Pros:** ample DVD library; honor bar with Antinori wines. **Cons:** staff goes home at 8; no credit cards accepted. $ *Rooms from: €200* ✉ *Via San Gallo 72, San Marco* ☎ *055/4627296* ⊕ *www.anticadimorafirenze. it* ⤳ *6 rooms* ☰ *No credit cards* ⦿ *Breakfast* ✛ *E1.*

$$
B&B/INN
Fodor'sChoice
★

🏨 **Antica Dimora Johlea.** Lively color runs rampant on the top floor of this 19th-century palazzo, with a charming flower-filled rooftop terrace where you can sip a glass of wine while taking in a view of Brunelleschi's cupola. **Pros:** great staff; cheerful rooms; honor bar. **Cons:** staff goes home at 7; narrow staircase to get to roof terrace. $ *Rooms from: €139* ✉ *Via San Gallo 80, San Marco* ☎ *055/4633292* ⊕ *www.johanna. it* ⤳ *6 rooms* ☰ *No credit cards* ⦿ *Breakfast* ✛ *E1.*

$$
HOTEL

🏨 **Hotel Casci.** In this refurbished 14th-century palace, the home of Giacchino Rossini in 1851–55, the friendly Lombardi family runs a hotel with spotless, functional rooms. **Pros:** helpful staff; good option for families; English-language DVD collection with good selections for kids. **Cons:** bit of a college-dorm atmosphere; small elevator. $ *Rooms from: €150* ✉ *Via Cavour 13, San Marco* ☎ *055/211686* ⊕ *www. hotelcasci.com* ⤳ *25 rooms* ⦿ *Breakfast* ✛ *E1.*

$$
HOTEL

🏨 **Il Guelfo Bianco.** The 15th-century building has all modern conveniences, but Renaissance charm still shines in the high-ceilinged rooms. **Pros:** stellar multilingual staff. **Cons:** rooms facing the street can be noisy. $ *Rooms from: €150* ✉ *Via Cavour 29, San Marco* ☎ *055/288330* ⊕ *www.ilguelfobianco.it* ⤳ *40 rooms* ⦿ *Breakfast* ✛ *F1.*

$
B&B/INN

🏨 **Residenza Johanna I.** Savvy travelers and those on a budget should look no further, as this *residenza* is a tremendous value for quality and location. **Pros:** great value. **Cons:** staff goes home at 7; no credit cards. $ *Rooms from: €93* ✉ *Via Bonifacio Lupi 14, San Marco* ☎ *055/481896* ⊕ *www.johanna.it* ⤳ *11 rooms* ☰ *No credit cards* ⦿ *No meals* ✛ *D1.*

SANTA MARIA NOVELLA

$$
B&B/INN

🏨 **Alessandra.** An aura of grandeur pervades these clean, ample rooms a block from the Ponte Vecchio. **Pros:** several rooms have views of the Arno; the spacious suite is a bargain. **Cons:** stairs to elevator; some rooms share bath. $ *Rooms from: €150* ✉ *Borgo Santi Apostoli 17, Santa Maria Novella* ☎ *055/283438* ⊕ *www.hotelalessandra.com* ⤳ *26 rooms, 19 with bath; 1 suite; 1 apartment* ⊘ *Closed Dec. 10–26* ⦿ *Breakfast* ✛ *D4.*

$$$
B&B/INN

🏨 **Antica Torre di Via Tornabuoni.** If you're looking for a room with a view, stop here, where just about every one has a window that frames the awe-inspiring Duomo or the Arno (some even have small terraces). **Pros:** views and terraces. **Cons:** no staff after 7; seemingly ongoing remodeling. $ *Rooms from: €280* ✉ *Via Tornabuoni 1, Santa Maria Novella* ☎ *055/2658161* ⊕ *www.tornabuoni1.com* ⤳ *11 rooms, 1 suite* ⦿ *Breakfast* ✛ *D4.*

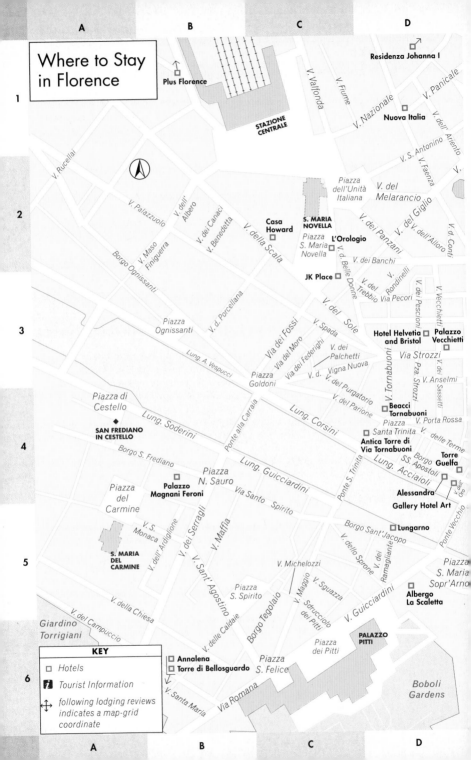

Where to Stay in Florence

KEY

☐ Hotels

🛈 Tourist Information

↕ following lodging reviews indicates a map-grid coordinate

Plus Florence

STAZIONE CENTRALE

Residenza Johanna I

V. Valfonda

V. Fiume

V. Nazionale

Nuova Italia

V. Panicale

V. dell' Arjeno

V. S. Antonino

V. S. Antonino

V. Faenza

Piazza dell'Unità Italiana

V. del Melarancio

V. dei Panzani

V. del Giglio

V. dell'Alloro

V. d. Conti

S. MARIA NOVELLA

Casa Howard

Piazza S. Maria Novella

L'Orologio

V. della Scala

V. dei Canaci

V. dei Benedetta

V. dell' Albero

V. Palazzuolo

V. Rucellai

V. Maso Finiguerra

Borgo Ognissanti

V. d. Porcellana

V. dei Fossi

V. del Moro

Piazza Ognissanti

Lung. A. Vespucci

Piazza Goldoni

V. Spada

V. del Sole

JK Place

V. d. Belle Donne

V. dei Banchi

V. del Trebbio

Via Pecori

V. Rondinelli

V. dei Pescioni

V. Vecchietti

V. dei Pecscioni

Hotel Helvetia and Bristol

Palazzo Vecchietti

Via Strozzi

V. dei Palchetti

V. dei Federighi

Via Vigna Nuova

V. d.

V. del Purgatorio

V. del Parione

V. Tornabuoni

Pza. Strozzi

V. d. Sassetti

V. Anselmi

Beacci Tornabuoni

Piazza Santa Trinita

V. Porta Rossa

Antica Torre di Via Tornabuoni

V. delle Terme

Piazza di Cestello

Lung. Soderini

SAN FREDIANO IN CESTELLO

Ponte alla Carraia

Lung. Corsini

Ponte S. Trinita

Lung. Acciaioli

SS. Apostoli

Borgo

Torre Guelfa

V. dell' Oro

Borgo S. Frediano

Piazza N. Sauro

Palazzo Magnani Feroni

Via Santo Spirito

Lung. Guicciardini

Alessandra

Gallery Hotel Art

Piazza del Carmine

S. MARIA DEL CARMINE

V. S. Monaca

V. dell'Ardiglione

V. dei Serragli

V. Sant'Agostino

V. Maffia

Piazza S. Spirito

V. Michelozzi

Borgo Sant'Jacopo

Lungarno

Ponte Vecchio

V. dello Sprone

V. dei Ramaglianti

Piazza S. Maria Sopr'Arno

Albergo La Scaletta

V. Maggio

V. Sguazza

Sdrucciolo dei Pitti

Borgo Tegolaio

V. delle Caldaie

V. Guicciardini

V. della Chiesa

V. del Campuccio

Giardino Torrigiani

Annalena

Torre di Bellosguardo

Piazza S. Felice

Via Romana

V. Santa Maria

Piazza dei Pitti

PALAZZO PITTI

Boboli Gardens

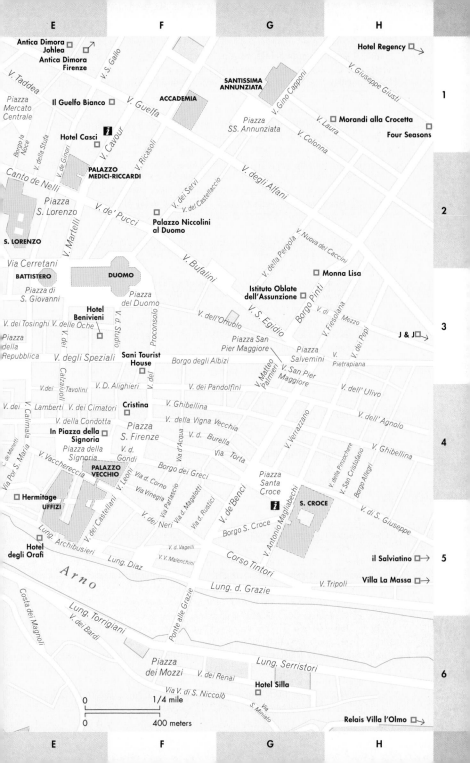

$$ 🏨 **Beacci Tornabuoni.** Florentine pensioni don't get any classier than this:
HOTEL old-fashioned style, enough modern comfort to keep you happy, and a 14th-century palazzo. **Pros:** multilingual staff; flower-filled terrace. **Cons:** hall noise can sometimes be a problem. $ *Rooms from: €200* ✉ *Via Tornabuoni 3, Santa Maria Novella* ☎ *055/212645* ⊕ *www. tornabuonihotels.com* ⟿ *37 rooms, 16 suites* ⦿ *Breakfast* ✣ *D4.*

$$ 🏨 **Casa Howard.** This unassuming little inn has no two rooms alike, and
HOTEL an aura of eclectic funk pervades: one room takes its inspiration from Japan; others are geared to families; others have access to a garden. **Pros:** great location near the basilica of Santa Maria Novella; good vibe. **Cons:** very limited concierge service; staff goes home early in the evening. $ *Rooms from: €161* ✉ *Via della Scala 18, Santa Maria Novella* ☎ *06/69924555* ⊕ *www.casahoward.com* ⟿ *13 rooms* ⦿ *No Meals* ✣ *C2.*

$$$ 🏨 **Gallery Hotel Art.** High design resides at this art showcase near the
HOTEL Ponte Vecchio, where sleek, uncluttered rooms are dressed mostly in neutrals and luxe touches, such as leather headboards and kimono robes, abound. **Pros:** cool atmosphere; beautiful people; miso soup on the breakfast menu; the in-house Fusion Bar, which pours delightful cocktails. **Cons:** sometimes elevator is slow; too cool for some. $ *Rooms from: €280* ✉ *Vicolo dell'Oro 5, Santa Maria Novella* ☎ *055/27263* ⊕ *www.lungarnohotels.com* ⟿ *65 rooms, 9 suites* ⦿ *Breakfast* ✣ *D4.*

$$ 🏨 **Hotel L'Orologio.** The owner of this quietly understated, elegant hotel
HOTEL has a real passion for watches, which is why he chose to name his hotel after them (and why you will see them in many places). **Pros:** location; great staff; stunning breakfast room; fantastic in-house bar. **Cons:** some folk think it too close to the train station. $ *Rooms from: €195* ✉ *Piazza Santa Maria Novella 24, Santa Maria Novella* ☎ *055/277 380* ⊕ *www. whythebesthotels.com* ⟿ *44 rooms, 8 suites* ⦿ *Breakfast* ✣ *C2.*

$$$$ 🏨 **JK Place.** Hard to spot from the street, these sumptuous appoint-
HOTEL ments provide all the comforts of a luxe home away from home—expect
Fodor'sChoice soothing earth tones in the guest rooms, free minibars, crisp linens, and
★ a room service menu with organic dishes. **Pros:** private, intimate feel; stellar staff; free minibar; organic meal choices. **Cons:** breakfast at a shared table (which can be easily gotten around with room service). $ *Rooms from: €380* ✉ *Piazza Santa Maria Novella 7* ☎ *055/2645181* ⊕ *www.jkplace.com* ⟿ *14 doubles, 6 suites* ⦿ *Breakfast* ✣ *C3.*

$ 🏨 **Nuova Italia.** The genial English-speaking Viti family oversees
HOTEL these clean and simple rooms near the train station and well within walking distance of the sights. **Pros:** reasonable rates. **Cons:** no elevator. $ *Rooms from: €89* ✉ *Via Faenza 26, Santa Maria Novella* ☎ *055/268430* ⊕ *www.hotel-nuovaitalia.com* ⟿ *20 rooms* ⊘ *Closed Dec. 8–Dec. 26* ⦿ *Breakfast* ✣ *D1.*

$$ 🏨 **Torre Guelfa.** If you want a taste of medieval Florence, try one of
B&B/INN these character-filled guest rooms—some with canopied beds, some with balconies—housed within a 13th-century tower. **Pros:** rooftop terrace with tremendous views; wonderful staff; some family-friendly triple and quadruple rooms. **Cons:** 72 steps to get to the terrace. $ *Rooms from: €190* ✉ *Borgo Santi Apostoli 8, Santa Maria Novella* ☎ *055/2396338* ⊕ *www.hoteltorreguelfa.com* ⟿ *28 rooms, 3 suites* ⦿ *Breakfast* ✣ *D4.*

THE OLTRARNO

$ **Albergo La Scaletta.** For a tremendous view of the Boboli Gardens,
HOTEL look no further than this exquisite pensione near the Ponte Vecchio
and Palazzo Pitti. **Pros:** fantastic terrace. **Cons:** small elevator; many
steps. $ *Rooms from: €119* ⊠ *Via Guicciardini 13, Palazzo Pitti*
☎ *055/283028* ⊕ *www.lascaletta.com* ⤳ *13 rooms* ⦿*Breakfast* ✦ *D5.*

$ **Annalena.** The story goes that Annalena, a 15th-century maiden, mar-
HOTEL ried a Medici; another man, smitten with her and angry at her refusal to
capitulate, murdered her husband and her young son. **Pros:** the triples and
quads are great for families. **Cons:** a hefty flight of stairs to get to reception.
$ *Rooms from: €119* ⊠ *Via Romana 34, Santo Spirito* ☎ *055/222402*
⊕ *www.annalenahotel.com* ⤳ *20 rooms* ⦿*Breakfast* ✦ *B6.*

$ **Hotel Silla.** Rooms in this 15th-century palazzo, entered through a
HOTEL courtyard lined with potted plants and sculpture-filled niches, are simply furnished and walls are papered; some have views of the Arno.
Pros: a Fodor's reader raves, "It's in the middle of everything except
the crowds." **Cons:** some readers complain of street noise and too-
small rooms. $ *Rooms from: €120* ⊠ *Via de' Renai 5, San Niccolò*
☎ *055/2342888* ⊕ *www.hotelsilla.it* ⤳ *35 rooms* ⦿*Breakfast* ✦ *G6.*

$$$$ **Lungarno.** Many rooms and suites here have private terraces that jut
HOTEL out right over the Arno, granting stunning views of the Palazzo Vecchio and the Lungarno. **Pros:** upscale without being stuffy. **Cons:** rooms
without Arno views feel less special. $ *Rooms from: €390* ⊠ *Borgo San
Jacopo 14, Oltrarno* ☎ *055/27261* ⊕ *www.lungarnohotels.com* ⤳ *59
rooms, 14 suites* ⦿*Breakfast* ✦ *D5.*

$$$ **Palazzo Magnani Feroni.** The perfect place to play the part of a Flo-
HOTEL rentine aristocrat is here at this 16th-century palazzo, which despite its
massive halls and sweeping staircase could almost feel like home. **Pros:**
24-hour room service; billiard room; Bulgari bath products; generous
buffet breakfast; terrific staff. **Cons:** a few steps up to the elevator;
many steps to the rooftop terrace; Wi-Fi's not free. $ *Rooms from:
€230* ⊠ *Borgo San Frediano 5, Santo Spirito* ☎ *055/2399544* ⊕ *www.
florencepalace.it* ⤳ *12 suites* ⦿*Breakfast* ✦ *B4.*

SANTA CROCE

$$$$ **The Four Seasons.** Seven years of restoration have turned this 15th-cen-
HOTEL tury palazzo in Florence's center into a luxury hotel where no two guest
rooms are alike; many have original 17th-century frescoes, some face the
garden, others quiet interior courtyards. **Pros:** a unique "city meets coun-
try" experience; the marvelous garden. **Cons:** for this price, breakfast really
should be included; some feel it's a little too removed from the historic cen-
ter. $ *Rooms from: €695* ⊠ *Borgo Pinti 99e, Santa Croce* ☎ *055/26261*
⊕ *www.fourseasons.com/florence* ⤳ *117 rooms* ⦿*No meals* ✦ *H1.*

$$$$ **Hotel Regency.** Rooms dressed in richly colored fabrics and antique-
HOTEL style furniture remain faithful to the premises' 19th-century origins as a
private mansion. **Pros:** faces one of the few green parks in the center of
Florence. **Cons:** a small flight of stairs takes you to reception. $ *Rooms
from: €365* ⊠ *Piazza d'Azeglio 3, Santa Croce* ☎ *055/245247* ⊕ *www.
regency-hotel.com* ⤳ *30 rooms, 4 suites* ⦿*Breakfast* ✦ *H1.*

$ ⌂ **Istituto Oblate dell'Assunzione.** Seven nuns run this convent, minutes from
B&B/INN   the Duomo, with spotlessly clean, simple rooms; some have views of the
cupola, and others look out onto a carefully tended garden where you
are welcome to relax. **Pros:** bargain price; great location; quiet rooms;
garden. **Cons:** curfew; no credit cards. $ *Rooms from: €90 ⌂ Borgo Pinti
15, Santa Croce* ☎ *055/2480582* ⊕ *www.sanctuarybbfirenze.com* ⌂ *28
rooms, 22 with bath* ☐ *No credit cards* ⦿ *No meals* ⊹ *G3.*

$$$ ⌂ **J&J.** On a quiet street within walking distance of the sights sits this
B&B/INN   unusual hotel, a converted 16th-century convent. **Pros:** large rooms.
Cons: one flight of steep stairs to get to rooms; Wi-Fi in public areas
only, for an hourly fee. $ *Rooms from: €290 ⌂ Via di Mezzo 20,
Santa Croce* ☎ *055/26312* ⊕ *www.jandjhotel.net* ⌂ *19 rooms, 7 suites*
⦿ *Breakfast* ⊹ *H3.*

$$$ ⌂ **Monna Lisa.** Though some rooms are small, they are tasteful, and best
HOTEL   of all, housed in a 15th-century palazzo that retains some of its wood-
Fodor's Choice   coffered ceilings from the 1500s, as well as its original staircase. **Pros:**
★   lavish buffet breakfast; cheerful staff; garden. **Cons:** rooms in annex
are less charming than those in palazzo; street noise in some rooms.
$ *Rooms from: €259 ⌂ Borgo Pinti 27, Santa Croce* ☎ *055/2479751*
⊕ *www.monnalisa.it* ⌂ *45 rooms* ⦿ *Breakfast* ⊹ *G3.*

$$ ⌂ **Morandi alla Crocetta.** You're made to feel like privileged friends of the
B&B/INN   family at this charming and distinguished residence, furnished comfort-
ably in the classic style of a gracious Florentine home. **Pros:** interest-
ing, offbeat location near the sights; terrific staff; great value. **Cons:**
two flights of stairs to reach reception and rooms. $ *Rooms from:
€150 ⌂ Via Laura 50, Santissima Annunziata* ☎ *055/2344747* ⊕ *www.
hotelmorandi.it* ⌂ *10 rooms* ⊹ *H1.*

BEYOND THE CITY CENTER

$$$$ ⌂ **Il Salviatino.** There's no reception area, but the intention is to make
HOTEL   you feel at home—that is, if home were a restored 14th-century villa at
the end of a cypress-studded winding drive. **Pros:** great views; attentive
staff. **Cons:** no reception area; some hall noise. $ *Rooms from: €458
⌂ Via del Salviatino 21, Santa Croce* ☎ *055/904111* ⊕ *www.salviatino.
com* ⌂ *23 rooms, 22 suites* ⦿ *Breakfast* ⊹ *H5.*

$$ ⌂ **Relais Villa l'Olmo.** Alberto and Claudia Giannotti have turned a for-
B&B/INN   mer 16th-century country villa into an elegantly comfortable agritu-
rismo 20 minutes south of the center of Florence. **Pros:** good for families
and groups; golf privileges. **Cons:** you need a car if you don't want to
depend on the city bus; breakfast must be ordered in advance; concierge
goes home at 7:30. $ *Rooms from: €170 ⌂ Via Imprunetana per Tavar-
nuzze 19, Impruneta* ☎ *055/2311311* ⊕ *www.relaisfarmholiday.it* ⌂ *8
apartments, 2 cottages, 1 farmhouse* ⦿ *Breakfast* ⊹ *H6.*

$$$ ⌂ **Torre di Bellosguardo.** *Bellosguardo* means "beautiful view"; given the
B&B/INN   view of Florence you get here, the name is fitting. **Pros:** great for escap-
FAMILY   ing heat of the city in summer; a villa experience with the city just min-
Fodor's Choice   utes away. **Cons:** a car is a necessity; breakfast is not included. $ *Rooms
★   from: €280 ⌂ Via Roti Michelozzi 2, Oltrarno* ☎ *055/2298145* ⊕ *www.
torrebellosguardo.com* ⌂ *9 rooms, 7 suites* ⊹ *B6.*

$$$$ HOTEL **Villa La Massa.** In this tall and imposing villa, 15 minutes out of town, public rooms are outfitted in Renaissance style and guest rooms have high ceilings, plush carpeting, and deep bathtubs. **Pros:** pleasing mix of city and country life; sumptuous buffet breakfast; views of the Tuscan hills; phenomenal staff. **Cons:** even with shuttle, a car is a necessity; not open year-round. [$] *Rooms from: €490* ✉ *Via della Massa 24, Candeli* ☎ *055/62611* 🌐 *www.villalamassa.com* 🛏 *19 rooms, 18 suites* 🕒 *Closed Dec.–Mar.* 🍴 *Breakfast* ✥ *H5.*

NIGHTLIFE AND THE ARTS

NIGHTLIFE

Florentines are rather proud of their nightlife options. Most bars now have some sort of happy hour, which usually lasts for many hours and often has snacks that can substitute for a light dinner. (Check, though, that the buffet is free or comes with the price of a drink.) Clubs typically don't open until very late in the evening, and don't get crowded until 1 or 2 in the morning.

DUOMO

il bar de l'O. This swanky, American-style bar is attached to the Hotel l'Orologio. It's a good spot for a well-executed cocktail with tasty snacks; when it's warm, you can sit outside and gaze at the beautiful facade of Santa Maria Novella. ✉ *Via delle Belle Donne 34/r* ☎ *055/277380* 🌐 *www.ilbardelo.com.*

SANTA MARIA NOVELLA

Harry's Bar. For a posh evening, lubricated with trademark Bellinis and the best martinis in Florence, head to Harry's Bar. ✉ *Lungarno Vespucci 22/r* ☎ *055/2396700* 🌐 *www.harrysbarfirenze.it.*

OLTRARNO

Montecarla. People sip cocktails against a backdrop of exotic flowers, leopard-print chairs and chintz, and red walls on the two crowded floors at Montecarla. ✉ *Via de' Bardi 2* ☎ *055/2340259.*

Negroni. Well-dressed young Florentines flock to Negroni at happy hour. ✉ *Via de' Renai 17/r* ☎ *055/243647* 🌐 *www.negronibar.it.*

Noir. Noir makes great Bloody Marys, and it's *the* place to be at cocktail time when young Florentines crowd the doors and spill out into the street. ✉ *Lungarno Corsini 12/14r, Lungarno Sud* ☎ *055/210751.*

Zoe. Though it's called a "caffetteria," and coffee is served (as well as terrific salads and burgers at lunchtime), Zoe's fine cocktails are the real draw for elegant youngish Florentines who come here to see and be seen. Here's people-watching at its very best, done while listening to the latest CDs imported from England. ✉ *Via de' Renai 13/r* ☎ *055/243111* 🌐 *www.zoebar.it.*

SAN LORENZO

Kitsch. Choose from indoor or outdoor seating and take advantage of the great list of wines by the glass. At aperitivo time €9 will buy you a truly tasty cocktail and give you access to the tremendous buffet; it's so good, you won't need dinner afterward—in fact, they called it "Apericena." That means, roughly, "drink and dinner." ⊠ *Via San Gallo 22/r* ☎ *328/9039289* ⊕ *www.kitschfirenze.com.*

SANTA CROCE

Jazz Club. Enjoy live music in this small basement club. ⊠ *Via Nuova de' Caccini 3, corner of Borgo Pinti, Santa Croce* ☎ *339/4980752.*

Rex. A trendy, artsy clientele frequents this bar at aperitivo time; around 10 o'clock, the place is packed with mostly young folks sipping artfully made cocktails. ⊠ *Via Fiesolana 23–25/r, Santa Croce* ☎ *055/2480331.*

Sant'Ambrogio Caffè. Come here in the summer for outdoor seating with a view of an 11th-century church (Sant'Ambrogio) directly across the street. ⊠ *Piazza Sant'Ambrogio 7–8/r, Santa Croce* ☎ *055/2477277* ⊕ *www.caffesantambrogio.it.*

PIAZZA DELLA REPUBBLICA

Hard Rock Cafe. Hard Rock packs in young Florentines and travelers eager to sample the iconic chain's take on classic American grub. ⊠ *Piazza della Repubblica* ☎ *055/2670499* ⊕ *www.hardrock.com.*

Yab. Yab never seems to go out of style, though it increasingly becomes the haunt of Florentine high schoolers and university students intent on dancing and doing vodka shots. ⊠ *Via Sassetti 5/r* ☎ *055/215160* ⊕ *www.yab.it.*

THE ARTS

Florence has a lively classical music scene. The internationally famous annual Maggio Musicale lights up the musical calendar in early spring, and continues throughout most of the rest of the year. Fans of rock, pop, and hip-hop might be somewhat surprised by the absence of live acts that make it to town (for such offerings, travel to Rome or Milan is often a necessity). What it lacks in contemporary music, however, is more than made up for with its many theatrical offerings.

FESTIVALS AND SPECIAL EVENTS

Festa di San Giovanni (*Feast of St. John the Baptist*). On June 24 Florence grinds to a halt to celebrate the Festa di San Giovanni in honor of its patron saint. Many shops and bars close, and at night a fireworks display lights up the Arno and attracts thousands.

Holy Thursday. At the Duomo on Holy Thursday, a centuries-old ritual is reenacted with members of the Compagnia della Misericordia, a lay association that during the Renaissance comforted those condemned to death and provided dowries for poor girls as well as other services for its members. (Today the confraternity runs an efficient ambulance service, as it has done since its inception.) A solemn procession of priests and confraternity members wends its way into the Duomo, then the priests wash the feet of those processing.

Scoppio del Carro (*Explosion of the Cart*). On Easter Sunday Florentines and foreigners alike flock to the Piazza del Duomo to watch as the Scoppio del Carro, a monstrosity of a carriage, pulled by two huge oxen decorated for the occasion, makes its way through the city center and ends up in the piazza. Through an elaborate wiring system, an object representing a "dove" is sent from inside the cathedral to the Baptistery across the way. The dove sets off an explosion of fireworks that come streaming from the carriage. You have to see it to believe it. If you don't like crowds, don't worry: video replays figure prominently on the nightly newscasts afterward.

FILM

British Institute of Florence. The British Institute of Florence runs several English-language film series; the programmer has a penchant for classic movies. Also on offer here are weekly lectures, courses mostly related to things Florentine or Italian, and a most wonderful library. ⊠ *Palazzo Lanfredini, Lungarno Guicciardini 9, Lungarno Sud* ☎ *055/26778270* ⊕ *www.britishinstitute.it.*

Festival dei Popoli. This weeklong documentary film festival happens in November or December with screenings at various venues around town. ⊠ *Borgo Pinti 82/r, Santa Croce* ☎ *055/244778* ⊕ *www. festivaldeipopoli.org.*

La Nazione. The daily Florentine newspaper *La Nazione* has movie listings. Note that most American films are dubbed into Italian rather than subtitled. ⊕ *www.lanazione.it.*

Odeon Firenze. This magnificent art deco theater shows first-run English-language films on Monday, Tuesday, and Thursday. ⊠ *Piazza Strozzi 2, Piazza della Repubblica* ☎ *055/295051* ⊕ *www.odeonfirenze.com.*

MUSIC

Accademia Bartolomeo Cristofori. Also known as the Amici del Fortepiano (Friends of the Fortepiano), the Accademia Bartolomeo Cristofori sponsors fortepiano concerts throughout the year. ⊠ *Via di Camaldoli 7/r, Santo Spirito/San Frediano* ☎ *055/221646* ⊕ *www.accademiacristofori.it.*

Amici della Musica. This organization sponsors classical and contemporary concerts at the **Teatro della Pergola** (*Box office* ⊠ *Via Alamanni 39, Lungarno North* ☎ *055/210804* ⊕ *www.teatrodellapergola.com*). ⊠ *Via Pier Capponi 41* ⊕ *www.amicimusica.fi.it.*

Maggio Musicale Fiorentino. At press time, construction had been halted due to lack of funds on the **Parco della Musica** (Music Park) designed by Paolo Desideri and associates. Three concert halls (two indoor, one outdoor) are planned, and only one has been completed. Maggio Musicale plans to relocate once construction is finished. In the meantime, it continues to be held at the **Teatro Comunale** (⊠ *Corso Italia 16, Lungarno North* ☎ *055/287222* ⊕ *www.maggiofiorentino.com*). Within Italy you can purchase tickets from late April through July directly at the box office or by phone at ☎ *055/2779350*. You can also buy them online. Call ahead to confirm if performances are taking place in this venue or have switched over to the new space. ⊠ *Via Alamanni 39* ☎ *055/210804* ⊕ *www.maggiofiorentino.it.*

OBIHALL. This large exhibition space, formerly Teatro Saschall, hosts many events throughout the year, including a large Christmas bazaar run by the Red Cross, visiting rock stars, and trendy bands from all over Europe. ⊠ *Lungarno Aldo Moro 3* ☎ *055/6503068* ⊕ *www.obihall.it.*

Orchestra da Camera Fiorentina. This orchestra performs various concerts of classical music throughout the year at Orsanmichele, the grain market–turned–church. ⊠ *Via Monferrato 2, Piazza della Signoria* ☎ *055/783374* ⊕ *www.orcafi.it.*

Orchestra della Toscana. The concert season of the Orchestra della Toscana runs from November to June. ⊠ *Via Ghibellina 101, Santa Croce* ☎ *055/2340710* ⊕ *www.orchestradellatoscana.it.*

THEATER

Teatro della Pergola. Theater lovers might want to try an evening at Teatro della Pergola. The season runs from mid-October to mid-April. If the idea of hearing a play in Italian is too forbidding, visit the lovely theater. Built in 1656 by Ferdinando Tacca, and once the private theater of the grand dukes, it was opened to the public in 1755. The theater has undergone several metamorphoses; its present incarnation dates to 1828, and the atrium was constructed nine years later. ⊠ *Via della Pergola 12/r, Santissima Annunziata* ☎ *055/2264353* ⊕ *www.teatrodellapergola.com.*

SHOPPING

Window-shopping in Florence is like visiting an enormous contemporary-art gallery. Many of today's greatest Italian artists are fashion designers, and most keep shops in Florence. Discerning shoppers may find bargains in the street markets. ⚠ **Do not buy any knockoff goods from any of the hawkers plying their fake Prada (or any other high-end designer) on the streets.** It's illegal, and fines are astronomical if the police happen to catch you. (You pay the fine, not the vendor.)

Shops are generally open 9 to 1 and 3:30 to 7:30, and are closed Sunday and Monday mornings most of the year. Summer (June to September) hours are usually 9 to 1 and 4 to 8, and some shops close Saturday afternoon instead of Monday morning. When looking for addresses, you'll see two color-coded numbering systems on each street. The red numbers are commercial addresses and are indicated, for example, as 31/r. The blue or black numbers are residential addresses. Most shops take major credit cards and ship purchases, but because of possible delays it's wise to take your purchases with you.

The usual fashion suspects—Prada, Gucci, Versace, to name but a few— all have shops in Florence. But if you want to buy Florentine in Florence, stick to Gucci, Pucci, Ferragamo, and Roberto Cavalli—they're either all native sons or adopted native sons (Salvatore Ferragamo).

The intrepid shopper might want to check out some other, lesser-known shops. For bargains on Italian designer clothing, you need to leave the city.

SHOPPING DISTRICTS

Florence's most fashionable shops are concentrated in the center of town. The fanciest designer shops are mainly on **Via Tornabuoni** and **Via della Vigna Nuova.** The city's largest concentrations of antiques shops are on **Borgo**

Ognissanti and the Oltrarno's **Via Maggio**. The **Ponte Vecchio** houses reputable but very expensive jewelry shops, as it has since the 16th century. The area near **Santa Croce** is the heart of the leather merchants' district.

PIAZZA DELLA REPUBBLICA

Fodor'sChoice **Bernardo.** Come here for men's trousers, cashmere sweaters, and shirts
★   with details like mother-of-pearl buttons. ⊠ *Via Porta Rossa 87/r* ☎ *055/283333.*

Cabó. Missoni knitwear is the main draw at Cabó. ⊠ *Via Porta Rossa 77–79/r* ☎ *055/215774.*

Furla. Internationally renowned Furla makes beautiful leather bags, shoes, and wallets in up-to-the-minute designs. ⊠ *Via Calzaiuoli 47/r* ☎ *055/2382883* ⊕ *www.furla.com.*

Liu-Jo. If you're looking for something hot to wear to the clubs, check out Liu-Jo. ⊠ *Via Calimala 14/r* ☎ *055/216164* ⊕ *www.liujo.com.*

Mercato dei Fiori (*flower market*). Every Thursday morning from September through June the covered loggia in Piazza della Repubblica hosts a Mercato dei Fiori; it's awash in a lively riot of plants, flowers, and difficult-to-find herbs. ⊠ *Piazza della Repubblica.*

Mercato del Porcellino. If you're looking for cheery, inexpensive trinkets to take home, you might want to stop and roam through the stalls under the loggia of the Mercato del Porcellino. ⊠ *Via Por Santa Maria at Via Porta Rossa.*

My Walit. Brightly colored wallets, purses, and other lovely leather accessories are on offer here at affordable prices. ⊠ *Via degli Speziali 10-12/r* ⊕ *www.mywalit.com.*

Spazio A. For cutting-edge fashion, these fun and funky window displays merit a stop. The shop carries such well-known designers as Alberta Ferretti and Moschino, as well as lesser-known Italian, English, and French designers. ⊠ *Via Porta Rossa 109–115/r* ☎ *055/212995.*

SAN LORENZO

Mercato Centrale. This huge indoor food market offers a staggering selection of all things edible. ⊠ *Piazza del Mercato Centrale.*

Mercato di San Lorenzo. The clothing and leather-goods stalls of the Mercato di San Lorenzo in the streets next to the church of San Lorenzo have bargains for shoppers on a budget. Do please remember that you get what you pay for.

SANTA CROCE

Libreria Salimbeni. One of Florence's best art-book shops has an outstanding selection. ⊠ *Via Matteo Palmieri 14–16/r* ☎ *055/2340905* ⊕ *www.libreriasalimbeni.com.*

Mercato di Sant'Ambrogio. It's possible to strike gold at this lively market, where clothing stalls abut the fruit and vegetables. ⊠ *Piazza Ghiberti, off Via dei Macci.*

The bounty at Florence's Mercato Centrale

Oreria. The two women who run Oreria create divine designs using silver and semiprecious stones. Send suitors to purchase significant gifts here. ✉ *Borgo Pinti 87/a* ☏ *055/244708.*

Piazza dei Ciompi flea market. You can find bargains here Monday through Saturday and on the last Sunday of the month. ✉ *Sant'Ambrogio.*

Sbigoli Terrecotte. Traditional Tuscan terra-cotta and ceramic vases, pots, and cups and saucers are on offer at this shop in the Santa Croce neighborhood. ✉ *Via Sant'Egidio 4/r* ☏ *055/2479713.*

Scuola del Cuoio. A consortium of leatherworkers plies its trade at La Scuola del Cuoio (Leather School), in the former dormitory of the convent of Santa Croce; high-quality, fairly priced jackets, belts, and purses are sold here. ✉ *Piazza Santa Croce 16* ☏ *055/244533* ⊕ *www.scuoladelcuoio.com.*

OLTRARNO

Galleria Luigi Bellini. This gallery claims to be Italy's oldest antiques dealer, which may be true, since father Mario Bellini was responsible for instituting Florence's international antiques biennial. ✉ *Lungarno Soderini 5, Oltrarno* ☏ *055/214031* ⊕ *www.bellinimuseum.org.*

Giulio Giannini e Figlio. One of Florence's oldest paper-goods stores is *the* place to buy the marbleized stock, which comes in many shapes and sizes, from flat sheets to boxes and even pencils. ✉ *Piazza Pitti 37/r, Oltrarno* ☏ *055/212621* ⊕ *www.giuliogiannini.it.*

Lorenzo Villoresi. Proprietor Lorenzo Villoresi makes one-of-a-kind fragrances, which he develops after meeting with you. Such personalized attention does not come cheap. ✉ *Via de'Bardi 14, Oltrarno* ☎ *055/2341187* ⊕ *www.lorenzovilloresi.it.*

PALAZZO PITTI

Geraldine Tayar. Eclectic fabric combinations are the focal point of Geraldine Tayar's unique clothing and accessories. ✉ *Sdrucciolo de' Pitti 6/r* ☎ *055/290405.*

Maçel. Browse collections by lesser-known Italian designers, many of whom use the same factories as the A-list, at this women's clothing shop. ✉ *Via Guicciardini 128/r* ☎ *055/287355.*

Madova. Complete your winter wardrobe with a pair of high-quality leather gloves, available in a rainbow of colors and a choice of linings (silk, cashmere, and unlined), from Madova. ✉ *Via Guicciardini 1/r* ☎ *055/2396526* ⊕ *www.madova.com.*

Paolo Paoletti. Look for Florentine antiques with an emphasis on Medici-era objects from the 15th and 16th centuries at Paolo Paoletti. ✉ *Via Maggio 30/r* ☎ *055/215487.*

Pitti Mosaici. Stones are worked into exquisite tables, pictures, and jewelry at Pitti Mosaici, which continues the pietre dure tradition that was all the rage of 16th-century Florence. ✉ *Piazza dei Pitti 23/r* ☎ *055/282127* ⊕ *www.pittimosaici.com.*

SANTO SPIRITO

Santo Spirito flea market. The second Sunday of every month brings the Santo Spirito flea market. On the third Sunday of the month, vendors at the Fierucola organic fest sell such delectables as honeys, jams, spice mixes, and fresh vegetables.

PIAZZA DELLA SIGNORIA

Carlo Piccini. Still in operation after several generations, this Florentine institution sells antique jewelry and makes pieces to order; you can also get old jewelry reset here. ✉ *Ponte Vecchio 31/r* ☎ *055/292030* ⊕ *www.carlopiccini.com.*

Cassetti. This jeweler combines precious and semiprecious stones and metals in contemporary settings. ✉ *Ponte Vecchio 54/r* ☎ *055/2396028* ⊕ *www.cassetti.it.*

Diesel. Trendy Diesel started in Vicenza; its gear is on the "must-have" list of many self-respecting Italian teens. ✉ *Via dei Lamberti 13/r* ☎ *055/2399963* ⊕ *www.diesel.com.*

Gherardi. Florence's king of coral, Gherardi has the city's largest selection of finely crafted pieces, as well as cultured pearls, jade, and turquoise. ✉ *Ponte Vecchio 5/r* ☎ *055/211809.*

Oro Due. Gold jewelry and other beauteous objects are priced according to the level of craftsmanship and the price of gold bullion that day. ✉ *Via Lambertesca 12/r* ☎ *055/292143.*

SAN NICCOLÒ

Il Torchio. Photograph albums, frames, diaries, and other objects dressed in handmade paper are high quality, and the prices lower than usual. ✉ *Via dei Bardi 17* ☎ *055/2342862* ⊕ *www.legatoriailtorchio.com.*

SANTA MARIA NOVELLA

Alberto Cozzi. You'll find an extensive line of Florentine papers and paper products here. The artisans in the shop rebind and restore books and works on paper. Their hours are tricky, so it's best to call first before stopping by. ✉ *Via del Parione 35/r* ☎ *055/294968.*

Fodor's Choice
★ **Angela Caputi.** Angela Caputi wows Florentine cognoscenti with her highly creative, often outsized plastic jewelry. A small, but equally creative, collection of women's clothing made of fine fabrics is also on offer. ✉ *Borgo Santi Apostoli 44/46* ☎ *055/292993* ⊕ *www.angelacaputi.com.*

Antica Officina del Farmacista Dr. Vranjes. Dr. Vranjes elevates aromatherapy to an art form, with scents for the body and for the house. ✉ *Via della Spada 9, Santa Maria Novella* ☎ *055/288796* ⊕ *www.drvranjes.it.*

Blue Home. This home goods store sells sumptuous fabrics that can be rendered into sofas, rugs, and other home furnishings to create divinely inspired interiors. Antique and contemporary rugs are also on hand. ✉ *Borgo Santi Apostoli 58/r* ☎ *055/2658262.*

Casadei. The ultimate fine leathers are crafted into classic shapes, winding up as women's shoes and bags. ✉ *Via Tornabuoni 33/r* ☎ *055/287240* ⊕ *www.casadei.com.*

Cellerini. In a city where it seems just about everybody wears an expensive leather jacket, Cellerini is an institution. ✉ *Via del Sole 37/r* ☎ *055/282533* ⊕ *www.cellerini.it.*

Emilio Pucci. The aristocratic Marchese di Barsento, Emilio Pucci, became an international name in the late 1950s when the stretch ski clothes he designed for himself caught on with the dolce vita crowd—his pseudo-psychedelic prints and "palazzo pajamas" became all the rage. ✉ *Via Tornabuoni 20–22/r* ☎ *055/2658082* ⊕ *www.emiliopucci.com.*

Emporio Armani. The sister store of the Giorgio Armani boutique has slightly more affordable nightclub- and office-friendly garb. ✉ *Piazza Strozzi 16/r* ☎ *055/284315.*

Ferragamo. This classy institution, in a 13th-century palazzo, displays designer clothing and accessories, though elegant footwear still underlies the Ferragamo success. ✉ *Via Tornabuoni 2/r* ☎ *055/292123* ⊕ *www.ferragamo.com.*

Gatto Bianco. This contemporary jeweler has breathtakingly beautiful pieces worked in semiprecious and precious stones. ✉ *Borgo Santi Apostoli 12/r* ☎ *055/282989.*

G.B. Frugone 1885. If you're looking for elegant cashmere, look no further. This Genoa-based company has been making scarves, dresses, and sweaters (among other things) for men and women since 1885. ✉ *Via delle Belle Donne 35/r* ☎ *055/287820.*

Giorgio Armani. The sleek, classic boutique Giorgio Armani is a centerpiece of the dazzling high-end shops clustered in this part of town. ✉ *Via Tornabuoni 48/r* ☎ *055/219041.*

Giorgio Vannini. You can take home a custom-made suit or dress from the designer, who has a showroom for his prêt-à-porter line. ✉ *Borgo Santi Apostoli 43/r* ☎ *055/293037* ⊕ *www.giorgiovannini.it.*

Gucci. Florentine perennial Gucci puts its famous initials on just about everything it sells. ✉ *Via Tornabuoni 73/r* ☎ *055/2645432.*

La Bottega dell'Olio. Experience olive oil in all its permutations at La Bottega dell'Olio. The shop, which is tucked into a small piazza, has a great collection of fine olive oils, as well as bath products made from olive oil. ✉ *Piazza del Limbo 2/r* ☎ *055/2670468.*

Loretta Caponi. Synonymous with Florentine embroidery, the luxury lace, linens, and lingerie have earned the eponymous signora worldwide renown. There's also beautiful (and expensive) clothing for children. ✉ *Piazza Antinori 4/r* ☎ *055/213668.*

Fodor's Choice ★ **Officina Profumo Farmaceutica di Santa Maria Novella.** The essence of a Florentine holiday is captured in the sachets of this art nouveau emporium of herbal cosmetics and soaps that are made following centuries-old recipes created by friars. It celebrated its 400th birthday in 2012. ✉ *Via della Scala 16* ☎ *055/216276* ⊕ *www.smnovella.it.*

Pineider. Though it has shops throughout the world, Pineider started out in Florence and still does all its printing here. Stationery and business cards are the mainstay, but the stores also sell fine leather desk accessories as well as a less stuffy, more lighthearted line of products. ✉ *via della Vigna Nuova 4-6/r, Santa Maria Novella* ☎ *055/284655* ⊕ *www.pineider.com.*

Prada. Known to mix schoolmarmish sensibility with sexy cuts and funky fabrics, Prada appeals to an exclusive clientele. ✉ *Via Tornabuoni 67/r* ☎ *055/267471.*

Principe. This Florentine institution sells casual clothes for men, women, and children at far-from-casual prices. It also has a great housewares department. ✉ *Via del Sole 2* ☎ *055/292764* ⊕ *www.principedifirenze.com.*

Roberto Cavalli. The sometimes outlandish designs of native son Roberto Cavalli appeal to Hollywood celebrities and to those who want a little bit of rock star in their wardrobe. ✉ *Via Tornabuoni 83/r* ☎ *055/2396226.*

Tiffany. One of Florence's oldest jewelers has supplied Italian (and other) royalty with finely crafted gems for centuries. Its selection of antique-looking classics has been updated with a selection of contemporary silver. ✉ *Via Tornabuoni 25/r* ☎ *055/215506* ⊕ *www.tiffany.it.*

Valli. Gifted seamstresses (and seamsters) should look no further than this place, which sells sumptuous silks, beaded fabrics, lace, wool, and tweeds by the meter. ✉ *Via della Vigna Nuova 81/r* ☎ *055/282485* ⊕ *www.tessutialtamodavalli.it.*

DUOMO

Luisa Via Roma. The surreal window displays at Luisa Via Roma hint at the trendy yet tasteful clothing inside this fascinating, *alta moda* (high-style) boutique, which stocks the world's top designers as well as Luisa's own line. ✉ *Via Roma 19–21/r* ☎ *055/217826* ⊕ *www.luisaviaroma.com.*

Mandragora Art Store. This is one of the first attempts in Florence to cash in on the museum-store craze. It's a lovely store with reproductions of valued works of art and jewelry. ✉ *Piazza del Duomo 50/r* ☎ *055/292559* ⊕ *www.mandragora.it.*

Patrizia Pepe. The Florentine designer has body-conscious clothes perfect for all ages, especially for women with a tiny streak of rebelliousness. Women who are not size zero—or close to it—need not apply. ✉ *via Strozzi 11/19r* ☎ *055/2302518* ⊕ *www.patriziapepe.com.*

Penko. Renaissance goldsmiths provide the inspiration for this dazzling jewelry with a contemporary feel. ✉ *Via F. Zannetti 14/16r* ☎ *055/211661* ⊕ *www.paolopenko.com.*

SANTA MARIA NOVELLA

Giotti. You'll find a full line of leather goods, including clothing, here. ✉ *Piazza Ognissanti 3–4/r, Santa Maria Novella* ☎ *055/294265* ⊕ *www. giotti.com.*

BEYOND THE CITY CENTER

Barberino Designer Outlet. Prada, Pollini, Missoni, and Bruno Magli, among others, are all found at Barberino Designer Outlet. To get here, take the A1 to the Barberino di Mugello exit, and follow signs to the mall. ✉ *Via Meucci snc, Florence* ☎ *055/842161* ⊕ *www.mcarthurglen.com.*

Le Cascine's open-air market. Held every Tuesday morning, this market includes stalls selling food, bargain clothing, and gadgets. It's an easy walk from the Centro Storico. ✉ *Florence.*

Mall. One-stop bargain shopping awaits at this collection of stores selling goods by such names as Bottega Veneta, Giorgio Armani, Loro Piana, Sergio Rossi, and Yves St. Laurent. ✉ *Via Europa 8, Florence* ☎ *055/8657775* ⊕ *www.themall.it.*

Prada Outlet. Cognoscenti drive 45 minutes (or take the train to Montevarchi, and then a taxi) to find a bargain here. ✉ *Levanella Spacceo, Estrada Statale 69* ☎ *055/9196528* ⊕ *www.prada.com.*

SIDE TRIPS FROM FLORENCE

FIESOLE

A half-day excursion to Fiesole, in the hills 8 km (5 miles) above Florence, gives you a pleasant respite from museums and a wonderful view of the city. From here the view of the Duomo gives you a new appreciation for what the Renaissance accomplished. Fiesole began life as an ancient Etruscan and later Roman village that held some power until it succumbed to barbarian invasions. Eventually it gave up its independence in exchange for Florence's protection. The medieval cathedral, ancient Roman amphitheater, and lovely old villas behind garden walls are clustered on a series of hilltops. A walk around Fiesole can take from one to two or three hours, depending on how far you stroll from the main piazza.

GETTING HERE AND AROUND

The trip from Florence by car takes 20 to 30 minutes. Drive to Piazza Liberta and cross the Ponte Rosso heading in the direction of the SS65/SR65. Turn right on to Via Salviati and continue on to Via Roccettini. Make a left turn to Via Vecchia Fiesolana, which will take you directly to the center of town. There are several possible routes for the two-hour walk from central Florence to Fiesole. One route begins in a residential area of Florence called Salviatino (Via Barbacane, near Piazza Edison, on the Bus 7 route), and after a short time, offers peeks over garden walls of beautiful villas, as well as the view over your shoulder at the panorama of Florence in the valley.

VISITOR INFORMATION

Fiesole tourism office ⊠ *Via Portigiani 3* ☎ *055/5961323* ⊕ *www.fiesoleforyou.it.*

EXPLORING

Anfiteatro Romano (*Roman Amphitheater*). The beautifully preserved 2,000-seat Anfiteatro Romano, near the Duomo, dates from the 1st century BC and is still used for summer concerts. To the right of the amphitheater are the remains of the **Terme Romani** (Roman Baths), where you can see the gymnasium, hot and cold baths, and rectangular chamber where the water was heated. A beautifully designed **Museo Archeologico,** its facade evoking an ancient Roman temple, is built amid the ruins and contains objects dating from as early as 2000 BC. The nearby **Museo Bandini** is filled with the private collection of Canon Angelo Maria Bandini (1726–1803); he fancied 13th- to 15th-century Florentine paintings, terra-cotta pieces, and wood sculpture, which he later bequeathed to the Diocese of Fiesole. ⊠ *Via Portigiani 1* ☎ *055/5961293* ⌑*€12, includes access to the archaeological park and museums* ⊙ *Apr.–Sept., daily 9:30–7; Oct.–Mar., Wed.–Mon. 10–4:30.*

Badia Fiesolana. From the church of San Domenico it's a five-minute walk northwest to the Badia Fiesolana, which was Fiesole's original cathedral. Dating to the 11th century, it was first the home of the Camaldolese monks. Thanks to Cosimo il Vecchio, the complex was substantially restructured. The facade, never completed owing to Cosimo's death, contains elements of its original Romanesque decoration. The attached convent once housed Cosimo's valued manuscripts. Its mid-15th-century cloister is well worth a look. ⊠ *Via della Badia dei Roccettini 11* ☎ *055/46851* ⊕ *www.iue.it* ⊙ *Weekdays 9–6, Sat. 9:30–12:30.*

Duomo. A stark medieval interior yields many masterpieces. In the raised presbytery, the **Cappella Salutati** was frescoed by 15th-century artist Cosimo Rosselli, but it was his contemporary, sculptor Mino da Fiesole (1430–84), who put the town on the artistic map. The Madonna on the altarpiece and the tomb of Bishop Salutati are fine examples of the artist's work. ✉ *Piazza Mino da Fiesole* ☎ *055/59400* 🕓 *Nov.–Mar., daily 7:30–noon and 2–5; Apr.–Oct., daily 7:30–noon and 3–6.*

San Domenico. If you really want to stretch your legs, walk 4 km (2½ miles) toward the center of Florence along Via Vecchia Fiesolana, a narrow lane in use since Etruscan times, to the church of San Domenico. Sheltered in the church is the *Madonna and Child with Saints* by Fra Angelico, who was a Dominican friar here. ✉ *Piazza San Domenico, off Via Giuseppe Mantellini* ☎ *055/59230* 🕓 *Mon.–Sat. 8–noon.*

San Francesco. This lovely hilltop church has a good view of Florence and the plain below from its terrace and benches. Off the little cloister is a small, eclectic museum containing, among other things, two Egyptian mummies. Halfway up the hill you'll see sloping steps to the right; they lead to a fragrant wooded park with trails that loop out and back to the church.

WHERE TO EAT AND STAY

For expanded hotel reviews, visit Fodors.com.

$$ ITALIAN Fodor's Choice ★ 🍴 **La Reggia degli Etruschi.** If you want a breath of fresh air—literally—this lovely little eatery is worth a detour. Stamina is necessary to get here, as it's on a steep hill on the way up to the church of San Francesco. The rewards upon arrival, in the form of inventive reworkings of Tuscan classics, are well worth it. The *mezzaluna di pera a pecorino* (little half moon pasta stuffed with pear and pecorino) is sauced with Roquefort and poppy seeds. Slivers of papaya—a rare commodity on restaurant menus in these parts—anoint the tasty carpaccio *di tonno affumicato* (smoked tuna). The wine list and the attentive service help make this a terrific place to have a meal. When it's warm, you can sit on the little terrace outside. [$] *Average main: €19* ✉ *Via San Francesco* ☎ *055/59385* 🌐 *www.lareggiadeglietruschi.com.*

$ TUSCAN 🍴 **Le Cave di Maiano.** If you're looking to get out of town, hop in your car (or take a taxi) to this simple trattoria in the hills just outside Florence. Italians flock here for the *buon rapporto fra qualità e prezzo* (the good rapport between quality and price). Tuscan staples are on hand, as is a fine plate of spaghetti with truffled asparagus. They grill well here, so consider something from the grill to follow. By all means leave room for dessert. Though the food is typical, they do it exceedingly well: the *zuppa cotta* should not be missed. [$] *Average main: €13* ✉ *Via Cave di Maiano 16* ☎ *055/59133.*

$$ HOTEL 🏨 **Villa Aurora.** The attractive hotel on the main piazza takes advantage of its hilltop spot, with beautiful views in many of the rooms, some of which are on two levels with beamed ceilings and balconies. **Pros:** some rooms have pretty views; air quality better than in Florence. **Cons:** a little worn at the edges. [$] *Rooms from: €149* ✉ *Piazza Mino da Fiesole 39* ☎ *055/59363* 🌐 *www.villaurorafiesole.com* 🛏 *23 rooms, 2 suites* 🍽 *Breakfast.*

$$$$ HOTEL 🏨 **Villa San Michele.** The cypress-lined driveway provides an elegant preamble to this incredibly gorgeous (and very expensive) hotel nestled in the hills of Fiesole. **Pros:** exceptional convent conversion. **Cons:** money must be no object. [$] *Rooms from: €890* ✉ *Via Doccia 4* ☎ *055/5678200* 🌐 *www.villasanmichele.com* 🛏 *21 rooms, 24 suites* 🕓 *Closed Nov.–Easter.*

CLOSE UP

Gardens Around Florence

Like any well-heeled Florentine, you, too, can get away from Florence's hustle and bustle by heading for the hills. Take a break from city sightseeing to enjoy gardens and villas. Villa di Castello and Villa La Petraia, both northwest of Florence's historic center, can be explored in one trip. The Italian garden at Villa Gamberaia is an 8-km (5-mile) jaunt east of the center near Settignano. Plan for a full-day excursion, picnic lunch included, if visiting all three gardens. Though Villa Demidoff, originally a Medici country house, is in somewhat dilapidated shape, it's worth a trip to see Giambologna's *Appenino*. For a prime taste of Medici living, venture farther afield to the family's Villa Medicea in Poggio a Caiano, south of Prato (⇨ Chapter 3, Northwest Tuscany).

Villa di Castello. A fortified residence in the Middle Ages, Villa di Castello was bought in 1477 by Lorenzo and Giovanni di Pierfrancesco de' Medici and significantly restructured by Cosimo I in the 16th century. The palace isn't open to the public; the gardens, however, are the main attraction.

Though the original garden design has been altered somewhat over the centuries, the allegorical theme of animals, devised by Tribolo in 1537, remains. The artificial cave, Grotta degli Animali (Animal Grotto), displays sculpted animals by Giambologna and his assistants. An Ammannati sculpture, a figure of an old man representing the Appenines, sits at the center of a pond on the terrace overlooking the garden. Two bronze sculptures by Ammannati, centerpieces of fountains studding the garden, can now be seen indoors in Villa La Petraia. Allow about 45 minutes to visit the garden;

you can easily visit Villa La Petraia from here, making for a four-hour trip in total.

To get to Villa di Castello by car, head northwest from Florence on Via Reginaldo Giuliani (also known as Via Sestese) to Castello, about 6 km (4 miles) northwest of the city center in the direction of Sesto Fiorentino; follow signs to Villa di Castello. Or take Bus 28 from the city center and tell the driver you want to get off at Villa di Castello; from the stop, walk north about ½ km (¼ mile) up the tree-lined allée from the main road. ⊠ *Via di Castello 47, Castello* ☎ *055/454791* 💲 *Free* ☉ *Garden: Nov.–Feb., daily 8:15–4:30; Mar., daily 8:15–5:30, Apr.– May and Sept.–Oct., daily 8:15–6:30; June–Aug., daily 8:15–7:30. Closed 2nd and 3rd Mon. of month; palace closed to public.*

Villa La Petraia. The splendidly planted gardens of Villa La Petraia sit high above the Arno with a sweeping view of Florence. The villa was built around a medieval tower and reconstructed after it was purchased by the Medici sometime after 1530. Virtually the only traces of their having lived here are the courtyard frescoes, some by Volterrano, executed between 1636 and 1648.

The garden and the vast park behind the palace suggest a splendid contrast between formal and natural landscapes. Allow 60 to 90 minutes to explore the park and gardens, plus 30 minutes for the guided tour of the so-called museum, the villa interior. This property is best visited after the Villa di Castello.

2

To get here by car, follow directions to Villa di Castello, but take the right off Via Reginaldo Giuliani, following the sign for Villa La Petraia. You can walk from Villa di Castello to Villa La Petraia in about 15 minutes; turn left beyond the gate of Villa di Castello and continue straight along Via di Castello and the imposing Villa Corsini; take Via della Petraia uphill to the entrance. ✉ *Via della Petraia 40, Località Castello* ☎ *055/451208* 🎫 *Free* 🕐 *Nov.–Feb., daily 8:15– 4:30; Mar.–May and Sept.–Oct., daily 8:15–6:30; June–Aug., daily 8:15–7:30. Closed 2nd and 3rd Mon. of month.*

Villa Gamberaia. Villa Gamberaia, near the village of Settignano on the eastern outskirts of Florence, was the rather modest 15th-century country home of Matteo di Domenico Gamberelli, the father of noted Renaissance sculptors Bernardo, Antonio, and Matteo Rossellino. In the early 1600s the villa passed into the hands of the wealthy Capponi family. They spared no expense in rebuilding it and, more important, creating its garden, one of the finest near Florence. Studded with statues and fountains, the garden suffered damage during World War II, but has been restored according to the original 17th-century design. This excursion takes about 1½ hours, allowing 45 minutes to visit the garden. Parts of the villa are open by appointment.

To get here by car, head east on Via Aretina, an extension of Via Gioberti, which is picked up at Piazza Beccaria; follow the sign to the turnoff to the north to Villa Gamberaia, about 8 km (5 miles) from the center. To go by bus, take Bus 10 to Settignano. From Settignano's main Piazza Tommaseo, walk east on Via di San Romano; the second lane on the right is Via del Rossellino, which leads southeast to the entrance of Villa Gamberaia. The walk from the piazza takes about 10 minutes. ✉ *Via del Rossellino 72, near Settignano* ☎ *055/697205* 🎫 *€15* 🕐 *Garden: daily 9–6.*

Villa Demidoff. Francesco I de' Medici commissioned the multitalented Bernardo Buontalenti in 1568 to build a villa and a grandiose park to accompany it. The park, particularly the colossal and whimsical sculpture of the *Fontana dell'Appenino* (*Fountain of the Appenines*), executed by Giambologna in 1579–89, is worth the price of admission alone. Besides providing a nice excursion from Florence, the villa is an excellent picnic spot.

To get here by car, head north from Florence on the SR65 toward Pratolino and follow signs to the villa. Or take Bus 25 from Piazza San Marco and get off at Pratolino. ✉ *Località Pratolino, Vaglia* ☎ *055/409427* 🎫 *Free* 🕐 *May– Oct., Thurs.–Sun. 10–7:30.*

NIGHTLIFE AND THE ARTS

Estate Fiesolana. From June through August, Estate Fiesolana, a festival of theater, music, dance, and film, takes place in Fiesole's churches and in the Roman amphitheater—demonstrating that the ancient Romans knew a thing or two about acoustics. ⊠ *Teatro Romano* ☎ *055/5961323* ⊕ *www.comune.fiesole.fi.it.*

SETTIGNANO

When Florence is overcrowded and hot—that is, for most of the summer—this village, a 20-minute car or bus trip east of Florence, is particularly appealing. It was the birthplace of many artists, including the sculptors Desiderio di Settignano (circa 1428–64), Antonio (1427–79) and Bernardo (1409–64) Rossellino, and Bartolomeo Ammannati (1511–92). Michelangelo's wet nurse was the wife of a stonecutter in Settignano, and to her he attributed his later calling in life. Alas, these artists' works no longer adorn their native town, but Settignano is worth a visit simply to breathe its fresh air, walk its tiny streets, and sit in its small **piazza** with an aperitivo.

GETTING HERE AND AROUND

To get to the village, take Bus 10 from the station at Santa Maria Novella or at Piazza San Marco, all the way to the end of the line, the *capolinea*. It will put you in the middle of Settignano's piazzetta.

WHERE TO EAT AND STAY

For expanded hotel reviews, visit Fodors.com.

$ ✕ **Osvaldo.** If you're making the trip to Settignano, this is a great dining
TUSCAN   option (get off Bus 10 at the stop called Ponte a Mensola). The small, unassuming family-run trattoria is situated along a street and a tiny stream; if you sit outside (there are no views, alas), you might hear the trickle of the stream. The food is terrific, and though it is described as *cucina casalinga* (home cooking), only the portions are home-style. Service is prompt and courteous. $ *Average main: €12* ⊠ *Via G. D'Annunzio 51/r* ☎ *055/603972* ☉ *Closed Wed. No lunch Tues.*

$$ ⊞ **Fattoria di Maiano.** In the foothills between Florence and Fiesole are
RENTAL   these lovely apartments, which sleep 4–11 people and rent by the week.
FAMILY   **Pros:** great way to have a country experience with the city nearby. **Cons:** requires a week's stay during high season (Dec.–Jan. 12, July–Sept.). $ *Rooms from: €126* ⊠ *Via Benedetto da Maiano 11* ☎ *055/599600* ⊕ *www.fattoriadimaiano.com* ⇴ *8 apartments* ℞ *No meals.*

PISA, LUCCA, AND NORTHWEST TUSCANY

WELCOME TO NORTHWEST TUSCANY

TOP REASONS TO GO

★ **Leaning Tower of Pisa:** It may be touristy, but it's still a whole lot of fun to climb to the top and admire the view.

★ **Olive-oil tasting in and around Lucca:** Italian olive oil is justifiably world famous, and cognoscenti insist that the best is found here.

★ **Cappella Maggiore, Duomo, Prato:** Filippo Lippi's solemn frescoes depicting scenes from the lives of John the Baptist and Saint Stephen positively glow.

★ **Bagni di Lucca:** This sleepy little town attracted the English Romantics, among others, who were drawn to its salubrious waters and air.

★ **Tomb of Ilaria del Carretto, Duomo, Lucca:** Check out this moving sculpture by Jacopo della Quercia commemorating a young woman who died in childbirth.

1 Towns west of Florence. At industrial centers from the Middle Ages such as Prato and Pistoia you can relax far from Florence's throngs and savor fine food and some art gems. Fragrant white truffles adorn many a restaurant menu in San Miniato.

2 Pisa. Thanks to an engineering mistake, the name Pisa is recognized the world over. The Leaning Tower, the baptistery, the Camposanto, and the cathedral make an impressive foursome on the Piazza del Duomo.

3 Lucca. This laid-back yet elegant town is surrounded by tree-bedecked 16th-century ramparts that are now a delightful promenade.

4 The Garfagnana. Sports enthusiasts and nature addicts flock to Abetone to ski in winter and refresh themselves with cool, mountain air in summer.

5 The Northwest Coast. Experience Italian beach culture at Forte dei Marmi, a crowded and expensive place to see and be seen. Farther west, it's a worthwhile side trip out of Tuscany to visit the coastal villages of the Cinque Terre.

TUSCANY   UMBRIA

EMILIA-
ROMAGNA

Abetone
12

4

San
Marcello

12

64

Bagni
di Lucca

66

A1

Borgo
San Lorenzo

EMILIA-
ROMAGNA

67

Pistoia

325

65

Pescia

Montecatini

1

Prato

65

67

A11

Mt
Albano

Florence

Vinci

Arno River

67

Mt
Pisano

Fucecchio

Empoli

Mantelupo

San
Miniato

Castelfiorentino

Impruneta

A1

C
H
A
N
T
I

Pontedera

2

222

429

Certaldo

Greve

Volterra

68

Poggibonsi

68

1

0   10 mi

0   10 km

Piombino

Golfo
di Follónica

GETTING
ORIENTED

The landscape west of
Florence is, for the most
part, flat and generally
unremarkable, but when
you reach the coast
there are beautiful sandy
beaches on the Tyrrhenian
Sea—and the almost
surreal charm of Pisa's
Piazza del Duomo, with the
Leaning Tower as the star
attraction. Heading north,
lush hills and olive trees
dot the countryside around
Lucca, and the elevation
climbs as you enter the
Garfagnana and its Alpi
Apuane—the Apuane Alps.

Updated
by Patricia
Rucidlo

LUCCA AND PISA ARE THE MOST-VISITED CITIES of northwest Tuscany, and with good reason: Lucca has a charming historic center set within its 16th-century walls, and Pisa is home to what may be the most famous tower in the world. Both cities are due west of Florence; the landscape along the way isn't Tuscany's finest, but it has several smaller cities with low-key appeal: good restaurants, a few noteworthy sights, and a taste of Italian life away from the main tourism centers.

Farther north the setting gets more impressive. Craggy, often snow-capped mountains rise above sparsely populated valleys, accessed by narrow winding roads. This is the Garfagnana, Tuscany's most mountainous territory, cut through by the majestic Alpi Apuane. The steep terrain rolls down into pine-forested hills and eventually meets the wide, sandy beaches of the Ligurian Sea. Along this stretch, known as the Versilian Coast, are the resort towns of Viareggio and Forte dei Marmi, both of which pack in Italian and other European beachgoers in the summer. Farther west, a hop over the border from Tuscany into Liguria brings you to the Cinque Terre—five tiny, cliff-hugging seaside villages that have become one of Italy's most popular destinations.

PLANNING

BEACH KNOW-HOW

You may not think of Tuscany as a beach destination, but its long coastline is popular with Italian vacationers. From June through August the resort towns of Viareggio, Forte dei Marmi, and Marina di Massa are packed with beachgoers. Bagni (bathhouses) open, and the sands fill with colorful umbrellas and beach chairs; you can rent your own for about €20 a day and upward.

MAKING THE MOST OF YOUR TIME

The majority of first-time visitors to Tuscany start out by exploring Florence, and then are lured south by the Chianti district and Siena. Heading west instead is an appealing alternative. **Pisa** is the main attraction, and it certainly isn't short on tourists. If that's all you want (or have time) to see here, you're probably best off doing it as a day trip from Florence. If you want to stick around for a while, consider making **Lucca** your base. It's a tremendously appealing town, with fine food and an easygoing atmosphere.

From Lucca you can discover the rest of the area on day trips. The **Garfagnana** has gorgeous mountain peaks and excellent hiking opportunities (as well as skiing in winter). You can follow a day in the mountains with a day along the coast, at the resort towns along the Ligurian Sea and the **Cinque Terre.**

GETTING HERE AND AROUND
BUS TRAVEL

Many of the cities in the region do have bus stations, but service is often sporadic or complicated; it's easier to take the train to Pisa, Prato, Pistoia, Lucca, Montecatini Terme, Livorno, and Empoli, where service is regular and trains run frequently. San Miniato and environs are best reached by car, as service is limited.

It's possible to take a bus from Pistoia or Florence to get to Abetone. A car is necessary to see Carrara and the rest of the Versilian Coast, because bus service is dicey. For the Cinque Terre, the Lazzi bus service will get you to La Spezia, and then you can take the train to Riomaggiore.

There are three primary bus lines.

COPIT. This bus service connects Empoli, Montelupo, Florence, Prato, and Pistoia; it also has Florence–Abetone service. ☎ *0573/3630 in Pistoia* ⊕ *www.copitspa.it.*

Lazzi. This bus service connects Florence, Pisa, Lucca, Pescia, Pistoia, and Montecatini. ☎ *0573/1937900* ⊕ *www.lazzi.it.*

SITA. This bus service connects Florence and Empoli. ☎ *055/47821 in Florence* ⊕ *www.busitalia.it.*

CAR TRAVEL

The best way to explore the region is by car—and part of the fun is stopping to take in the scenery. In the northern part of the region, towns are spread out and driving the winding mountain roads adds to your travel time.

The A1 autostrada connects Florence to Prato; for Pistoia, Montecatini, and Lucca, follow signs for Firenze Nord, which connects to the A11. For Empoli, Pisa, and hill towns west, take the Strada Grande Communicazione Firenze-Pisa-Livorno, commonly known as the Fi-Pi-Li and sometimes indicated on signage as S.G.C. Firenze-Pisa-Livorno, from Scandicci, just outside Florence. (Note that the Fi-Pi-Li is notorious for its frequent delays due to accidents and construction.) The A12 will take you from near Pisa along the Versilian Coast to La Spezia, entryway to the Cinque Terre. The Cinque Terre itself is impractical for car travel because of the narrow roads and lack of parking (although better access and parking are available at the northern and southern towns of Monterosso al Mare and Riomaggiore); from La Spezia you can take the train, which is the main means of access to the area.

TRAIN TRAVEL

Two main train lines run from Florence's Santa Maria Novella station into northwest Tuscany—one traveling through Prato, Pistoia, Montecatini, and Lucca; the other through Empoli and Pisa. The two lines meet up on the coast with a line that runs through Livorno, Viareggio, and La Spezia.

Trains are a viable option if you're going to any of these cities. For the rest of northwest Tuscany, train connections are extremely limited or nonexistent. To get to the Cinque Terre, you can take a train to La Spezia and then pick up a local train to any of the five towns.

HOTELS

Excluding the beach resort towns, lodging is generally a better deal here than in much of the rest of Tuscany; some real bargains can be found in off-the-beaten-path towns. Consider staying at an *agriturismo*, a farm or vineyard with guest accommodations, which can range from rustic to stately. Many area hotel restaurants serve excellent food, and meal plans are usually available as supplements to your room rate. In summer, when Florence is hot and crowded, it's not a bad plan to base yourself in one of the surrounding towns and use the train to make day trips into the city.

ALONG THE ARNO FROM FLORENCE TO PISA

Off the beaten path in Empoli, San Miniato, and the neighboring hill towns are fine examples of art—especially in Empoli and Carmignano—and stirring views. The terrific restaurants in this area are often less expensive than those in the larger surrounding cities, and this is also a good place to find local handmade products—ceramics in Montelupo, glass and leather in the Empoli–Vinci area.

MONTELUPO

30 km (19 miles) southwest of Florence, 6 km (4 miles) east of Empoli.

This small town, which straddles the Arno, and its surrounding villages have been producing ceramics for centuries. A ceramics museum proudly displays the work of the past, but the finest tribute to the tradition is the fact that top-quality ceramics are still handmade in the region. Montelupo's *centro storico* (historic center) is filled with shops selling the finished product.

GETTING HERE

Train service does run from Florence's Santa Maria Novella to Montelupo. It's also an easy drive on the Fi-Pi-Li highway.

VISITOR INFORMATION

Montelupo tourism office ⊠ *Piazza Vittorio Veneto 8–10* ☏ *0571/51352* ⊕ *www.museomontelupo.it.*

EXPLORING

Museo della Ceramica (*Museum of Archaeology and Ceramics*). The Museo della Ceramica has some 3,000 pieces of majolica, a type of glazed pottery made in this region since the early 14th century. The museum is beautifully lit; objects dating from the early 14th century to the late 18th century are well labeled and arranged, and provide a good overview of the region's ceramics-making history. There's also an interesting display of the coats of arms of important Renaissance families such as the Medici and Strozzi. ⊠ *Piazza Vittorio Veneto 10* ☏ *0571/51087* ☏ *€5, combination ticket €8 (includes Museo Leonardiano in Vinci and Collegiata di Sant'Andrea in Empoli)* ☉ *Tues.–Sun. 10–6.*

WHERE TO EAT

$ ✕**Osteria BoNanni.** A short drive from Montelupo, this osteria is well
TUSCAN worth the detour—if you don't drive right past it by mistake. Its plain exterior—and interior, for that matter—belies the glories coming from the kitchen; the menu depends heavily upon seasonal ingredients, and it's a blessed event if you arrive during porcini season. Locals come to eat large portions of grilled meats and to drink the local wine; if you opt for their outstanding bistecca fiorentina, the tab might jump to the next price category. The osteria has been in the hands of the BoNanni

family since it opened in 1920, and ebullient service contributes to the sheer enjoyment of the meal. $ *Average main: €8* ⊠ *Via Turbone 9* ☎ *0571/913477* ⊘ *No lunch Sun. Closed Mon.*

FESTIVAL

Festa della Ceramica. Every June, Montelupo hosts the weeklong Festa della Ceramica, a ceramics festival that includes exhibitions of local and international art, demonstrations of techniques new and

ancient, street theater and music—and, of course, sales of ceramics from around the world. Additional information about the ceramics festival is available from the Montelupo Fiorentino tourist office. ☎ *0571/518993, 0571/51352 tourist office.*

SHOPPING

Many of the pieces for sale at Montelupo's ceramics shops follow traditional styles, but some artists bring modern inspiration to their wheels. Note that not all of the stores will ship items home for you.

Ceramica ND Dolfi. Ceramica ND Dolfi has been in the family for three generations. It's a ceramics-making compound located 3 km (2 miles) from Montelupo on the road heading east toward Florence, where you'll find a sun-drenched *spazio aziendale* (selling floor), a factory workshop, the family residence, and a yard where terra-cotta planters are displayed. The ceramics, all priced reasonably given the high-quality handcrafted work, include large vases, plates suitable for hanging, and brightly colored serving pieces for the table. ⊠ *Via Toscoromagnola 1, Località Antinoro* ☎ *0571/51264* ⊘ *Daily 9–8.*

EMPOLI

33 km (21 miles) west of Florence, 50 km (31 miles) east of Pisa.

Empoli, roughly halfway between Florence and Pisa, is a small town with a long history. References to the city first appear in documents from the 800s. By the late 12th century it was under the control of Florence. It was here in 1260, after the Battle of Montaperti, that Farinata degli Uberti, leader of the Ghibellines, decided not to burn Florence to the ground. Dante immortalized this decision in Canto X of his *Inferno*.

Now Empoli is a sleepy little town a quick train ride from Florence. If you're traveling in summer, when Florence is at its hottest and most crowded, you might consider staying here and hopping on the train for day trips into the city. But don't overlook the sights of Empoli itself—they're worth seeing.

GETTING HERE

Empoli is an easy 20-minute train ride from Florence's Santa Maria Novella station. If you're driving, take the Fi-Pi-Li—and head out armed with patience. The road is regularly under construction, and

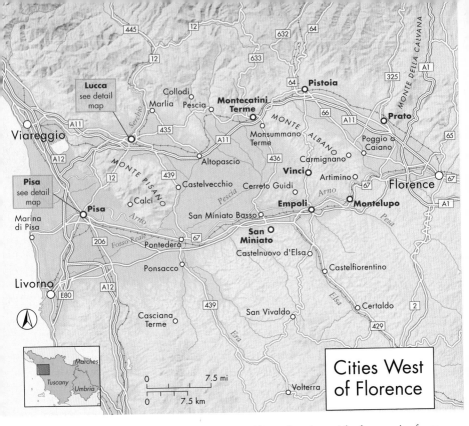

Cities West
of Florence

there are often delays due to accidents. Lazzi provides bus service from Florence to Empoli.

VISITOR INFORMATION

Empoli tourism office ⊠ *Piazza Farinata degli Uberti 3* ☎ *0571/757729* ⊕ *www.terredelrinascimento.it.*

EXPLORING

Collegiata di Sant'Andrea. The Collegiata di Sant'Andrea is a jewel of a museum, filled with terra-cotta sculptures from the della Robbia school, including one by Andrea della Robbia. There's also a magnificent 15th-century fresco pietà by Masolino (circa 1383–1440), as well as a small work by Fra Filippo Lippi (1406–69) and a wonderful tabernacle attributed to Francesco Botticini (circa 1446–97) and Antonio Rossellino (1427–79). ⊠ *Just off Piazza Farinata degli Uberti* ☎ *0571/76284* 💶 *€3.10, combination ticket €8 (includes Museo Leonardiano in Vinci and Museo della Ceramica in Montelupo)* 🕘 *Tues.–Sun. 9–noon and 2–7.*

NEED A BREAK?

Vinegar. This bar near the train station sells all sorts of panini as well as coffee and *aperitivi* (cocktails). It's a great spot to grab a sandwich before hopping on the bus to Vinci. ⊠ *Piazza della Vittoria 36–37* ☎ *0571/74630.*

San Michele in Pontorme. A short but not very scenic walk from the center of town brings you to the little church of San Michele in Pontorme, chiefly notable for the gorgeous *St. John the Baptist* and *St. Michael the Archangel,* two works dating from about 1519 by native son Jacopo Carrucci (1494–1556), better known as Pontormo. ⊠ *Piazza San Michele* 🔳 *Free* ⊙ *Ring bell for sacristan; no set hrs, but most consistently open in morning.*

Santo Stefano. Originally founded by Augustinians in the 11th century, the church of Santo Stefano can be visited only by requesting a tour in the Collegiata di Sant'Andrea. It's worth the walk around the corner and down the street to see the *sinopie* (preparatory drawings) by Masolino depicting scenes from the *Legend of the True Cross.* He left without actually frescoing them; it may be that the Augustinian friars were late in making payment. ⊠ *Via de' Neri* 🕾 *0571/76284* 🔳 *Free with admission to the Collegiata* ⊙ *Tues.–Sun. 9–noon and 2–7.*

**OFF THE
BEATEN
PATH**

Villa Medicea. On the night of July 15, 1576, Isabella de' Medici, daughter of the all-powerful Cosimo I, grand duke of Tuscany, was murdered by her husband in the Villa Medicea in the town of Cerreto Guidi for "reasons of honor"—that is, she was suspected of adultery. These days, although the villa's formal garden is in somewhat imperfect condition, the vast halls and chambers within remain majestic. Copies of portraits of various Medici, including Isabella, cover the walls. The villa sits atop the highest point in Cerreto Guidi, encircled by two narrow streets where the daily business of the town goes on. As you stand on the wide, flat front lawn, high above the streets of the town, with the villa behind you and terraced hillsides of olive groves and vineyards stretching into the distance, you can imagine what it was like to be a Medici. To see the villa, ring the bell for the custodian. ⊠ *8 km (5 miles) west of Empoli, Cerreto Guidi* 🕾 *0571/55707* 🔳 *Free* ⊙ *Daily 8:15–6:30. Closed 2nd and 3rd Mon. of each month.*

WHERE TO EAT

$$$
ITALIAN

✕**Il Galeone.** This relaxed and friendly place is known for its fish, but the meat dishes are just as good. Pale-pink walls and pink tablecloths play off the gray-and-white tile floors. Give the *moscardini con fagioli e rucola* (baby squid gently cooked with cannellini beans, diced tomatoes, and olive oil, served on a bed of arugula) a try; the *spiedini di seppioline e gamberoni* (kebabs of squid with shrimp) are terrific, too. Pizza is also served here. 💲 *Average main: €28* ⊠ *Via Curtatone e Montanara 67* 🕾 *0571/72826* ⊙ *Closed Sun. and Aug.*

VINCI

10 km (6 miles) north of Empoli, 45 km (28 miles) west of Florence.

The small hill town from which Leonardo da Vinci derived his name is a short drive or bus ride north of Empoli. At the church of Santa Croce, near the town square, you can see the baptismal font in which Leonardo was baptized. But if you want to see the house where he was born, you'll have to travel to Anchiano, 3 km (2 miles) north of Vinci. Though it's somewhat of a tourist trap, a trip to Vinci is worth the effort for the views alone.

GETTING HERE

To get to Vinci via public transportation, take the train to Empoli, then catch a Lazzi bus to Vinci.

VISITOR INFORMATION

Vinci tourism office ✉ *Via delle Torre 11* ☎ *0571/568012* 🌐 *www.terredelrinascimento.it.*

> **WORD OF MOUTH**
>
> "I would recommend Vinci, which is only 30–40 minutes outside Florence. Great museum of Leonardo's inventions and a beautiful little town." —sandi travelnut

EXPLORING

Museo Leonardiano. Museo Leonardiano, atop the castle belonging to the Guidi family in the historic center of Vinci, has replicas of many of Leonardo's machines and gadgets. The stunning country views most likely influenced the artist, as some of his painted backgrounds suggest the hills of Vinci. ✉ *Via della Torre 2* ☎ *0571/933251* 🎫 *€7, €8 combination ticket (includes Collegiata di Sant'Andrea in Empoli and Museo della Ceramica in Montelupo)* 🕓 *Daily 9:30–7.*

OFF THE BEATEN PATH

Casa Natale di Leonardo. No one knows the precise location of Leonardo da Vinci's birthplace, but this typical 15th-century Tuscan house is in the general vicinity and probably shares much in common with the house where he was born. It's in Anchiano, 3 km (2 miles) from Vinci, and can be reached easily on foot or by car. It has a primitive interior—it hasn't been gussied up for tourists. Note the printed inventory of Leonardo's library. His tastes in literature were wide-ranging, from the ancients to contemporary (15th-century) authors. At press time, the house was undergoing restoration and was closed to the public. ✉ *Località Anchiano* ☎ *0571/56519* 🎫 *€1* 🕓 *Mar.–Oct., daily 9:30–7; Nov.–Feb., daily 9:30–6.*

WHERE TO STAY

For expanded hotel reviews, visit Fodors.com.

$ 🏨 **Il Fondaccio.** The Falzari family operates this moderately priced agriturismo overlooking the hills near Vinci. **Pros:** central location; good for kids; dog-friendly. **Cons:** one-week stay required. [$] *Rooms from: €107* ✉ *Via del Fondaccio 19* ☎ *0571/559511* 🌐 *www.fondaccio.it* 🛏 *5 apartments* 💳 *No credit cards* 🍴 *No meals.*

SAN MINIATO

20 km (12 miles) southwest of Vinci, 43 km (27 miles) west of Florence.

San Miniato has a history dating to Etruscan and Roman times; today it's a tiny, pristine hill town of narrow streets lined with austere 13th- to 17th-century facades, some covering buildings that are centuries older. The Holy Roman Empire had very strong ties here—the local castle was built in 962 under the aegis of Otto I (912–973). Eventually the town, with its Ghibelline (pro-imperial) sympathies, passed into the hands of the Florentines. San Miniato's artistic treasures are limited by Tuscan standards, but the town's prettiness makes a visit worthwhile. On three weekends in November an annual truffle festival adds to San Miniato's allure; it's well worth visiting if you're in the area. The food stalls teem

Going Local at Festivals

A great way to get a feel for the region and its people is to attend a local *sagra* (festival). During the summer there's one taking place nearly every weekend in some small town or village, usually with a food theme, such as a *sagra dei funghi* (mushroom festival) or *sagra della zuppa* (soup festival). Held at night, the events dish out plenty to eat and drink, and there's usually dancing, sometimes with live music.

Old-school ballroom moves are the norm; you're likely to see couples fox-trotting or doing the tango.

These are village affairs, with few people speaking English. There are no numbers to call for information. The festivals are advertised only by crudely printed signs on the side of the road. Attending a sagra is a unique opportunity to experience small-town Italian culture.

3

---

with fantastic local stuff, while restaurants are crammed with locals and visitors chowing down on truffled things.

GETTING HERE

The easiest way to get to San Miniato is by car via the Fi-Pi-Li. The San Miniato train station is far from the centro storico.

VISITOR INFORMATION

San Miniato tourism office ⊠ *Piazza del Popolo 3* ☎ *0571/418739* ⊕ *www.sanminiatopromozione.it.*

EXPLORING

Convento di San Francesco (*Convent and Church of St. Francis*). In 1211 Saint Francis founded the Convento di San Francesco, which contains two cloisters and an ornate wooden choir. For a dose of monastic living, you can stay overnight (€39 for a double room). ⊠ *Piazza San Francesco* ☎ *0571/43051* ⊠ *Free* ☉ *Daily 9–noon and 3–7 (or ring bell).*

Convento e Chiesa di Santi Jacopo e Lucia (*Convent and Church of Sts. Jacob and Lucia*). The Convento e Chiesa di Santi Jacopo e Lucia is also oddly known as the church of San Domenico, which refers to the fact that the Dominicans took over the church in the 14th century. Most of the interior suffers from too much Baroque, but there is a lovely sculpted tomb by Bernardo Rossellino for Giovanni Chellini, a doctor who died in 1461. You'll find it on the right-hand nave close to the high altar. ⊠ *Piazza del Popolo* ☎ *0571/43150* ☉ *Daily 8:30–noon and 3:30–6.*

NEED A BREAK?

Bar Cantini. This social hub for San Miniatans serves wonderful panini that are made with bread baked on-site. There is also pizza by the slice, tasty *granita* (flavored ice), and homemade ice cream. ⊠ *Via Conti 1* ☎ *0571/43030.*

Duomo. The only thing remarkable about San Miniato's Duomo, set in a pretty piazza, is its 13th-century facade, which has been restored. The interior is largely uninteresting, though there's a poignant plaque commemorating the 55 citizens who were killed in this church in July 1944 by German occupying forces. (The Taviani brothers' 1982 movie, *The Night of San Lorenzo,* was about this tragedy.) ✉ *Piazza del Castello* 🕓 *Daily 8–12:30 and 3–6:30.*

Museo Diocesano. Although the Museo Diocesano is small, the modest collection incorporates a number of subtle and pleasant local works of art. Note the rather odd *Crucifixion* by Fra Filippo Lippi, Verrocchio's *Il Redentore,* and the small but exquisite *Education of the Virgin* by Tiepolo. ✉ *Piazza del Castello* ☎ *0571/406700* 🎫 *€2.50* 🕓 *Apr.–Oct., weekends 10–1 and 2–6; Nov.–Mar., Tues.– Sun. 11–5.*

Torre di Federico II. Dating from the time of Frederick II (1194–1250), the Torre di Federico II was destroyed during World War II. A point of civic pride for San Miniatans and visible for miles, the tower was rebuilt and reopened in 1958. The hapless, ill-fated Pier della Vigna, chancellor and minister to Frederick II, leaped to his death from the tower, earning a mention in Dante's *Inferno.* The hill on which the tower stands—a surprisingly large oval of green grass—is one of the loveliest places in the area to have a picnic, enjoy the 360-degree view, and perhaps join local children in a pickup game of *calcio* (soccer). ✉ *Piazza la Torre* ☎ *0571/42745* 🎫 *€3.50* 🕓 *Apr.–Oct., Tues.–Sun. 11–6; Nov.–Mar., Tues.–Sun. 11–5.*

WHERE TO EAT AND STAY

For expanded hotel reviews, visit Fodors.com.

$$ TUSCAN 🍴 **Il Convio.** A short drive down a steep, serpentine road from San Miniato brings you to this rustic country *ristorante* with sponged walls, stenciled decorations, and checkered tablecloths. The main courses are mostly Tuscan classics, such as *bistecca fiorentina* (a generous cut of grilled steak). White truffles, the local specialty, are showcased—you can get them with pasta, *crespelle* (thin pancakes filled with ricotta), tripe, eggs, beef fillet, and even with a postprandial truffled grappa. All this good fare pairs marvelously with their fine selection of local, lesser-known wines. If truffles don't float your boat, there are untruffled things on the menu and, at night, they fire up the pizza oven. [$] *Average main: €15* ✉ *Via San Maiano 2* ☎ *0571/408114* 🕓 *Closed Wed.*

$ B&B/INN 🏨 **Convento di San Francesco.** For a complete change of pace, you can stay in this 13th-century convent in the company of five Franciscan friars. **Pros:** great price; tranquility. **Cons:** rooms are rather spartan; most of staff speaks only Italian. [$] *Rooms from: €39* ✉ *Piazza San Francesco* ☎ *0571/43051* 🛏 *30 rooms* 💳 *No credit cards* 🍽 *No meals.*

PISA

If you can get beyond the kitsch of the stalls hawking cheap souvenirs around the Leaning Tower, you'll find that Pisa has much to offer. Its treasures aren't as abundant as those of Florence, to which it is inevitably compared, but the cathedral-baptistery-tower complex of Piazza del Duomo, known collectively as the Campo dei Miracoli (Field of Miracles), is among the most dramatic settings in Italy.

Pisa may have been inhabited as early as the Bronze Age. It was certainly populated by the Etruscans and, in turn, became part of the Roman

Empire. In the early Middle Ages it flourished as an economic power-house—along with Amalfi, Genoa, and Venice, it was one of the four maritime republics. The city's economic and political power ebbed in the early 15th century as it fell under Florence's domination, though it enjoyed a brief resurgence under Cosimo I in the mid-16th century. Pisa sustained heavy damage during World War II, but the Duomo and Tower were spared, along with some other grand Romanesque structures.

GETTING HERE

Pisa is an easy hour's train ride from Florence. By car it's a straight shot on the Fi-Pi-Li autostrada. The Pisa–Lucca train runs frequently and takes about 30 minutes.

VISITOR INFORMATION

Pisa Tourism Office ⊠ *Piazza Vittorio Emanuele II* ☎ *050/42291* ⊕ *www.pisaunicaterra.it.*

EXPLORING PISA

Pisa, like many Italian cities, is best explored on foot, and most of what you'll want to see is within walking distance. The views along the Arno River are particularly grand and shouldn't be missed—there's a feeling of spaciousness that isn't found along the Arno in Florence.

As you set out, note that there are various combination-ticket options for sights on the Piazza del Duomo.

TOP ATTRACTIONS

Battistero. This lovely Gothic baptistery, which stands across from the Duomo's facade, is best known for the pulpit carved by Nicola Pisano (circa 1220–84; father of Giovanni Pisano) in 1260. Every half hour, an employee will dramatically close the doors, then intone and chant, thereby demonstrating how remarkable the acoustics are in the place. ⊠ *Piazza del Duomo* ☎ *050/835011* ⊕ *www.opapisa.it* ✆ *€5, discounts available if bought in combination with tickets for other monuments* ⊙ *Nov.–Feb., daily 10–5; Mar., daily 9–6; Apr.–Sept., daily 8–8; Oct., daily 9–7.*

Duomo. Pisa's cathedral brilliantly utilizes the horizontal marble-stripe motif (borrowed from Moorish architecture) that became common to Tuscan cathedrals. It is famous for the Romanesque panels on the transept door facing the tower that depict scenes from the life of Christ. The beautifully carved 14th-century pulpit is by Giovanni Pisano (son of Nicola). ⊠ *Piazza del Duomo* ☎ *050835011* ⊕ *www.opapisa.it* ✆ *€5* ⊙ *Nov.–Feb., daily 10–12:45 and 2–5; Mar., daily 10–6; Apr.–Sept., daily 10–8; Oct., daily 10–7.*

Fodor's Choice ★ **Leaning Tower (Torre Pendente).** Legend holds that Galileo conducted an experiment on the nature of gravity by dropping metal balls from the top of the 187-foot-high Leaning Tower of Pisa. Historians, say this legend has no basis in fact—which isn't quite to say that it's false. Work on this tower, built as a campanile (bell tower) for the Duomo, started in 1173: the lopsided settling began when construction reached the third story. The tower's architects attempted to compensate

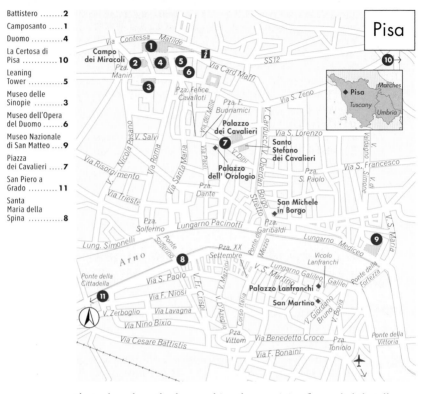

through such methods as making the remaining floors slightly taller on the leaning side, but the extra weight only made the problem worse. The settling continued, and by the late 20th century it had accelerated to such a point that many feared the tower would simply topple over, despite all efforts to prop it up. The structure has since been firmly anchored to the earth. The final phase to restore the tower to its original tilt of 300 years ago was launched in early 2000 and finished two years later. The last phase removed some 100 tons of earth from beneath the foundation. Reservations, which are essential, can be made online or by calling the Museo dell'Opera del Duomo; it's also possible to arrive at the ticket office and book for the same day. Note that children under eight years of age are not allowed to climb. ⊠ *Piazza del Duomo* ☏ *050/835011* ⊕ *www.opapisa.it* ⊠ *€18* ⊘ *Dec. and Jan., daily 10–5; Nov. and Feb., daily 9:40–5:40; Mar., daily 9–6; Apr.–Sept., daily 8:30–8; Oct., daily 9–7.*

WORTH NOTING

Camposanto. According to legend, the cemetery—a walled structure on the western side of the Campo dei Miracoli—is filled with earth that returning Crusaders brought back from the Holy Land. Contained within are numerous frescoes, notably *The Drunkenness of Noah* by Renaissance artist Benozzo Gozzoli (1422–97), presently under restoration; and the disturbing *Triumph of Death* (14th century; artist uncertain), whose subject matter shows what was on people's minds in a century that saw the ravages of the Black Death. ⊠ *Piazza del Duomo* ☎ *050/835011* ⊕ *www.opapisa.it* ✉ *€5, discounts available if bought in combination with tickets for other monuments* ⊙ *Nov.–Feb., daily 10–5; Mar., daily 9–6; Apr.–Sept., daily 8:30–8; Oct., daily 9–7.*

Museo delle Sinopie. The well-arranged museum on the south side of the Piazza del Duomo holds the *sinopie* (preparatory drawings) for the Camposanto frescoes. Though the exhibits are mostly of interest to specialists, some didactic audio-visual material provides a good introduction to the whole religious complex. ⊠ *Piazza del Duomo* ☎ *050/835011* ⊕ *www.opapisa.it* ✉ *€5, discounts available if bought in combination with tickets for other monuments* ⊙ *Nov.–Feb., daily 10–5; Mar., daily 9–6; Apr.–Sept., daily 8:30–8; Oct., daily 9–7.*

Museo dell'Opera del Duomo. At the southeast corner of the sprawling Campo dei Miracoli, this museum holds a wealth of medieval sculptures and the ancient Roman sarcophagi that inspired Nicola Pisano's figures. ⊠ *Piazza del Duomo* ☎ *050/835011* ⊕ *www.opapisa.it* ✉ *€5, discounts available if bought in combination with tickets for other monuments* ⊙ *Nov.–Feb., daily 10–5; Mar., daily 9–6; Apr.–Sept., daily 8:30–8; Oct., daily 9–7.*

Museo Nazionale di San Matteo. On the north bank of the Arno, this museum contains some beautiful examples of local Romanesque and Gothic art. ⊠ *Lungarno Mediceo* ☎ *050/541865* ✉ *€5* ⊙ *Tues.–Sat. 9–7, holidays 9–2.*

Piazza dei Cavalieri. The piazza, with its fine Renaissance **Palazzo dei Cavalieri, Palazzo dell'Orologio,** and Chiesa di **Santo Stefano dei Cavalieri,** was laid out by Giorgio Vasari in about 1560. The square was the seat of the Ordine dei Cavalieri di San Stefano (Order of the Knights of St. Stephen), a military and religious institution meant to defend the coast from possible invasion by the Turks. Also in this square is the prestigious **Scuola Normale Superiore,** founded by Napoléon in 1810 on the French model. Here graduate students pursue doctorates in literature, philosophy, mathematics, and science. In front of the school is a large statue of Ferdinando I de' Medici dating from 1596. On the extreme left is the tower where the hapless Ugolino della Gherardesca (died 1289) was imprisoned with his two sons and two grandsons; legend holds that he ate them. Dante immortalized him in Canto XXXIII of his *Inferno*. Duck into the **Church of Santo Stefano** (if you're lucky enough to find it open) and check out Bronzino's splendid *Nativity of Christ* (1564–65).

San Piero a Grado. This 11th-century basilica, located 8 km (5 miles) southwest of Pisa along the Arno, was built over the remains of two earlier churches. According to legend, it was here that St. Peter the Apostle stepped off the boat in AD 42—his first step on Italian soil. (It would have made more sense for him to land on the Adriatic Coast, as he was coming from Antioch.) The structure is a lovely example of Romanesque architecture, and it's not without its quirks: it has two apses, one at each end. On the walls are some crumbling, but still

DID YOU KNOW?

Pisa's Leaning Tower was already beginning to tilt by the time construction was underway on its third story.

vibrant, frescoes dating from the 12th and 13th centuries. Thirty-one of these frescoes depict scenes from the lives of Saints Peter and Paul, an uncommon subject in Tuscan wall painting. ✉ *Via Vecchia di Marina* ☎ *050/960065* ⏲ *Daily 9–5:30.*

WORD OF MOUTH

"At Pisa we discovered a peaceful haven with relatively few tourists compared with Florence, and a magnificent lawn you could actually walk and sit on. I lay down in the lovely grass and slept in the sun until I was awakened by the cool shadow of the Leaning Tower. It was magic and peaceful and beautiful." —Jo

Santa Maria della Spina. Originally an oratory dating from the 13th century, this gem of a church has been restored several times, most recently in 1996–98 (due to flood damage). It's a delicate, tiny church, and a fine example of Tuscan Gothic architecture. The church is only open when special exhibitions are on; however, the view from outside is well worth the trip. ✉ *Lungarno Gambacorti* 🎫 *€2.50* ⏲ *Apr.–Oct., Tues.–Fri. 10–1:15 and 2:30–5:45; Nov.–Mar., Tues.–Sun. 10–1 and 3–6.*

OFF THE BEATEN PATH

La Certosa di Pisa. A *certosa* is a monastery whose monks belong to the strict Carthusian order. This vast and sprawling complex, begun in 1366, was suppressed by Napoléon in the early 1800s, and then again in 1866. Most of the art and architecture you see dates from the 17th and 18th centuries. The Carthusians returned here, only to leave it permanently in 1969. Also within it is the **Museo di Storia Naturale e del Territorio.** This museum of natural history contains fossils, 24 whale skeletons that serve to trace the mammal's development over the millennia, and some exhibits of local minerals. ✉ *10 km (6 miles) east of Pisa via road north of Arno, through Mezzana and then toward Calci and Montemagno* ☎ *050/938430* 🎫 *€5* ⏲ *Tues.–Sat. 8:30–6:30, Sun. 8:30–12:30, with tours on half hr.*

WHERE TO EAT

$$ TUSCAN Fodor's Choice ★

🍴 **Beny.** Apricot walls hung with etchings of Pisa make this small, single-room restaurant warmly romantic. Husband and wife Damiano and Sandra Lazzerini have been running the place for two decades, and it shows in their obvious enthusiasm while talking about the menu and daily specials (which often astound). Fish is a specialty here: the *ripieno di polpa di pesce a pan grattato con salsa di seppie e pomodoro* (fish-stuffed ravioli with tomato-octopus sauce) delights. Seasonal ingredients are key throughout the menu; Sandra works wonders with *tartufi estivi* (summer truffles), artichokes, and market fish of the day. [$] *Average main: €21* ✉ *Piazza Gambacorti 22* ☎ *050/25067* ⏲ *Closed Sun. and 2 wks in mid-Aug. No lunch Sat.*

$$ TUSCAN

🍴 **La Pergoletta.** On an old town street named for its beautiful towers, this small, simple restaurant is in one such tower itself. There's also a shady garden for outdoor dining. Emma Forte, the proprietor and chef, cooks such Tuscan classics as *minestra di farro* (spelt soup) and choice interpretations of *grigliata* (grilled beef, veal, or lamb). Her sense of whimsy accounts for some of the non-Italian ingredients, such as ginger, that find their way into her dishes. Parents with small children may be pleased to find that there's a children's menu, and couples looking for a romantic spot could find no better place in Pisa. [$] *Average main: €15* ✉ *Via delle Belle Torri 40* ☎ *050/542458* 🌐 *www.ristorantelapergoletta.com* 🕒 *Closed Mon. and 1 wk in Aug. No lunch Sat.*

$ ITALIAN 🍴 **Osteria dei Cavalieri.** This charming white-wall restaurant, a few steps from Piazza dei Cavalieri, is reason enough to come to Pisa. They can do it all here—serve up exquisitely grilled fish dishes, please vegetarians, and prepare *tagliata* (thin slivers of rare beef) for meat lovers. Three set menus, from the sea, garden, and earth, are available, or you can order à la carte. For dinner there's an early seating (around 7:30) and a later one (around 9); opt for the later one if you want time to linger over your meal. [$] *Average main: €14* ✉ *Via San Frediano 16* ☎ *050/580858* ✍ *Reservations essential* 🕒 *Closed Sun., 2 wks in Aug., and Dec. 29–Jan. 7. No lunch Sat.*

$ ITALIAN 🍴 **Trattoria la Faggiola.** It's only seconds away from the Leaning Tower, which probably explains the "No Pizza" sign written in big, bold letters on the blackboard outside. Inside, another blackboard lists two or three primi and secondi. The amiable Carlo Silvestrini presides over this little eatery, and he cares if you don't clean your plate. That's not a problem though, because everything's good, from the *pasta pasticciata con speck e carciofi* (oven-baked penne with cured ham and artichokes) to the finishing touch of *castagnaccio con crema di ricotta* (a chestnut flan topped with ricotta cream). [$] *Average main: €9* ✉ *Via della Faggiola 1* ☎ *050/556179* ✍ *Reservations essential* 💳 *No credit cards.*

WHERE TO STAY

For expanded hotel reviews, visit Fodors.com.

$ Fodor's Choice ★ 🏨 **Fattoria di Migliarino.** Martino Salviati and his wife Giovanna have turned their working *fattoria* (farm)—on which they raise soybeans, corn, and sugar beets—into an inn. **Pros:** near Pisa airport; a good choice for a tranquil last night in Italy. **Cons:** mandatory one-week apartment stay during high season. [$] *Rooms from: €110* ✉ *Via dei Pini 289, 10 km (6 miles) northwest of Pisa, Migliarino* ☎ *050/803046, 335/6608411 mobile* 🌐 *www.fattoriadimigliarino.it* 🛏 *10 rooms in B&B, 13 apartments* 🍽 *Breakfast.*

$$$ HOTEL 🏨 **Hotel Relais dell'Orologio.** What used to be a private family palace is now an intimate hideaway where 18th-century antiques fill the rooms and public spaces and some rooms have stenciled walls and wood-beam ceilings. **Pros:** location—in the center of town, but on a quiet side street. **Cons:** breakfast costs extra; a bit pricey. [$] *Rooms from: €300* ✉ *Via della Faggiola 12/14, off Campo dei Miracoli, Santa Maria* ☎ *050/830361* 🌐 *www.hotelrelaisorologio.com* 🛏 *16 rooms, 5 suites* 🍽 *No meals.*

$ HOTEL 🏨 **Royal Victoria.** In a pleasant palazzo facing the Arno, a 10-minute walk from the Campo dei Miracoli, room styles range from the 1800s, complete with frescoes, to the 1920s; the most charming are in the old tower. **Pros:** friendly staff; lovely views of the Arno from many rooms. **Cons:** rooms vary significantly in size; all are a little worn.

Ⓢ *Rooms from: €78* ✉ *Lungarno Pacinotti 12* ☎ *050/940111* ⊕ *www.* *royalvictoria.it* ⤳ *48 rooms, 40 with bath* ⦿ *Breakfast.*

NIGHTLIFE AND THE ARTS

Fondazione Teatro di Pisa. Pisa has a lively performing-arts scene, most of which happens at the 19th-century Teatro Verdi. Music and dance performances are presented from September through May. Contact Fondazione Teatro di Pisa for schedules and information. ✉ *Via Palestro 40, Lungarni* ☎ *050/941111* ⊕ *www.teatrodipisa.pi.it.*

Luminaria. Pisa at its best during the Luminaria feast day, on June 16. The day honors Saint Ranieri, the city's patron saint. Palaces along the Arno are lit with white lights, and there are plenty of fireworks.

THE ROAD FROM FLORENCE TO LUCCA

The cities along the route between Florence and Lucca are primarily industrial—and they've been that way for a long time. Prato has been producing textiles since the Middle Ages; Renaissance art lovers should pay a visit to the Duomo, with its magnificent Filippo Lippi frescoes. Farther northwest, Pistoia's historic center abounds with art treasures. If you're looking for a spa treatment, or if you want to experience a bit of kitsch, Italian style, visit Montecatini Terme, where the clock seems to have stopped sometime in the 1950s.

PRATO

19 km (12 miles) northwest of Florence, 60 km (37 miles) east of Lucca.

The wool industry in this city, one of the world's largest producers of cloth, was famous throughout Europe as early as the 13th century. Business was further stimulated in the late 14th century by a local cloth merchant, Francesco di Marco Datini, who built his business, according to one of his surviving ledgers, "In the name of God and of profit." One thing that distinguishes Prato from other Italian towns of its size is the presence of modern public art—most notably Henry Moore's mammoth, marble *Square Form with Cut* in Piazza San Marco. ■ TIP→ Most of Prato's major museums are closed Tuesday.

GETTING HERE

Prato is a quick train ride from Florence. By car it's a 45-minute trip on the A11/E76 toll road.

VISITOR INFORMATION

Prato tourism office ✉ *Piazza del Duomo 8* ☎ *0574/24112* ⊕ *www.* *pratoturismo.it.*

EXPLORING

Carmignano. Pontormo's *Visitation* is in this small village a short drive from Poggio a Caiano. The Franciscan church of **San Michele**, dedicated in 1211, houses the work. The painting dates from 1527–30, and it may well be Pontormo's masterpiece. The luminous colors, flowing drapery, and steady gaze shared between the Virgin and St. Elizabeth are breathtaking. The church's small cloister, shaded by olive trees, is always open, and offers a quiet place to sit. ⊠ *15 km (9 miles) south of Prato, through Poggio a Caiano, up Mt. Albano* ☎ *055/8712046* ⊙ *Oct.–Apr., daily 7:30–5; May–Sept., daily 7:30–6.*

Castello (*Castle*). The formidable Castello, near Santa Maria delle Carceri, is an impressive sight. The (Sicilian) Holy Roman Emperor Frederick II (1194–1250) built the seat of his authority in Tuscany in this somewhat unlikely spot. Frederick's castles were designed to echo imperial Rome, and the many columns, lions, and porticoes testify to his ambition. This is the only castle he built outside of Sicily and Puglia in southern Italy. ⊠ *Piazza Santa Maria delle Carceri* ☎ *0574/38207* ☞ *Free* ⊙ *Wed.–Mon. 9:30–1 and 3–7.*

Duomo. Prato's Romanesque Duomo, reconstructed from 1211, is famous for its **Pergamo del Sacro Cingolo** (Chapel of the Holy Girdle), to the left of the entrance, which enshrines the sash of the Virgin Mary. It is said that the girdle was given to the apostle Thomas by the Virgin Mary when she miraculously appeared after her Assumption into heaven. The Duomo also contains 15th-century frescoes by Prato's most famous son, Fra Filippo Lippi. His scenes from the life of Saint Stephen are on the left wall of the **Cappella Maggiore** (Main Chapel); those from the life of John the Baptist are on the right. ⊠ *Piazza del Duomo* ☎ *0574/26234* ⊕ *www.diocesiprato.it* ☞ *€3 to visit Cappella Maggiore* ⊙ *Daily 10–1 and 3–5:30.*

NEED A BREAK? **Antonio Mattei.** Prato's *biscotti* (literally "twice-cooked" cookies) have an extra-dense texture, lending themselves to submersion in your caffè or vin santo. The best biscotti in town are at Antonio Mattei. Their *brutti buoni* (ugly but good) almond-laced cookies are especially delicious. ⊠ *Via Ricasoli 20/22* ☎ *0574/25756* ⊕ *www.antoniomattei.it.*

Museo del Tessuto (*Textile Museum*). Preserved in the Museo del Tessuto is what made this city a Renaissance economic powerhouse. The collection includes clothing, fabric fragments, and the machines used to make them, all dating from the 14th to the 20th centuries. Check out the 15th-century fabrics with pomegranate prints, a virtuoso display of Renaissance textile wizardry. The well-designed museum (objects are clearly labeled in English) is within the medieval walls of the city in the old Cimatoria, a 19th-century factory that finished raw fabrics. The temporary exhibitions are usually noteworthy; check with the Prato tourist office to see what's on display when you visit. ⊠ *Via Santa Chiara 24* ☎ *0574/611503* ⊕ *www.museodeltessuto.it* ☞ *€3* ⊙ *Daily 10–6.*

Museo dell'Opera del Duomo. A sculpture by Donatello (circa 1386–1466) that originally adorned the Duomo's exterior pulpit is now on display in the Museo dell'Opera del Duomo. The museum also includes such 15th-century gems as Fra Filippo Lippi's *Madonna and Child,* Giovanni Bellini's (circa 1432–1516) *Christ on the Cross,* and Caravaggio's (1571–1610) *Christ Crowned with Thorns.* ⊠ *Piazza del Duomo 49* ☎ *0574/29339* ⊕ *www.diocesiprato.it* ☞ *€5, combination ticket €8 (includes Museo di Pittura Murale and il Castello)* ⊙ *Mon., Thurs., and Fri. 9–1 and 2:30–6:30, Sat. 10–1 and 2–6:30, Sun. 10–1.*

Museo di Pittura Murale (*Museum of Mural Painting*). The permanent collection in the Museo di Pittura Murale contains frescoes and altarpieces (removed from sites in and around Prato) by artists such as Filippo Lippi, Agnolo Gaddi, Nicolo Gerini, and Il Volterrano, among others. ⊠ *Piazza San Domenico 8* ☎ *0574/440501* 🖃 *€5, combination ticket €8 (includes Museo dell'Opera del Duomo and il Castello)* ⊙ *Mon., Wed.–Fri., and Sun. 9–1, Sat. 9–1 and 3–6.*

Poggio a Caiano. For a look at gracious country living Renaissance style, take a detour to the Medici villa in Poggio a Caiano. Lorenzo "il Magnifico" (1449–92) commissioned Giuliano da Sangallo (circa 1445–1516) to redo the villa, which was lavished with frescoes by important Renaissance painters such as Pontormo (1494–1556), Franciabigio (1482–1525), and Andrea del Sarto (1486–1531). You can walk around the austerely ornamented grounds while waiting for one of the hourly villa tours, which start on the half-hour. The guides do not speak, but follow you around the place. ⊠ *Piazza dei Medici 14, 7 km (4½ miles) south of Prato (follow signs)* ☎ *055/877012* 🖃 *Free* ⊙ *Sept. and Oct., daily 8:30–5:30; Nov.–Feb., daily 8:30–3:30; Mar., daily 8:30–4:30; Apr. and May, daily 8:30–5:30; June–Aug., daily 8:30–6:30.*

Santa Maria delle Carceri. The church of Santa Maria delle Carceri was built by Giuliano Sangallo in the 1490s, and is a landmark of Renaissance architecture. ⊠ *Piazza Santa Maria delle Carceri, off Via Cairoli and southeast of the cathedral* ☎ *0574/27933* ⊙ *Daily 7–noon and 4–7.*

OFF THE BEATEN PATH

Villa Medicea La Ferdinanda di Artimino. In the small town of **Artimino**, next door to Carmignano, is the Villa Medicea La Ferdinanda di Artimino. Built by Ferdinando I de' Medici (1549–1609) in the 1590s, it was originally used as a hunting lodge. Though it's closed to the public (except for special occasions or by prior arrangement), it's simply a stunning villa to look at. ⊠ *11 km (7 miles) south of Prato (head east from Carmignano or south from Poggio a Caiano, up Mt. Albano)* ☎ *055/875141.*

WHERE TO EAT

$$
TUSCAN
Fodor'sChoice
★

Baghino. In the heart of the historic center, Baghino is the best restaurant in town. It's been serving since 1870, capably run by five generations of the Pacetti family (daughters Guja and Silvia are presently in charge). Part of the building dates to the 15th century, when it was a convent; later it was the seat of the Freemasons. The food lives up to the building's colorful history. Do not miss the *sedano ripieno alla pratese* (stuffed celery), in which celery is pressed, stuffed with a minced veal and mortadella filling, coated in flour and egg, and fried in olive oil. A tasty ragù crowns the dish. Another house specialty is the *filetto al pepe verde* (beef filet in a creamy green peppercorn sauce). The wine list boasts local favorites, which are among the best in Tuscany. 💲 *Average main: €17* ⊠ *Via dell'Accademia 9* ☎ *0574/27920* ⊙ *Closed Aug. No lunch Mon. No dinner Sun.*

$$
TUSCAN
Fodor'sChoice
★

Da Delfina. Delfina Cioni began cooking many years ago for hungry hunters in the town of Artimino, 20 km (12 miles) south of Prato; now her son Carlo maintains the culinary legacy. Dishes celebrate Tuscan food, with an emphasis on fresh local ingredients. Secondi such as *coniglio con olive e pignoli* (rabbit sautéed with olives and pine nuts—the house specialty) are a real treat. The seasonal menu is complemented by a fine wine list, and service is gracious. From the restaurant's four comfortably rustic rooms (and outside terrace when it's warm) you have a glorious view of the Tuscan countryside, including a Medici villa. $ *Average main: €17* ✉ *Via della Chiesa 1, Artimino* ☎ *055/8718074* 🔖 *Reservations essential* ▭ *No credit cards* ☾ *Closed Mon. No lunch Tues. No dinner Sun.*

$

TUSCAN

✕**La Vecchia Cucina di Soldano.** This place could be mistaken for a grandmother's kitchen: it's completely unpretentious, with red-and-white-checked tablecloths and a waitstaff who treat you like an old friend. The restaurant teems with locals who appreciate fine dining at rock-bottom prices. Typical Tuscan specialties are on hand, including a superb *tagliolini sui fagioli* (thin noodles with beans). $ *Average main: €7* ✉ *Via Pomeria 23* ☎ *0574/34665* ▭ *No credit cards* ☾ *Closed Sun.*

$$

TUSCAN

✕**Osteria da i'Peruzzi.** If you've just visited the Medici Villa at Poggio a Caiano, wander down the street to this intimate restaurant, the rooms of which date to the 16th century. Here you'll find hearty, wonderful food, a great wine list, and lovely staff. The osteria's version of *peposo*, a local specialty, is a small masterpiece: a beef stew, laced with black pepper and a little bit of red wine, served on creamy polenta. The chef has an equally deft touch with vegetables; the *carciofi al tegame con olive nere* contains gently stewed artichokes, their flavor sharpened by the addition of black olives. Biscotti di Prato (the twice-baked cookie) dipped in vin santo provides a fitting conclusion. $ *Average main: €20* ✉ *Via Cancellieri 29, Poggio a Caiano* ☎ *055/8798692* ☾ *Closed Mon.*

WHERE TO STAY

For expanded hotel reviews, visit Fodors.com.

$$

HOTEL

🛏 **Hotel Paggeria Medicea.** Ferdinando I de'Medici loved to hunt, and so erected his villa to accommodate this whim. **Pros:** peace and tranquility; spectacular views. **Cons:** a car is essential. $ *Rooms from: €160* ✉ *Viale Papa Giovanni XXIII 1* ☎ *055/875141* ⊕ *www.artimino.com* ↪ *37 rooms.*

PISTOIA

18 km (11 miles) northwest of Prato, 43 km (27 miles) east of Lucca, 37 km (23 miles) northwest of Florence.

Founded in the 2nd century BC as a support post for Roman troops, Pistoia grew over the centuries into an important trading center. In the Middle Ages it was troubled by civic strife and eventually fell to the Florentines, who imposed a pro-Guelf government in 1267; it lost its last vestiges of independence to Florence in 1329.

Reconstructed after heavy bombing during World War II, it has preserved some fine Romanesque architecture. Modern-day Pistoia's major industries include the manufacture of rail vehicles (including the cars for Washington, D.C.'s Metro) and tree and plant nurseries, which flourish on the alluvial plain around the city.

GETTING HERE

From Florence or Lucca, Pistoia is an easy train ride; trains run frequently. By car, take the A11/E76.

VISITOR INFORMATION

Pistoia tourism office ✉ *Palazzo dei Vescovi* ☎ *0573/21622* ⊕ *www. pistoia.turismo.toscana.it.*

EXPLORING

Duomo. The Romanesque Duomo, the Cattedrale di San Zeno, dates from as early as the 5th century. It houses a magnificent silver altar dedicated to Saint James. The two half-figures on the left are by Filippo Brunelleschi (1377–1446), the first Renaissance architect (and designer of Florence's magnificent Duomo cupola). The octagonal **Battistero,** with green-and-white-stripe marble cladding, dates from the middle of the 14th century. Three of its eight sides have doorways; the main door facing the piazza is crowned with a rose window. Note the lovely little lantern crowning the top of the building. ✉ *Piazza del Duomo* ☎ *0573/25095* 🕮 *Free; access to altarpiece €2* ۞ *Church: Oct.–Apr., Mon.–Sat. 8–12:30 and 3:30–7, Sun. 8–1 and 3:30–7; May–Sept., daily 8–1 and 3:30–7. Altar: Mon.–Sat. 10–12:30 and 3–5:30, Sun. 8–9:30, 11–11:30, and 4–5:30.*

Fondazione Marino Marini. Lest you think that Tuscany produced only Renaissance artists, the Fondazione Marino Marini presents many works from its namesake modern native Pistoian (1901–80). Sculpture, etchings, paintings, engravings, and mixed media have all been installed in the elegantly renovated 14th-century Convento del Tau. ✉ *Corso Silvano Fedi 30* ☎ *0573/30285* 🕮 *€3.50, combination ticket €6 (includes Museo Civico)* ۞ *Oct.–Mar., Mon.–Sat. 10–5; Apr.–Sept., Mon.–Sat. 10–6.*

FAMILY **Giardino Zoologico.** A 20-minute drive out of town brings you to the Giardino Zoologico, a small zoo laid out to accommodate the wiles of both animals and children. ✉ *Via Pieve a Celle 160/a, take Bus 29 from train station* ☎ *0573/911219* 🕮 *€14.50* ۞ *Oct.–Mar., daily 9–5, Apr.–Sept., daily 9–7.*

Musei dell'Antico Palazzo dei Vescovi (*Old Bishop's Palace*). At the end of the 11th century, the bishop of Pistoia began construction on this palace. One thousand years later, it houses several collections including the **Museo della Cattedrale di San Zeno,** which contains spectacular treasures from Pistoia's cathedral—including ornate pieces in gold, rings with jewels the size of small eggs, and solemn, powerful statuary. Below, however, is the **Percorso Archeologico**—Roman, medieval, and Etruscan archaeological sites uncovered during a 1970s renovation. The warren of corridors and caves below and the plain, spare rooms above both show off their treasures with simple elegance. Also in the complex is the **Museo Tattile,** which allows visitors to touch various local buildings built to scale. A guide accompanies you while you wander, and wandering days and times are limited. ✉ *Piazza del Duomo* ☎ *0573/369272* 🕮 *€4* ۞ *Tues., Thurs., and Fri. 10, 11:30, and 3.*

Museo Civico. The Palazzo del Comune, begun around 1295, houses the Museo Civico, containing works by local artists from the 13th to 19th centuries. ⊠ *Piazza del Duomo 1* ☎ *0573/371296* 🎫 *€3.50, combination ticket €6 (includes Fondazione Marino Marini)* ⊘ *Apr.–Oct., Tues.–Sun. 10–6; Nov.–Mar., Tues.–Sun. 10–5.*

Ospedale del Ceppo. Founded in the 13th century and still a functioning hospital, the Ospedale del Ceppo has a facade with a superb early-16th-century exterior terra-cotta frieze. It was begun by Giovanni della Robbia (1469–1529) and completed by the workshop of Santi and Benedetto Buglioni between 1526 and 1528. Though the inside is closed to the public, catch a glimpse of the 17th-century graffiti on the columns outside. ⊠ *Piazza Giovanni XIII, down Via Pacini from Piazza del Duomo.*

San Giovanni Fuorcivitas. An architectural gem in green-and-white marble, the medieval church of San Giovanni Fuorcivitas holds a *Visitation* by Luca della Robbia (1400–82), a painting attributed to Taddeo Gaddi, and a holy-water font that may have been made by Fra Guglielmo around 1270. ⊠ *Via Cavour* ☎ *0573/24784* ⊘ *Daily 7:30–noon and 5–6:30.*

Sant'Andrea. In the 12th-century church of Sant'Andrea, the fine pulpit by Giovanni Pisano (circa 1250–1314) depicts scenes from the life of Christ in a series of high-relief, richly sculpted marble panels. ⊠ *Piazzetta Sant'Andrea, Via Sant'Andrea* ☎ *0573/21912* ⊘ *Daily 7:30–12:30 and 3:30–6.*

WHERE TO EAT

$ ✕ **La Botte Gaia.** Jazz plays softly in the background as patrons sip wine
WINE BAR   at rustic tables in rooms with exposed brick-and-stone walls. In warm weather you can also dine alfresco with a splendid view of the Piazza del Duomo. Typical wine-bar fare, such as plates of cured ham and cheese, shares the menu with a surprisingly sophisticated list of daily specials. For example, you might try *insalatina con foie gras condita con vinaigrette* (foie gras with dressed greens). 💲 *Average main: €13* ⊠ *Via del Lastrone 17* ☎ *0573/365602* ⊕ *www.labottegaia.it* ⌚ *Reservations essential* ⊘ *Closed Mon. and last 3 wks in Aug. No lunch Sun.*

$ ✕ **MagnoGaudio.** It bills itself as a *caffetteria/ristorante*, which means
ITALIAN   it opens at 7 in the morning for coffee, serves lunch and dinner, and then closes well after dinner is over. Warm sponged colored walls and simple wooden tables and chairs provide the backdrop for some tasty fare. They're particularly big on fish here; if it's available, order the *calamari spadellati su crema di fagioli alla paprika e valeriana* (pan-fried squid on a creamy bean puree spiced with paprika and garnished with delicate green leaves). Their ample portion of lasagna is cheesy and thoroughly satisfying. Service is great, and the wine list (strong on local wines) equally so. 💲 *Average main: €11* ⊠ *Via Curtatone e Montanara 12* ☎ *0573/26905* ⌚ *Reservations essential.*

$$ ✕ **Trattoria dell'Abbondanza.** Entering from a quiet side street, you walk
TUSCAN   into a small place with cream-colored walls that's busy but not noisy.

Run by husband and wife team Patrizio (affectionately known by all as "Iccio") and Rosella Meuci, the trattoria serves traditional dishes like *minestra di farro* (a hearty soup made with farro) and *maccheroni all'anatra* (pasta in a duck sauce). For seconds, the house specialties of *baccalà alla Livornese* (salt cod in a tomato sauce) and *fritto di pollo con verdure* (fried chicken with vegetables) are standouts. *Torta rustica,* a cake of cornmeal and cream, makes a fine dessert. $ *Average main: €16* ⊠ *Via dell'Abbondanza 10/14, off Via degli Orafi* ☎ *0573/368037* ⊗ *Closed Wed. No lunch Thurs.*

NIGHTLIFE AND THE ARTS

La Giostra dell'Orso (*Bear Joust*). On July 25, La Giostra dell'Orso celebrates Saint James, Pistoia's patron saint. During the staged event three knights from each section of the city fight a "bear" (actually a target shaped like a bear that they strike, on horseback). The visitor center has more information on the event.

Pistoia Blues. In mid-July Pistoia Blues brings international blues artists and rock-and-rollers to town for performances in the main square. ☎ *0573/994659* ⊕ *www.pistoiablues.com.*

MONTECATINI TERME

15 km (9 miles) west of Pistoia, 49 km (30 miles) west of Florence, 29 km (18 miles) northeast of Lucca.

Immortalized in Fellini's film 8½, Montecatini Terme is the home of Italy's premier *terme* (spas). Known for their curative powers—and, at least once upon a time, for their great popularity among the wealthy—the mineral springs flow from five sources and are taken for a variety of ailments, including liver and skin disorders. Those "taking the cure" report each morning to one of the town's *stabilimenti termali* (thermal establishments) to drink their prescribed cupful of water. Afterward, guests can enjoy a leisurely breakfast, read the newspaper, recline and listen to music, or walk in the parks that surround these grand old spas.

Montecatini Terme's wealth of art nouveau buildings dates to the town's most active period of development at the beginning of the 20th century. Like most other well-heeled resort towns, Montecatini attracts the leisured traveler, conventioneer, and senior citizen on a group tour; it's trimmed with a measure of neon and glitz; aside from taking the waters and people-watching in Piazza del Popolo, there's not a whole lot to do here. There are, however, plenty of places to stay, making the town a good base from which to explore the region.

GETTING HERE

Montecatini Terme is one of the stops on the Florence–Lucca train line, and getting to the centro storico is an easy walk from the station. The A11/E76 will get you here by car.

VISITOR INFORMATION

Montecatini Terme tourism office ⊠ *Viale Verdi 66–68* ☎ *0572/772244* ⊕ *www.pistoia.turismo.toscana.it.*

Pistoia's medieval skyline

Terme di Montecatini. The umbrella group Terme di Montecatini has information on the town's nine thermal spas. ⊠ *Viale Verdi 43* ☎ *0572/7781* ⊕ *www.termemontecatini.it.*

EXPLORING

Excelsior. For traditional beauty treatments, the Excelsior offers manicures, facials, and massage therapies with mud, algae, and oils. ⊠ *Viale Verdi 61* ☎ *0572/778518* ⊕ *www.termemontecatini.it.*

Montecatini Alto. The older town, Montecatini Alto, sits atop a hill nearby, and is reached by a funicular from Viale Diaz. Though there isn't much to do once you get up there, the medieval square is lined with restaurants and bars, the air is crisp, and the views of the Nievole, the valley below, are gorgeous.

Piazza del Popolo. The town's main square teems with cafés and bars. It's an excellent spot for people-watching; in the evening and on weekends it seems like everyone is out walking, seeing, and being seen.

NEED A BREAK?

Bargilli. *Cialde,* a local specialty, are circular wafers made with flour, sugar, eggs, and almonds from Puglia. The Bargilli family has been serving them with their terrific ice cream since 1936. Try them at Bargilli, the family's shop and probably the best gelateria in town. ⊠ *Viale Grocco 2* ☎ *0572/79459* ⊕ *www.cialdedimontecatini.it.*

Terme Tettuccio. The most attractive art nouveau structure in town, Terme Tettuccio, has lovely colonnades. Here fountains set up on marble counters dispense mineral water, bucolic scenes painted on tiles decorate walls, and an orchestra plays under a frescoed dome. ⊠ *Viale Verdi 71* ☎ *0572/778501* 🎟 *€6, €10 to take the waters* ⊗ *Mar.–Oct., daily 8–noon and 3–5:30.*

WHERE TO STAY

For expanded hotel reviews, visit Fodors.com.

$$ 🏨 **Grand Hotel Croce di Malta.** Taste and sophistication have been the
HOTEL calling cards of this hotel since 1911. **Pros:** good location; attentive staff. **Cons:** attracts many tour groups. $ *Rooms from: €160* ⊠ *Viale IV Novembre 18* ☎ *0572/9201* ⊕ *www.crocedimalta.com* 🛏 *122 rooms, 22 suites* ⍾ *Breakfast.*

LUCCA

Ramparts built in the 16th and 17th centuries enclose a charming fortress town filled with churches (99 of them), terra-cotta–roofed buildings, and narrow cobblestone streets, along which locals maneuver bikes to do their daily shopping. Here Caesar, Pompey, and Crassus agreed to rule Rome as a triumvirate in 56 BC; Lucca was later the first Tuscan town to accept Christianity. The town still has a mind of its own, and when most of Tuscany was voting communist as a matter of course, Lucca's citizens rarely followed suit. The famous composer Giacomo Puccini (1858–1924) was born here; he is celebrated during the summer Opera Theater and Music Festival of Lucca. The ramparts circling the centro storico are the perfect place to stroll, bicycle, or just admire the view.

GETTING HERE

You can reach Lucca easily by train from Florence; the historic center is a short walk from the station. If you're driving, take the A11/E76.

VISITOR INFORMATION

Lucca Tourism Office ⊠ *Piazza Santa Maria* ☎ *0583/91991* ⊕ *www. luccaturismo.it.*

EXPLORING LUCCA

Traffic (including motorbikes) is restricted in the walled historic center of Lucca. Walking is the best, most enjoyable way to get around. Or you can rent a bicycle; getting around on bike is easy, as the center is quite flat.

TOP ATTRACTIONS

Duomo. The blind arches on the cathedral's facade are a fine example of the rigorously ordered Pisan Romanesque style, in this case happily enlivened by an extremely varied collection of small, carved columns. Take a closer look at the decoration of the facade and that of the portico below; they make this one of the most entertaining church exteriors in Tuscany. The Gothic interior contains a moving Byzantine crucifix—called the Volto Santo, or Holy Face—brought here, according to legend, in the 8th century (though it probably dates from between the 11th and early 13th centuries). The masterpiece of the Sienese sculptor Jacopo della Quercia (circa 1371–1438) is the marble *Tomb of Ilaria del Carretto* (1407–08). ⊠ *Piazza del Duomo* ☎ *0583/490530* ⊕ *www.museocattedralelucca.it* ✉ *Church free, tomb €3* ☉ *Duomo: Nov. 3–Mar. 14, weekdays 9:30–4:45, Sat. 9:30–6:45, Sun. 9:30–10:45 and noon–5; Mar. 15–Nov. 2, weekdays 9:30–5:45, Sat. 9–6:45, Sun. 9:30–10:45 and 11:30–6.*

NEED A BREAK? **Stella Polare.** Stella Polare bills itself as a "classic bar and bistrot." In this case, that means expertly mixed cocktails, wines by the glass, and light meals at lunch and dinner. Because it's on Piazza Napoleone (the city's largest and prettiest square), it's a great spot for people-watching. On weekends Stella offers an English breakfast, which means bacon and eggs. ⊠ *Via Vittorio Veneto 21* ☎ *0583/496332.*

Passeggiata delle Mura. Any time of day when the weather is nice, you can find the citizens of Lucca cycling, jogging, strolling, or kicking a soccer ball in this green, beautiful, and very large park—neither inside nor outside the city but rather right atop and around the ring of ramparts that defines Lucca. Sunlight streams through two rows of tall plane trees to dapple the *passeggiata delle mura* (walk on the walls), which is 4.2 km (2½ miles) in length. Ten bulwarks are topped with lawns, many with picnic tables and some with play equipment for children. Be aware at all times of where the edge is—there are no railings, and the drop to the ground outside the city is a precipitous 40 feet. ⊕ *www.lemuradilucca.it.*

Piazza dell'Anfiteatro Romano. Here's where the ancient Roman amphitheater once stood; some of the medieval buildings built over the amphitheater retain its original oval shape and brick arches. ⊠ *Off Via Fillungo, near north side of old town.*

San Frediano. A 14th-century mosaic decorates the facade of this church just steps from the Anfiteatro. Inside are works by Jacopo della Quercia (circa 1371–1438) and Matteo Civitali (1436–1501), as well as the lace-clad mummy of Saint Zita (circa 1218–78), the patron saint of household servants. ⊠ *Piazza San Frediano* ☎ *No phone* ☉ *Mon.–Sat. 8:30–noon and 3–5, Sun. 10:30–5.*

San Michele in Foro. The facade here is even more fanciful than that of the Duomo. Its upper levels have nothing but air behind them (after the front of the church was built, there were no funds to raise the nave), and the winged Archangel Michael, who stands at the very top, seems precariously poised for flight. The facade, heavily restored in the 19th century, displays busts of such 19th-century Italian patriots as Garibaldi and Cavour. Check out the superb Filippino Lippi (1457/58–1504) panel painting of Saints Jerome, Sebastian, Rocco, and Helen in the right transept. ⊠ *Piazza San Michele* ☉ *Nov.–Mar., daily 9–noon and 3–5; Apr.–Oct., daily 9–noon and 3–6.*

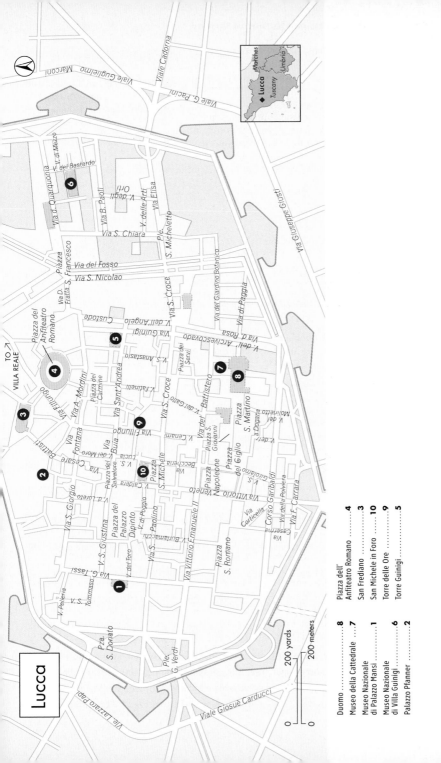

Lucca

FAMILY **Torre Guinigi.** The tower of the medieval Palazzo Guinigi contains one of the city's most curious sights: a grove of ilex trees has grown at the top of the tower, and their roots have pushed their way into the room below. From the top you have a magnificent view of the city and the surrounding countryside.

(Only the tower is open to the public, not the palazzo.) ✉ *Palazzo Guinigi, Via Sant'Andrea* ☎ *0583/583 086* ⊕ *www.lemuradilucca.it* 🖾 *€4* ⊙ *Nov.–Feb., daily 9:30–4:30; Mar. and Oct., daily 9:30–5:30; Apr.–Sept., daily 9:30–7:30.*

WORTH NOTING

Museo della Cattedrale. The cathedral museum exhibits many items too precious to be in the church, most notably the finely worked golden decorations of the Volto Santo, the Byzantine crucifix that remains in the Duomo. ✉ *Piazza Antelminelli* ☎ *0583/490530* ⊕ *www. museocattedralelucca.it* 🖾 *€4, combination ticket €5 (includes tomb in Duomo)* ⊙ *Mid-Mar.–mid-Nov., daily 10–6; mid-Nov.–mid-Mar., weekdays 10–2, weekends 10–5.*

Museo Nazionale di Palazzo Mansi. Highlights here include the lovely *Portrait of a Youth* by Pontormo; portraits of the Medici painted by Bronzino (1503–72); and paintings by Tintoretto, Vasari, and others. ✉ *Palazzo Mansi, Via Galli Tassi 43, near west walls of old city* ☎ *0583/55570* 🖾 *€4, combination ticket €6.50 (includes Museo Nazionale di Villa Guinigi)* ⊙ *Tues.–Sat. 8:30–7, Sun. 8:30–1:30.*

Museo Nazionale di Villa Guinigi. On the eastern end of the historic center, this sadly overlooked museum has an extensive collection of local Etruscan, Roman, Romanesque, and Renaissance art. The museum represents an overview of Lucca's artistic traditions from Etruscan times until the 17th century, housed in the former 15th-century villa of the Guinigi family. ✉ *Villa Guinigi, Via della Quarquonia* ☎ *0583/496033* 🖾 *€4* ⊙ *Tues.–Sat. 9–7, Sun. 9–2.*

Palazzo Pfanner. Here you can rest your feet and let time pass, surrounded by a harmonious arrangement of sun, shade, blooming plants, water, and mysterious statuary. The palazzo's well-kept formal garden, which abuts the city walls, centers on a large fountain and pool. Allegorical statues line pebbled paths that radiate outward. The palazzo, built in the 17th century, was purchased in the 19th century by the Pfanners, a family of Swiss brewers. The family, which eventually gave the town a mayor, still lives here. ✉ *Via degli Asili 33* ☎ *0583/954029* ⊕ *www. palazzopfanner.it* 🖾 *Garden €4.50, palazzo €4.50, garden and palazzo €6* ⊙ *Mar. 25–Oct. 31, daily 10–6. Nov. 1–15, Thurs.–Mon, 11–4.*

NEED A BREAK? **Gelateria Veneta.** Gelateria Veneta makes outstanding gelato, sorbet, and ices (some sugar-free). They prepare their confections three times a day, using the same recipes with which the Brothers Arnoldo opened the place in 1927. The pièces de résistance are frozen fruits stuffed with

creamy filling: don't miss the apricot sorbet-filled apricot. Note that they close up shop in October and reopen around Easter. ✉ ***Via V. Veneto 74*** ☎ ***0583/467037.***

FAMILY **Torre delle Ore** (*Tower of the Hours*). The highest spot in Lucca is the top of this tower, which had its first mechanical clock in 1390. It's since contained several clocks over the centuries; the current timepiece was installed in 1754. The reward for climbing 207 steps to the top is a panoramic view of the town. ✉ *Via Fillungo at Via dell'Arancio* ☎ *0583/316846* 🎟 *€4* 🕒 *Mar.–Nov., daily 9–7.*

OFF THE BEATEN PATH

Villa Reale. Eight kilometers (5 miles) north of Lucca in Marlia, this villa was once the home of Napoléon's sister, Princess Elisa. Restored by the Counts Pecci-Blunt, the estate is celebrated for its spectacular gardens, laid out in the 16th century and redone in the middle of the 17th. Gardening buffs adore the legendary *teatro di verdura*, a theater carved out of hedges and topiaries; concerts are occasionally held here. During the summer, concerts are held in the gardens of other famous Lucca villas as well. Contact the Lucca tourist office (☎ *0583/91991*) for details. ✉ *North of Lucca along river Serchio, in direction of Barga and Bagni di Lucca, Marlia* ☎ *0583/30108* 🎟 *€7* 🕒 *Guided visits: Mar.–Nov., Tues.–Sun. at 10, 11, noon, 3, 4, and 5.*

WHERE TO EAT

$$ TUSCAN Fodor's Choice ★

🍴 **Buca di Sant'Antonio.** The staying power of Buca di Sant'Antonio—it's been around since 1782—is the result of superlative Tuscan food brought to the table by waitstaff who doesn't miss a beat. The menu includes the simple but blissful, like *tortelli lucchesi al sugo* (meat-stuffed pasta with a tomato-and-meat sauce), and more daring dishes such as roast *capretto* (kid) with herbs. A white-wall interior hung with copper pots and brass musical instruments creates a classy but comfortable dining space. [$] *Average main: €15* ✉ *Via della Cervia 3* ☎ *0583/55881* 🕒 *Closed Mon., 1 wk in Jan., and 1 wk in July. No dinner Sun.*

$$$ TUSCAN

🍴 **Il Giglio.** This place for all seasons, with a big fireplace for chilly weather and an outdoor terrace in summer, has quiet, late-19th-century charm and classic cuisine. If mushrooms are in season, try the *tacchoni con funghi*, a homemade pasta with mushrooms and a local herb called *nepitella*. A local favorite during winter is the *coniglio con olive* (rabbit stew with olives). [$] *Average main: €34* ✉ *Piazza del Giglio 2* ☎ *0583/494508* 🕒 *Closed Wed. and 15 days in Nov. No dinner Tues.*

$ ITALIAN

🍴 **La Pecora Nera.** This lively, gaily colored little trattoria (the name means "black sheep") with a high-vaulted ceiling is staffed by *giovani disabili* (both mentally challenged and learning-disabled young people), who wait tables under the supervision of a non-disabled companion. The food's terrific, from the made-in-house *tordelli lucchesi* (meat-stuffed tortelli sauced with a fragrant meat ragù) to the tasty crostata. Great care is taken with sourcing, when possible, local organic ingredients, and such care translates into a lovely meal. [$] *Average main: €10* ✉ *Piazza San Francesco 4* ☎ *0583/469738* 🌐 *www.lapecoraneralucca.it* 🕒 *Closed Mon.–Tues. No lunch Wed.–Fri.*

$ ✕**Port Ellen Clan.** This somewhat odd name refers to a town on the
TUSCAN   Scottish island of Islay, in the Hebrides, where the proprietor and his
family vacation. It calls itself a restaurant and a wine bar, and it also
is a whiskey bar serving up fine single malts and blends. The interesting and short menu offers a selection of primi and secondi, as well as
some tasty antipasti like the *panino di magro di lesso con salsa verde e
tazzina di consommé* (a boiled beef sandwich with a herby green sauce
served with a little cup of consommé). All secondi come with a side
dish, which is somewhat of a novelty on Italian menus. Eclectic desserts
such as the *pera cotta nel wine con gelato* (pears poached in red wine
served with ice cream) provide a lovely final note. The place is small,
intimate, and candle-lighted: perfect for a romantic meal. $ *Average
main: €12* ✉ *via, del Fosso 120* ☎ *0583/493 952* ⊕ *www.portellenclan.
com* ⌫ *Reservations essential* ⊙ *Closed Mon. Lunch Tues., Sat. and
Sun. Dinner Wed.–Sun.*

$ ✕**Trattoria da Leo.** A few short turns away from the facade of San
ITALIAN   Michele, this noisy, informal, traditional trattoria delivers *cucina alla
casalinga* (home cooking) in the best sense. Try the typical minestra di
farro to start or just go straight to *secondi piatti* (entrées); in addition
to the usual roast meats, there's excellent chicken with olives and a
good cold dish of boiled meats served with a sauce of parsley and pine
nuts. Save some room for a dessert, such as the rich, sweet, fig-and-
walnut torte or the lemon sorbet brilliantly dotted with bits of sage,
which tastes almost like mint, and is indescribably delicious. So, too, is
the chestnut ice cream. $ *Average main: €9* ✉ *Via Tegrimi 1, at corner
of Via degli Asili* ☎ *0583/492236* ▭ *No credit cards* ⊙ *No lunch Sun.
Closed Sun. Nov.–Mar.*

WHERE TO STAY

For expanded hotel reviews, visit Fodors.com.

$ ⊡ **Albergo San Martino.** The brocade bedspreads are fresh and crisp; the
HOTEL   proprietor friendly; the breakfast, served in a cheerful apricot room,
more than ample. **Pros:** comfortable beds; great breakfast (extra). **Cons:**
parking is difficult; surroundings are pleasant and stylish though not
luxurious. $ *Rooms from: €110* ✉ *Via della Dogana 9* ☎ *0583/469181*
⊕ *www.albergosanmartino.it* ⤳ *6 rooms, 2 suites* ⦿ *No meals.*

$$ ⊡ **Alla Corte degli Angeli.** This charming hotel with a friendly staff is right
B&B/INN   off the main shopping drag, Via Fillungo. **Pros:** many rooms are connect-
ing, making them good for families. **Cons:** some rooms have tubs but no
showers. $ *Rooms from: €140* ✉ *Via degli Angeli 23* ☎ *0583/469204*
⊕ *www.allacortedegliangeli.com* ⤳ *12 rooms* ⦿ *Breakfast.*

$$ ⊡ **Hotel Ilaria.** The former stables of the Villa Bottini have been trans-
HOTEL   formed into a modern hotel with stylish rooms done in a warm wood
veneer with blue-and-white fittings. **Pros:** a Fodor's reader sums it up
as a "nice, modern small hotel"; free bicycles. **Cons:** though in the city
center, it's a little removed from main attractions. $ *Rooms from: €138*
✉ *Via del Fosso 26* ☎ *0583/47615* ⊕ *www.hotelilaria.com* ⤳ *36 rooms,
5 suites* ⦿ *Breakfast.*

$$ **La Luna.** On a quiet, airy courtyard close to the Piazza del Mer-
B&B/INN cato, this hotel, run by the Barbieri family for more than four decades,
occupies two renovated wings of an old building. **Pros:** professional
staff; the annex has wheelchair-accessible rooms. **Cons:** some rooms
feel dated. $ *Rooms from: €140* ⊠ *Corte Compagni 12, at Via Fil-
lungo* ☎ *0583/493634* ⊕ *www.hotellaluna.com* ↷ *27 rooms, 2 suites*
⊙ *Closed Jan. 7–31* ⊖ *No meals.*

$$ **Locanda l'Elisa.** Surrounded by rosemary, lavender, and azaleas, this
B&B/INN hotel preserves the intimacy of a well-furnished home; it's decorated in
Empire style, with 19th-century furniture, prints, and fabrics. **Pros:** multilingual staff; top-notch restaurant. **Cons:** a car is essential. $ *Rooms
from: €150* ⊠ *Via Nuova per Pisa 1952, Massa Pisana* ☎ *0583/379737*
⊕ *www.locandalelisa.it* ↷ *3 rooms, 7 suites* ⊙ *Closed Jan. 7–Feb. 11*
⊖ *No meals.*

$$ **Palazzo Alexander.** The building, dating from the 12th century, has
HOTEL been restructured to create the ease common to Lucchesi nobility: tim-
bered ceilings, warm yellow walls, and brocaded chairs adorn the pub-
lic rooms, and guest rooms have high ceilings and that same glorious
damask. **Pros:** intimate feel; gracious staff; bacon and eggs included
in the buffet breakfast; a short walk from San Michele in Foro. **Cons:**
some Fodor's readers complain of too-thin walls. $ *Rooms from: €200*
⊠ *Via S. Giustina 48* ☎ *0583/583571* ⊕ *www.palazzoalexander.it* ↷ *9
rooms, 3 suites, 1 apartment* ⊖ *Breakfast.*

$ **Piccolo Hotel Puccini.** Steps away from the busy square and church
HOTEL of San Michele, this little hotel is quiet and calm—and a great deal.
Pros: cheery, English-speaking staff. **Cons:** breakfast costs extra; some
rooms are on the dark side. $ *Rooms from: €80* ⊠ *Via di Poggio 9*
☎ *0583/55421* ⊕ *www.hotelpuccini.com* ↷ *14 rooms* ⊖ *No meals.*

NIGHTLIFE AND THE ARTS

Estate Musicale Lucchese. Throughout the summer there are jazz, pop, and
rock concerts in conjunction with the Estate Musicale Lucchese music
festival. It happens in the large, beautiful Piazza Napoleone.

Lucca Comics and Games. During the first weekend of November, the
city's piazzas are filled with tents featuring exhibitions and games, and
the streets are invaded with comic-book fans and gamesters for Lucca
Comics and Games. During the last week of October, and continuing
through the Comics festival, a *mostra mercato* (market show) takes
place as well. ☎ *0583/48522* ⊕ *www.luccacomicsandgames.com.*

Lucca Tourist Office. Schedule and ticket information for many local
events, including the Opera Theater and Estate Musicale Lucchese fes-
tivals, is available at the Lucca Tourist Office. ⊠ *Piazza Santa Maria
35, San Michele* ☎ *0583/583150* ⊕ *www.luccaturismo.it.*

Opera Theater and Music Festival of Lucca. Sponsored by the Opera The-
ater of Lucca and the music college of the University of Cincinnati, the
Opera Theater and Music Festival of Lucca runs from mid-June to mid-
July; performances are staged in open-air venues. Call the Lucca tourist
office or the Opera Theater of Lucca (☎ *0583/46531*) for information.

Teatro del Giglio. From September through April you can see operas, plays, and concerts staged at the Teatro del Giglio. ⊠ *Piazza del Giglio, Duomo* ☎ *0583/46531* ⊕ *www.teatrodelgiglio.it.*

SPORTS AND THE OUTDOORS

A good way to spend the afternoon is to go biking around the large path atop the city's ramparts. There are two good spots right next to each other where you can rent bikes. The prices are about the same (about €12.50 for the day and €2.50 per hour for city bikes) and they are centrally located, just beside the town wall.

Berutto Nedo. The vendors at Berutto Nedo, which sell bikes near the Piazza dell'Anfiteatro, are friendly and speak English. ⊠ *Via dei Gaspari Alcide 83/r, Anfiteatro* ☎ *0583/517073* ⊕ *www.beruttonedo.com.*

Poli Antonio Biciclette. This is the best option for bicycle rental on the east side of town. ⊠ *Piazza Santa Maria 42, Lucca East* ☎ *0583/493787* ⊕ *www.biciclettepoli.com.*

SHOPPING

CLOTHING

Benetton Stock Outlet. Bargain hunters won't want to miss Benetton Stock Outlet, with its brightly colored garments at reduced prices. ⊠ *Via Mordini 17/19, Anfiteatro* ☎ *0583/464533.*

Mode Mignon. Come here for one-stop high-end designer shopping, including Prada, Miu-Miu, Gucci, Dolce e Gabbana, Jil Sander, and Tod's—among others. ⊠ *Piazza Bernardini 1-2-3* ☎ *0583/491217.*

My Walit. Brightly colored wallets, purses, and other lovely leather accessories are on offer here at affordable prices. ⊠ *Piazza Anfiteatro 40* ☎ *0583/491375* ⊕ *www.mywalit.com.*

FOOD

Lucca is known for its farro, an ancient barleylike grain that has found its way into regional specialties such as *zuppa* (or *minestra*) *di farro* (farro soup). It's available in food shops all over the city. Lucca is most famous for its olive oil, however, which is exported throughout the world. Look for extra-virgin oil whose label clearly indicates that it is entirely from Tuscany or, better yet, entirely from a local *fattoria,* or farm. *Olio nuovo* (new oil) is available for a few weeks in November, when the olive-picking season begins. This new oil is strong-flavored and peppery—great for drizzling on soup, pasta, and bread—and it's also nearly impossible to find in North America. Wine from small Lucca producers is also difficult to find abroad.

Antica Bottega di Prospero. Stop by this shop for top-quality local products, including farro, dried porcini mushrooms, olive oil, and wine. ⊠ *Via San Lucia 13.*

Caniparoli. Chocolate lovers will be pleased with the selection of artisanal chocolates. This artisanal shop is so serious about their sweets that they do not make them from June to August, because of the heat. ⊠ *Via San Paolino 96* ☎ *0583/53456* ⊕ *www.caniparolicioccolateria.it.*

Enoteca Vanni. A huge selection of wines, as well as an ancient cellar, makes this a place worth stopping at. For the cost of the wine only, tastings can be organized through the shopkeepers and are held in the cellar. ✉ *Piazza del Salvatore 7* ☎ *0583/491902* ⊕ *www.enotecavanni.com.*

Massei Ugo. This small shop offers great wine prices and assorted local delicacies. The store's owner, Ugo Massei, doesn't speak English, but he's friendly and helpful. ✉ *Via S. Andrea 19* ☎ *0583/467656.*

MARKETS

antiques market. On the third weekend of the month an antiques market happens in Piazza San Martino. Vendors unveil their wares around 8:30, and start packing up around dusk. There's something for everyone, including old-fashioned glassware, ancient coins, and furniture—some antique, some just old. Check out the 19th-century tools and collections of fascist memorabilia.

bookstalls. Looking for old prints? Old postcards? Old comic books? Just behind the church of San Giusto (off Via Beccheria, which runs for about two blocks between Piazza Napoleone and Piazza San Michele) are bookstalls that open their cupboard doors on clement days (including Sunday), from about 10 to 7. You may discover anything from hand-tinted prints of orchids to back issues of *Uomo Ragno* (Spiderman looks and acts just the same even when he's speaking Italian).

PASTRIES

Pasticceria Pinelli. For a broad selection of scrumptious pastries, visit this favorite haunt of Lucca's senior citizens, who frequently stop in after Sunday Mass. ✉ *Via Beccheria 28* ☎ *0583/496119.*

Pasticceria Taddeucci. A particularly delicious version of *buccellato*—the sweet, anise-flavor bread with raisins that is a Luccan specialty—is baked at Pasticceria Taddeucci. ✉ *Piazza San Michele 34* ☎ *0583/494933.*

THE GARFAGNANA

In the heart of the Alpi Apuane, the Garfagnana is one of the most visually stunning regions in Tuscany. Roads wind around precipitous, jagged peaks and through old stone villages. Cool mountain air tempers even the sultriest summer. Most of the major cities and towns are found along the Serchio, Italy's third-largest river, which runs north–south. The Val di Lima (Lima Valley), formed by the Lima River, has for centuries been known for its curative thermal waters and its lush chestnut groves.

As you plan your travels through the area, keep in mind that you'll encounter winding two-lane mountain roads—driving 16 km (10 miles) may take longer than you'd expect. Pass through in October, though, and you'll be rewarded with bursts of yellow and splashes of red as the leaves change color.

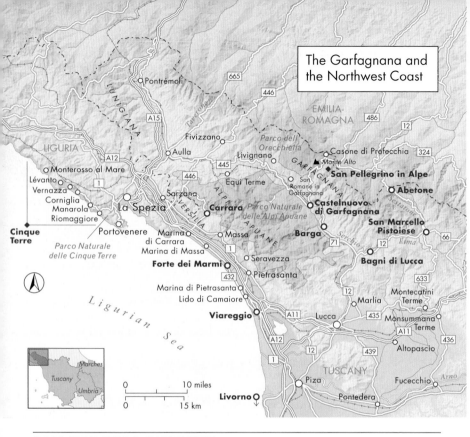

The Garfagnana and
the Northwest Coast

SAN MARCELLO PISTOIESE

*33 km (21 miles) northwest of Pistoia, 66 km (41 miles) northwest of
Florence.*

This small town—small, but still the largest in the area—bustles in
summer and winter (when it's one of Tuscany's few ski destinations),
but calms down in spring and fall. It's set amid spectacular scenery;
you can drive across a dramatic suspension bridge over the Lima River.

GETTING HERE

By car, you're likely to approach San Marcello Pistoiese from Pistoia;
take the SS435 to the SS66, which takes you right into town (follow
the signs). COPIT provides frequent bus service as well. There is no
train service.

VISITOR INFORMATION

San Marcello Pistoiese ✉ *Piazza del Duomo, Pistoia* ☎ *0573/21622*
🌐 *www.turismo.pistoia.it.*

EXPLORING

Pieve di San Marcello. This church dates from the 12th century, though
the interior was redone in the 18th century and most of the art inside
is from that period. ✉ *Piazza Arcangeli* 🎫 *Free* 🕐 *Daily 9–1 and 3–6.*

SPORTS AND THE OUTDOORS

Nonsolovolo. You can rent mountain bikes and equipment for paragliding from Nonsolovolo. ⊠ *Via XXIV Maggio 10, Lizzano Pistoiese* ☏ *0573/677700* ⊕ *www.nonsolovolo.com.*

ABETONE

20 km (12 miles) northwest of San Marcello Pistoiese, 53 km (33 miles) northwest of Pistoia, 86 km (53 miles) northwest of Florence.

Abetone is one of the most-visited vacation spots in the Apennine Mountains, where Tuscans, Emilia-Romagnans, and others come to ski. Set above two valleys, the resort town is on the edge of a lush and ancient forest of more than 9,000 acres. The numerous ski trails are mostly for beginners and intermediate skiers (the entire area has only two expert slopes). Summer is the time to trek or mountain bike in and around the beautiful hills and mountains.

GETTING HERE

By car from Pistoia, take the SS435/SR436 and follow signs for Abetone-Modena. You'll exit onto the SS66/SR66; continue for some 30 km (18 miles) to the SS12, which will take you into Abetone. COPIT buses run to Abetone, but there is no train service.

VISITOR INFORMATION

San Marcello Pistoiese tourism office ⊠ *Piazza del Duomo, Pistoia* ☏ *0573/630145* ⊕ *www.turismo.provincia.pistoia.it.*

WHERE TO EAT AND STAY

For expanded hotel reviews, visit Fodors.com.

$

ITALIAN

✕ **Ciuste.** If you're hankering for a finely crafted sandwich (they have 18 different varieties on the menu), or something more substantial like the *crostone ai funghi* (a very large portion of toasted bread topped with local, fragrant porcini mushrooms), this is the place to be. The friendly, youthful staff is only too happy to bring artisanal beers from nearby La Petrognola, or serve a glass of wine to pair nicely with their *carpaccio di manzo di affumicato in salsa d'arancia* (thinly sliced smoked beef with an orange sauce). Tiny local blueberries, in season, appear in numerous guises on the dessert menu. At aprés-ski time, the place positively hums as the pizza oven is fired up, and happy skiers seat themselves on furniture that looks as if an Alpine Fred Flinstone designed it. $ *Average main: €13* ⊠ *via, dell'Uccellaria 22, Abetone* ☏ *0573/60504* ⊕ *www. weloveabetone.it.*

$$

ITALIAN

✕ **La Capannina.** Duccio Ugolini is in the kitchen, and his wife Miriam Manni runs this large, one-room trattoria, which has a grand view of beautiful woods and ski slopes. In the middle of the room is a fireplace, which casts a lovely glow in cooler months. Local ingredients like mushrooms and chestnuts take center stage here. The chef has a deft touch with mushrooms; his *insalatina di porcini e grana* (salad of raw, shaved porcini and cheese) is delicate; his *flan di finferli e crema di tartufo* (an eggy dish with fine, thin mushrooms), sublime. Sommeliers abound in the couple's extended family, and it shows in the exquisite

wine list. $ *Average main: €16*
✉ *Via Brennero 256* ☎ *0573/60562*
⊘ *Closed Mon. and 2 wks in May and Oct.*

$ ⚐ **Hotel Bellavista.** Originally a 19th-
HOTEL   century villa belonging to Marchesa Guendalina Strozzi—her ancestors were powerful bankers in Renaissance Florence—this is now a contemporary inn. **Pros:** you can ski from hotel to chairlift. **Cons:** attracts a younger; sometimes rowdy crowd. $ *Rooms from: €90* ✉ *Via Brennero 383* ☎ *0573/60028* ⊕ *www.bellavista-abetone.it* ⇨ *40 rooms, 2 suites* ⊘ *Closed May, Oct., and Nov.* ☉ *Breakfast.*

SKIING

Consorzio Impianti. This group manages the ski facilities in Abetone and has information on the Multipass, as well as maps, directions, and area information. ✉ *Via Brennero 429* ☎ *0573/60557* ⊕ *www. multipassabetone.it.*

Pistoiese ski area. The area has 37 ski slopes, amounting to about 50 km (31 miles) of ski surface, all accessible through the purchase of a single Multipass. You can check the Abetone section of the Pistoiese ski area website for details on the Multipass. ⊕ *www.lamontagnapistoiese.it.*

EN
ROUTE   **San Pellegrino in Alpe.** Stop at the San Pellegrino in Alpe monastery en route from Abetone to Castelnuovo di Garfagnana to see the staggering view and the large wooden cross. Story has it that a 9th-century Scot, Pellegrino ("Little Pilgrim") by name, came to this spot to repent. ✉ *Via del Voltone 14, Off SR12, 16 km (10 miles) northeast of Castelnuovo di Garfagnana, 28 km (17 miles) northwest of Abetone, San Pellegrino in Alpe* ☎ *0583/649072* 🎫 *Free* ⊘ *Tues.–Sat. 9:30–12:30, Sun. 9:30–12:30 and 2–5.*

BAGNI DI LUCCA

36 km (22 miles) southwest of Abetone, 27 km (17 miles) north of Lucca, 101 km (63 miles) northwest of Florence.

Pretty Bagni di Lucca was a fashionable spa town in the early 19th century—in part because of its thermal waters. The Romantic poet Percy Bysshe Shelley (1792–1822) installed his family here during the summer of 1818. He wrote to a friend in July of that year that the waters here were exceedingly refreshing: "My custom is to undress and sit on the rocks, reading Herodotus, until perspiration has subsided, and then to leap from the edge of the rock into this fountain." In 1853, Robert and Elizabeth Browning spent the summer in a house on the main square. Its heyday behind it, the town is now a quiet, charming place where elegant thermal spas still soothe on temperate summer days.

GETTING HERE

By car from Florence, take the A11 and exit at Capannori. Take the SS439 in the direction of Lucca. From Lucca, take the SS12/Via del Brennero. This leads to the SP18, which takes you directly into Bagni di Lucca. Lazzi bus lines also operate from Lucca and Florence. Trains run nearly every hour from Lucca and take about 25 minutes.

VISITOR INFORMATION

Bagni di Lucca tourism office ✉ *Via Umberto I 139* ☎ *0583/805754* 🌐 *www.prolocobagnidilucca.it.*

OFF THE BEATEN PATH

Centro Termale Bagni di Lucca. Here you'll find two natural steam-room caves, as well as spa services such as mud baths, massage, hydrotherapy, and facials. ✉ *Piazza San Martino 11* ☎ *0583/87221* 🌐 *www.termebagnidilucca.it* 🎟 *€12 for thermal pool weekdays, €15 weekends; spa services vary* 🕒 *Daily 9–6.*

Il Ponte della Maddalena (*The Magdalen's Bridge*). Il Ponte della Maddalena is, oddly, also known as the Devil's Bridge. Commissioned in all likelihood by Matilde di Canossa (1046–1115), it was restructured by the petty despot Castruccio Castracani in the early 14th century. It's worth the climb to the middle—the bridge is narrow, steep, and pedestrians-only—to check out the view. Despite 1836 flood damage and early-20th-century alterations, it seems little changed from the Middle Ages. If you're heading north along the Serchio from Lucca to Bagni di Lucca, you will see the bridge on your left.

WHERE TO EAT

$ TUSCAN 🍴 **Osteria i Macelli.** Honest Tuscan cooking prevails at this simple trattoria next to a large parking lot. No matter that there's no view: the terrific food and pleasing service—all of it served in a typical Tuscan dining room with high timbered ceilings—make a stop here well worth the detour. Locals swear by the *affettati misti* (sliced cured meats), which include the stellar *biroldo* (cured pork from nearby Garfagnana). The ravioli *di castagne* (stuffed with chestnut puree, sauced with radicchio and pancetta bits) should not be missed. [$] *Average main: €12* ✉ *Piazza i Macelli, Borgo a Mozzano21 km (13 miles) north of Lucca on the SS12* ☎ *0583/88700* 🕒 *Closed Jan. 1–15 and Sept. 1–15.*

BARGA

17 km (11 miles) northwest of Bagni di Lucca, 111 km (69 miles) northwest of Florence.

Barga is a lovely little city (one of Italy's smallest under that classification) with a finely preserved medieval core. It produced textiles—mostly silk—during the Renaissance and wool in the 18th century. You won't find textiles here today; now the emphasis is on tourism. Here the African-American troops known as the Buffalo Soldiers are remembered by the locals for their bravery in defending this mountainous area during World War II.

Walking around Barga is not for the faint of heart: it's one steep uphill after another to get to the tiny centro storico, and more steps to get to Piazza del Duomo.

DID YOU KNOW?

The mountains of the Garfagnana provide some of Tuscany's best hiking opportunities, particularly in the Parco Naturale delle Alpi Apuane.

GETTING HERE

By car from Lucca, take the SS12/Via del Brennero directly to Barga. Though there is train service to Barga, the station is far away from the centro storico. The only bus option is the small CLAP line (✉ *Via Roma 7* ☎ *0583/723050*), which runs between here and Castelnuovo di Garfagnana.

WORD OF MOUTH

"Barga is a lovely hill town, with a beautiful Romanesque style Duomo on the top of the hill, the view of . . . the surrounding mountains is breathtaking." —JudyC

3

VISITOR INFORMATION

Barga tourism office ✉ *Via di Mezzo 45* ☎ *0583/72471* 🌐 *www.comune.barga.lu.it.*

EXPLORING

Duomo. Dedicated to Saint Christopher, the Duomo is a Romanesque cathedral, made from elegant limestone (quarried from nearby caves), which saw four separate building campaigns. The first began in the 9th century, and it was only finished in the 15th. Inside, the intricately carved pulpit, one of the finest examples of mid-12th-century Tuscan sculpture, commands center stage. The view from the Duomo is incredible: Tuscan mountains have never looked so good. ✉ *Via del Duomo* 🕓 *Daily 9–7.*

OFF THE BEATEN PATH

Grotta del Vento. About 14 km (9 miles) southwest of Barga, after following a winding road flanked by both sheer cliffs and fantastic views, you come to Tuscany's Cave of the Wind. As the result of a steady internal temperature of 10.7°C (about 51°F), the wind is sucked into the cave in the winter and blown out in the summer. It has a long cavern with stalactites, stalagmites, "bottomless" pits, and subterranean streams. One-, two-, and three-hour guided tours of the cave are given. (The one-hour tour is offered only from November through March.) ✉ *SP 39, west at Galliciano, Vergemoli* ☎ *0583/722024* 🌐 *www.grottadelvento.com* 🎟 *€9 for 1 hr, €14 for 2 hrs, €20 for 3 hrs* 🕓 *Daily 10–6.*

WHERE TO STAY

For expanded hotel reviews, visit Fodors.com.

$$ B&B/INN 🏨 **Casa Fontana.** Ron and Susi Gaud have transformed an 18th-century town house into a cozy little B&B nestled in the heart of Barga. [$] *Rooms from: €140* ✉ *via, di Mezzo 77, Barga* ☎ *0039/3496842721* 🌐 *www.casa-fontana.com* 🛏 *6 rooms* 🕓 *Closed Nov.–mid-Mar.*

NIGHTLIFE AND THE ARTS

Barga Jazz. Listen to the newest music during Barga Jazz, a jazz orchestra competition (in July and August). The scores presented each year are selected by a special committee, and a winner is selected by an international jury. ✉ *Teatro dell'Accademia dei Differenti, Piazza Angelio 4* 🌐 *www.bargajazz.it.*

Opera Barga. From mid-July to mid-August, the stony streets of Barga come alive as opera fans come to Opera Barga. This highly regarded opera festival takes place at the **Teatro dell'Accademia dei Differenti** (Theater of the Academy of the Different). The Opera Barga began in 1967 as a workshop for young singers and musicians. Now it stages lesser-known baroque operas, as well as contemporary works. Check their website for current information. ✉ *Teatro dell'Accademia dei Differenti, Piazza Angelio 4* ⊕ *www.operabarga.it.*

CASTELNUOVO DI GARFAGNANA

13 km (8 miles) northwest of Barga, 47 km (27 miles) north of Lucca, 121 km (75 miles) northwest of Florence.

Castelnuovo di Garfagnana might be the best base for exploring the Garfagnana, because it's central with respect to the other towns. During the Renaissance the town's fortunes were frequently tied to those of the powerful Este family of Ferrara. It's now a bustling town with a lovely historic center.

GETTING HERE

By car from Lucca, take the SS12/Via del Brennero, follow signs to Borgo a Mozzano; then take the SS445, which leads directly into town.

CLAP buses. Buses run between Castelnuovo di Garfagnana and Barga. You can purchase tickets at Paolini, the tobacconist's shop in Piazza della Repubblica. ✉ *Piazza della Repubblica.*

There is no train service.

VISITOR INFORMATION

Castelnuovo di Garfagnana tourism office ✉ *Piazza della Erbe* ☎ *0583/641007* ⊕ *www.castelnuovogarfagnana.org.*

EXPLORING

Duomo. Dedicated to Saint Peter, the Duomo was begun in the 11th century and was reconstructed in the early 1500s. Inside is a crucifix dating from the 14th to 15th century. There's also an early-16th-century terra-cotta attributed to the school of the della Robbia. ✉ *Piazza del Duomo* ☎ *0583/62170* ⊙ *Daily 9–7.*

La Rocca (*The Fortress*). Dating from the 13th century, *La Rocca* (The Fortress) has a plaque commemorating writer Ludovico Ariosto's brief tenure here as commissar general for the Este. Ariosto (1474–1533) wrote the epic poem *Orlando Furioso* (1516), among other works. You can only see the impressive walls and great entryway of the fort from the outside—at press time, entry into La Rocca was not allowed. ✉ *Piazza Umberto.*

Parco Naturale delle Alpi Apuane. Preserved ancient forests and barren rocky peaks create dramatic scenery in the Parco Naturale delle Alpi Apuane (Natural Park of the Apuane Alps), a national park that encompasses several towns. Its highest peak, Monte Pisanino, rises more than 6,000 feet, and towers over an artificial lake, Lago di Vagli, which covers the submerged village of Fabbricca. The tiny stone villages of Vagli di Sotto and Vagli di Sopra sit alongside the lake. Plan on a half or full day of hiking in the park. Remember to wear comfortable sports shoes or hiking boots and bring plenty of drinking water. A two-lane winding road through the park (SP13) connects Castelnuovo di Garfagnana to the sea. To get to Vagli di Sotto and Vagli di Sopra, go north of Castelnuovo di Garfagnana on SR445 to Poggio and then turn west on SP50. ☎ *0583/644478* ⊕ *www.parcapuane.it* ✂ *Free.*

3

WHERE TO EAT

$$ ✕ **Osteria Vecchio Mulino.** "The old mill" has an antique marble serv-
TUSCAN
Fodor'sChoice
★
ing counter filled with free nibbles and two large wooden tables in a room lined with wine bottles. The enthusiastic host, Andrea Bertucci, proudly touts local products on his simple menu, which usually consists of superior cheese and *affettati misti* (mixed sliced cured meats). Traditional local dishes with farro grain, polenta, pecorino cheese, and salami round out the selections. Finish your meal with their famous *caffè al vetro con miele di castagno* (coffee in a glass with chestnut honey). This osteria is open from 7:30 am to 8 pm in the warmer months, and from 11 to 8 in winter. $ *Average main: €20* ⊠ *Via Vittorio Emanuele 12* 📞 *0583/62192* ⊕ *www.vecchiomulino.info* ☽ *Closed Mon. and 3 wks in Oct. or Jan.*

SPORTS AND THE OUTDOORS

HIKING AND
CLIMBING
Centro Accoglienza Parco. Stop here for help with hiking information, particularly for the Parco Naturale delle Alpi Apuane. ⊠ *Piazza Erbe 1* 📞 *0583/644242* ✉ *garfagnana@tin.it.*

Club Alpino Italiano (*Italian Alpine Club*). For detailed maps and information about trekking in the mountains surrounding Castelnuovo di Garfagnana, contact the Club Alpino Italiano. ⊠ *Via Vittorio Emanuele* ⊕ *www.cai.it.*

THE NORTHWEST COAST

Livorno has been a port town since the 16th century, and continues to host countless cruise and cargo ships from around the world. It has a gritty, lively feel. Heading up the coast you'll pass lots of beaches (both sandy and rocky, but none all that inviting) until you hit the popular destinations of Viareggio and swank, expensive Forte dei Marmi. The air gets clearer if you head up the hills toward Carrara, a lively, beautiful, rarely visited town.

On the Ligurian coast west of Tuscany are the five seaside villages that make up the Cinque Terre. They're a hugely popular side trip for visitors to northwest Tuscany.

LIVORNO

24 km (15 miles) south of Pisa, 187 km (116 miles) west of Florence.

Livorno is a gritty city with a long and interesting history. In the early Middle Ages it alternately belonged to Pisa and Genoa. In 1421 Florence, seeking access to the sea, bought it. Cosimo I (1519–74) started construction of the harbor in 1571, putting Livorno on the map. After Ferdinando I de' Medici (1549–1609) proclaimed Livorno a free city, it became a haven for people suffering from religious persecution; Roman Catholics from England and Jews and Moors from Spain and Portugal, among others, settled here. The *Quattro Mori* (Four Moors), also known as the Monument to Ferdinando I, commemorates this. (The statue of Ferdinando I dates from 1595, the bronze Moors by Pietro Tacca from the 1620s.)

In the following centuries, and particularly in the 18th, Livorno boomed as a port. In the 19th century the town drew a host of famous Britons passing through on their grand tours. Its prominence continued up to World War II, when it was heavily bombed. Much of the town's architecture, therefore, postdates the war, and it's somewhat difficult to imagine what it might have looked like before. Livorno has recovered from the war, however, as it's become a huge point of departure for container ships, as well as the only spot in Tuscany for cruise ships to dock for the day.

Most of Livorno's artistic treasures date from the 17th century and aren't all that interesting unless you dote on obscure baroque artists. Livorno's most famous native artist, Amedeo Modigliani (1884–1920), was of much more recent vintage. Sadly, there's no notable work by him in his hometown.

There may not be much in the way of art, but it's still worth strolling around the city. The **Mercato Nuovo,** which has been around since 1894, sells all sorts of fruits, vegetables, grains, meat, and fish. Outdoor markets nearby are also chock-full of local color. The presence of Camp Darby, an American military base just outside town, accounts for the availability of many American products.

If you have time, Livorno is worth a stop for lunch or dinner at the very least.

GETTING HERE

Livorno is easily reached by rail; trains from Florence run hourly. By car it's about an hour west of Florence on the Fi-Pi-Li.

VISITOR INFORMATION

Livorno tourism office ✉ *via Pieroni 18/20* ☎ *0586/894236* 🌐 *www.costadeglietruschi.it.*

WHERE TO EAT

$ ITALIAN 🍴 **Cantina Nardi.** It's only open for lunch, and it's well off the beaten path (even if it is in the center of Livorno's shopping district). But getting here is worth the trouble: this tiny place, lined with bottles of wine, has a small menu that changes daily, a superb wine list, and gregarious staff. Their *baccalà alla livornese* (deep-fried salt cod served with chickpeas) is succulently crisp; soups, such as ribollita, are very soothing. [$] *Average main: €10* ✉ *Via Cambini 6/8* ☎ *0586/808006* 🕒 *Closed Sun. No dinner.*

$$ TUSCAN 🍴 **L'Ostricaio.** Locals crowd into this tiny place with a lovely view at lunch and dinner to feast on treats from the sea. The place is lively and full of folks enjoying the terrific food on offer here. Antipasti such as raw oysters, *code di manzancolle* (deep fried shrimp), or the *antipasti misti* (a marvelous assemblage with fried baccalà and a lima beans and shrimp salad, among other things) provide the perfect kick-off to what follows. It's hard to decide between the succulent mixed fry, the perfectly mixed grill (including scampi, shrimp, and squid), or any of the pasta dishes. Finish your meal with *sgroppino* (lemon sorbet pureed with vodka) to help cleanse the palate. [$] *Average main: €15* ✉ *viale, Italia 100, Livorno* ☎ *0586/581 345* ✍ *Reservations essential.*

$$$ SEAFOOD 🍴 **Osteria del Mare.** Husband and wife Claudio and Marila run this fish restaurant across the (busy) street from the docks. The decor's nothing to write home about (paneled walls with framed prints and navigational coats of arms), but it doesn't much matter once you get into the essentials of tucking into the food. Order the fish of the day, and the waiter will bring the fish to the table for approval; then order it cooked *all'isolana* (baked whole with tomatoes and potatoes). Marila has created a one-of-a-kind dessert, a cross between a cheesecake and a semifreddo. It's heavenly, especially when sauced with either a chocolate, caramel, or strawberry concoction. Polite service and an affable wine list make eating here a pleasure. [$] *Average main: €27* ✉ *Borgo Cappuccini 5* ☎ *0586/881027.*

WORD OF MOUTH

"The beaches in northern Tuscany are sandy, i.e., Marina di Massa, Forte de Marmi, Lido di Camaiore, Viareggio, Marina di Pisa, Tirrenia, Castiglioncello (a really nice undiscovered beach town), Rosignano Solway, Vada, and Marina di Cecina. They really are sandy beaches rather than the rocky beaches in other parts of Italy." —Dona

VIAREGGIO

8 km (5 miles) south of Pietrasanta, 25 km (15 miles) northwest of Lucca, 97 km (60 miles) northwest of Florence.

Tobias Smollett (1721–71), the English novelist, wrote in the 1760s that Viareggio was "a kind of sea-port on the Mediterranean. . . . The roads are indifferent and the accommodation is execrable." Much has changed here since Smollett's time. For one, this beach town becomes very crowded in summer, so accommodations are plentiful. It can also be loud and brassy at the height of the season, though there's peace and quiet in the autumn and early spring.

Viareggio has numerous buildings decorated in the 1920s Liberty style, characterized by colorful wood and some with ornate exterior decoration. Locals and tourists alike stroll along the town's wide seaside promenade lined with bars, cafés, and some very fine restaurants. If you can't make it to Venice for *Carnevale* (Carnival), come here, where the festivities are in some ways more fun than in Venice. The city is packed with revelers from all over Tuscany, taking part in the riot of colorful parades with giant floats. Book lodging far in advance, and be aware that hotels charge top prices during Carnevale.

GETTING HERE

Trains run frequently from Florence on the Lucca line. By car from Lucca, take the A11 and follow the signs for Viareggio. Exit at Massarosa and take the SS439 to the SP5, which goes into the center of town.

VISITOR INFORMATION

Viareggio tourism office ✉ *Viale Carducci 10* ☎ *0584/962233* 🌐 *www.turismo.intoscana.it or www.aptversilia.it.*

3

WHERE TO EAT AND STAY

For expanded hotel reviews, visit Fodors.com.

$$$ TUSCAN Fodor's Choice ★ **Pino Ristorante.** Locals swear by this unpretentious trattoria a couple of blocks away from the beach. The Artizzu family has been serving specialties from the sea since 1979 in their small eatery with yellow-sponged walls. The menu notes that the availability of various dishes changes due to conditions at sea: you get the idea that what you're eating just came off the boat (and you are). The house specialty is the pricey but divine *aragosta alla catalana con verdure* (Mediterranean lobster with steamed and raw vegetables). The *spiedino di sogliola* (sole kebab) arrives with silken mashed potatoes topped with *bottarga* (a smoked tuna product); the unoily, crunchy *fritto misto* (mixed fish fry) is a joy. If you can't decide, order the tasting menu, which gives you a little bit of a lot of the menu. Patrizia makes all the desserts; remember to leave room for them. *Average main: €35 Via Matteotti 18 0584/961356 Closed Wed.*

$$$$ SEAFOOD **Romano.** The Franceschini family has been running this swank seafood eatery since the 1970s. Ebullient host Romano Franceschini is justifiably proud of the food produced by his wife and daughter, Franca and Cristina; son Roberto, an accomplished sommelier, presides over the floor. Don't miss the *fantasia di pesce crudo* (fantasy of raw fish), which arrives at the table with an aroma redolent of the sea, and follow up with any of the marvelous fish seconds. Or you can leave everything in the Franceschinis' hands and order the tasting menu (€95 without wine). *Average main: €70 Via Mazzini 122 0584/31382 Reservations essential Closed Mon. and Jan. No lunch Tues. in July and Aug.*

$$$ HOTEL **Hotel Plaza e de Russie.** Opened in 1871, this was Viareggio's first hotel, playing host to those on the Grand Tour. **Pros:** proximity to beach; excellent restaurant. **Cons:** some rooms facing street can get street noise. *Rooms from: €234 Piazza d'Azeglio 1 0584/31714 www.plazaederussie.com 50 rooms, 3 suites Breakfast.*

NIGHTLIFE AND THE ARTS

Carnevale. For four Sundays and Shrove Tuesday preceding Lent, this little seaside town produces its world-famous Carnevale, with intricate floats, or *carri,* representing Italy's most influential celebrities and politicians and sometimes the famous and infamous from around the world. Started in the late 1800s, the Viareggio Carnevale differs from the carnival held in Venice because of its parades of huge and fantastical floats. Traditionally, they were put together by Viareggio's shipbuilders, and in the beginning the masked celebrants were civil and political protesters, and the floats were, and often still are, used as a vehicle to lampoon popular figures of the day. Other events—music, parties, and art displays—also take place during Carnevale. The crowds are huge, with many attending in costume. *0584/962568 www.viareggio.ilcarnevale.com.*

SPORTS AND THE OUTDOORS

Club Nautico Versilia. Sailors who wish to tour the coastal waters should contact Club Nautico Versilia for assistance with maps, port and docking information, charter and craft-rental resources, and information about craft repair and refueling. ✉ *Piazza Artiglio* ⊕ *www.cnv-viareggio.it.*

FORTE DEI MARMI

3

8 km (5 miles) south of Massa, 37 km (27 miles) northwest of Lucca, 106 km (66 miles) northwest of Florence.

Forte dei Marmi is a playground for wealthy Italians and equally well-heeled visitors. Its wide, sandy beaches—strands are 6 km (4 miles) long—have the Alpi Apuane as a dramatic backdrop. The town was, from Roman times, the port for marble quarried in Carrara. In the 1920s the Agnelli family (of Fiat fame) began summering here, and other tycoons followed suit. It remains the East Hampton of Italy; everyone seems to be dripping in gold, and prices are very, very high. In winter the town's population is about 7,000; in summer, it swells to about 150,000, most of those folks staying in their own private villas.

GETTING HERE

By car from Florence, take the A11, following signs for Viareggio. From there, take the A12/E80 following signs for Genova. Exit at Versilia, and take the SP70 directly into town. Arriving by train isn't a good option; the station is far from the center of town, and the taxi ride in is expensive.

VISITOR INFORMATION

Forte dei Marmi tourism office ✉ *Piazza Garibaldi 1* ☎ *0584/280292.*

WHERE TO EAT AND STAY

For expanded hotel reviews, visit Fodors.com.

$$$$
SEAFOOD

✕ **Lorenzo.** The affable Lorenzo Viani has presided here for more than 30 years, and his restaurant still draws a well-heeled, sophisticated crowd. Start with the chilled raw oysters before moving on to seafood pasta, sea bass with chopped tomatoes, or a fish tartare. Or request the *menu degustazione* (tasting menu) and let chef Gioacchino Pontrelli prepare the freshest items of the day. You can also choose vegetarian and *terra* (meat) tasting menus. $ *Average main: €70* ✉ *Via Carducci 61* ☎ *0584/874030* ⌂ *Reservations essential* ⊗ *Closed mid-Dec.–Jan. and Mon. No lunch July and Aug.*

$$$$
HOTEL
Fodor's Choice
★

🏨 **Byron.** The pale yellow exterior only hints at the elegance inside the hotel created by joining two Liberty villas from 1899 and 1902. **Pros:** cutting-edge chef Andrea Mattei at the hotel restaurant; golf and tennis privileges; sunny staff. **Cons:** one-week minimum stay. $ *Rooms from: €525* ✉ *Viale Morin 46* ☎ *0584/787052* ⊕ *www.hotelbyron.net* ⌂ *29 rooms, 3 suites* ⊗ *Closed Oct.–Easter* ❙⊙❙ *Multiple meal plans.*

$$$$
HOTEL

🏨 **Hotel Ritz.** The Biagi family lovingly restored this 1920s beaux arts villa, and opened it to the public in 1980. **Pros:** multilingual staff; award-winning barman Lorenzo mixing drinks in the hotel bar; the Beemousine (a free pick-up and drop-off service for points in town),

Outrageous is the rule at Viareggio's Carnevale festivities.

the hotel's very own Mercedes to take you or pick you up at at the airport. **Cons:** beach costs extra (you have to join a beach club); sea-view rooms can pick up some street noise. $\boxed{\$}$ *Rooms from: €399* $\boxtimes$ *Via Flavio Gioia 2* ☎ *0584/787531* ⊕ *www.ritzfortedeimarmi.com* ↰ *32 rooms* ⏐⊙⏐ *Multiple meal plans.*

NIGHTLIFE AND THE ARTS

Almarosa Art Music and Bar. After a day at the beach, the place to see and be seen is Almarosa Art Music and Bar. The clientele during high season frequently includes Italian soccer players and young, good-looking celebrities and politicians. $\boxtimes$ *Viale Morin 89/a* ☎ *0584/82503* ⊕ *www. almarosa.it.*

SPORTS AND THE OUTDOORS

BIKING **Claudio Maggi Cicli.** This shop has been selling bicycle equipment and renting bikes since 1906. From May through September it's open daily 8 to 1 and 3 to 8; from October through April it's closed Wednesday and Sunday. $\boxtimes$ *Viale Morin 85* ☎ *0584/89529* ⊕ *www.ciclimaggi.it.*

Coppa Bikes. Right on the beach, Coppa rents bicycles and keeps late hours: 8 am to midnight daily from May through August, 8 to 8 daily the rest of the year. $\boxtimes$ *Via A. Franceschi 4/d* ☎ *0584/83528.*

HIKING AND CLIMBING **Forte dei Marmi Club Alpino Italiano.** This group can provide guided tours, as well as information on area hiking, spelunking, and rock climbing. $\boxtimes$ *Via Buonarroti 47* ☎ *No phone* ⊕ *www.caifortedeimarmi.it.*

SCUBA DIVING **Associazione Subacquei Versilia.** For information about the best places to scuba dive on the Versilian and Ligurian coasts, contact the Associazione Subacquei Versilia. ✉ *Via S. Allende 38* ☏ *0584/82070* ⊕ *www. subversilia.it.*

CARRARA

45 km (28 miles) southeast of Riomaggiore, 126 km (79 miles) northwest of Florence.

Carrara, from which the famous white marble takes its name, lies in a beautiful valley midway up a spectacular mountain in the Apuane Alps. The surrounding peaks are free of foliage and white as snow, even in summer, because they are full of marble stone. Marble has been quarried in the area for the past 2,000 years. The art historian Giorgio Vasari (1511–74) recorded that Michelangelo came to Carrara with two apprentices to quarry the marble for the never-completed tomb of Julius II (1443–1513). According to Vasari, Michelangelo spent eight months among the rocks conceiving fantastical ideas for future works.

GETTING HERE
By car, take the A11, following signs for Lucca, then at Viareggio take the A12. Trains run frequently from Florence, but a change of trains is almost always required, and the Carrara station is not centrally located. Coming from Lucca, you usually have to change trains at Viareggio.

VISITOR INFORMATION
Carrara tourism office ✉ *Lungomare A. Vespucci 24, Marina di Massa* ☏ *0585/240063* ⊕ *www.aptmassacarrara.it.*

EXPLORING
Accademia di Belle Arti. During the 19th and 20th centuries Carrara became a hotbed for anarchism, and during World War II it put up fierce resistance to the Nazis. The town is still lively thanks to its art institute. The Accademia di Belle Arti, founded by Maria Teresa Cybo Malaspina d'Este in 1769, draws studio art students from all over Italy. This may explain why there are many good bars and cafés in many of the town's squares.

Duomo. Work began on the Duomo in the 11th century and continued into the 14th. The cathedral, dedicated to Saint Andrew, is the first church of the Middle Ages constructed entirely of marble. Most of it comes from the area (the white, light blue-gray, black, and red). The tremendous facade is a fascinating blend of Pisan Romanesque and Gothic influences. Note the human figures and animals on Corinthian capitals. ✉ *Piazza del Duomo* ⊙ *Daily 9–7.*

Marble quarries. The area around Carrara has a lot of still-active quarries—well over 100 at last count. Most of them are not open to the public for safety reasons. However, it is possible to tour specific marble caves. The Carrara tourism office, 7 km (4½ miles) away in Marina di Massa, has details about which areas you can visit. ✉ *Carrara tourism office:, Lungomare A. Vespucci 24, Marina di Massa* ☏ *0585/240063.*

Museo Civico del Marmo (*Marble Museum*). Carrara's history as a marble-producing center is well documented in the Museo del Marmo, beginning with early works from the 2nd century. Exhibits detail the working of marble, from quarrying and transporting it to sculpting

it. ⊠ *Viale XX Settembre 85* ☎ *0585/845746* ⊕ *www.carraramarble.
it* 🗖 *€4.50* ◷ *Oct.–Apr., Mon.–Sat. 9–12:30 and 2:30–5; May–Sept.
9:30–1 and 3:30–6.*

San Francesco. The lovely baroque church of San Francesco is a study in
understated elegance. It dates from the 1620s to 1660s, and even though
it was built during the peak years of the baroque, the only excess can be
found in the twisting marble columns embellishing the altars. ⊠ *Piazza
XXVII Aprile* ◷ *Daily 9–7.*

WHERE TO EAT AND STAY
For expanded hotel reviews, visit Fodors.com.

$ ✗ **Ristorante Venanzio.** *Lardo di colonnata*, treated pork fat, is a gastro-
TUSCAN nomic specialty in Italy, and there's no place better to try it than the
place from which it hails. From the center of Carrara, the restaurant is
a 15-minute drive up winding roads cut through marble-filled mountains. Chef Alessio Lucchetti works wonders in the kitchen; if you're
undecided on where to start, the €40 tasting menu with four courses is
a great deal. The succulent primi are also impressive, such as the house
specialty ravioli *di carne ed erbette di montagne* (mixed meat and lardo
ravioli with a simple tomato ragù). Most of the secondi feature the
local product; the *coniglio farcito con mandorle e verdure* (stuffed rabbit with almonds and Savoy cabbage) is a heavenly marriage between
rabbit and pork. Do save room for dessert: they do terrific semifreddi
here. 💲 *Average main: €14* ⊠ *Piazza Palestro 3, Colonnata Carrara, 1
mile from Carrara* ☎ *0585/758033* ◷ *Closed Thurs. No dinner Sun.*

CINQUE TERRE

EXPLORING
Manarola. Enchanting pastel houses spill down a steep hill overlooking a spectacular turquoise swimming cove and a bustling harbor. The
whole town is built on black rock. Above the town, ancient terraces
still protect abundant vineyards and olive trees. This village is the center
of the wine and olive-oil production of the region, and its streets are
lined with shops selling local products. ⊕ *www.aptcinqueterre.sp.it* and
www.parconazionale5terre.it.

Riomaggiore. This village at the eastern end of the Cinque Terre is built
into a river gorge (thus the name, which means "river major"). It has
a tiny harbor protected by large slabs of alabaster and marble, which
serve as tanning beds for sunbathers, as well as being the site of several outdoor cafés with fine views. According to legend, the settlement of Riomaggiore dates as far back as the 8th century, when Greek
religious refugees came here to escape persecution by the Byzantine
emperor. ⊠ *Stazione Ferroviaria, Riomaggiore* ☎ *0187/762287* ⊕ *www.
aptcinqueterre.sp.it* and *www.parconazionale5terre.it.*

Vernazza. With narrow streets and small squares, the village that many
consider to be the most charming of the five towns has the best access
to the sea—a geographic reality that made the village wealthier than its
neighbors, as evidenced by the elaborate arcades, loggias, and marble-
work. The village's pink, slate-roof houses and colorful squares contrast

Continued on page 185

HIKING THE CINQUE TERRE

FIVE REMOTE VILLAGES MAKE ONE MUST-SEE DESTINATION

"Charming" and "breathtaking" are adjectives that get a workout when you're traveling in Italy, but it's rare that both apply to a single location. The Cinque Terre is such a place, and this combination of characteristics goes a long way toward explaining its tremendous appeal.

The area is made up of five tiny villages (Cinque Terre literally means "Five Lands") clinging to the cliffs along a gorgeous stretch of the Ligurian coast. The terrain is so steep that for centuries footpaths were the only way to get from place to place. It just so happens that these paths provide beautiful views of the rocky coast tumbling into the sea, as well as access to secluded beaches and grottoes.

Backpackers "discovered" the Cinque Terre in the 1970s, and its popularity has been growing ever since. Despite summer crowds, much of the original appeal is intact. Each town has maintained its own distinct charm, and views from the trails in between are as breathtaking as ever.

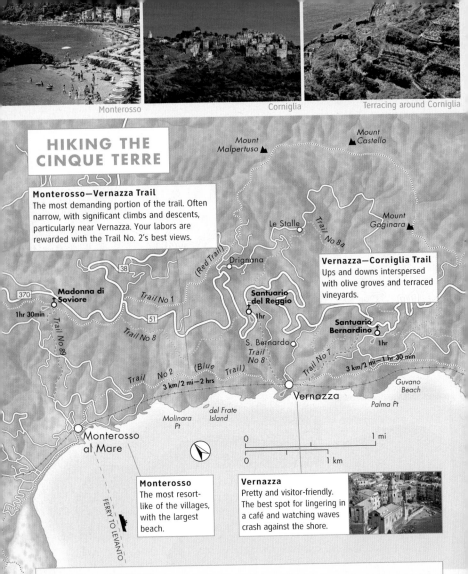

Monterosso

Corniglia

Terracing around Corniglia

HIKING THE CINQUE TERRE

Mount Malpertuso

Mount Castello

Monterosso—Vernazza Trail
The most demanding portion of the trail. Often narrow, with significant climbs and descents, particularly near Vernazza. Your labors are rewarded with the Trail No. 2's best views.

Le Stalle

Trail No 8a

Mount Gaginara

(Red Trail)

Drignana

Vernazza—Corniglia Trail
Ups and downs interspersed with olive groves and terraced vineyards.

38

Madonna di Soviore

Trail No 1

Santuario del Reggio

1hr

Santuario Bernardino

370

51

1hr 30min

Trail No 89

Trail No 8

S. Bernardo
Trail No 8

Trail No 7

1hr

3 km/2 mi – 1 hr 30 min

Trail No 2 (Blue Trail)

3 km/2 mi – 2 hrs

Guvano Beach

Vernazza

Palma Pt

del Frate Island

Molinara Pt

Monterosso al Mare

0   1 mi

0   1 km

FERRY TO LEVANTO

Monterosso
The most resort-like of the villages, with the largest beach.

Vernazza
Pretty and visitor-friendly. The best spot for lingering in a café and watching waves crash against the shore.

THE CLASSIC HIKE

Hiking is the most popular way to experience the Cinque Terre, and Trail No. 2, the Sentiero Azzurro (Blue Trail), is the most traveled path. To cover the entire trail is a full day: it's approximately 13 km (8 miles) in length, takes you to all five villages, and requires about five hours, not including stops, to complete. The best approach is to start at the eastern-most town of Riomaggiore and warm up your legs on the easiest segment of the trail. As you work your way west, the hike gets progressively more demanding. For a less strenuous experience, you can choose to skip a leg or two and take the ferry (which provides its own beautiful views) or the inland train running between the towns instead.

Manarola

Along Trail No.2

Via dell'Amore

Corniglia–Manarola Trail
Runs through the hills near Manarola, descends to rocky beach near Corniglia.

Manarola–Riomaggiore Trail
Known as the Via dell'Amore (Lovers' Lane). A wide, paved, flat path with fine views.

KEY

::::::::::::::::::	*Major footpaths*
-----------	*Sanctuary footpaths*
-----------	*Connecting footpaths*
45min ▶	*Hiking times*
⚲	*Sanctuaries*

Mount Capri

No 1 (Red Trail)

Mount Cuna

Trail No 6

Mount Galera

Mount Grosso

Trail No 7a

1hr 30min

Madonna della Salute

Trail No 02

Trail No 6d

1hr

Volastra

3 km/2 mi – 1 hr
Trail No 2 (Blue Trail)

51

Trail No 3

Madonna di Montenero
⚲ 45min

370

370
TO ➚
LA SPEZIA

Spiaggione di Corniglia

Corniglia

el Luogo Pt

Ligurian Sea

Manarola

Buonfiglio Pt

30min

Via dell' Amore

Riomaggiore

Trail No 2 (Blue Trail)

Torre Guardiola

C di M Nero

Corniglia
Perched on a cliff 500 ft. above the sea, reached by a switchback path (or by shuttle bus).

Manarola
The most photogenic of the villages, best seen from the cemetery a few minutes up the path toward Corniglia.

Riomaggiore
Cliff-clinging buildings are almost as striking as those in Manarola. Stairs to the left of the train station entrance cross over the tracks and lead to the trailhead.

BEYOND TRAIL NO.2

Trail No. 2 is just one of a network of trails crisscrossing the hills. If you're a dedicated hiker, spend a few nights and try some of the other routes. Trail No. 1, the Sentiero Rosso (Red Trail), climbs from Portovenere (east of Riomaggiore) and returns to the sea at Levanto (west of Monterosso al Mare). To hike its length takes from 9 to 12 hours; the ridge-top trail provides spectacular views from high above the villages, each of which can be reached via a steep path. Other shorter trails go from the villages up into the hills, some leading to religious sanctuaries. Trail No. 9, for example, starts from the old section of Monterosso and ends at the Madonna di Soviore Sanctuary.

WELCOME TO HIKING HEAVEN

While often described as beautiful, relaxing, and easy, it would be fair to say that the first applies to anywhere in Le Cinque Terre, but best to leave the other two for your time after hiking between the villages. Many people do not realize just how "demanding" parts of these trails can be; it's best to come prepared. We recommend bringing: a Cinque Terre Card, see below, and cash (smaller shops, eateries, as well as the park entrances do not accept credit cards).

A hike through the entire region takes about 4–5 hours plus time for exploring each village and taking a lunch break. It's an all-day, if not two-day trek. We recommend an early start, especially in summer when midday temperatures can rise to 90 degrees. Note that only "Sentiero Azzuro" (Trail No. 2)requires the Cinque Terre Card. The other 20–plus trails in the area, including the famous "Via dell'Amore," or Lovers' Lane, are free. All trails are well marked with a red and white hiking trail sign. The trails from village to village get progressively steeper as you move from south (Riomaggiore) to the north (Monterosso). If you're a day-tripper arriving by car, use the new underground lot at the La Spezia Centrale train station (€1.50/hour in summer) and take the train to Riomaggiore (6–8 minutes) to begin your hiking adventure.

FOR MORE INFO

⊕ *www.cinqueterre.com*; ⊕ *www.lecinqueterre.org*; ⊕ *www.parconazionale-5terre.it*; ⊕ *www.rebuildmonterosso.com*; ⊕ *savevernazza.com*; ⊕ *www.littleparadiso.com* (blog); ⊕ *lifeinliguria.blogspot.it* (blog).

PRECAUTIONS

If you're hitting the trails, you'll want to carry water with you, wear sturdy shoes (hiking boots are best), and have a hat and sunscreen handy. ⚠ Check weather reports; especially in late fall and winter, thunderstorms can make the shelterless trails slippery and dangerous. Rain in October and November can cause landslides and close the trails. Note that the lesser-used trails aren't as well maintained as Trail No. 2. If you're undertaking the full Trail No. 1 hike, bring something to snack on as well as your water bottle.

ADMISSION

Entrance tickets for use of the trails are available at ticket booths located at the start of each section of Trail No. 2, and at information offices in the Levanto, Monterosso, Vernazza, Corniglia, Manarola, Riomaggiore, and La Spezia train stations.

A one-day pass costs €5, which includes a trail map and an information leaflet. A one-day Cinque Terre Card costs €4, €12 for the weekend. The card combines park entrance fees with unlimited daily use of the regional train between villages.

WHEN TO GO

The ideal times to visit the Cinque Terre are September and May, when the weather is mild and the summer tourist season isn't in full swing.

GETTING HERE AND AROUND

The local train on the Genoa–La Spezia line stops at each of the Cinque Terre villages, and runs approximately every 30 minutes. Tickets for each leg of the journey (€1.80–2) are available at the five train stations. In Corniglia, the only one of the Cinque Terre that isn't at sea level, a shuttle service (€1) is provided for those who don't wish to climb (or descend) 300-plus steps that link the train station with the cliff-top town.

Strolling the Via dell'Amore, also known as Lovers' Lane.

Along the Cinque Terre coast two ferry lines operate. From June to September, Golfo Paradiso runs from Genoa and Camogli to Monterosso al Mare and Vernazza. The smaller but more frequent Golfo dei Poeti stops at each village from Lerici (east of Riomaggiore) to Monterosso, with the exception of Corniglia, four times a day. A one-day ticket costs €22.

OUR FAVORITES

Each town has something that passes for a beach, but there are only two options for both sand and decent swimming. The more accessible is in Monterosso, opposite the train station; it's equipped with chairs, umbrellas, and snack bars. The other is the secluded, swimwear-optional Guvano Beach, between Corniglia and Vernazza. To reach it from the Corniglia train station, bypass the steps leading up to the village, instead following signs to an abandoned train tunnel. Ring a bell at the tunnel's entrance, and the gate will automatically open; after a dimly lit 10-minute walk, you'll emerge at the beach. Both beaches have a nomi-

nal admission fee. Other trails to consider include: Monterosso to Santuario Madonna di Soviore, a fairly strenuous but rewarding 1½ hours up to a lovely 8th–century sanctuary. There is also a restaurant and a priceless view. Riomaggiore to Montenero and Portovenere is 1 hour up to the sanctuary and another 3 on to Portovenere, passing through some gorgeous, less traveled terrain. Manarola to Volastra to Corniglia runs high above the main trail and through vineyards and lesser-known villages. Monterosso to Levanto is a good 2½-hour hike, passing over Punta Mesco with glorious views of Cinque Terre to the south, Corsica to the west, and the Alps to the north.

Monterosso al Mare

DID YOU KNOW?

Manarola is the best spot for purchasing the wine and olive oil produced in the Cinque Terre.

with the remains of the medieval fort and castle, including two towers, in the Old Town. The Romans first inhabited this rocky spit of land in the 1st century. Today Vernazza has a fairly lively social scene. It's a great place to refuel with a hearty seafood lunch or linger in a café between links of the seaside hike. ✉ *Vernazza* 🌐 *www.aptcinqueterre.sp.it and and www.parconazionale5terre.it.*

WHERE TO EAT

$$ WINE BAR 🍴 **Enoteca Internazionale.** Located on the main street in Centro, this wine bar offers a large variety of vintages, both local and from further afield, plus delicious light fare; its umbrella-covered patio is a perfect spot to recuperate after a day of hiking. The owner, Susanna, is a certified sommelier who's always forthcoming with helpful suggestions on local wines. [$] *Average main: €20* ✉ *Via Roma 62, Monterosso al Mare* ☎ *0187/817278* 🕓 *Closed Tues. and Jan–Mar.*

$$$$ LIGURIAN 🍴 **Gambero Rosso.** Relax on Vernazza's main square at this fine trattoria looking out at a church. Enjoy such delectable dishes as shrimp salad, vegetable torte, and squid-ink risotto. The creamy pesto, served atop spaghetti, is some of the best in the Cinque Terre. End your meal with Cinque Terre's own *sciacchetrà*, a dessert wine served with semisweet biscotti. Don't drink it out of the glass—dip the biscotti in the wine instead. [$] *Average main: €45* ✉ *Piazza Marconi 7, Vernazza* ☎ *0187/812265* 🌐 *www.ristorantegamberorosso.net* 🕓 *Closed Mon., Jan., and Feb.*

$$$$ LIGURIAN 🍴 **La Lanterna.** Colorful chalkboards out in front of this small trattoria by the harbor list the day's selection of fresh fish; the set-up might sound modest, but this is arguably the finest restaurant in the Cinque Terre. During the winter, Chef Massimo serves as a teacher at the Culinary Academy in Switzerland, and he always returns with new ideas for his menu. When available, the *cozze ripiene* (stuffed mussels) shouldn't be missed. Other offerings may be a touch exotic, such as stingray with Ligurian herbs and white wine. [$] *Average main: €40* ✉ *Via San Giacomo 10, Riomaggiore* ☎ *0187/920589* 🕓 *Closed Jan. and 2 wks in Nov.*

$$$$ SEAFOOD 🍴 **Miki.** Miki has a beautiful little garden in the back, perfect for lunch on a sunny day, where you can enjoy the seafood specialties Miki is known for, including an *insalata di mare* (seafood salad), with squid and fish, that is more than tasty. If you're not up for grilled fish or calamari, opt for a pizza. [$] *Average main: €45* ✉ *Via Fegina 104, Monterosso al Mare* ☎ *0187/817608* 🕓 *Closed Nov. and Dec. and Tues. Sept.–July.*

WHERE TO STAY

For expanded hotel reviews, visit Fodors.com.

$$ HOTEL 🏨 **Ca' d'Andrean.** If you want to stay in one of the less crowded Cinque Terre offerings, this tiny, simple hotel is one of your best options. **Pros:** quiet location; lovely garden. **Cons:** rooms are comfy, but basic. [$] *Rooms from: €130* ✉ *Via Discovolo 101, Manarola* ☎ *0187/920040* 🌐 *www.cadandrean.it* 🛏 *10 rooms* 💳 *No credit cards* 🕓 *Closed mid-Nov.–mid-Dec.* 🍽 *No meals.*

$ HOTEL 🏨 **Cecio.** Many of the spotless rooms at this family-run inn at the edge of Corniglia have spectacular views of the town clinging to the cliffs above the bay. **Pros:** stunning views; good value. **Cons:** rooms are very basic; nearby bell tower may distract light sleepers. [$] *Rooms from: €60* ✉ *Via Serra 58, toward Vernazza, Corniglia* ☎ *0187/812043* 🛏 *12 rooms* 🍴 *Breakfast.*

$$ B&B/INN Fodor's Choice ★ **Il Giardino Incantato.** With wood-beam ceilings and stone walls, the stylishly restored and updated rooms in this 16th-century house in the historic center of Monterosso ooze comfort and Old World charm. **Pros:** spacious rooms; gorgeous garden; excellent hosts. **Cons:** located towards the upper end of town; no views. [$] *Rooms from: €170* ✉ *Via Mazzini 18, Monterosso al Mare* ☎ *0185/818315* 🌐 *www.ilgiardinoincantato.net* 🛏 *3 rooms, 1 junior suite* ⏲ *Closed Nov.–Mar.* 🍴 *Breakfast.*

$$ B&B/INN Fodor's Choice ★ **La Malà.** A cut above other lodging options in the Cinque Terre, these small guest rooms are equipped with flat-screen TVs, a/c, marble showers, comfortable bedding, and have views of the sea or the port, which can also be enjoyed at their most bewitching from the shared terrace literally suspended over the Mediterranean. **Pros:** clean, fresh-feeling rooms; attentive staff; oh, the views. **Cons:** there are some stairs involved; breakfast (extra) is served at a local bar and is not abundant. [$] *Rooms from: €160* ✉ *Giovanni Battista 29, Vernazza* ☎ *334/2875718* 🌐 *www.lamala.it* 🛏 *4 rooms* ⏲ *Closed Jan. 10–Mar.* 🍴 *No meals.*

4

CHIANTI, SIENA, AND CENTRAL TUSCANY

4

Visit Fodors.com for advice, updates, and bookings

WELCOME TO CENTRAL TUSCANY

TOP REASONS TO GO

★ **The Piazza del Campo, Siena:** Sip a cappuccino or enjoy some gelato as you take in this spectacular shell-shaped piazza.

★ **San Gimignano:** Grab a spot at sunset on the steps of the Collegiata as flocks of swallows swoop in and out of the famous medieval towers.

★ **Cheering the Palio in Siena:** Vie for a spot among thousands to salute the winners of this race, which takes over Siena's main square twice each year.

1 Chianti. The heart of Italy's most famous wine region is dotted with appealing towns. The largest, Greve, comes alive with a bustling local market in its town square every Saturday, while Radda sits on a hilltop in classic Tuscan style, ringed by a 14th-century walkway. Cutting through the region is the Strada Chiantigiana, one of Italy's great drives.

2 Siena. Throughout the Middle Ages Siena competed with Florence for regional supremacy. Today it remains one of Italy's most enchanting medieval towns, with an exceptional Gothic cathedral and a main square, il Campo, that has an almost magical charm.

3 Monteriggioni and Colle di Val d'Elsa. These two sleepy hill towns are pleasing, laid-back stops on the road between Siena and San Gimignano.

4 San Gimignano. From miles away you can spot San Gimignano's soaring medieval "skyscrapers"— towers that were once the ultimate status symbols of the aristocracy.

5 **Volterra.** Etruscan artifacts and Roman ruins are highlights of this city set in a rugged moonscape of a valley.

GETTING ORIENTED

Undulating hills blanketed with vineyards, groves of silver-green olive trees, and enchanting towns perched on hilltops are the essence of central Tuscany. Siena, with its extraordinary piazza and magnificent cathedral, anchors the southern end of the region. Cypress-lined roads wind their way west to San Gimignano and Volterra, and north through the Chianti district.

4

Updated
by Peter
Blackman

COUNTRY ROADS WIND AROUND CYPRESS trees on hilltops that often appear to catch and hold onto the clouds. Planted vineyards, fields, and orchards turn those curving hills into a patchwork of colors and textures that have inspired artists and delighted travelers for centuries. Sitting majestically in the midst of all this natural splendor is Siena, longtime rival of Florence and one of Italy's best-preserved medieval cities. Other hilltop towns will beckon you as well: San Gimignano, with its lofty towers; the ancient city of Volterra, once capital of a flourishing Etruscan state; and myriad charming villages dotting the rolling hills of Chianti.

The rolling hills are the region's most famous geographic feature, and you can expect to do a lot of winding up and down on the beautifully panoramic roads that link the area's hill towns. The narrow medieval streets of these old town centers are mostly closed to traffic. Park outside the city walls and walk in. Keep in mind that roads often lack shoulders in these parts, and that gas stations are rarely open Sunday.

Siena fills to the brim in the weeks surrounding the running of the Palio on July 2 and August 16, when prices, crowds, and commotion are at their highest. Between May and late September hotels and restaurants throughout the region fill up and foreign license plates and rental cars cram the roads. There's a reason for the crush: summer is a glorious time to be driving in the hills and sitting on terraces. If you want fewer crowds, try visiting during spring or fall. Spring can be especially spectacular, with blooming poppy fields, bursts of yellow broom, and wild irises growing by the side of the road. Fall is somewhat more soothing, when all those colors typically associated with Tuscany—burnt sienna, warm ocher, mossy forest greens—predominate.

In the winter months you may have towns mostly to yourself, although the choices for hotels and restaurants can be a bit more limited than when the season is in full swing. From November through mid-March it's fairly difficult to find a room in San Gimignano and Volterra: plan accordingly.

PLANNING

MAKING THE MOST OF YOUR TIME

Central Tuscany has an enticing landscape, one that invites you to follow its meandering roads to see where they might lead. Perhaps you'll come to a farmhouse selling splendid olive oil or one of the superb wines produced in the region; or perhaps you'll arrive at a medieval *pieve* (country church), an art-filled abbey, a *castello* (castle), or a restaurant where a flower-bedecked terrace looks out on a spectacular panorama.

Whatever road you take, **Siena**, Italy's most enchanting medieval city, is the one stop that's mandatory. The perfectly preserved *centro storico*, with its medieval palaces, is a delight to walk around; vehicle traffic is banned. Once in the region, however, there are plenty of other places to explore: **San Gimignano** is known as the "medieval Manhattan" because of its enormous towers, built by rival families, that still stand today. Like Siena, it benefited from commerce and trade along the pilgrimage routes, as the wonderful art in its churches and museums attests. With

The classic rolling hills of central Tuscany

additional time, consider venturing farther afield to **Volterra,** with a stop in **Colle di Val d'Elsa** along the way.

GETTING HERE AND AROUND

BICYCLE TRAVEL

In spring, summer, and fall, cyclists are as much a part of the landscape as the cypress trees. Many are on weeklong tours, but it's also possible to rent bikes or to join afternoon or day tours.

I Bike Italy. I Bike Italy leads one-day rides through the Chianti countryside. ⊠ *Via di Santa Lucia 16, Florence* ☎ *342 9352395* ⊕ *www. ibikeitaly.com.*

Marco Ramuzzi. Marco Ramuzzi rents bikes by the day or week from his shop in Greve, and organizes tours in the surrounding area. ⊠ *Via Stecchi 23, Greve in Chianti* ☎ *055/853037* ⊕ *www.ramuzzi.com.*

BUS TRAVEL

Buses are a reliable but time-consuming means of getting around the region because they often stop in every town.

CPT. CPT has infrequent buses between Volterra and Colle di Val d'Elsa, and also connects Volterra with the nearest train station in Saline. ☎ *050/884111, 199/120150 toll-free in Italy* ⊕ *www.cpt.pisa.it.*

SENA. The trip between Siena and Rome takes three hours on regular service provided by SENA. ☎ *0861/1991900* ⊕ *www.sena.it.*

SITA. From Florence, SITA buses serve Siena (one hour) and numerous towns in Chianti. ☎ *0577/204328, 800/373760 toll-free in Italy.*

Tra-In. There are three primary bus services in Tuscany: Tra-In covers much of the territory south of Florence, and the province of Siena.

✉ *Strada Statale 73, Levante 23, Località Due Ponti* ☎ *0577/204111, 800/922984 toll-free in Italy* ⊕ *www.trainspa.it.*

CAR TRAVEL

The best way to discover central Tuscany is by car, as its beauty often reveals itself along the road less traveled. The Certosa exit from the A1 highway (the Autostrada del Sole, running between Rome and Florence) provides direct access to the area. The Florence–Siena Superstrada (no number) is a four-lane, divided road with exits onto smaller country roads. The Via Cassia (SR2) winds its way south from Florence to Siena, along the western edge of the Chianti region. The superstrada is more direct, but much less scenic, than the SR2, and it can have a lot of traffic, especially on Sunday evenings. The Strada Chiantigiana (SR222) cuts through Chianti, east of the superstrada, in a curvaceous path past vineyards and countryside.

From Poggibonsi, a modern town to the west of the superstrada, you can quickly reach San Gimignano and then take the SR68 toward Volterra. The SR68 continues westward to join the Via Aurelia (SR1), linking Pisa with Rome.

TRAIN TRAVEL

Traveling between Florence and Siena by train is quick and convenient; trains make the 80-minute trip several times a day, with a change in Empoli sometimes required. Train service also runs between Siena and Chiusi–Chianciano Terme, where you can make Rome–Florence connections. Siena's train station is 2 km (1 mile) north of the centro storico, but cabs and city buses are readily available.

Other train service within the region is limited. For instance, the nearest station to Volterra is at Saline di Volterra, 10 km (6 miles) to the west. From Siena, trains run north to Poggibonsi and southeast to Sinalunga. Trains run from Chiusi–Chianciano Terme to Siena (one hour) with stops in Montepulciano Scalo, Sinalunga, and Asciano. There are no trains to San Gimignano, Monteriggioni, or the Chianti wine region.

Ferrovie dello Stato. You can check the website of the state railway, the Ferrovie dello Stato, for information. You can also get information and tickets at most travel agencies. ☎ *892021 toll-free within Italy* ⊕ *www. trenitalia.com.*

HOTELS

Siena, San Gimignano, and Volterra are among the most-visited towns in Tuscany, so there's no lack of choice for hotels across the price ranges. You can often stay right on the main square. The best accommodations, however, are often a couple of miles outside town. If you're staying a week, you have enough time to rent an *agriturismo* (working farm) apartment. Stock up your refrigerator with local groceries and wines, go for hikes in the hills, and take leisurely day trips to the main towns of the region.

VISITOR INFORMATION

The tourist information office in Greve is an excellent source for general information about the Chianti wine region and its hilltop towns. In Siena the centrally located tourist office, in Piazza del Campo, has

CENTRAL TUSCANY, PAST AND PRESENT

It may be hard to imagine that much of central Tuscany was once the battleground of warring Sienese and Florentine armies, but until Florence finally defeated Siena in 1555, the enchanting walled cities of this gentle area were strategic-defensive outposts in a series of seemingly never-ending wars.

Since the 1960s many British and northern Europeans have relocated here: they've been drawn to the unhurried life, balmy climate, and old villages. They've bought and restored farmhouses, many given up by the young heirs who decided not to continue life on the farm and instead found work in cities. There are so many Britons, in fact, that the area has been nicknamed Chiantishire. But don't let this be a deterrent to a visit: the whole area still proudly exerts its strongly Tuscan character.

information about Siena and its province. Both offices book hotel rooms for a nominal fee. Offices in smaller towns can also be a good place to check if you need last-minute accommodations.

Tourist bureaus in larger towns are typically open from 8:30 to 1 and 3:30 to 6 or 7; bureaus in villages are generally open from Easter until early November, but usually remain closed Saturday afternoon and Sunday.

CHIANTI

This is the heartland: both sides of the Strada Chiantigiana, or SR222, are embraced by glorious panoramic views of vineyards, olive groves, and castle towers. Traveling south from Florence, you first reach the aptly named one-street-town of Strada in Chianti. Farther south, the number of vineyards on either side of the road dramatically increases— as do the signs inviting you in for a free tasting of wine. Beyond Strada lies Greve in Chianti, completely surrounded by wineries and filled with wineshops. There's art to be had as well: Passignano, west of Greve, has an abbey that shelters a 15th-century *Last Supper* by Domenico and Davide Ghirlandaio. Farther still, along the Strada Chiantigiana, are Panzano and Castellina in Chianti, both hill towns. It's from near Panzano and Castellina that branch roads head to the other main towns of eastern Chianti: Radda in Chianti, Gaiole in Chianti, and Castelnuovo Berardenga.

The Strada Chiantigiana gets crowded during the high season, but no one is in a hurry. The slow pace gives you time to soak up the beautiful scenery.

GREVE IN CHIANTI

40 km (25 miles) north of Siena, 28 km (17½ miles) south of Florence.

If there is a capital of Chianti, it is Greve, a friendly market town with no shortage of cafés, *enoteche* (wine bars), and crafts shops lining its streets.

GETTING HERE

Driving from Florence or Siena, Greve is easily reached via the Strada Chiantigiana (SR222). SITA buses travel frequently between Florence and Greve. Tra-In and SITA buses connect Siena and Greve, but a direct trip is virtually impossible. There is no train service to Greve.

VISITOR INFORMATION

Greve in Chianti Tourism Office ✉ *Piazza Matteotti 8/11* ☎ *055/8546299.*

EXPLORING

Chiesa di San Donato a Lamole. The tiny village of Lamole contains this Romanesque church that was greatly modified in 1860; the only remnant of its earlier incarnation can be found in its simple facade. Inside is a 14th-century altarpiece, as well as a curious side chapel on the right that is decorated with rather garish 20th-century religious works. From Greve in Chianti, drive south on SR222 for about 1 km (½ mile); take a left and follow signs for Lamole. It's about 10 km (6 miles) southeast of Greve. ✉ *Località Lamole in Chianti 1* ☎ *055/8547015* 🕒 *Daily 9–12:30 and 4–6:30.*

Montefioralle. A tiny hilltop hamlet, about 2 km (1 mile) west of Greve in Chianti, Montefioralle is the ancestral home of Amerigo Vespucci (1454–1512), the mapmaker, navigator, and explorer who named America. (His niece Simonetta may have been the inspiration for Sandro Botticelli's *Birth of Venus,* painted sometime in the 1480s.)

Piazza Matteotti. Greve's gently sloping and asymmetrical central piazza is surrounded by an attractive arcade with shops of all kinds. In the center stands a statue of the discoverer of New York harbor, Giovanni da Verrazano (circa 1480–1527). Check out the lively market held here on Saturday morning.

WHERE TO EAT

$$ TUSCAN 🍴 **Da Padellina.** Locals don't flock to this restaurant on the outskirts of Strada in Chianti for the art on the walls, some of it questionable, most of it kitsch, but for the *bistecca fiorentina* (Florentine beefsteak). As big as a breadboard and served rare, one of these justly renowned steaks is enough to feed a family of four, with doggy bags willingly provided if required! First courses are typical, desserts are standard, but the wine list is a varied and extensive surprise. Outdoor seating on the upstairs terrace provides great views of the surrounding countryside. [$] *Average main: €15* ✉ *Via Corso del Popolo 54, 10 km (6 miles) north of Greve, Località Strada in Chianti* ☎ *055/858388* 🌐 *www.ristorantedapadellina.com* 🕒 *Closed Tues.*

$ TUSCAN 🍴 **Enoteca Fuoripiazza.** Detour off Greve's flower-strewn main square for food that relies heavily on local ingredients (like cheese and salami produced nearby). The lengthy wine list provides a bewildering array of choices to pair with *affettati misti* (a plate of cured meats) or one of their primi—the *pici* (a thick, short noodle) is deftly prepared here. All the dishes are made with great care. [$] *Average main: €12* ✉ *Via I Maggio* ☎ *055/8546313* 🕒 *Closed Mon.*

$$ TUSCAN 🍴 **Il Caminetto.** The pasta is all homemade at this small, cozy country restaurant; the *pici al sugo d'anatra* (thick spaghetti with duck sauce) is a real treat. There's a terrace for summer dining under the shade of

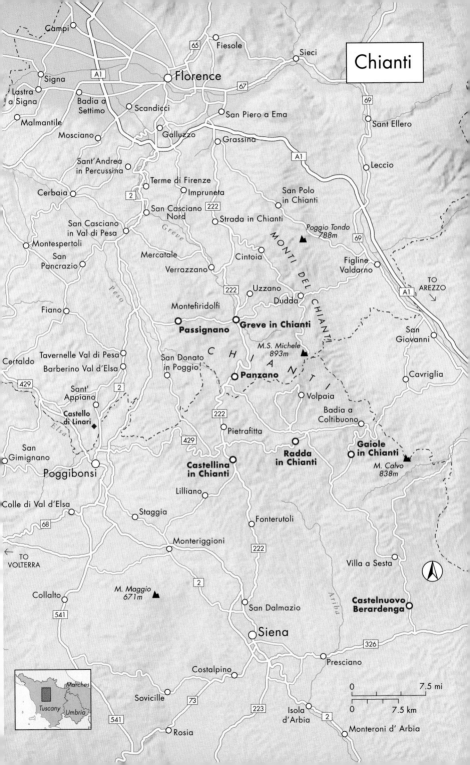

Chianti

Campi
Fiesole
65
Florence
67
Sieci
Signa
A1
Badia a Settimo
Scandicci
San Piero a Ema
69
Lastra a Signa
Malmantile
Mosciano
Galluzzo
Grassina
Sant Ellero
Sant'Andrea in Percussina
Terme di Firenze
Impruneta
San Polo in Chianti
A1
Leccio
Cerbaia
2
San Casciano Nord
Strada in Chianti
Poggio Tondo 788m
69
San Casciano in Val di Pesa
222
Figline Valdarno
Montespertoli
Greve
Mercatale
Cintoia
MONTI DEL CHIANTI
San Pancrazio
Verrazzano
222
Uzzano
TO AREZZO
A1
Peso
Montefiridolfi
Dudda
Fiano
Passignano
Greve in Chianti
San Giovanni
M.S. Michele 893m
Tavernelle Val di Pesa
San Donato in Poggio
C H I A N T I
Cavriglia
Certaldo
Barberino Val d'Elsa
2
Panzano
Sant' Appiano
Volpaia
429
Castello di Linari
222
Badia a Coltibuono
Elsa
Pietrafitta
San Gimignano
429
Radda in Chianti
Gaiole in Chianti
San Giminiano
Castellina in Chianti
M. Calvo 838m
Poggibonsi
Lilliano
Colle di Val d'Elsa
Staggia
Fonterutoli
68
222
Monteriggioni
TO VOLTERRA
2
Villa a Sesta
M. Maggio 671m
Collalto
Arbia
Castelnuovo Berardenga
541
San Dalmazio
Siena
326
Presciano
Costalpino
0   7.5 mi
Sovicille
73
0   7.5 km
541
223
Isola d'Arbia
2
Rosia
Monteroni d' Arbia

Marches
Tuscany
Umbria

lime trees. $ *Average main: €16* ⊠ *Via della Montagnola 52, 11 km (7 miles) north of Greve, Località Strada in Chianti* ☎ *055/8588909* ⊕ *www.ilcaminettodelchianti.com* ⊘ *Closed Tues.*

$ × **Locanda il Gallo.** Terrific thin-crust pizzas come out of the wood-burn-
TUSCAN ing oven here, but the menu also includes Tuscan favorites, such as Florentine beefsteak and pasta with mushrooms or truffles. The large, informal, country dining rooms have stone walls and wood-beam ceilings, and there's a veranda for dining outside in summer. The restaurant is about 4 km (2½ miles) north of Greve in Chianti. $ *Average main: €12* ⊠ *Via Lando Conti 18, Località Chiocchio* ☎ *055/8572266* ⊕ *www.locandailgallo.it* ⊘ *Closed Tues. and Nov.–Mar.*

$$$ × **Ristoro di Lamole.** Although off the beaten path up a winding road
TUSCAN lined with olive trees and vineyards, this place is worth the effort to find. The view from the outdoor terrace is divine, as is the simple, exquisitely prepared Tuscan cuisine. Start with the bruschetta drizzled with olive oil or the sublime *verdure sott'olio* (marinated vegetables) before moving on to any of the fine secondi. The kitchen has a way with *coniglio* (rabbit); don't pass it up if it's on the menu. $ *Average main: €35* ⊠ *Via di Lamole 6, Località Lamole in Chianti* ☎ *055/8547050* ⊕ *www.ristorodilamole.it* ⊘ *Closed Wed. and Nov.–Apr.*

WHERE TO STAY
For expanded hotel reviews, visit Fodors.com.

$ ⊞ **Albergo del Chianti.** Simply but pleasantly decorated bedrooms with
B&B/INN plain modern cabinets and wardrobes and wrought-iron beds have views of the town square or out over the tile rooftops toward the surrounding hills. **Pros:** central location; best value in Greve. **Cons:** rooms facing the piazza can be noisy; small bathrooms. $ *Rooms from: €100* ⊠ *Piazza Matteotti 86* ☎ *055/853763* ⊕ *www.albergodelchianti.it* ↶ *16 rooms* ⊘ *Closed Jan.* ⦿ *Breakfast.*

$$ ⊞ **Castello Vicchiomaggio.** Stay in a fortified castle built more than a
B&B/INN millennium ago (and rebuilt during the Renaissance). **Pros:** spacious rooms; spectacular views; very helpful staff. **Cons:** some rooms lack a/c; you need a car to get around; a minimum stay of two nights may be required. $ *Rooms from: €130* ⊠ *Via Vicchiomaggio 4, Località Vicchiomaggio* ☎ *055/854079* ⊕ *www.vicchiomaggio.it* ↶ *7 rooms, 8 apartments, 1 house* ⦿ *Breakfast.*

$$$ ⊞ **Villa Bordoni.** David and Catherine Gardner, Scottish expats, have
B&B/INN transformed a ramshackle 16th-century villa into a stunning little
Fodor'sChoice retreat where no two rooms are alike—all have stenciled walls; some
★ have four-poster beds, others small mezzanines. **Pros:** splendidly isolated in the hills above Greve; beautiful decor; wonderful hosts. **Cons:** on a long and bumpy dirt road; need a car to get around. $ *Rooms from: €245* ⊠ *Via San Cresci 31/32, Località Mezzuola* ☎ *055/8547453* ⊕ *www.villabordoni.com* ↶ *8 rooms, 3 suites* ⊘ *Closed 3 wks in Jan. and Feb.* ⦿ *Breakfast.*

$$ ⊞ **Villa Il Poggiale.** Renaissance gardens, beautiful rooms with high ceil-
B&B/INN ings and elegant furnishings, a panoramic pool, and expert staff are just
Fodor'sChoice a few of the things that make a stay at this 16th-century villa memo-
★ rable. **Pros:** beautiful gardens and panoramic setting; elegant historical building; exceptionally professional staff. **Cons:** a little isolated, making

private transportation necessary; some rooms face a country road and may be noisy during the day. $ *Rooms from: €160* ⊠ *Via Empolese 69, 20 km (12 miles) northwest of Greve, San Casciano Val di Pesa* ☎ *055/828311* ⊕ *www.villailpoggiale.it* ⇋ *20 rooms, 4 suites* ☉ *Closed Jan.–Feb.* ⊚| *Breakfast.*

$$
B&B/INN

⊡ **Villa Vignamaggio.** Reputed to be the birthplace of the woman made famous by Leonardo da Vinci's *Mona Lisa*, and used as the setting of Kenneth Branagh's 1993 film, *Much Ado About Nothing*, Villa Vignamaggio has origins in the 14th century. **Pros:** unbeatable views; informative wine tastings. **Cons:** no elevator to third floor; private transportation required. $ *Rooms from: €200* ⊠ *Via Petriolo 5, Località Vicchiomaggio* ☎ *055/854661* ⊕ *www.vignamaggio.com* ⇋ *9 rooms, 16 suites, 13 apartments, 2 cottages* ☉ *Closed mid-Nov.–mid-Mar.* ⊚| *Breakfast.*

PASSIGNANO

8 km (5 miles) south of Mercatale, 29 km (18 miles) south of Florence.

Other than its Romanesque abbey and the few houses clustered around it, there is very little to actually see in this tiny hamlet. But the panoramic setting and the beautiful natural surroundings do make a short side-trip recommendable.

GETTING HERE

By car, take the Tavernelle exit from the Florence–Siena Superstrada. Direct bus or train service is not available.

EXPLORING

Badia a Passignano (*Abbey of Passignano*). The dining hall of the towering 11th-century Abbey of Passignano houses a stunningly massive, 21-foot-wide *Last Supper* (1476) by Domenico and Davide Ghirlandaio, and the monastery's church of has a 13th-century sculpture of Saint Michael slaying the dragon. At this writing, the Ghirlandaio fresco was undergoing extensive restoration, but even if you can't get to see the *Last Supper,* it's still worth the drive to visit the rest of the abbey and to walk in the beautiful countryside. ⊠ *Via Passignano 20* ☎ *055/8071622* ☉ *Daily 10:30–noon and 3–5:30.*

WHERE TO EAT

$
ITALIAN

✕ **La Cantinetta di Rignana.** On Sunday afternoons this old-fashioned trattoria is teeming with lively Italian families. Grilled meats are the specialty of the house. If you have room for dessert, the kitchen whips up a mean tiramisu. Enjoy the farmhouse feel of the dining room, or choose a shady table in the garden overlooking the vineyards. The restaurant is 4 km (2 miles) west of Passignano. $ *Average main: €13* ⊠ *Via di Rignana 15, 4, Località Rignana* ☎ *055/852601* ⊕ *www.lacantinettadirignana. it* ⌂ *Reservations essential* ☉ *Closed Tues.*

$$$
ITALIAN

✕ **Osteria di Passignano.** In an ancient wine cellar owned by the Antinori family—who also happen to own much of what you see in these parts—is a sophisticated restaurant ably run by chef Marcello Crini and his attentive staff. The menu changes seasonally; traditional Tuscan cuisine is given a delightful twist through the use of unexpected herbs.

EATING WELL IN CENTRAL TUSCANY

Chianti restaurants serve Tuscan dishes similar to those in Florence, but they also have local specialties, such as pasta creations made with *pici* (a long, thick, hand-rolled spaghetti). You'll find other pasta dishes, like *pappardelle alla lepre* (a long, flat type of pasta noodle with hare sauce), and soups, such as *pappa al pomodoro* (a thick tomato soup) and *ribollita* (Tuscan bread soup), on most menus.

Panzanella, a salad of tomato, basil, bread, and onion, is a common first course on summer menus. Many recipes are from the *nonna* (grandmother) of the restaurant's owner, handed down through time but never written down.

The so-called *tonno del Chianti* (Chianti tuna) is really a dish of tender flakes of rabbit meat that look and, believe it or not, taste like tuna—it's actually delicious. Pecorino, a soft sheep's-milk cheese, makes it onto many menus in pasta dishes and appetizers.

The Sienese often add a subtle flair of extra herbs and garlic to their rendition of traditional Tuscan fare. Antipasti (usually made of the simplest ingredients) are extremely satisfying.

A typical starter might be a plate of excellent locally cured meats, such

as those made from *cinta senese*, a species of domestic pig rescued from near extinction. *Verdure sott'olio* (marinated vegetables) are usually artichokes, red peppers, carrots, celery, cauliflower, olives, and capers marinated in olive oil. Second courses are traditionally game meats, and *piccione* (pigeon), served either roasted or stuffed and baked, is commonly on the menu.

After your meal, try some delicious amber-color *vin santo*, a sweet dessert wine with *cantuccini* (hard almond cookies), which are dunked once or twice in the glass. The wine is made from choice white Trebbiano Toscano or Malvasia del Chianti grapes and is aged in small, partially filled oak barrels. Other favorite Sienese sweets include *ricciarelli*, succulent almond-flavor cookies.

Excellent extra-virgin olive oil is produced throughout the region, and the best way to taste it is in the form of a *fettunta* (oily slice), a thick slice of toasted Tuscan bread rubbed with garlic, sprinkled with salt, and dripping with olive oil. Asking for a plate or bowl to sample olive oil with bread before a meal is a dead giveaway that you're a tourist—it's the invention of American restaurateurs.

When porcini mushrooms are in season, a particularly tantalizing treat is the *filetto di vitello in panura di funghi secchi e noci al sedano rapa e porcini* (veal sirloin in a crust of dried mushrooms, walnuts, celeriac, and fresh porcini). The extensive wine list includes local vintages as well as numerous international labels. Day-long cooking courses are also available. $ *Average main: €35* ✉ *Via Passignano 33* ☎ *055/8071278* ⊕ *www.osteriadipassignano.com* ⊗ *Closed Sun., 3 wks in Jan., and 1 wk in Aug.*

$$$ ✕ **Ristoro L'Antica Scuderia.** Across the street from the abbey and run
TUSCAN   by the same family for more than 30 years, this once simple eatery in what were once the monk's stables has undergone a complete facelift.

Continued on page 205

GRAPE ESCAPES
THE PLEASURES OF TUSCAN WINE

The vineyards stretching across the landscape
of Tuscany may look like cinematic backdrops,
but in fact they're working farms, and they
produce some of Italy's best wines. No matter
whether you're a wine novice or a connoisseur,
there's great pleasure to be had from exploring this
lush terrain, visiting the vineyards, and uncorking a bottle
for yourself.

GETTING TO KNOW TUSCAN WINE

Most of the wine produced in Tuscany is red (though there are some notable whites as well), and most Tuscan reds are made primarily from one type of grape, sangiovese. That doesn't mean, however, that all wines here are the same. God (in this case Bacchus) is in the details: differences in climate, soil, and methods of production result in wines with several distinct personalities.

Chianti

Chianti is the most famous name in Tuscan wine, but what exactly the name means is a little tricky. It once identified wines produced in the region extending from just south of Florence to just north of Siena. In the mid-20th century, the official Chianti zone was expanded to include a large portion of central Tuscany. That area is divided into eight subregions. **Chianti Classico** is the name given to the original zone, which makes up 17,000 of the 42,000 acres of Chianti-producing vineyards.

Classico wines, which bear the *gallo nero* (black rooster) logo on their labels, are the most highly regarded Chiantis (with **Rùfina** running second), but that doesn't mean Classicos are always superior. All Chiantis are strictly regulated (they must be a minimum 75% to 80% sangiovese, with other varieties blended in to add nuance), and they share a strong, woodsy character that's well suited to Tuscan food. It's a good strategy to drink the local product—**Colli Senesi Chianti** when in Siena, for example. The most noticeable, and costly, difference comes when a Chianti is from *riserva* (reserve) stock, meaning it's been aged for at least two years.

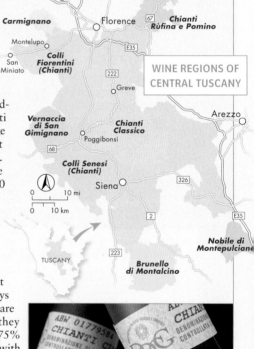

WINE REGIONS OF CENTRAL TUSCANY

DOC & DOCG The designations "DOC" and "DOCG"—Denominazione di Origine Controllata (e Garantita)—mean a wine comes from an established region and adheres to rigorous standards of production. Ironically, the esteemed Super Tuscans are labeled *vini da tavola* (table wines), the least prestigious designation, because they don't use traditional grape blends.

Brunello di Montalcino

The area surrounding the hill town of Montalcino, to the south of Siena, is drier and warmer than the Chianti regions, and it produces the most powerful of the sangiovese-based wines. Regulations stipulate that Brunello di Montalcino be made entirely from sangiovese grapes (no blending) and aged at least four years. **Rosso di Montalcino** is a younger, less complex, less expensive Brunello.

The Super Tuscans

Beginning in the 1970s, some winemakers, chafing at the regulations imposed on established Tuscan wine varieties, began blending and aging wines in innovative ways. Thus were born the so-called Super Tuscans. These pricey, French oak–aged wines are admired for their high quality, led by such star performers as **Sassicaia**, from the Maremma region, and **Tignanello**, produced at the Tenuta Marchesi Antinori near Badia a Passignano. Purists, however, lament the loss of local identity resulting from the Super Tuscans' use of nonnative grape varieties such as cabernet sauvignon and merlot.

Vino Nobile di Montepulciano

East of Montalcino is Montepulciano, the town at the heart of the third, and smallest, of Tuscany's top wine districts.

Blending regulations aren't as strict for Vino Nobile as for Chianti and Brunello, and as a result it has a wider range of characteristics. Broadly speaking, though, Vino Nobile is a cross between Chianti and Brunello—less acidic than the former and softer than the latter. It also has a less pricey sibling, **Rosso di Montepulciano.**

The Whites

Most whites from Tuscany are made from **trebbiano** grapes, which produce a wine that's light and refreshing but not particularly aromatic or flavorful—it may hit the spot on a hot afternoon, but it doesn't excite connoisseurs.

Golden-hewed **Vernaccia di San Gimignano** is a local variety with more limited production but greater personality—it's the star of Tuscan whites. Winemakers have also brought chardonnay and sauvignon grapes to the region, resulting in wines that, like some Super Tuscans, are pleasant to drink but short on local character.

TOURING & TASTING IN TUSCAN WINE COUNTRY

Strade del Vino di Toscana Tuscany has visitor-friendly wineries, but the way you go about visiting is a bit different here from what it is in California or France. Many wineries welcome drop-ins for a tasting, but for a tour you usually need to make an appointment a few days in advance. There are several approaches you can take, depending on how much time you have and how serious you are about wine:

PLAN 1: FULL IMMERSION. Make an appointment to tour one of the top wineries (see our recommendations on the next page), and you'll get the complete experience: half a day of strolling through vineyards, talking grape varieties, and tasting wine, often accompanied by food. Groups are small; in spring and fall, it may be just you and the winemaker. The cost is usually €10 to €15 per person, but can go up to €40 if a meal is included. Remember to specify a tour in English.

PLAN 2: SEMI-ORGANIZED. If you want to spend a few hours going from vineyard to vineyard, make your first stop one of the local tourist information offices—they're great resources for maps, tasting itineraries, and personalized advice about where to visit. The offices in **Greve, Montalcino,** and **Montepulciano** are the best equipped. **Enoteche** (for more about them, turn the page) can also be good places to pick up tips about where to go for tastings.

PLAN 3: SPONTANEOUS. Along Tuscany's country roads you'll see signs for wineries offering **vendita diretta** (direct sales) and **degustazioni** (tastings). For a taste of the local product with some atmosphere thrown in, a spontaneous visit is a perfectly viable approach. You may wind up in a simple shop or an elaborate tasting room; either way, there's a fair chance you'll sample something good. Expect a small fee for a three-glass tasting.

THE PICK OF THE VINEYARDS

Within the Chianti Classico region, these wineries should be at the top of your to-visit list, whether you're dropping in for a taste or making a full tour. (Tours require reservations unless otherwise indicated.)

CHIANTI CLASSICO

Badia a Coltibuono

(✉ Gaiole in Chianti ☎ 0577/749498 ⊕ www.coltibuono.com). Along with an extensive prelunch tour and tasting, there are shorter afternoon tours, no reservation required, starting on the hour from 2 to 5. (See "Radda in Chianti" in this chapter.)

Castello di Fonterutoli

(✉ Castellina in Chianti ☎ 0577/73571 ⊕ www.fonterutoli.it). Hour-long tours include a walk through the neighboring village.

Castello di Volpaia

(✉ Radda in Chianti ☎ 0577/738066 ⊕ www.volpaia.com). The castle is part of the tiny town of Volpaia, perched above Radda.

Castello di Verrazzano

(✉ Via S. Martino in Valle 12, Greve in Chianti ☎ 055/854243 ⊕ www.verrazzano.com). Tours here take you down to the cellars, through the gardens, and into the woods in search of wild boar.

Villa Vignamaggio

(✉ Via Petriolo 5, Greve in Chianti ☎ 055/854661 ⊕ www.vignamaggio.com). Along with a wine tour, you can spend the night at this villa where Mona Lisa is believed to have been born. (See "Where to Stay" under "Greve in Chianti" in this chapter.)

Rocca delle Màcie

(✉ Località Le Macìe 45, Castellina in Chianti ☎ 0577/732236 ⊕ www.roccadellemacie.com). A full lunch or dinner can be incorporated into your tasting here.

Castello di Brolio

(✉ Gaiole in Chianti ☎ 0577/730220 ⊕ www.ricasoli.it). One of Tuscany's most impressive castles also has a centuries-old winemaking tradition. (See "Radda in Chianti" in this chapter.)

4

IN FOCUS GRAPE ESCAPES

MORE TUSCAN WINE RESOURCES

Enoteche: Wine Shops

The word *enoteca* in Italian can mean "wine store," "wine bar," or both. In any event, *enoteche* (the plural, pronounced "ay-no-*tek*-ay") are excellent places to sample and buy Tuscan wines, and they're also good sources of information about local wineries. There are scores to choose from. These are a few of the best:

Enoteca Italiana, Siena (Fortezza Medicea, Viale Maccari ☎ 0577/288497 ⊕ www. enoteca-italiana.it). The only one of its kind, this *enoteca* represents all the producers of DOC and DOCG wines in Italy and stocks over 400 labels. Wine by the glass and snacks are available.

Enoteca Osticcio, Montalcino (✉ Via Matteotti 23 ☎ 0577/848271 ⊕ www. osticcio.com). There are more than one thousand labels in stock. With one of the best views in Montalcino, it is also a very pleasant place to sit and meditate over a glass of Brunello.

Enoteca del Gallo Nero, Greve in Chianti (✉ Piazzetta S. Croce 8 ☎ 055/853297). This is one of the best stocked *enoteche* in the Chianti region.

La Dolce Vita, Montepulciano (Via di Voltaia nel Corso 80/82 ☎ 0578/757872). An elegantly restored monastery is home to the excellent enoteca in the upper part of Montepulciano, which has a wide selction of wines by the glass.

Wine on the Web

Tuscan wine country is well represented on the Internet. A good place for an overview is ⊕ www.terreditoscana.regione. toscana.it. (Click on "Le Strade del Vino"; the page that opens next will give you the option of choosing an English-language version.) This site shows 14 *strade del vino* (wine roads) that have been mapped out by consortiums representing major wine districts (unfortunately, Chianti Classico isn't included), along with recommended itineraries. You'll also find links to the consortium Web sites, where you can dig up more detailed information on touring. The Chianti Classico consortium's site is ⊕ www.chianticlassico.com. The Vino Nobile di Montepulciano site is ⊕ www.vinonobiledimontepulciano.it, and Brunello di Montalcino is ⊕ www. consorziobrunellodimontalcino.it. All have English versions.

The interior is decorated along modern-elegant lines, and the menu, while thoroughly based on traditional cuisine, is filled with creative interpretations. The *taglierini al tartuffo* (pasta with truffles) is delicious, the *tagliata al ginepro* (grilled sliced beef with juniper berries) excellent, and the wine list superb. Pizza is also available, but only at dinnertime. Shaded, outdoor seating on the restaurant's stepped terrace provides a pleasant setting for dinner on a warm summer's evening. [$] *Average main: €25* ✉ *Via di Passignano 17* ☎ *055/80716233* 🌐 *www.ristorolanticascuderia.com* 🕓 *Closed Tues.*

PANZANO

4

7 km (4½ miles) south of Greve in Chianti, 36 km (22 miles) south of Florence.

The magnificent views of the valleys of the Pesa and Greve rivers easily make Panzano one of the prettiest stops in Chianti. The triangular Piazza Bucciarelli is the heart of the new town. A short stroll along Via Giovanni da Verrazzano brings you up to the old town, Panzano Alto, which is still partly surrounded by medieval walls. The town's 13th-century castle is now almost completely absorbed by later buildings (its central tower is now a private home).

GETTING HERE

From Florence or Siena, Panzano is easily reached by car along the Strada Chiantigiana (SR222). SITA buses travel frequently between Florence and Panzano. From Siena, the journey by bus is extremely difficult because SITA and Tra-In do not coordinate their schedules. There is no train service to Panzano.

EXPLORING

San Leolino. Ancient even by Chianti standards, this hilltop church probably dates from the 10th century, but was completely rebuilt in the Romanesque style sometime in the 13th century. It has a 14th-century cloister worth seeing. The 16th-century terra-cotta tabernacles are attributed to Giovanni della Robbia, and there's also a remarkable triptych (attributed to the Master of Panzano) that was executed sometime in the mid-14th century. Open days and hours are unpredictable; check with the tourist office in Greve in Chianti for the latest. ✉ *Località San Leolino, 3 km (2 miles) south of Panzano* ☎ *055/8546299.*

Santa Maria Assunta. Situated next to the castle in the upper part of town, this church was completely rebuilt in the 19th century. In the small chapel to the right of the nave is an Annunciation attributed to Michele di Ridolfo del Ghirlandaio (1503–77). ✉ *Via Castellana 6* 🕓 *Daily 7–noon and 4–6.*

WHERE TO EAT

$ WINE BAR 🍴 **Enoteca Baldi.** Sample the local *vino* while satisfying your appetite with simply prepared and presented bruschetta, soups, and pastas. In summer a few tables are set in the shade under the trees in the town's main square. [$] *Average main: €8* ✉ *Piazza Bucciarelli 26* ☎ *055/852843.*

$$ INTERNATIONAL 🍴 **Mac Dario.** Local butcher and restaurateur, Dario Cecchini, has extended his empire of meat to include this space located directly above

his butcher's shop. Here, you'll find only three items on the menu: the *Mac Dario*, a half-pound burger in a crisp crumb crust served with roast potatoes and onions; the *Super Dario*, the former with salad and beans added; and the *Welcome*, four different dishes of beef and pork served with fresh garden vegetables. All are a nice change from the more standard options found at restaurants throughout Chianti. Outdoor seating is available in summer, but get here early—it's enormously popular. Enter from the public parking area behind the restaurant. $ *Average main: €15 ⊠ Via XX Luglio 11 ☎ 055/852176 ⊕ www.dariocecchini. com ⩜ Reservations not accepted ⊗ Closed Sun.*

$$
TUSCAN
✕ **Montagliari.** This ancient stone farmhouse is the place to go for very tasty Tuscan food. Enjoy your meal in the courtyard, or, when the temperature drops, the main dining room with a farm-style fireplace. The *peposo* (beef stew laced with black pepper) is particularly piquant; the *papardelle al cinghiale* (flat noodles with a wild boar sauce) delightfully fragrant. The wine list, particularly strong on local varieties, includes the farm's own Chianti Classico. $ *Average main: €18 ⊠ Via Montagliari 29 ☎ 055/852014 ⊕ www.montagliari.it ⊗ Closed Mon. and early Jan.–late Feb.*

$$$
TUSCAN
✕ **Solociccia.** "Abandon all hope, ye who enter here," announces the menu, "you're in the hands of a butcher." Indeed you are, for this restaurant is the creation of Dario Cecchini, Panzano's local merchant of meat. Served at communal tables, the set meal consists of no less than six meat courses, chosen at Dario's discretion. They are accompanied by seasonal vegetables, white beans with olive oil, and focaccia bread. Though Cecchini emphasizes that steak is never on the menu, this lively, crowded place is definitely not for vegetarians. The entrance is on Via XX Luglio. $ *Average main: €30 ⊠ Via Chiantigiana 5 ☎ 055/852727 ⊕ www.solociccia.it ⩜ Reservations essential ⊗ Closed Mon.–Wed. No dinner Sun.*

WHERE TO STAY
For expanded hotel reviews, visit Fodors.com.

$$$
B&B/INN
Fodor'sChoice
★
🛏 **Villa Le Barone.** Once the home of the Viviani della Robbia family, this 16th-century villa in a grove of ancient cypress trees retains many aspects of a private country dwelling, complete with homey guest quarters. **Pros:** beautiful location; wonderful restaurant; great base for exploring the region. **Cons:** rooms vary in size; 15-minute walk to nearest town. $ *Rooms from: €280 ⊠ Via San Leolino 19 ☎ 055/852621 ⊕ www.villa-lebarone.com ⤵ 28 rooms ⊗ Closed Nov.– Easter ⦿❘ Breakfast.*

$$
B&B/INN
🛏 **Villa Sangiovese.** On the town's main square, this simple, well-run hotel has rooms that look out to the hillside or face the piazza. **Pros:** immaculate rooms; pool area great for kids; great location for exploring Chianti. **Cons:** front rooms can be noisy; lots of stairs. $ *Rooms from: €150 ⊠ Piazza Bucciarelli 5 ☎ 055/852461 ⊕ www.villasangiovese.it ⤵ 19 rooms ⊗ Closed mid-Dec.–mid-Mar. Restaurant closed Wed. ⦿❘ Breakfast.*

SHOPPING

Antica Macelleria Cecchini. This just might be the world's most dramatic butcher shop. Here, amid classical music and lively conversation, owner Dario Cecchini holds court: while quoting Dante, he serves samples of his very fine *sushi di Chianina* (raw slices of Chianina beef gently salted and peppered). He has researched recipes from the 15th century, and sells pâtés and herb concoctions found nowhere else. Serious food enthusiasts should not miss the place. ⊠ *Via XX Luglio 11* ☎ *055/852020.*

CASTELLINA IN CHIANTI

13 km (8 miles) south of Panzano, 59 km (35 miles) south of Florence, 22 km (14 miles) north of Siena.

Castellina in Chianti—or simply Castellina—is on a ridge above three valleys: the Val di Pesa, Val d'Arbia, and Val d'Elsa. No matter what direction you turn, the panorama is bucolic. The strong 15th-century medieval walls and fortified town gate give a hint of the history of this village, which was an outpost during the continuing wars between Florence and Siena. In the main square, the Piazza del Comune, there's a 15th-century palace and a 15th-century fort constructed around a 13th-century tower. It now serves as the town hall.

GETTING HERE

As with all the towns along the Strada Chiantigiana (SR222), Castellina is an easy drive from either Siena or Florence. From Siena, Castellina is well served by the local Tra-In bus company. However, only one bus a day travels here from Florence. The closest train station is at Castellina Scalo, some 15 km (9 miles) away.

VISITOR INFORMATION

Castellina in Chianti Tourism Office ⊠ *Via Ferruccio 40* ☎ *0577/741392.*

NEED A BREAK?

L'Antica Delizia. Treat yourself to one of the terrifically fragrant ice creams at this *gelateria* just outside the town center. The fruit flavors—*fragola* (strawberry), *melone* (cantaloupe), and *limone* (lemon)—are all homemade and particularly good. ⊠ *Via Fiorentina 4* ☎ *0577/741337.*

WHERE TO EAT

$$$
TUSCAN

✕ **Albergaccio.** The fact that the dining room can seat only 35 guests makes a meal here an intimate experience. The ever-changing menu mixes traditional and creative dishes. In late September and October *zuppa di funghi e castagne* (mushroom and chestnut soup) is a treat; grilled meats and seafood are on the list throughout the year. There's also an excellent wine list. When the weather is warm, make sure you dine on the terrace. $ *Average main: €25* ⊠ *Via Fiorentina 63* ☎ *0577/741042* ⊕ *www.albergacciocast.com* ⟋ *Reservations essential* ▭ *No credit cards* ⊙ *Closed Sun. No lunch Wed. and Thurs.*

$$
ITALIAN

✕ **Osteria alla Piazza.** Relax amid vineyards on a countryside terrace with one of Chianti's most spectacular views of the vineyards in the valley of the River Pesa. Enjoy the sophisticated menu: the *girasole ai quattro sapori,* a giant vegetable-filled ravioli flavored with fresh tomato sauce and a few drops of cream, arrives at the table looking much like a *girasole* (sunflower). For pistachio fans, the *raviolo con pistacchi di Bronte, ragù e nocciole* (pistachio ravioli with meat sauce and hazlenuts) is a must. And certainly, try any of the delicious desserts. It's in La Piazza, 15 km (8 miles) north of Castellina. $ *Average main: €20* ⊠ *Località La Piazza* ☎ *0577/733580* ⊕ *www.osteriaallapiazza.com* ☚ *Reservations essential* ⊙ *Closed Mon. and Jan. and Feb.; closed weekdays Mar., Nov., and Dec.*

$$ ✕ **Ristorante Le Tre Porte.** Grilled meat dishes are the specialty at this
TUSCAN popular restaurant, with a Florentine beefsteak (served very rare) taking pride of place. Paired with grilled fresh porcini mushrooms when in season (in spring and fall), it's a particularly heady dish. The panoramic terrace is a good choice for dining in summer. Inside, the upper floor offers an unmistakably Tuscan setting, while the downstairs is more modern and intimate. Reservations are essential in July and August. $ *Average main: €20* ⊠ *Via Trento e Trieste 4* ☎ *0577/741163* ⊕ *www.ristoranteinchianti.com* ⊙ *Closed Tues.*

$$ ✕ **Sotto Le Volte.** As the name suggests, you'll find this small restaurant
TUSCAN under the arches of Castellina's medieval walkway. The restaurant has vaulted ceilings, which make for a particularly romantic setting. The menu is short and eminently Tuscan, with typical soups and pasta dishes. The *costolette di agnello alle erbe* (herbed lamb chops) are especially tasty. $ *Average main: €20* ⊠ *Via delle Volte 14–16* ☎ *0577/056530* ⊕ *www.ristorantesottolevolte.it* ☰ *No credit cards* ⊙ *Closed Wed.*

WHERE TO STAY
For expanded hotel reviews, visit Fodors.com.

$ ⛱ **Colle Etrusco Salivolpi.** The family that owns this farmhouse took spe-
B&B/INN cial care not to change too much when they began accepting guests: faded family photos, mementos of long-past journeys, and bric-a-brac of all kinds decorate the common areas. **Pros:** tranquil location; 10-minute walk to nearest town. **Cons:** some stairs to climb; no a/c in some rooms. $ *Rooms from: €115* ⊠ *Via Fiorentina 89* ☎ *0577/740484* ⊕ *www.hotelsalivolpi.com* ⤴ *19 rooms* ⫶⊙⫶ *Breakfast.*

$$ ⛱ **Hotel Belvedere di San Leonino.** Stroll around the wonderful gardens on
B&B/INN this restored country estate dating from the 14th century. **Pros:** great family atmosphere; lovely old house; central location. **Cons:** stairs to climb; need a car to get around. $ *Rooms from: €130* ⊠ *Località San Leonino* ☎ *0577/740887* ⊕ *www.hotelsanleonino.com* ⤴ *28 rooms* ⊙ *Closed mid-Nov.–mid-Apr.* ⫶⊙⫶ *Breakfast.*

$$$ ⛱ **Locanda Le Piazze.** This old farmhouse has been transformed into
B&B/INN a marvelous hotel in the midst of vineyards. **Pros:** pastoral setting; fun cooking classes; luxurious bathrooms. **Cons:** no a/c; need a car to get around. $ *Rooms from: €230* ⊠ *Località Le Piazze 41* ☎ *0577/743190* ⊕ *www.locandalepiazze.it* ⤴ *20 rooms* ⊙ *Closed Nov.–Apr.* ⫶⊙⫶ *Breakfast.*

$ ⛱ **Palazzo Squarcialupi.** In this lovely 15th-century palace rooms are
B&B/INN spacious, with high ceilings, tile floors, and 18th-century furnishings,
Fodor's Choice and many have views of the valley below. **Pros:** great location in town
★ center; elegant public spaces; nice spa, pool, and grounds. **Cons:** on a street with no car access; across from a busy restaurant. $ *Rooms from:*

€120 ⊠ Via Ferruccio 22 ☎ 0577/741186 ⊕ www.palazzosquarcialupi. com ⤶ 17 rooms ☉ Closed Nov.–Mar. ⦿ Breakfast.

SHOPPING

Castellina is a small town, with most of its shops located either along Via Ferruccio or on the Piazza del Comune. But don't miss the specialty stores hidden away on Via delle Volte, which runs inside the eastern medieval walls of the town—you can reach it from either end of Via Ferruccio.

Bottega Antichità. Antiquario Mario Cappelletti carries interesting prints and reproductions of well-known Renaissance artworks. ⊠ *Via Ferruccio 39* ☎ *0577/740980.*

Laboratorio di Ceramica. Lucia Volentieri has a delightful selection of delicately hand-painted ceramics in her studio/shop. ⊠ *Via Trento e Trieste 24* ☎ *0577/741133* ⊕ *www.luciavolentieri.com.*

Le Volte Enoteca. On Castellina's main street, Aleandro and his daughter Roberta stock an ample and well-chosen supply of local wines produced by small estates. On request, they can also organize visits to nearby wineries. ⊠ *Via Ferruccio 12* ☎ *0577/741314* ⊕ *www.enotecalevolte.com.*

RADDA IN CHIANTI

10 km (6 miles) east of Castellina in Chianti, 55 km (34 miles) south of Florence.

Radda in Chianti sits on a ridge stretching between the Val di Pesa and Val d'Arbia. It is easily reached by following the SR429 from Castellina. It's another one of those tiny villages with steep streets for strolling; follow the signs that point you toward the *camminamento medioevale,* a covered 14th-century walkway that circles part of the city inside the walls.

GETTING HERE

Radda can be reached by car from either Siena or Florence along the SR222 (Strada Chiantigiana), and from the A1 highway. Three Tra-In buses make their way from Siena to Radda. One morning SITA bus travels from Florence to Radda. There is no train service convenient to Radda.

VISITOR INFORMATION

Radda in Chianti Tourism Office ⊠ *Piazza Castello 6* ☎ *0577/738494.*

EXPLORING

Palazzo del Podestà. Radda's town hall (aka Palazzo Comunale), in the middle of town, was built in the second half of the 14th century and has served the same function ever since. Fifty-one coats of arms (the largest is the Medici's) are imbedded in the facade, representing the past governors of the town, but unless you have official business, the building is closed to the public. ⊠ *Piazza Ferrucci 1.*

Volpaia. This tiny town, with a population of roughly 50, is perched on a hill 10 km (6 miles) north of Radda. During the wars between Florence and Siena it served as a key castle and military outpost, but lost its importance when the Florentines defeated Siena in 1555.

Approximately three-quarters of the town are now given over to the production of wine and olive oil.

Castello di Volpaia. At this small enoteca on Piazza della Cisterna you can sample and purchase the fine wines, olive oil, and flavored vinegars made by Castello di Volpaia. Booked in advance, tours in English of the winery and olive press are also available. ✉ *Piazza della Cisterna 1* 🌐 *www.volpaia.it.*

WHERE TO EAT AND STAY

For expanded hotel reviews, visit Fodors.com.

$$ TUSCAN Fodor's Choice ★ 🍴 **Osteria Le Panzanelle.** Silvia Bonechi's experience in the kitchen—with the help of a few precious recipes handed down from her grandmother—is one of the reasons for the success of this small restaurant. The other is the front-room hospitality of Nada Michelassi. These two *panzanelle* (women from Panzano) serve a short menu of tasty and authentic dishes at what the locals refer to as *il prezzo giusto* (the right price). Both the *pappa al pomodoro* (tomato soup) and the *peposo* (peppery beef stew) are exceptional. Whether you are eating inside or under large umbrellas on the terrace near a tiny stream, the experience is always congenial. "The best food we had in Tuscany," writes one member of Fodors.com. Reservations are essential in July and August. [$] *Average main: €15* ✉ *Località Lucarelli 29, 8 km (5 miles) northwest of Radda on the road to Panzano* ☎ *0577/733511* 🌐 *www.osteria.lepanzanelle.it* 🕒 *Closed Mon. and Jan. and Feb.*

$$ B&B/INN 🏨 **Il Borgo di Vescine.** At this former Etruscan settlement a series of low-slung medieval stone buildings with barrel-tile roofs are connected by cobbled paths and punctuated by cypress trees. **Pros:** set in a lovely park; cozy public rooms. **Cons:** long walk to nearest town; isolated location. [$] *Rooms from: €160* ✉ *Località Vescine, 5 km (3 miles) west of Radda in Chianti* ☎ *0577/741144* 🌐 *www.vescine.it* 🛏 *19 rooms, 7 suites* 🕒 *Closed Nov.–Apr., except at Christmas* 🍽 *Breakfast.*

$ B&B/INN 🏨 **La Bottega di Giovannino.** This is a fantastic place for the budget-conscious traveler, as rooms are immaculate and most have a stunning view of the surrounding hills. **Pros:** great location in the center of town; close to restaurants and shops; super value. **Cons:** some rooms are small; some bathrooms are down the hall; basic decor. [$] *Rooms from: €70* ✉ *Via Roma 6–8* ☎ *0577/738056* 🌐 *www.labottegadigiovannino.it* 🛏 *9 rooms, 1 apartment* 🍽 *No meals.*

$$$ B&B/INN 🏨 **La Locanda.** At an altitude of more than 1,800 feet, this converted farmhouse is probably the loftiest luxury inn in Chianti. **Pros:** idyllic setting; panoramic views; wonderful hosts. **Cons:** on a very rough gravel access road; isolated location; need a car to get around. [$] *Rooms from: €220* ✉ *Località Montanino di Volpaia, off Via della Volpaia, 13 km (8 miles) northwest of Radda* ☎ *0577/738833* 🌐 *www.lalocanda.it* 🛏 *6 rooms, 1 suite* 🕒 *Closed Nov.–Mar.* 🍽 *Breakfast.*

$$ HOTEL 🏨 **Palazzo San Niccolò.** The wood-beamed ceilings, terra-cotta floors, and some of the original frescoes of a 19th-century town palace remain, but the marble bathrooms have all been updated, some with Jacuzzi tubs. **Pros:** central location; friendly service. **Cons:** some rooms face a main street; room sizes vary. [$] *Rooms from: €140* ✉ *Via Roma 16*

Tuscany in its autumn gold

📠 *0577/735666* 🌐 *www.hotelsanniccolo.com* ⤴ *17 rooms, 1 suite* 🕙 *Closed Nov.–Mar.* 🍽️ *Breakfast.*

$$ 🏨 **Relais Fattoria Vignale.** A refined and comfortable country house offers
B&B/INN numerous sitting rooms with terra-cotta floors and attractive stonework
and wood-beamed guest rooms filled with simple wooden furnishings
and handwoven rugs. **Pros:** intimate public spaces; excellent restaurant;
helpful and friendly staff; nice grounds and pool. **Cons:** north-facing
rooms blocked by tall cypress trees; single rooms are small; annex across
a busy road. 💲 *Rooms from: €185* ✉️ *Via Pianigiani 9* 📠 *0577/738300
hotel, 0577/738094 restaurant* 🌐 *www.vignale.it* ⤴ *42 rooms, 5 suites*
🕙 *Closed Nov.–Mar. 15* 🍽️ *Breakfast.*

SHOPPING

Ceramiche Rampini. With a shop also in Florence, this kiln and painting
studio, 5 km (3 miles) south of Radda in Chianti, produces exquisite
(and expensive) hand-painted ceramic objects, including plates, bowls,
and candlesticks. The firm ships anywhere in the world and keeps its
customers' information on file. If you break a plate or want to buy more,
they'll know exactly what your pattern is. ✉️ *Casa Beretone, Località
Beretone di Vistarenni* 📠 *0577/738043* 🌐 *www.rampiniceramics.com.*

La Bottega delle Fantasie. Colorful pillows and carefully crafted linens
in sun-drenched Tuscan hues are the specialty of this centrally located
shop. ✉️ *Via Roma 47* 📠 *0577/738978.*

Tecno-Casa. Locals come here to buy their nuts, bolts, and small tools,
but visitors will also find a surprisingly varied assortment of traditional
Italian household items, including coffeemakers and cups, wine decant-
ers, and decorative bottle stoppers. ✉️ *Via Roma 20/22* 📠 *0577/738613.*

GAIOLE IN CHIANTI

9 km (5½ miles) southeast of Radda in Chianti, 69 km (43 miles) south of Florence.

A market town since 1200, Gaiole is now a central destination for touring southern Chianti. A stream runs through its center, and flowers adorn many of its window boxes. The surrounding area is dotted with castles perched on hilltops (the better to see the approaching enemy): they were of great strategic importance during the Renaissance, and still make dazzling lookout points.

GETTING HERE

To get here by car from the A1, take the Val d'Arno exit and follow signs for Gaiole on the SR408. Gaiole is relatively well connected to Siena by Tra-In buses, but cannot be reached by train.

EXPLORING

Badia a Coltibuono (*Abbey of the Good Harvest*). North of Gaiole a turn-off leads to this Romanesque abbey that has been owned by Lorenza de' Medici's family for more than a century and a half (the family isn't closely related to the Renaissance-era Medici). Wine has been produced here since the abbey was founded by Vallombrosan monks in the 11th century. Today the family continues the tradition, making Chianti Classico and other wines, along with cold-pressed olive oil and various flavored vinegars and floral honeys. A small church with campanile is surrounded by 2,000 acres of oak, fir, and chestnut woods threaded with walking paths—open to all—that pass two small lakes. Though the abbey itself, built between the 11th and 18th centuries, serves as the family's home, parts are open for tours (in English, German, or Italian). Visit the jasmine-draped main courtyard, the inner cloister with its antique well, the musty old aging cellars, and the Renaissance-style garden redolent of lavender, lemons, and roses. In the shop, **L'Osteria,** you can taste wine and honey, as well as pick up other items like homemade beeswax hand lotion in little ceramic dishes. The Badia is closed on public holidays. ✉ *Località Badia a Coltibuono, 4 km (2½ miles) north of Gaiole* ☎ *0577/74481 for tours, 0577/749479 for shop* ⊕ *www.coltibuono.com* ✆ *Abbey €5* ☉ *Tours: Apr.–Oct., daily at 2, 3, 4, and 5; shop: Mar.–mid-Jan., daily 9–1 and 2–7.*

Fodor's Choice ★   **Castello di Brolio.** If you have time for only one castle in Tuscany, this is it. At the end of the 12th century, when Florence conquered southern Chianti, Brolio became Florence's southernmost outpost, and it was often said, "When Brolio growls, all Siena trembles." Brolio was built about AD 1000 and owned by the monks of the Badia Fiorentina; the "new" owners, the Ricasoli family, have been in possession since 1141. Bettino Ricasoli (1809–80), the so-called Iron Baron, was one of the founders of modern Italy, and is said to have invented the original formula for Chianti wine. Brolio, one of Chianti's best-known labels, is still justifiably famous. Its cellars may be toured by appointment. The grounds are worth visiting, though the 19th-century manor house is not open to the public. A small museum, where the Ricasoli Collection is housed in a 12th-century tower, displays objects that relate the long history of the family and the origins of Chianti. Two apartments here are available for rent by the week. ⊠ *Località Brolio, 2 km (1 mile) southeast of Gaiole* ☎ *0577/730280* ⊕ *www.ricasoli. it* ⚏ *€5 gardens, €8 gardens and museum, €10 guided tours* ⊙ *Apr.– Oct., daily 10–7; ticket sales until 6.*

Castello di Meleto. It's a pretty drive up winding roads to this 13th-century fortress. Attached is an 18th-century villa; more importantly, there's a wineshop that serves locally produced wine. It's worth touring the castle to get a sense of

how 18th-century aristocrats lived; if that doesn't interest you, proceed directly to the enoteca for a tasting. Six apartments are available for rent. ⊠ *Località Meleto, 5 km (3 miles) south of Gaiole* ☎ *0577/749217 castle, 0577/749129 enoteca* ⊕ *www.castellomeleto.it* ⚏ *€10* ⊙ *Tours: Mon. 3 and 4:30; Tues.–Sat. 11:30, 3, and 4:30; Sun. 11:30, 4, and 5. Wineshop: mid-Mar–mid-Nov., daily 11:30–4:30.*

Vertine. Dating back to the 10th century, this walled town is oval in shape and has a tall watchtower guarding the entrance gate. A walk along the streets gives you a glimpse of life in a Tuscan hill town as it once was, and the views of the undulating countryside from the occasional opening in the walls are simply spectacular. ⊠ *Località Vertine, 2 km (1 mile) west of Gaiole.*

WHERE TO EAT

$$ ✕ **Badia a Coltibuono.** Outside the walls of Badia a Coltibuono is the
ITALIAN abbey's pleasant restaurant, with seating on a terrace or in rooms divided by ancient brick arches. The *pappardelle con sugo di cinghiale, uvetta, pinoli e fave di cacao* (pasta with braised wild boar sauce, raisins, pine nuts, and cocoa beans) is as delicious as it is unusual; the *costata di manzo nostrano* (locally raised T-bone steak) for two is particularly flavorful. It all pairs marvelously with the abbey's wines. $ *Average main: €20* ⊠ *Località Badia a Coltibuono, 4 km (2½ miles) north of Gaiole* ☎ *0577/749031* ⊕ *www.coltibuono.com* ⊙ *Closed Mon. and Nov.–Feb.*

$$ ✕ **La Grotta della Rana.** A perfect stop for lunch while exploring the
ITALIAN region's wineries, this trattoria offers *cucina casalinga* (home cooking) that can be eaten in the dining room or outdoor patio. (If you time dinner right, you might get to watch the sunset.) Outstanding primi include *maccheroni alla nonna* (macaroni with asparagus in cream sauce dotted with truffle oil). The *misto alla griglia* (mixed grilled meats) includes succulent pork. Also notable is the *filetto al pepe verde* (Chianina beef in a creamy green-peppercorn sauce). $ *Average main: €15* ⊠ *Località San Sano 8 km (5 miles) south of Gaiole* ☎ *0577/746020* ⊕ *www. lagrottadellarana.it* ⊙ *Closed Wed. and Feb.–mid-Mar.*

$ ✕ **Lo Sfizio di Bianchi.** A pleasant restaurant with outdoor seating on
ITALIAN Gaiole's main square, this spot is as popular with the locals as it is with travelers. The menu, presented on small blackboards, has unexpected

items like the plate of perfectly grilled vegetables, listed as an anti-pasto. The kitchen also makes delicious pastries and ice cream, so skipping dessert is difficult. Reservations are essential on weekends. $ *Average main: €10* ⊠ *Via Ricasoli 44/46* ☎ *0577/749501* ⊕ *www.losfiziodibianchi.it* ⊘ *Closed Wed.*

WHERE TO STAY
For expanded hotel reviews, visit Fodors.com.

$$
B&B/INN
Fodor's Choice
★

▭ **Borgo Argenina.** Elena Nappa, a former interior designer, is now the consummate hostess at this centuries-old villa. **Pros:** homemade buffet breakfasts; off-the-beaten-path feel. **Cons:** no pool; need a car to get around. $ *Rooms from: €170* ⊠ *Località Borgo Argenina, 15 km (9 miles) south of Gaiole* ☎ *0577/747117* ⊕ *www.borgoargenina.it* ⇦ *5 rooms, 2 suites, 3 houses* ⊘ *Closed mid-Nov.–mid-Mar.* ⑂ *Breakfast.*

$$$
B&B/INN
Fodor's Choice
★

▭ **Castello di Spaltenna.** This rustic yet elegant lodging includes a former convent (dating to the 1300s) and a Romanesque church. **Pros:** romantic setting; excellent restaurant; discreet and professional service. **Cons:** some rooms are reached via narrow stairways; some rooms look over the interior courtyard. $ *Rooms from: €230* ⊠ *Pieve di Spaltenna 13* ☎ *0577/749483* ⊕ *www.spaltenna.it* ⇦ *32 rooms, 5 suites, 2 apartments* ⊘ *Closed early Jan.–mid-Mar.* ⑂ *Breakfast.*

$
B&B/INN

▭ **Hotel Residence San Sano.** An open-hearth fireplace and hand-hewn stone porticoes hark back to the 13th century, when this was a fortress. **Pros:** good base for exploring Chianti; great family atmosphere; warm and friendly hosts. **Cons:** need a car to get around; furnishings, in true Tuscan style, are very plain. $ *Rooms from: €120* ⊠ *Località San Sano 21, 10 km (6 miles) south of Gaiole* ☎ *0577/746130* ⊕ *www.sansanohotel.it* ⇦ *16 rooms* ⊘ *Closed Jan.–Feb.* ⑂ *Breakfast.*

CASTELNUOVO BERARDENGA

20 km (12 miles) southeast of Gaiole in Chianti, 90 km (56 miles) southeast of Florence, 23 km (14 miles) east of Siena.

The southernmost village in Chianti has a compact center with hilly, curving streets. A plethora of piazzas invite wandering.

GETTING HERE
Castelnuovo is easily reached by car from Siena via the SS73. Tra-In buses run infrequently from Siena. Castelnuovo's train station, Castelnuovo Berardenga Scalo, is 8 km (5 miles) away.

VISITOR INFORMATION
Castelnuovo Berardenga tourism office ⊠ *Via Chianti 61* ☎ *0577/351337.*

EXPLORING
San Giusto e San Clemente. Built in the 1840s on a Greek-cross plan, this neoclassical church contains a Madonna and Child with angels by an anonymous 15th-century master. Also inside is the *Holy Family with St. Catherine of Siena*, attributed to Arcangelo Salimbeni (1530/40–79). ⊠ *Piazza Matteotti 4* ⊘ *Daily 7:30–7.*

San Gusmè. The oldest and most interesting of the hilltop medieval towns that surround Castelnuovo Berardenga, this village still retains its early 1400s layout, with arched passageways, gates topped with coats of arms, narrow squares, and steep streets. You can walk through the entire village in 20 minutes, but in those 20 minutes you may feel as if you have stepped back in time some 600 years. ✉ *SR484 5 km (3 miles) north of Castelnuovo Berardenga.*

Villa Chigi. Peek at the gardens of Villa Chigi, a 19th-century villa built on the site of a 14th-century castle (actually the "new castle" from which Castelnuovo got its name). The villa is closed to the public, but its manicured gardens are open on Sunday and holidays. ✉ *Via Berardenga 20* 🎫 *Free* 🕒 *Apr.–Sept., Sun. 10–8; Oct.–Mar., Sun. 10–5.*

WHERE TO STAY

For expanded hotel reviews, visit Fodors.com.

$$$$ B&B/INN 🏨 **Borgo San Felice.** Spread across five buildings, this elegant lodging used to be a small medieval town. **Pros:** beautiful buildings; romantic setting; heated pool. **Cons:** service is sometimes lax; need a car to get around. [$] *Rooms from: €400* ✉ *Località San Felice, 8 km (5 miles) northwest of Castelnuovo Berardenga* ☎ *0577/3964* 🌐 *www.borgosanfelice.com* 🛏 *28 rooms, 15 suites* 🕒 *Closed Nov.–Mar.* 🍴 *Breakfast.*

4

SIENA

With its narrow streets and steep alleys, a Gothic Duomo, a bounty of early Renaissance art, and the glorious Palazzo Pubblico overlooking its magnificent Campo, Siena is often described as Italy's best-preserved medieval city. It is also remarkably modern: many shops sell clothes by up-and-coming designers. Make a point of catching the *passeggiata* (evening stroll), when locals throng the Via di Città, Banchi di Sopra, and Banchi di Sotto, the city's three main streets.

Sienese mythology holds that the city shares common ancestry with Rome: the legendary founder, Senius, was said to be the son of Remus, the twin brother of Rome's founder, Romulus. The city emblem—a she-wolf and suckling twins—promulgates the claim. Archaeological evidence suggests there were prehistoric as well as Etruscan settlements here, which undoubtedly made way for Saena Julia, the Roman town established by Augustus in the 1st century BC.

Siena rose to prominence as an essential stop on that most important of medieval roads, the Via Francigena (or Via Romea), prospering from the yearly flow of thousands of Christian pilgrims coming south to Rome from northern Europe. Siena developed a banking system—one of Europe's oldest banks, the Monte dei Paschi, is still very much in business—and dominated the wool trade, thereby establishing itself as a rival to Florence. The two towns became regional powers and bitter enemies, each taking a different side in the struggle that divided the peninsula between the Guelphs (loyal to the Pope) and Ghibellines (loyal to the Holy Roman Emperor). Siena aligned itself with the latter.

Victory over Florence in 1260 at Montaperti marked the beginning of Siena's golden age. Even though Florentines avenged the loss nine years later, Siena continued to prosper. During the following decades Siena erected its greatest buildings (including the Duomo); established a model city government presided over by the Council of Nine; and

Siena's frenetic Palio

became a great art, textile, and trade center. All of these achievements came together in the decoration of the Sala della Pace in Palazzo Pubblico. It makes you wonder what greatness the city might have gone on to achieve had its fortunes been different, but in 1348 a plague decimated the population, brought an end to the Council of Nine, and left Siena economically vulnerable. Siena succumbed to Florentine rule in the mid-16th century, when a yearlong siege virtually eliminated the native population. Ironically, it was precisely this decline that, along with Sienese pride, prevented further development, to which we owe the city's marvelous medieval condition today.

But although much looks as it did in the early 14th century, Siena is no museum. Walk through the streets and you can see that the medieval *contrade,* 17 neighborhoods into which the city has been historically divided, are a vibrant part of modern life. You may see symbols of the *contrada*—Tartuca (turtle), Oca (goose), Istrice (porcupine), Torre (tower)—emblazoned on banners and engraved on building walls. The Sienese still strongly identify themselves by the contrada where they were born and raised; loyalty and rivalry run deep. At no time is this more visible than during the centuries-old Palio, a twice-yearly horse race held in the Piazza del Campo, but you need not visit then to come to know the rich culture of Siena, evident at every step.

GETTING HERE
From Florence, the quickest way to Siena is via the Florence–Siena Superstrada. Otherwise, take the Via Cassia (SR2), for a scenic route. Coming from Rome, leave the A1 at Valdichiana, and follow the Siena–Bettole Superstrada. SITA provides excellent bus service between

Florence and Siena. Because buses are direct and speedy, they are preferable to the train, which sometimes involves a change in Empoli.

VISITOR INFORMATION

Siena Tourism Office ✉ *Piazza del Campo 56* ☎ *0577/280551* ⊕ *www. terresiena.it.*

EXPLORING SIENA

If you come by car, you're better off leaving it in one of the parking lots around the perimeter of town. Driving is difficult or impossible in most parts of the city center. Practically unchanged since medieval times, Siena is laid out in a "Y" over the slopes of several hills, dividing the city into *terzi* (thirds). Although the most interesting sites are in a fairly compact area around the Campo at the center of town, be sure to leave some time to wander into the narrow streets that rise and fall steeply from the main thoroughfares, giving yourself at least two days to explore the town. At the top on the list of things to see is the Piazza del Campo, considered by many to be the finest public square in Italy. The Palazzo Pubblico at the lower end of the square is worth a visit. The Duomo is a must-see, as is the nearby Cripta.

Tra-In. City buses run frequently within and around Siena, including the centro storico. Tickets cost €1.30 and should be bought in advance at tobacconists or newsstands. Routes are marked with signposts. ☎ *0577/204111* ⊕ *www.trainspa.it.*

TIMING It's a joy to walk in Siena—hills notwithstanding—as it's a rare opportunity to stroll through a medieval city rather than just a town. (There is quite a lot to explore, in contrast to tiny hill towns that can be crossed in minutes.) The walk can be done in as little as a day, with minimal stops at the sights. But stay longer and take time to tour the church building and museums, and to enjoy the streetscapes themselves. Several of the sites have reduced hours Sunday afternoon and Monday.

TOP ATTRACTIONS

Fodor'sChoice **Cripta.** After it had lain unseen for possibly 700 years, a crypt was redis-
★ covered under the grand *pavimento* (floor) of the Duomo during routine excavation work and was opened to the public in 2003. An unknown master executed the breathtaking frescoes here sometime between 1270 and 1280; they retain their original colors and pack an emotional punch even with sporadic damage. The *Deposition/Lamentation* gives strong evidence that the Sienese school could paint emotion just as well as the Florentine school—and did it some 20 years before Giotto. Guided tours in English take place more or less every half hour and are limited to no more than 35 persons. ✉ *Piazza del Duomo, entrance on the right side of the cathedral, Città* ☎ *0577/286300* ⊕ *www.operaduomo. siena.it* 🎟 *€6; €12 combined ticket includes the Duomo, Battistero, and Museo dell'Opera Metropolitana* ☉ *Mar.–Oct., daily 10:30–7; Nov.– Feb., daily 10:30–5:30.*

Fodor'sChoice **Duomo.** Siena's cathedral is beyond question one of the finest Gothic
★ churches in Italy. The multicolored marbles and painted decoration are typical of the Italian approach to Gothic architecture—lighter and

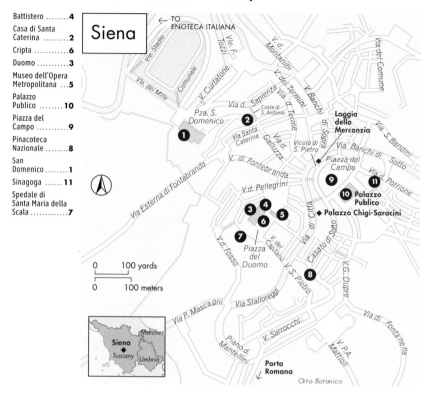

much less austere than the French. The amazingly detailed facade has few rivals in the region, although it's quite similar to the Duomo in Orvieto. It was completed in two brief phases at the end of the 13th and 14th centuries. The statues and decorative work were designed by Nicola Pisano and his son Giovanni, although most of what we see today are copies, the originals having been removed to the nearby Museo dell'Opera Metropolitana. The gold mosaics are 18th-century restorations. The Campanile (no entry) is among central Italy's finest, the number of windows increasing with each level, a beautiful and ingenious way of reducing the weight of the structure as it climbs to the heavens.

The Duomo's interior, with its black-and-white striping throughout and finely coffered and gilded dome, is simply striking. Step in and look back up at Duccio's (circa 1255–1319) panels of stained glass that fill the circular window. Finished in 1288, it's the oldest example of stained glass in Italy. The Duomo is most famous for its unique and magnificent inlaid-marble floors, which took almost 200 years to complete; more than 40 artists contributed to the work, made up of 56 separate compositions depicting biblical scenes, allegories, religious symbols, and civic emblems. The floors are covered for most of the year for conservation purposes, but are unveiled during September and October. The

Duomo's carousel pulpit, also much appreciated, was carved by Nicola Pisano (circa 1220–84) around 1265; the *Life of Christ* is depicted on the rostrum frieze. In striking contrast to all the Gothic decoration in the nave are the magnificent Renaissance frescoes in the **Biblioteca Piccolomini,** off the left aisle. Painted by Pinturicchio (circa 1454–1513) and completed in 1509, they depict events from the life of native son Aeneas Sylvius Piccolomini (1405–64), who became Pope Pius II in 1458. The frescoes are in excellent condition, and have a freshness rarely seen in work so old.

The Duomo is grand, but the medieval Sienese people had even bigger plans. They wanted to enlarge the building by using the existing church as a transept for a new church, with a new nave running toward the southeast, to make what would be the largest church in the world. But only the side wall and part of the new facade were completed when the Black Death struck in 1348, decimating Siena's population. The city fell into decline, funds dried up, and the plans were never carried out. (The dream of building the biggest church was actually doomed to failure from the start—subsequent attempts to get the project going revealed that the foundation was insufficient to bear the weight of the proposed structure.) The beginnings of the new nave, extending from the right side of the Duomo, were left unfinished, perhaps as a testament to unfulfilled dreams, and ultimately enclosed to house the adjacent **Museo dell'Opera Metropolitana.** The **Cripta** was discovered during routine preservation work on the church and has been opened to the public. ✉ *Piazza del Duomo, Città* ☎ *0577/286300* ⊠ *€4 Nov.–Aug.; €7 Sept. and Oct.; €12 combined ticket includes the Cripta, Battistero, and Museo dell'Opera Metropolitana* ☉ *Mar.–Oct., Mon.–Sat. 10:30–7, Sun. 1:30–6; Nov.–Feb., Mon.–Sat. 10:30–5:30, Sun. 1:30–5:30.*

Fodor'sChoice ★ **Museo dell'Opera Metropolitana.** Part of the unfinished nave of what was to have been a new cathedral, the museum contains the Duomo's treasury and some of the original decoration from its facade and interior. The first room on the ground floor displays weather-beaten 13th-century sculptures by Giovanni Pisano (circa 1245–1318) that were brought inside for protection and replaced by copies, as was a tondo of the *Madonna and Child* (now attributed to Donatello) that once hung on the door to the south transept. The masterpiece is unquestionably Duccio's *Maestà,* one side with 26 panels depicting episodes from the Passion, the other side with a *Madonna and Child Enthroned.* Painted between 1308 and 1311 as the altarpiece for the Duomo (where it remained until 1505), its realistic elements, such as the lively depiction of the Christ child and the treatment of interior space, proved an enormous influence on later painters. The second floor is divided between the treasury, with a crucifix by Giovanni Pisano and several statues and busts of biblical characters and classical philosophers, and La Sala della Madonna degli Occhi Grossi (the Room of the Madonna with the Big Eyes), named after the namesake painting it displays by the Maestro di Tressa, who painted in the early 13th century. The work originally decorated the Duomo's high altar, before being displaced by Duccio's *Maestà.* There is a fine view from the tower inside the museum. ✉ *Piazza del Duomo 8, Città* ☎ *0577/286300* ⊕ *www.operaduomo.siena.it*

Continued on page 224

Climbing the 400 narrow steps of the **Torre del Mangia** rewards you with unparalleled views of Siena's rooftops and the countryside beyond.

The **Palazzo Pubblico**, Siena's town hall since the 14th century.

Something about the fan-shaped, sloping design of **Il Campo** encourages people to sit and relax (except during the Palio, when they stand and scream). The communal atmosphere here is unlike that of any other Italian piazza.

PIAZZA DEL CAMPO

9 The fan-shaped **Piazza del Campo,** known simply as il Campo (The Field), is one of the finest squares in Italy. Constructed toward the end of the 12th century on a market area unclaimed by any contrada, it's still the heart of town. The bricks of the Campo are patterned in nine different sections—representing each member of the medieval Government of Nine. At the top of the Campo is a copy of the **Fonte Gaia,** decorated in the early 15th century by Siena's greatest sculptor, Jacopo della Quercia, with 13 sculpted reliefs of biblical events and virtues. Those lining the rectangular fountain are 19th-century copies; the originals are in the Spedale di Santa Maria della Scala. On Palio horse race days (July 2 and August 16), the Campo and all its surrounding buildings are packed with cheering, frenzied locals and tourists craning their necks to take it all in.

Fodor'sChoice ★

10 The Gothic **Palazzo Pubblico,** the focal point of the Piazza del Campo, has served as Siena's town hall since the 1300s. It now also contains the **Museo Civico,** with walls covered in early Renaissance frescoes. The nine governors of Siena once met in the Sala della Pace, famous for Ambrogio Lorenzetti's frescoes called *Allegories of Good and Bad Government,* painted in the late 1330s to demonstrate the dangers of tyranny. The good government side depicts utopia, showing first the virtuous ruling council surrounded by angels and then scenes of a perfectly running city and countryside. Conversely, the bad government fresco tells a tale straight out of Dante. The evil ruler and his advisers have horns and fondle strange animals, and the town scene depicts the seven mortal sins in action. Interestingly, the bad government fresco is severely damaged, and the good government fresco is in terrific condition. The **Torre del Mangia,** the palazzo's famous bell tower, is named after one of its first bell ringers, Giovanni di Duccio (called Mangiaguadagni, or earnings eater). The climb up to the top is long and steep, but the view makes it worth every step. ⊠ *Piazza del Campo 1, Città* ☎ *0577/41169* 🎫 *Museo €7, Torre €6, combined ticket €10* ⊗ *Museo Nov.–Mar. 15, daily 10–6:30; Mar. 16–Oct., daily 10–7. Torre Nov.–Mar. 15, daily 10–4; Mar. 16–Oct., daily 10–7.*

THE PALIO

The three laps around a makeshift racetrack in Piazza del Campo are over in less than two minutes, but the spirit of Siena's Palio— a horse race held every July 2 and August 16—lives all year long.

The Palio is contested between Siena's contrade, the 17 neighborhoods that have divided the city since the Middle Ages. Loyalties are fiercely felt. At any time of year you'll see on the streets contrada symbols—Tartuca (turtle), Oca (goose), Istrice (porcupine), Torre (tower)—emblazoned on banners and engraved on building walls. At Palio time, simmering rivalries come to a boil.

It's been that way since at least August 16, 1310, the date of the first recorded running of the Palio. At that time, and for centuries to follow, the race went through the streets of the city. The additional July 2 running was instituted in 1649; soon thereafter the location was moved to the Campo and the current system for selecting the race entrants established. Ten of the contrade are chosen at random to run in the July Palio. The August race is then contested between the 7 contrade left out in July, plus 3 of the 10 July participants, again chosen at random. Although the races are in theory of equal importance, Sienese will tell you that it's better to win the second and have bragging rights for the rest of the year.

The race itself has a raw and arbitrary character—it's no Kentucky Derby. There's barely room for the 10 horses on the makeshift Campo course, so falls and collisions are inevitable. Horses are chosen at random three days before the race, and jockeys (who ride bareback) are mercenaries hired from surrounding towns. Almost no tactic is considered too underhanded. Bribery, secret plots, and betrayal are commonplace—so much so that the word for "jockey," *fantino,* has come to mean "untrustworthy" in Siena. There have been incidents of drugging (the horses) and kidnapping (the jockeys); only sabotaging a horse's reins remains taboo.

Above: The tension of the starting line. Top left: The frenzy of the race. Bottom left: A solemn flag bearer follows in the footsteps of his ancestors.

AQUILA	BRUCO	CHIOCCIOLA

17 MEDIEVAL CONTRADE

Festivities kick off three days prior to the Palio, with the selection and blessing of the horses, trial runs, ceremonial banquets, betting, and late-night celebrations. Residents don their contrada's colors and march through the streets in medieval costumes. The Campo is transformed into a racetrack lined with a thick layer of sand. On race day, each horse is brought to the church of the contrada for which it will run, where it's blessed and told, "Go little horse and return a winner." The Campo fills through the afternoon, with spectators crowding into every available space until bells ring and the piazza is sealed off. Processions of flag wavers in traditional dress march to the beat of tambourines and drums and the roar of the crowds. The *palio* itself—a banner for which the race is named, dedicated to the Virgin Mary—makes an appearance, followed by the horses and their jockeys.

The race begins when one horse, chosen to ride up from behind the rest of the field, crosses the starting line. There are always false starts, adding to the frenzied mood. Once underway, the race is over in a matter of minutes. The victorious rider is carried off through the streets of the winning contrada (where in the past tradition dictated he was entitled to the local girl of his choice), while winning and losing sides use television replay to analyze the race from every possible angle. The winning contrada will celebrate into the night, at long tables piled high with food and drink. The champion horse is guest of honor.

Reserved seating in the stands is sold out months in advance of the races; contact the Siena Tourist Office (✉ Piazza del Campo 56 ☎ 0577/280551) to find out about availability, and ask your hotel if it can procure you a seat. The entire area in the center is free and unreserved, but you need to show up early in order to get a prime spot against the barriers.

CIVETTA	DRAGO
GIRAFFA	ISTRICE
LEOCORNO	LUPA
NICCHIO	OCA
ONDA	PANTERA
SELVA	TARTUCA
TORRE	VALDIMONTONE

4

IN FOCUS PIAZZA DEL CAMPO

🖼 *€7; €12 combined ticket includes the Duomo, Cripta, and Battistero* ⏱ *Mar.–Oct., daily 10:30–7; Nov.–Feb., daily 10:30–5:30.*

Pinacoteca Nazionale. The superb collection of five centuries of local painting in Siena's national picture gallery can easily convince you that the Renaissance was by no means just a Florentine thing—Siena was arguably just as important a center of art and innovation as its rival to the north, especially in the mid-13th century. Accordingly, the most interesting section of the collection, chronologically arranged, has several important "firsts." Room 1 contains a painting of the *Stories of the True Cross* (1215) by the so-called Master of Tressa, the earliest identified work by a painter of the Sienese school, and is followed in Room 2 by late-13th-century artist Guido da Siena's *Stories from the Life of Christ,* one of the first paintings ever made on canvas (earlier painters used wood panels). Rooms 3 and 4 are dedicated to Duccio, a student of Cimabue (circa 1240–1302) and considered to be the last of the proto-Renaissance painters. Ambrogio Lorenzetti's landscapes in Room 8 are the first truly secular paintings in Western art. Among later works in the rooms on the floor above, keep an eye out for the preparatory sketches used by Domenico Beccafumi (1486–1551) for the 35 etched marble panels he made for the floor of the Duomo. ✉ *Via San Pietro 29, Città* ☎ *0577/286143* ⊕ *www.pinacotecanazionale.siena. it* 🖼 *€4* ⏱ *Tues.–Sat. 8:15–7:15; Sun. and Mon. 9–1; last entrance ½ hr before closing.*

Fodor'sChoice   **Spedale di Santa Maria della Scala.** For more than a thousand years, this
★   complex across from the Duomo was home to Siena's hospital, but now it serves as a museum to display some terrific frescoes and other Sienese Renaissance treasures. Restored 15th-century frescoes in the Sala del Pellegrinaio (once the emergency room) tell the history of the hospital, which was created to give refuge to passing pilgrims and to those in need, and to distribute charity to the poor. Incorporated into the complex is the church of the Santissima Annunziata, with a celebrated *Risen Christ* by Vecchietta (also known as Lorenzo di Pietro, circa 1412–80). Down in the dark Cappella di Santa Caterina della Notte is where Saint Catherine went to pray at night. The subterranean archaeological museum contained within the *ospedale* (hospital) is worth seeing even if you're not particularly taken with Etruscan objects: the interior design is sheer brilliance—it's beautifully lighted, eerily quiet, and an oasis of cool on hot summer days. The displays—including the *bucchero* (dark, reddish clay) ceramics, Roman coins, and tomb furnishings— are clearly marked and can serve as a good introduction to the history of regional excavations. Don't miss della Quercia's original sculpted reliefs from the Fonte Gaia. Although the fountain has been faithfully copied for the Campo, there's something incomparably beautiful about the real thing. ✉ *Piazza del Duomo 1, Città* ☎ *0577/534571* ⊕ *www. santamariadellascala.com* 🖼 *€6* ⏱ *Mid-Mar.–mid-Oct., daily 10:30– 6:30; mid-Oct.–mid-Mar., daily 10:30–4:30; ticket office closes 1 hr before closing.*

WORTH NOTING

Battistero. The Duomo's 14th-century Gothic Baptistery was built to prop up the apse of the cathedral. There are frescoes throughout, but the highlight is a large bronze 15th-century baptismal font designed by Jacopo della Quercia (1374–1438). It's adorned with bas-reliefs by various artists, including two by Renaissance masters: the *Baptism of Christ* by Lorenzo Ghiberti (1378–1455) and the *Feast of Herod* by Donatello. ⊠ *Piazza San Giovanni* ☎ *0577/286300* ⊕ *www. operaduomo.siena.it* 🖅 *€4; €12 combined ticket includes the Duomo, Cripta, and Museo dell'Opera del Duomo* ⊙ *Mar.–Oct., daily 10:30–7; Nov.–Feb., daily 10:30–5:30.*

Casa di Santa Caterina. Caterina Benincasa was born here in 1347, and although she took the veil of the Dominican Tertiary order at age eight, she remained here, devoting her life to the sick and poor in the aftermath of the devastating plague of 1348. She had divine visions and received the stigmata, but is most famous for her words and her argumentative skills. Her letters—many of which are preserved in the Biblioteca Comunale—were dictated because she did not know how to write. She is credited with convincing Pope Gregory XI (1329–78) to return the papacy to Rome after 70 years in Avignon and French domination, ending the Western Schism. Caterina died in Rome in 1380 and was canonized in 1461. A few years later the city purchased the family house and turned it into a shrine, one of the first examples of its kind in Italy. The rooms of the house, including her cell and the kitchen, were converted into a series of chapels and oratories and decorated by noteworthy artists over the following centuries with scenes from Caterina's life. In 1939 she was made a patron saint of Italy, along with Saint Francis of Assisi. In 1970 she was elevated to Doctor of the Church, the highest possible honor in Christendom. She has been named a patron saint of Europe but, strangely enough, never of her hometown. ⊠ *Costa di Sant'Antonio 6, Camollia* ☎ *0577/288175* 🖅 *Free* ⊙ *Daily 9:30–7.*

San Domenico. Although the Duomo is celebrated as a triumph of 13th-century Gothic architecture, this church, built at about the same time, turned out to be an oversize, hulking brick box that never merited a finishing coat in marble, let alone a graceful facade. Named for the founder of the Dominican order, the church is now more closely associated with Saint Caterina of Siena. Just to the right of the entrance is the chapel in which she received the stigmata. On the wall is the only known contemporary portrait of the saint, made in the late 14th century by Andrea Vanni (circa 1332–1414). Farther down is the famous **Cappella di Santa Caterina,** the church's official shrine. Caterina, or bits and pieces of her, was literally spread all over the country—a foot is in Venice, most of her body is in Rome, and only her head (kept in a reliquary on the chapel's altar) and her right thumb are here. She was revered throughout the country long before she was officially named a patron saint of Italy in 1939. On either side of the chapel are well-known frescoes by Sodoma (aka Giovanni Antonio Bazzi, 1477–1549) of *St. Catherine in Ecstasy*. Don't miss the view of the Duomo and town center from the apse-side terrace. ⊠ *Piazza San Domenico, Camollìa* 📷 *0577/280893* ⊕ *www.basilicacateriniana.com* ⊙ *Mar.–Oct., daily 7–6:30; Nov.–Feb., daily 9–6.*

Sinagoga. Down a small street around the corner from Il Campo, this synagogue is worth a visit simply to view the two sobering plaques that adorn its facade. One commemorates June 28, 1799, when 13 Jews were taken from their homes by a fanatic mob and burned in the square. The other memorializes the Sienese Jews who were deported during World War II. Guided tours in English are available by arrangement. ⊠ *Vicolo delle Scotte 14, San Martino* 📷 *0577/271345* 🎫 *€4* ⊙ *Weekdays 10:30–3 and Sun. 10:30–5:30.*

WHERE TO EAT

$

ITALIAN

✕ **Hosteria il Carroccio.** Angle for one of the few seats here to have an intimate meal and to try dishes both creative and deliciously simple. The *palline di pecorino con lardo e salsa di pere* (pecorino cheese balls wrapped with pork fat and briefly grilled), for instance, are sublime. So, too, are the amply portioned primi—the *pici* (a local pasta specialty resembling a thick spaghetti) is especially good. Sit at tables outside in summer. $ *Average main: €12* ⊠ *Via Casato di Sotto 32, Città* 📷 *0577/41165* ⊙ *Closed Wed., 2 wks in Jan., and 2 wks in July.*

$$$

TUSCAN

Fodor's Choice

★

✕ **Le Logge.** Bright flowers provide a dash of color at this classic Tuscan dining room, and stenciled designs on the ceilings add some whimsy. The wooden cupboards (now filled with wine bottles) lining the walls recall its past as a turn-of-the-19th-century grocery store. The menu, with four or five primi and secondi, changes regularly, but almost always includes their classic *malfatti all'osteria* (ricotta and spinach dumplings in a cream sauce). Desserts such as *coni con mousse al cioccolato e gelato allo zafferano* (two diminutive ice-cream cones with chocolate mousse and saffron ice cream) provide an inventive ending to the meal. When not vying for one of the outdoor tables, make sure to ask for one in the main downstairs room. $ *Average main: €25* ⊠ *Via del Porrione 33, San Martino* 📷 *0577/48013* ⊕ *www.osterialelogge.it* ⚏ *Reservations essential* ⊙ *Closed Sun. and 3 wks in Jan.*

$

TUSCAN

✕ **Osteria Castelvecchio.** On the daily menu you're likely to find both Sienese standards, such as spaghetti *saporiti con gli aromi* (with tomatoes and herbs), as well as more offbeat selections like *bocconcini di pollo alla mediterranea* (tender chicken cooked in a robust tomato-and-olive sauce). Husband-and-wife team Simone Romi and Sabrina Fabi are committed to including *piatti di verdura* (vegetarian dishes) among the choices, and they've put together a great wine list. A tasting menu allows you to sample just about all the daily specials. The little restaurant with high vaulted ceilings is in the oldest part of town. $ *Average main: €14* ⊠ *Via Castelvecchio 65, Città* 📷 *0577/49586* ⊙ *Closed Tues.*

$

TUSCAN

✕ **Osteria Il Grattacielo.** Wiped out from too much sightseeing? Consider a meal at this hole-in-the-wall restaurant where locals congregate for

Ricciarelli, delicate almond cookies native to Siena

a simple lunch over a glass of wine. There's a collection of *verdure sott'olio* (marinated vegetables), a wide selection of *affettati misti* (cured meats), and various types of frittatas. All off this can be washed down with the cheap, yet eminently drinkable, house red. A couple of bench tables provide outdoor seating in summer. Don't be put off by the absence of a written menu. All the food is displayed at the counter, so you can point if you need to. $ *Average main: €10* ✉ *Via Pontani 8, Camollia* ☎ *0577/289326* 📖 *Reservations not accepted* 🚫 *No credit cards* 🕙 *Closed Sun.*

$ ✕ **Trattoria Papei.** The menu hasn't changed for years, and why should it?
TUSCAN The *pici al cardinale* (handmade spaghetti with a duck and bacon sauce) is wonderful, and all the other typically Sienese dishes are equally delicious. Grilled meats are the true speciality; the *bistecca di vitello* (grilled veal steak) is melt-in-your-mouth wonderful. Tucked away behind the Palazzo Pubblico in a square that serves as a parking lot for most of the day, the restaurant's location isn't great, but the food is. Thanks to portable heaters, there is outdoor seating all year-round. $ *Average main: €14* ✉ *Piazza del Mercato 6, Città* ☎ *0577/280894* 🕙 *Closed Mon.*

WHERE TO STAY

For expanded hotel reviews, visit Fodors.com.

$$ 🛏 **Antica Torre.** The cordial Landolfo family has carefully evoked a pri-
B&B/INN vate home with their eight guest rooms inside a restored 16th-century tower. **Pros:** near the town center; charming atmosphere. **Cons:** narrow stairway up to the rooms; low ceilings; cramped bathrooms. $ *Rooms*

from: €125 ✉ *Via Fieravecchia 7, San Martino* ☎ *0577/222255* ⊕ *www.anticatorresiena.it* 🛏 *8 rooms* ⦿*Breakfast.*

$$$$
B&B/INN
🛏 **Certosa di Maggiano.** A 14th-century monastery has been converted into this upscale country hotel. **Pros:** elegant service; luxurious rooms. **Cons:** some find the atmosphere too formal; located outside of town. ⓢ *Rooms from: €370* ✉ *Siena Sud exit off Superstrada, Strada di Certosa 82, ½ km (¼ mile) east of Siena* ☎ *0577/288180* ⊕ *www.certosadimaggiano.com* 🛏 *9 rooms, 8 suites* ⦿*Some meals.*

$$
B&B/INN
🛏 **Chiusarelli.** Caryatids stud the grounds of this well-kept neoclassical villa; a small garden invites reading. **Pros:** near the main bus terminal; spacious rooms; quiet garden. **Cons:** on a busy street; bland furnishings. ⓢ *Rooms from: €150* ✉ *Viale Curtatone 15, Camollìa* ☎ *0577/280562* ⊕ *www.chiusarelli.com* 🛏 *48 rooms, 1 suite* ⦿*Breakfast.*

$$$$
HOTEL
🛏 **Grand Hotel Continental.** Pope Alexander VII of the famed Sienese Chigi family gave this palace to his niece as a wedding present in 1600; through the centuries it has been a private family home as well as a grand hotel. **Pros:** luxurious accommodations; great location on the main drag; first-rate concierge. **Cons:** sometimes stuffy atmosphere; rooms show signs of wear. ⓢ *Rooms from: €540* ✉ *Banchi di Sopra 85, Camollìa* ☎ *0577/56011* ⊕ *www.royaldemeure.com* 🛏 *40 rooms, 11 suites* ⦿*Breakfast.*

$$
B&B/INN
🛏 **Hotel Santa Caterina.** Manager Lorenza Capannelli and her fine staff are welcoming, hospitable, enthusiastic, and go out of their way to ensure a fine stay in rooms where dark, straight-lined wood furniture stands next to beds with floral spreads. **Pros:** friendly staff; a short walk to center of town; breakfast in the garden. **Cons:** on a busy intersection; outside city walls. ⓢ *Rooms from: €185* ✉ *Via Piccolomini 7, San Martino* ☎ *0577/221105* ⊕ *www.hscsiena.it* 🛏 *22 rooms* ⦿*Breakfast.*

$$
HOTEL
Fodor's Choice
★
🛏 **Palazzo Ravizza.** This romantic palazzo exudes a sense of genteel shabbiness, and lovely guest rooms have high ceilings, antique furnishings, and bathrooms decorated with hand-painted tiles. **Pros:** 10-minute walk to the center of town; pleasant garden with a view beyond the city walls; professional staff. **Cons:** not all rooms have views; some rooms are a little cramped. ⓢ *Rooms from: €180* ✉ *Pian dei Mantellini 34, Città* ☎ *0577/280462* 🖷 *0577/221597* ⊕ *www.palazzoravizza.it* 🛏 *38 rooms, 4 suites* ⦿*Breakfast.*

NIGHTLIFE AND THE ARTS

THE ARTS

Estate Musicale Chigiana. Master classes and workshops held by internationally famous musicians result in top-notch performances in Siena between July and September. Age-old venues such as the Accademia Musicale Chigiana, the Spedale di Santa Maria della Scala, the church of Sant'Agostino, and Piazza Duomo are used for these exceptional concerts. It is best to book well in advance as tickets are usually in high demand. ✉ *Accademia Musicale Chigiana, Via di Città 89, Città* ☎ *0577/22091* ⊕ *www.chigiana.it.*

Settimane Musicali Senesi festival. Performances by local and national classical musicians take place during a series of concerts held in churches and courtyards during the Settimane Musicali Senesi festival in mid-July. ⊕ *www.chigiana.it.*

NIGHTLIFE

Caffè del Corso. Join the locals for *aperitivi* (apertifs) at this very popular bar, where aspiring artists and savvy students hobnob until 3 am. ⊠ *Banchi di Sopra 25, Camollìa* ☎ *0577/226656.*

Sapordivino. This wine bar at the Grand Hotel Continental has live piano music most evenings. A well-stocked liquor collection includes a well-thought-out list of whiskeys. ⊠ *Banchi di Sopra 85, Città* ☎ *0577/56011.*

SPORTS AND THE OUTDOORS

4

Fodor's Choice ★ **Palio.** Siena's thrilling horse race takes place every year on July 2 and August 16. Three laps around the track in the Piazza del Campo earn the victor the *palio* (a hand-painted banner, unique to each event), and the respect or scorn of the remaining 16 contrade. Tickets usually sell out months in advance; call the Siena tourist office for more information. Note that some hotels reserve a number of tickets for guests. It's also possible you might luck out and get an unclaimed seat or two. The standing-room center of the piazza is free to all on a first-come, first-served basis, until just moments before the start. If you opt for this option, beware of the summer heat, and take water with you. The entry of the horses into the starting gate can sometimes be a lengthy process—they are easily spooked and it can take up to several hours to get things ready—all-in-all, you might be better off finding a comfortable seat in front of a TV. ⊠ *Siena tourist office, Piazza del Campo 56, Città* ☎ *0577/280551.*

SHOPPING

Siena is known for a delectable variety of cakes and cookies with recipes dating to medieval times. Some Sienese sweets are *cavallucci* (sweet spice biscuits), *panforte* (a traditional Christmas delicacy, literally "strong bread," with honey, hazelnuts, almonds, and spices), *ricciarelli* (almond-paste cookies), and *castagnaccio* (a baked Tuscan flat cake made in fall and winter from a batter of chestnut flour topped with pine nuts and rosemary).

ARTS AND CRAFTS

Antiche Dimore. Embroidered linens, curtains, and sheets made by Sienese artisans are among the housewares sold at this store run by Debora Loreni. ⊠ *Via di Città 115, Città* ☎ *0577/45337.*

Bottega dell'Arte. If you've always wanted a 14th- or 15th-century painting to hang on your wall, but the cost of acquiring one is prohibitive, consider purchasing one of the superb copies at this shop made by Chiara or her brother Michelangelo Casoni. Their work in tempera and in gold leaf is of the highest quality. ⊠ *Via Stalloreggi 47, Città* ☎ *0577/40755* ⊕ *www.arteinsiena.it.*

Fioretta Bacci. Wool, mohair, silk, linen, and cotton are woven on-site, and turned into sweaters and jackets in the colors of the rainbow. ⊠ *Via San Pietro 7, Città* ☎ *0577/282200* ⊕ *www.fiorettabacci.it.*

Siena Ricama. Siena has been famous for centuries for its fine embroidery work, and Bruna Brizza continues the tradition in her tiny shop. Hand stitching, usually on simple white and cream-color linen, adorns lamp shades, tablecloths, and other housewares. ⊠ *Via di Città 61, Città* ☎ *0577/288339.*

Vetrate Artistiche Toscane. Stained-glass artists create and sell contemporary secular and religious works here. If you want to learn the technique, they also offer workshops and apprenticeship programs. ⊠ *Via della Galluzza 5, Camollìa* ☎ *0577/48033* ⊕ *www.glassisland.com.*

FOOD AND DRINK

Antico Pizzicheria. There has been a *salumeria* (delicatessen) here since 1889. The cheeses, cured meats, and made-to-order panini are top-notch. ⊠ *Via di Città 93–95, Città* ☎ *0577/289164.*

Enoteca Italiana. Italy's only state-sponsored enoteca has a vast selection of wines from all parts of the country. Housed in the fortress that the Florentines built to dominate Siena after they conquered the town in 1555, it's a must for any lover of Italian wines. ⊠ *Fortezza Medicea 1, Camollìa* ☎ *0577/228832* ◷ *Mon.–Sat., noon–1 am.*

La Bottega dei Sapori Antichi. Bruno De Miccoli stocks an impressive array of verdure sott'olio, local wines, and dried herbs in his food and wine bar. ⊠ *Via delle Terme 39–41, Camollìa* ☎ *0577/285501.*

Nannini. Locals flock to this central cafè to quaff a cappuccino and pick up panforte (the chocolate panforte is a real treat) and ricciarelli to go. ⊠ *Banchi di Sopra 24, Camollìa* ☎ *0577/236009.*

MONTERIGGIONI AND COLLE DI VAL D'ELSA

From Siena the Via Cassia (SR2) heading north passes through two pretty towns, Monteriggioni and Colle di Val d'Elsa. Both are well worth visiting: Monteriggioni, for its spectacularly well-preserved ring of medieval walls, and Colle di Val d'Elsa, for the elegance of its 15th-century upper town.

MONTERIGGIONI

19 km (12 miles) northwest of Siena, 55 km (34 miles) south of Florence.

Tiny Monteriggioni makes a nice stop on the way north to Colle di Val d'Elsa, San Gimignano, or Volterra. It's hard to imagine that this little town surrounded by poppy fields was ever anything but sleepy, but in the 13th century Monteriggioni served as Siena's northernmost defense against impending Florentine invasion. (It's likely that the residents of the town spent many a sleepless night.) The town's formidable walls are in good condition, although the 14 square towers are not as tall as in Dante's (1265–1321) time, when the poet likened them to giants guarding the horrifying central pit of hell. The town empties of day-trippers at sundown, and this hamlet becomes very tranquil.

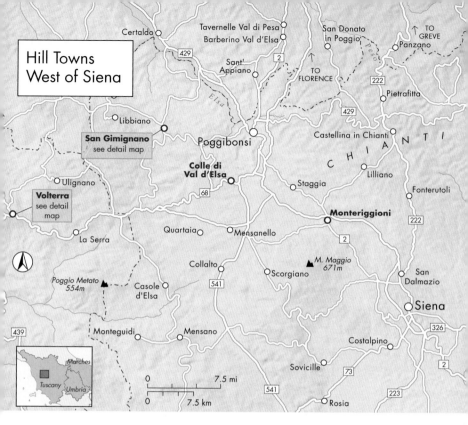

Hill Towns
West of Siena

Certaldo • Tavernelle Val di Pesa • San Donato in Poggio → TO GREVE

Barberino Val d'Elsa • Panzano

Sant' Appiano • TO FLORENCE

Pietrafitta •

Libbiano •

San Gimignano see detail map

Poggibonsi

Castellina in Chianti •

C H I A N T I

Ulignano •

Colle di Val d'Elsa

Staggia •

Lilliano •

Fonterutoli •

Volterra see detail map

La Serra •

Quartaia •

Mensanello •

Monteriggioni

Collalto •

Scorgiano •

M. Maggio 671m ▲

San Dalmazio •

Poggio Metato 554m ▲

Casole d'Elsa •

Siena

Monteguidi •

Mensano •

Costalpino •

Marches

Tuscany Umbria

0 ———— 7.5 mi

0 ———— 7.5 km

Sovicille •

Rosia •

GETTING HERE

You can reach Monteriggioni by car on either the SR2 or the Florence–Siena Superstrada. Buses run frequently to and from Siena. The closest train station to Monteriggioni, with frequent service to and from Siena, is in Castellina Scalo. You will then have to reach Monteriggioni on foot—it's a 4-km (2½-mile) walk.

VISITOR INFORMATION

Monteriggioni tourism office ⊠ *Piazza Roma 23, Monteriggioni* ☎ *0577/304834* ⊕ *www.monteriggioniturismo.it.*

WHERE TO EAT AND STAY

For expanded hotel reviews, visit Fodors.com.

$$ ✕ **Il Pozzo.** Famous for its preparation of a 16th-century recipe of *cing-*

TUSCAN *hiale al cioccolato* (wild boar stewed in chocolate sauce), this restaurant is a popular spot. Tamer specialties include a range of homemade fresh pastas, *filetto alla boscaiola* (fillet of beef with porcini mushrooms), *piccione ripieno* (stuffed squab), and a long list of homey desserts. $ *Average main: €18* ⊠ *Piazza Roma 2* ☎ *0577/304127* ⊕ *www.ilpozzo.net* ⊗ *Closed Mon., last 3 wks in Jan.–mid-Feb. No dinner Sun.*

$$ 🛏 **Borgo San Luigi.** This 17th-century villa lined with lavender bushes

HOTEL and cypress trees sits just outside Monteriggioni. **Pros:** good base for exploring Siena; some rooms have kitchens; excellent gym and pool. **Cons:** somewhat isolated; few restaurants are within walking distance. [$] *Rooms from: €190* ✉ *Strada della Cerretta 7, 4 km (2½ miles) southwest of Monteriggioni, Località San Luigi Strove* ☎ *0577/301055* 🌐 *www.borgosanluigi.it* 🛏 *54 rooms, 10 apartments* 🍴 *Breakfast.*

$$$ B&B/INN 🏨 **Hotel Monteriggioni.** A sense of freshness comes from the terracotta floors, high wood-beamed ceilings, and soothing whitewashed walls in the hotel's guest rooms. **Pros:** great location inside town walls; well-appointed rooms; peaceful setting. **Cons:** no views beyond the walls; no nightlife to speak of. [$] *Rooms from: €230* ✉ *Via I Maggio 4* ☎ *0577/305009* 🌐 *www.hotelmonteriggioni.net* 🛏 *12 rooms* ⏲ *Closed Jan. 9–Feb. 28* 🍴 *Breakfast.*

WORD OF MOUTH

"What Tuscany has to offer is beautiful vistas and winding roads that take you to small towns and villages—like Monteriggioni. We found it on the way to Siena from Florence. It was a charming walled village. When we got home, we found out that Dante described the well in the center of the piazza as the entrance to hell in his *Divine Comedy*." —tony

COLLE DI VAL D'ELSA

12 km (7 miles) west of Monteriggioni, 25 km (16 miles) northwest of Siena, 51 km (32 miles) south of Florence.

Most people pass through on their way to and from popular tourist destinations Volterra and San Gimignano—a shame, since Colle di Val d'Elsa has a lot to offer. It's another town on the Via Francigena that benefited from trade along the pilgrimage route to Rome. Colle got an extra boost in the late 16th century when it was given a bishopric, probably related to an increase in trade when nearby San Gimignano was cut off from the well-traveled road. The town is arranged on two levels, and from the 12th century onward the flat lower portion was given over to a flourishing papermaking industry; today the area is mostly modern, and efforts have shifted toward the production of fine glass and crystal.

Make your way from the newer lower town (Colle Bassa) to the prettier, upper part of town (Colle Alta); the best views of the valley are to be had from Viale della Rimembranza, the road that loops around the western end of town, past the church of San Francesco. The early-16th-century Porta Nuova was inserted into the preexisting medieval walls, just as several handsome Renaissance palazzos were placed into the medieval neighborhood to create what is now called the Borgo. The Via Campana, the main road, passes through the facade of the surreal Palazzo Campana, an otherwise unfinished building that serves as a door connecting the two parts of the upper town. Via delle Volte, named for the vaulted arches that cover it, leads straight to Piazza del Duomo. There is a convenient parking lot off the SS68, with stairs leading up the hill. Buses arrive at Piazza Arnolfo, named after the town's favorite son, Arnolfo di Cambio (circa 1245–1302), the early-Renaissance architect who designed Florence's Duomo and Palazzo Vecchio (but sadly nothing here).

GETTING HERE

You can reach Colle di Val d'Elsa by car on either the SR2 from Siena or the Florence–Siena Superstrada. Bus service to and from Siena and Florence is frequent.

VISITOR INFORMATION

Colle di Val d'Elsa Tourism Office ⊠ *Via del Castello 33/b* ☏ *0577/922791.*

EXPLORING

Chiesa di Santa Caterina. Visit this 15th-century church to view the excellent stained-glass window in the apse, executed by Sebastiano Mainardi (circa 1460–1513), as well as a haunting *Pietà* created by local artist Zacchia Zacchi (1473–1544). ⊠ *Via Campana 35* ☏ *0577/920647* ⊘ *Daily 8–noon and 3–6.*

Duomo. Several reconstructions have left little to admire of the once-Romanesque Duomo. Inside is the **Cappella del Santo Chiodo** (Chapel of the Holy Nail), built in the 15th century to hold a nail allegedly from the cross upon which Christ was crucified. (Perhaps it inspired the locals to go into the nail-making business, which became another of the town's flourishing industries.) ⊠ *Piazza del Duomo, on Via del Castello* ⊘ *Daily 8–noon and 4–6.*

Museo Civico e d'Arte Sacra. The museum of sacred art displays religious relics as well as triptychs from the Sienese and Florentine schools dating from the 14th and 15th centuries. It also contains the town's tribute to Arnolfo di Cambio, with photos of the buildings he designed for other towns. Down Via del Castello, at No. 63, is the house-tower where Arnolfo was born in 1245. (It's not open to the public.) ⊠ *Via del Castello 31* ☏ *0577/923888* ⊒*€6, includes the Museo Archeologico and the Museo del Cristallo* ⊘ *Fri.–Sun. 11:30–5.*

WHERE TO EAT

$$
TUSCAN

✕ **L'Angolo di Sapia.** A short and simple set menu that changes with the seasons is one of the reasons to eat here. The other is the sweeping view from the terrace of the countryside below. You might want to start with the *piatto misto* (mixed plate, which in this case includes a slice of vegetable tart and mozzarella and tomatoes) and then continue with one of the house specialties like the *topini della torre* (gnocchi in a vibrant saffron sauce). Every evening there's a cocktail hour with an ample free buffet. $ *Average main: €15* ⊠ *Via del Castello 4* ☏ *0577/921453* ⊘ *No lunch. Closed Mon.–Wed. and Oct.–Apr.*

$$
TUSCAN

✕ **L'Antica Trattoria.** Residents of Colle di Val d'Elsa hold this trattoria in high esteem, even though it's a little overpriced. Tuscan classics fill the large menu, which concentrates on game, particularly pheasant, pigeon, and quail. Some of the pastas, such as *tortelli di sedano in purea di fagioli* (stuffed pasta with creamy celery and topped with a light bean puree) differ from the usual fare. The decor is simple; in warmer months outdoor seating on a square is a possibility. The service is first-rate. $ *Average main: €22* ⊠ *Piazza Arnolfo di Cambio 23* ☏ *0577/923747* ⊠ *Reservations essential* ⊘ *Closed Tues. and last wk in Aug.*

$$
TUSCAN

✕ **Molino il Moro.** The early-12th-century grain mill, now a romantic restaurant, is perched over a rushing river. The chef concocts sophisticated spins on traditional dishes, such as the divine *filetto di coniglio* *in crosta con purè di pruge* (rabbit loin with a prune puree). The wine list is short but sweet, the service note-perfect. [$] *Average main: €20* ✉ *Via della Ruota 2* ☎ *0577/920862* 🌐 *www.molinoilmoro.it* ⏲ *Closed Mon. No lunch Tues.*

$$$$ MODERN ITALIAN Fodor's Choice ★ 🍴 **Ristorante Arnolfo.** Food lovers should not miss Arnolfo, one of Tuscany's most highly regarded restaurants. Chef Gaetano Trovato sets high standards of creativity; his dishes daringly ride the line between innovation and tradition, almost always with spectacular results. The menu changes frequently but you are always sure to find fish and lots of fresh vegetables in the summer. You're in for a treat if the specials include *carrè di agnello al vino rosso e sella alle olive* (rack of lamb in a red wine sauce and lamb saddle with olives). [$] *Average main: €75* ✉ *Via XX Settembre 52* ☎ *0577/920549* 🌐 *www.arnolfo.com* ✍ *Reservations essential* ⏲ *Closed Tues. and Wed., last wk in Jan. and Feb., and last wk in Aug.*

WHERE TO STAY

For expanded hotel reviews, visit Fodors.com.

$$$ 🏨 **La Suvera.** Pope Julius II once owned this luxurious estate in the valley of the River Elsa. **Pros:** luxurious accommodations; historic setting; far from the madding crowd. **Cons:** out-of-the-way location; showing its age; some bristle at the extremely formal service. [$] *Rooms from: €300* ✉ *Off SS541 15 km (9 miles) south of Colle di Val d'Elsa, Pievescola* ☎ *0577/960300* 🌐 *www.lasuvera.it* 🛏 *36 rooms, 12 suites* ⏲ *Closed Nov.–Easter* 🍽 *Breakfast.*

$$ B&B/INN 🏨 **Palazzo San Lorenzo.** A 17th-century palace in the historic center of Colle boasts rooms that exude warmth and comfort, with light-color wooden floors, soothingly tinted fabrics, and large windows. **Pros:** central location; spotless; extremely well maintained. **Cons:** caters to business groups; some of the public spaces feel rather sterile. [$] *Rooms from: €125* ✉ *Via Gracco del Secco 113* ☎ *0577/923675* 🌐 *www.palazzosanlorenzo.it* 🛏 *43 rooms, 6 suite, 6 apartments* 🍽 *Breakfast.*

SHOPPING

La Moleria Gelli. Art meets contemporary design in the glass objects here. The slanted champagne flutes are a marvel of engineering, as are the wine carafes, shaped like a child's top, that perfectly balance and gently spin. ✉ *Via delle Romite 26* ☎ *0577/920163* 🌐 *www.lamoleriagelli.com.*

SAN GIMIGNANO

Fodor's Choice ★ *14 km (9 miles) northwest of Colle di Val d'Elsa, 38 km (24 miles) northwest of Siena, 54 km (34 miles) southwest of Florence.*

When you're on a hilltop surrounded by soaring medieval towers silhouetted against the sky, it's difficult not to fall under the spell of San Gimignano. Its tall walls and narrow streets are typical of Tuscan hill towns, but it's the medieval "skyscrapers" that set the town apart from its neighbors. Today 14 towers remain, but at the height of the Guelph–Ghibelline conflict there was a forest of more than 70, and it was possible to cross the town by rooftop rather than by road. The towers were built partly for defensive purposes—they were a safe refuge and useful

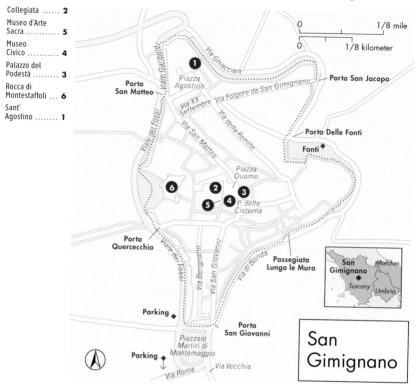

San Gimignano

for pouring boiling oil on attacking enemies—and partly for bolstering the egos of their owners, who competed with deadly seriousness to build the highest tower in town.

The relative proximity of San Gimignano, arguably Tuscany's best-preserved medieval hill town, to Siena and Florence also makes it one of Italy's most-visited ones. But the traffic is hardly a new thing; the Etruscans were encamped here, and the Romans made it an outpost. With the yearly flow of pilgrims to and from Rome in the Middle Ages, the town—then known as Castel di Selva—became a prosperous market center. When locals prayed to a martyred bishop from Modena for relief from invading barbarians, relief they got, and in gratitude they rechristened the town in his honor as San Gimignano. Devastated by the Black Death of 1348, the town subsequently fell under Florentine control. Things got going again in the Renaissance, with some of the best and brightest painters in the area—Ghirlandaio (1449–94), Benozzo Gozzoli (1420–97), and Pinturicchio (circa 1454–1513)—coming to work, but soon after, the main road was moved, cutting San Gimignano off from the main trade route and sending it into decline.

Today San Gimignano isn't much more than a gentrified walled city, touristy but still very much worth exploring because, despite the profusion of cheesy souvenir shops lining the main drag, there's some serious

Renaissance art to be seen here. Tour groups arrive early and clog the wine-tasting rooms—San Gimignano is famous for its light white Vernaccia—and art galleries for much of the day, but most sights stay open through late afternoon, when all the tour groups have long since departed.

GETTING HERE

You can reach San Gimignano by car from the Florence–Siena Superstrada. Exit at Poggibonsi Nord and follow signs for San Gimignano. Although it involves changing buses in Poggibonsi, getting to San Gimignano by bus from Florence is a relatively straightforward affair. SITA operates the service between Siena or Florence and Poggibonsi. From Siena, Tra-In offers direct service to San Gimignano several times daily. You cannot reach San Gimignano by train.

VISITOR INFORMATION

San Gimignano Tourism Office ✉ *Piazza Duomo 1* ☎ *0577/940008* ⊕ *www.sangimignano.com.*

EXPLORING SAN GIMIGNANO

The center of San Gimignano is closed to traffic. If you arrive by car, there are parking lots next to the Parco della Rimembranza, near Porta San Giovanni, the main pedestrian entrance into town. Buses from Florence and Siena all stop at Porta San Giovanni. Follow Via San Giovanni a short way to the center of town. Souvenir shops lining the way leave no doubt about the lifeblood of the town, but better things lie ahead. Pass under Arco dei Becci, a leftover from the city's Etruscan walls, to Piazza della Cisterna, a square named for the cistern at its center. The Piazza del Duomo, where you'll find the Museo Civico, lies just beyond the two towers built by the Ardinghelli family. Continue along Via San Matteo and turn right just before Porta San Matteo to reach Sant'Agostino.

TIMING   You can see all of San Gimignano's main sights in a single day. But, if you arrive in the morning and leave in the afternoon, you miss the town at its best. From 9 to 5 tourists on jaunts from Florence and Siena swarm San Gimignano's streets, filling the shops and museums. In the evening, when all the day-trippers have departed, the town is transformed. Reclaiming its serenity, San Gimignano takes on a magically medieval air that, if you can possibly stay the night in or near town, is not to be missed.

TOP ATTRACTIONS

Fodor's Choice ★   **Collegiata.** The town's main church is not officially a *duomo* (cathedral), because San Gimignano has no bishop. But behind the simple facade of the Romanesque Collegiata lies a treasure trove of fine frescoes, covering nearly every part of the interior. Bartolo di Fredi's 14th-century fresco cycle of Old Testament scenes extends along one wall. Their distinctly medieval feel, with misshapen bodies, buckets of spurting blood, and lack of perspective, contrasts with the much more reserved scenes from the *Life of Christ* (attributed to 14th-century artist Lippo Memmi), painted on the opposite wall just 14 years later. Taddeo di Bartolo's otherworldly *Last Judgment* (late 14th century), with its distorted and suffering nudes, reveals the great influence of Dante's horrifying imagery in *The Inferno* and was surely an inspiration for later painters. Proof that the town had more than one protector, Benozzo Gozzoli's arrow-riddled *St. Sebastian* was commissioned in gratitude after the locals prayed to the saint for relief from plague. The Renaissance **Cappella di Santa Fina** is decorated with a fresco cycle by Domenico Ghirlandaio illustrating the life of Saint Fina. A small girl who suffered from a terminal disease, Fina repented for her sins—among them having accepted an orange from a boy—and in penance lived out the rest of her short life on a wooden board, tormented by rats. The scenes depict the arrival of Saint Gregory, who appeared to assure her that death was near; the flowers that miraculously grew from the wooden plank; and the miracles that accompanied her funeral, including the healing of her nurse's paralyzed hand and the restoration of a blind choirboy's vision. ⊠ *Piazza Pecori 1–2* ☎ *0577/940316* 💷 *€3.50; €5.50 including the Museo d'Arte Sacra* ⊙ *Apr.–Oct., weekdays 10–7:10, Sat. 10–5:10, Sun. 12:30–7:10; Nov. 1–15, Dec. 1–Jan. 15, and Feb. 1–Mar., Mon.–Sat. 10–4:40, Sun. 12:30–4:40. Closed Nov. 16–30 and Jan. 16–31.*

Museo Civico. The impressive civic museum occupies what was the "new" Palazzo del Popolo; the Torre Grossa is adjacent. Dante visited San Gimignano for only one day as a Guelph ambassador from Florence to ask the locals to join the Florentines in supporting the pope—just long enough to get the main council chamber, which now holds a 14th-century *Maestà* by Lippo Memmi, named after him. Off the stairway is a small room containing the racy frescoes by Memmo di Filippuccio (active 1288–1324), depicting the courtship, shared bath, and wedding of a young, androgynous-looking couple. That the space could have been a private room for the commune's chief magistrate may have something to do with the work's highly charged eroticism.

Upstairs, paintings by famous Renaissance artists Pinturicchio (*Madonna Enthroned*) and Benozzo Gozzoli (*Madonna and Child*), and two large *tondi* (circular paintings) by Filippino Lippi (circa 1457–1504) attest to the importance and wealth of San Gimignano. Also worth seeing are Taddeo di Bartolo's *Life of San Gimignano*, with the saint holding a model of the town as it once appeared; Lorenzo di Niccolò's gruesome martyrdom scene in the *Life of St. Bartholomew* (1401); and scenes from the *Life of St. Fina* on a tabernacle that was designed to hold her head. Admission includes the steep climb to the top of the Torre Grossa, which on a clear day has spectacular views. ⊠ *Piazza Duomo 2* ☎ *0577/990312* 💷 *€5* ⊙ *Apr.–Sept., daily 9:30–7; Oct.–Mar., daily 11–5:30.*

NEED A BREAK?

Enoteca Gustavo. There's no shortage of places to try Vernaccia di San Gimignano, the justifiably famous white wine with which San Gimignano would be singularly associated—if it weren't for all those towers. At this wine bar, run by energetic Maristella Becucci, you can buy a glass of Vernaccia di San Gimignano and sit down with a cheese plate or with one of the fine crostini. ⊠ *Via San Matteo 29* ☎ *0577/940057.*

DID YOU KNOW?

San Gimignano, sometimes called "the medieval Manhattan," once had more than 70 towers. Today 14 remain standing.

Sant'Agostino. Make a beeline for Benozzo Gozzoli's superlative 15th-century fresco cycle depicting scenes from the life of Saint Augustine. The saint's work was essential to the early development of church doctrine. As thoroughly discussed in his autobiographical *Confessions* (an acute dialogue with God), Augustine, like many saints, sinned considerably in his youth before finding God. But unlike the lives of other saints, where the story continues through a litany of deprivations, penitence, and often martyrdom, Augustine's life and work focused on philosophy and the reconciliation of faith and thought. Benozzo's 17 scenes on the choir wall depict Augustine as a man who traveled and taught extensively in the 4th and 5th centuries. The 15th-century altarpiece by Piero del Pollaiolo (1443–96) depicts *The Coronation of the Virgin* and the various protectors of the city. On your way out of Sant'Agostino, stop in at the **Cappella di San Bartolo,** with a sumptuously elaborate tomb by Benedetto da Maiano (1442–97). ✉ *Piazza Sant'Agostino 10* ☎ *0577/907012* 🔳 *Free* 🕙 *Apr.–Oct., daily 7–noon and 3–7; Nov.–Mar., daily 7–noon and 3–6.*

> ### WORD OF MOUTH
>
> "It's nice to arrive in San Gimignano after the bus tours leave for the day. Make sure you take a walk around the walls of the town. . . . it's lovely in the morning. There's a path to follow and the views are jaw dropping."
> —CRAZY4TRAVEL

WORTH NOTING

Museo d'Arte Sacra. Even with all the decoration in the Collegiata, the fine collection of various religious articles in the church museum, across the pretty courtyard, is still worth a look. The highlight is a *Madonna and Child* by Bartolo di Fredi. Other pieces include several busts, wooden statues of Christ, the Virgin Mary, and the angel Gabriel, and several illuminated songbooks. ✉ *Piazza Pecori 4* ☎ *0577/940316* 🔳 *€3; €5.50 includes the Collegiata and the Santa Fina chapel* 🕙 *Apr.–Oct., weekdays 10–7:10, Sat. 10–5:10, Sun. 12:30–7:10; Nov. 1–15, Dec. 1–Jan. 15, and Feb. and Mar., Mon.–Sat. 10–4:40, Sun. 12:30–4:40. Closed Nov. 16–30 and Jan. 16–31.*

Palazzo del Podestà. Across the piazza from the Collegiata is the "old" town hall built in 1239. Its tower was erected by the municipality in 1255 to settle the raging "my-tower-is-bigger-than-your-tower" contest—as you can see, a solution that just didn't last long. The palace is closed to visitors. ✉ *Piazza Duomo.*

Rocca di Montestaffoli. If you want to see more of that quintessential Tuscan landscape, walk up to the Rocca di Montestaffoli, which sits at the highest point in San Gimignano. Built after the Florentine conquest to keep an eye on the town, and dismantled a few centuries later, it's now a public garden. ✉ *Via della Rocca* 🔳 *Free* 🕙 *Daily dawn–dusk.*

WHERE TO EAT

$$ ✗ **La Mangiatoia.** Multicolor gingham tablecloths provide an interesting
TUSCAN juxtaposition with rib-vaulted ceilings dating from the 13th century. The lighthearted touch might be explained by the influence of chef Susi

Cuomo, who has been presiding over the kitchen for more than 20 years. The menu is seasonal—in autumn, don't miss her *tonnarelli cacio e pepe* (thick spaghetti with cheese and pepper). In summer, eat lighter fare on the intimate, flower-bedecked terrace in the back. $ *Average main: €18 ⊠ Via Mainardi 5 ☎ 0577/941528 ⊕ www.ristorantelamangiatoia. it* ⊙ *Closed Tues., 3 wks in Nov., and 1 wk in Jan.*

$$ ✕**Osteria del Carcere.** Though it calls itself an *osteria* (a tavern), this
ITALIAN   place much more resembles a wine bar, with a bill of fare that includes several different types of pâtés and a short list of seasonal soups and salads. The sampler of goat cheeses, which can be paired with local wines, should not be missed. Operatic arias play softly in the background, and service is courteous. $ *Average main: €15 ⊠ Via del Castello 13 ☎ 0577/941905* ▭ *No credit cards* ⊙ *Closed Wed. and early Jan.–Mar. No lunch Thurs.*

WHERE TO STAY

For expanded hotel reviews, visit Fodors.com.

$ ⛻ **Bel Soggiorno.** If you're looking for a place within the town walls, this
B&B/INN   is a fine choice. **Pros:** inside the ancient walls of San Gimignano; magnificent views; some rooms have small terraces facing the countryside. **Cons:** plain decor; somber public spaces. $ *Rooms from: €95 ⊠ Via San Giovanni 91 ☎ 0577/940375 ⊕ www.hotelbelsoggiorno.it* ⟳ *21 rooms* ⊙ *Closed late Nov.–late Dec.* ⦿| *Breakfast.*

$$$ ⛻ **La Collegiata.** After serving as a Franciscan convent and then the
HOTEL   residence of the noble Strozzi family, the Collegiata has been converted into a fine hotel, with no expense spared in the process. **Pros:** gorgeous views from terrace; elegant rooms in main building. **Cons:** long walk into town; service can be impersonal; some rooms are dimly lit. $ *Rooms from: €210 ⊠ Località Strada 27, 1 km (½ mile) north of San Gimignano town center ☎ 0577/943201 ⊕ www.lacollegiata.it* ⟳ *20 rooms, 1 suite* ⊙ *Closed Nov.–Mar.* ⦿| *Breakfast.*

$ ⛻ **Pescille.** A rambling farmhouse has been transformed into a hand-
B&B/INN   some hotel with understated contemporary furniture in the bedrooms and country-classic motifs such as farm implements hanging on the walls in the bar. **Pros:** splendid views; quiet atmosphere; 10-minute walk to town. **Cons:** furnishings a bit austere; there's an elevator for luggage but not for guests. $ *Rooms from: €95 ⊠ Località Pescille, 4 km (2½ miles) south of San Gimignano ☎ 0577/940186 ⊕ www.pescille.it* ⟳ *38 rooms, 12 suites* ⊙ *Closed Nov.–Mar.* ⦿| *Breakfast.*

$$ ⛻ **Torraccia di Chiusi.** A perfect retreat for families, this tranquil hilltop
B&B/INN   *agriturismo* (farm stay) offers simple, comfortably decorated accommodations on extensive grounds 5 km (3 miles) from the hubbub of San Gimignano. **Pros:** tranquil haven close to San Gimignano; great walking possibilities; family-run hospitality; delightful countryside views. **Cons:** 30 minutes from the nearest town on a windy gravel road; need a car to get here. $ *Rooms from: €140 ⊠ Località Montauto ☎ 0577/941972 ⊕ www.torracciadichiusi.com* ⟳ *8 rooms, 3 apartments* ⦿| *Breakfast.*

NIGHTLIFE AND THE ARTS

Carnevale. San Gimignano is one of the few small towns in the area that make a big deal out of carnival festivities, with locals dressing up in colorful costumes and marching through the streets from 3:30 to 6:30 on the four Sundays preceding Shrove Tuesday.

Estate San Gimignanese. If you visit in summer, check with the tourist office about concerts and performances related to San Gimignano's arts festival, one of Tuscany's oldest. It's held mid-June to August each year. ⊠ *Piazza Duomo 1* ☎ *0577/940008* ⊕ *www.sangimignano.com.*

SHOPPING

Antica Latteria di Maurizio e Tiziana. Maurizio and Tiziana's shop has an arresting array of cheeses, and perhaps the best array of verdure sott'olio in town. They also make top-notch panini. ⊠ *Via San Matteo 19* ☎ *0577/941952.*

Mercato. As everywhere else, the town brightens on *mercato* (open-air market) mornings, every Thursday and Saturday, in Piazza del Duomo. It's the place to pick up fresh fruits and other snacks.

VOLTERRA

30 km (18 miles) southwest of San Gimignano.

As you approach the town through bleak, rugged terrain, you can see that not all Tuscan hill towns rise above rolling green fields. Volterra stands mightily over Le Balze, a stunning series of gullied hills and valleys formed by erosion that has slowly eaten away at the foundation of the town—now considerably smaller than it was during its Etruscan glory days 25 centuries ago. The town began as the northernmost city of the 12 that made up the Etruscan League, and excavations in the 18th century revealed a bounty of relics, which are on exhibit at the impressively overstocked Museo Etrusco Guarnacci. The Romans and later the Florentines laid siege to the town to secure its supply of minerals and stones, particularly alabaster, which is still worked into handicrafts on sale in many of the shops around town.

GETTING HERE

By car, the best route from San Gimignano follows the SP1 south to Castel San Gimignano and then the SS68 all the way to Volterra. Coming from the west, take the SS1, a coastal road to Cecina, then follow the SS68 to Volterra. Either way, there's a long, winding climb at the end of your trip. Traveling to Volterra by bus or train is complicated; avoid it if possible, especially if you have lots of luggage. From Florence or Siena the journey is best made by bus and involves a change in Colle di Val d'Elsa. From Rome or Pisa, it is best to take the train to Cecina and then take a bus to Volterra or a train to the Volterra-Saline station. The latter is 10 km (6 miles) from town.

VISITOR INFORMATION

Volterra Tourism Office ⊠ *Piazza dei Priori 20* ☎ *0588/87257* ⊕ *www.volterratur.it.*

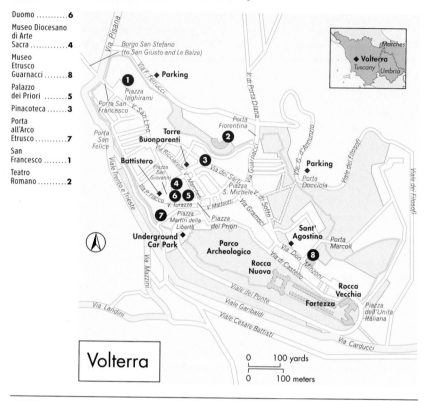

EXPLORING VOLTERRA

Driving in the old town is forbidden. There are several parking lots around the perimeter of the city walls, the most convenient of which is the underground parking lot at Piazza Martiri della Libertà. Begin your exploration of Volterra from Piazza Martiri della Libertà and take Via Marchesi to Piazza dei Priori. It's lined with an impressive collection of medieval buildings, including the imposing Palazzo dei Priori, the seat of city government for more than seven centuries. Across the piazza is the Palazzo Pretorio topped by the Torre del Porcellino, named after the sculpted little boar mounted at the upper window. Walk down Via Turazza along the side of the Duomo to the triangular Piazza San Giovanni, and head out the left corner of the piazza to steal a look at the ancient Porta all'Arco Etrusco.

TIMING   Allow at least three hours to see the town. Off-season, it's best to make an early start in order to have time in the museums before they close. The whole town can easily be seen in a day, although its distance from everything else makes it a good stopover as well.

TOP ATTRACTIONS

Duomo. Behind the textbook 13th-century Pisan–Romanesque facade is proof that Volterra counted for something during the Renaissance, when many important Tuscan artists came to decorate the church. Three-dimensional stucco portraits of local saints are on the gold, red, and blue ceiling (1580) designed by Francesco Capriani, including Saint Linus, the successor to Saint Peter as pope and claimed by the Volterrans to have been born here. The highlight of the Duomo is the brightly painted 13th-century wooden life-size *Deposition* in the chapel of the same name. The unusual Cappella dell'Addolorata (Chapel of the Grieved) has two terra-cotta Nativity scenes; the depiction of the arrival of the Magi has a background fresco by Benozzo Gozzoli. The 16th-century pulpit in the middle of the nave is lined with fine 14th-century sculpted panels, attributed to a member of the Pisano family. Across from the Duomo in the center of the piazza is the **Battistero**, with stripes that match the Duomo. Evidently this baptistery got a lot of use, as the small marble baptismal font carved by Andrea Sansovino in 1502 was moved to the wall to the right of the entrance in the mid-18th century to make room for a much larger one. ⊠ *Piazza San Giovanni* 🕾 *0588/88524* ⊙ *Daily 9:30–noon and 3:30–6:30.*

Museo Etrusco Guarnacci. An extraordinarily large and unique collection of Etruscan relics is made all the more interesting by clear explanations in English. The bulk of the collection is comprised of roughly 700 carved funerary urns: the oldest, dating from the 7th century BC, were made from tufa (volcanic rock); a handful are made of terra-cotta; and the vast majority—from the 3rd to 1st century BC—are alabaster. The urns are grouped by subject and taken together form a fascinating testimony about Etruscan life and death. Some illustrate domestic scenes, others the funeral procession. Greek gods and mythology, adopted by the Etruscans, also figure prominently. Particularly well known is *Gli Sposi (Husband and Wife)*, a haunting, elderly duo in terra-cotta. Also on display are Attic vases, bucchero ceramics, jewelry, and household items. ⊠ *Via Don Minzoni 15* 🕾 *0588/86347* 🗺 *€8; €10 including the Museo Diocesano di Arte Sacra and the Pinacoteca* ⊙ *Mid-Mar.–Oct., daily 9–7; Nov.–mid-Mar., daily 9:10–4:30.*

Pinacoteca. One of Volterra's best-looking Renaissance buildings contains an impressive collection of Tuscan paintings arranged chronologically on two floors. Head straight for Room 12, with Luca Signorelli's (circa 1445–1523) *Madonna and Child with Saints* and Rosso Fiorentino's *Deposition*. Though painted just 30 years apart, they serve to illustrate the shift in style from the early-16th-century Renaissance ideals to full-blown mannerism. Other important paintings include Ghirlandaio's *Apotheosis of Christ with Saints* and a polyptych of the *Madonna and Saints* by Taddeo di Bartolo. ⊠ *Via dei Sarti 1* 🕾 *0588/87580* 🗺 *€8; €10 including the Museo Etrusco Guarnacci and the Museo Diocesano di Arte Sacra* ⊙ *Mid-Mar.–Oct., daily 9–7; Nov.–mid-Mar., daily 10–4:30.*

Porta all'Arco Etrusco. Even if a good portion of the arch was rebuilt by the Romans, three dark and weather-beaten 4th-century BC heads (thought to represent Etruscan gods) still face outward to greet those who enter here. A plaque on the outer wall recalls the efforts of the locals who saved the arch from destruction by filling it with stones during the German withdrawal at the end of World War II.

Teatro Romano. Just outside the walls past Porta Fiorentina are the ruins of the 1st-century BC Roman theater, one of the best-preserved in Italy, with adjacent remains of the Roman *terme* (baths). You can enjoy an excellent bird's-eye view of the theater from Via Lungo le Mura. ⊠ *Viale Francesco Ferrucci* 🗐 *€3.50* ⊙ *Mid.-Mar.–Oct., daily 10:30–3:30; Nov.–mid. Mar., daily 10–4.*

> **WORD OF MOUTH**
>
> "We found Volterra charming, and it was not as crowded as San Gim, Siena, or Florence (July). The countryside is different than the typical Tuscan hills, but lovely all the same. They are known for their alabaster, and I picked up some lovely little dishes."
> —walkteach48

WORTH NOTING

Museo Diocesano di Arte Sacra. The religious-art collection housed in the Bishop's Palace was collected from local churches, and includes an unusual reliquary by Antonio Pollaiolo with the head of Saint Octavian in silver resting on four golden lions. There's also a fine terra-cotta bust of Saint Linus by Andrea della Robbia (1435–1525/28). Two paintings are noteworthy: Rosso Fiorentino's (1495–1540) *Madonna di Villamagna* and Daniele da Volterra's (1509–66) *Madonna di Ulignano*, named for the village churches in which they were originally placed. ⊠ *Palazzo Vescovile, Via Roma 13* 🗐 *0588/86290* 🗐 *€8, includes admission to Museo Etrusco Guarnacci and Pinacoteca* ⊙ *Mid-Mar.–Oct., daily 9–1 and 3–6; Nov.–mid-Mar., daily 9–1.*

Palazzo dei Priori. Tuscany's first town hall was built between 1208 and 1254, with a no-nonsense facade, fortresslike crenellations, and a five-sided tower. Such fortifications served as a model for other similar structures throughout the region, including Florence's Palazzo Vecchio. The Florentine medallions that adorn the facade were added after the Florentines conquered Volterra. The town leaders still meet on the first floor in the Sala del Consiglio; the room is open to the public and has a 14th-century fresco of the *Annunciation.* ⊠ *Piazza dei Priori* 🗐 *0588/86099* 🗐 *€1.50* ⊙ *Mid-Mar.–Oct., daily 10:30–5:30; Nov.–mid-Mar., weekends 10–5.*

San Francesco. Look inside the church for the celebrated early-15th-century frescoes of the *Legend of the True Cross* by a local artist. It traces the history of the wood used to make the cross upon which Christ was crucified. From Piazza San Giovanni, take Via Franceschini (which becomes Via San Lino) to the church. ⊠ *Piazza Inghirami, off Via San Lino* ⊙ *Daily 8–noon and 3–6.*

LE BALZE

Walk along Via San Lino, through Porta San Francesco, and out Borgo Santo Stefano into Le Balze—an undulating landscape of yellow earth drawn into crags and gullies as if worn down by a desert torrent. This area was originally part of the Etruscan town (called Velathri; as usual, the current name is closer to the Roman name, Volaterrae), as evidenced

Volterra's Porta all'Arco Etrusco

by walls that extend 1 km (½ mile) toward the old Porta Menseri. Toward the end of the road, on the right, is the church of San Giusto (with terra-cotta statues of the town's patron saints). The church was built to replace an earlier church under which the earth had eroded. The haunting landscape is thought to be the result of rainwater wearing down the soil substructure. The bus for Borgo San Giusto, leaving from Piazza Martiri, goes through Le Balze (about 10 runs per day).

WHERE TO EAT AND STAY

For expanded hotel reviews, visit Fodors.com.

$ ✕ **Da Badò.** This is the best place in town to eat traditional food elbow-
TUSCAN to-elbow with the locals. Da Badò is family-run, with Lucia in the kitchen and her sons Giacomo and Michele waiting tables. Lucia likes to concentrate on just a few dishes: *zuppa alla volterrana* (a soup made with vegetables and bread), *pappardelle alla lepre* (wide fettuccine with rabbit sauce), and a stew of either rabbit or wild boar. A slice of home-made almond tart is a must. $ *Average main: €12* ✉ *Borgo San Lazzaro 9* ☎ *0588/86477* ⊕ *www.trattoriadabado.com* ✆ *Closed Wed.*

$$ ✕ **Il Sacco Fiorentino.** Start with the *antipasti del Sacco Fiorentino*—a
TUSCAN medley of sautéed chicken liver, porcini mushrooms, and polenta drizzled with balsamic vinegar. The meal gets better when you move on to the *tagliatelle del Sacco Fiorentino*, curried spaghetti with chicken and roasted peppers. The well-priced wine list is a marvel. $ *Average main: €16* ✉ *Piazza XX Settembre 18* ☎ *0588/88537* ✆ *Closed Wed.*

$ ⌂ **Etruria.** The rooms are modest and there's no elevator, but the central
B&B/INN location, the ample buffet breakfast, and the modest rates make this a

good choice for those on a budget. **Pros:** great central location; friendly staff; tranquil garden. **Cons:** some rooms can be noisy during the day; no a/c. $ *Rooms from: €99 ⊠ Via Matteotti 32 ☎ 0588/87377 ⊕ www. albergoetruria.it ↩ 21 rooms* ¶⊙¶ *Breakfast.*

$ 🏨 **San Lino.** Within the town's medieval walls, this convent-turned-
HOTEL   hotel has wood-beam ceilings, graceful archways, and terra-cotta floors, with contemporary furnishings. **Pros:** steps away from center of town; friendly and helpful staff; convenient parking. **Cons:** rooms facing the street can be noisy; breakfast is adequate, but nothing to write home about. $ *Rooms from: €90 ⊠ Via San Lino 26 ☎ 0588/85250 ⊕ www.hotelsanlino.com ↩ 43 rooms ⊙ Closed Nov. and Jan.–Feb.* ¶⊙¶ *Breakfast.*

FESTIVALS

Astiludio festival. On the first Sunday in September the Astiludio festival celebrates a flag-throwing tradition that dates to 1406. Performances and processions are part of the activities.

SHOPPING

Anna Maria Molesini. A large loom dominates this tiny workshop/show-room where scarves, shawls, throws, and jackets are woven. Anna Maria's work, mostly in mohair, is done in lively hues. ⊠ *Via Gramsci 45* ☎ *0588/88411.*

Camillo Rossi. At Camillo Rossi you can watch the artisans create household items in alabaster, and then buy their wares. ⊠ *Piazza della Peschiera 3* ☎ *0588/86133.*

Cooperativa Artieri Alabastro. The two large showrooms here are housed in medieval buildings and contain a large number of alabaster objects for sale, including bookends, ashtrays, and boxes. ⊠ *Piazza dei Priori 5* ☎ *0588/87590.*

Mercato (*market*). Volterra's market is held on Saturday morning from November to April in Piazza dei Priori, and on Viale Ferrucci (just outside the city walls) from May through October. On hand is a selection of fresh fruits and vegetables, as well as vendors selling everything from corkscrews to *intimi* (underwear).

AREZZO, CORTONA, AND EASTERN TUSCANY

WELCOME TO EASTERN TUSCANY

TOP REASONS TO GO

★ **Driving through the Parco Nazionale Casentino:** The vistas along the winding road of this park in the Casentino will not disappoint.

★ **Piero della Francesca's True Cross frescoes:** If your holy grail is great Renaissance art, seek out these 12 silently enigmatic scenes in Arezzo's Basilica di San Francesco.

★ **Santa Maria al Calcinaio:** The interior of this Cortona church is much like that of Florence's Duomo, and it's a prime example of Renaissance architecture.

★ **Shopping for jewelry in Arezzo:** Gold has been part of Arezzo's economy since Etruscan times, and today the town is well known worldwide for jewelry design.

1 Arezzo. Tuscany's third-largest city feels a touch more cosmopolitan than the neighboring hill towns—meaning among other things that it has the best shopping in the region. The real draw, though, is the Basilica di San Francesco, adorned with frescoes by Piero della Francesca.

2 Cortona. This ancient stone town, made famous by the book *Under the Tuscan Sun,* sits high above the perfectly flat Valdichiana valley, offering great views of beautiful countryside.

3 Sansepolcro. Lovers of Renaissance painting make pilgrimages to out-of-the-way Sansepolcro, birthplace of Piero della Francesca. He often worked in, or near, his hometown, finding inspiration for the landscapes in his often enigmatic paintings.

4 The Casentino. A short distance north of Arezzo, the Casentino region is highlighted by the Parco Nazionale Casentino—a drive through the park reveals one gorgeous view after another. Dante, exiled here from Florence, recorded his love of the countryside in *The Divine Comedy*.

GETTING ORIENTED

The hill towns of Arezzo and Cortona are the main attractions of eastern Tuscany; despite their appeal, this part of the region gets less tourist traffic than its neighbors to the west. You'll truly escape the crowds if you venture north to the Casentino, which is backwoods Tuscany—tiny towns and abbeys are sprinkled through beautiful forestland, some of which is set aside as a national park.

Updated
by Peter
Blackman

CLOSER TO ITALY'S RUGGED APENNINES than any other part of the region, eastern Tuscany hides its secrets in the valleys of the upper Arno and Tiber rivers, and among mountains covered with forests of chestnut, fir, and beech: it was here, at La Verna, that Saint Francis founded a sanctuary and received the signs of Christ's wounds, and here that Michelangelo first saw the light of day. One of Tuscany's best "off-the-beaten-path" experiences, Parco Nazionale Casentino, is also here, with mountain scenery that has been safeguarded by monks for eight centuries. The area invites visitors seeking an experience far from the madding crowd.

The hill towns of **Arezzo** and **Cortona** serve as introductions to the area. They carry on age-old local traditions—each June and September Arezzo's Romanesque and Gothic churches are enlivened by the Giostra del Saracino, a medieval pageant. Since ancient times, Arezzo has been home to important artists: from the Etruscan potters who produced those fiery-red vessels to the poet Petrarch and the writer, architect, and painter Giorgio Vasari. Cortona, magnificently situated, with olive groves and vineyards creeping up to its walls, commands sweeping views over Lago Trasimeno and the plain of the Valdichiana. The medieval streets are a pleasure to wander, and the town has two galleries and a scattering of churches that are worth a visit.

PLANNING

MAKING THE MOST OF YOUR TIME

Plan on spending a good four days to tour the area. Arezzo and Cortona each merit a full day, and if you stay in the vicinity you'll have a good base from which to explore the countryside. Both towns are close to the A1 (Autostrada del Sole) and are on main train lines.

GETTING HERE AND AROUND

BUS TRAVEL

Baschetti. The bus company provides regular service between Arezzo and Sansepolcro. ☎ *0575/749816 in Sansepolcro* ⊕ *www.baschetti.it.*

Etruria Mobilità. All bus service in the province of Arezzo is coodinated by Etruria Mobilità, a cooperative of seven different transport companies, including SITA and Baschetti; it's the best source for information about bus service to outlying towns in the region. ☎ *0575/39881 in Arezzo* ⊕ *www.etruriamobilita.it.*

SITA. Bus service between Florence and Arezzo is provided three times daily by SITA, which also provides regular connections between Arezzo and Cortona. ☎ *055/47821 in Florence, 0575/74361 in Sansepolcro, 800/373760 toll-free in Italy* ⊕ *www.sitabus.it.*

CAR TRAVEL

The best way to travel within the region, making it possible to explore tiny hill towns and country restaurants, is by car. The roads are better north–south than east–west, so allow time for excessively winding roads when heading east or west. Sometimes it's faster to go out of your way and get on one of the bigger north–south routes.

The A1 highway, which runs from Florence to Rome, passes close to Arezzo. Cortona is just off the main road linking Perugia to the A1, and Sansepolcro can be reached from Arezzo on the SR73, with Monterchi a short 3-km (2-mile) detour along the way.

Though Arezzo is the third-largest city in Tuscany (after Florence and Pisa), the old town is small, and is on a low hill almost completely closed to traffic. Look for parking along the roads that circle the lower part of town, near the train station, and walk up into town from there.

In Cortona, the city center is completely closed to traffic and the few parking areas sprinkled outside the city walls don't make it easy to park. The majority of Cortona's streets are steep. Fortunately, most of the main sights are grouped near the Duomo in the lower part of town, but if you want to visit the upper town, be prepared for a stiff climb.

For visits to the mountainous National Park of the Casentino and the smaller towns and villages farther to the east, such as Sansepolcro and Monterchi, a car is almost a necessity: bus schedules can be difficult to plan around, and train service is either infrequent or nonexistent. All make for rewarding day trips, though a fair part of your time will be spent on winding, beautiful, country roads. If you want time to explore, plan to stay the night.

TRAIN TRAVEL

Ferrovia dello Stato. The national railway service, Ferrovia dello Stato, has frequent trains between Florence and Arezzo. A regular service links Arezzo with Cortona, and with Poppi and the Casentino. ☎ *892021 toll-free in Italy ⊕ www.trenitalia.com.*

HOTELS

A visit to Tuscany is a trip to the country. There are good hotels in Arezzo and Cortona, but for a classic experience stay in one of the rural accommodations—often converted villas, sometimes working farms or vineyards (known as *agriturismi*).

AREZZO

Arezzo is best known for the magnificent Piero della Francesca frescoes in the church of San Francesco. It's also the birthplace of the poet Petrarch (1304–74), the Renaissance artist and art historian Giorgio Vasari, and Guido d'Arezzo (aka Guido Monaco), the inventor of contemporary musical notation. Arezzo dates from pre-Etruscan times, when around 1000 BC the first settlers erected a cluster of huts. Arezzo thrived as an Etruscan capital from the 7th to the 4th century BC, and was one of the most important cities in the Etruscans' anti-Roman 12-city federation, resisting Rome's rule to the last.

The city eventually fell and in turn flourished under the Romans. In 1248 Guglielmino degli Ubertini, a member of the powerful Ghibelline family, was elected bishop of Arezzo. This sent the city headlong into the enduring conflict between the Ghibellines (pro-emperor) and the Guelphs (pro-pope). In 1289 Florentine Guelphs defeated Arezzo in a famous battle at Campaldino. Among the Florentine soldiers was Dante Alighieri (1265–1321), who often referred to Arezzo in his *Divine*

Comedy. Guelph–Ghibelline wars continued to plague Arezzo until the end of the 14th century, when Arezzo lost its independence to Florence.

GETTING HERE

Arezzo is easily reached by car from the A1, the main highway running between Florence and Rome. Direct trains connect Arezzo with Rome (2½ hours) and Florence (1 hour). Direct bus service is available from Florence, but not from Rome.

VISITOR INFORMATION

Arezzo Tourism Office ✉ *Piazza della Libertà 3* ☎ *0575/392274* ⊕ *arezzo. intoscana.it.*

EXPLORING AREZZO

Sitting on a low hill in a wide plain, Arezzo, especially the bell tower of its Duomo, is visible from afar. Surrounding the older town is an area of urban sprawl. As you begin to walk along the narrow pedestrian streets inside the walls, however, the standard stores of the lower town are gradually replaced by the exclusive antiques and jewelry shops for which Arezzo is known, and the anonymous buildings of the new town give way to Renaissance town palaces, Romanesque and Gothic churches, and the medieval squares of the upper town—all of which is crowned, quite naturally, by the Duomo itself.

TOP ATTRACTIONS

Fodor'sChoice
★

Basilica di San Francesco. The famous Piero della Francesca frescoes depicting *The Legend of the True Cross* (1452–66) were executed on the three walls of the Capella Bacci, the main apse of this 14th-century church. What Sir Kenneth Clark called "the most perfect morning light in all Renaissance painting" may be seen in the lowest section of the right wall, where the troops of Emperor Maxentius flee before the sign of the cross. The rest of the church is decorated with 14th-, 15th- and 16th-century frescoes. Reservations are recommended June through September. ✉ *Piazza San Francesco* ☎ *0575/352727* ⊕ *www. pierodellafrancesca.it* 🎟 *€8* ⊗ *Weekdays 9–6:30, Sat. 9–5:30, Sun. 1–5:30.*

Duomo. Arezzo's medieval cathedral at the top of the hill contains an eye-level fresco of *Maria Maddalena* by Piero della Francesca (1420–92); look for it in the north aisle next to the marble tomb near the organ. Construction of the Duomo began in 1278, but twice came to a halt, and the church wasn't completed until 1510. The ceiling decorations and the stained-glass windows date from the 16th century. The facade was added later (1901–14). ✉ *Piazza del Duomo 1* ☎ *0575/23991* ⊗ *Daily 6:30–12:30 and 3–6:30.*

Piazza Grande. With its irregular shape and sloping brick pavement, framed by buildings of assorted centuries, Arezzo's central piazza echoes Siena's Piazza del Campo. Though not quite so magnificent, it's lively enough during the outdoor antiques fair the first weekend of the month and when the **Giostra del Saracino** (Saracen Joust), featuring medieval costumes and competition, is held here on the third Saturday of June and on the first Sunday of September.

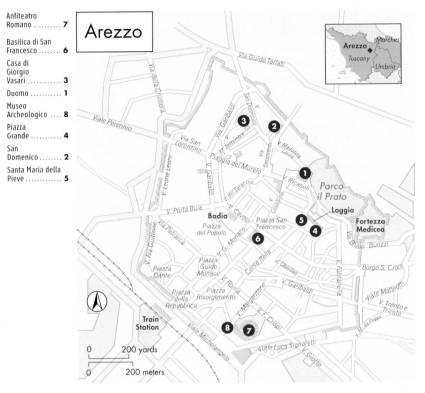

FodorśChoice **Santa Maria della Pieve** (*Church of Saint Mary of the Parish*). The curv-
★ ing, tiered apse on Piazza Grande belongs to a fine Romanesque church
that was originally an Early-Christian structure, which had been constructed over the remains of a Roman temple. The church was rebuilt
in Romanesque style in the 12th century. The splendid facade dates
from the early 13th century, but includes granite Roman columns. A
magnificent polyptych, depicting the Madonna and Child with four
Saints, by Pietro Lorenzetti (circa 1290–1348), embellishes the high
altar. ⊠ *Corso Italia 7* ☎ *0575/22629* ☼ *May–Sept., daily 8–7; Oct.–
Apr., daily 8–noon and 3–6.*

WORTH NOTING

Anfiteatro Romano. Periodic excavations since 1950 have brought to
light segments of Arezzo's Roman amphitheater, which was probably
built during the early 2nd century AD. The entire perimeter has been
exposed, and you can see some of the entrance passages and the structures that supported the amphitheater's central arena. ⊠ *Via Margaritone 10* ☎ *0575/20882* ⊠*Free* ☼ *Daily 8:30–7:30.*

**NEED A
BREAK?** **Caffè dei Costanti.** Outdoor seating on Arezzo's main pedestrian square
and a tasty range of chef's salads (named after the waitresses that serve
here) make this a very pleasant spot for a light lunch during a tour of town.

In continuous operation since 1886, it's the oldest café in Arezzo, and the charming old-world interior served as backdrop to scenes in Roberto Benigni's 1997 film, *Life is Beautiful.* If you're here in the early evening, the dei Costanti serves up an ample buffet of snacks to accompany pre-dinner aperitifs. ✉ *Piazza San Francesco 19* ☎ *0575/1824075.*

Casa di Giorgio Vasari. Giorgio Vasari (1511–74), the region's leading mannerist artist, architect, and art historian, designed and decorated this house after he bought it in 1540. He ended up not spending much time here, since he and his wife moved to Florence in 1554. Today the building houses archives on Vasari, and underwhelming works by the artist and his peers are on view. In the first room, which Vasari called the "Triumph of Virtue Room," a richly ornamented wooden ceiling shows Virtue combating Envy and Fortune in a central octagon. Frescoes on the walls depict, among other things, Extravagance, Charity, the Fire of Troy, and a panorama of a Rome cow field. ✉ *Via XX Settembre 55* ☎ *0575/409040* 🎟 *€4* 🕒 *Mon. and Wed.–Sat. 8:30–7:30, Sun. 8:30–1:30.*

Museo Archeologico. The Archaeological Museum in the **Convento di San Bernardo,** just outside the **Anfiteatro Romano,** exhibits a fine collection of Etruscan bronzes. ✉ *Via Margaritone 10* ☎ *0575/20882* 🎟 *€6* 🕒 *Daily 8:30–7:30.*

San Domenico. Inside the northern city walls, this church was begun by Dominican friars in 1275 and completed in the 14th century. The walls were once completely frescoed and decorated with niches and chapels. Very little remains of the original works, but a famous 13th-century crucifix by Cimabue (circa 1240–1302) and frescoes by Spinello Aretino (1350–1410) still remain. ✉ *Piazza San Domenico 7* ☎ *0575/22906* 🕒 *Daily 8:30–1 and 3:30–7.*

WHERE TO EAT

$$ SEAFOOD 🍴 **I Tre Bicchieri.** Chef Luigi Casotti hails from Amalfi and this shows through in his fine adaptations of dishes more commonly served near the Bay of Naples. The *raviolone farcito con gamberi rossi di Sicilia e tonno* (a large raviolo stufffed with Sicilian prawns and tuna served with a sauce of tomatoes, capers, and olives) and the *filetto di Branzino in panuria di erbe* (breaded filet of sea bass) are particularly delicious. [$] *Average main: €15* ✉ *Piazzetta Sopra i Ponti 3–5* ☎ *0575/26557.*

$ ITALIAN 🍴 **La Torre di Gnicche.** Wine lovers shouldn't miss this wine bar/eatery, just off Piazza Grande, with more than 700 labels on the list. Seasonal dishes of traditional fare, such as *acquacotta del casentino* (porcini mushroom soup) and *baccalà in umido* (salt-cod stew), are served in the simply decorated, vaulted dining room. You can accompany your meal with one, or more, of the almost 30 wines that are available by the glass. Limited outdoor seating is available in warm weather. [$] *Average main: €14* ✉ *Piaggia San Martino 8* ☎ *0575/352035* 🌐 *www.latorredignicche.it* 🕒 *Closed Wed., Jan., and 2 wks in July.*

WHERE TO STAY

For expanded hotel reviews, visit Fodors.com.

$$ B&B/INN **Calcione.** The elegant Marchesa Olivella Lotteringhi della Stufa has turned her six-century-old family estate (circa 1483) into a top-notch agriturismo. **Pros:** houses can sleep up to 17; large swimming pools; quiet, beautiful, remote setting. **Cons:** private transportation is a must: nearest village is 8 km (5 miles) away; no a/c. [$] *Rooms from: €150* ✉ *Calcione, 26 km (15 miles) southwest of Arezzo, Lucignano* ☎ *0575/837153* 🌐 *www.calcione.com* 🛏 *2 houses, 1 cottage, 6 apartments* 💳 *No credit cards* ⏲ *Closed Oct.–mid-Mar.* 🍴 *No meals.*

$$ HOTEL **Castello di Gargonza.** Enchantment reigns at this tiny 13th-century countryside hamlet, part of the fiefdom of the aristocratic Florentine Guicciardini and reinvented by the modern Count Roberto Guicciardini as an agriturismo. **Pros:** romantic, one-of-a-kind accommodation in a medieval castle; peaceful, isolated setting. **Cons:** standard rooms are extremely basic; a little out of the way for exploring the region; private transportation is a necessity. [$] *Rooms from: €160* ✉ *SR73 28 km (17 miles) southwest of Arezzo, Località Gargonza, Monte San Savino* ☎ *0575/847021* 🌐 *www.gargonza.it* 🛏 *37 rooms, 8 apartments* ⏲ *Closed last 3 wks in Jan. and Feb.* 🍴 *Breakfast.*

$$$$ HOTEL **Il Borro.** The location has been described as "heaven on earth," and a stay at Salvatore Ferragamo's estate is sure to bring similar descriptions to mind. **Pros:** superlative service; great location for exploring eastern Tuscany; unique setting and atmosphere. **Cons:** off the beaten track making private transport a must; not all suites have country views; ultramodern spa facility seems out of place. [$] *Rooms from: €320* ✉ *Località Il Borro (outside the village of San Giustino Valdarno, 20 km /12 miles northwest of Arezzo)* ☎ *055/977053* 🌐 *www.ilborro.com* 🛏 *16 suites, 3 villas, 7 farmhouses, 4 apartments* 🍴 *Breakfast.*

SHOPPING

Ever since Etruscan goldsmiths set up their shops here more than 2,000 years ago, Arezzo has been famous for its jewelry. Today the town lays claim to being one of the world's capitals of jewelry design and manufacture, and you can find an impressive display of big-time baubles in the town center's shops. Arezzo is also famous, at least in Italy, for its antiques dealers.

ANTIQUES

The first weekend of every month, between 8:30 and 5:30 each day, a colorful flea market selling antiques and not-so-antiques takes place in the town's main square, **Piazza Grande.**

Grace Gallery. Look for antique jewelry, furniture, and paintings at this gallery. ✉ *Via Cavour 30* ☎ *0575/354963.*

La Belle Epoque. Specialties here include period clothing, antique lace, and embroidered linens. ✉ *Piazza San Francesco 18* ☎ *0575/355495.*

CORTONA

Cortona is called "Mother of Troy and Grandmother of Rome" in popular speech, and may be one of Italy's oldest towns. Tradition claims it was founded by Dardanus, the founder of Troy (after whom the Dardanelles are named). He was fighting a local tribe, the story goes, when he lost his helmet (*corythos* in Greek) on Cortona's hill. In time a town grew up that took its name (Corito) from the missing headgear. By the 4th century BC the Etruscans had built town walls, the traces of which can still be seen in the 3-km (2-mile) sweep of the present fortifications. As a member of the Etruscans' 12-city league, Cortona became one of the federation's leading northern cities. The area's major road, the Via Cassia, passed the foot of Cortona's hill, maintaining the town's importance under the Romans. Medieval fortunes waned, however, as the plain below reverted to marsh. After holding out against Perugia, Arezzo, and Siena, the *commune* was captured by King Ladislas of Naples in 1409 and sold to the Florentines.

GETTING HERE

Cortona is easily reached by car from the A1 highway: take the Valdichiana exit toward Perugia, then follow signs for Cortona. Regular bus service, provided by Etruria Mobilità, is available between Arezzo and Cortona (one hour). Train service to Cortona is made inconvenient by the location of the train station, in the valley 3 km (2 miles) steeply below the town itself. From there, you have to rely on bus or taxi service to get up to Cortona.

VISITOR INFORMATION

Cortona Tourism Office ⊠ *Piazza Signorelli 9* ☏ *0575/637223* ⊕ *arezzo. intoscana.it.*

EXPLORING CORTONA

Brought into the limelight by Frances Mayes's book *Under the Tuscan Sun* and a subsequent movie, Cortona is no longer the destination of just a few specialist art historians and those seeking reprieve from busier tourist venues. The main street, Via Nazionale, is now lined with souvenir shops and crowds during summer. Though the main sights of Cortona make braving the crowds worthwhile, much of the town's charm lies in its maze of quiet backstreets. It's here that you will see laundry hanging from windows and children playing, and catch the smell of simmering pasta sauce. Wander off the beaten track and you won't be disappointed.

TOP ATTRACTIONS

Duomo. Cortona's cathedral stands on an edge of the city, next to what's left of the Etruscan and medieval walls running from Porta Santa Maria to Porta Colonia. It was built on the site of an old Romanesque church, but the present Renaissance church was begun in 1480 and finished in 1507. An arcade along the outside wall was erected in the 16th century. The interior is a mixture of Renaissance and baroque styles featuring an exquisite 1664 baroque tabernacle on the high altar by Francesco Mazzuoli. ⊠ *Piazza Duomo 1* ☏ *0575/62830* ☙ *Daily 10–12:30 and 3–5.*

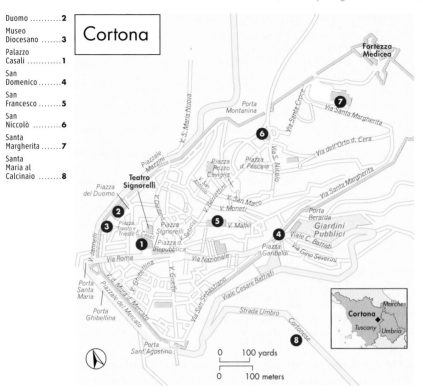

Museo Diocesano. Housed in part of the original cathedral structure, this nine-room museum houses an impressive number of paintings by native son Luca Signorelli (1445–1523), as well as the *Annunciation* by Fra Angelico (1387/1400–1455). The former oratory of the Compagnia del Gesù, reached by descending the 1633 staircase opposite the Duomo, is part of the museum. The church was built between 1498 and 1505 and restructured by Giorgio Vasari in 1543. Frescoes depicting sacrifices from the Old Testament by Doceno (1508–56), based on designs by Vasari, line the walls. ⊠ *Piazza Duomo 1* ☎ *0575/62830* ⊠ *€5* ⊗ *Apr.– Oct., daily 10–7; Nov.–Mar., Tues.–Sun. 10–5.*

Santa Maria al Calcinaio. Legend has it that the image of the Madonna appeared on a wall of a medieval *calcinaio* (lime pit used for curing leather), the site on which the church was then built between 1485 and 1513. The linear gray-and-white interior recalls Florence's Duomo. Sienese architect Francesco di Giorgio (1439–1502) most likely designed the sanctuary. ⊠ *Località Il Calcinaio 227, 3 km (2 miles) southeast of Cortona's center* ☎ *0575/604830* ⊗ *Mon.–Sat. 3:30–6, Sun. 10–12:30.*

WORTH NOTING

Palazzo Casali. Built originally by the Casali family, who lived here until 1409, this palace combines 13th- to 17th-century architectural styles. Today it is home to the Accademia Etrusca, with an extensive library;

La Biblioteca Comunale; and the Museo dell'Accademia Etrusca e della Città di Cortona (aka MAEC). A mix of Egyptian objects, Etruscan and Roman bronzes and statuettes, and paintings is on display in the museum. Perhaps the most famous piece is the Tabula Cortonensis,

WORD OF MOUTH

"If you stay overnight, you can watch the mist rising from the valley below Cortona, and watch the churches emerge from the mist." —cmt

an Etruscan contract written on bronze that was found in 1922 but dates back to the second century BC. In the basement, sections of the Etruscan and Roman buildings that form the foundations of the palace have been exposed. Look for work by Renaissance artists such as Luca Signorelli and Pinturicchio (circa 1454–1513). From May through September, guided tours are available in English. Accompanied visits with Italian guides to the Etruscan tombs on the slopes below Cortona may also be booked. ⊠ *Piazza Signorelli 9* ☎ *0575/630415* ⊕ *www.cortonamaec.org* ⊠ *Museo €10, €13 in combination with the Museo Diocesano, Biblioteca free* ⊗ *Apr.–Oct., daily 10–7; Nov.–Mar., Tues.–Sun. 10–5.*

San Domenico. Inside this anonymous-looking 14th-century church, just outside Cortona's walls, is an altarpiece depicting the Coronation of the Virgin against a sparkling gold background by Lorenzo di Niccolò Gerini (active late 14th–early 15th centuries). Among the other works is a Madonna and Child by Luca Signorelli. ⊠ *Largo Beato Angelico 1* ☎ *0575/603217* ⊗ *Daily 9–6.*

NEED A BREAK?

Caffe degli Artisti. If you need a break from sightseeing, this is a pleasant place to stop for a cappuccino, sandwiches at lunchtime, or the array of appetizers set out during the cocktail hour. In the summer months a few outdoor tables are set up directly on Via Nazionale, Cortona's main pedestrian street, and provide a great perch for those who love to people-watch. ⊠ *Via Nazionale 18* ☎ *0575/601237.*

San Francesco. In the mid-13th century, this Gothic-style church was built on the site of Etruscan and Roman baths. It is decorated with frescoes that date from 1382, a 17th-century crucifix by Giuseppe Piamontini of Florence, and houses a Relic of the Santa Croce, a vestige of the True Cross apparently given to Brother Elia when he served as an envoy for Federico II in Constantinople. The church's rather beautiful organ was unfortunately badly damaged during WWII. ⊠ *Via Berrettini 4* ☎ *0575/603205* ⊗ *Daily 9–7.*

San Niccolò. A small, cypress-lined courtyard and porch stand in front of this delightful Renaissance church. On the main altar is a fresco by Luca Signorelli, the *Deposition of Christ*, painted around 1510. On the left wall is another fresco by Signorelli of the Madonna and Child, which was plastered over in 1768 and rediscovered in 1847. To visit the church, ring the custodian's doorbell on the left-hand side of the building. ⊠ *Via S. Niccolò* ☎ *0575/604591* ⊠ *By donation* ⊗ *Daily 9–noon and 3–5.*

Santa Margherita. The large 1897 basilica was constructed over the foundation of a 13th-century church dedicated to the same saint. What makes the 10-minute uphill walk worthwhile is the richly decorated interior. The body of the 13th-century Saint Margherita—clothed but with skull and bare feet clearly visible—is displayed in a case on the main altar. ✉ *Piazzale Santa Margherita 1* ☎ *0575/603116* 🕓 *Daily 8–noon and 3–6.*

WHERE TO EAT AND STAY

For expanded hotel reviews, visit Fodors.com.

$$ TUSCAN 🍴 **Osteria del Teatro.** Photographs from theatrical productions spanning many years line the walls of this tavern off Cortona's large Piazza del Teatro. The food is simply delicious—try the *filetto al lardo di colonnata e prugne* (beef cooked with bacon and prunes); service is warm and friendly. [$] *Average main: €20* ✉ *Via Maffei 2* ☎ *0575/630556* 🌐 *www.osteria-del-teatro.it* 🕓 *Closed Wed., Feb., and 2 wks in Nov.*

$$$ B&B/INN 🏨 **Il Falconiere.** Accommodation options here include rooms in an 18th-century villa, suites in the *chiesetta* (chapel, or little church), or for more seclusion, Le Vigne del Falco suites at the far end of the property. **Pros:** attractive setting in the valley beneath Cortona; excellent service; elegant, but relaxed. **Cons:** a car is a must; some find rooms in main villa a little noisy; a bit fancy for the environs. [$] *Rooms from: €290* ✉ *Località San Martino 370, 3 km (1½ miles) north of Cortona* ☎ *0575/612679* 🌐 *www.ilfalconiere.com* 🛏 *13 rooms, 7 suites* 🕓 *Hotel closed last 3 wks in Jan.–mid-Feb.* 🍽 *Breakfast.*

SHOPPING

Antico Cocciaio. For nice ceramics, with many pieces depicting the brilliant sunflowers that blanket local fields, check here. ✉ *Via Benedetti 24* ☎ *0575/605294.*

SANSEPOLCRO AND THE CASENTINO

Sansepolcro, as far east as you can go in Tuscany without entering either Umbria or the Marches, sits in the upper valley of the Tiber River. Once a provincial Roman town, and then a medieval city, Sansepolcro has now developed an urban sprawl that almost masks its real treasures. Pass the 'burbs, enter the ancient walls, and you'll find narrow streets, Romanesque and Gothic churches, Renaissance palazzi, and city squares. All roads in Sansepolcro eventually lead to the small Museo Civico, where works by Piero della Francesca, the town's most famous artist, adorn the walls—a must-visit for any lover of Italian Renaissance art.

The sparsely populated region of the Casentino—defined as the upper valley of the Arno, the Val d'Arno—contains enough castles, Romanesque parish churches, and unspoiled villages to keep you exploring for days. But the jewels in its crown are contained within the Parco Nazionale Casentino, an 89,000-acre preserve. The heart of the park,

Piazza Signorelli, Cortona

on an Apennine ridge between the Arno and the Tiber, is the antique forest tended for eight centuries by the monks of the Abbazia Camaldoli, designers of the world's first forestry code. Every year they have planted 4,000–5,000 saplings. Eventually they planted only firs, creating majestic stands of the trees whose 150-foot trunks were once floated down the Arno to be used for the masts of warships.

SANSEPOLCRO

40 km (25 miles) northeast of Arezzo.

Originally called *Borgo San Sepolcro* (City of the Holy Sepulchre), this sprawling agricultural town takes its name from relics brought here from the Holy Land by two pilgrims in the 10th century. Today, inside a circle of 15th-century walls, the gridlike street plan hints at the town's ancient Roman origins. Known as the birthplace of Piero della Francesca—several of his paintings are displayed in the town's Civic Museum—the old center of Sansepolcro retains a distinctly medieval air, with narrow streets lined with churches and 15th-century palaces.

GETTING HERE

Traveling to Sansepolcro by either car or bus from Arezzo is to be preferred over the journey by train, which can take up to four hours. By car, follow the SS73; if traveling by bus (one hour), check with Etruria Mobilità for the schedule, though service is infrequent.

VISITOR INFORMATION

Sansepolcro tourism office ✉ *Via Matteotti 8* ☎ *0575/740536* ⊕ *www. apt.arezzo.it.*

EXPLORING

Museo Civico. Piero della Francesca is the star at this small provincial museum. Three—possibly four—of his works are on display: the reassembled altarpiece of the *Misericordia* (1445–62) and frescoes depicting the *Resurrection* (circa 1460), *Saint Julian,* and the disputed *Saint Louis of Toulouse,* which is possibly the work of a close follower of the artist. Other works of interest are those by Santi di Tito (1536–1603), also from Sansepolcro, and Pontormo's *San Quintino* (1517–18). ✉ *Via Aggiunti 65* ☎ *0575/732218* 🌐 *www.museocivicosansepolcro.it* 🎟 *€8* 🕒 *June 15–Sept. 15, daily 9:30–1:30 and 2:30–7; Sept. 16–June 14, daily 9:30–1 and 2:30–6.*

OFF THE BEATEN PATH

Monterchi. This sleepy town, sitting on a small knoll about 15 km (9 miles) south of Sansepolcro, would probably attract little attention if it were not for the fact that Piero della Francesca stopped here to paint one of his greatest masterpieces in the 1450s.

Museo "Madonna del Parto". Not surprisingly, only one painting is displayed here, Piero's *Madonna del Parto* (circa 1455), a fresco depicting the expectant Virgin flanked by two angels. Originally painted for the small chapel of Santa Maria a Momentana in Monterchi's cemetery, the work was restored in 1992–93 and moved, shortly thereafter, into the museum. ✉ *Via Reglia 1* ☎ *0575/70713* 🎟 *€3.50; pregnant women are admitted free of charge* 🕒 *Apr.–Oct., Tues.–Sun. 9–1 and 2–7; Nov.–Mar., Tues.–Sun. 9–1 and 2–5.*

WHERE TO EAT

$ TUSCAN

🍴 **Taverna Toscana.** An exceptionally tasty *panzanella* (Tuscan bread salad) might start off your meal at this authentic trattoria in the center of Sansepolcro. Follow it with a homemade pasta, accompanied by a glass of house wine, a Banfi Cabernet Sauvignon from Montalcino. A complimentary glass of *vin santo* is offered with your choice of dessert. [$] *Average main: €12* ✉ *Via Luca Pacioli 50/a* ☎ *0575/742017* 🌐 *www.tavernatoscana.it* 🕒 *Closed Tues.*

5

PARCO NAZIONALE CASENTINO

Pratovecchio: 55 km (34 miles) north of Arezzo, 50 km (31 miles) east of Florence.

GETTING HERE

You'll need a car to explore this area: getting here by bus, though surprisingly easier from Florence than it is from Arezzo, is a complicated process; it's impossible by train.

VISITOR INFORMATION

Park information office. In addition to this office, there are branch offices at Camaldoli (✉ *Località Camaldoli 19* ☎ *0575/556130*) and Stia (✉ *Piazza Tanucci, no phone*). ✉ *Via Giodo Brocchi 7* ☎ *0543/50301* 🌐 *www.parcoforestecasentinesi.it.*

EXPLORING

Parco delle Foreste Casentinesi. A drive through the park, especially on the winding 34-km (21-mile) road between the Monastero di Camaldoli and Santuario della Verna, passing through the abbey town of

Badia Prataglia, reveals one satisfying vista after another, from walls of firs to pillows of pastureland. In autumn the beeches add a mass of red-brown to the palette, and in spring torrents of golden broom pour off the hillsides with a profusion and fragrance. Walking the forests is the best way to see the wild creatures, from deer and mouflon (wild sheep imported from Sardinia starting in 1872) to eagles and many other birds, as well

> **WORD OF MOUTH**
>
> "I suggest the area east of Florence and south of Ravenna, known as the Casentino. Fairly mountainous, it has a number of famous monasteries including the one at La Verna (St Francis) and Camaldoli. There's also the hilltown of Poppi and its castello."
> —TuckH

as 1,000 species of flora, including many rare and endangered plants and an orchid found nowhere else. The **Grande Escursione Apenninica** (GEA) hiking route, which is accessible from both the Monastero di Camaldoli and the Sanutario della Verna, runs along a winding ridge. The park organizes walks in summer and provides English-speaking guides with advance notice. ✉ *Via Centro, Campigna* ☎ *0575/0543 980231* ⊕ *www.parcoforestecasentinesi.it.*

MONASTERO DI CAMALDOLI

20 km (12 miles) northeast of Pratovecchio, 55 km (34 miles) north of Arezzo.

GETTING HERE
As with the Casentino National Park in general, the only practical way to reach the monastery is by car: take SP71 to Serravalle, then follow the signs. Bus service is infrequent and the schedule is tortuous; train service is nonexistent.

EXPLORING
Monastero di Camaldoli. In 1012 Saint Romualdo, scion of a noble Ravenna family, came upon the forests of the Casentino and found their remoteness conducive to religious contemplation. He stayed and founded a hermitage, Monastero Camaldoli (named for Count Maldoli, who donated the land), which became the seat of a new Benedictine order. Four centuries after the order's founding by Saint Benedict, Romualdo felt it had become too permissive. An important requirement of the order was preserving its ascetic atmosphere: "If the hermits are to be true devotees of solitude, they must take the greatest care of the woods." When the flow of pilgrims began to threaten that solitude, Romualdo had a monastery and hospital built 1 km (½ mile) down the mountain to create some distance. Today the hermitage, **Sacro Eremo di Camaldoli**—where the monks live in complete silence in 20 cottages, each with its own walled garden—can be seen through gates, and the church and original cell of Romualdo, the model for all the others, can be visited. The church, rebuilt in the 13th century and transformed in the 18th to its present appearance, strikes an odd note in connection with such an austere order because it's done up in gaudy baroque style.

Its most appealing artwork is the glazed terra-cotta relief *Madonna and Child with Saints* by Andrea della Robbia.

Within the monastery half a mile away is a church containing 14th-century frescoes by Spinello Aretino, seven 16th-century panel paintings by Giorgio Vasari, and a lovely monastic choir. The choir has 18th-century walnut stalls, more Vasari paintings, and a serene fresco of Saint Romualdo instructing his white-robed disciples. In a hospital built for sick villagers in 1046 is the 1543 **Antica Farmacia** (Old Pharmacy), with original carved walnut cabinets. Here you can buy herbal teas, liqueurs, and toiletries made by the monks from centuries-old recipes as part of their daily routine balancing prayer, work, and study (the monastery is self-supporting). In the back room is an exhibit of the early pharmacy's equipment with which the monks made herbs into medicines. You can attend spiritual retreats organized by the monks: contact the *foresteria* (visitors lodge) for details. ⊠ *Località Camaldoli, Poppi* ☎ *0575/556021 Monastero, 0575/556013 Foresteria* ⊕ *www. camaldoli.it* 🔲 *Free* ⊙ *Daily 6:30–12:30 and 3–7.*

SANTUARIO DELLA VERNA

34 km (21 miles) southeast of Monastero di Camaldoli and of Pratovecchio.

GETTING HERE

The only practical way to reach the sanctuary is by car—it's 21 km (13 miles) east of Bibbiena on SP208. There is no direct bus service, and train service is nonexistent.

EXPLORING

Santuario della Verna. A few hills away from the Monastero di Camaldoli, perched on a sheer-walled rock surrounded by firs and beeches, is La Verna, founded by Saint Francis of Assisi in 1214. Ten years later, after a 40-day fast, Saint Francis had a vision of Christ crucified, and when it was over, Francis had received the stigmata, the signs of Christ's wounds, on his hands, feet, and chest. A stone in the floor of the 1263 Chapel of the Stigmata marks the spot. A corridor through which the monks pass, chanting in a solemn procession each afternoon at 3 on the way to Mass, is lined with frescoes of the *Life of St. Francis*. The true artistic treasures of the place, though, are 15 della Robbia glazed terra-cottas. Most, like a beautiful Annunciation, are in the 14th- to 15th-century basilica, which has a 5,000-pipe organ.

Several chapels, each with its own story, can be visited, and some natural and spiritual wonders can also be seen. A walkway along the 230-foot-high cliff leads to an indentation where the rock is said to have miraculously melted away to protect Saint Francis when the devil tried to push him off the edge. Most touching is the enormous Sasso Spicco (Projecting Rock), where Saint Francis meditated. You can also view the Letto di San Francesco (Saint Francis's Bed), a slab of rock in a damp cave with an iron grate on which he prayed and slept. A 40-minute walk through the woods to the top of Mt. Penna passes some religious sites and ends in panoramic views of the Arno Valley, but those from the cliff-edge terrace are equally impressive, including the tower of the castle in Poppi, the Prato Magno (great meadow), and the olive groves on the lower slopes. Santuario della Verna's foresteria also has simple, comfortable rooms with or without bath. A restaurant ($) with basic fare is there, and a shop sells the handiwork of the monks.

As you leave La Verna, be glad you needn't do it as Edith Wharton (1862–1937) did on a 1912 visit during a drive across the Casentino. As she wrote, her car "had to be let down on ropes to a point about ¾ mile below the monastery, Cook [her chauffeur] steering down the vertical descent, and twenty men hanging on to a funa [rope] that, thank the Lord, didn't break." ⊠ *21 km (13 miles) east of Bibbiena on the Sp 208, Via del Santuario 45* ☎ *0575/5341* ⊕ *www.santuariolaverna.org* ⊗ *Apr.–Oct., daily 6:30 am–10 pm; Nov.–Mar., daily 6:30 am–7:30 pm.*

OFF THE BEATEN PATH

Caprese Michelangelo. Some 10 km (6 miles) south of La Verna on SR54 is the small hilltop town where Michelangelo Buonarroti, sculptor, painter, architect, and poet, was born on March 6, 1475.

Museo Michelangelo. Opened in 1964 to honor the 400th anniversary of Michelangelo's death, the museum displays photographs, plaster casts, and documents relating to the artist's work. ⊠ *Via Capoluogo 3* ☎ *0575/793912* 🎫 *€5* ⊗ *Apr. and May, Mon.–Sat. 11–6, Sun. 11–7; June, July, and Sept., Mon.–Sat. 10–7, Sun. 9:30–7:30; Aug., daily 9:30–7:30; Oct., Mon.–Sat. 10:30–5:30, Sun. 10:30–6:30; Nov.–Mar., Mon.–Sat. 11–5, Sun. 11–6.*

Sagra della Castagna (*Chestnut Festival*). During two weekends in mid-October, Caprese Michelangelo's very lively Sagra della Castagna (*Chestnut Festival*) takes place. Among the many other chestnut-based delights that feature in the fair, the freshly made *castagnaccia* (a typically Tuscan dessert made with chestnut flour, pine nuts, and rosemary) is a must-try. ⊠ *Tourist office, Via Capoluogo 46* ☎ *0575/793760* ⊕ *www.capresemichelangelo.net.*

SOUTHERN
TUSCANY

WELCOME TO SOUTHERN TUSCANY

TOP REASONS TO GO

★ **Pienza's urban renewal:** A 15th-century makeover turned this otherwise unpretentious village into a model Renaissance town.

★ **Saturnia's hot water:** The gods themselves reportedly had a hand in creating the springs at this world-famous spa town.

★ **Napoléon's home in exile:** The island of Elba, where the French leader was once imprisoned, is the prettiest island in the Tuscan archipelago.

★ **Wine tastings in Montepulciano:** This gorgeous town also happens to be the home of one of Italy's finest wines—Vino Nobile di Montepulciano.

★ **A stroll through Abbazia di Sant'Antimo:** This 12th-century Romanesque abbey shows French, Lombard, and even Spanish influences.

1 Val d'Orcia. In the area surrounding this lush valley you'll find some of southern Tuscany's most attractive towns. Montalcino and Montepulciano are famed for their wine, Pienza for its urban planning and its pecorino cheese.

2 Le Crete. South of Siena, the stark clay landscape and unassuming towns are interrupted by Abbazia di Monte Oliveto Maggiore, the most-visited abbey in Tuscany.

3 The Maremma. Tuscany's deep south may not conform to your expectations for the region; it's best known for its cattle ranches and its coastline. "Discovering" the Maremma has become popular with off-the-beaten-path travelers, though you hardly have to rough it here—you'll find exceptional food and wine, and the spa town of Saturnia is all about indulgence.

TUSCANY

UMBRIA

GETTING ORIENTED

Southeast of Siena, not far from the Umbrian border, the towns of Montepulciano, Montalcino, and Pienza are Tuscan classics—perched on hills, constructed during the Middle Ages and the Renaissance, and saturated with fine wine. Venture farther south and you encounter Tuscany with a rougher edge: the Maremma region is populated by cowboys, and a good portion of the landscape remains wild. But you won't forget you're in Italy here; the wine is still excellent, and some locals store their supply in Etruscan tombs.

6

4 Elba and the Surrounding Islands. It's a short hop from the coast to the islands of the Tuscan archipelago. Several of them—most notably Elba—have long been vacation getaways.

Updated
by Peter
Blackman

AS DIVERSE AS ITALY ITSELF, southern Tuscany ranges from the green knolls of the Val d'Orcia to the sandy beaches at Punta Ala. It contains the wildest parts of Tuscany—the Maremma, once a malaria-ridden swampland where the *butteri*, Italy's cowboys, rounded up their cattle, now a peaceful woodland fringed with beaches; Monte Amiata, a scruffy mountain landscape where goats gnaw at clumps of brown grass among scattered rocks; and the still-wild islands of the Tuscan archipelago. Some of Tuscany's best-kept secrets lie here in the south, among them the Abbazia di San Galgano, which is open to the sky, and the cool mountain enclaves of Monte Amiata. This is Etruscan country, where the necropolis near Sovana hints at a rich and somewhat mysterious pre-Roman civilization.

Apart from the occasional rocky promontory, the coast of southern Tuscany is virtually one long stretch of fine-sand beach. Private beach areas are common near the resort towns south of Livorno and just north of Monte Argentario, where there are chairs and umbrellas for rent, shower facilities, and bars. Along the rest of the coast, the beaches are public. They're particularly pleasant in the nature reserve at Monti dell'Uccellina and along the sandbars that connect Monte Argentario to the mainland. On the islands, rocky shores predominate, although Elba has a few sandy beaches on its southern side.

You can visit the whole region in about five days. Keep in mind that southern Tuscany isn't well served by trains, so if you aren't renting a car you'll have to plan around sometimes difficult bus schedules, and the going will be slow. The A1 (Autostrada del Sole), which runs from Florence to Rome, passes near the Val d'Orcia. SS1 (the Via Aurelia) follows the western coastline for much of the way, before jutting inland at Grosseto.

PLANNING

MAKING THE MOST OF YOUR TIME

The towns in southern Tuscany are fairly close together, so it's possible to pick one of them as your base and take day trips to almost everywhere else in the region. **Pienza,** in the middle of the **Val d'Orcia,** makes an excellent place to begin your trip. Other good choices include **Montepulciano** and **Montalcino.** From any of these it's only a short drive to all the other towns in the Val d'Orcia, as well as the famous abbeys in and around **Le Crete.**

If your main reason for visiting this region is a dip in the hot springs, you should stay in **Saturnia** or one of the surrounding villages. (Because so many people go there for a soak, Saturnia has the most luxurious lodgings.)

If your destination is the Tuscan archipelago, you'd do best to choose one island, as there is no ferry service between them. **Elba** is more famous, but it's hard to find a place to lay your towel in the summer months. **Giglio** has less-crowded beaches, and a few accessible on foot or by boat that you might have to yourself.

GETTING HERE AND AROUND
BUS TRAVEL
Although tortuous roads and circuitous routes make bus travel in southern Tuscany slow, it's a reliable way to get around if you don't have a car. Schedules are always changing, so plan your trip carefully with the aid of local tourist offices. (They're more likely to have an English-speaking staff than are bus stations.) The major bus stations for the region are in Siena and Grosseto, but most towns have bus service even if they don't have actual bus stations.

ATL. With an office in Portoferraio, the company provides bus service around Elba. ☎ *0565/915704, 800/371560 toll-free in Italy* ⊕ *www.atl.livorno.it.*

RAMA. Based in Grosseto, the company provides bus service throughout the Maremma region. ☎ *0564/475111, 199/848787 toll-free in Italy* ⊕ *www.griforama.it.*

SITA. This bus company provides regular rapid service between Florence and Siena. ☎ *0577/204259 in Siena, 800/570530 toll-free in Italy.*

Tra-In. Bus service thoughout the province of Siena is provided by Tra-In. ☎ *0577/204246* ⊕ *www.trainspa.it.*

CAR TRAVEL
The area is easily reached by car on the A1 highway (Autostrada del Sole), which runs between Rome and Florence—take the Chiusi–Chianciano Terme exit for Montepulciano, Pienza, and San Quirico Val d'Orcia. From Florence the fastest route to southern Tuscany is via the Florence–Siena Superstrada and then the Via Cassia (SR2) from Siena for Buonconvento and Montalcino. There is also a good road (SR223) linking Siena and Grosseto, for outings to the Parco Naturale della Maremma and Monte Argentario.

From Genoa or the northern Tuscan coast, follow the coastal highway (A12) to reach Livorno and its ferry service to Capraia. For direct ferry service to Elba, continue south on the SS1 (the Via Aurelia) to reach Piombino. Past Piombino, the SS1 passes Grosseto, the Parco Naturale della Maremma, and Monte Argentario, before continuing south toward Rome.

TRAIN TRAVEL
Train service within this region is slow; in many cases buses are quicker. Trains run from Chiusi–Chianciano Terme to Siena (one hour) with stops in Montepulciano and Asciano.

Ferrovie dello Stato. You can check the website of the state railway for train schedules, or stop in any travel agency— many speak English and will book and print train tickets for you. ☎ *892021 toll-free in Italy* ⊕ *www.trenitalia.com.*

HOTELS
Southern Tuscany is a great place to enjoy the *agriturismo* (agrotourism) lifestyle: if you have a week to stay in one of these rural farmhouses, pick someplace central, such as Pienza, and explore the region from that base. It may be so relaxing and the food so good that you might have trouble wandering away.

You will also find many hotels in this region: modern affairs in cities, surfside beach resorts, and timeworn villas.

VAL D'ORCIA

The Val d'Orcia (Orcia Valley) is a sumptuous green valley with breathtaking views of the Orcia River, which runs through it. The area's long-standing agricultural tradition has left it utterly undeveloped, and so the vistas here are classic Tuscany—rolling hills topped by villages, wide plains, swaths of blooming fields punctuated by vineyards and olive groves. Picture-perfect Pienza, medieval San Quirico d'Orcia, and Bagno Vignoni are great photo-op stops; amateur archaeologists will enjoy pondering Chiusi's painted Etruscan tombs; and Chianciano Terme's thermal baths can provide a sybaritic treat during your stay. Hills near Montalcino border the valley in the west, and it's in that hilltop town that Siena chose to make a last desperate stand against the invading Florentines. Not to be missed is the superbly positioned Abbazia di Sant'Antimo to the south. Montepulciano, filled with town palaces and Renaissance churches—and fortified by some great red wine—is at the valley's boundary in the east.

CHIUSI

40 km (25 miles) south of Cortona, 84 km (50 miles) southeast of Siena, 126 km (78 miles) southeast of Florence.

Chiusi was once one of the most powerful of the ancient cities of the Etruscan League, and it's now a valuable source of information about that archaic civilization. Fifth-century BC tombs found in the nearby hills have provided archaeologists with a wealth of artifacts. On the route of the ancient Via Cassia, Chiusi became a major Roman center and an important communication hub that linked Rome with the agriculturally rich Chiana Valley to the east, with Siena to the northwest, and to other major cities in central and northern Italy. When the Chiana Valley became a malaria-ridden swamp during the Middle Ages, Chiusi's importance declined, and it was not until the Medici devised a scheme to drain the valley (with plans supplied by Leonardo da Vinci) in the early 15th century that the town began to reestablish itself.

GETTING HERE

Chiusi is easily reached by car on the A1 highway (Autostrada del Sole), which runs between Rome and Florence. Tra-In buses link Chiusi with Siena, but train service is faster and more frequent. Chiusi is on a main rail line between Florence and Rome, and can be reached from either city.

VISITOR INFORMATION

Chiusi tourism office ✉ *Via Porsena 79* ☎ *0578/227667* ⊕ *www. prolocochiusi.it.*

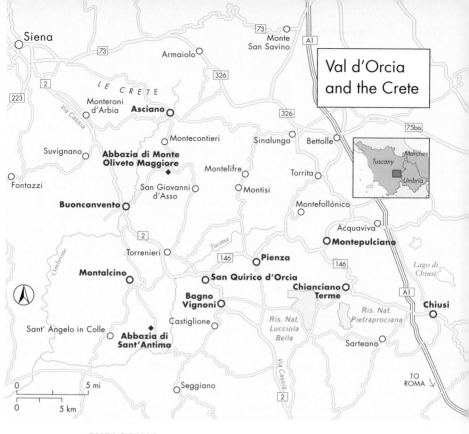

Val d'Orcia
and the Crete

EXPLORING

Museo Nazionale Etrusco. Most of the artifacts found during the excavations of Chiusi's Etruscan sites are now on display in this small but expertly laid out museum. Relics include elegant Etruscan and Greek vases, carved Etruscan tomb chests, and a number of the strange canopic jars with anthropomorphic shapes that are particular to this area. The tombs themselves can be seen by arrangement with the museum; visits are accompanied by a member of the museum staff. These underground burial chambers are still evocative of ancient life, particularly in the Tomba della Scimmia (Tomb of the Monkey), where well-preserved frescoes depict scenes from ordinary life 2,500 years ago. The Tomba del Leone (Tomb of the Lion) and Tomba della Pellegrina (Tomb of the Pilgrim) are open at set times during museum hours. ⊠ *Via Porsenna 93* ☎ *0578/20177* 🖼 *Museum €6, with the Tombs of the Lion and of the Pilgrim; Tomb of the Monkey €3* 🕙 *Museum: daily 9–8 (last entrance 7:30). Tomba della Scimmia: by appointment Apr.–Oct.,*

WORD OF MOUTH

"Chiusi is very easy to train to, has car-rental places, and is within easy reach of charming towns where you might want to base yourselves. It's very well placed for the Val d'Orcia and other beauty spots in Tuscany."
—tuscanlifeedit

Tues., Thurs., and Sat. at 11 and 4; Nov.–Mar., Tues., Thurs., and Sat. at 11 and 2:30.

CHIANCIANO TERME

11 km (7 miles) northwest of Chiusi, 73 km (44 miles) southeast of Siena.

People from around the world come to the *città del fegato sano* (city of the healthy liver) to experience the curative waters. The area's innumerable mineral-water springs are reputed to restore and maintain the health of the skin, among other things. This is nothing new; as early as the 5th century BC Chianciano Terme was the site of a temple to Apollo the Healer. It's no secret, either—the Terme di Chianciano spa alone claims to draw 120,000 visitors a year, and Italian state health insurance covers visits to the baths and springs for qualified patients. But you can test the waters yourself at a number of springs. If you're not here for the waters, probably the most interesting part of Chianciano is the old town, which lies to the north. The modern town, stretching along a hillside to the south, is a series of hotels, shops, and restaurants catering to spa aficionados.

GETTING HERE

From Rome or Florence, Chiusi is easily reached by car on the A1 highway (Autostrada del Sole). Tra-In buses link Chianciano with Siena. The closest train station to Chianciano Terme is in Chiusi, about 15 km (9 miles) away.

VISITOR INFORMATION

Chianciano Terme tourism office ✉ *Piazza Italia 67* ☎ *0578/671122* ⊕ *www.chianciano.com.*

EXPLORING

Chianciano. This walled medieval town, 3 km (2 miles) northeast of Chianciano Terme, is best known for its proximity to the nearby spas; nevertheless, the well-preserved center has an appeal all of its own. ✉ *Chianciano.*

Museo Civico Archeologico. This museum contains a good collection of Etruscan and Roman sculpture and pottery excavated from around the area. ✉ *Via Dante 80, Chianciano* ☎ *0578/30471* ⊕ *www. museoetrusco.it* 🖭 *€5* ☼ *Apr.–July and Sept.–Oct., Tues.–Sun. 10–1 and 4–7; Aug., daily 10–1 and 4–7; Nov.–Mar., weekends 10–1 and 4–7.*

Sarteano. To the southeast of Chianciano, 10 km (6 miles) along SP19, lies this relatively unspoiled village that dates from the 12th and 13th centuries. The town's narrow streets, which wind slowly up toward an imposing fortress, now privately owned, make for very pleasant strolling.

San Martino in Foro. Don't miss this small church, which houses a striking Annunciation by the important Sienese painter Domenico Beccafumi (1486–1551). ✉ *Piazza San Martino, Sarteano* ☼ *Daily 9–12:30 and 4–7:30.*

Terme di Chianciano. This organization represents three spas in Chianciano: Acqua Santa, Acqua Fucoli, and Acqua Sillene, where mud baths are also available. The Terme website lists the varied spa treatments available. Perhaps to offset the clinical coldness of the actual treatment centers, each spa is surrounded by a large park filled with trees, flower gardens, and reflecting pools. There are facilities for such light sporting activities as tennis and boccie, and dance floors are available for musical events on summer evenings. The all-important water is served up at long counters, where the spa staff is always ready to refill your glass. Be warned: The mineral water can have a cleansing effect on your system that may come on suddenly. ⊠ *Via delle Rose 12* ☎ *848/800243* ⊕ *www.termechianciano.it.*

Terme Sant'Elena. The waters here are said to help with kidney and urinary-tract ailments and all manner of digestive disorders; there are boccie courts and a pretty park to stroll in while you sip. On summer afternoons you can dance to live orchestra music in the park. ⊠ *Viale dell Libertà 112* ☎ *0578/31141* ⊕ *www.acquasantelena.it* ⊠ *Mid-Apr.– May and last two weeks in Oct., €6.50; June–mid-Oct., €8* ⊙ *Mid-Apr.– Oct., weekdays 8–noon and 4:30–7:30, Sat. 9–noon.*

OFF THE
BEATEN
PATH

Cetona. Follow SP19 past Sarteano and continue on SP21 to reach this delightful village. Time may seem to have stopped as you walk along the quiet, narrow, medieval lanes and back alleys. Peer through the locked gate for a glimpse of the privately owned castle, and take in splendid views of olive orchards, cypress groves, and the quiet wooded slopes of Mt. Cetona from the town's terraced streets. ⊠ *20 km (12 miles) southeast of Chianciano Terme.*

MONTEPULCIANO

10 km (6 miles) northeast of Chianciano Terme, 65 km (40 miles) southeast of Siena, 114 km (70 miles) southeast of Florence.

Perched on a hilltop, Montepulciano is made up of a pyramid of red-brick buildings set within a circle of cypress trees. At an altitude of almost 2,000 feet, it is cool in summer and chilled in winter by biting winds sweeping down its spiraling streets. The town has an unusually harmonious look, the result of the work of three architects: Antonio da Sangallo "il Vecchio" (circa 1455–1534), Vignola (1507–73), and Michelozzo (1396–1472). The group endowed it with fine palaces and churches in an attempt to impose Renaissance architectural ideals on an ancient Tuscan hill town.

GETTING HERE

From Rome or Florence, take the Chiusi–Chianciano exit from the A1 highway (Autostrada del Sole). From Siena, take the SR2 south to San Quirico and then the SP146 to Montepulciano. Tra-In offers bus service from Siena to Montepulciano several times a day. Montepulciano's train station is in Montepulciano Stazione, 10 km (6 miles) away.

VISITOR INFORMATION

Montepulciano Tourism Office ⊠ *Piazza Don Minzoni 1* ☎ *0578/757341* ⊕ *www.prolocomontepulciano.it.*

EXPLORING

Duomo. On the Piazza Grande the unfinished facade of Montepulciano's cathedral doesn't measure up to the beauty of its neighboring palaces. On the inside, however, its Renaissance roots shine through. The high altar has a splendid triptych painted in 1401 by Taddeo di Bartolo (ca. 1362–1422), and you can see fragments of the tomb of Bartolomeo Aragazzi, secretary to Pope Martin V, which was sculpted by Michelozzo between 1427 and 1436. ✉ *Piazza Grande* ☎ *0578/757341* 🕐 *Daily 9–12:30 and 3–6.*

Palazzo Comunale. Montepulciano's town hall dates to the late 13th century, though it was restructured in the 14th century and again in the mid-15th century. Michelozzo oversaw this last phase, using the Palazzo Vecchio in Florence as his inspiration. From the tower, a commanding view of Siena, Mt. Amiata (the highest point in Tuscany), and Lake Trasimeno (the largest lake on the Italian peninsula) can be enjoyed on a clear day. ✉ *Piazza Grande 1* ☎ *0578/757341* 🎟 *Free* 🕐 *Tower: Apr.–Oct., Mon.–Sat. 9–1.*

Piazza Grande. Filled with handsome buildings, this large square on the heights of the old historic town is Montepulciano's pièce de résistance.

Fodor's Choice ★ **San Biagio.** Designed by Antonio da Sangallo il Vecchio, and considered his masterpiece, this church sits on the hillside below the town walls and is a model of High Renaissance architectural perfection. Inside the church is a painting of the Madonna that according to legend, was the only thing remaining in an abandoned church that two young girls entered on April 23, 1518. The girls saw the eyes of the Madonna moving, and that same afternoon so did a farmer and a cow, who knelt down in front of the painting. In 1963 the image was proclaimed the Madonna del Buon Viaggio (Madonna of the Good Journey), the protector of tourists in Italy. ✉ *Via di San Biagio* ☎ *0578/757164* 🕐 *Daily 9–12:30 and 3:30–7:30.*

Sant'Agostino. Michelozzo had a hand in creating the beautiful travertine facade on the church of Sant'Agostino, which was built in 1285 and renovated in the early 1400s. He also sculpted the terra-cotta relief of the Madonna and Child above the entrance. ✉ *Piazzale Pasquino da Montepulciano 6* ☎ *0578/757341* 🕐 *Daily 9–12:30 and 3:30–7:30.*

WHERE TO EAT

$$$ TUSCAN Fodor's Choice ★ 🍴 **La Grotta.** You might be tempted to pass right by the innocuous entrance across the street from San Biagio, but you'd miss some fantastic food. Try the *pici fatti a mano con ragù di anatra e lenticchie* (homemade noodles with duck sauce and lentils) or *carrè di agnello alle erbe aromatiche con verdure al forno* (rack of lamb with herbs and baked vegetables). Wash it down with the local wine, which just happens to be one of Italy's finest—Vino Nobile di Montepulciano. The desserts, such as an extravagantly rich triple-chocolate flan, are prepared with particular flair. [$] *Average main: €30* ✉ *Via di San Biagio 15* ☎ *0578/757479* 🌐 *www.lagrottamontepulciano.it* 🕐 *Closed Wed. and Jan.–mid-Mar.*

$$ TUSCAN 🍴 **Osteria del Conte.** As high in Montepulciano as you can get, just behind the Duomo, this small and intimate restaurant is expertly run by the mother and son team of Lorena and Paolo Brachi. Passionate about

Summer in Valle d'Orcia

the food they prepare, both have a flair for the region's traditional dishes—the *pici all'aglione* (handmade spaghetti with garlic sauce) and the *filetto ai funghi porcini* (steak with porcini mushrooms) are mouth-wateringly good. The wine list, though limited in range, presents a decent selection of wines from both Montepulciano and Montalcino. For a change from the usual Tuscan meat dishes, fresh fish is served on Friday. Outdoor seating is limited. [$] *Average main: €15* ✉ *Via di San Donato 19* ☎ *0578/756062* 🌐 *www.osteriadelconte.it* ✍ *Reservations essential* 🕑 *Closed Wed.*

WHERE TO STAY

For expanded hotel reviews, visit Fodors.com.

$ B&B/INN 🏨 **La Terrazza.** On a quiet street in the upper part of town, these unpretentious lodgings are given sparkle by the welcoming and friendly service of the owners, Roberto and Vittoria Giardinelli. **Pros:** friendly family atmosphere; quiet central location. **Cons:** no a/c; no service at night. [$] *Rooms from: €90* ✉ *Via del Piè al Sasso 16* ☎ *0578/757440* 🌐 *www.laterrazzadimontepulciano.it* 🛏 *12 rooms* 🍴 *Breakfast.*

$$$$ B&B/INN Fodor's Choice ★ 🏨 **Podere Dionora.** At this secluded and serene country inn, earth-tone fabrics complement antiques in the individually decorated rooms, all of which have functioning fireplaces. **Pros:** secluded setting; great views; attentive service. **Cons:** long walk to the nearest town; need a car to get around. [$] *Rooms from: €330* ✉ *Via Vicinale di Poggiano 9, 3 km (2 miles) east of Montepulciano town center* ☎ *0578/717496* 🌐 *www.dionora.it* 🛏 *6 rooms* 🕑 *Closed mid-Dec.–mid-Feb.* 🍴 *Breakfast.*

$$$ B&B/INN Fodor's Choice ★ 🏨 **Relais San Bruno.** Alberto Pavoncelli converted his family's summer home, just minutes from the town center, into a splendid inn where well-appointed rooms are filled with views. **Pros:** king-size beds in most rooms; functioning fireplaces; relaxed but attentive service. **Cons:** cottages can be chilly; need a car to get around. [$] *Rooms from: €250* ✉ *Via di Pescaia 5/7* ☎ *0578/716222* 🌐 *www.sanbrunorelais.com* 🛏 *7 rooms, 2 suites, 1 cottage* 🍴 *Breakfast.*

$$ B&B/INN 🏨 **San Biagio.** A five-minute walk from the church of the same name, this family-run inn makes a great base for exploring Montepulciano and the surrounding countryside. **Pros:** heated indoor pool; family-friendly atmosphere. **Cons:** some rooms face a busy road; lots of tour groups. [$] *Rooms from: €135* ✉ *Via San Bartolomeo 2* ☎ *0578/717233* 🌐 *www.albergosanbiagio.it* 🛏 *27 rooms* 🍴 *Breakfast.*

NIGHTLIFE AND THE ARTS

Cantiere Internazionale d'Arte. This festival of art, music, and theater takes place in a variety of venues during July and August, ending with a dramatic stage production in the Piazza Grande. ✉ *Via del Teatro 4* ☎ *0578/758473 ticket office.*

PIENZA

12 km (7 miles) west of Montepulciano, 52 km (31 miles) southeast of Siena, 120 km (72 miles) southeast of Florence.

Pienza owes its appearance to Pope Pius II (1405–64), who had grand plans to transform his hometown of Corsignano—its former name—into a compact model Renaissance town. The man entrusted with the transformation was Bernardo Rossellino (1409–64), a protégé of the great Renaissance architectural theorist Leon Battista Alberti (1404–72). His mandate was to create a cathedral, a papal palace, and a town hall that adhered to the vainglorious pope's principles. Gothic and Renaissance styles were fused, and the buildings were decorated with Sienese paintings. The net result was a project that expressed Renaissance ideals of art, architecture, and civilized good living in a single scheme: it stands as an exquisite example of the architectural canons that Alberti formulated in the early Renaissance and that were utilized by later architects, including Michelangelo, in designing many of Italy's finest buildings and piazzas. Today the cool nobility of Pienza's center seems almost surreal in this otherwise unpretentious village, renowned for its smooth sheep's-milk pecorino cheese.

GETTING HERE

From Siena, drive south along the SR2 to San Quirico d'Orcia and then take the SP146. The trip should take just over an hour. Tra-In shuttles passengers between Siena and Pienza. There is no train service to Pienza.

VISITOR INFORMATION

Pienza Tourism Office ✉ *Piazza Dante 18* ☎ *0578/749071* 🌐 *www.pienza.info.*

EXPLORING

Duomo. This 15th-century cathedral was built by the architect Rossellino under the influence of Alberti. The travertine facade is divided in three parts, with Renaissance arches under the pope's coat of arms encircled by a wreath of fruit. Inside, the cathedral is simple but richly decorated with Sienese paintings. The building's perfection didn't last long—the first cracks appeared immediately after the building was completed, and its foundations have shifted slightly ever since as rain erodes the hillside behind. You can see this effect if you look closely at the base of the first column as you enter the church and compare it with the last. ⊠ *Piazza Pio II* ☏ *0578/749071* ⊗ *Daily 10–1 and 3–7.*

Museo Diocesano. This museum sits to the left of Pienza's Duomo. It's small but has a few interesting papal treasures and rich Flemish tapestries. The most precious piece is a rare mantle woven in gold with pearls and embroidered religious scenes that belonged to Pope Pius II. ⊠ *Corso Il Rossellino 30* ☏ *0578/749905* ⊠ *€4* ⊗ *Mar.–Oct., Wed.–Mon. 10–1 and 3–7; Nov.–Mar., weekends 10–1 and 3–7.*

Palazzo Piccolomini. In 1459 Pius II commissioned Rossellino to design the perfect palazzo for his papal court. The architect took Florence's Palazzo Rucellai by Alberti as a model and designed this 100-room palace. Three sides of the building fit perfectly into the urban plan around it, while the fourth, looking over the valley, has a lovely loggia uniting it with the gardens in back. Guided tours departing every 30 minutes take you to visit the papal apartments, including a beautiful library, the Sala delle Armi (with an impressive weapons collection), and the music room, with its extravagant wooden ceiling forming four letter Ps, for Pope, Pius, Piccolomini, and Pienza. The last tour departs 30 minutes before closing. ⊠ *Piazza Pio II* ☏ *0578/748392* ⊕ *www. palazzopiccolominipienza.it* ⊠ *€7* ⊗ *Mid-Mar.–mid-Oct., Tues.–Sun. 10–6:30; mid-Oct.–mid-Mar., Tues.–Sun. 10–4:30. Last entrance 30 mins before closing.*

Sant'Anna in Camprena. Part of the acclaimed 1996 film *The English Patient* was filmed at this former Benedictine monastery where you can view frescoes by Sodoma (1477–1549) in the dining hall and in the room where the eponymous patient lay in bed. It's best reached by car or bicycle, as public transportation isn't available. For the world-weary, extremely plain rooms are available in the austere silence of the monastery. Double rooms with private bathroom and breakfast are €80 per night; those without private bathroom are €65. To get here from Pienza, take the road to San Quirico for 1 km (½ mile), then turn right at the sign for the monastery. ☏ *0578/748037, 338/4079284* ⊕ *www. camprena.it* ⊗ *Apr.–Oct., daily 4–6.*

WHERE TO EAT AND STAY

For expanded hotel reviews, visit Fodors.com.

$$ ✕**La Chiocciola.** Take the few minutes to walk from the old town for
TUSCAN   typical Pienza fare, including homemade *pici* (thick, short spaghetti) with hare or wild-boar sauce. The restaurant's version of *formaggio in forno* (baked cheese) with assorted accompaniments such as fresh porcini mushrooms is reason enough to venture here. $ *Average*

main: €15 ✉ *Viale Mencatelli 2* ☎ *0578/748683* 🌐 *www.trattorialachiocciola.it* ⏲ *Closed Wed. and 2 wks in Feb.*

$ TUSCAN 🍴 **Osteria Sette di Vino.** Tasty dishes based on the region's cheeses are the specialty at this simple and inexpensive *osteria* (tavern) on a quiet, pleasant square in the center of Pienza. Try versions of pici or the starter of radicchio baked quickly to brown the edges. The local pecorino cheese appears often on the menu—the pecorino *grigliata con pancetta* (grilled with cured bacon) is divine. Can't decide? Try the pecorino tasting menu. [$] *Average main: €10* ✉ *Piazza di Spagna 1* ☎ *0578/749092* 💳 *No credit cards* ⏲ *Closed Wed., July 1–15, and Nov.*

WORD OF MOUTH

"We rented an apartment in the Pienza area—arguably the most scenic area of Tuscany. From our apartment, we were able to explore the surrounding hill villages, the St. Antimo Abby, and also do a little hiking and biking. Just realize that maps can be deceiving—getting from one village to another can take a lot more time than it appears due to the narrow, twisting roads." —zootsi

$ B&B/INN Fodor's Choice ★ 🏨 **Agriturismo Cerreto.** Built a short distance from Pienza in the 18th and 19th centuries, this grouping of farm buildings is now done in traditional Tuscan decor with terra-cotta flooring, wood beams, wrought-iron beds, and heavy oak furniture. **Pros:** peaceful country setting; great for families and small groups; good base for exploring the Val d'Orcia. **Cons:** private transportation a must; closest restaurants and town 5 km (3 miles) away. [$] *Rooms from: €110* ✉ *Strada Provinciale per Sant'Anna in Camprena, 5 km (3 miles) north of Pienza* ☎ *0578/749121* 🌐 *www.agriturismocerreto.com* 🛏 *9 rooms* 🍽 *Breakfast.*

SAN QUIRICO D'ORCIA

9½ km (5½ miles) southwest of Pienza, 43 km (26 miles) southeast of Siena, 111 km (67 miles) southeast of Florence.

San Quirico d'Orcia, on the modern Via Cassia (SR2) south from Siena toward Rome, has almost-intact 15th-century walls topped with 14 turrets. The pleasantly crumbling appearance of the town recalls days of yore. It's well suited for a stop to enjoy a gelato or a meal and to see its Romanesque church.

GETTING HERE

From Siena, San Quirico d'Orcia is an hour-long drive on the SR2. Tra-In provides buses from Siena to San Quirico. There is no train service to San Quirico.

VISITOR INFORMATION

San Quirico d'Orcia tourism office ✉ *Piazza Chigi 2* ☎ *0577/897211* 🌐 *www.comunesanquirico.it.*

EXPLORING

Collegiata. The 13th-century Collegiata church has three majestic portals, one possibly the work of Giovanni Pisano (circa 1245/48–1318). Behind the high altar are some fine examples of inlaid woodwork by

Antonio Barilli (1482–1502). In the floor of the left aisle, look for the tomb slab of Henry of Nassau, a pilgrim knight who died here in 1451. ✉ *Piazza Chigi* 🕒 *Daily 8:30–12:30 and 3–7.*

Horti Leonini. Against the walls of San Quirico d'Orcia, these Italian-style gardens retain merely a shimmer of their past opulence. They were planted in 1581 by Diomede Leoni—hence the name of the park. In the center there's a 17th-century statue of Cosimo III, one of the last of the Medici dukes of Tuscany. ✉ *Off Piazza della Libertà.*

Palazzo Chigi. Near the Collegiata stands this splendid town palace, named after the family to whom the Medici bestowed San Quirico in 1667. Small art exhibitions are occasionally displayed in the palace courtyard, and the tourist office is here. The rest of the building is closed to the public. ✉ *Piazza Chigi 2.*

WHERE TO EAT AND STAY

For expanded hotel reviews, visit Fodors.com.

$$ TUSCAN 🍴 **Trattoria al Vecchio Forno.** A meal here is always special. Don't miss the dishes accented with porcini mushrooms, such as the excellent mushroom soup. You might also try *pici* with tomato or boar sauce, and roast boar and game. The menu is rounded out by a varied wine selection. There's a nice garden out back. [$] *Average main: €15* ✉ *Via Piazzola 8* ☎ *0577/897380* 🕒 *Closed Feb.*

$ B&B/INN 🏨 **Palazzo del Capitano.** The guest rooms at this 14th-century palace are named for signs of the zodiac, but the astrological reference stops at the painted symbol on the door. **Pros:** central location; elegant furnishings; secluded garden. **Cons:** rooms are on the small side; some street noise; getting here by car is difficult. [$] *Rooms from: €120* ✉ *Via Poliziano 18* ☎ *0577/899028, 0577/899421* 🌐 *www.palazzodelcapitano.com* 🛏 *14 rooms, 8 suites* 🍽 *Breakfast.*

BAGNO VIGNONI

5 km (3 miles) south of San Quirico d'Orcia, 48 km (29 miles) southeast of Siena, 116 km (70 miles) southeast of Florence.

Bagno Vignoni has been famous since Roman times for the mildly sulfurous waters that come bubbling up into the large rectangular pool that forms the town's main square, Piazza delle Sorgenti (Square of the Springs). Medieval pilgrims and modern hikers alike have soothed their tired feet in the pleasantly warm water that flows through open channels on its way to the River Orcia. Of particular interest are the ruins of an 18th-century bathhouse on the edge of town and the Chapel of Saint Catherine, who, it seems, came here often.

GETTING HERE

Bagno Vignoni is off the SR2, about an hour from Siena. Tra-In provides bus service from Siena to Bagno Vignoni. There is no train station nearby.

VISITOR INFORMATION

Bagno Vignoni tourism office ✉ *Località Bagno Vignoni 2* ☎ *0577/888975* 🌐 *www.comunesanquirico.it.*

EXPLORING

Piscina Val di Sole. Bagno Vignoni's public hot-spring pool provides warm-water relaxation for more than just your feet. Stand under the waterfall to massage and soothe weary shoulder muscles. Though the facility remains open, there's no swimming permitted between 1 and 2 from April to September. The last admission is one hour before closing. ✉ *Via Ara Urcea 43* ☎ *0577/887112* ⊕ *www.piscinavaldisole.it* 💶 *€15* ⊗ *Jan.–Mar., daily 10–5; Apr.–Sept., daily 9:30–6; Oct.–Dec., daily 10–5.*

OFF THE BEATEN PATH

Vignoni Alto. A steep gravel road leads north out of Bagno Vignoni for 2 km (1 mile) to the town's upper village, a tiny grouping of buildings huddled at the base of a 13th-century tower. The tower, now a private home, was built to watch over the Via Francigena. A spectacular view of the entire Val d'Orcia opens up from the eastern gate.

WHERE TO EAT

$ × **Bottega di Cacio.** Lots of shaded outdoor seating makes this a pleasant place for lunch on a warm day. Pecorino cheese, spicy salami, and grilled vegetables *sott'olio* (preserved in olive oil) are served cafeteria-style. And, if you want something even spicier, the stuffed hot peppers are delicious. There is a good selection of wine, but the choice of desserts is limited and they don't serve coffee. $ *Average main: €10* ✉ *Piazza del Moretto 31* ☎ *0577/887477* ⊟ *No credit cards* ⊗ *Closed Thurs.*

TUSCAN

6

MONTALCINO

19 km (12 miles) northeast of Bagno Vignoni, 41 km (25½ miles) south of Siena, 109 km (68 miles) south of Florence.

Tiny Montalcino, with its commanding view from high on a hill, can claim an Etruscan past. It saw a fair number of travelers, as it was directly on the road from Siena to Rome. During the early Middle Ages it enjoyed a brief period of autonomy before falling under the orbit of Siena in 1201. Now Montalcino's greatest claim to fame is that it produces Brunello di Montalcino, one of Italy's most esteemed reds. Driving to the town, you pass through the Brunello vineyards. You can sample the excellent but expensive red in wine cellars in town or visit a nearby winery, such as Fattoria dei Barbi, for a guided tour and tasting; you must call ahead for reservations.

GETTING HERE

By car, follow the SR2 south from Siena, then follow the SP45 to Montalcino. Several Tra-In buses travel between Siena and Montalcino daily, making a tightly scheduled day trip possible. There is no train service available.

VISITOR INFORMATION

Montalcino Tourism Office ✉ *Costa del Municipio 1* ☎ *0577/849331* ⊕ *www.prolocomontalcino.it.*

EXPLORING

Fattoria dei Barbi. The cellars of this venerable winery date from the 17th century and hold almost 200 oak wine barrels. Some of Italy's most famous wines are produced here, including an excellent range of Brunellos, a fine Rosso di Montalcino, and the estate's special Super Tuscan brands: Brusco dei Barbi and Bruscone dei Barbi. Olive oil, salami, and pecorino cheese are made at the winery's organic farm. Guided tours of the cellars are followed by wine tastings, during which you can also sample the other products. ✉ *Località Podernovi 1* ☎ *0577/841111* 🌐 *www.fattoriadeibarbi.it* 🎟 *€5* 🕒 *Tours weekdays at noon and 3.*

La Fortezza. Providing refuge for the last remnants of the Sienese army during the Florentine conquest of 1555, the battlements of this 14th-century fortress are still in excellent condition. Climb up the narrow, spiral steps for the 360-degree view of most of southern Tuscany. An enoteca for tasting wines is on-site. ✉ *Piazzale Fortezza* ☎ *0577/849211* 🎟 *€3* 🕒 *Nov.–Mar., Tues.–Sun. 9–6; Apr.–Oct., daily 9–8.*

Museo Civico e Diocesano d'Arte Sacra. This fine museum is housed in a building that once belonged to 13th-century Augustinian monks. The ticket booth is in the glorious refurbished cloister, and the sacred art collection, gathered from churches throughout the region, is displayed on two floors in former monastic quarters. Though the art here might be called "B-list," a fine altarpiece by Bartolo di Fredi (circa 1330–1410), the *Coronation of the Virgin,* makes dazzling use of gold. In addition, there's a striking 12th-century crucifix that originally adorned the high altar of the church of Sant'Antimo. Also on hand are many wood sculptures, a typical medium in these parts during the Renaissance. ✉ *Via Ricasoli 31* ☎ *0577/846014* 🎟 *€8* 🕒 *Nov.–Mar., Tues.–Sun. 10–1 and 2–4; Apr.–Oct., Tues.–Sun. 10–6.*

WHERE TO EAT AND STAY

For expanded hotel reviews, visit Fodors.com.

$ WINE BAR 🍴 **Enoteca Osteria Osticcio.** Tullio and Francesca Scrivano have beautifully remodeled this restaurant and wineshop. Upon entering, you descend a staircase to a tasting room filled with rustic wooden tables. Adjacent is a small dining area with a splendid view of the hills far below, and outside is a lovely little terrace perfect for sampling Brunello di Montalcino when the weather is warm. The menu is light and pairs nicely with the wines, which are the main draw. The *acciughe sotto pesto* (anchovies with pesto) is a particularly fine treat. [$] *Average main: €12* ✉ *Via Matteotti 23* ☎ *0577/848271* 🌐 *www.osticcio.it* 🕒 *Closed Sun.*

$$$ TUSCAN 🍴 **Fattoria dei Barbi.** Set among the vineyards that produce excellent Brunello—as well as its younger cousin, Rosso di Montalcino—is this rustic taverna with a large stone fireplace. The estate farm produces many of the ingredients used in such traditional specialties as *stracotto nel brunello* (braised beef cooked with beans in Brunello wine). This eatery is a few minutes south of Montalcino, in the direction of Sant'Antimo. [$] *Average main: €25* ✉ *Podere Podernuovo 170* ☎ *0577/847117* 🌐 *www.fattoriadeibarbi.it* ✍ *Reservations essential* 🕒 *Closed Wed. and mid-Jan.–mid-Feb.*

$ ✗ **Il Grappolo Blu.** Any one of this restaurant's *piatti tipici* (typical plates)
ITALIAN is worth trying: the local specialty, *pici all'aglione* (thick, long noodles served with sautéed cherry tomatoes and many cloves of garlic), is done particularly well. The chef also has a deft touch with vegetables; if there's fennel on the menu, make sure to try it. The interior, with white walls, low ceilings, and old wood tables, is cozy and the service is warm and friendly. ⓢ *Average main: €14* ✉ *Scale di Via Moglio 1* ☎ *0577/847150* 🖃 *Reservations essential* ⊘ *Closed Fri.*

$$$$ 🏨 **Castiglion del Bosco.** This estate, one of the largest still in private hands
HOTEL in Tuscany, was purchased by Massimo Ferragamo at the beginning of
Fodor's Choice this century and meticulously converted into a second-to-none resort
★ that incorporates a medieval borgo (village) and surrounding farmhouses. **Pros:** extremely secluded; exclusive and tranquil location; top-notch service; breathtaking scenery. **Cons:** well off the beaten track, the nearest town is 12 km (7½ miles) away; private transportation required. ⓢ *Rooms from: €570* ✉ *Località Castiglion del Bosco* ☎ *0577/1913111* ⊕ *www.castigliondelbosco.com* 🛏 *23 suites, 9 villas* �🍴 *Breakfast.*

$ 🏨 **La Crociona.** A quiet and serene family-owned farm in the middle
B&B/INN of a small vineyard with glorious views houses guests in lovely apartments that can sleep up to five people. **Pros:** peaceful location; great for families; friendly atmosphere. **Cons:** no a/c; need a car to get around. ⓢ *Rooms from: €120* ✉ *Località La Croce 15* ☎ *0577/848007* ⊕ *www. lacrociona.com* 🛏 *11 apartments* �🍴 *No meals.*

ABBAZIA DI SANT'ANTIMO

10 km (6 miles) south of Montalcino, 51 km (32 miles) south of Siena, 119 km (74 miles) south of Florence.

GETTING HERE

Abbazia di Sant'Antimo is a 15-minute drive from Montalcino. Tra-In bus service is extremely limited. The abbey cannot be reached by train.

EXPLORING

Fodor's Choice **Abbazia di Sant'Antimo.** It's well worth your while to go out of your
★ way to visit this 12th-century Romanesque abbey, as it's a gem of pale stone in the silvery green of an olive grove. The exterior and interior sculpture is outstanding, particularly the nave capitals, a combination of French, Lombard, and even Spanish influences. The sacristy (seldom open) forms part of the primitive Carolingian church (founded in AD 781), its entrance flanked by 9th-century pilasters. The small vaulted crypt dates from the same period. Above the nave runs a *matroneum* (women's gallery), an unusual feature once used to separate the congregation. Equally unusual is the ambulatory, for which the three radiating chapels were almost certainly copied from a French model. Stay to hear the canonical hours celebrated in Gregorian chant. On the road that leads up toward Castelnuovo dell'Abate is a small shop that sells souvenirs and has washrooms.

> **WORD OF MOUTH**
>
> "We stopped in at Sant'Antimo when the monks were conducting their Gregorian chants and it was one of the loveliest moments to experience." —caroltis

6

A 2½-hour hiking trail (signed as #2) leads to the abbey from Montalcino. Starting near Montalcino's small cemetery, the trail heads south through woods, along a ridge road to the tiny hamlet of Villa a Tolli, and then downhill to Sant'Antimo. ⊠ *Castelnuovo dell'Abate* ☎ *0577/835659* ⊕ *www.antimo.it* ⊘ *Daily 6 am–9 pm.*

LE CRETE

Van Gogh never saw the area south of Siena known as Le Crete (*creta* means "clay" in Italian), but in the bare, moonstone-color clay hills around Asciano—the rolling wheat fields, the warm light, the dramatic gullies and ravines cut by centuries of erosion—he would have perhaps found worthy subjects, as these landscapes seem carved into the earth much like how the furrows of paint layer his canvases.

BUONCONVENTO

27 km (17 miles) southeast of Siena, 80 km (50 miles) south of Florence.

Buonconvento dates back to the 12th century, though it was surrounded by defensive walls in the later middle ages. Though the name means "happy place" in Latin, it was here that Holy Roman Emperor Henry VII died in 1313, cutting short his ill-fated attempt to establish imperial rule in Italy.

GETTING HERE

By car, Buonconvento is a 30-minute drive south from Siena on the SR2. Tra-In buses travel daily between Siena and Buonconvento several times a day, making a carefully scheduled day trip quite possible. A train connects Siena with Buonconvento, Monte Amiato Scalo, Asciano, and Arbia.

VISITOR INFORMATION

Buonconvento tourism office ⊠ *Piazzale Garibaldi 1* ☎ *0577/807181* ⊕ *www.turismobuonconvento.it.*

EXPLORING

Fodor's Choice ★ **Museo d'Arte Sacra.** Today quiet Buonconvento is worth a stop for a look at its tiny museum, a two-room picture gallery with more than its fair share of works by Tuscan artists such as Duccio and Andrea di Bartolo. A triptych with the *Madonna and Saints Bernardino and Catherine* by Sano di Pietro stands out amongst other gems by Sienese painters of the 14th and 15th centuries, and Donatello tops a list of the Renaissance sculptors also represented. ⊠ *Via Soccini 18* ☎ *0577/807181* 🎫 *€5* ⊘ *Apr.–Oct., Tues.–Sun. 10–1 and 3–6; Nov.–Mar., weekends 10–1 and 3–5.*

EN ROUTE **Murlo.** If you're heading northwest to Siena, stray 9 km (5½ miles) west of the Via Cassia to Vescovado and then follow the signs 2 km (1 mile) south to this tiny fortified medieval *borgo* (village) that has been completely restored.

Antiquarium Poggio Civitate. An imposing bishop's palace holds this unique museum of Etruscan relics. Although there are many beautiful pieces displayed in an intelligent and well-documented fashion, the

Continued on page 293

SIMPLY PERFECT
*The Basic Goodness
of Tuscan Food*

**THE CUISINE OF TUSCANY ISN'T COM-
PLICATED.** In fact, every dish follows the
same basic recipe:

■ Begin with fresh, high-quality ingredients, preferably produced within walking distance of the kitchen.

■ Prepare them using techniques that
have been refined over centuries, ideally
by members of the chef's family.

■ Serve the finished dish unpretentiously
("plate" is not a verb here), accompanied by a glass of good local wine.

The recipe looks simple, but executing
it is not so easy. Some of the staples
of "fine dining" that chefs elsewhere
depend upon are pointedly missing.

There's nothing exotic: it would violate
the "walking distance" principle of
fresh, local ingredients. There's nothing
ostentatious: showiness would distract
from the basic beauty of the food. And
innovation is looked on with a skeptical
eye: if a new recipe or a new technique
were really so good, surely someone in
the preceding ten generations would have
already thought of it.

The result is a cuisine that's inextricably
tied to the place where it's made. There
may now be Tuscan restaurants all over
the globe, but you can still only eat genuine Tuscan food in Tuscany. It's home
cooking that's worth traveling halfway
around the world to taste.

EXPLORING THE TUSCAN MENU

Menu Basics

A meal in Tuscany (and elsewhere in Italy) traditionally consists of five courses, and every menu you encounter will be organized along this five-course plan:

First up is the **antipasto** (appetizer), often consisting of cured meats or marinated vegetables. Next to appear is the **primo**, usually pasta or soup, and after that the **secondo**, a meat or fish course with, perhaps, a **contorno** (vegetable dish) on the side. A simple **dolce** (dessert) rounds out the meal.

This, you've probably noticed, is a lot of food. Italians have noticed as well—a full, five-course meal is an indulgence usually reserved for special occasions. Instead, restaurant meals are a mix-and-match affair: you might order a primo and a secondo, or an antipasto and a primo, or a secondo and a contorno.

■ TIP→ The crucial rule of restaurant dining is that you should **order at least two courses**. It's a common mistake for tourists to order only a secondo, thinking they're getting a "main course" complete with side dishes. What they wind up with is one lonely piece of meat.

After you've eaten at a couple of restaurants, you may feel you're experiencing déjà vu: many of the same dishes are served almost everywhere. This is a by-product of the devotion to local, traditional cuisine, and part of the pleasure of dining in Tuscany is seeing how preparations vary from region to region and restaurant to restaurant.

What follows is a rundown, course by course, of classic dishes. The ones highlighted as "quintessential" are the epitome of Tuscan cooking. They shouldn't be missed.

Clockwise from bottom left: A well-worn menu; preparing *ribollita*; a typical food shop.

ANTIPASTI: APPETIZERS

The quintessential antipasto
Affettati misti

The name, roughly translated, means "mixed cold cuts," and it's something Tuscans do exceptionally well. The platter of cured meats is sure to include ***prosciutto crudo*** (ham, cut paper thin) and ***salame*** (dry sausage, prepared in dozens of ways, some spicy, some sweet). The most distinctly Tuscan *affettati* are made from ***cinta senese*** (a once nearly extinct pig found only in the heart of the region) and ***cinghiale*** (wild boar, which roam all of central Italy). You can eat these delicious slices unadorned or layered on a piece of bread.

From left: A typical affettati misti plate; two butchers; artichokes cured in olive oil

Other classics
Crostini
Toasted slices of bread with toppings—most commonly *fegatini* (chicken liver pâté), though other meat and vegetable concoctions also appear

Verdure sott'olio
Peppers, carrots, artichokes, and other vegetables cured in olive oil

Lardo di Colonnata
Not to be confused with lard (rendered fat), *lardo* is pig back fat that's seasoned with herbs, soaked in brine, and cured for months. Sliced thin and served over bread, it's a melt-in-your-mouth delicacy.

A WELL-OILED CUISINE

Olive oil is far and away the most important ingredient in Tuscan kitchens: it's a condiment, a cooking oil, a marinade, a salad dressing, a bread topping—one way or another, it makes its way into every meal.

The oil from Tuscany is frequently lauded as the best in the world. Open a bottle and you'll immediately know why: the aroma reaches out and grabs

you. Like wine connoisseurs, oil lovers struggle for words to describe the experience—"spicy," "fruity," "herby," "redolent of artichokes"—but the sensual character of Tuscan oils defies description.

Which area in Tuscany produces the best oil is the subject of a never-ending debate. Sample as you go and decide for yourself—or simply enjoy the fact that there is no right answer. It's all good.

6

IN FOCUS SIMPLY PERFECT

PRIMI: FIRST COURSES

The quintessential primo
Ribollita

A vegetable soup thickened with cannellini beans and stale bread—a classic example of how Tuscans make great things from humble ingredients. *Cavolo nero* (black cabbage, sometimes called Tuscan kale in the U.S.) is another key element—it gives the flavor a little kick. Upon serving, the soup is "christened" with a generous swirl of olive oil. In southern Tuscany, ribollita sometimes comes with chopped red onions on the side.

Other classics

Panzanella
A summer salad made of bread, tomatoes, basil, cucumbers, and olive oil

Pappa al pomodoro
Pureed tomato soup, thickened with bread

Zuppa alla frantoiana
Another bean, bread, and vegetable soup, this time run through a food mill

Pappardelle col sugo di cinghiale
Fresh pasta cut in wide strips with wild boar sauce

Ravioli di ricotta e spinaci
Spinach and cheese ravioli

Local specialties
(and the town or region where they're found)

Pici all'aglione
Hand-rolled pasta with garlic sauce (Siena and Montalcino)

Linguine alla granseola
Linguine with stone crab (a staple on Elba)

Minestra al farro
Soup made with *farro*, a barley-like grain (Lucca and the Garfagnana)

Ignudi
"Naked" ravioli-spinach and cheese dumplings minus the pasta (Florence and Chianti)

Crespelle
Crepe-like pancakes, stuffed with spinach and cheese and topped with a bechamel sauce (Florence)

Polenta di castagne
Chestnut polenta (the Garfagnana)

Acquacotta
"Cooked water"—thick vegetable soup (a specialty of the Maremma)

Tordelli di carne al ragù
Meat-stuffed tortelli pasta with a meat sauce (Lucca, where they prefer the spelling with a "d")

SECONDI: SECOND COURSES

The quintessential secondo
Bistecca alla fiorentina

You can get grilled steak everywhere from Texas to Tokyo, but in Tuscany they've found a way to make it their own. *Bistecca alla fiorentina* is an extra-thick T-bone that comes from ox-like Chianina cattle, a carefully nurtured Tuscan breed. It's seasoned with salt, pepper, and olive oil, and always served rare; cooking it longer is considered a travesty. Maybe it's the high quality of the beef, maybe it's the wonderful oil—whatever the reason, *bistecca alla fiorentina* truly is exceptional.

Other classics

Arista di maiale
Roast pork with sage and rosemary

Calamari all'inzimino
Squid and spinach stew

Tagliata di manzo
Thin slices of roasted beef, drizzled with oil

Fritto di pollo e coniglio
Fried chicken and rabbit

Salsiccia e fagioli
Pork sausage with beans

Local specialties

Frittura di paranza
Mixed fish fry (found all along the coast, but best in Livorno)

Peposo
A peppery beef stew (Impruneta)

Piccione
Pigeon—it can be roasted, stuffed, or baked (southern Chianti)

Baccalà con ceci
Salt cod with chickpeas (much beloved by the Livornesi)

Trippa alla fiorentina
Tripe stewed in a tomato sauce (Florence)

Ricotta cheese, Vitereta, Tuscany

A TASTE OF THE TYPICAL

While "typical" can be a disparaging term in English, its Italian equivalent, *"tipico,"* is high praise. Whether you're talking about a type of cheese, a variety of wine, or a particular cut of pasta, *"tipico"* indicates something that's traditional to the location where you find it. Which means it's been perfected over the course of centuries. And that means, whatever it is, you won't get it better anywhere else.

CONTORNI: VEGETABLES

The quintessential contorno

Fagioli all'olio

Tuscans are known among fellow Italians as *"mangiafagioli"* (bean eaters), and with good reason. White cannellini beans are the standard, usually boiled with fresh sage, drained, and liberally laced with olive oil. Another preparation is *fagioli all'uccelletto,* in which the beans are cooked with tomato and sage. **Fagioli al fiasco** are slow-cooked in a glass bottle.

Other classics

Virtually any fresh vegetable, either briefly boiled or sautéed in oil, possibly with a touch of garlic. Greens are especially popular—look for *cime di rape* (turnip greens) as well as *spinaci* (spinach). Other seasonal favorites are *carciofi* (artichokes), *asparagi* (asparagus) *piselli* (peas), *zucchini*, *peperoni* (peppers), and *fave* (fava beans).

DOLCI: DESSERTS

The quintessential dolce

Cantuccini con vin santo

These hard little almond cookies, also known as **biscotti di Prato**, are virtually inedible when dry, but dip them into sweet vin santo wine, and the result is delectable.

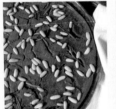  

From left: Castagnaccio; cantucci and vin santo; buccellato

Other classics

Tuscan cuisine is not particularly noted for its desserts. Meals often end with an unadorned piece of fruit. Here and there, though, you'll find exceptions.

Local specialties

Buccellato	*Ricciarelli*	*Brigidini*
An anise-flavored sweet bun (Lucca)	Delicate almond cookies (Siena)	Sugary wafers, best when topped with gelato (Montecatini)
Castagnaccio	*Panforte*	
A flat chestnut-flour cake (Lucca)	Candied fruit and nut cake (Siena)	

almost complete roof and pediment from a 5th-century BC Etruscan house stand out as rare and precious artifacts. The so-called "Cowboy of Murlo," a large-hatted figure from the same roof, is the star of the collection but anyone interested in ancient Etruscan culture will be well rewarded by a visit here. The museum is named after the nearby site from which most of the artifacts were excavated. ⊠ *Piazza della Cattedrale 4, Murlo* ☎ *0577/814099* ⊒ *€5* ⊘ *Mar. and Oct., Tues.–Sun. 10–1 and 3–5; Apr.–June and Sept., Tues.–Sun. 10–1 and 3–7; July and Aug., Tues.–Sun. 10–7; Nov.–Feb., Tues.–Fri. 10–1, weekends 10–1 and 3–5.*

ABBAZIA DI MONTE OLIVETO MAGGIORE

9 km (5½ miles) northeast of Buonconvento, 37 km (23 miles) southeast of Siena.

GETTING HERE

From Siena, the abbey is a 45-minute drive on the SR2 south to Buonconvento and then the SP451 to Monte Oliveto. Bus and train service are not available.

EXPLORING

Fodor's Choice ★ **Abbazia di Monte Oliveto Maggiore.** Tuscany's most-visited abbey sits in an oasis of olive and cypress trees amid the harsh landscape of Le Crete. It was founded in 1313 by Giovanni Tolomei, a rich Sienese lawyer who, after miraculously regaining his lost sight, changed his name to Bernardo in homage to Saint Bernard of Clairvaux, who is sometimes credited with the creation of medieval monasticism. Bernardo then founded a monastic order dedicated to the restoration of Benedictine principles. The name of the order—the White Benedictines—refers to a vision that Bernardo had in which Jesus, Mary, and his own mother were all clad in white. The monks are sometimes also referred to as Olivetans, which is the name of the hill where the monastery was built. Famous for maintaining extreme poverty—their feast-day meal consisted of two eggs—they slept on straw mats and kept a vow of silence. Although the monks look like they are eating a little better these days and are not afraid to strike up a conversation, the monastery still operates, and most of the area is off limits to visitors. One of Italy's most important book restoration centers is here, and the monks still produce a wide variety of traditional liqueurs (distilled from herbs that grow on the premises), which are available in the gift shop along with enough food products to fill a pantry, all produced by monks in various parts of Italy.

From the entrance gate a tree-lined lane leads down to the main group of buildings, with paths veering off to several shrines and chapels dedicated to important saints of the order. The church itself is not particularly memorable, but the exquisite choir stalls (1503–05) by Fra Giovanni da Verona are among the country's finest examples of *intarsia* (wood inlay). Forty-eight of the 125 stalls have inlaid decoration, each set up as a window or arched doorway that opens onto a space (a town, a landscape) or an object (a musical instrument, a bird), rendered in marvelous perspective. Check at the entrance for the schedule of Masses, as the monks often chant the liturgy.

6

In the abbey's main cloister, frescoes by Luca Signorelli and Sodoma depict scenes from the life of St. Benedict. Signorelli began the cycle by painting scenes from the saint's adult life as narrated by Saint Gregory the Great, and although his nine scenes are badly worn, the individual expressions are fittingly austere and pensive, full of serenity and religious spirit, and as individualized as those he painted in the San Brizio chapel in Orvieto's Duomo. Later Sodoma filled in the story with scenes from the saint's youth and the last years of his life. The results are also impressive, but in this case what stands out are the use of color and earthier imagery. Note the detailed landscapes, the rich costumes, the animals (similar to those Sodoma was known to keep as pets), and the scantily clad boys he apparently preferred (for this he was called "the Sodomist" and described by Vasari as "a merry and licentious man of scant chastity"). ⊠ *Località Monteoliveto Maggiore 1, Chiusure, Asciano* ☎ *0577/707611* ⊕ *www.monteolivetomaggiore.it* ⊠ *By donation* ☉ *Nov.–Mar., daily 9:15–noon and 3:15–5; Apr.–Oct., daily 9:15–noon and 3:15–6.*

WHERE TO EAT AND STAY
For expanded hotel reviews, visit Fodors.com.

$ ✕ **La Torre.** You can enjoy straightforward Tuscan fare in the massive
TUSCAN tower at the abbey's entrance, or, when it's warm, on a flower-filled terrace. The *pici ai funghi* (extra-thick handmade spaghetti with mushroom sauce) or *zuppa di funghi* (mushroom soup) take the sting out of a crisp winter day, and the grilled meats are a good bet at any time of year. If you want lighter fare, there's a bar serving panini that has outdoor seating. ⓢ *Average main: €12* ⊠ *Località Monteoliveto Maggiore 2, 8 km (5 miles) south of Asciano on SS451, Asciano* ☎ *0577/707022* ☉ *Closed Tues.*

$$ ⊡ **Fattoria del Colle.** Amid rolling vineyards and olive trees, this *fattoria*
B&B/INN (farmhouse) produces fine wine and olive oil. **Pros:** great for families; beautiful location. **Cons:** no a/c; no phones in rooms; 30-minute walk to nearest town. ⓢ *Rooms from: €140* ⊠ *Località Il Colle, 12 km (7 miles) east of Abbazia di Monte Oliveto Maggiore, Trequanda* ☎ *0577/662108* ⊕ *www.cinellicolombini.it* ↝ *2 rooms, 19 apartments, 2 villas* ⦿❙ *Breakfast.*

$$ ⊡ **La Chiusa.** Dania and Umberto Lucherini bought this old farmhouse in
B&B/INN 1974 and turned it into a significant restaurant ($$$$) with emphasis on Tuscan classics. **Pros:** delightful setting; excellent restaurant; personal service. **Cons:** standard rooms are on the small side; need a car to get around. ⓢ *Rooms from: €200* ⊠ *Via della Madonnina 88, 25 km (15 miles) east of Abbazia di Monte Oliveto Maggiore, Montefollonico* ☎ *0577/669668* ⊕ *www.ristorantelachiusa.it* ↝ *15 rooms* ☉ *Closed Tues. and mid-Jan.–Mar.* ⦿❙ *Breakfast.*

$$$ ⊡ **Locanda dell'Amorosa.** What was a self-sufficient hamlet with its own
B&B/INN chapel in the 14th century is now a refined inn. **Pros:** romantic setting;
Fodor'sChoice excellent restaurant; luxurious rooms. **Cons:** standard rooms are small;
★ need a car to get around. ⓢ *Rooms from: €270* ⊠ *Località L'Amorosa 1, 23 km (14 miles) east of Abbazia di Monte Oliveto Maggiore, Sinalunga* ☎ *0577/67721* ⊕ *www.amorosa.it* ↝ *17 rooms, 8 suites* ☉ *Closed Jan. and Feb.*

ASCIANO

8 km (5 miles) north of Abbazia di Monte Oliveto Maggiore, 25 km (16 miles) southeast of Siena, 124 km (77 miles) southeast of Florence.

Founded by the Etruscans around the 5th century BC, Asciano is now a sleepy little town surrounded by 13th-century walls. The tiny centro storico (historic center) is eminently bike-friendly; any serious cyclist should consider a pit stop here.

GETTING HERE

From Siena, driving to Asciano on the SP438 takes about 40 minutes. Tra-In has limited bus service, making the train, with five or six daily departures, a better option.

VISITOR INFORMATION

Asciano tourism office ⊠ *Via Amos Cassioli 2* ☎ *0577/718666.*

EXPLORING

Farmacia De Munari. The basement of the local pharmacy holds the town's most important Roman artifact, a polychrome Roman mosaic from the 1st to 2nd centuries AD. To see the mosaic, you must ask for the keys at the tourist information office. ⊠ *Corso Matteotti 82* ☎ *0577/718124* 🎟 *Free* ⊙ *Weekdays 9–1 and 4–8, Sat. 9–1.*

Fodor's Choice ★ **Museo d'Arte Sacra e Archeologico.** Palazzo Corboli, a magnificent palace dating from the 12th century, has been refurbished and houses the Museo d'Arte Sacra e Archeologico. The collection of Etruscan artifacts is worth a visit, though the real highlight is the collection of lesser-known 13th- and 14th-century paintings from the Sienese school. ⊠ *Corso Matteotti 122* ☎ *0577/719524* 🎟 *€5* ⊙ *Tues.–Fri. 10–1 and 2:30–5, weekends 10–1 and 2:30–6.*

THE MAREMMA

The wildest part of Tuscany is here in its southern heart. And it's here that you get a sense of what the region looked like before Tuscany became a must-see on the grand tour. The landscape alternates between rolling hills and tufa cliffs; hill towns abound, linked by narrow, winding roads. Saturnia—with its superior hotels, restaurants, and one-of-a-kind hot springs—makes a good base to explore and sample the best of what the south has to offer: ancient Etruscan tombs and caverns at Sovana and Sorano, the famous white wine of Pitigliano, and wild mushrooms and chestnut honey from the rugged slopes of Monte Amiata, which presides over Tuscany with views from Arezzo to the sea.

MONTE AMIATA

16 km (10 miles) south of Abbazia di Sant'Antimo, 86 km (52 miles) southeast of Siena, 156 km (94 miles) southeast of Florence.

GETTING HERE

Monte Amiata can be reached by car from Siena on the SR2 (Via Cassia). Bus service is extremely limited. There is a train station at Monte Amiata Scalo, but it is at the base of the mountain and not well served by local buses.

In Search of Etruscan Artifacts

To fully appreciate the strangely quixotic relationship that the ancient Etruscan culture had with the tufa rock that provided the fabric of the civilization, you must visit southern Tuscany. The houses and tombs, and sometimes even the roads, were carved from this soft volcanic stone, making it impossible to think about the Etruscans without also imagining the dark sandy tufa that surrounded them.

Some of the best-preserved, and most mysterious, of all their monumental tombs are in the area of Pitigliano, Sorano, and Sovana. In the necropolis of the latter, you can actually walk on a section of Etruscan road that is almost 2,500 years old.

Chiusi should not be missed if you are interested in things Etruscan: several tombs that still retain their brightly colored decorations and a particularly fine and thoughtfully organized archaeological museum await you there.

VISITOR INFORMATION
Monte Amiata tourism office ✉ *Via Adua 25, Abbadia San Salvatore* ☎ *0577/775811* ⊕ *www.webamiata.it.*

EXPLORING
Monte Amiata. At 5,702 feet, this benign volcano is one of Tuscany's few ski slopes, but it's no Mont Blanc. Come in warmer months to take advantage of an abundance of hiking trails that cross wide meadows full of wildflowers and slice through groves of evergreens. Panoramic views of all of Tuscany present themselves on the winding road up to the summit. Along the way, you pass through a succession of tiny medieval towns, including Castel del Piano, Arcidosso, Santa Flora, and Piancastagnaio, where you can pick up picnic supplies and sample the chestnuts and game for which the mountain is famous.

Abbadia San Salvatore. This thousand-year-old village is worth a stop—skip the nondescript new town and head straight to the centro storico to explore winding stone streets with tiny churches around every corner. The abbey for which the town was named was founded in 743; its current appearance reflects an 11th-century renovation, but the original crypt remains intact. The tourist office in town has hiking-trail maps for Monte Amiata. ✉ *Tourist office, Via Adua 25, Abbadia San Salvatore* ☎ *0577/775811.*

SORANO

38 km (23 miles) south of Abbadia San Salvatore on Monte Amiata, 138 km (86 miles) southeast of Siena, 208 km (130 miles) southeast of Florence.

GETTING HERE
Being in the southern part of Tuscany, Sorano is most easily reached from Rome. From the A1 highway, take the Orvieto exit. There are no practical ways to arrive here by bus or train.

EXPLORING

Sorano's history follows the pattern of most settlements in the area: it was an ancient Etruscan citadel, built up in the 15th century and fortified by one of the many warring families of Tuscany (in this case, the Orsini). It's the execution that sets it apart. With its tiny, twisted streets and stone houses connected by wooden stairways and ramps, Sorano looks as if it was carved from the tufa beneath it—and that's because it was. Underneath the town, visible as you approach, is a vast network of *colombari*, Etruscan-era rooms lined with hundreds of niches carved into stone walls, dating from the 1st century BC. The colombari aren't yet open to the public, but Sorano is worth a visit regardless, if only to walk its medieval alleyways and to watch old-style artisans at work. Views of the densely forested hills around town will have you reaching for your camera.

WHERE TO STAY

For expanded hotel reviews, visit Fodors.com.

$
B&B/INN
Della Fortezza. High above Sorano, this austere-looking 11th-century Orsini castle boasts spectacular views of the town and surrounding countryside. **Pros:** rooms have great views of Sorano; romantic location. **Cons:** very basic decor; no a/c in rooms. $ *Rooms from: €120* ⊠ *Piazza Cairoli 5* ☎ *0564/632010* ⊕ *www.fortezzahotel.it* ➔ *14 rooms, 1 suite* ⓞ *Breakfast.*

PITIGLIANO

10 km (6 miles) south of Sorano, 147 km (92 miles) southeast of Siena, 217 km (136 miles) southeast of Florence.

From a distance, the medieval stone houses of Pitigliano look as if they melt into the cliffs upon which they are perched. Etruscan tombs, which locals use to store wine, are connected by a network of caves and tunnels. At the beginning of the 14th century the Orsini family moved its base from Sovana to the better-fortified Pitigliano. They built up the town's defenses and fortified their home, Palazzo Orsini. Later, starting in 1543, Antonio da Sangallo the Younger added to the town's fortress, building bastions and towers throughout the town and adding the aqueduct as well.

Pitigliano has become a trendy locale for Italian vacation rentals, making the town center lively in summer. Restaurants serve up good meals that, as a result of the tourist boom, have inflated prices. Bianco di Pitigliano (Pitigliano white wine) is a fresh and light, dry wine produced from the vines that thrive in the tufa soil of the area.

GETTING HERE

Pitigliano is best reached by car along the SR74 from either the Via Aurelia to the west or the A1 highway to the east. Plan on a journey of about an hour. Pitigliano cannot be reached directly by train, but bus service is available from the train station in Grosseto.

VISITOR INFORMATION

Maremma regional tourism office ⊠ *Piazza Garibaldi 12* ☎ *0564/617111.*

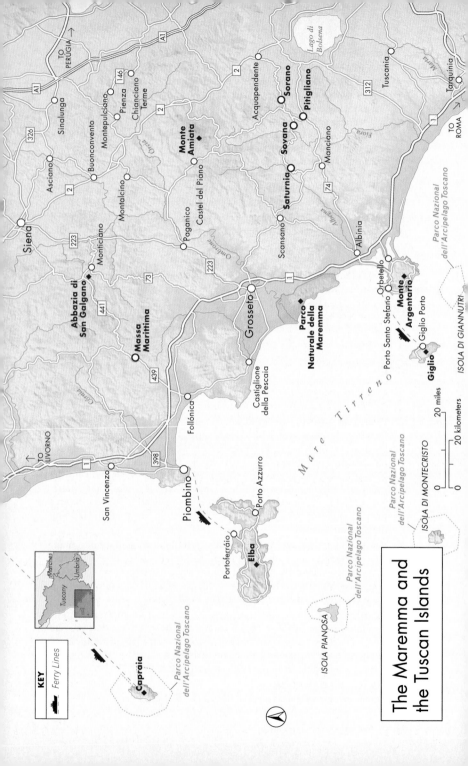

The Maremma and the Tuscan Islands

KEY

Ferry Lines

Parco Nazional dell'Arcipelago Toscano

Capraia

Parco Nazional dell'Arcipelago Toscano

ISOLA PIANOSA

ISOLA DI MONTECRISTO

Parco Nazional dell'Arcipelago Toscano

Parco Nazional dell'Arcipelago Toscano

Mare Tirreno

ISOLA DI GIANNUTRI

Marche

Umbria

Tuscany

TO LIVORNO

San Vincenzo

Piombino

Portoferráio

Elba

Porto Azzurro

Castiglione della Pescaia

Follónica

Siena

Asciano

Sinalunga

Buonconvento

Montepulciano

Pienza

Chianciano Terme

Montalcino

Monticiano

Monteriggioni

Abbazia di San Galgano

Massa Maríttima

Paganico

Castel del Piano

Monte Amiata

Acquapendente

Lago di Bolsena

Sorano

Pitigliano

Sovana

Saturnia

Scansano

Manciano

Tuscania

TO PERÚGIA →

TO ROMA

Tarquinia →

Grosseto

Parco Naturale della Maremma

Albinia

Orbetello

Porto Santo Stefano

Monte Argentario

Giglio Porto

Giglio

Paganico

Ombrone

Orcia

Fiora

Albegna

Merse

Cecina

Cornia

326

2

146

2

2

312

74

223

73

441

223

1

1

439

398

A1

A1

TO LIVORNO

20 miles

20 kilometers

0

0

The Maremma and
the Tuscan Islands

EXPLORING

Duomo. This 18th-century baroque cathedral has a single nave with chapels and paintings on the sides. There are two altarpieces by local artist Francesco Zuccarelli (1702–88), a rococo landscape artist, favorite of George III, and one of the founders of the British Royal Academy. ✉ *Piazza S. Gregorio 1* ☎ *0564/616090* 🕒 *Daily 9–7.*

> **WORD OF MOUTH**
>
> "Pitigliano is a truly special town. The very old, lovingly restored synagogue is a sight to be seen. The town itself is perched high on a hill, built on tufa rocks, which in itself makes it quite unique, I think." —Flame123

Museo di Arte Sacra. The museum, housed in the Palazzo Orsini, has several rooms featuring paintings by Zuccarelli, who was born in Pitigliano in 1702. Other works include a Madonna carved in wood by Jacopo della Quercia (1371/74–1438), a 14th-century crucifix, period furniture, and a numismatic collection. ✉ *Piazza Fortezza Orsini 4* ☎ *0564/616074* 🌐 *www.palazzo-orsini-pitigliano.it* 🎫 *€4* 🕒 *Apr.–July, Tues.–Sun. 10–1 and 3–7; Aug., daily 10–7; Sept.–Oct., Tues.–Sun. 10–1 and 3–7; Nov.–Mar., Tues.–Fri. 10–1 and 3–5.*

6

Piccola Gerusaleme di Pitigliano. Now a museum of Jewish culture, the ghetto where Jews took refuge from 16th-century Catholic persecution was a thriving community until the beginning of World War II. Inside the precinct today are the remains of ritual bathing basins, a wine cellar, a kosher butcher shop and bakery, and the restored synagogue, where religious services are held on the Sabbath. ✉ *Vicolo Marghera* ☎ *0564/614230* 🌐 *www.lapiccolagerusalemme.it* 🎫 *€3* 🕒 *Apr.–Sept., Sun.–Fri. 10–1:30 and 2:30–6:30; Oct.–Mar., Sun.–Fri. 10–12:30 and 3–5:30.*

WHERE TO EAT AND STAY

For expanded hotel reviews, visit Fodors.com.

$$ TUSCAN 🍴 **Il Tufo Allegro.** The name means Happy Tufa; you would be happy, too, if you ate at this fine restaurant cut directly into the tufa rock plateau upon which old Pitigliano sits. The cuisine is local and regional: pappardelle *al ragù di cinghiale* (with wild boar sauce) is particularly tasty, and fish also figures on the menu from time to time. For the particularly hungry, there are usually several four-course, fixed price menus to choose from. [$] *Average main: €15* ✉ *Vicolo della Costituzione 5* ☎ *0564/616192* 🌐 *www.iltufoallegro.com* 🕒 *Closed Tues. and mid-Jan.–mid-Feb. No lunch Wed. Oct.–July.*

$ B&B/INN 🏨 **Locanda Il Tufo Rosa.** The space for part of this tiny guesthouse has been carved out of the tufa rock beneath the aqueduct at the entrance to the old town. **Pros:** excellent location; best value in town. **Cons:** rooms are small; getting here is difficult, narrow stairways to climb. [$] *Rooms from: €75* ✉ *Piazza Petruccioli 97* ☎ *0564/617019* 🌐 *www.iltuforosa.com* 🛏 *6 rooms, 1 apartment* 🍽 *No meals.*

SOVANA

5 km (3 miles) north of Pitigliano, 155 km (97 miles) southeast of Siena, 225 km (141 miles) southeast of Florence.

This town of Etruscan origin was once the capital of the area in southern Tuscany dominated by the Aldobrandeschi family, whose reign was at its height in the 11th and first half of the 12th centuries. One member of the family, Hildebrand, was the 11th-century Catholic reformer Pope Gregory VII (circa 1020–85). The 13th- to 14th-century Romanesque fortress known as the Rocca Aldobrandesca is now in ruins. Via di Mezzo, with stones arranged in a fish-scale pattern, is the main street running the length of the town.

GETTING HERE

Like Sorano and Pitigliano, Sovana is best reached by car along the SR74, either from the Via Aurelia to the west or the A1 highway to the east. Sovana cannot be reached by train or bus.

EXPLORING

Duomo. Sovana extends from the Rocca Aldobrandesca at the eastern end of town to the imposing cathedral, built between the 10th and 14th centuries, in the west. The church, dedicated to Saints Peter and Paul, is Romanesque in style but, atypically, the main entrance is on the lefthand side of the building. ⊠ *Piazza del Duomo* ⊙ *Daily 10–1 and 2:45–5:45.*

Etruscan necropolis. Some of Italy's best-preserved monumental rock tombs, dating from the 2nd to the 3rd centuries BC, are found just outside the town at the Etruscan necropolis. Some of the tombs, such as the so-called Tomba Sirena (Siren's Tomb), preserve clear signs of their original and elaborately carved decorations. Others, like the Tomba Ildebranda (Hildebrand Tomb), are spectacular evidence of the architectural complexity sometimes achieved. Don't forget to walk along the section of an Etruscan road carved directly into the tufa stone. ⊠ *1½ km (1 mile) west of town center* ☎ *0564/633099* ☒ *€5* ⊙ *Daily 9–sunset.*

Piazza del Pretorio. Here, in the central town square, you'll find the 13th-century Palazzo Pretorio, which has a facade adorned with crests of Sovana's captains of justice; and the Renaissance Palazzo Bourbon dal Monte.

Santa Maria Maggiore. This little 14th-century church on the main square has frescoes from the late-15th-century Sienese Umbrian school and a ciborium dating back to the 8th century. ⊠ *Piazza del Pretorio* ⊙ *Daily 8:30–12:30 and 4–6:30.*

WHERE TO EAT

$$
TUSCAN
Fodor's Choice
★

✕ **La Taverna Etrusca.** Elaborately prepared Tuscan fare is served at this elegant restaurant on Sovana's central square. For your starter, try the *tortino di pecorino maremmano con miele di castagno, gelatina di pere e cialda croccante* (local sheep cheese tart with chestnut honey, pear gelatine, and a Parmesan crisp). Grilled meat and some fish dishes highlight the list of second courses, but a well-priced fixed menu might be a good way to go for the indecisive. Service is prompt and highly professional. A pleasant outdoor terrace provides plenty of fresh air in the summer months. $ *Average main: €20* ⊠ *Piazza del Pretorio 16* ☎ *0564/616183* ⊕ *www.tavernaetrusca.com* ⊙ *Closed Wed.*

SATURNIA

25 km (15 miles) east of Sovana, 129 km (77 miles) south of Siena, 199 km (119 miles) south of Florence.

Saturnia was settled even before the Etruscan period, but nowadays it's best known not for what lies buried beneath the ground but for what comes up from it: hot, sulfurous water that supplies the town's world-famous spa. According to an oft-repeated legend, the thermal waters were created when Saturn, restless with earth's bickering mortals, threw down a thunderbolt and created a hot spring whose miraculously calming waters created peace among them. Today these magnesium-rich waters bubble forth from the clay, drawing Italians and non-Italians alike seeking relief for skin and muscular ailments as well as a bit (well, a lot) of relaxation. Unlike better-known spa centers such as Montecatini Terme, nature still has her place here.

GETTING HERE

Saturnia is a 30-minute drive from Pitigliano. Follow the SS74 to Manciano, then the SS322 to Montemerano, and then turn right onto the Strada Saturnia–La Croce. The RAMA bus company travels from Grosseto to Saturnia, but three changes make the journey particularly arduous. There is no train service to Saturnia.

EXPLORING

Cascate del Gorello (*Gorello Falls*). Outside Saturnia, the hot, sulfurous waters cascade over natural limestone shelves at the Cascate del Gorello, affording bathers a sweeping view of the open countryside. The falls are on public land and can be enjoyed 24 hours a day. They get extremely crowded—day and night—during August. ⊠ *2 km (1 mile) south of Saturnia, on road to Montemerano* 🆓 *Free.*

Necropoli del Puntone. Pre-Etruscan tombs at this necropolis aren't kept up well, but they're interesting simply for their age, as they're even older than Saturnia's legendary baths. ⊠ *1 km (½ mile) north of Saturnia, on road to Poggio Murello, turn left and follow signs* 🆓 *Free* ⊙ *Daily 24 hrs.*

Terme di Saturnia. The swimming pools and treatments at Terme di Saturnia spa and resort are open to the public. You might make an appointment for a thermal mud therapy or rent a lounge chair and umbrella to sit by the pools. ⊠ *3 km (2 miles) east of Saturnia on road to Montemerano, after Gorello Falls* ☎ *0564/600111* ⊕ *www.termedisaturnia. it* 🆓 *Full day €22, half day €17* ⊙ *Apr.–Oct., daily 9:30–7; Nov.–Mar., daily 9:30–5.*

WHERE TO EAT

$$$$
TUSCAN

✕ **Da Caino.** At this excellent restaurant in the nearby town of Montemerano, specialties include roast veal tongue with blueberry-flavored onions, saffron, and capers, *tortelli di cinta senese in brodetto di castagne e gallina* (pasta filled with Sienese pork in a chicken and chesnut

6

CLOSE UP

Terme, Wrath of the Gods

In a country known for millennia as a hotbed of seismic activity, Tuscany seems to have gotten a lucky break. Although Campania and Sicily are famous for active volcanoes, and Umbria and the Marches stand on notoriously shaky ground, Tuscany's underground activity makes itself known in the form of steamy and sulfurous hot springs that have earned the region a name as a spa-goer's paradise.

Tuscany is dotted throughout with small *terme* (thermal baths), where hot waters flow from natural springs deep under the earth's surface. Since the time of the Etruscans, these hot springs have been valued for their curative properties. The Romans attributed the springs' origins to divine thunderbolts that split the earth open and let flow the miraculous waters. Regardless of their origin, their appeal endures, as the presence of thousands of people taking the waters in the Maremma attests.

Each of the springs has different curative properties, attributable to the various concentrations of minerals and gases that individual water flows pick up on their way to the surface. Carbon dioxide, for example, is said to strengthen the immune system, and sulfur, its characteristic rotten-egg smell notwithstanding, is said to relieve pain and aid in relaxation.

Although customs and conventions vary between spas, you generally pay an admission fee to swim in baths that range from hot natural lakes and waterfalls (with accompanying mud) to giant limestone swimming pools filled with cloudy, bright blue, steaming water. Larger establishments have treatments that can range from mineral mud baths to steam inhalations.

Believers swear that Tuscany's hot springs have a positive effect on everything from skin disorders to back pain to liver function to stress. Whatever your opinion, a good soak in a Tuscan spring is a relaxing way to take a break, and as far as geological phenomena go, it beats an earthquake or a volcanic eruption any day.

A few of the region's spas, notably the world-famous Montecatini Terme (⇨ *See Chapter 3)*, are well known outside Tuscany. For the most part, however, the local establishments that run the springs are not well publicized, which can mean a more local flavor, lower prices, and fewer crowds: Terme di Bagni di Lucca is near Lucca; Terme di Chianciano is near Chiusi; Bagno Vignoni is just south of San Quirico d'Orcia; and Terme di Saturnia is not too far from Grosseto.

Local tourist offices have the most up-to-date information on smaller springs, many of which are open for only part of the year.

broth), and such hearty dishes as *cinghiale lardolato con finocchi, arance e olive* (larded wild boar with fennel, orange, and olives). Prices are among the highest in the region; locals consider it a serious splurge. [$] *Average main: €50* ✉ *Via della Chiesa 4, 7 km (4½ miles) south of Saturnia on road to Scansano, Montemerano* ☎ *0564/602817* 🌐 *www.dacaino.it* ✍ *Reservations essential* 🕓 *Closed Wed., Jan., and 2 wks in July. No lunch Thurs.*

$$
TUSCAN

✕**I Due Cippi–Da Michele.** Owner Michele Aniello captivates with a creative menu that emphasizes local ingredients like wild boar and duck. Try the *tortelli di castagne al seme di finocchio* (chestnut-stuffed pasta with butter sauce and fennel seeds). In good weather you can enjoy your meal on a terrace overlooking the town's main square. $ *Average main: €15* ⊠ *Piazza Vittorio Veneto 26a* ☎ *0564/601074* ⚑ *Reservations essential* ⊘ *Closed Dec. 20–26, Jan. 10–25, and Tues. Oct.–June.*

WHERE TO STAY
For expanded hotel reviews, visit Fodors.com.

$$$$
RESORT

Terme di Saturnia. Spa living might not get any more top-notch than this: roam the spa resort in a plush white bathrobe (waiting in your room) before dipping into the 37.5°C (100°F) sulfurous thermal pools. **Pros:** luxurious setting; excellent service; wide range of treatments. **Cons:** on the pricey side; aseptic atmosphere. $ *Rooms from: €320* ⊠ *3 km (2 miles) east of Saturnia on road to Montemerano, past Gorello Falls* ☎ *0564/600111* ⊕ *www.termedisaturnia.it* ⬐ *124 rooms, 2 suites* ⦿*Breakfast.*

$$
B&B/INN

Villa Acquaviva. An elegant villa painted antique rose appears at the end of a tree-lined driveway perched on top of a hill off the main road 1 km (½ mile) before Montemerano. **Pros:** near the hot springs; lovely views; family-friendly atmosphere. **Cons:** attendants can be hard to find during the day; need a car to get around. $ *Rooms from: €130* ⊠ *Strada Scansanese 6 km (4 miles) south of Saturnia, Montemerano* ☎ *0564/602890* ⊕ *www.relaisvillaacquaviva.com* ⬐ *23 rooms, 2 suites* ⦿*Breakfast.*

$
B&B/INN

Villa Clodia. Situated in the oldest part of town, the villa has splendid views over the nearby hills and the steamy clouds coming from the hot springs. **Pros:** excellent location on edge of town; great views; cozy environment. **Cons:** some rooms are small; need a car to get around. $ *Rooms from: €120* ⊠ *Via Italia 43* ☎ *0564/601212* ⊕ *www.hotelvillaclodia.com* ⬐ *8 rooms, 2 suites* ⊘ *Closed Dec.* ⦿*Breakfast.*

EN
ROUTE

Grosseto. The largest town in southern Tuscany, Grosseto is the capital of the Maremma. First recorded in the 9th century as a *castellum* (castle) built to defend a bridge and a port on the nearby River Ombrone, the town is now a thriving agricultural center. Badly damaged during World War II, it has been largely rebuilt since the 1950s, but a small *centro storico* (historic center), protected by defensive walls that follow a hexagonal plan, is worth a short visit on your way to the coast.

A field of sunflowers in the Maremma

PARCO NATURALE DELLA MAREMMA

10 km (6 miles) south of Grosseto, 88 km (55 miles) southwest of Siena, 156 km (97 miles) south of Florence.

GETTING HERE
The park is best reached by car from the Via Aurelia (SS1), which runs between Rome and Pisa. Local bus service connects the park with the train station in nearby Grosseto.

VISITOR INFORMATION
Parco Naturale della Maremma tourism office ⊠ *Via del Bersgliere 7/9, Alberese* ☏ *0564/407098* ⊕ *www.parco-maremma.it.*

EXPLORING
Parco Naturale della Maremma. The well-kept nature preserve at **Monti dell'Uccellina** is an oasis of green hills sloping down to small, secluded beaches on protected coastline. Wild goats and rabbits, foxes and wild boars, as well as horses and a domesticated long-horned white ox unique to this region, make their home among miles of sea pines, rosemary plants, and juniper bushes. The park also has scattered Etruscan and Roman ruins and a medieval abbey, the **Abbazia di San Rabano.** Enter from the south at Talamone (turn right 1 km [½ mile] before town) or from Alberese, both reachable from the SS1 (Via Aurelia). Daily limits restrict the number of cars that can enter, so in summer it's best to either reserve ahead or to leave your car in Alberese and use the regular bus service; contact the park's information office for bookings, and to secure English-language guides. ⊠ *Park Office, Via Bersagliere 7/9, Alberese* ☏ *0564/407098* ⊠ *Free* ☉ *Daily 9–1 hr before sunset.*

MONTE ARGENTARIO

Porto Santo Stefano 60 km (37 miles) southwest of Saturnia, 118 km (74 miles) southwest of Siena, 186 km (116 miles) southwest of Florence.

Connected to the mainland only by two thin strips of land and a causeway, Monte Argentario feels like an island. The north and south isthmuses, La Giannella and La Feniglia, have long sandy beaches popular with families, but otherwise the terrain is rugged, dotted with luxurious vacation houses. There are beautiful views from the panoramic mountain road encircling the promontory, and a drive here is a romantic sunset excursion. The mountain itself rises 2,096 feet above the sea, and it's ringed with rocky beaches and sheer cliffs that afford breathtaking views of the coast.

GETTING HERE

The Monte Argentario peninsula lies just off the SS1 (Via Aurelia), which connects Rome and Pisa. It's a two-hour drive from either city. Intercity buses are not a viable option. The closest train station is in Orbetello Scalo, with local bus service available to both Porto Ercole and Porto Santo Stefano.

VISITOR INFORMATION

Monte Argentario tourism office ✉ *Piazza delle Repubblica 3, Orbetello* ☎ *0564/860447* 🌐 *www.prolocomonteargentario.com.*

EXPLORING

Porto Ercole. On the southeastern side of Monte Argentario, this small port town is the haunt of the rich and famous, with top-notch hotels and restaurants perched on the cliffs.

Porto Santo Stefano. On the north side, busy and colorful Porto Santo Stefano is Monte Argentario's main center, with markets, hotels, restaurants, and ferry service to Giglio and Giannutri, two of the Tuscan islands.

WHERE TO EAT AND STAY

For expanded hotel reviews, visit Fodors.com.

$$ SEAFOOD 🍴 **Gambero Rosso.** Right on the waterfront at Porto Ercole, this classic Italian restaurant offers simple preparations of locally caught fresh fish. Try the antipasto *sorpresa del Gambero* (surprise of the house), an ever-changing array of six, sometimes seven, different fish dishes (fried, chilled, or baked, for example). The chef lets his imagination run wild, and it's only to the benefit of the happy diners. It's even better if you enjoy it on the terrace with a view. [$] *Average main: €20* ✉ *Lungomare Doria 70, Porto Ercole* ☎ *0564/832650* ✍ *Reservations essential* 🕒 *Closed Wed. (except in Jul.–Aug.), and mid-Nov.–mid-Jan.*

$$$ SEAFOOD 🍴 **La Fontanina di San Pietro.** Grape vines climbing up a trellis, cherry trees in the countryside overlooking the port—the scene here is romantic. Dine on scampi with zucchini and spaghetti *allo scoglio* (with fresh clams and mussels in a light tomato sauce), while enjoying a fruity white from the well-matched wine list. The catch of the day can be prepared a number of ways, and is priced by weight; the *pesce spada* (swordfish) is terrific. [$] *Average main: €25* ✉ *Località San Pietro, Porto*

Santo Stefano ☎ *0564/825261* 🌐 *www.lafontanina.com* ⏲ *Closed Wed. and Jan.*

$ B&B/INN 🏨 **Hotel Don Pedro.** The private beach more than makes up for the lack of a pool at this hotel in Porto Ercole. **Pros:** panoramic views of port; private beach; family-friendly atmosphere. **Cons:** not all rooms have sea views; uninspired decor. [$] *Rooms from: €110* ✉ *Via Panoramica 7, Porto Ercole* ☎ *0564/833914* 🌐 *www.hoteldonpedro.it* 🛏 *60 rooms* ⏲ *Closed Nov.–Easter* 🍴 *No meals.*

$$$$ RESORT Fodor's Choice ★ 🏨 **Il Pellicano.** Worldly cares are softly washed away by the comforts of the rooms (some damask linens, tapestry-like canopies, marble highboys), the superlative attentiveness of the staff, and the hotel's magnificent garden setting. **Pros:** spectacular setting and gardens; superlative service; excellent dining options. **Cons:** isolated location; on a long dirt road; beach is rocky. [$] *Rooms from: €640* ✉ *Località Lo Sbarcatello, 5 km (3 miles) west of Porto Ercole* ☎ *0564/858111* 🌐 *www.pellicanohotel.com* 🛏 *40 rooms, 10 suites* ⏲ *Closed Nov.–Mar.* 🍴 *Breakfast.*

MASSA MARITTIMA

111 km (69 miles) southeast of Livorno, 48 km (30 miles) east of Piombino, 66 km (42 miles) southwest of Siena, 132 km (82 miles) southwest of Florence.

Massa Marittima is a charming medieval hill town with a rich mining and industrial heritage—pyrite, iron, and copper were found in these parts. After a centuries-long slump (most of the minerals having been depleted), the town is now popular simply for its old streets.

GETTING HERE

From Siena, the easiest way to reach Massa Marittima is to take the SP73bis, then the SP441. Bus service from Siena, provided by Tra-In, is not timed to make day trips feasible. Massa Marittima cannot be reached by train.

VISITOR INFORMATION

Massa Marittima tourism office ✉ *Via Todini 3/5* ☎ *0566/902756* 🌐 *www.altamaremmaturismo.it.*

EXPLORING

Duomo. The central Piazza Garibaldi, dating from the 13th to the early 14th centuries, contains this Romanesque cathedral, with sculptures of the life of patron saint Cerbone above the door. ✉ *Via della Libertà 1* ☎ *0566/902237* ⏲ *Daily 8–noon and 3–6.*

Museo Archeologico. The 13th-century Palazzo Pretorio, on Piazza Garibaldi, is home to this fascinating museum with plenty of Etruscan artifacts. A number of displays reconstruct the nature of daily life for the Etruscans who once inhabited the hills in this area. ✉ *Piazza Garibaldi 1* ☎ *0566/902289* 🎟 *€3* ⏲ *Apr.–mid-July, Tues.–Sun. 10–12:30 and 3:30–7; mid-July–end Aug., Tues.–Sun. 10–12:30 and 4–8; end Aug.–Oct., Tues.–Sun. 10–12:30 and 3:30–7; Nov.–Mar., Tues.–Sun. 10–12:30 and 3–5.*

Museo Arte e Storia della Miniera (*Museum of the Art and History of Mining*). This museum, in the upper part of town, shows how dependent Massa Marittima has been since Etruscan times on the mining of copper, lead, and silver. Exhibits trace the history of the local mining industry. Across the street, you can even visit a real mine. ✉ *Palazzetto delle Armi, Piazza Matteotti* ☎ *0566/902289* 🎟 *Museum €1.50; museum and mine €5* 🕒 *Museum: Apr.–mid-July, Tues.–Sun. 3–5:30; mid-July–Aug., Tues.–Sun. 10:30–1 and 3–5:30; Sept.–Mar. by appointment for groups. Mine visits: Apr.–Oct., Tues.–Sun. at 10, 11, noon, 12:45, 3:30, 4:30, 5, and 5:45; Nov.–Mar. at 10, 11, noon, 12:45, 3, 4, and 4:30.*

Museo di Arte Sacra. In the converted convent church of San Pietro all'Orto, this museum houses a large number of medieval paintings and sculptures gathered from churches in and around Massa Marittima. Perhaps the most important piece, Ambrogio Lorenzetti's early-14th-century *Maestà*, was discovered in the storage room of the church in 1866. ✉ *Corso Diaz 37* ☎ *0566/901954* 🎟 *€5* 🕒 *Apr.–Oct., Tues.–Sun. 10–1 and 3–6; Nov.–Mar., Tues.–Sun. 11–1 and 3–5.*

Torre del Candeliere (*Tower of the Candlemaker*). Built to both defend and control their new possession after the Sienese conquered Massa Marittima in 1335, the **Fortezza dei Senesi** crowns the upper part of town. Just inside the imposing Sienese gate is the so-called Tower of the Candle Holder, a massive bastion that is connected to the outer walls by the **Arco Senese,** a high arched bridge. A visit to the tower gives access to the arch and to the upper city walls, where commanding views open before you. ✉ *Piazza Matteotti* ☎ *0566/902289* 🎟 *€2.50* 🕒 *Apr.–mid-July, Tues.–Sun. 3–5:30; mid-July–Aug., daily 10:30–1 and 3–5:30; Sept.–Mar., by appointment for groups.*

WHERE TO STAY

For expanded hotel reviews, visit Fodors.com.

$ B&B/INN 🏨 **Rifugio Prategiano.** Horseback trail rides through Tuscany's cowboy country are an integral part of the experience at this family-run country inn. **Pros:** great for families with children; plenty of outdoor sports activities; peaceful setting. **Cons:** very simple furnishings; no a/c in rooms; need a car to get around. [$] *Rooms from: €124* ✉ *Via dei Platani 3b, Località Prategiano 17 km (11 miles) west of Abbazia San Galgano, Montieri* ☎ *0566/997700* 🌐 *www.prategiano.com* 🛏 *24 rooms* 🕒 *Closed Nov.–mid-Mar.* 🍴 *Breakfast.*

NIGHTLIFE AND THE ARTS

Balestro del Girifalco (*Falcon Crossbow Contest*). On the fourth Sunday of May, and again on the second Sunday in August, Massa Marittima's three traditional neighborhood groups dress in medieval costumes and parade through the town with much fanfare and flag throwing. The pinnacle of the event is a shooting competition between the town's districts using arrows and crossbows.

ABBAZIA DI SAN GALGANO

32 km (20 miles) northeast of Massa Marittima, 33 km (20 miles) southwest of Siena, 87 km (54 miles) south of Florence.

GETTING HERE

You'll need a car to get here, as bus and train service is not available. From Siena, follow the SP73bis, then take the SP441 south.

EXPLORING

Fodor'sChoice   **Abbazia di San Galgano.** Time has had its way with this Gothic cathedral
★   without a rooftop, a hauntingly beautiful sight well worth a detour. The church was built in the 13th century by Cistercian monks, who designed it after churches built by their order in France. But starting in the 15th century it fell into ruin, declining gradually over centuries. Grass has grown through the floor, and the roof and windows are gone. What's left of its facade and walls makes a grandiose and desolate picture. In July and August the scene is enlivened by evening concerts arranged by the Accademia Musicale Chigiana in Siena. Contact the tourist information office at the abbey for details. ⊠ *Off SP441* ☎ *0577/756738 for tourist office* ⊕ *www.prolocochiusdino.it* ☜€2 ☉ *Apr.–Oct., daily 9–8; Nov.–Mar., daily 9–6.*

Eremo di Montesiepi. Behind the church of San Galgano, a short climb brings you to this charming little chapel with frescoes by painter Ambrogio Lorenzetti (documented 1319–48), and a sword in a stone. Legend has it that Galgano, a medieval warrior and bon vivant, was struck by a revelation on this spot in which an angel told him to give up his fighting and frivolous ways forever. As a token of his conversion, he plunged his sword into the rock, where it still remains today. ⊠ *Above Abbazia di San Galgano* ☎ *0577/756700* ☜ *Free* ☉ *Daily 9–sunset.*

ELBA AND THE SURROUNDING ISLANDS

The Tuscan archipelago is a wide semicircle of islands that traces a path, in the crystal-clear sea, between Livorno and Monte Argentario. All of the larger islands in the group can be reached by ferry service from the mainland, whereas the smaller islands, like the charmingly named Formiche di Grosseto (Ants of Grosseto) and the Formica di Montecristo (Ant of Montecristo), can only be reached by private boat. The largest, and most famous, of the islands is Elba, with several large towns and its own airport. Equally popular as a summer destination is Giglio. Other islands, like Capraia, Pianosa, and Montecristo, more closely guard their natural beauty, offering visitors few or no hotels or restaurants. The peak season is in July and August—book your ferry journey well in advance.

GIGLIO

60 km (36 miles) south of Massa Marittima, 90 km (55 miles) south of Siena, 145 km (87 miles) south of Florence.

GETTING HERE

To get to Giglio, take one of the Toremar car ferries that run between Porto Santo Stefano on the Monte Argentario peninsula and Giglio Porto. The trip, which costs €6.30 for passengers and €30 for cars, takes about an hour.

VISITOR INFORMATION

Giglio tourism office ✉ *Via Provinciale 9, Giglio Porto* ☎ *0564/809400* 🌐 *www.isoladelgiglio.it.*

EXPLORING

Isola del Giglio. This rocky, romantic isle, whose name translates to "Island of the Lily," is an hour by ferry from Porto Santo Stefano—but a world away from the mainland's hustle and bustle. The island's three towns—**Giglio Porto,** the charming harbor where the ferry arrives; **Giglio Castello,** a walled village at Giglio's highest point; and **Giglio Campese,** a modern town on the west side of the island—are connected by one long, meandering road. But to really explore Giglio you need a good pair of hiking boots. A network of rugged trails climbs up the steep hills through clusters of wild rosemary and tiny daffodils, and once you leave town, chances are your only company will be the goats who thrive on Giglio's sun-baked hills.

The island's main attraction, however, is at sea level—a sparkling array of lush coves and tiny beaches, most accessible only on foot or by boat. With the exception of Giglio Campese, where the sandy beach is as popular in summer as any mainland resort, most of the little island's coastline is untouched, leaving plenty of room for peaceful sunning for those willing to go off the beaten path.

WHERE TO STAY

For expanded hotel reviews, visit Fodors.com.

$$ B&B/INN 🏨 **Hotel Arenella.** Sitting above the sea, this isolated hotel has a private rocky beach reachable by a steep 60-foot descent. **Pros:** magnificent views; peaceful location; shuttle service to the port. **Cons:** long walk to nearest restaurants; modern decor geared to a business clientele. [$] *Rooms from: €150* ✉ *Via Arenella 5, Giglio Porto* ☎ *0564/809340* 🌐 *www.hotelarenella.com* 🛏 *26 rooms* ⏲ *Closed Nov.–Easter* 🍴 *Breakfast.*

SPORTS AND THE OUTDOORS

HIKING For day-trippers, the best hike is the 1,350-foot ascent from Giglio Porto to Giglio Castello. It's a 4-km (2½-mile) trek that takes about an hour and affords marvelous views of the island's east coast. Frequent bus service to and from Castello allows the option of walking just one way. The rest of the island's trails are reasonably well marked. Pick up maps at the tourist office in Giglio Porto.

WATER SPORTS **Boatmen.** Rent motorboats for exploring the island's innumerable coves at this kiosk on the waterfront. Look for signs reading *noleggio barche*

GETTING HERE AND AROUND: THE ISLANDS

Passenger and car ferries link the Tuscan islands with the mainland.

Moby Lines. From Piombino, this company provides one-hour ferry service to Portoferraio on Elba. ⊠ *Via Ninci 1, Portoferraio* ☎ *0565/916758, 199/303040 toll-free in Italy* ⊕ *www.mobylines.it.*

Toremar. This ferry service provides transportation between Piombino and Elba's main ports as well as to the smaller islands: from Livorno to Capraia; from Piombino to Pianosa; and from Porto Santo Stefano to Giglio. ⊠ *Piazzale Premuda 13, Nuova Stazione Marittima, Piombino* ☎ *0565/31100* ⊕ *www.toremar.it.*

Prices can differ drastically, so comparison shop before buying your tickets. Reserve your seat ahead of time in the peak-season months of July and August.

Baby Rent. On Elba there are numerous places to rent bikes, scooters, motorcycles, or cars: here you can choose, all of the above as well as dune buggies and convertibles. ⊠ *Piazza Marinai d'Italia 9, Portoferraio* ☎ *329/3631291 mobile.*

Chiappi. Honda and Yamaha scooters as well as campers, cars, and boats can be rented here. ⊠ *Calata Italia 38, Elba, Portoferraio* ☎ *0565/914366* ⊕ *www.rentchiappi.it.*

(boat rentals) near the ferry dock. ⊠ *On port, Via Umberto I, Giglio Porto* ☎ *347/0547755* ⊕ *www.boatmen.it.*

Spiaggia Arenella. You can charter your own snorkeling or beach excursion and let someone else do the piloting through Marco Bartoletti. You'll find him at the Arenella beach. ⊠ *Località Arenella, 2½ km (1 mile) north of Giglio Porto* ☎ *336/535054 Marco.*

ELBA

40 km (24 miles) southwest of Massa Marittima, 80 km (48 miles) southwest of Siena, 120 km (72 miles) southwest of Florence.

Elba is the Tuscan archipelago's largest island, but it resembles nearby verdant Corsica more than it does its rocky Italian sisters, thanks to a network of underground springs that keep it lush and green. It's this combination of semitropical vegetation and dramatic mountain scenery—unusual in the Mediterranean—that has made Elba so prized for so long, and the island's uniqueness continues to draw boatloads of visitors throughout the warm months. A car is very useful for getting around the island, but public buses stop at most towns several times a day; the tourist office has timetables.

GETTING HERE

Toremar car ferries make the one-hour trip between Portoferraio and Piombino on the mainland. The cost is €10.50 for foot passengers, €39 for cars with two passengers.

VISITOR INFORMATION

For information about the flora and fauna to be found on Elba, as well as throughout the Tuscan archipelago, contact the Parco Nazionale dell'Arcipelago Toscano. The tourism office also has detailed walking and hiking maps.

Elba tourism office ⊠ *Viale Elba 4, Portoferraio* ☎ *0565/914671* ⊕ *www.aptelba.it.*

Parco Nazionale dell'Arcipelago Toscano tourism office. For information about the flora and fauna to be found on Elba, as well as throughout the Tuscan archipelago, contact the park board. ⊠ *Via Guerazzi 1, Portoferraio* ☎ *0565/919411* ⊕ *www.islepark.it.*

WORD OF MOUTH

"The beaches on Elba are wonderful and you can swim, snorkel or just relax. We were there in off season, but I expect they get really crowded. The times we went out to eat were wonderful. Simple pizzas and fish and inexpensive wine. What a place!"
—applejax

EXPLORING

Marina di Campo. On the south side of Elba, this small town with a long sandy beach and protected cove is a classic summer vacationer's spot. The laid-back marina is full of bars, boutiques, and restaurants.

Monte Capanne. The highest point on Elba, Monte Capanna is crossed by a twisting road that provides magnificent vistas at every turn; the tiny towns of **Poggio** and **Marciana** have enchanting little piazzas full of flowers and trees. You can hike to the top of the mountain, or take an unusual open-basket cable car from just above Poggio.

Montecristo. The most famous prisoner of the island, about 50 km (30 miles) south of Elba, was fictional: Alexandre Dumas's legendary count. Today the island is a well-protected nature preserve with wild Montecristo goats and vipers, peregrine falcons, and rare Corsican seagulls who make their home amid rosemary bushes and stunted pine trees. Scientific-research teams are given priority for permission to land on the island, and an annual quota of 1,000 visitors strictly limits even their number.

  Corpo Forestale. Montecristo is monitored by the National Forestry Service. Contact them for access permits to the island. ⊠ *Via Bicocchi 2, Follonica* ☎ *0566/40019* ⊕ *www.corpoforestale.it.*

Museo Archeologico. Exhibits at this museum reconstruct the island's ancient history through a display of Etruscan and Roman artifacts recovered from shipwrecks. ⊠ *Località Linguella, Calata Buccari, Portoferraio* ☎ *0565/944024* ⊠ *€3* ☉ *June 15–Sept. 15, daily 9:30–2:30 and 5–midnight; Sept. 16–June 14, Thurs. 10:30–1:30 and 4–8.*

Palazzina dei Mulini. During Napoléon's famous exile on Elba in 1814–15, he built this residence out of two windmills. It still contains furniture from the period and Napoléon's impressive library, with the more than 2,000 volumes that he brought here from France. ⊠ *Piazzale Napoleone 1, Portoferraio* ☎ *0565/915846* ⊠ *€7, €13 with admission to Villa San Martino* ☉ *Mon. and Wed.–Sat. 9–7, Sun. 9–1.*

Porto Azzurro. The waters of the port at Elba's eastern end are noticeably *azzurro* (sky-blue). It's worth a stop for a walk and a gelato along the rows of yachts harbored here.

Portoferraio. The lively port town where Victor Hugo (1802–85) spent his boyhood makes a good base for visiting Elba. Head right when you get off the ferry to get to the centro storico, fortified in the 16th century by the Medici grand duke Cosimo I (1519–74). Most of the pretty, multicolor buildings that line the old harbor date from the 18th and 19th centuries when the boats in the port were full of mineral exports rather than tourists.

Rio Marina. Elba's quietest town is an old-fashioned port on the northeastern edge of the island. Here you'll find a pebble beach, an old mine, a leafy public park, and ferry service to Piombino.

Villa San Martino. A couple of miles outside Portoferraio, this splendid villa was Napoléon's summer home during his 10-month exile on Elba. Temporary exhibitions are held in a gallery attached to the main building. The Egyptian Room, decorated with idealized scenes of the Egyptian campaign, may have provided Napoléon the consolation of glories past. The villa's classical facade was added by a Russian prince, Anatolia Demidoff, after he bought the house in 1852. ⊠ *Località San Martino* ☎ *0565/914688* 💰€*7, €13 with admission to Palazzina dei Mulini* ⊙ *Tues.–Sat. 9–7 and Sun. 9–1.*

WHERE TO EAT

$ ╳**Il Cantuccio.** This small, simple eatery is a standout in the touristy
SEAFOOD Marina di Campo. Shady outdoor tables on a backstreet keep diners cool on warm nights. If the long menu seems daunting, focus on the list of specials, which often includes such local delicacies as spaghetti *alle uova di pesce* (with sea-bream caviar). The staff is friendly and well informed, particularly about wine. 💲 *Average main: €15* ⊠ *Via Garibaldi 6, Marina di Campo* ☎ *0565/976775* ⊕ *www. ristoranteilcantuccio.eu.*

$ ╳**Il Mare.** Homemade pastas and fresh seafood are served here with a
ITALIAN dash of style. The chef puts a creative spin on the classics, coming up with such delights as homemade vegetable gnocchi with scampi in a butter and saffron sauce. The *semifreddi* (desserts made with ice cream and eggs) are particularly good. Just a few steps from Rio Marina's pretty port, this is an easy stop on your way to or from the ferry. 💲 *Average main: €14* ⊠ *Via del Pozzo 16, Rio Marina* ☎ *0565/962117.*

$$$ ╳**La Canocchia.** In the center of Rio Marina sits this breezy restaurant.
SEAFOOD Seafood takes center stage: specialties include *gran risotto di mare con crostacei e astice* (seafood risotto with lobster) and the fresh catch of the day, prepared to order.The *frittura di paranza* (mixed fried fish) is crisp and light, and the *involtini di pesce spada* (swordfish rolls) melt in your mouth. Book ahead in summer, as it can get very crowded. 💲 *Average main: €25* ⊠ *Via Palestro 3, Rio Marina* ☎ *0565/962432* ⊕ *www.lacanocchia.com* 🥢 *Reservations essential* ⊙ *Closed Mon. and Nov.–mid-Feb.*

$$ ╳**Trattoria da Lido.** Come here for commendable *gnocchetti di pesce*
SEAFOOD (bite-size potato-and-fish dumplings) with a white cream sauce and

A cove on Elba

fresh *pesce all'elbana* (whitefish baked with vegetables and potatoes). The bustling, casual trattoria is in the old center of Portoferraio, at the beginning of the road to the old Medici walls. $ *Average main: €20* ⊠ *Salita del Falcone 2, Portoferraio* ☎ *0565/914650* ⊕ *www. ristorantelido.org* ☉ *Closed mid-Dec.–mid-Feb.*

WHERE TO STAY

For expanded hotel reviews, visit Fodors.com.

$$$$
HOTEL
⌂ **Hermitage.** You have private access to a white sandy beach at this hotel on a private bay. **Pros:** wide range of sports equipment; several good restaurants; on a private beach and bay. **Cons:** half-board is mandatory in high season; can get very crowded. $ *Rooms from: €440* ⊠ *Strada della Biodola 1, 8 km (5 miles) west of Portoferraio, Portoferraio* ☎ *0565/9740* ⊕ *www.hotelhermitage.it* ⇴ *114 rooms, 16 suites* ☉ *Closed Oct.–Mar.*

$$
B&B/INN
⌂ **Rio sul Mare.** Convenient to Rio Marina's charming town center and gravel beach, this comfortable hotel has pretty sea views. **Pros:** close to town center; very attractive sea views from all rooms. **Cons:** not all rooms have a/c; the nearby beach is rocky. $ *Rooms from: €160* ⊠ *Via Palestro 31, Rio Marina* ☎ *0565/924225* ⊕ *www.hotelriomarina.com* ⇴ *35 rooms* ☉ *Closed Nov.–Mar.* ⦿ *Breakfast.*

SPORTS AND THE OUTDOORS

BEACHES Elba's most celebrated beaches are the sandy stretches at **Biodola, Procchio,** and **Marina di Campo,** but the entire island—and particularly the westernmost section, encircling Monte Capanne—is ringed with beautiful coastline. Indeed, it seems every sleepy town has its own perfect tiny beach. Try **Cavoli** and **Fetovaia** anytime but July and August, when the car-accessible beaches on the island are packed (there are also some accessible only by boat, such as the black-sand beach of **Punta Nera**).

Il Viottolo. Adventurous types can rent sea kayaks and mountain bikes from this tour operator, or participate in three-day guided excursions on land or by sea. ⊠ *Via Fucini 279, Marina di Campo* ☎ *0565/978005* ⊕ *www.ilviottolo.it.*

Spaziomare. If you are hoping to rent a motorboat for a half- or full-day, this is the place. Sailboats to rent by the week are also available. ⊠ *Via Vittorio Veneto 13, Porto Azzurro* ☎ *0565/95112, 348/6017862* ⊕ *www.spaziomare.it.*

Subnow. Contact this group of experienced divers for information on diving excursions in the waters of Elba's National Marine Park. ⊠ *Via della Foce 32, Località La Foce, Marina di Campo* ☎ *0565/979051* ⊕ *www.subnow.it.*

CAPRAIA

60 km (35 miles) west of Massa Marittima, 90 km (55 miles) west of Siena, 110 km (66 miles) southwest of Florence.

GETTING HERE

Car ferry service from Livorno is provided by Toremar. The trip takes 2½ hours.

VISITOR INFORMATION

Capraia tourism office ⊠ *Via Assunzione 72* ☎ *0586/905138* ⊕ *www.prolococapraiaisola.it.*

EXPLORING

Capraia. Only a handful of people actually live on the island of Capraia, which is frequented mainly by sailors. It's a rocky and hilly unspoiled national park, with only one sandy beach, **Cala della Mortola,** on the northern end of the island; the rest of the coast is a succession of cliffs and deep green coves with pretty rock formations. The 2½-hour ferry trip departs from Livorno and pulls in at the town of **Capraia Isola,** dominated by the Fortezza di San Giorgio up above. Nearby, an archway leads to an area that was once a prison.

SPORTS AND THE OUTDOORS

Capraia Diving Club. Capraia's clear waters and undersea life draw raves from scuba divers. Scuba-diving equipment, boats for rent, and the guidance of qualified instructors are available through this diving service. ⊠ *Via Assunzione 100/B, Capraia Isola* ☎ *0586/905137* ⊕ *www.capraiadiving.it.*

UMBRIA AND THE MARCHES

WELCOME TO UMBRIA AND THE MARCHES

TOP REASONS TO GO

★ **Palazzo Ducale, Urbino:** A visit here reveals more about the ideals of the Renaissance than a shelf of history books could.

★ **Assisi, shrine to Saint Francis:** Recharge your soul in this rose-color hill town with a visit to the gentle saint's majestic basilica, adorned with great frescoes.

★ **Spoleto, Umbria's musical Mecca:** Crowds may descend and prices ascend here during summer's Festival dei Due Mondi, but Spoleto's hushed charm enchants year-round.

★ **Tantalizing truffles:** Are Umbria's celebrated "black diamonds" coveted for their pungent flavor, their rarity, or their power in the realm of romance?

★ **Orvieto's Duomo:** Arresting visions of heaven and hell on the facade and brilliant frescoes within make this Gothic cathedral a dazzler.

1 Perugia. Umbria's largest town is easily reached from Rome, Siena, or Florence. Home to some of Perugino's great frescoes and a hilltop *centro storico* (historic center), it's also favored by chocolate lovers, who celebrate their passion at October's Eurochocolate Festival.

2 Assisi. The city of Saint Francis is a major pilgrimage site, crowned by one of Italy's greatest churches. Despite the throngs of visitors, it still maintains its medieval hill-town character.

3 Northern Umbria. The quiet towns lying around Perugia include Deruta, which produces exceptional ceramics. A trip through the rugged terrain of northeast Umbria takes you to Gubbio, where from the Piazza della Signoria you can admire magnificent views of the countryside below.

4 Spoleto. Though it's known to the world for its annual performing-arts festival, Spoleto offers much more than Puccini in its Piazza del Duomo. There are Filippo Lippi frescoes in the cathedral, a massive castle towering over the town, and a bridge across the neighboring valley that's an engineering marvel.

5 Southern Umbria.
Of central Italy's many hill towns, none has a more impressive setting than Orvieto, perched on a plateau 1,000 feet above the surrounding valley. Its cathedral ranks with Assisi's as the most spectacular in Umbria. Between Spoleto and Orvieto there's a collection of quiet, laid-back towns, including the jewel of the area, Todi.

GETTING ORIENTED

Central Italy doesn't begin and end with Tuscany; the pastoral, hilly provinces of Umbria and the Marches pick up where the more famous neighbor leaves off. Divided by the Apennine range, both regions are studded with Renaissance-era villages and fortresses—a landscape hallowed by Saint Francis and immortalized in the works of native son Raphael.

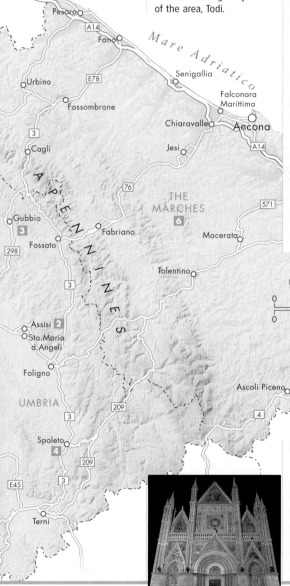

6 The Marches. East of Umbria, the steep, twisting roads of this region lead to well-preserved medieval towns before settling down to the sandy beaches of the Adriatic. The main attraction is Urbino, the best surviving example of the ideal Renaissance city.

EATING AND DRINKING WELL IN UMBRIA AND THE MARCHES

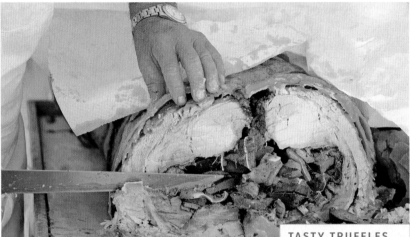

Central Italy is mountainous, and its food is hearty and straightforward, with a stick-to-the-ribs quality that sees hardworking farmers and artisans through a long day's work and helps them make the steep climb home at night.

In restaurants here, as in much of Italy, you're rewarded for seeking out the local cuisines, and you'll often find better and cheaper food if you're willing to stray a few hundred yards from the main sights. Spoleto is noted for its good food and service, probably a result of high expectations from the international arts crowd. For gourmets, however, it's hard to beat Spello, which has both excellent restaurants and first-rate wine merchants.

A rule of thumb for eating well throughout Umbria is to order what's in season; the trick is to stroll through local markets to see what's for sale. A number of restaurants in the region offer *degustazione* (tasting) menus, which give you a chance to try different local specialties without breaking the bank.

TASTY TRUFFLES

More truffles are found in Umbria than anywhere else in Italy. Spoleto and Norcia are prime territory for the *tartufo nero* (reddish-black interior and fine white veins), pictured below right, prized for its extravagant flavor and intense aroma.

The mild summer truffle, *scorzone estivo* (black outside and beige inside), is in season from May through December. The *scorzone autunnale* (burnt brown color and visible veins inside) is found from October through December. Truffles can be shaved into omelets or over pasta, pounded into sauces, or chopped and mixed with oil.

OLIVE OIL

Nearly everywhere you look in Umbria, olive trees grace the hillsides. The soil of the Apennines allows the olives to ripen slowly, guaranteeing low acidity, a cardinal virtue of fine oil. Look for restaurants that proudly display their own oil, often a sign that they care about their food.

Umbria's finest oil is found in Trevi, where the local product is intensely green and fruity. You can sample it in the town's wine bars, which often do double duty, offering olive-oil tastings.

PORK PRODUCTS

Much of traditional Umbrian cuisine revolves around pork. It can be cooked in wood-fire stoves, sometimes basted with a rich sauce made from innards and red wine. The roasted pork known as *porchetta (pictured at left)* is grilled on a spit and flavored with fennel and herbs, leaving a crisp outer sheen.

The art of pork processing has been handed down through generations in Norcia, so much so that charcuterie producers throughout Italy are often known as *norcini*. Don't miss *prosciutto di Norcia*, which is aged for two years.

LENTILS AND SOUPS

The town of Castelluccio di Norcia is particularly known for its lentils and its *farro* (an ancient grain used by the Romans, similar to wheat), and a variety of beans used in soups. Throughout

Umbria, look for *imbrecciata*, a soup of beans and grains, delicately flavored with local herbs. Other ingredients that find their way into thick Umbrian soups are wild beet, sorrel, mushrooms, spelt, chickpeas, and the elusive, fragrant saffron, grown in nearby Cascia.

WINE

Sagrantino grapes are the star in Umbria's most notable red wines. For centuries they've been used in Sagrantino *passito*, a semisweet wine made by leaving the grapes to dry for a period after picking in order to intensify their sugar content. In recent decades, the *secco* (dry) Sagrantino has occupied the front stage. Both passito and secco have a deep red-ruby color, with a full body and rich flavor.

In the past few years the phenomenon of the *enoteca* (wineshop and wine bar) has taken off, making it easier to arrange wine tastings. Many also let you sample different olive oils on toasted bread, known as bruschetta. Some wine information centers, such as La Strada del Sagrantino in the town of Montefalco, will help set up appointments for tastings.

7

Updated
by Jonathan
Willcocks

BIRTHPLACE OF SAINTS AND HOME TO some of the country's greatest artistic treasures, central Italy is a collection of misty green valleys and picture-perfect hill towns laden with centuries of history.

Umbria and the Marches are the Italian countryside as you've imagined it: verdant farmland, steep hillsides topped with medieval fortresses, and winding country roads. No single town here has the extravagant wealth of art and architecture of Florence, Rome, or Venice, but this works in your favor: small jewels of towns feel knowable, not overwhelming. And the cultural cupboard is far from bare. Orvieto's cathedral and Assisi's basilica are two of the most important sights in Italy, while Perugia, Todi, Gubbio, and Spoleto are rich in art and architecture.

East of Umbria, the Marches (Le Marche to Italians) stretch between the Apennines and the Adriatic Sea. It's a region of great turreted castles on high peaks defending passes and roads—a testament to the centuries of battle that have taken place here. Rising majestically in Urbino is a splendid palace, built by Federico da Montefeltro, where the humanistic ideals of the Renaissance came to their fullest flower, while the town of Ascoli Piceno can lay claim to one of the most beautiful squares in Italy. Virtually every small town in the region has a castle, church, or museum worth a visit—but even without them, you'd still be compelled to stop for the interesting streets, panoramic views, and natural beauty.

PLANNING

MAKING THE MOST OF YOUR TIME

Umbria is a nicely compact collection of character-rich hill towns; you can settle in one, then explore the others, as well as the countryside and forest in between, on day trips.

Perugia, Umbria's largest and most lively city, is a logical choice for your base, particularly if you're arriving from the north. If you want something a little quieter, virtually any other town in the region will suit your purposes; even Assisi, which overflows with bus tours during the day, is delightfully quiet in the evening and early morning. Spoleto and Orvieto are the most developed towns to the south, but they're still of modest proportions.

If you have the time to venture farther afield, consider trips to Gubbio, northeast of Perugia, and Urbino, in the Marches. Both are worth the time it takes to reach them, and both make for pleasant overnight stays. In southern Umbria, Valnerina and the Piano Grande are out-of-the-way spots with the region's best hiking.

FESTIVALS

Festival dei Due Mondi. Each summer Umbria hosts one of Italy's biggest arts festivals: Spoleto's Festival dei Due Mondi, the Festival of the Two Worlds. Starting out as a classical music festival, it has now evolved into one of Italy's brightest gatherings of arts aficionados. Running from late June through early July, it features modern and classical music, theater, dance, and opera. Increasingly there are also a number of small cinema producers and their films. ⊕ *www.festivaldispoleto.com.*

Umbria Jazz Festival. Perugia is hopping for 10 days in July, when more than a million people flock to see famous names in contemporary music perform at the Umbria Jazz Festival. In recent years the stars have included B.B.King, Wynton Marsalis, Sting, Eric Clapton, and Elton John. ⊕ *www.umbriajazz.com.*

If you want to attend either event, you should make arrangements in advance. And if you don't want to attend, you should plan to avoid the cities during festival time, when hotel rooms and restaurant tables are at a premium. A similar caveat applies for Assisi during religious festivals at Christmas, Easter, the feast of Saint Francis (October 4), and Calendimaggio (May 1), when pilgrims arrive en masse.

Eurochocolate Festival. If you've got a sweet tooth and are visiting in fall, book up early and head to Perugia for the Eurochocolate Festival. This is one of the biggest chocolate festivals in the world, with a million visitors, and is held in the third week of October. ⊕ *www. eurochocolate.com.*

GETTING HERE AND AROUND
BUS TRAVEL
Perugia's bus station is in Piazza Partigiani, which you can reach by taking the escalators from the town center.

Sulga Line. Perugia is served by the Sulga Line, which has daily departures to Rome's Stazione Tiburtina and to Florence's Piazza Adua. ☎ *075/5009641* ⊕ *www.sulga.it.*

Bucci. Connections between Rome, Spoleto, and the Marches are provided by the bus company Bucci. ☎ *0721/32401* ⊕ *www.autolineebucci.com.*

Local bus services between all the major and minor towns of Umbria are good. Some of the routes in rural areas are designed to serve as many places as possible and are, therefore, quite roundabout and slow. Schedules change often, so consult with local tourist offices before setting out.

CAR TRAVEL
On the western edge of the region is the Umbrian section of the Autostrada del Sole (A1), Italy's principal north–south highway. It links Florence and Rome with Orvieto and passes near Todi and Terni. The S3 intersects with A1 and leads on to Assisi and Urbino. The Adriatica superhighway (A14) runs north–south along the coast, linking the Marches to Bologna and Venice.

The steep hills and deep valleys that make Umbria and the Marches so idyllic also make for challenging driving. Fortunately, the area has an excellent, modern road network, but be prepared for tortuous mountain roads if your explorations take you off the beaten track. Central Umbria is served by a major highway, the S75bis, which passes along the shore of Lake Trasimeno and ends in Perugia. Assisi is served by the modern highway S75; the S75 connects to the S3 and S3bis, which cover the heart of the region. Major inland routes connect coastal A14 to large towns in the Marches, but inland secondary roads in mountain areas can be winding and narrow. Always carry a good map, a flashlight, and, if possible, a cell phone in case of a breakdown.

TRAIN TRAVEL

Several direct daily trains run by the Italian state railway, **Ferrovia dello Stato** (☎ *892021 toll-free in Italy* ⊕ *www.trenitalia.com*), link Florence and Rome with Perugia and Assisi, and local service to the same area is available from Terontola (on the Rome–Florence line) and from Foligno (on the Rome–Ancona line). Intercity trains between Rome and Florence make stops in Orvieto, and the main Rome–Ancona line passes through Narni, Terni, Spoleto, and Foligno.

Within Umbria, a small, privately owned railway operated by **Ferrovia Centrale Umbra** (☎ *024/73000541*) runs from Città di Castello in the north to Terni in the south via Perugia. Note: train service isn't available to either Gubbio or Urbino.

HOTELS

Virtually every older town, no matter how small, has some kind of hotel. A trend, particularly around Gubbio, Orvieto, and Todi, is to convert old villas, farms, and monasteries into first-class hotels. The natural splendor of the countryside more than compensates for the distance from town—provided you have a car. Hotels in town tend to be simpler than their country cousins, with a few notable exceptions in Spoleto, Gubbio, and Perugia.

Hotel reviews have been condensed for this book. Please go to Fodors. com for expanded reviews of each property.

VISITOR INFORMATION

Umbria's Regional Tourism Office. Umbria's regional tourism office is in Perugia. The staff is well informed about the area and can give you a wide selection of leaflets and maps to assist you during your trip. It's open daily 9–7. ⊠ *Piazza Matteotti 18, Perugia* ☎ *075/5736458* ⊕ *www.regioneumbria.eu.*

PERUGIA

Perugia is a majestic, handsome, wealthy city, and with its trendy boutiques, refined cafés, and grandiose architecture, it doesn't try to hide its affluence. A student population of more than 30,000 means that the city is abuzz with activity throughout the year. Umbria Jazz, one of the region's most important music festivals, attracts music lovers from around the world every July, and Eurochocolate, the international chocolate festival, is an irresistible draw each October for anyone with a sweet tooth.

GETTING HERE

The best approach to the city is by train. The area around the station doesn't attest to the rest of Perugia's elegance, but buses running from the station to Piazza d'Italia, the heart of the old town, are frequent. If you're in a hurry, take the minimetro, a one-line subway, to Stazione della Cupa. If you're driving to Perugia and your hotel doesn't have parking facilities, leave your car in one of the lots close to the center. Electronic displays indicate the location of lots and the number of spaces free. If you park in the Piazza Partigiani, take the escalators that

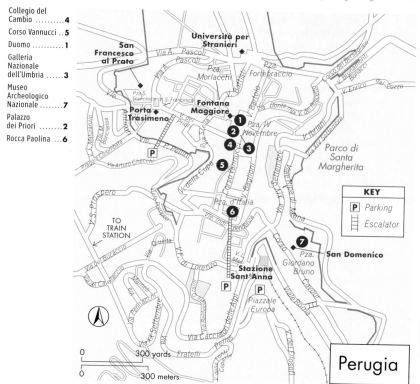

Perugia

KEY	
P	Parking
	Escalator

pass through the fascinating subterranean excavations of the Roman foundations of the city and lead to the town center.

EXPLORING PERUGIA

Thanks to Perugia's hilltop position, the medieval city remains almost completely intact. It's the best-preserved hill town of its size, and few other places in Italy better illustrate the model of the self-contained city-state that so shaped the course of Italian history.

TOP ATTRACTIONS

Collegio del Cambio (*Bankers' Guild Hall*). These elaborate rooms, on the ground floor of the **Palazzo dei Priori,** served as the meeting hall and chapel of the guild of bankers and moneychangers. Most of the frescoes were completed by the most important Perugian painter of the Renaissance, Pietro Vannucci, better known as Perugino. He included a remarkably honest self-portrait on one of the pilasters. The iconography includes common religious themes, such as the Nativity and the Transfiguration seen on the end walls. On the left wall are female figures representing the virtues, and beneath them are the heroes and sages of antiquity. On the right wall are figures presumed to have been painted in part by Perugino's most famous pupil, Raphael. (His hand, experts say, is most apparent in the figure of Fortitude.) The *cappella* (chapel) of San Giovanni Battista has frescoes painted by Giannicola di Paolo, another student of Perugino's. ✉ *Corso Vannucci 25* ☎ *075/5728599* 💶 *€4.50 with Collegio della Mercanzia* 🕙 *Mon.–Sat. 9–12:30 and 2:30–5:30, Sun. 9–1.*

Corso Vannucci. A string of elegantly connected *palazzi* (palaces) expresses the artistic nature of this city center, the heart of which is concentrated along Corso Vannucci. Stately and broad, this pedestrians-only street runs from Piazza Italia to Piazza IV Novembre. Along the way, the entrances to many of Perugia's side streets might tempt you to wander off and explore. But don't stray too far as evening falls, when Corso Vannucci fills with Perugians out for their evening *passeggiata*, a pleasant pre-dinner stroll that may include a pause for an aperitif at one of the many bars that line the street.

Fodor's Choice
★
Galleria Nazionale dell'Umbria. The region's most comprehensive art gallery is housed on the fourth floor of the **Palazzo dei Priori.** Enhanced by skillfully lit displays and computers that allow you to focus on the works' details and background information, the collection includes work by native artists—most notably Pintoricchio (1454–1513) and Perugino (circa 1450–1523)—and others of the Umbrian and Tuscan schools, among them Gentile da Fabriano (1370–1427), Duccio (circa 1255–1318), Fra Angelico (1387–1455), Fiorenzo di Lorenzo (1445–1525), and Piero della Francesca (1420–92). In addition to paintings, the gallery has frescoes, sculptures, and some superb examples of crucifixes from the 13th and 14th centuries. Some rooms are dedicated to Perugia itself, showing how the medieval city evolved. ✉ *Corso Vannucci 19, Piazza IV Novembre* ☎ *075/58668410* ⊕ *www. gallerianazionaleumbria.it* 💶 *€6.50* 🕙 *Tues.–Sun. 8:30–7:30; last admission ½ hr before closing.*

Palazzo dei Priori (*Palace of Priors*). A series of elegant connected buildings, the palazzo serves as Perugia's city hall and houses three of the city's museums. The buildings string along Corso Vannucci and wrap around the Piazza IV Novembre, where the original entrance is located. The steps here lead to the **Sala dei Notari** (Notaries' Hall). Other entrances lead to the **Galleria Nazionale dell'Umbria,** the **Collegio del Cambio,** and the **Collegio della Mercanzia.** The Sala dei Notari, which dates back to the 13th century and was the original meeting place of the town merchants, had become the seat of the notaries by the second half of the 15th century. Wood beams and an interesting array of frescoes attributed to Maestro di Farneto embellish the room. Coats of arms and crests line the back and right lateral walls; you can spot some famous figures from Aesop's *Fables* on the left wall. The palazzo facade is adorned with symbols of Perugia's pride and past power: the griffin is the city symbol, and the lion denotes Perugia's allegiance to the Guelph (or papal) cause. ✉ *Piazza IV Novembre 25* 💶 *Free* 🕙 *Tues.– Sun. 9–1 and 3–7.*

Rocca Paolina. A labyrinth of little streets, alleys, and arches, this underground city was originally part of a fortress built at the behest of Pope Paul III between 1540 and 1543 to confirm papal dominion over the city. Parts of it were destroyed after the end of papal rule, but much still

UMBRIA THROUGH THE AGES

The earliest inhabitants of Umbria, the Umbri, were thought by the Romans to be the most ancient inhabitants of Italy. Little is known about them; with the coming of Etruscan culture the tribe fled into the mountains in the eastern portion of the region. The Etruscans, who founded some of the great cities of Umbria, were in turn supplanted by the Romans. Unlike Tuscany and other regions of central Italy, Umbria had few powerful medieval families to exert control over the cities in the Middle Ages—its proximity to Rome ensured that it would always be more or less under papal domination.

In the center of the country, Umbria has for much of its history been a battlefield where armies from north and south clashed. Hannibal destroyed a Roman army on the shores of Lake Trasimeno, and the bloody course of the interminable

Guelph–Ghibelline conflict of the Middle Ages was played out here. Dante considered Umbria the most violent place in Italy. Trophies of war still decorate the Palazzo dei Priori in Perugia, and the little town of Gubbio continues a warlike rivalry begun in the Middle Ages—every year it challenges the Tuscan town of Sansepolcro to a crossbow tournament. Today the bowmen shoot at targets, but neither side has forgotten that 500 years ago they were shooting at each other. In spite of—or perhaps because of—this bloodshed, Umbria has produced more than its share of Christian saints. The most famous is Saint Francis, the decidedly pacifist saint whose life shaped the Church of his time. His great shrine at Assisi is visited by hundreds of thousands of pilgrims each year. Saint Clare, his devoted follower, was Umbria-born, as were Saint Benedict, Saint Rita of Cascia, and the patron saint of lovers, Saint Valentine.

remains. Begin your visit by taking the escalators that descend through the subterranean ruins from Piazza Italia down to Via Masi. In the summer this is the coolest place in the city. ⊠ *Piazza Italia* 🎫 *€3.50* ⊙ *Tues.–Sun. 10–1:30 and 2:30–6.*

WORTH NOTING

Duomo. Severe yet mystical, the Cathedral of San Lorenzo is most famous for being the home of the wedding ring of the Virgin Mary, stolen by the Perugians in 1488 from the nearby town of Chiusi. The ring, kept high up in a red-curtained vault in the chapel immediately to the left of the entrance, is stored under lock—15 locks, to be precise—and key most of the year. It's shown to the public on July 30 (the day it was brought to Perugia) and the second-to-last Sunday in January (Mary's wedding anniversary). The cathedral itself dates from the Middle Ages, and has many additions from the 15th and 16th centuries. The most visually interesting element is the altar to the Madonna of Grace; an elegant fresco on a column at the right of the entrance of the altar depicts *La Madonna delle Grazie* and is surrounded by prayer benches decorated with handwritten notes to the Holy Mother. Around the column are small amulets—symbols of gratitude from those whose prayers were answered. There are also elaborately carved choir stalls, executed by Giovanni Battista Bastone in 1520. The altarpiece (1484), an early masterpiece by Luca Signorelli (circa 1441–1523), shows the Madonna with Saint John the Baptist, Saint Onophrius, and Saint Lawrence. Sections of the church may be closed to visitors during religious services.

The **Museo Capitolare** displays a large array of precious objects associated with the cathedral, including vestments, vessels, and manuscripts. Outside the Duomo is the elaborate **Fontana Maggiore,** which dates from 1278. It's adorned with zodiac figures and symbols of the seven arts. ✉ *Piazza IV Novembre* ☏ *075/5723832* 🖼 *Museum €3.50* ⊙ *Duomo: Mon.–Sat. 7:30–12:30 and 4–6, Sun. 8–12 and 4–6:30. Museum: Tues.–Sun. 9–5; last admission ½ hr before closing.*

Museo Archeologico Nazionale. An excellent collection of Etruscan artifacts from throughout the region sheds light on Perugia as a flourishing Etruscan city long before it fell under Roman domination in 310 BC. Little else remains of Perugia's mysterious ancestors, although the Arco di Augusto, in Piazza Fortebraccio, the northern entrance to the city, is of Etruscan origin. ✉ *Piazza G. Bruno 10* ☏ *075/5727141* ⊕ *www.archeopg.arti.beniculturali.it* 🖼 *€4* ⊙ *Mon. 10–7:30, Tues.–Sun. 8:30–7:30.*

WORD OF MOUTH

"Two things you must not fail to do in Perugia are to (a) join the evening walk on the Corso Vannucci beginning at about 5 pm and (b) take the escalators that go up and down and through the historic city walls. Also: Hang out as often as you dare at Sandri's, one of Italy's most marvelous cafe/pastry shops, on the Corso Vannucci." —nessundorma

WHERE TO EAT

$$
UMBRIAN
✕ **Antica Trattoria San Lorenzo.** Brick vaults are not the only distinguishing feature of this small, popular eatery next to the Duomo, as both the food and the service are outstanding. Particular attention is paid to adapting traditional Umbrian cuisine to the modern palate. There's also a nice variety of seafood dishes on the menu. The *trenette alla farina di noce con pesce di mare* (flat noodles made with walnut flour topped with fresh fish) is a real treat. 💲 *Average main: €18* ✉ *Piazza Danti 19-A* ☏ *075/5721956* ⊕ *www.anticatrattoriasanlorenzo.com* ⊙ *Closed Sun.*

$$
UMBRIAN
✕ **Dal Mi' Cocco.** A great favorite with Perugia's university students, it is fun, crowded, and inexpensive. You may find yourself seated at a long table with other diners, but some language help from your neighbors could come in handy—the menu is in pure Perugian dialect. The fixed-price meals change with the season, and each day of the week brings some new creation *dal cocco* (from the "coconut," or head) of the chef. 💲 *Average main: €17* ✉ *Corso Garibaldi 12* ☏ *075/5732511* ⌁ *Reservations essential* ▭ *No credit cards* ⊙ *Closed late July–mid-Aug.*

$
UMBRIAN
✕ **Il Falchetto.** Exceptional food at reasonable prices makes this Perugia's best bargain. Service is smart but relaxed in the two medieval dining rooms that put the chef on view. The house specialty is *falchetti* (home-

made gnocchi with spinach and ricotta cheese). $ *Average main: €14* ⊠ *Via Bartolo 20* ☎ *075/5731775* ⊗ *Closed Mon. and last 2 wks in Jan.*

$$ ✕ **La Rosetta.** The dining room of the hotel of the same name is a peace-
ITALIAN   ful, elegant spot. In winter you dine inside under medieval vaults; in summer, in the cool courtyard. The food is simple but reliable, and flawlessly served. The restaurant caters to travelers seeking to get away from the bustle of central Perugia. $ *Average main: €18* ⊠ *Piazza d'Italia 19* ☎ *075/5720841* ⌂ *Reservations essential.*

$$ ✕ **La Taverna.** Medieval steps lead to a rustic two-story space where wine
UMBRIAN   bottles and artful clutter decorate the walls. Good choices from the regional menu include *caramelle al gorgonzola* (pasta rolls filled with red cabbage and mozzarella and topped with a Gorgonzola sauce) and grilled meat dishes, such as the *medaglioni di vitello al tartuffo* (grilled veal with truffles). $ *Average main: €18* ⊠ *Via delle Streghe 8, off Corso Vannucci* ☎ *075/5724128* ⊗ *Open daily.*

WHERE TO STAY

For expanded hotel reviews, visit Fodors.com.

$$ ⛫ **Castello dell'Oscano.** A splendid neo-Gothic castle, a late-19th-century
HOTEL   villa, and a converted farmhouse hidden in the tranquil hills north of Perugia offer a wide range of accommodations. **Pros:** quiet elegance; fine gardens; Umbrian wine list. **Cons:** distant from Perugia; not easy to find. $ *Rooms from: €200* ⊠ *Strada della Forcella 37, Cenerente* ☎ *075/584371* ⊕ *www.oscano.com* ⟿ *24 rooms, 8 suites, 13 apartments* ⦶ *Breakfast.*

$$ ⛫ **Hotel Fortuna.** The elegant decor in the large rooms, some with balco-
HOTEL   nies, complements the frescoes, which date from the 1700s. **Pros:** central but quiet; cozy, friendly atmosphere; elevator. **Cons:** some small rooms; no restaurant. $ *Rooms from: €130* ⊠ *Via Bonazzi 19, Corso Vannucci* ☎ *075/5722845* ⊕ *www.hotelfortunaperugia.com* ⟿ *51 rooms* ⦶ *Breakfast.*

$$ ⛫ **Locanda della Posta.** Renovations have left the lobby and other public
HOTEL   areas rather bland, but the rooms in this converted 18th-century palazzo are soothingly decorated in muted colors. **Pros:** some fine views; central position. **Cons:** some street noise; some small rooms; no restaurant. $ *Rooms from: €150* ⊠ *Corso Vannucci 97* ☎ *075/5728925* ⟿ *38 rooms, 1 suite* ⦶ *Breakfast.*

$$ ⛫ **Posta dei Donini.** Beguilingly comfortable guest rooms are set on lovely
HOTEL   grounds, where gardeners go quietly about their business. **Pros:** plush atmosphere; a quiet and private getaway. **Cons:** outside Perugia; uninteresting village. $ *Rooms from: €150* ⊠ *Via Deruta 43, San Martino in Campo* ☎ *075/609132* ⊕ *www.postadonini.it* ⟿ *33 rooms* ⦶ *No meals.*

$$ ⛫ **Tre Vaselle.** Rooms spread throughout four stone buildings are spa-
HOTEL   cious and graced with floors of typical red-clay Tuscan tiles. **Pros:** perfect for visiting Torgiano wine area and Deruta; friendly staff; nice pool. **Cons:** somewhat far from Perugia; in center of uninspiring village. $ *Rooms from: €150* ⊠ *Via Garibaldi 48, Torgiano* ☎ *075/9880447* ⊕ *www.3vaselle.it* ⟿ *47 rooms* ⦶ *No meals.*

7

NIGHTLIFE AND THE ARTS

With its large student population, the city has plenty to offer in the way of bars and clubs. The best ones are around the city center, off Corso Vannucci. *Viva Perugia* is a good source of information about nightlife. The monthly, sold at newsstands, has a section in English.

MUSIC FESTIVALS

Sagra Musicale Umbra. Held from mid-August to mid-September, the Sagra Musicale Umbra celebrates sacred music. ☎ *075/5722271* ⊕ *www.perugiamusicaclassica.com.*

SHOPPING

Take a stroll down any of Perugia's main streets, including Corso Vannucci, Via dei Priori, Via Oberdan, and Via Sant'Ercolano, and you'll see many well-known designer boutiques and specialty shops.

The most typical thing to buy in Perugia is some Perugina chocolate, which you can find almost anywhere. The best-known chocolates made by Perugina are the chocolate-and-hazelnut-filled nibbles called Baci (literally, "kisses"). They're wrapped in silver paper that includes a sliver of paper, like the fortune in a fortune cookie, with multilingual romantic sentiments or sayings.

ASSISI

The small town of Assisi is one of the Christian world's most important pilgrimage sites and home of the Basilica di San Francesco—built to honor Saint Francis (1182–1226) and erected in swift order after his death. The peace and serenity of the town is a welcome respite after the hustle and bustle of some of Italy's major cities.

Like most other towns in the region, Assisi began as an Umbri settlement in the 7th century BC and was conquered by the Romans 400 years later. The town was Christianized by Saint Rufino, its patron saint, in the 3rd century, but it's the spirit of Saint Francis, a patron saint of Italy and founder of the Franciscan monastic order, that's felt throughout its narrow medieval streets. The famous 13th-century basilica was decorated by the greatest artists of the period.

GETTING HERE

Assisi lies on the Terontola–Foligno rail line, with almost hourly connections to Perugia and direct trains to Rome and Florence several times a day. The Stazione Centrale is 4 km (2½ miles) from town, with a bus service about every half hour. Assisi is easily reached from the A1 Motorway (Rome–Florence) and the S75b highway. The walled town is closed to traffic, so cars must be left in the parking lots at Porta San

WORD OF MOUTH

"Assisi is surrounded by gorgeous walks. The side road from the Basilica around to the Rocca is absolutely wonderful. The same can be said for a walk out to the Eremo delle Carceri, and further into the woods past the Eremo."
—tuscanlifeedit

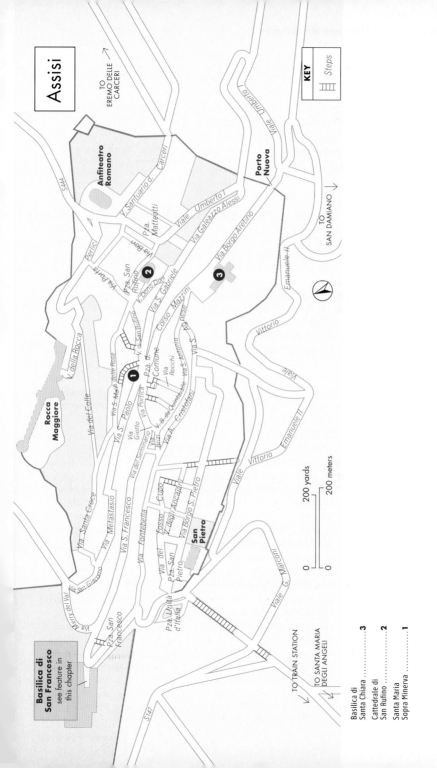

Assisi

Basilica di
San Francesco
see feature in
this chapter

TO
EREMO DELLE
CARCERI →

Anfiteatro
Romano

Porto
Nuova

TO
SAN DAMIANO →

KEY

⊞⊞ Steps

Rocca
Maggiore

San
Pietro

TO TRAIN STATION →

TO SANTA MARIA
DEGLI ANGELI →

0   200 yards

0   200 meters

V. della Rocca

Via del Colle

Via S. Croce

Via Metastasio

Via S. Francesco

Via Fontebella

Via del
Seminario

Via Portica

Via Giotto

Via S. Paolo

Via S. M. delle Rose

V. di Santuario

Perlici

Via Porta

Pza. San
Rufino

V. Santuario d. Carceri

V. Bovi

Pza.
Matteotti

Viale Umberto I

Via Galeazzo Alessi

Via Borgo Aretino

Corso Mazzini

V. Dono Doni

Via S. Gabriele

Via
Rocchi

Pza. d.
Comune

V. d. del Quintavalle

Via
Bini

Via S. Antonio

Via S.

Via A. Cristofani

Viale Vittorio Emanuele II

Viale Vittorio Emanuele II

Viale Umberto I

Viale G. Marconi

Via Borgo S. Pietro

Pza.-San
Pietro

Via del Fosso

V. degli Anciaiani

Cupo

Pza. Unità
d'Italia

Via S. Giacomo

Via Merry del Val

Pza. San
Francesco

S444

S147

1

2

3

Basilica di
Santa Chiara 3

Cattedrale di
San Rufino 2

Santa Maria
Sopra Minerva 1

Pietro, near Porta Nuova, or beneath Piazza Matteotti. Pay your parking fee at the *cassa* (ticket booth) before you return to your car to get a ticket to insert in the machine that will allow you to exit. It's a short but sometimes steep walk into the center of town; frequent minibuses (buy tickets from a newsstand or tobacco shop near where you park your car) make the rounds for weary pilgrims.

VISITOR INFORMATION
Assisi Tourism Office ⊠ *Piazza del Commune 22* ☎ *075/8138680* ⊕ *www. regioneumbria.eu.*

EXPLORING ASSISI

Assisi is pristinely medieval in architecture and appearance, owing in large part to relative neglect from the 16th century until 1926, when the celebration of the 700th anniversary of Saint Francis's death brought more than 2 million visitors. Since then, pilgrims have flocked here in droves, and today several million arrive each year to pay homage. But not even the constant flood of visitors to this town of just 3,000 residents can spoil the singular beauty of this significant religious center, the home of some of the Western tradition's most important works of art. The hill on which Assisi sits rises dramatically from the flat plain, and the town is dominated by a medieval castle at the very top.

Even though Assisi is sometimes besieged by busloads of sightseers who clamor to visit the famous basilica, it's difficult not to be charmed by the tranquillity of the town and its medieval architecture. Once you've seen the basilica, stroll through the town's narrow winding streets to see beautiful vistas of the nearby hills and valleys peeking through openings between the buildings.

TOP ATTRACTIONS

Basilica di Santa Chiara. The lovely, wide piazza in front of this church is reason enough to visit. The red-and-white-striped facade frames the piazza's panoramic view over the Umbrian plains. Santa Chiara is dedicated to Saint Clare, one of the earliest and most fervent of Saint Francis's followers and the founder of the order of the Poor Ladies—or Poor Clares—which was based on the Franciscan monastic order. The church contains Clare's body, and in the **Cappella del Crocifisso** (on the right) is the cross that spoke to Saint Francis. A heavily veiled nun of the Poor Clares order is usually stationed before the cross in adoration of the image. ⊠ *Piazza Santa Chiara* ☎ *075/812282* ☉ *Nov.–mid-Mar., daily 7–noon and 2–6; mid-Mar.–Oct., daily 7–noon and 2–7.*

Cattedrale di San Rufino. Saint Francis and Saint Clare were among those baptized in Assisi's Cattedrale, which was the principal church in town until the 12th century. The baptismal font has since been redecorated, but it's possible to see the crypt of Saint Rufino, the bishop who brought Christianity to Assisi and was martyred on August 11, 238 (or 236 by some accounts). Admission to the crypt includes the small **Museo Capitolare,** with its detached frescoes and artifacts. ⊠ *Piazza San Rufino* ☎ *075/5812283* ⊕ *www.sistemamuseo.it* 🎫 *Crypt and Museo Capitolare €3* ☉ *Cathedral: daily 7–noon and 2–6. Crypt and Museum: mid-*

Continued on page 335

ASSISI'S BASILICA DI SAN FRANCESCO

The legacy of St. Francis, founder of the Franciscan monastic order, pervades Assisi. Each year the town hosts several million pilgrims, but the steady flow of visitors does nothing to diminish the singular beauty of one of Italy's most important religious centers. The pilgrims' ultimate destination is the massive Basilica di San Francesco, which sits halfway up Assisi's hill, supported by graceful arches.

The basilica is not one church but two. The Romanesque **Lower Church** came first; construction began in 1228, just two years after St. Francis's death, and was completed within a few years. The low ceilings and candlelit interior make an appropriately solemn setting for St. Francis's tomb, found in the crypt below the main altar. The Gothic **Upper Church,** built only half a century later, sits on top of the lower one, and is strikingly different, with soaring arches and tall stained-glass windows (the first in Italy). Inside, both churches are covered floor to ceiling with some of Europe's finest frescoes: the Lower Church is dim and full of candlelit shadows, and the Upper Church is bright and airy.

VISITING THE BASILICA

THE LOWER CHURCH

The most evocative way to experience the basilica is to begin with the dark Lower Church. As you enter, give your eyes a moment to adjust. Keep in mind that the artists at work here were conscious of the shadowy environment—they knew this was how their frescoes would be seen.

In the first chapel to the left, a superb fresco cycle by Simone Martini depicts scenes from the life of St. Martin. As you approach the main altar, the vaulting above you is decorated with the *Three Virtues of St. Francis* (poverty, chastity, and obedience) and *St. Francis's Triumph*, frescoes attributed to Giotto's followers. In the transept to your left, Pietro Lorenzetti's *Madonna and Child with St. Francis and St. John* sparkles when the sun hits it. Notice Mary's thumb; legend has it Jesus is asking which saint to bless, and Mary is pointing to Francis. Across the way in the right transept, Cimabue's *Madonna Enthroned Among Angels and St. Francis* is a famous portrait of the saint. Surrounding the portrait are painted scenes from the childhood of Christ, done by the assistants of Giotto.

Nearby is a painting of the crucifixion attributed to Giotto himself.

You reach the crypt via stairs midway along the nave—on the crypt's altar, a stone coffin holds the saint's body. Steps up from the transepts lead to the cloister, where there's a gift shop, and the treasury, which contains holy objects.

THE UPPER CHURCH

The St. Francis fresco cycle is the highlight of the Upper Church. (See facing page.) Also worth special note is the 16th-century choir, with its remarkably delicate inlaid wood. When a 1997 earthquake rocked the basilica, the St. Francis cycle sustained little damage, but portions of the ceiling above the entrance and altar collapsed, reducing their frescoes (attributed to Cimabue and Giotto) to rubble. The painstaking restoration is ongoing. ⚠ The dress code is strictly enforced—no bare shoulders or bare knees. Piazza di San Francesco, 075/819001, Lower Church Easter–Oct., Mon.–Sat. 6 AM–6:45 PM, Sun. 6:30 AM–7:15 PM; Nov.–Easter, daily 6:30–6. Upper Church Easter–Oct., Mon.–Sat. 8:30–6:45, Sun. 8:30–7:15; Nov.–Easter, daily 8:30–6.

FRANCIS, ITALY'S PATRON SAINT

PREGANDO ASPETTERO CHE TORNI

St. Francis was born in Assisi in 1181, the son of a noblewoman and a well-to-do merchant. His troubled youth included a year in prison. He planned a military career, but after a long illness Francis heard the voice of God, renounced his father's wealth, and began a life of austerity. His mystical embrace of poverty, asceticism, and the beauty of man and nature struck a responsive chord in the medieval mind; he quickly attracted a vast number of followers. Francis was the first saint to receive the stigmata (wounds in his hands, feet, and side corresponding to those of Christ on the cross). He died on October 4, 1226, in the Porziuncola, the secluded chapel in the woods where he had first preached the virtue of poverty to his disciples. St. Francis was declared patron saint of Italy in 1939, and today the Franciscans make up the largest of the Catholic orders.

THE UPPER CHURCH'S ST. FRANCIS FRESCO CYCLE

The 28 frescoes in the Upper Church depicting the life of St. Francis are the most admired works in the entire basilica. They're also the subject of one of art history's biggest controversies. For centuries they thought to be by Giotto (1267-1337), the great early Renaissance innovator, but inconsistencies in style, both within this series and in comparison to later Giotto works, have thrown their origin into question. Some scholars now say Giotto was the brains behind the cycle, but that assistants helped with the execution; others claim he couldn't have been involved at all.

Two things are certain. First, the style is revolutionary—which argues for Giotto's in-volvement. The tangible weight of the figures, the emotion they show, and the use of perspective all look familiar to modern eyes, but in the art of the time there was nothing like it. Second, these images have played a major part in shaping how the world sees St. Francis. In that respect, who painted them hardly matters.

Starting in the transept, the frescoes circle the church, showing events in the saint's life (and afterlife). Some of the best are grouped near the church's entrance—look for the nativity at Greccio, the miracle of the spring, the death of the knight at Celano, and, most famously, the sermon to the birds.

The St. Francis fresco cycle

1. Homage of a simple man
2. Giving cloak to a poor man
3. Dream of the palace
4. Hearing the voice of God
5. Rejection of worldly goods
6. Dream of Innocent III
7. Confirmation of the rules
8. Vision of flaming chariot
9. Vision of celestial thrones
10. Chasing devils from Arezzo
11. Before the sultan
12. Ecstasy of St. Francis
13. Nativity at Greccio
14. Miracle of the spring
15. Sermon to the birds
16. Death of knight at Celano
17. Preaching to Honorius III
18. Apparition at Arles
19. Receiving the stigmata
20. Death of St. Francis
21. Apparition before Bishop Guido and Fra Agostino
22. Verification of the stigmata
23. Mourning of St. Clare
24. Canonization
25. Apparition before Gregory IX
26. Healing of a devotee
27. Confession of a woman
28. Repentant heretic freed

FODOR'S FIRST PERSON

Sister Marcellina,
Order of St. Bridget

Sister Marcellina of the Order of St. Bridget talks about her life in Assisi, where she and 11 other sisters live in a convent and guesthouse on the outskirts of the town:

"Before coming to Assisi, I lived in various countries. I've lived in India, and in England, and been to Holland, to Sweden, and to Finland, as well as lived in Rome. But Assisi is the place that I would never want to change for any other. I don't know, I think there is something very special about this place. I've been here 13 years now, and each year I pray that I won't be sent somewhere else. I'm very happy here.

"I like the atmosphere of Assisi, it's very friendly, and of course with St. Francis and St. Claire, but especially St. Francis, there is a simplicity to life that I like very much. Even though I'm in the Order of St. Bridget, living here I feel very much a part of Franciscan spirituality. There is also a very strong ecumenical feeling to Assisi and this is very nice. There are over 60 different religious

communities, with people from all over the world. And even though they come from different religious backgrounds they still feel a part of Assisi. Living here, you don't see the people of Assisi, you see people who have come from all over the world.

"There is something you feel when you come to Assisi, something you feel in your heart that makes you want to come back. And people do return! They feel the peacefulness and tranquility. Not that there aren't other aspects, like the commercialism—but these things happen. People return for the simplicity of this place. People feel attracted to Assisi. There's always something that people feel when they come here—even the hard-hearted ones!"

Asked if she thinks Assisi is changing, Sister Marcellina answers, with laughter in her voice, "When they wanted to make all the changes in the year 2000, the Jubilee Year, our Lord said, 'I must stop everything.' They had lots of projects to build new accommodations to house the people coming for the Jubilee Year, but the Lord said, 'No!'"

Mar.–mid-Oct., daily 10–1 and 3–6; mid-Oct.–mid-Mar., daily 10–1 and 2:30–6.

WORTH NOTING

Santa Maria Sopra Minerva. Dating from the time of the Emperor Augustus (27 BC–AD 14), this structure was originally dedicated to the Roman goddess of wisdom, in later times used as a monastery and prison before being converted into a church in the 16th century. The expectations raised by the perfect classical facade are not met by the interior, which was subjected to a thorough Baroque transformation in the 17th century. ✉ *Piazza del Comune* ☎ *075/812268* 🕘 *Daily 7:30–7:30.*

OFF THE BEATEN PATH

Eremo delle Carceri. About 4 km (2½ miles) east of Assisi is a monastery set in a dense wood against Monte Subasio. The "Hermitage of Prisons" was the place where Saint Francis and his followers went to "imprison" themselves in prayer. The only site in Assisi that remains essentially unchanged since Saint Francis's time, the church and monastery are the kinds of tranquil places that Saint Francis would have appreciated. The walk out from town is very pleasant, and many trails lead from here across the wooded hillside of Monte Subasio (now a protected forest), with beautiful vistas across the Umbrian countryside. True to their Franciscan heritage, the friars here are entirely dependent on alms from visitors. ✉ *Via Santuario delle Carceri 4 km (2½ miles) east of Assisi* ☎ *075/812301* 🎫 *Donations accepted* 🕘 *Nov.–Mar., daily 8:30–6:30; Apr.–Oct., daily 8:30–5:30.*

7

WHERE TO EAT

Assisi isn't a late-night town, so don't plan on any midnight snacks. What you can count on is the ubiquitous *stringozzi* (thick spaghetti), as well as the local specialty *piccione all'assisana* (roasted pigeon with olives and liver). The locals eat *torta al testo* (a dense flatbread, often stuffed with vegetables or cheese) with their meals.

$$ UMBRIAN

🍴 **Buca di San Francesco.** In summer, dine in a cool green garden; in winter, under the low brick arches of the cozy cellars. The unique settings and the first-rate fare make this central restaurant Assisi's busiest. Try homemade spaghetti *alla buca,* served with a roasted mushroom sauce. [$] *Average main: €16* ✉ *Via Eugenio Brizi 1* ☎ *075/812204* 🕘 *Closed Mon. and 10 days in late July.*

$$ UMBRIAN Fodor's Choice ★

🍴 **La Pallotta.** At this homey, family-run trattoria with a crackling fireplace and stone walls, the women do the cooking and the men serve the food. Try the *stringozzi alla pallotta* (thick spaghetti with a pesto of olives and mushrooms). Connected to the restaurant is an inn whose eight rooms have firm beds and some views across the rooftops of town. [$] *Average main: €17* ✉ *Vicolo della Volta Pinta 3* ☎ *075/812649* 🌐 *www.hotelpallotta.it* 🕘 *Closed Tues. and 2 wks in Jan. or Feb.*

$$ UMBRIAN

🍴 **Osteria Piazzetta dell'Erba.** Hip service and sophisticated presentations attract locals, who enjoy a wide selection of appetizers, including smoked goose breast, and four or five types of pasta, plus various salads and a good selection of torta al testo. For dessert, try the homemade biscuits, which you dunk in sweet wine. The owners carefully select wine at local vineyards, buy it in bulk, and then bottle it themselves, resulting in high quality and reasonable prices. Outdoor seating is available. $ *Average main: €15* ⊠ *Via San Gabriele dell'Addolorata 15a* ☎ *075/815352* ⊘ *Closed Mon. and a few wks in Jan. or Feb.*

$$ ✕ **San Francesco.** An excellent view of the Basilica di San Francesco from
UMBRIAN   the covered terrace is just one reason to enjoy the best restaurant in town, where creative Umbrian dishes are made with aromatic locally grown herbs. The seasonal menu might include gnocchi topped with a sauce of wild herbs and *oca stufata di finocchio selvaggio* (goose stuffed with wild fennel). Appetizers and desserts are especially good. $ *Average main: €22* ⊠ *Via di San Francesco 52* ☎ *075/812329* ⊘ *Closed Wed. and July 15–30.*

WHERE TO STAY

Advance reservations are essential at Assisi's hotels between Easter and October and over Christmas. Latecomers are often forced to stay in the modern town of Santa Maria degli Angeli, 8 km (5 miles) away. As a last-minute option, you can always inquire at restaurants to see if they're renting out rooms.

Until the early 1980s, pilgrim hostels outnumbered ordinary hotels in Assisi, and they present an intriguing and economical alternative to conventional lodgings. They're usually called *conventi* or *ostelli* ("convents" or "hostels") because they're run by convents, churches, or other Catholic organizations. Rooms are spartan but peaceful. Check with the tourist office for a list.

For expanded hotel reviews, visit Fodors.com.

$$ 🏨 **Castello di Petrata.** Wood beams and sections of exposed medieval
HOTEL   stonework add a lot of character to this fortress built in the 14th
Fodor'sChoice   century, while comfortable couches turn each individually decorated
★   room into a delightful retreat. **Pros:** great views of town and countryside; medieval character; pool. **Cons:** slightly isolated; far from Assisi town center. $ *Rooms from: €130* ⊠ *Via Petrata 25, Località Petrata* ☎ *075/815451* ⊕ *www.castellopetrata.com* ⬑ *16 rooms, 7 suites* ⊘ *Closed Jan.–Mar.* ❝❙ *Breakfast.*

$ 🏨 **Hotel Umbra.** Rooms on the upper floors of this charming 16th-
HOTEL   century town house near Piazza del Comune look out over the Assisi rooftops to the valley below, as does a sunny terrace. **Pros:** friendly welcome; pleasant small garden. **Cons:** difficult parking; some small rooms. $ *Rooms from: €90* ⊠ *Via degli Archi 6* ☎ *075/812240* ⊕ *www.hotelumbra.it* ⬑ *25 rooms* ⊘ *Closed Dec. and Jan.* ❝❙ *Breakfast.*

$ 🏨 **San Francesco.** Rooms and facilities range from simple to dreary,
HOTEL   but you can't beat the location—the roof terrace and some of the rooms look out onto the basilica. **Pros:** excellent location; great views and breakfast. **Cons:** simple rooms; sometimes noisy in peak season. $ *Rooms from: €120* ⊠ *Via San Francesco 48* ☎ *075/812281* ⊕ *www.hotelsanfrancescoassisi.it* ⬑ *44 rooms* ❝❙ *Breakfast.*

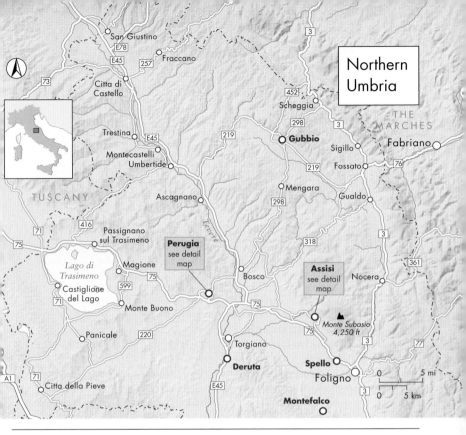

NORTHERN UMBRIA

To the north of Perugia, placid, walled Gubbio watches over green countryside, true to its nickname, City of Silence—except for its fast and furious festivals in May, as lively today as when they began more than 800 years ago. To the south, along the Tiber River valley, are the towns of Deruta and Torgiano, best known for their hand-painted ceramics and wine—as locals say, go to Deruta to buy a pitcher and to Torgiano to fill it.

GUBBIO

35 km (22 miles) southeast of Città di Castello, 39 km (24 miles) northeast of Perugia, 92 km (57 miles) east of Arezzo.

There's something otherworldly about this jewel of a medieval town tucked away in a mountainous corner of Umbria. Even at the height of summer, the cool serenity and quiet of Gubbio's streets remain intact. The town is perched on the slopes of Monte Ingino, meaning the streets are dramatically steep. Gubbio's relatively isolated position has kept it free of hordes of high-season visitors, and most of the year the city lives up to its Italian nickname, *La Città del Silenzio* (City of Silence). Parking in the central Piazza dei Quaranta Martiri—named for 40 hostages murdered by the Nazis in 1944—is easy and secure, and it's wise to leave your car in the piazza and explore the narrow streets on foot.

At Christmas, kitsch is king. From December 7 to January 10, colored lights are strung down the mountainside in a shape resembling an evergreen, the world's largest Christmas tree.

GETTING HERE

The closest train station is Fossato di Vico, about 20 km (12 miles) from Gubbio. Ten daily buses connect the train station with the city, a 30-minute trip. If you're driving from Perugia, take the SS298, which rises steeply up toward the Gubbio hills. The trip will take you one hour. There are also 10 buses a day that leave from Perugia's Piazza Partigiani, the main Perugia bus terminal.

VISITOR INFORMATION

Gubbio Tourism Office ✉ *Via della Repubblica 15* ☎ *075/9220693.*

EXPLORING

Basilica di Sant'Ubaldo. Gubbio's famous *ceri*—three 16-foot-tall pillars crowned with statues of Saints Ubaldo, George, and Anthony—are housed in this basilica atop Monte Ingino. The pillars are transported to the Palazzo dei Consoli on the first Sunday of May, in preparation for the Festa dei Ceri, one of central Italy's most spectacular festivals. ✉ *Monte Ingino* ☎ *075/9273872* ☉ *Daily 8:30–noon and 4–7.*

Duomo. On a narrow street on the highest tier of the town, the Duomo dates from the 13th century, with some baroque additions—in particular, a lavishly decorated bishop's chapel. ✉ *Via Ducale* ☉ *Daily 8–12:30 and 3–7.*

Funicular. For a bracing ride to the top of Monte Ingino, hop on the funicular that climbs the hillside just outside the city walls at the eastern end of town. It's definitely not for those who suffer from vertigo. ✉ *Follow Corso Garibaldi or Via XX Settembre to end* ⊕ *www.funiviagubbio.it* 🎫 *€4, €5 round-trip* ☉ *Sept.–June, daily 10–1:15 and 2:30–6; July and Aug., daily 9–7.*

Palazzo dei Consoli. Gubbio's striking Piazza Grande is dominated by this medieval palazzo, attributed to a local architect known as Gattapone, who is still much admired by today's residents (though some scholars have suggested that the palazzo was in fact the work of another architect, Angelo da Orvieto). In the Middle Ages the Parliament of Gubbio assembled in the palace, which has become a symbol of the town and now houses a museum with a collection famous chiefly for the Tavole Eugubine. These seven bronze tablets are written in the ancient Umbrian language, employing Etruscan and Latin characters, and provide the best key to understanding this obscure tongue. Also in the museum is a fascinating miscellany of rare coins and earthenware pots. A lofty loggia provides exhilarating views over Gubbio's roofscape and beyond. For a few days at the beginning of May, the palace also displays the famous *ceri,* the ceremonial wooden pillars at the center of Gubbio's annual festivities. ✉ *Piazza Grande* ☎ *075/9274298* 🌐 *www.comune.gubbio.pg.it* 🎟 *€5* 🕒 *Apr.–Oct., daily 10–1 and 3–6; Nov.–Mar., daily 10–1 and 2:30–5:30.*

Palazzo Ducale. This scaled-down copy of the Palazzo Ducale in Urbino (Gubbio was once the possession of that city's ruling family, the Montefeltro) contains a small museum and a courtyard. Some of the public rooms offer magnificent views. ✉ *Via Ducale* ☎ *075/9275872* 🎟 *€5* 🕒 *Tues.–Sun. 8:30–7:30.*

WHERE TO EAT

$$ UMBRIAN 🍴 **Grotta dell'Angelo.** The rustic trattoria sits in the lower part of the old town near the main square. The menu features simple local specialties, including *capocollo* (a type of salami), *stringozzi* (thick spaghetti), and lasagne *tartufata* (with truffles). The few outdoor tables are in high demand in the summer. The restaurant also offers a few small, basically furnished guest rooms, which should be booked in advance. [$] *Average main: €18* ✉ *Via Gioia 47* ☎ *075/9271747* ✍ *Reservations essential* 🕒 *Closed Tues. and Jan. 7–Feb. 7.*

$$ UMBRIAN Fodor's Choice ★ 🍴 **Taverna del Lupo.** One of the city's most famous taverns gets hectic on weekends and during the high season. Lasagne made in the Gubbian fashion, with ham and truffles, is an unusual indulgence, and the *suprema di faraono* (guinea fowl in a delicately spiced sauce) is a specialty. The restaurant has two fine wine cellars and an extensive wine list. Save room for the excellent desserts. [$] *Average main: €23* ✉ *Via Ansidei 21* ☎ *075/9274368* 🕒 *Closed Mon. Oct.–June.*

$$ UMBRIAN 🍴 **Ulisse e Letizia.** A stone-and-wood structure from the 1300s (once an important ceramics factory) is the setting for flavorful seasonal menus. The creative fare might include tagliatelle *al tartuffo* (in a truffle sauce), *gnochetti al finocchio selvatico* (potato dumplings with wild fennel), and *raviolini di faro con asparagi* (tiny ravioli with spelt and asparagus). [$] *Average main: €20* ✉ *Via Mastro Giorgio 2* ☎ *075/9221970* 🕒 *Closed Mon.*

WHERE TO STAY

For expanded hotel reviews, visit Fodors.com.

$ HOTEL 🏨 **Hotel Bosone Palace.** A former palace is now home to an elegant hotel, where elaborate frescoes grace the ceilings of the two enormous suites and delightful breakfast room. **Pros:** friendly welcome; excellent location. **Cons:** some noise in tourist season; simple lobby. [$] *Rooms from: €120* ✉ *Via XX Settembre 22* ☎ *075/9220688* 🌐 *www.hotelbosone.com* 🛏 *28 rooms, 2 suites* 🕒 *Closed 3 wks in Jan.* 🍽 *Breakfast.*

DERUTA

7 km (4½ miles) south of Torgiano, 19 km (11 miles) southeast of Perugia.

This 14th-century medieval hill town is most famous for its ceramics. A drive through the countryside to visit the ceramics workshops is a good way to spend a morning, but be sure to stop in the town itself.

GETTING HERE

From Perugia follow the directions for Rome and the E45 highway; Deruta has its own exits. There are also trains from the smaller St. Anna train station in Perugia. Take the train in the direction of Terni, and get off at Deruta.

VISITOR INFORMATION

Deruta Tourism Office ⊠ *Piazza dei Consoli 4* ☎ *075/9711559.*

EXPLORING

Museo Regionale della Ceramica (*Regional Ceramics Museum*). It's only fitting that Deruta is home to an impressive ceramics museum, part of which extends into the adjacent 14th-century former convent of San Francesco. The museum tells the history of ceramics, with panels (in Italian and English) explaining artistic techniques and production processes, and also holds the country's largest collection of Italian ceramics—nearly 8,000 pieces are on display. The most notable are the Renaissance vessels using the *lustro* technique, which originated in Arab and Middle Eastern cultures some 500 years before coming into use in Italy in the late 1400s. Lustro, as the name sounds, gives the ceramics a rich finish, which is accomplished with the use of crushed precious materials such as gold and silver. ⊠ *Largo San Francesco* ☎ *075/9711000* ⊕ *www.comunederuta.gov.it/cultura-e-territorio/museo-regionale-della-ceramica* ⛊ *€5, includes admission to Pinoteca Comunale* ⊗ *Wed.–Sun. 10:30–1 and 2:30–5.*

SHOPPING

Deruta is home to more than 70 ceramics shops. They offer a range of ceramics, including extra pieces from commissions for well-known British and North American tableware manufacturers. If you ask, most owners will take you to see where they actually throw, bake, and paint their wares. A drive along Via Tiberina Nord takes you past one shop after another.

SPELLO

12 km (7 miles) southeast of Assisi, 33 km (21 miles) north of Spoleto.

Spello is a gastronomic paradise, especially compared to Assisi. Only a few minutes from Assisi by car or train, this hilltop town at the edge of Monte Subasio makes an excellent strategic and culinary base for exploring nearby towns. Its hotels are well appointed and its restaurants serve some of the best cuisine and wines in the region—sophisticated in variety and of excellent quality. Spello's art scene includes first-rate frescoes by Pinturicchio and Perugino and contemporary artists who can be observed at work in studios around town. If antiquity is your passion, the town also has some intriguing Roman ruins. And the warm, rosy-beige tones of the local *pietra rossa* stone on the buildings brighten even cloudy days.

GETTING HERE

Spello is an easy half-hour drive from Perugia. From the E45 highway, take the exit toward Assisi and Foligno. Merge onto the SS75 and take the Spello exit. There are also regular trains on the Perugia–Assisi line. Spello is 1 km (½ mile) from the train station, and buses run every 30 minutes for Porta Consolare. From Porta Consolare continue up the steep main street that begins as Via Consolare and changes names several times as it crosses the little town, following the original Roman road. As it curves around, notice the winding medieval alleyways to the right and the more uniform Roman-era blocks to the left.

VISITOR INFORMATION

Spello Tourism Office ✉ *Piazza Matteotti 3* ☎ *0742/301009* 🌐 *www.prospello.it* 🕓 *Daily 9:30–12:30 and 3:30–5:30.*

EXPLORING

Santa Maria Maggiore. The two great Umbrian artists hold sway in this 16th century basilica. Pinturicchio's vivid frescoes in the Cappella Baglioni (1501) are striking for their rich colors, finely dressed figures, and complex symbolism. Among Pinturicchio's finest works are the *Nativity, Christ Among the Doctors* (on the far left side is a portrait of Troilo Baglioni, the prior who commissioned the work), and the *Annunciation* (look for Pinturicchio's self-portrait in the Virgin's room). The artist painted them after he had already won great acclaim for his work in the Palazzi Vaticani in Rome for Borgia Pope Alexander VI. Two pillars on either side of the apse are decorated with frescoes by Perugino (circa 1450–1523). ✉ *Piazza Matteotti 18* ☎ *0742/301792* 🌐 *www.smariamaggiore.com* 🕓 *Daily 9–12:30 and 3–7.*

7

WHERE TO EAT AND STAY

For expanded hotel reviews, visit Fodors.com.

$$ UMBRIAN Fodor's Choice ★ 🍴 **Il Molino.** A former mill is one of the region's best restaurants. Appetizers are varied, and often highlight foods found only here, like the *risina*, a tiny white bean. The meat is first-rate, either elaborately prepared or grilled and topped with a signature sauce, and for any dish, the type of olive oil and the names of the local farmers who grew the produce are noted on the menu. Service is attentive and the wine list has plenty of local and Italian options, including the pungent Sagrantino di Montefalco and fresh Orvieto whites. Outside seating lets you soak up the passing street scene; inside is a series of impressive 14th-century arches. [$] *Average main: €22* ✉ *Piazza Matteotti 6/7* ☎ *0742/301021* 🕓 *Closed Tues.*

$$ HOTEL 🏨 **Hotel Palazzo Bocci.** Lovely sitting areas, a reading room, bucolic ceiling and wall frescoes, and a garden terrace all add quiet and elegant charm to this 14th-century building, where several rooms have valley views. **Pros:** central location; splendid views of the valley from public areas and some rooms. **Cons:** noisy in summer months; not all rooms have views. [$] *Rooms from: €140* ✉ *Via Cavour 17* ☎ *0742/301021* 🌐 *www.palazzobocci.com* 🛏 *23 rooms* 🍽 *Breakfast.*

$ HOTEL **La Bastiglia.** Polished wood planks and handwoven rugs have replaced the rustic flooring of a former grain mill, and comfortable sitting rooms and cozy bedrooms are filled with a mix of antique and modern pieces. **Pros:** lovely terrace restaurant; cozy rooms; fine views from top-floor rooms, some with terraces. **Cons:** some shared balconies; breakfast is underwhelming; no elevator and plenty of steps, so pack light. [$] *Rooms from: €120* ✉ *Via Salnitraria 15* ☎ *0742/651277* 🌐 *www.labastiglia.com* 🛏 *31 rooms, 2 suites* ⏲ *Closed early Jan.–early Feb.* 🍴 *Breakfast.*

MONTEFALCO

6 km (4 miles) southeast of Bevagna, 34 km (21 miles) south of Assisi.

Nicknamed the "balcony over Umbria" for its high vantage point over the valley that runs from Perugia to Spoleto, Montefalco began as an important Roman settlement situated on the Via Flaminia. The town owes its current name—which means "Falcon's Mount"—to Emperor Frederick II (1194–1250). Obviously a greater fan of falconry than Roman architecture, he destroyed the ancient town, which was then called Coccorone, in 1249, and built in its place what would later become Montefalco. Aside from a few fragments incorporated in a private house just off Borgo Garibaldi, no traces remain of the old Roman center. However, Montefalco has more than its fair share of interesting art and architecture and is well worth the drive up the hill.

GETTING HERE

If you're driving from Perugia, take the E45 toward Rome. Take the Foligno exit, then merge onto the SP445 and follow it into Montefalco. The drive takes around 50 minutes. The nearest train station is in Foligno, about 7 km (4½ miles) away. From there you can take a taxi or a bus into Montefalco.

VISITOR INFORMATION

La Strada del Sagrantino ✉ *Piazza del Comune 17* ☎ *0742/378490* 🌐 *www.stradadelsagrantino.it.*

WHERE TO EAT AND STAY

For expanded hotel reviews, visit Fodors.com.

Montefalco is a good stop for sustenance: here you need go no farther than the main square to find a restaurant or bar with a hot meal, and most establishments—both simple and sophisticated—offer a splendid combination of history and small-town hospitality.

$$ WINE BAR ✕ **L'Alchemista.** "The Alchemist" is an apt name, as the chef's transformations are magical. Try the *fiore molle della Valnerina,* baked saffron cheese, bacon, and zucchini—served only here. In summer, cold dishes to try are *panzanella,* vegetable salad mixed with bread, or the barley salad tossed with vegetables. The *farro* (spelt) soup made with Sagrantino wine is a local specialty. The desserts are delicious: all are made on the premises and not too sweet. [$] *Average main: €16* ✉ *Piazza del Comune 14* ☎ *0742/378558* ⏲ *Closed Tues. and Jan.–Mar.*

CLOSE UP

The Sagrantino Story

Sagrantino grapes have been used for the production of red wine for centuries. The wine began centuries ago as Sagrantino *passito,* a semisweet version in which the grapes are left to dry for a period after picking to intensify the sugar content. One theory traces the origin of Sagrantino back to ancient Rome in the works of Pliny the Elder, the author of the *Natural History,* who referred to the Itriola grape that some researchers think may be Sagrantino. Others believe that in medieval times Franciscan friars returned from Asia Minor with the grape. ("Sagrantino" perhaps derives from *sacramenti,* the religious ceremony in which the wine was used.)

The passito is still produced today, and is preferred by some. But the big change in Sagrantino wine production came in the past decades, when Sagrantino *secco* (dry) came onto the market. Both passito and secco have a deep ruby-red color that tends toward garnet highlights, with a full body and rich flavor.

For the dry wines, producers not to be missed are Terre di Capitani, Antonelli, Perticaia, and Caprai. Try those labels for the passito as well, in addition to Ruggeri and Scacciadiavoli. Terre di Capitani is complex and has vegetable and mineral tones that join tastes of wild berries, cherries, and chocolate—this winemaker hand-pampers his grapes and it shows. Antonelli is elegant, refined, and rich. The Ruggeri passito is one of the best, so don't be put off by its homespun label. Caprai is bold and rich in taste, and has the largest market share, including a high percentage exported to the United States. Perticaia has a full, rounded taste.

Some wineries are small and not equipped to receive visitors.

At La Strada del Sagrantino in Montefalco's main square, you can pick up a map of the wine route and set up appointments, book accommodations, and then visit local enoteche. At the enoteca, ask the sommelier to guide you to some smaller producers you'll have difficulty finding elsewhere.

Salute!

7

$$ HOTEL Fodor's Choice ★ 🏨 **Villa Pambuffetti.** If you want to be pampered in the refined atmosphere of a private villa, this is the spot, with the warmth of a fireplace in the winter, a pool to cool you down in summer, and cozy reading nooks and guest rooms year-round. **Pros:** peaceful gardens; refined furnishings; excellent dining room. **Cons:** outside the town center; can get crowded on weekends. [$] *Rooms from: €190* ✉ *Viale della Vittoria 20* ☎ *0742/379417* 🌐 *www.villapambuffetti.it* 🛏 *15 rooms, 3 suites* 🍴 *Breakfast.*

SPOLETO

For most of the year, Spoleto is one more in a pleasant succession of sleepy hill towns, resting regally atop a mountain. But for three weeks every summer the town shifts into high gear for a turn in the international spotlight during the Festival dei Due Mondi (Festival of Two

Worlds), an extravaganza of theater, opera, music, painting, and sculpture. As the world's top artists vie for honors, throngs of art aficionados vie for hotel rooms. If you plan to spend the night in Spoleto during the festival, make sure you have confirmed reservations, or you may find yourself scrambling at sunset.

Spoleto has plenty to lure you during the rest of the year as well: the final frescoes of Filippo Lippi, beautiful piazzas and streets with Roman and medieval attractions, and superb natural surroundings with rolling hills and a dramatic gorge. Spoleto makes a good base for exploring all of southern Umbria, as Assisi, Orvieto, and the towns in between are all within easy reach.

GETTING HERE

Spoleto is an hour's drive from Perugia. From the E45 highway, take the exit toward Assisi and Foligno, then merge onto the SS75 until you reach the Foligno Est exit. Merge onto the SS3, which leads to Spoleto. There are regular trains on the Perugia–Foligno line. From the train station it's a 15-minute uphill walk to the center, so you'll probably want to take a taxi.

VISITOR INFORMATION

Spoleto Tourism Office ⊠ *Piazza della Libertà 7* ☎ *0743/218620* ⊕ *www.regioneumbria.eu.*

EXPLORING SPOLETO

The walled city is set on a slanting hillside, with the most interesting sections clustered toward the upper portion. Parking options inside the walls include Piazza Campello (just below the Rocca) on the southeast end, Via del Trivio to the north, and Piazza San Domenico on the west end. You can also park at Piazza della Vittoria farther north, just outside the walls. There are also several well-marked lots near the train station. If you arrive by train, you can walk 1 km (½ mile) from the station to the entrance to the lower town. Regular bus connections are every 15 to 30 minutes. You can also use the *trenino,* as locals call the shuttle service, from the train station to Piazza della Libertà, near the upper part of the old town, where you'll find the tourist office.

Like most other towns with narrow, winding streets, Spoleto is best explored on foot. Bear in mind that much of the city is on a steep slope, so there are lots of stairs and steep inclines. The well-worn stones can be slippery even when dry; wear rubber-sole shoes for good traction. Several pedestrian walkways cut across Corso Mazzini, which zigzags up the hill. A €12 combination ticket purchased at the tourist office allows you entry to all the town's museums and galleries.

TOP ATTRACTIONS

Duomo. The 12th-century Romanesque facade received a Renaissance face-lift with the addition of a loggia in a rosy pink stone, creating a stunning contrast in styles. One of the finest cathedrals in the region is lit by eight rose windows that are especially dazzling in the late afternoon sun. The original floor tiles date from an earlier church that was destroyed by Frederick I (circa 1123–90).

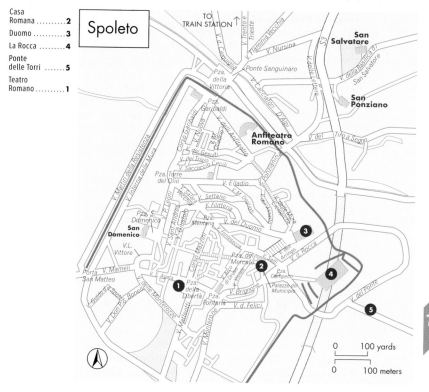

Above the church's entrance is Bernini's bust of Pope Urban VIII (1568–1644), who had the church redecorated in 17th-century baroque; fortunately he didn't touch the 15th-century frescoes painted in the apse by Fra Filippo Lippi (circa 1406–69) between 1466 and 1469. These immaculately restored masterpieces—the *Annunciation, Nativity,* and *Dormition*—tell the story of the life of the Virgin. The *Coronation of the Virgin,* adorning the half dome, is the literal and figurative high point. Portraits of Lippi and his assistants are on the right side of the central panel. The Florentine artist priest "whose colors expressed God's voice" (the words inscribed on his tomb) died shortly after completing the work. His tomb, which you can see in the right transept (note the artist's brushes and tools), was designed by his son, Filippino Lippi (circa 1457–1504).

Another fresco cycle, including work by Pinturicchio, is in the Cappella Eroli, off the right aisle. Note the grotesques in the ornamentation, then very much in vogue with the rediscovery of ancient Roman paintings. The bounty of Umbria is displayed in vivid colors in the abundance of leaves, fruits, and vegetables that adorn the center seams of the cross vault. In the left nave, not far from the entrance, is the well-restored 12th-century crucifix by Alberto Sozio, the earliest known example of this kind of work, with a painting on parchment attached to a wood cross. To the right of the presbytery is the Cappella della Santissima Icona (Chapel of the Most Holy Icon), which contains a small Byzantine painting of a Madonna given to the town by Frederick Barbarossa as a peace offering in 1185, following his destruction of the cathedral and town three decades earlier. ⊠ *Piazza del Duomo* ☎ *0743/231063* ⏱ *Apr.–Oct., daily 8:30–12:30 and 3:30–6; Nov.–Mar., daily 8:30–12:30 and 3:30–5.*

Ponte delle Torri (*Bridge of the Towers*). Standing massive and graceful through the deep gorge that separates Spoleto from Monteluco, this 14th-century bridge is one of Umbria's most photographed monuments, and justifiably so. Built over the foundations of a Roman-era aqueduct, it soars 262 feet above the forested gorge—higher than the dome of St. Peter's in Rome. Sweeping views over the valley and a pleasant sense of vertigo make a walk across the bridge a must, particularly on a starry night. ⊠ *Via del Ponte.*

WORTH NOTING

Casa Romana. Spoleto became a Roman colony in the 3rd century BC, but the best excavated remains date from the 1st century AD. Best preserved among them is the Casa Romana. According to an inscription, it belonged to Vespasia Polla, the mother of Emperor Vespasian (one of the builders of the Colosseum and perhaps better known by the Romans for taxing them to install public toilets, later called "Vespasians"). The rooms, arranged around a large central atrium built over an *impluvium* (rain cistern), are decorated with black-and-white geometric mosaics. ⊠ *Palazzo del Municipio, Via Visiale 9* ☎ *0743/234250* ⊕ *www.spoletocard.it* ☑ *€3, €6 combination ticket includes Pinacoteca Comunale and Galleria d'Arte Moderna* ⏱ *Daily 11–7; closed Tues. and last wk of Dec.*

La Rocca. Built in the mid-14th century for Cardinal Egidio Albornoz, this massive fortress served as a seat for the local pontifical governors, a tangible sign of the restoration of the Church's power in the area when the pope was ruling from Avignon. Several popes spent time here, and one of them, Alexander VI, in 1499 sent his capable teenage daughter Lucrezia Borgia (1480–1519) to serve as governor for three months. The Gubbio-born architect Gattapone (14th century) used the ruins of a Roman acropolis as a foundation and took materials from many Roman-era sites, including the Teatro Romano. La Rocca's plan is long and rectangular, with six towers and two grand courtyards, an upper loggia, and inside some grand reception rooms. In the largest tower, Torre Maestà, you can visit an apartment with some interesting frescoes. A small shuttle bus gives you that last boost up the hill from the ticket booth to the entrance of the fortress. If you phone in advance, you may be able to secure an English-speaking guide. ⊠ *Piazza Campello* ☎ *0743/224952* ⊕ *www.spoletocard.it* ☑ *€7.50* ⏱ *Apr.–Oct., daily 9:30–7:30.*

Teatro Romano. The Romans who colonized the city in 241 BC constructed this small theater in the 1st century AD; for centuries afterward it was used as a quarry for building materials. The most intact portion is the hallway that passes under the *cavea* (stands). The rest was heavily restored in the early 1950s and serves as a venue for Spoleto's Festival dei Due Mondi. The theater was the site of a gruesome episode in Spoleto's history: during the medieval struggle between Guelph (papal) and Ghibelline (imperial) forces, Spoleto took the side of the Holy Roman Emperor. Afterward, 400 Guelph supporters were massacred in the theater, their bodies burned in an enormous pyre. In the end, the Guelphs were triumphant, and Spoleto was incorporated into the states of the Church in 1354. Through a door in the west portico of the adjoining building is the **Museo Archeologico,** with assorted artifacts found in excavations primarily around Spoleto and Norcia. The collection contains Bronze Age and Iron Age artifacts from Umbrian and pre-Roman eras. Another section contains black-glaze vases from the Hellenistic period excavated from the necropolis of Saint Scolastica in Norcia. The highlight is the stone tablet inscribed on both sides with the Lex Spoletina (Spoleto Law). Dating from 315 BC, this legal document prohibited the desecration of the woods on the slopes of nearby Monteluco. ✉ *Piazza della Libertà* ☎ *0743/223277* 🎫 *€4* 🕒 *Daily 8:30–7:30.*

WHERE TO EAT

$$ UMBRIAN 🍴 **Apollinare.** Low wooden ceilings and flickering candlelight make this monastery from the 10th and 11th centuries Spoleto's most romantic spot. The kitchen serves sophisticated, innovative variations on local dishes. Sauces of cherry tomatoes, mint, and a touch of red pepper, or of porcini mushrooms, top the long, slender strangozzi. The *caramella* (light puff-pastry cylinders filled with local cheese and served with a creamy Parmesan sauce) is popular. In warm weather you can dine under a canopy on the piazza across from the archaeological museum. [$] *Average main: €20* ✉ *Via Sant'Agata 14* ☎ *0743/223256* 🕒 *Closed Tues.*

$$ UMBRIAN 🍴 **Il Tartufo.** As the name indicates, dishes prepared with truffles are the specialty here—don't miss the risotto al tartufo. Incorporating the ruins of a Roman villa, the surroundings are rustic on the ground floor and more modern upstairs. In summer, tables appear outdoors and the traditional fare is spiced up to appeal to the cosmopolitan crowd attending (or performing in) the Festival dei Due Mondi. [$] *Average main: €20* ✉ *Piazza Garibaldi 24* ☎ *0743/40236* ✍ *Reservations essential* 🕒 *Closed Mon. and last 2 wks in July. No dinner Sun.*

$$ UMBRIAN 🍴 **Osteria del Trivio.** Everything is made on the premises and the menu changes daily, depending on what's in season. Dishes might include stuffed artichokes, pasta with local mushrooms, or chicken with artichokes. For dessert, try the homemade biscotti, made for dunking in sweet wine. There's a printed menu, but the owner can explain the dishes in a number of languages. [$] *Average main: €18* ✉ *Via del Trivio 16* ☎ *0743/44349* 🕒 *Closed Tues. and 3 weeks in Jan.*

$$ UMBRIAN 🍴 **Ristorante Panciolle.** A small garden filled with lemon trees in the heart of Spoleto's medieval quarter provides one of the most appealing

CLOSE UP

A Taste of Truffles

Umbria is rich with truffles—more are found here than anywhere else in Italy—and those not consumed fresh are processed into pastes or flavored oils. The primary truffle areas are around the tiny town of Norcia, which holds a truffle festival every February, and near Spoleto, where signs warn against unlicensed truffle hunting at the base of the Ponte delle Torri.

Although grown locally, the rare delicacy can cost a small fortune, up to $200 for a quarter pound—fortunately, a little goes a long way. At such a price there's great competition among the nearly 10,000 registered truffle hunters in the province, who use specially trained dogs to sniff them out among the roots of several types of trees, including oak and ilex. Despite a few incidents involving inferior tubers imported from China, you can be reasonably assured that the truffle shaved onto your pasta has been unearthed locally. Don't pass up the opportunity to try this delectable treat. The intense aroma of a dish perfumed with truffles is unmistakable and the flavor memorable.

settings you could wish for. Dishes change throughout the year, and may include pastas served with asparagus or mushrooms, as well as grilled meats. More expensive dishes prepared with fresh truffles are also available in season. [$] *Average main: €20* ✉ *Via Duomo 3/5* ☎ *0743/45677* ✍ *Reservations essential* ⏲ *Closed Wed.*

WHERE TO STAY

For expanded hotel reviews, visit Fodors.com.

$$ HOTEL 🏨 **Cavaliere Palace Hotel.** A sense of old-world comfort pervades the 17th-century home of an influential cardinal, and many rooms retain their sumptuous frescoed ceilings. **Pros:** quiet elegance; central position. **Cons:** finding parking can be a problem; crowded in summer. [$] *Rooms from: €180* ✉ *Corso Garibaldi 49* ☎ *0743/220350* 🌐 *www.hotelcavaliere.eu* 🛏 *29 rooms, 2 suites* 🍴 *Breakfast.*

$ HOTEL 🏨 **Hotel Clitunno.** Cozy guest rooms and intimate public rooms, some with timbered ceilings, give the sense of a traditional Umbrian home—albeit one with a good restaurant. **Pros:** friendly staff; good restaurant. **Cons:** difficult to find a parking space; some small rooms. [$] *Rooms from: €90* ✉ *Piazza Sordini 6* ☎ *0743/223340* 🌐 *www.hotelclitunno.com* 🛏 *45 rooms* 🍴 *Breakfast.*

$$ HOTEL Fodor's Choice ★ 🏨 **Hotel San Luca.** Hand-painted friezes decorate the walls of the spacious guest rooms, and elegant comfort is the gracenote throughout—you can sip afternoon tea in oversize armchairs by the fireplace, or take a walk in the sweet-smelling rose garden. **Pros:** very helpful staff; peaceful location. **Cons:** outside the town center; a long walk to the main sights. [$] *Rooms from: €150* ✉ *Via Interna delle Mura 19* ☎ *0743/223399* 🌐 *www.hotelsanluca.com* 🛏 *33 rooms, 2 suites* 🍴 *Breakfast.*

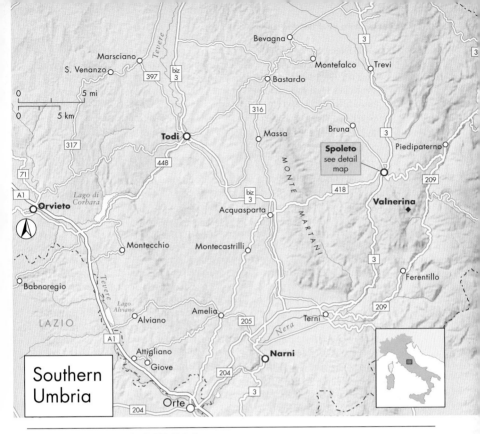

SOUTHERN UMBRIA

Orvieto, built on a tufa mount, produces one of Italy's favorite white wines and has one of the country's greatest cathedrals and most compelling fresco cycles. Nearby Narni and Todi are pleasant medieval hill towns. The former stands over a steep gorge, its Roman pedigree evident in dark alleyways and winding streets; the latter is a fairy-tale village with incomparable views and one of Italy's most perfect piazzas.

TODI

34 km (22 miles) south of Perugia, 34 km (22 miles) east of Orvieto.

As you stand on Piazza del Popolo, looking out onto the Tiber Valley below, it's easy to see why Todi is often described as Umbria's prettiest hill town. Legend has it that the town was founded by the Umbri, who followed an eagle who had stolen a tablecloth. They liked this lofty perch so much that they settled here for good. The eagle is now perched on the insignia of the medieval palaces in the main piazza.

GETTING HERE

Todi is best reached by car, as the town's two train stations are way down the hill and connected to the center by infrequent bus service. From Perugia, follow the E45 toward Rome. Take the Todi/Orvieto exit, then follow the SS79bis into Todi. The drive takes around 40 minutes.

VISITOR INFORMATION

Todi Tourism Office ✉ *Piazza del Popolo 38-39* ☎ *075/8942526* ⊕ *www. regioneumbria.eu.*

EXPLORING

Duomo. One end of the Piazza del Popolo is dominated by this 12th-century Romanesque-Gothic masterpeice, built over the site of a Roman temple. The simple facade is enlivened by a finely carved rose window. Look up at that window as you step inside and you'll notice its peculiarity: each "petal" of the rose has a cherub's face in the stained glass. Also take a close look at the capitals of the double columns with pilasters: perched between the acanthus leaves are charming medieval sculptures of saints—Peter with his keys, George and the dragon, and so on. You can see the rich brown tones of the wooden choir near the altar, but unless you have binoculars or request special permission in advance, you can't get close enough to see all the exquisite detail in this Renaissance masterpiece of woodworking (1521–30). The severe, solid mass of the Duomo is mirrored by the Palazzo dei Priori (1595–97) across the way. ✉ *Piazza del Popolo* ☎ *075/8943041* ☉ *Daily 8–1 and 3–6.*

Piazza del Popolo. Built above the Roman Forum, Piazza del Popolo is Todi's high point, a model of spatial harmony with stunning views onto the surrounding countryside. In the best medieval tradition, the square was conceived to house both the temporal and the spiritual centers of power.

WHERE TO EAT AND STAY

For expanded hotel reviews, visit Fodors.com.

$$ ✕ **Ristorante Umbria.** Todi's most popular restaurant for more than four
UMBRIAN   decades is reliable for its sturdy country food and the wonderful view from the terrace. Since it has only 16 tables outside, make sure you reserve ahead. In winter, try legume soup, homemade pasta with truffles, or *palombaccio alla ghiotta* (roasted squab). Steaks, accompanied by a rich dark-brown wine sauce, are good as well. Ⓢ *Average main: €19* ✉ *Via San Bonaventura 13* ☎ *075/8942737* ☉ *Closed Tues.*

$ ☷ **San Lorenzo 3.** Surrounded by antique furniture, paintings, and period
HOTEL   knickknacks, you will be as charmed by a sense of being in the 19th century as you are by the magnificent views over valleys and hills. **Pros:** Old World atmosphere; excellent central location. **Cons:** few modern amenities; basic furnishings; some shared bathrooms. Ⓢ *Rooms from: €110* ✉ *Via San Lorenzo 3* ☎ *075/8944555* ⊕ *www.sanlorenzo3.it* ⇱ *6 rooms, 3 with bath* ▬ *No credit cards* ☉ *Closed Jan. and Feb.* ❑ *Breakfast.*

ORVIETO

30 km (19 miles) southwest of Todi, 81 km (51 miles) west of Spoleto.

Carved out of an enormous plateau of volcanic rock high above a green valley, Orvieto has natural defenses that made the high walls seen in many Umbrian towns unnecessary. The Etruscans were the first to settle here, digging a honeycombed network of more than 1,200 wells and storage caves out of the soft stone. The Romans attacked, sacked, and destroyed the city in 283 BC; since then, it has grown up out of the rock into an enchanting maze of alleys and squares. Orvieto was solidly Guelph in the Middle Ages, and for several hundred years popes sought refuge in the city, at times needing protection from their enemies, at times seeking respite from the summer heat of Rome.

When painting his frescoes inside the Duomo, Luca Signorelli asked that part of his contract be paid in Orvietan wine, and he was neither the first nor the last to appreciate the region's popular white. In past times the caves carved underneath the town were used to ferment the Trebbiano grapes used in making Orvieto Classico; now local wine production has moved out to more traditional vineyards, but you can still while away the afternoon in tastings at any number of shops in town.

GETTING HERE

Orvieto is well connected by train to Rome, Florence, and Perugia. It's also adjacent to the A1 Superstrada that runs between Florence and Rome. Parking areas in the upper town tend to be crowded. A better idea is to follow the signs for the Porta Orvietana parking lot, then take the funicular that carries people up the hill.

VISITOR INFORMATION

Orvieto Tourism Office ⊠ *Piazza del Duomo 24* ☎ *0763/341772* ⊕ *www.regioneumbria.eu.*

A *Carta Orvieto Unica* (single ticket) is expensive but a great deal if you want to visit everything; for €18 you get admission to the three major sights in town—Cappella di San Brizio (at the Duomo), Museo Claudio Faina, and Orvieto Underground *(see below)*—along with entry to the Torre del Moro; with views of Orvieto, plus a combination bus-funicular pass or five hours of free parking.

EXPLORING

Fodor's Choice ★ **Duomo.** Orvieto's stunning cathedral was built to commemorate the Miracle at Bolsena. In 1263 a young priest who questioned the miracle of transubstantiation (in which the Communion bread and wine become the flesh and blood of Christ) was saying mass at nearby Lago di Bolsena. His doubts were put to rest, however, when a wafer he had just blessed suddenly started to drip blood, staining the linen covering the altar. The cloth and the host were taken to the pope, who proclaimed a miracle and a year later provided for a new religious holiday—the Feast of Corpus Domini. Thirty years later, construction began on a *duomo* in Orvieto to celebrate the miracle and house the stained altar cloth.

It's thought that Arnolfo di Cambio (circa 1245–1302), the famous builder of the Duomo in Florence, was given the initial commission, but the project was soon taken over by Lorenzo Maitani (circa 1275–1330), who consolidated the structure and designed the monumental facade. Maitani also made the bas-relief panels between the doorways, which graphically tell the story of the Creation (on the left) and the Last Judgment (on the right). The lower registers, now protected by Plexiglas, succeed in conveying the horrors of hell as few other works of art manage to do, an effect made all the more powerful by the worn gray marble. Above, gold mosaics are framed by finely detailed Gothic decoration.

Inside, the cathedral is rather vast and empty; the major works are in the transepts. To the left is the **Cappella del Corporale,** where the square linen cloth (corporale) is kept in a golden reliquary that's modeled on the cathedral and inlaid with enamel scenes of the miracle. The cloth is removed for public viewing on Easter and on Corpus Domini (the ninth Sunday after Easter). In the right transept is the **Cappella di San Brizio,** or Cappella Nuova. In this chapel is one of Italy's greatest fresco cycles, notable for its influence on Michelangelo's *Last Judgment,* as well as for the extraordinary beauty of the figuration. In these works, a few by Fra Angelico and the majority by Luca Signorelli, the damned fall to hell, demons breathe fire and blood, and Christians are martyred. Some scenes are heavily influenced by the imagery in Dante's (1265–1321) *Divine Comedy.* ⊠ *Piazza del Duomo* ☏ *0763/342477* 📠 *Cappella Nuova €3* ⊗ *Mar.–Oct., daily 9:30–7; Nov.–Feb., daily 9:30–1 and 2:30–5.*

Museo Archeologico Claudio Faina. This superb private collection, beautifully arranged and presented, goes far beyond the usual museum offerings of a scattering of local remains. The collection is particularly rich in Greek- and Etruscan-era pottery, from large Attic amphorae (6th–4th century BC) to Attic black- and red-figure pieces to Etruscan *bucchero* (dark-reddish clay) vases. Other interesting pieces in the collection include a 6th-century sarcophagus and a substantial display of Roman-era coins. ⊠ *Piazza del Duomo 29* ☏ *0763/341511* ⊕ *www.museofaina. it* 📠 *€4* ⊗ *Apr.–Sept., daily 9:30–6; Oct.–Mar., Tues.–Sun. 10–5.*

Orvieto Underground. More than just about any other town, Orvieto has grown from its own foundations. The Etruscans, the Romans, and those who followed dug into the tufa (the same soft volcanic rock from which catacombs were made) to create more than 1,000 separate cisterns, caves, secret passages, storage areas, and production areas for wine and olive oil. Much of the tufa removed was used as building blocks for the city that exists today, and some was partly ground into *pozzolana,* which was made into mortar. You can see the labyrinth of dugout chambers beneath the city on the **Orvieto Underground tour** (*Orvieto tourism office, Piazza del Duomo 24* ☏ *0763/341772*) run daily at 11, 12:15, 4, and 5:15. Admission for the hour-long English tour is €6. 🌐 *www.orvietounderground.it.*

Pozzo della Cava. If you're short on time but want a quick look at the cisterns and caves beneath the city, head for the Pozzo della Cava, an Etruscan well for spring water. ✉ *Via della Cava 28* ☎ *0763/342373* 🎟 *€3* 🕐 *Tues.–Fri. 9–8.*

WHERE TO EAT

The streets around the Duomo are lined with all types of bars and restaurants where you can eat simple or elaborate food and try wines by the glass.

$$ UMBRIAN Fodor's Choice ★ 🍴 **Il Giglio D'Oro.** A great view of the Duomo is coupled with superb food. Eggplant is transformed into an elegant custard with black truffles in the *sformatino di melenzane con vellutata al tartuffo nero.* Pastas, like *ombrichelli al pesto umbro,* are traditional, but perhaps with a new twist like fresh coriander leaves instead of the usual basil. Lamb roasted in a crust of bread is delicately seasoned with a tomato cream sauce. The wine cellar includes some rare vintages. [$] *Average main: €20* ✉ *Piazza Duomo 8* ☎ *0763/341903* 🕐 *Closed Wed.*

$$ UMBRIAN 🍴 **Le Grotte del Funaro.** Dine inside tufa caves under central Orvieto, where the two windows afford splendid views of the hilly countryside. The traditional Umbrian food is reliably good, with simple grilled meats and vegetables and pizzas. Oddly, though, the food is outclassed by an extensive wine list, with top local and Italian labels and quite a few rare vintages. [$] *Average main: €19* ✉ *Via Ripa Serancia 41* ☎ *0763/343276* ✍ *Reservations essential* 🕐 *Closed 1 wk in July.*

$$ UMBRIAN 🍴 **Trattoria La Grotta.** Franco, the owner, has been in this location for more than 20 years and has attracted a steady American clientele without losing his local following—or his touch with homemade pasta, perhaps with a duck or wild-boar sauce. Roast lamb, veal, and pork are all good, and the desserts are homemade. Franco knows the local wines well and has a carefully selected list, including some from smaller but excellent wineries, so ask about them. [$] *Average main: €18* ✉ *Via Luca Signorelli 5* ☎ *0763/341348* 🕐 *Closed Tues.*

WHERE TO STAY

For expanded hotel reviews, visit Fodors.com.

$$ HOTEL 🏨 **Hotel Palazzo Piccolomini.** A 16th-century family palazzo has been beautifully restored, with inviting public spaces and handsome guest quarters where contemporary surroundings are accented with old beams, vaulted ceilings, and other distinctive touches. **Pros:** peaceful atmosphere; efficient staff; good location. **Cons:** slightly overpriced. [$] *Rooms from: €150* ✉ *Piazza Ranieri 36* ☎ *0763/341743* 🌐 *www.palazzopiccolomini.it* 🛏 *28 rooms, 3 suites* 🍽 *Breakfast.*

NARNI

13 km (8 miles) southwest of Terni, 46 km (29 miles) southeast of Orvieto.

Once a bustling and important town at a major crossroads on the Via Flaminia, Narni is now a quiet backwater with only the occasional

CLOSE UP

Hiking the Umbrian Hills

Magnificent scenery makes the heart of Italy excellent walking, hiking, and mountaineering country. In Umbria, the area around Spoleto is particularly good; several pleasant, easy, and well-signed trails begin at the far end of the Ponte alle Torri bridge over Monteluco. From Cannara, an easy half-hour walk leads to the fields of Pian d'Arca, the site of Saint Francis's sermon to the birds. For slightly more arduous walks, you can follow the saint's path, uphill from Assisi to the Eremo delle Carceri, and then continue along the trails that crisscross Monte Subasio. At 4,250 feet, the Subasio's treeless summit affords views of Assisi, Perugia, far-off Gubbio, and the distant mountain ranges of Abruzzo.

For even more challenging hiking, the northern reaches of the Valnerina are exceptional; the mountains around Norcia should not be missed. Throughout Umbria and the Marches, you'll find that most recognized walking and hiking trails are marked with the distinctive red-and-white blazes of the Club Alpino Italiano. Tourist offices are a good source for walking and climbing itineraries to suit all ages and levels of ability, while bookstores, *tabacchi* (tobacconists), and *edicole* (newsstands) often have maps and hiking guides that detail the best routes in their area. Depending on the length and location of your walk, it can be important that you have comfortable walking shoes or boots, appropriate attire, and plenty of water to drink.

tourist invading its hilltop streets. Modern development is kept out of sight in the new town of Narni Scalo, below. This means that you'll find the older neighborhood safely preserved behind, and in the case of Narni's subterranean Roman ruins, beneath, the town's sturdy walls.

GETTING HERE

From Perugia, take the E45 highway toward Rome. Merge onto the SS675, then take the exit to San Gemini and follow signs for Narni Scalo. The drive takes around 1½ hours. There are also regular trains from Perugia.

VISITOR INFORMATION

Terni Tourism Office. Stop here for information about Narni and a number of other smaller towns. ⊠ *Via Cassian Bon 4, Terni* ☎ *0744/423047* ⊕ *www.regioneumbria.eu.*

EXPLORING

Roman Aqueduct. You can take a unique tour of Narni's underground Roman aqueduct—the only one open to the public in all of Italy—but it's not for the claustrophobic. Contact Narni Sotterranea at least ten days ahead to book a visit. ⊠ *Narni Sotterranea, Via San Bernardo 12* ☎ *0744/722292* ⊕ *www.narnisotterranea.it* ⊠ *€20* ☼ *Apr.–Oct., by appointment.*

WHERE TO EAT

$$ UMBRIAN 🍴 **Il Cavallino.** Run by the third generation of the Bussetti family, this trattoria is south of Narni on the Via Flaminia. The most dependable menu selections are the grilled meats. Rabbit roasted with rosemary and sage and juicy grilled T-bone steaks are house favorites; in the winter, phone ahead to request the wild pigeon. The wine list has a limited selection of dependable local varieties. [$] *Average main: €15* ✉ *Via Flaminia Romana 220, 3 km (2 miles) south of center* ☎ *0744/761020* ⏲ *Closed Tues. and Dec. 20–26.*

VALNERINA

Terni is 13 km (8 miles) northeast of Narni, 27 km (17 miles) southeast of Spoleto.

The Valnerina (the valley of the River Nera, to the east of Spoleto) is the most beautiful of central Italy's many well-kept secrets. The twisting roads that serve the rugged landscape are poor, but the drive is well worth the effort for its forgotten medieval villages and dramatic mountain scenery.

GETTING HERE

You can head into the area from Terni on the S209, or on the SP395bis north of Spoleto, which links the Via Flaminia (S3) with the middle reaches of the Nera Valley through a tunnel.

EXPLORING

Cascata delle Marmore. The road east of Terni (SS Valnerina) leads 10 km (6 miles) to the Cascata delle Marmore (Waterfalls of Marmore), which, at 541 feet, are the highest in Europe. A canal was dug by the Romans in the 3rd century BC to prevent flooding in the nearby agricultural plains. Nowadays the waters are often diverted to provide hydroelectric power for Terni, reducing the roaring falls to an unimpressive trickle, so check with the information office at the falls (there's a timetable on their website in English) or with Terni's tourist office before heading here. On summer evenings, when the falls are in full spate, the cascading water is floodlit to striking effect. The falls are usually at their most energetic at midday and at around 4 pm. This is a good place for hiking, except in December and January, when most trails may be closed. ✉ *SP79 10 km (6 miles) east of Terni* ☎ *0744/62982* 🌐 *www.marmorefalls.it* 🎟 *€9* ⏲ *May, weekends noon–1 and 4–5; June–Aug., daily 11–10; mid-Mar.–Apr. and Sept., weekends noon–9; Jan.–mid-Mar., weekends noon–4.*

Norcia. The birthplace of Saint Benedict, Norcia is best known for its Umbrian pork and truffles. Norcia exports truffles to France and hosts a truffle festival, the Sagra del Tartufo, every February. The surrounding mountains provide spectacular hiking. ✉ *67 km (42 miles) northeast of Terni.*

Piano Grande. A mountain plain 25 km (15 miles) to the northeast of the valley, Piano Grande is a hang glider's paradise and a wonderful place for a picnic or to fly a kite. It's also nationally famous for the quality of the lentils grown here, which are a traditional part of every Italian New Year's feast.

7

THE MARCHES

An excursion from Umbria into the Marches region allows you to see a part of Italy rarely visited by foreigners. Not as wealthy as Tuscany or Umbria, the Marches has a diverse landscape of mountains and beaches, and marvelous views. Like that of neighbors to the west, the patchwork of rolling hills of Le Marche (as it's known in Italian) is stitched with grapevines and olive trees, bearing luscious wine and olive oil.

Traveling here isn't as easy as in Umbria or Tuscany. Beyond the narrow coastal plain and away from major towns, the roads are steep and twisting. An efficient bus service connects the coastal town of Pesaro to Urbino. Train travel in the region is slow, however, and stops are limited—although you can reach Ascoli Piceno by rail.

URBINO

75 km (47 miles) north of Gubbio, 116 km (72 miles) northeast of Perugia, 230 km (143 miles) east of Florence.

Majestic Urbino, atop a steep hill with a skyline of towers and domes, is something of a surprise to come upon. Although quite remote, it was once a center of learning and culture almost without rival in Western Europe. The town looks much as it did in the glory days of the 15th century: a cluster of warm brick and pale stone buildings, all topped with russet-color tile roofs. The focal point is the immense and beautiful Palazzo Ducale.

The city is home to the small but prestigious Università di Urbino—one of the oldest in the world—and the streets are usually filled with students. Urbino is very much a college town, with the usual array of bookshops, bars, and coffeehouses. In summer the Italian student population is replaced by foreigners who come to study Italian language and arts at several prestigious private fine-arts academies.

Urbino's fame rests on the reputation of three of its native sons: Duke Federico da Montefeltro (1422–82), the enlightened warrior-patron who built the Palazzo Ducale; Raffaello Sanzio (1483–1520), or Raphael, one of the most influential painters in history and an embodiment of the spirit of the Renaissance; and the architect Donato Bramante (1444–1514), who translated the philosophy of the Renaissance into buildings of grace and beauty. Unfortunately there's little work by either Bramante or Raphael in the city, but the duke's influence can still be felt strongly.

GETTING HERE

Take the SS3bis from Perugia, and follow the directions for Gubbio and Cesena. Exit at Umbertide and take the SS219, then the SS452, and at Calmazzo, the SS73bis to Urbino.

VISITOR INFORMATION

Urbino Tourism Office ✉ *Piazza de Rinascimento 1* ☎ *0722/2613* ⊕ *www.comune.urbino.ps.it.*

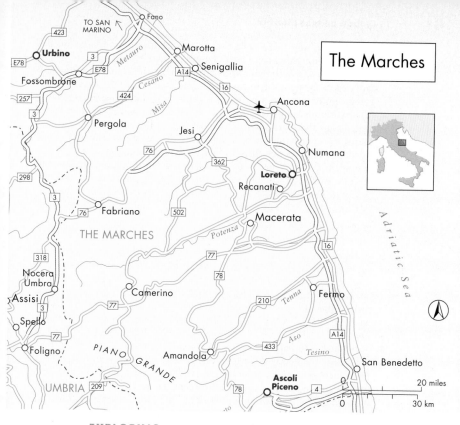

EXPLORING

Casa Natale di Raffaello (*House of Raphael*). This is the house in which the painter was born and where he took his first steps in painting, under the direction of his artist father. There's some debate about the fresco of the Madonna here; some say it's by Raphael, whereas others attribute it to the father—with Raphael's mother and the young painter himself standing in as models for the Madonna and Child. ⊠ *Via Raffaello 57* ☎ *0722/320105* 🖃 *€3.50* ⊙ *Mon.–Sat. 9–2, Sun. 10–1.*

Fodor'sChoice
★
Palazzo Ducale (*Ducal Palace*). The Palazzo Ducale holds a place of honor in the city. If the Renaissance was, ideally, a celebration of the nobility of man and his works, of the light and purity of the soul, then there's no place in Italy, the birthplace of the Renaissance, where these tenets are better illustrated. From the moment you enter the peaceful courtyard, you know you're in a place of grace and beauty, the harmony of the building reflecting the high ideals of the time. Today the palace houses the **Galleria Nazionale delle Marche** (National Museum of the Marches), with a superb collection of paintings, sculpture, and other objets d'art. Some works were originally the possessions of the Montefeltro family; others were brought here from churches and palaces throughout the region. Masterworks in the collection include Paolo Uccello's *Profanation of the Host,* Titian's *Resurrection* and

Last Supper, and Piero della Francesca's *Madonna of Senigallia.* But the gallery's highlight is Piero's enigmatic work long known as *The Flagellation of Christ.* Much has been written about this painting, and few experts agree on its meaning. Legend had it that the figures in the foreground represent a murdered member of the Montefeltro family (the barefoot young man) and his two killers. However, Sir John Pope-Hennessy—the preeminent scholar of Italian Renaissance art—argues that they represent the arcane subject of the vision of Saint Lawrence. Academic debates notwithstanding, the experts agree that the work is one of the painter's masterpieces. Piero himself thought so: it's one of the few works he signed (on the lowest step supporting the throne). ⊠ *Piazza Duca Federico* ☎ *0722/322625* ⊕ *www.comune.urbino.ps.it* ⊠ *€5* ⊙ *Mon. 8:30–2, Tues.–Sun. 8:30–7:15; ticket office closes at 6.*

WHERE TO EAT AND STAY

For expanded hotel reviews, visit Fodors.com.

$ ✕ **Angolo Divino.** At this osteria in the center of Urbino, tradition reigns
ITALIAN   supreme: the menu is written in local dialect, flanked by Italian and English translations. Dishes range from the deliciously simple spaghetti *col pane grattugiato* (with bread crumbs) to the temptingly rich *filetto al tartufo* (beef fillet with truffles). $ *Average main: €14* ⊠ *Via S. Andrea 14* ☎ *0722/327559* ⊙ *Closed Mon. and mid-Oct.–mid-Nov. No dinner Sun.*

$ ✕ **La Vecchia Fornarina.** Locals often crowd this small, two-room trat-
ITALIAN   toria near the Piazza della Repubblica. The specialty is meaty country fare, such as *coniglio* (rabbit) and *vitello alle noci* (veal cooked with walnuts) or *ai porcini* (with mushrooms). There's also a good selection of pasta dishes. $ *Average main: €12* ⊠ *Via Mazzini 14* ☎ *0722/320007* ⚐ *Reservations essential.*

$$ ⊡ **Hotel Bonconte.** Pleasant rooms just inside the city walls and close
HOTEL   to the Palazzo Ducale are decorated with a smattering of antiques, and those in front have views of the valley below Urbino. **Pros:** some nice views; away from the bustle. **Cons:** an uphill walk to town center; service can be sleepy. $ *Rooms from: €170* ⊠ *Via delle Mura 28* ☎ *0722/2463* ⊕ *www.viphotels.it* ⇆ *23 rooms, 2 suites* ⊙ *No meals.*

LORETO

31 km (19 miles) south of Ancona, 118 km (73 miles) southeast of Urbino.

There's a strong Renaissance feel about this hilltop town, which is home to one of the most important religious sites in Europe, the Santuario della Santa Casa (House of the Virgin Mary). Bramante and Sansovino gave the church its Renaissance look, although many other artists helped create its special atmosphere. Today the town revolves around the religious calendar; if you can be here on December 10, you will witness the Feast of the Translation of the Holy House, when huge bonfires are lighted to celebrate the miraculous arrival of the house in 1294.

GETTING HERE

If you're driving from Perugia, take the SS318 and then the SS76 highway to Fabriano and then on to Chiaravalle, where it merges with the A14 autostrada. The drive takes around 2½ hours. Trains also go to Loreto, but the station is about a mile outside the town center. Regular buses leave from the station to the center.

VISITOR INFORMATION

Loreto Tourism Office ☒ *Via Solari 3* ☏ *071/970276* ⊕ *www.turismo. marche.it.*

EXPLORING

Basilica della Santa Casa. Loreto is famous for one of the best-loved shrines in the world, that of the **Santuario della Santa Casa** (House of the Virgin Mary), within the Basilica della Santa Casa. Legend has it that angels moved the house from Nazareth, where the Virgin Mary was living at the time of the Annunciation, to this hilltop in 1295. The reason for this sudden and divinely inspired move was that Nazareth had fallen into the hands of Muslim invaders, whom the angelic hosts viewed as unsuitable keepers of this important shrine. Excavations made at the behest of the Catholic Church have shown that the house did once stand elsewhere and was brought to the hilltop—by either crusaders or a family named Angeli—around the time the angels (*angeli*) are said to have done the job.

The house itself consists of three rough stone walls contained within an elaborate marble tabernacle. Built around this centerpiece is the giant basilica of the Holy House, which dominates the town. Millions of visitors come to the site every year (particularly at Easter and on the December 10 Feast of the Holy House), and the little town of Loreto can become uncomfortably crowded with pilgrims. Many great Italian architects, including Bramante, Antonio da Sangallo the Younger (1483–1546), Giuliano da Sangallo (circa 1445–1516), and Sansovino (1467–1529), contributed to the design of the basilica. It was begun in the Gothic style in 1468 and continued in Renaissance style through the late Renaissance. The bell tower is by Luigi Vanvitelli (1700–73). Inside the church are a great many mediocre 19th- and 20th-century paintings but also some fine works by Renaissance masters such as Luca Signorelli and Melozzo da Forlì (1438–94).

If you're a nervous air traveler, you can take comfort in the fact that the Holy Virgin of Loreto is the patron saint of air travelers and that Pope John Paul II composed a prayer for a safe flight—available here in a half-dozen languages. ☒ *Piazza della Madonna* ☏ *071/970104* ⊕ *www. santuarioloreto.it* ☉ *Apr.–Sept., daily 6 am–8 pm; Oct.–Mar., daily 6:30 am–7:30 pm. Santuario della Santa Casa closed daily 12:30–2:30.*

ASCOLI PICENO

88 km (55 miles) south of Loreto, 105 km (65 miles) south of Ancona.

Ascoli Piceno sits in a valley ringed by steep hills and cut by the Tronto River. In Roman times it was one of central Italy's best-known market towns, and today, with almost 60,000 residents, it's a major fruit and olive producer, making it one of the most important towns in the region. Despite growth during the Middle Ages and at other times, the streets in the town center continue to reflect the grid pattern of the ancient Roman city. You'll even find the word *rua*, from the Latin *ruga*, used for "street" instead of the Italian *via*. Now largely closed to traffic, the city center is great to explore on foot.

GETTING HERE

From Perugia take the SS75 to Foligno, then merge onto the SS3 to Norcia. From here take the SS4 to Ascoli Piceno. There are also trains, but the journey would be quite long, taking you from Perugia to Ancona before changing for Ascoli Piceno.

VISITOR INFORMATION

Ascoli Piceno Tourism Office ⊠ *Piazza Aringo 7* ☎ *0736/253045* ⊕ *www. comune.ascolipiceno.it.*

EXPLORING

Piazza del Popolo. The heart of the town is the majestic Piazza del Popolo, dominated by the Gothic church of **San Francesco** and the **Palazzo del Popolo**, a 13th-century town hall that contains a graceful Renaissance courtyard. The square functions as the living room of the entire city and at dusk each evening is packed with people strolling and exchanging news and gossip—the sweetly antiquated ritual called the *passeggiata*, performed all over the country.

WHERE TO STAY

For expanded hotel reviews, visit Fodors.com.

$ **Il Pennile.** A modern, family-run hotel in a quiet residential area outside the old city center is pleasantly set amid a grove of olive trees. **Pros:** peaceful; a good budget option. **Cons:** distance from town center; basic rooms. $ *Rooms from: €70* ⊠ *Via G. Spalvieri* ☎ *0736/41645* ⊕ *www. hotelpennile.it* ⤴ *33 rooms* ⦿| *Breakfast.*

UNDERSTANDING FLORENCE & TUSCANY

Vocabulary

ITALIAN VOCABULARY

	ENGLISH	ITALIAN	PRONUNCIATION
BASICS			
	Yes/no	Sí/No	see/no
	Please	Per favore	pear fa-**vo**-ray
	Yes, please	Sí grazie	see **grah**-tsee-ay
	Thank you	Grazie	**grah**-tsee-ay
	You're welcome	Prego	**pray**-go
	Excuse me, sorry	Scusi	**skoo**-zee
	Sorry!	Mi dispiace!	mee dis-spee-**ah**-chay
	Good morning/ afternoon	Buongiorno	bwohn-**jor**-no
	Good evening	Buona sera	**bwoh**-na **say**-ra
	Good-bye	Arrivederci	a-ree-vah-**dare**-chee
	Mr. (Sir)	Signore	see-**nyo**-ray
	Mrs. (Ma'am)	Signora	see-**nyo**-ra
	Miss	Signorina	see-nyo-**ree**-na
	Pleased to meet you	Piacere	pee-ah-**chair**-ray
	How are you?	Come sta?	**ko**-may **stah**
	Very well, thanks	Bene, grazie	**ben**-ay **grah**-tsee-ay
	Hello (phone)	Pronto?	**proan**-to
NUMBERS			
	one	uno	**oo**-no
	two	due	**doo**-ay
	three	tre	Tray
	four	quattro	**kwah**-tro
	five	cinque	**cheen**-kway
	six	sei	Say
	seven	sette	**set**-ay
	eight	otto	**oh**-to
	nine	nove	**no**-vay
	ten	dieci	dee-**eh**-chee
	twenty	venti	**vain**-tee

ENGLISH	ITALIAN	PRONUNCIATION
thirty	trenta	**train**-ta
forty	quaranta	kwa-**rahn**-ta
fifty	cinquanta	cheen-**kwahn**-ta
sixty	sessanta	seh-**sahn**-ta
seventy	settanta	seh-**tahn**-ta
eighty	ottanta	o-**tahn**-ta
ninety	novanta	no-**vahn**-ta
one hundred	cento	**chen**-to
one thousand	mille	**mee**-lay
ten thousand	diecimila	dee-eh-chee-**mee**-la

USEFUL PHRASES

Do you speak English?	Parla inglese?	**par**-la een-**glay**-zay
I don't speak Italian	Non parlo italiano	non **par**-lo ee-tal-**yah**-no
I don't understand	Non capisco	non ka-**peess**-ko
Can you please repeat?	Può ripetere?	pwo ree-**pet**-ay-ray
Slowly!	Lentamente!	**len**-ta-men-tay
I don't know	Non lo so	non lo **so**
I'm American	Sono americano(a)	**so**-no a-may-ree-**kah**-no(a)
I'm British	Sono inglese	so-no een-**glay**-zay
What's your name?	Come si chiama?	**ko**-may see kee-**ah**-ma
My name is . . .	Mi chiamo . . .	mee kee-**ah**-mo
What time is it?	Che ore sono?	kay **o**-ray **so**-no
How?	Come?	**ko**-may
When?	Quando?	**kwan**-doe
Yesterday/today/tomorrow	Ieri/oggi/domani	**yer**-ee/**o**-jee/do-**mah**-nee
This morning	Stamattina/Oggi	sta-ma-**tee**-na/**o**-jee
afternoon	pomeriggio	po-mer-**ee**-jo

ENGLISH	ITALIAN	PRONUNCIATION
Tonight	Stasera	sta-**ser**-a
What?	Che cosa?	kay **ko**-za
Why?	Perché?	pear-**kay**
Who?	Chi?	Kee
Where is . . .	Dov'è . . .	doe-**veh**
the bus stop?	la fermata dell'autobus?	la fer-**mah**-tadel ow-toe-**booss**
the train station?	la stazione?	la sta-tsee-**oh**-nay
the subway	la metropolitana?	la may-tro-po-lee-**tah**-na
the terminal?	il terminale?	eel ter-mee-**nah**-lay
the post office?	l'ufficio postale?	loo-**fee**-cho po-**stah**-lay
the bank?	la banca?	la **bahn**-ka
the . . . hotel?	l'hotel . . .?	lo-**tel**
the store?	il negozio?	eel nay-**go**-tsee-o
the cashier?	la cassa?	la **kah**-sa
the . . . museum?	il museo . . .?	eel moo-**zay**-o
the hospital?	l'ospedale?	lo-spay-**dah**-lay
the elevator?	l'ascensore?	la-shen-**so**-ray
the restrooms?	Dov'è il bagno?	do-**vay** eel **bahn**-yo
Here/there	Qui/là	kwee/la
Left/right	A sinistra/a destra	a see-**neess**-tra/a **des**-tra
Straight ahead	Avanti dritto	a-**vahn**-tee **dree**-to
Is it near/far?	È vicino/lontano?	ay vee-**chee**-no/ lon-**tah**-no
I'd like . . .	Vorrei . . .	vo-**ray**
a room	una camera	**oo**-na **kah**-may-ra
the key	la chiave	la kee-**ah**-vay
a newspaper	un giornale	oon jor-**nah**-lay
a stamp	un francobollo	oon frahn-ko-**bo**-lo
I'd like to buy . . .	Vorrei comprare . . .	vo-**ray** kom-**prah**-ray

ENGLISH	ITALIAN	PRONUNCIATION
How much is it?	Quanto costa?	**kwahn**-toe **coast**-a
It's expensive/ cheap	È caro/economico	ay **car**-o/ ay-ko-**no**-mee-ko
A little/a lot	Poco/tanto	**po**-ko/**tahn**-to
More/less	Più/meno	pee-**oo**/**may**-no
Enough/too (much)	Abbastanza/troppo	a-bas-**tahn**-sa/tro-po
I am sick	Sto male	sto **mah**-lay
Call a doctor	Chiama un dottore	kee-**ah**-mah oondoe-**toe**-ray
Help!	Aiuto!	a-**yoo**-toe
Stop!	Alt!	ahlt
Fire!	Al fuoco!	ahl **fwo**-ko
Caution/Look out!	Attenzione!	a-ten-**syon**-ay

DINING OUT

A bottle of . . .	Una bottiglia di . . .	**oo**-na bo-**tee**-lee-ahdee
A cup of . . .	Una tazza di . . .	**oo**-na **tah**-tsa dee
A glass of . . .	Un bicchiere di . . .	oon bee-key-**air**-ay dee
Bill/check	Il conto	eel **cone**-toe
Bread	Il pane	eel **pah**-nay
Breakfast	La prima colazione	la **pree**-ma ko-la-**tsee**-oh-nay
Cocktail/aperitif	L'aperitivo	la-pay-ree-**tee**-vo
Dinner	La cena	la **chen**-a
Fixed price menu	Menù a prezzo fisso	may-**noo** a **pret**-so **fee**-so
Fork	La forchetta	la for-**ket**-a
I am diabetic	Ho il diabete	o eel dee-a-**bay**-tay
I am vegetarian	Sono vegetariano(a)	**so**-no vay-jay-ta-ree-**ah**-no/a
I'd like . . .	Vorrei . . .	vo-**ray**
I'd like to order	Vorrei ordinare	vo-**ray** or-dee-**nah**-ray
Is service included?	Il servizio è incluso?	eel ser-**vee**-tzee-o ay een-**kloo**-zo

ENGLISH	ITALIAN	PRONUNCIATION
It's good/bad	È buono/cattivo	ay **bwo**-no/ka-**tee**-vo
It's hot/cold	È caldo/freddo	ay **kahl**-doe/**fred**-o
Knife	Il coltello	eel kol-**tel**-o
Lunch	Il pranzo	eel **prahnt**-so
Menu	Il menù	eel may-**noo**
Napkin	Il tovagliolo	eel toe-va-lee-**oh**-lo
Please give me . . .	Mi dia . . .	mee **dee**-a
Salt	Il sale	eel **sah**-lay
Spoon	Il cucchiaio	eel koo-kee-**ah**-yo
Sugar	Lo zucchero	lo **tsoo**-ker-o
Waiter/Waitress	Cameriere/ cameriera	ka-mare-**yer**-ay/ ka-mare-**yer**-a
Wine list	La lista dei vini	la **lee**-sta **day**-ee **vee**-nee

TRAVEL SMART
FLORENCE &
TUSCANY

GETTING HERE AND AROUND

▌ AIR TRAVEL

If you want to fly into Florence from the United States, you'll have to make connections in any number of major European cities (like Paris, Frankfurt, or London). Delta Airlines has a (seasonal) nonstop flight from New York's JFK to Pisa's Galileo Galilei. Florence is one hour away by train, and the train stops at the airport. At least, it used to: at press time, service from Pisa Aeroporto to Pisa Centrale has been temporarily halted. It is unclear when service will resume.

Airline Security Issues Transportation Security Administration ⊕ *www.tsa.gov.*

AIRPORTS

The major gateways to Italy include Rome's Aeroporto Leonardo da Vinci (airport code FCO), better known as Fiumicino, and Milan's Aeroporto Malpensa (MIL). Flights to Florence make connections at Fiumicino and Malpensa.

Florence is served by Aeroporto A. Vespucci (FLR), also called Peretola, and by Aeroporto Galileo Galilei (PSA), which is about a mile outside the center of Pisa and about one hour from Florence.

Perugia is served by Aeroporto S. Egidio (PEG), a small airport that receives connecting flights from Milan's Malpensa airport and London's Stansted airport.

Italy's airports have restaurants, snack bars and Internet or Wi-Fi access. Each airport has at least one nearby hotel—the city centers of Florence and Pisa are only 15 minutes away by taxi, so if you encounter a long delay, spend it in town.

Airports in Italy have been ramping up security measures, which include random baggage inspections and the presence of bomb-sniffing dogs.

Airport Information Aeroporto A. Vespucci (*FLR, usually called Peretola*) ☎ *055/30615* ⊕ *www.aeroporto.firenze.it.* **Aeroporto Galileo Galilei** (*PSA*) ☎ *050/849300*

⊕ *www.pisa-airport.com.* **Aeroporto Leonardo da Vinci** (*FCO, more commonly known as Fiumicino*) ☎ *06/65951* ⊕ *www.adr.it.* **Aeroporto Malpensa** (*MIL*) ☎ *02/232323* ⊕ *www.sea-aeroportimilano.it.* **Aeroporto S. Egidio** (*PEG*) ☎ *075/592141* ⊕ *www.airport.umbria.it.*

▌TIP→ Ask the local tourist board about hotel and local transportation packages that include tickets to major museum exhibits or other special events.

GROUND TRANSPORTATION

It takes about 20 minutes to get from **Aeroporto A. Vespucci** into Florence. Taxis are readily available, charging about €25, with a €1 surcharge for each bag and a €3 surcharge for nighttime trips. Outside the main terminal to the right is a bus stop where the SITA bus leaves every 30 minutes, making its final stop at the main Florence train station (Santa Maria Novella)—a ticket costs €6.

Taxis from **Aeroporto Galileo Galilei** to central Pisa cost about €20. At press time, train service from the airport to Pisa Centrale was suspended. A train ride from Pisa to Florence takes just over an hour (€7.90). You can also reach Florence from the Pisa airport by taxi (about €200) or by bus—the Terravision service runs from the Pisa airport to the train station in Florence (70 minutes; one-way €4.99, round-trip €9.98).

The train from **Aeroporto Leonardo da Vinci** stops at five stations in Rome and takes one hour (cost: €14) to get to the city. A taxi from the airport to the central train station costs about €60.

Metered taxis are available outside both Arrivals and Departures areas of **Aeroporto Malpensa.** The journey time to central Milan is around 50 minutes; the taxi fare is anywhere from €75 to €90. The Malpensa Shuttle departs every half hour from the train station at Milano Centrale; it's €10 one-way and takes about an hour.

FLIGHTS

TO FLORENCE, TUSCANY, AND UMBRIA

Air travel to Italy is frequent and virtually problem-free (excepting frequently delayed luggage from Paris transfers). Sometimes, however, airport- or airline-related union strikes may cause delays. These delays are usually reported in advance. Alitalia, Italy's national flag carrier, has the most nonstop flights to Rome and Milan. Frequent flights are available from the United States aboard Lufthansa, Air France, United, US Airways, and Delta; these stop once in Europe before they or their code-sharing partners continue on to Florence or Pisa.

WITHIN ITALY

Alitalia—in addition to other major European airlines and smaller, privately run companies such as Ryanair, Meridiana, and Air One—has an extensive network of flights within Italy. Ask your domestic or Italian travel agent about discounts.

Information Air One ☎ 892/444 in Italy, 39/0912551047 elsewhere ⊕ www.flyairone. it. **Alitalia** ☎ 39/0665649 elsewhere, 89/2010 in Italy ⊕ www.alitalia.com. **American Airlines** ☎ 800/433–7300 ⊕ www.aa.com. **Delta Airlines** ☎ 800/221–1212 for U.S. reservations ⊕ www.delta.com. **Meridiana** ☎ 0789/52600 in Italy ⊕ www.meridiana.it. **Ryanair** ☎ 0900/1000550 ⊕ www.ryanair.com. **United Airlines** ☎ 800/864–8331 for U.S. reservations, 800/538–2929 for international reservations ⊕ www.united.com. **US Airways** ☎ 800/428–4322 for U.S. and Canada reservations ⊕ www.usairways.com.

▮ BOAT AND FERRY TRAVEL

Ferries (*traghetti*) connect the mainland with the Tuscan islands, including Elba, Capraia, Pianosa, Giglio, and Giannutri. Hydrofoil (*aliscafo*) service goes to many destinations; it is generally twice as fast as the ferries—and double the price. All ferry service is considerably more frequent in summer.

Passenger and car ferries serve Elba. If you're traveling in July or August, try to make reservations at least a month in advance. Two ferry lines operate along the coast of Cinque Terre: Golfo Paradiso, which operates from June to September from Genoa and Camogli to the Cinque Terre villages of Monterosso al Mare and Vernazza; and the smaller, but more frequent, Golfo dei Poeti, which stops at each village (from Portovenere to Riomaggiore, except for Corniglia) four times a day.

The easiest place to find schedules and fare information for Tuscany ferry service is on each company's website. If you are already in the area, local tourist information offices, tourist agencies, and the ticket offices at the port will have printed schedules. Most ferry operators accept credit cards or cash, but no traveler's checks (the Toremar and Moby Lines ferry companies definitely do not accept traveler's checks).

Information Golfo dei Poeti ☎ 0187/732987 ⊕ www.navigazionegolfodeipoeti.it. **Golfo Paradiso** ☎ 0185/772091 ⊕ www. golfoparadiso.it. **Moby Lines** ☎ 199/303040 ⊕ www.mobylines.it. **Toremar** ☎ 0586/896 113 ⊕ www.toremar.it.

▮ BUS TRAVEL

Italy's bus network is extensive, but because of its low cost and convenience train travel is usually a more attractive option. Bus schedules are often drawn up with commuters and students in mind, and service may be sporadic on Sunday. That said, regional bus companies often provide the only means (not including car travel) of getting to out-of-the-way places. Even when this isn't the case, buses can be faster and more direct than local trains, so it's a good idea to compare bus and train schedules.

CLASSES

Both public and private buses offer only one class of service. Cleanliness and comfort levels are high on private buses, which have comfortable seats, but no toilets.

CUTTING COSTS

Public bus lines offer student and monthly passes. Private lines offer one-, three-, and six-month passes. Children under 3 feet in height ride free if they're traveling with an adult and don't require their own seat. Infant car seats are permitted on private bus lines.

DISCOUNT PASSES

None of the cities in Tuscany and Umbria are big enough to make the various discount bus pass schemes that appear and disappear with regularity worth the trouble. Most weeklong tourists to Florence, the largest city, will ride the city buses no more than four times at a cost of €1.20 per ticket. There is a 24-hour pass (€5) and a three-day pass (€12). A month-long pass is available for €35. Students staying for a semester in Florence may wish to look into an ATAF Student Pass, a month-long pass costing €23. Passes are available at the central bus station located at the side of the train station, and may be renewed at newsstands. See ⊕ *www.ataf. net* for information.

ATAF has an arrangement with Firenze City Sightseeing, a red open-top sightseeing bus in Florence. For €18.50 (€9 for children under 15) you can ride both it and all of the city buses for a 24-hour period, hopping on and off at your whim. Pisa also has a City SightSeeing hop-on/off tour bus that runs from April to November (€14 adults/€6.50 children).

In Perugia the public bus system is operated by APM, with the fare of €1 for a 70-minute ticket.

FARES AND SCHEDULES

You may purchase tickets for city buses with cash at newsstands or tobacco shops. The Florence public bus service ATAF allows customers to buy tickets, with a surcharge, in cash, on the bus from the driver—exact fare is necessary, as no change is given. You must validate the bus ticket in the machine on the bus. For private lines, tickets may be purchased with cash at the bus station or at travel agencies bearing the bus line's logo. Be sure to validate the ticket either at the bus station or on the bus as soon as you board. Bus schedules for private lines may be obtained online or at the bus station; city bus schedules for Florence (ATAF) are available online at ⊕ *www.ataf.net*.

PAYING

Credit cards and traveler's checks are generally not accepted for private-line bus tickets (some travel agencies may accept them), and public bus tickets purchased at newsstands and tobacco shops must be paid for in cash.

RESERVATIONS

Public bus lines do not issue reservations. For some private bus line direct routes (i.e., during commute hours) reservations are required.

Bus Information APM Perugia
☎ *075/506781* ⊕ *www.umbriamobilita.it.*
ATAF ✉ *Stazione Centrale di Santa Maria Novella* ☎ *055/5650642* ⊕ *www.ataf.net.*
Firenze City SightSeeing ⊕ *www.city-sightseeing.com.* **Lazzi Eurolines** ✉ *Via Mercadante 2* ☎ *0573/1937 900* ⊕ *www.lazzi. it.* **SITA** ✉ *Via Santa Caterina da Siena 17/r* ☎ *no phone* ⊕ *www.sitabus.it.*

▌ CAR TRAVEL

Tuscany and Umbria have an extensive network of *autostrade* (toll highways), complemented by equally well-maintained but free *superstrade* (expressways). The ticket you are issued upon entering an autostrada must be returned when you exit and pay the toll; on some shorter autostrade, mainly connecting highways, the toll is paid upon entering. Telepass, debit payment cards on sale at many autostrada locations (€25 at tollbooths), make paying tolls easier and faster by avoiding the hunt for change to pay the toll. A *raccordo* is a ring road surrounding a city. *Strade regionale* and *strade provinciale* (regional and provincial highways, denoted by *S, SS, SR,* or *SP* numbers) are usually two-lane roads, as are all secondary roads; directions and turnoffs on toll roads and expressways are frequent and clear; secondary roads aren't always clearly marked. Be prepared for fast and impatient fellow drivers.

GASOLINE

Gas stations are located at frequent intervals along the main highways and autostrade. In case you run out of gas along the toll roads or the main free superstrade, emergency telephones are provided. To find the phone, look on the pavement at the shoulder of the highway where painted arrows and the term "SOS" point in the direction of the nearest phone.

Gas stations on autostrade are usually open 24 hours. Gas stations in towns and cities are usually located on the periphery; they're rarely found in the city center. These stations are generally open Monday through Saturday 7–7 with a break at lunchtime.

Many stations have automatic self-service pumps that accept only bills of €5, €10, €20, and €50 and don't give change; if you want a receipt (*ricevuta*), you have to push a button before starting the process. Full-service stations or those with an attendant take both cash and credit cards. It's not customary to tip the attendant when full service is provided.

As of this writing, gas (*benzina*) costs about €1.80 a liter. It's available in unleaded (*verde*) and super unleaded (*super*). Many rental cars in Italy take only diesel (*gasolio*), which costs less per liter; ask about the fuel type before you leave the rental office.

PARKING

Parking is at a premium in most towns and cities, but especially in the *centri storici* (historic centers), which are filled with narrow streets and restricted circulation zones. It's advisable to leave your car only in guarded parking areas. In Florence such indoor parking costs about €23–€30 for 12–24 hours; outside attended parking costs about €10–€20. Parking in an area signposted "zona disco" (disk zone), usually found only in small towns, is allowed for limited periods (from 30 minutes to two hours or more—the limit is posted); if you don't have the cardboard disk (located in the glove box of your rental car) to show what time you parked, you can use a piece of paper. The *parcometro*, the Italian version of metered parking in which you put coins into a machine for a stamped ticket that you leave on the dashboard, has been introduced in most large towns and cities.

Parking regulations are strictly enforced both in the cities and small towns. Fines run as high as €70 (more for taking a space designated for people with disabilities), and towing (or tire clamps) is a possible penalty in Florence. Car-rental companies may use your credit card to be reimbursed for any fines you incur during your rental period. In Tuscany and Umbria vandalism and theft of cars are rare. Nevertheless, don't leave luggage or valuables in your car, especially in cities and large towns where thieves target rental cars.

ROAD CONDITIONS

Driving on the back roads of Tuscany and Umbria isn't difficult as long as you're on the alert for bicycles, scooters, and passing cars. In addition, street and road signs are often missing or placed in awkward spots, so a good map and patience are essential. Be aware that some maps may not use the *SR* or *SP* (*stradale regionale* and *stradale provinciale*) highway designations, which took the place of the old *SS* designations in 2004. They may use the old *SS* designation or no numbering at all. Autostrade are well maintained, as are most interregional highways. The condition of provincial (county) roads varies, but road maintenance at this level is generally good. In many small hill towns the streets are winding and extremely narrow; consider parking at the edge of town and exploring on foot.

Most autostrade have two lanes in both directions; the left lane is used only for passing. Italians drive fast and are impatient with those who don't, so tailgating is the norm here; the only way to avoid it is to get out of the way.

ROAD MAPS

Michelin and Touring Club Italiano, which have shops in major Italian cities, both produce good road maps. The Michelin website (⊕ *www.viamichelin. com*) is a good source of driving instructions and maps. Do note their highly optimistic travel times. You can also get free street maps for most Tuscan and Umbrian towns at local information offices.

RULES OF THE ROAD

Driving is on the right. Regulations largely resemble those in the United States, except that the police have the power to levy on-the-spot fines. In some Italian towns the use of the horn is forbidden in certain, if not all, areas; a large sign, "zona di silenzio" (silent zone), indicates where this is the case. Speed limits are 130 kph (80 mph) on autostrade and 100 kph (60 mph) on state and provincial roads, unless otherwise marked. Enforcement of speed limits varies from region to region. If you are driving on superstrade, pay particular attention to the gray machines that appear periodically along the road. They snap photos if you're exceeding the speed limit, and the rental-car company will eventually catch up with you to pay the fine. Stiff penalties include high fines and suspension of driving privileges. Penalties for driving after drinking are heavy, too, including license suspension and the additional possibility of six months' imprisonment. The legal maximum blood-alcohol level is 0.05.

Right turns on red lights are forbidden. Headlights are required to be on day and night while driving on all roads (large or small) outside of municipalities. Seat belts are required for adults, and infant and children's car seats are compulsory for babies and toddlers.

CAR RENTAL

When you reserve a car, ask about cancellation penalties, taxes, drop-off charges (if you're planning to pick up the car in one city and leave it in another), and surcharges (for being under or over a certain age, for additional drivers, or for driving across state or country borders or beyond a specific distance from your point of rental). All these things can add substantially to your costs. Request child car seats and extras, such as GPS, when you book. Rates are sometimes—but not always—better if you book in advance or reserve through a rental agency's website. There are other reasons to book ahead, though: for popular destinations, during busy times of the year, or to ensure that you get certain types of cars (vans, SUVs, exotic sports cars).

▓ TIP➔ Make sure that a confirmed reservation guarantees you a car. Agencies sometimes overbook, particularly for busy weekends and holiday periods.

Florence, Tuscany, and Umbria have an intricate network of autostrade routes, good highways, and secondary roads, making renting a car a better but expensive alternative (because of high gas prices and freeway tolls) to public transportation. A rental car can be a good investment for carefree countryside rambles, offering time to explore more remote towns.

Having a car in major cities, however, often leads to parking and traffic headaches, plus the additional expense of garage and parking fees. In major cities, such as Florence, Siena, and Perugia, there are restricted zones for cars. These areas are camera-monitored. If you drive to your hotel in the city center of these cities, inquire at the front desk of your hotel as to whether your rental car's license tag number must be submitted by the hotel to the police or traffic authority. Failure to do this may result in a large fine being levied on your car-rental company and passed on to you.

Major car-rental companies offer Ford-type cars (such as the Ford Fusion) and Fiats in various sizes and in good condition, all with air-conditioning. The local rental companies provide good service and, depending on the time of year, may have greater availability than the well-known international companies. Because most Italian cars have standard transmissions, automatics are more expensive and must be reserved well in advance. Mileage is usually unlimited, although certain offers limit included mileage to 150 km (93 miles) a day, after which you must pay for additional miles.

Most major U.S. car-rental companies have offices or affiliates in Italy, but the rates are generally better if you make a reservation from abroad rather than from within Italy. Each company's rental prices are uniform throughout Italy, so you won't save money by, for example, picking up a vehicle from a city rental office rather than from an airport location.

In Italy a U.S. driver's license is acceptable to rent a car, but you might also want to consider getting an International Driver's Permit (IDP). Italy, by law at least, requires non-Europeans to carry an IDP along with their domestic license because the IDP states in Italian (and a dozen other languages) that your license is valid. In practice, it depends on the police officer who pulls you over whether you will be penalized for not carrying the IDP.

In Italy you must be 18 years old to drive a car. Most rental companies will not rent to someone under age 21, refuse to rent any car larger than an economy or subcompact car to anyone under age 23, and further require customers under age 23 to pay by credit card. Additional drivers must be identified in the contract and must meet age requirements. There may be an additional daily fee for more than one driver. Upon rental, all companies require credit cards as a warranty; to rent bigger cars (2,000 cc or more), you must often show two credit cards. There are no special restrictions on senior-citizen drivers. Book car seats, required for children under age three, in advance. The cost is generally about €36 for the duration of the rental.

Hiring a car with a driver can come in handy, particularly if you plan to do some wine tasting. Ask at your hotel for recommended drivers, or inquire at the local tourist-information office. Typically, drivers are paid by the day, and are usually rewarded with a tip of about 15% on completion of the journey.

CAR-RENTAL INSURANCE

Italy requires car-rental companies to include Collision Damage Waiver (CDW) coverage in quoted rates. Ask your rental company about other coverage when you reserve the car and/or pick it up.

Everyone who rents a car wonders whether the insurance that the rental companies offer is worth the expense. No one has a simple answer. It all depends on how much regular insurance you have, how comfortable you are with risk, and whether or not money is an issue.

▌ TRAIN TRAVEL

The fastest trains on the Ferrovie dello Stato (FS), the Italian State Railways, are the Eurostar trains, operating on several main lines, including Rome–Milan via Florence and Bologna. A new high-speed Eurostar called Alta Velocita runs between Milan and Naples, stopping in Florence. Seat reservations are mandatory on Eurostar trains. Some Eurostar trains (the ETR 460 trains) have little aisle and luggage space (though there is a space near the door where you can put large bags). To avoid having to squeeze through narrow aisles, board only at your car (look for the number on the reservation ticket and match it to the number on the exterior of the car; it's usually on the door). The next-fastest trains are the Intercity (IC) trains, for which you pay a supplemental fee and seat reservations may be required (which is always advisable, especially during high season). *Interregionale* trains usually make more stops and are a little slower. *Regionale* and *locale* trains are the slowest and the most unpleasant—most cars are covered in graffiti, dirty, crowded, and geared to commuters. When train workers go on strike (which is often), the *regionali* trains are the ones that stop running.

There is refreshment service on all long-distance trains, with mobile carts and a cafeteria or dining car. Tap water on trains is not drinkable.

Traveling overnight can be efficient but it's not inexpensive (compared to the cost of a hotel room); never leave your belongings unattended (even for a minute), and make sure the door of your compartment is locked.

Train service between Milan, Florence, Rome, and Naples is frequent throughout the day. For the most part, trains stick to the schedule, although delays may occur during peak tourist season. Train strikes of various kinds are also frequent, so it's a good idea to make sure the train you want to take is in fact running.

The train from Rome to Florence takes 90 minutes; Rome to Perugia takes 2½ hours; Milan to Florence takes about 3 hours (it's another 2 hours by train from Florence to Perugia).

CLASSES

Many Italian trains have first and second classes, but regional trains frequently don't have first class. On interregional trains the higher first-class fare gets you little more than a clean doily (metaphorically speaking) on the headrest of your seat, but on long-distance trains you get wider seats, more legroom, and better ventilation and lighting. At peak travel times first-class train travel is worth the difference. One advantage of traveling first class is that the cars are almost always uncrowded—or, at the very least, less crowded than the second-class compartments. A first-class ticket, in Italian, is *prima classe*; second is *seconda classe*. Remember always to make seat reservations in advance, for either class, on Eurostar or Intercity (IC) trains.

CUTTING COSTS

If you're traveling only in Tuscany and Umbria, rail passes won't save you money. If Italy is your only destination in Europe, consider purchasing a Eurail Italy Pass, which allows a limited number of travel days within one month. Four days of travel cost about €208 (first class) or about €169 (second class); for further details, access Eurail's website. Note that you must purchase your Eurail Italy Pass before arriving in Italy.

Don't assume that a rail pass guarantees a seat on the trains you wish to ride; you need to reserve seats ahead even if you use a rail pass. There's a nominal fee (usually €5) for the reservation.

Information and Passes Eurail Italy Pass ☎ *800/6228600* ⊕ *www.eurail.com/eurail-countries-italy.* **RailPass** ⊕ *www.railpass.com.*

FARES AND SCHEDULES

You can buy train tickets for nearby destinations (within a 200-km [124-mile] range) at newsstands or tobacconists (usually only those inside the station) and at ticket machines in stations, as well as at the ticket windows at the station or at travel agencies in town. Tickets are good for two months after the date of issue, but right before departure you must validate tickets in the yellow machines in the departure area. Once stamped, tickets are valid for 6 hours on distances of less than 200 km (124 miles) or for 24 hours on longer distances. If you wish to stop along the way and your final destination is more than 200 km [124 miles] away, you can stamp the ticket a second time before it expires so as to extend its validity to a maximum of 48 hours from the time it was first stamped. If you forget to stamp your ticket in the machine, or you didn't make it to the station in time to buy the ticket, you must immediately seek out a conductor. Don't wait for the conductor to find out that you're without a valid ticket (unless the train is over-crowded and walking becomes impossible), as he or she might charge you a hefty fine. However, you often can avoid getting fined if you immediately write the time, date, and name of the departure station on the back of the ticket and sign it—essentially "validating" it and making it unusable for another trip.

Kilometric tickets—tickets priced according to kilometer amounts instead of specific destinations—are sold at newsstands and can be a great time-saver if the line at the official ticket booth is too long. Note, however, that you may have to round up amounts, and therefore pay more for your trip than if you purchased a destination-specific ticket. (For example, it's only 70 km [43 miles] from Florence to Pisa, but if the ticket amounts only come in 20-km [12-mile] denominations, you'd have to pay for an extra 10 km [6 miles].)

PAYING

You can pay for destination-specific train tickets in cash or with any major credit card such as American Express, Diners Club, MasterCard, and Visa. Newsstands only accept cash for kilometric tickets.

RESERVATIONS

Trains can be very crowded; it is always a good idea to make a reservation. In summer it's fairly common to stand for a good part of the journey, especially if you are coming off a cruise ship and heading to Florence. On the fast, direct Eurostar trains reservations are mandatory. To avoid long lines at station windows, buy tickets and make seat reservations up to two months in advance at travel agencies in Italy displaying the FS emblem or from a travel agent or website (⊕ *www. railpass.com*) before you leave home. Tickets can be purchased at the last minute, but seat reservations can be made only at agencies (or the train station) up until about three hours before the train departs from its city of origin. For trains that require a reservation (all Eurostar and some Intercity), you may be able to get a seat assignment just before boarding the train; look for the conductor on the platform, but do this only as a last resort. If you plan on traveling around August 15, make sure to book your tickets well in advance. Italians make a mass exodus to the sea or mountains, and sardinelike conditions prevail in many cases.

Train Information Trenitalia ☏ *892021 in Italy (fee charged)* ⊕ *www.trenitalia.com.*

ESSENTIALS

∎ ACCOMMODATIONS

Florence, Tuscany, and Umbria have a varied and abundant number of hotels, B&Bs, *agriturismi* (farm stays), and rental properties. In both the cities and the country you can find very sophisticated, luxurious palaces and villas as well as rustic farmhouses and small hotels.

Throughout the region you'll find historic properties, such as 600-year-old palazzi and former monasteries, which have been restored as luxurious hotels while retaining their original mystique. On the other hand, modern Italian design has swept the world, and many boutique hotels in historic buildings have favored chic modern interior design. Increasingly, the famed Tuscan and Umbrian wineries are creating rooms and apartments for three-day to weeklong stays. Tuscan and Umbrian establishments are generally run with pride and are very clean. Although Italy has a star system for rating hotels, it is based on amenities provided and is not a definitive indication of an establishment's quality.

Most hotels and other lodgings require credit-card details before they will confirm your reservation. If you don't feel comfortable emailing this information, ask if you can fax it (some places even prefer faxes). However you book, get confirmation in writing and have a copy of it handy when you check in.

Be sure you understand the hotel's cancellation policy. Some places allow you to cancel without any kind of penalty—even if you prepaid to secure a discounted rate—if you cancel at least 24 hours in advance. Others require you to cancel a week in advance or penalize you the cost of one night. Small inns and B&Bs are most likely to require you to cancel far in advance.

Some hotels allow children under a certain age to stay in their parents' room at no extra charge, but others charge for them as extra adults; find out the cutoff age for discounts.

APARTMENT AND HOUSE RENTALS

Italy gave birth to the Slow Food movement, and it appears to be at the start of the Slow Travel phenomenon also. More and more, travelers are turning away from the three-countries-in-two-weeks style of touring and choosing to spend a week in one city or a month in the countryside.

Often the most economical way to spend time in one place is to rent an apartment, a farmhouse, or a villa, even if you're traveling alone or with one other person.

These are readily available in Tuscany and Umbria. Most are owned by individuals and managed by rental agents who advertise available properties on the Internet. Many properties are represented by more than one rental agent, and thus the same property is frequently renamed ("Chianti Bella Vista" and "Tuscan Sun Home" and "Casa Toscana Sole" are all names of the same farmhouse) on various online rental sites. The rental agent may meet you at the property for the initial check-in, or the owner may be present, with the rental agent only handling the online reservation and financial arrangements.

Things to inquire about when renting an apartment in a city or town include: the type of neighborhood (ask about street noise, safety, and general ambience), the availability of an elevator or the number of stairs you'll have to climb, the available furnishings (including pots and pans and linens), where the nearest grocery store is, and the cost of utilities (included in the rental cost or not?). Inquiries about countryside properties should include all of that information plus an idea of how isolated the property is—do you have to drive for 45 minutes to reach the nearest town?

BED-AND-BREAKFASTS

You can find cozy B&Bs in Florence, Perugia, Assisi, and Siena, as well as in more rural areas. In towns and villages B&Bs tend to be personal, homey, simple, and clean. In the Tuscan countryside you can find private villas that offer B&B accommodations; many are very upscale.

Reservation Services Bed & Breakfast.com ☎ *512/322–2710* ⊕ *www.bedandbreakfast. com.* **BnB Finder.com** ☎ *888/469-6663* ⊕ *www.bnbfinder.com.*

CONVENTS AND MONASTERIES

Throughout Tuscany and Umbria tourists looking for lodging at a reasonable price seek out convents, monasteries, and religious houses. Religious orders usually charge €30–€60 per person per night for rooms that are clean, comfortable, and convenient. Most have private bathrooms; spacious lounge areas and secluded gardens or terraces are standard features. A Continental breakfast ordinarily comes with the room. Sometimes, for an extra fee, family-style lunches and dinners are available.

Be aware of three issues when considering a convent or monastery stay: most have a curfew of 11 pm or midnight; you need to book in advance, because they fill up quickly; and your best means of booking is usually email or fax—the person answering the phone may not speak English. For a list of convents in most cities in Tuscany and Umbria, go to ⊕ *www. hospites.it.*

Religious Guest Houses in Florence
Casa Santo Nome di Gesù ✉ *Piazza del Carmine 21* ☎ *055/213856* ⊕ *www.fmmfirenze. it.* **Istituto Gould/Foresteria Valdese di Firenze** ✉ *Via dei Serragli 49* ☎ *055/212576* ✎ *foresteriafirenze@diaconiavaldese.org* ⊕ *www.istitutogould.it/foresteria.* **Istituto Oblate Dell'Assunzione** ✉ *Borgo Pitti 15* ☎ *055/2480582, 055/2346291* ⊕ *www.sanctuarybbfirenze.com.*

Religious Guest Houses in Assisi
Albergo Ancajani ✉ *Via Ancajani 16, Assisi* ☎ *075/815128* ✎ *albergoancajani@libero. it* ⊕ *www.albergoassisi.it.* **St. Anthony Guest House** ✉ *Via Galeazzo Alessi 10, Assisi* ☎ *075/812542* ✎ *atoneassisi@tiscali.it.*

FARM HOLIDAYS AND AGRITOURISM

Rural accommodations in the *agriturismo* (agricultural tourism) category are increasingly popular with both Italians and visitors—you stay on a working farm or vineyard.

Accommodations vary in size and range from luxury apartments, farmhouses, and villas to very basic facilities. Agriturist has compiled *Agriturismo,* which is available only in Italian but includes more than 1,600 farms in Italy; pictures and the use of international symbols to describe facilities make the guide a good tool. Local APT tourist offices also have information.

Agencies Agriturismo.net ⊕ *www. agriturismo.net.* **Agriturist** ⊕ *www.agriturist. it.* **Italy Tourist: Farm Holiday** ⊕ *www. italyfarmholidays.com.*

HOME EXCHANGES

With a direct home exchange you stay in someone else's home while they stay in yours. Some outfits also deal with vacation homes, so you're not actually staying in someone's full-time residence, just their vacant weekend place.

Exchange Clubs Home Exchange.com. This agency charges $95.40 for a 1-year online listing. ☎ *800/877-8723* ⊕ *www. homeexchange.com.* **HomeLink International.** Web-only membership costs $89 per year. ☎ *800/638-3841* ⊕ *www.homelink.org.*

HOSTELS

Hostels in Florence, Tuscany, and Umbria run the gamut from low-end hotels to beautiful villas. In Florence the campground and hostel near Piazzale Michelangelo has a better view of the city than any luxury hotel in town (though there's also a really nice hostel in the centro storico). Hostels in these two regions are not just for student travelers; they are good budget accommodations for couples and families.

Hostels In Italy Hostelling International— USA ☎ *240/650-2100 national office* ⊕ *www.hiusa.org.* **Hostel World** ⊕ *www.hostelworld.com.*

HOTELS

Italian hotels are awarded stars (one to five) based on their facilities and services. Keep in mind, however, that these are general indications and that a charming three-star might make for a better stay than a more expensive four-star. In major cities room rates are on a par with other European capitals: five- and four-star rates can be downright extravagant. In those categories, ask for one of the better rooms, because the less desirable rooms—and there usually are some—don't give you what you're paying for. Even in some five- and four-star hotels, rooms may be very small by U.S. standards, and equally small bathrooms usually have showers rather than bathtubs. Hotels with three or more stars always have bathrooms in all rooms.

In all hotels a rate card inside the door of your room or inside the closet door tells you the maximum rate that can be legally charged for that particular room (rates in the same hotel may vary according to the location and type of room). On this card, breakfast and any other options must be listed separately. Any discrepancy between the basic room rate and that charged on your bill is cause for complaint to the manager and to the police.

High season in Italy, when rooms are at a premium, generally runs from Easter through the middle of June, from early September to the middle of October, and then for two weeks at Christmas. During low season and whenever a hotel isn't full, it's often possible to negotiate a discounted rate. Major cities have no official off-season as far as hotel rates go, but some hotels do offer substantial discounts during the slower parts of the year and on weekends. Always inquire about special rates. Major cities have hotel-reservation service booths in train stations. It's always a good idea to confirm your reservation, dates, and rate by fax or email.

Although by law breakfast is supposed to be optional, most hotels quote room rates including breakfast. When you book a room, specifically ask whether the rate includes breakfast (*colazione*). The trick is to "offer" guests "complimentary" breakfast and have its cost built into the rate. However, it's encouraging to note that many of the hotels we recommend provide generous buffet breakfasts instead of simple, even skimpy, "Continental" breakfasts. Remember, if the latter is the case, you can eat for less at the nearest coffee bar.

Hotels in the $$ and $ categories may charge extra for air-conditioning. In older hotels the quality of the rooms may be very uneven; if you don't like the room you're given, request another. This applies to noise, too. Front rooms may be larger or have a view, but they also may have a lot of street noise. If you're a light sleeper, request a quiet room when making reservations. Rooms in lodgings listed in this guide have a shower and/or bath, unless noted otherwise. (All hotels listed have private bath unless otherwise noted.) Remember to specify whether you care to have a bath or shower—not all rooms have both.

▌ COMMUNICATIONS

INTERNET

Getting online in Italian cities isn't difficult: public Internet stations and Internet cafés, some open 24 hours, are common, and many bars and cafés have Wi-Fi available.

Some hotels have in-room modem lines, but, as with phones, using the hotel's line is relatively expensive. Always check modem rates before plugging in.

You may need an adapter for your computer for the European-style plugs. If you are traveling with a laptop, carry a spare battery and an adapter. Never plug your computer into any socket before asking about surge protection. IBM sells a tiny modem tester that plugs into a telephone jack to check whether the line is safe to use.

Contacts Cybercafes. This website lists more than 4,000 Internet cafés worldwide. ⊕ *www.cybercafes.com.*

LOCAL DO'S AND TABOOS

Social behavior in Tuscany and Umbria tends to be more conservative and formal than in other parts of Italy.

GREETINGS

Upon meeting and leave-taking, both friends and strangers wish each other good day or good evening (*buon giorno, buona sera*); *ciao* isn't used between strangers. "Please" is *per favore*, "thank you" is *grazie*, and "you're welcome" is *prego*. When meeting, strangers shake hands. Italians who are friends greet each other with a kiss, usually first on the left cheek, and then on the right.

SIGHTSEEING

Italy is full of churches, and many of them contain significant works of art. They are places of worship, so care should be taken to dress appropriately. Shorts, miniskirts, tank tops, spaghetti straps, and sleeveless garments are taboo; short shorts are inappropriate anywhere. When touring churches—especially in summer when it's hot and no sleeves are desirable—carry a sweater, large scarf, or a light shawl to wrap around your shoulders before entering the church, and always remember to take off your hat. Do not enter a church with food, and don't drink from your water bottle while inside. If a service is in progress, don't go inside. And if you have a cell phone, turn it off before entering.

OUT ON THE TOWN

Table manners are formal; rarely do Italians share food from their plates. Flowers, dessert (in the form of a cake or torte from a pasticceria), or a bottle of wine are appropriate hostess gifts when invited to dinner.

Wiping your bowl clean with a small piece of bread is considered a sign of appreciation, and not bad manners. Spaghetti should be eaten with a fork only, although a little help from a spoon won't horrify locals the way cutting spaghetti into little pieces might. Order your espresso (Italians don't usually drink cappuccino after breakfast) after dessert, not with it. Don't ask for a doggy bag unless you really have a dog.

DOING BUSINESS

Showing up on time for business appointments is the norm and expected in Italy. There are more business lunches than business dinners, and even business lunches aren't common, as Italians view mealtimes as periods of pleasure and relaxation. Business cards are used throughout Italy, and business suits are the norm for both men and women.

LANGUAGE

One of the best ways to avoid being an Ugly American is to learn a little of the local language. You need not strive for fluency; even just mastering a few basic words and terms is bound to make chatting with the locals more rewarding.

In the main tourist cities, such as Florence, most hotels have English speakers at their reception desks, and you can always find someone who speaks at least a little English otherwise. Remember that the Italian language is pronounced exactly as it is written. You may run into a language barrier in the countryside, but a phrase book and the use of pantomime and expressive gestures will go a long way. Try to master a few phrases for daily use and familiarize yourself with the terms you'll need for deciphering signs, menus, and museum labels.

A phrase book and language-CD set can help get you started. *Fodor's Italian for Travelers* (available at bookstores everywhere) provides a terrific starting point.

PHONES

Telephone service in Tuscany and Umbria is efficient. Cell phones, however, are widely used by Italians, resulting in a decrease in the number of public pay phones. Calling from a hotel landline phone is almost always the most expensive option; hotels usually add huge surcharges to all calls, particularly international ones.

The country code for Italy is 39. Area codes for major cities are as follows: Florence, 055; Perugia, 075; Pisa, 050; Siena, 0577. For example, a call from New York City to Florence would be dialed as 011 + 39 + 055 + phone number.

When dialing an Italian number from abroad, do not drop the initial 0 from the local area code.

CALLING WITHIN ITALY

For all calls within Italy—local and long distance—you must dial the regional area code (*prefisso*), which begins with a 0, such as 055 for Florence. If you are calling from a public phone, you must deposit a coin or use a calling card to get a dial tone. Some of the newer public phones don't accept coins. Local calling cards are available at newsstands or tobacco shops. Rates on landline phones vary during the day; it's less expensive to call within Italy during nonworking hours (before 9 am and after 7 or 8 pm).

CALLING OUTSIDE ITALY

The country code for the United States is 1, so from most phones in Italy you will dial 001 + area code + phone number. To place international telephone calls and collect calls via an English-speaking operator-assisted service, dial 170 (available only on landline phones) or an international carrier's long-distance access code, or use an international prepaid calling card.

You can also place a direct call to the United States using your U.S. phone calling-card number, through which you automatically reach a U.S. operator and thereby avoid all language difficulties.

Access Codes AT&T USADirect
🌐 *www.att.com.*

CALLING CARDS

Prepaid *carte telefoniche* (calling cards) for intra-country calls are prevalent throughout Italy and more convenient than coins. You buy the card (values vary) at post offices, tobacconists, most newsstands, and bars. Tear off the corner of the card and insert it in the slot on a public pay phone. When you dial, its value appears in the window. After you hang up, the card is returned so you can use it until its value runs out.

International phone cards offer good value, allowing you to call Europe and the United States for less than 20 European cents a minute during peak hours. Follow the directions on the back of the card. These will include revealing the identification number on the card and calling an "800" number or other free number. If you wish to use this card at a public phone, you may need a local calling card (*see above*) to activate the public phone. If you are using your hotel phone, the call should be charged as any other "800" number call.

MOBILE PHONES

If you have a multiband phone (some countries use different frequencies from those used in the United States) and your service provider uses the world-standard GSM network (as do T-Mobile, AT&T, and Verizon), you can probably use your phone abroad. Roaming fees can be steep, however: 99¢ a minute is considered reasonable. And overseas you normally pay the toll charges for incoming calls. It's almost always cheaper to send a text message than to make a call, since text messages have a very low set fee (often less than 5¢).

If you just want to make local calls, consider buying a new SIM card (note that your provider may have to unlock your phone for you to use a different SIM card) and a prepaid service plan in the destination. You'll then have a local number and can make local calls at local rates. If your trip is extensive, you could also simply buy a new cell phone in your destination, as the initial cost will be off-set over time.

■TIP→ If you travel internationally frequently, save one of your old mobile phones or buy a cheap one on the Internet; ask your cell-phone company to unlock it for you, and take it with you as a travel phone, buying a new SIM card with pay-as-you-go service in each destination.

The cost of cell phones is dropping, and you can purchase a cell phone with a prepaid calling card (no monthly service plan) in Italy for around €35. Inexpensive cell phones are dual band and will not allow you to call the United States, but using an international calling card and the cell phone solves that problem in a very inexpensive manner. Most medium-size to large towns in Tuscany and Umbria (Florence, Siena, Lucca, Pisa, and Perugia) have stores dedicated to selling cell phones. You will need to present your passport to purchase the SIM card that goes with the phone.

Rental cell phones are available in cities and large towns. Most rental contracts require a refundable deposit that covers the cost of the cell phone (€75–€125) and then the purchase of a monthly service plan that is automatically charged to your credit card. Frequently, rental cell phones will be triple band and allow you to call the United States. Be sure to check the rate schedule before you rent a cell phone and commence calling to prevent a nasty surprise when you receive your credit-card bill two or three months later.

■TIP→ Beware of cell-phone (and PDA) thieves. Keep your phone or PDA in a secure pocket or purse. Do not lay it on the bar when you stop for an espresso. Do not zip it into the outside pocket of your backpack in crowded cities. Do not leave it in your hotel room. If you are using a phone with a monthly service plan, notify your provider immediately if it is lost or stolen.

Contacts **Cellular Abroad**. This company rents and sells GMS phones and sells SIM cards that work in many countries. ☏ 800/287–5072 ⊕ www.cellularabroad.com. **Mobal**. Rent mobiles and buy GSM phones (starting at $29) that will operate in 190 countries from Mobal. Per-call rates vary throughout the world. ⊕ www.mobalrental.com. **Planet Fone**. Cell phones are available for rent through Planet Fone, but the per-minute rates are expensive. ☏ 888/988–4777 ⊕ www.planetfone.com.

■ CUSTOMS AND DUTIES

Travelers from the United States should experience little difficulty clearing customs at any airports in Italy.

Of goods obtained anywhere outside the EU, the allowances are (1) 200 cigarettes or 100 cigarillos (under 3 grams) or 50 cigars or 250 grams of tobacco; (2) 2 liters of still table wine or 1 liter of spirits over 22% volume; and (3) 50 milliliters of perfume and 250 milliliters of toilet water.

Of goods obtained (duty and tax paid) within another EU country, the allowances are (1) 800 cigarettes or 400 cigarillos (under 3 grams) or 200 cigars or 1 kilogram of tobacco; and (2) 90 liters of still table wine or 10 liters of spirits over 22% volume or 20 liters of spirits under 22% volume or 110 liters of beer.

There is no quarantine period in Italy, so if you want to travel with Fido, it's possible. Contact your nearest Italian consulate to find out what paperwork is needed for entry into Italy; generally, it is a certificate noting that the animal is healthy and up-do-date on its vaccinations. Keep in mind, however, that the United States has some stringent laws about reentry: pets must be free of all diseases, especially those communicable to humans, and they must be vaccinated against rabies at least 30 days before returning. This means that if you are in Italy for a short-term stay, you must find a veterinarian or have your pet vaccinated before departure. (This law does not apply to puppies less than three months old.) Pets should arrive at the point of entry with a statement, in English, attesting to this fact.

Information in Italy Dogana Sezione Viaggiatori ⊕ *www.agenziadogane.it.* **Ministero delle Finanze, Direzione Centrale dei Servizi Doganali, Divisione I** ⊕ *www.finanze.it.*

U.S. Information U.S. Customs and Border Protection ⊕ *www.cbp.gov.*

▊ EATING OUT

The restaurants we list are the cream of the crop in each price category.

Not too long ago, ristoranti tended to be more elegant and expensive than trattorie and osterie, which serve traditional, home-style fare in an atmosphere to match. But the distinction has blurred considerably, and an osteria in the center of town might be far fancier (and pricier) than a ristorante across the street. Although most restaurants in Tuscany and Umbria serve traditional local cuisine, you can find Asian and Middle Eastern alternatives in Florence, Perugia, and other cities (though they are often pale imitations of what you would get in other American and European cities). Menus are posted outside most restaurants (in English in tourist areas); if not, you might step inside and ask to take a look at the menu (but don't ask for a table unless you intend to stay).

Italians take their food as it is listed on the menu, never making special requests such as "dressing on the side" or "hold the olive oil." If you have special dietary needs, however, make them known; they can usually be accommodated. Although mineral water makes its way to almost every table, you can order a carafe of tap water (*acqua di rubinetto* or *acqua semplice*) instead, but keep in mind that such behavior is sneered at by just about everyone, who all deem it *brutta figura* (bad form).

The handiest and least expensive places for a quick snack between sights are bars, cafés, and pizza *al taglio* (by the slice) spots. Bars in Italy are primarily places to get a coffee and a bite to eat, rather than drinking establishments. Most have a selection of panini, and sometimes you'll find the very Roman *tramezzini* (sandwiches served on triangles of white bread). In larger cities, bars also serve prepared salads, fruit salads, and cold and hot pasta dishes. Most bars offer beer and a variety of alcohol, as well as wines by the glass. A café (*caffè* in Italian) is like a bar but usually with more tables. If you place your order at the counter, ask whether you can sit down: some places charge extra for table service. In self-service bars and caffè, cleaning up your table before you leave is considered good manners. Note that in some places you have to pay before you place an order and then show your *scontrino* (receipt) when you move to the counter. Pizza al taglio shops are easy to negotiate. They sell pizza by weight: just point out which kind you want and how much. Very few pizza al taglio shops have seats.

MEALS AND MEALTIMES

The Italian breakfast (*la colazione*) is typically a cappuccino and a sweet roll (usually a brioche) served at the local bar. For lunch, Italians may eat a panino with a glass of wine while standing at a local bar. A more substantial lunch (*il pranzo*) consists of one or two courses at a trattoria. Dinner (*la cena*) is likely to be two or three courses at a restaurant or trattoria, or pizza and beer at a pizzeria.

Menus separate dishes into *antipasti* (starters), *primi piatti* (first courses), *secondi piatti* (second courses), *contorni* (side dishes), and *dolci* (desserts). At ristoranti, trattorie, and osterie, you're generally expected to order at least a two-course meal: a *primo* and a *secondo*; an antipasto followed by either primo or secondo; or, perhaps, a secondo and a dolce. Italian cuisine is still largely regional, so ask about the local specialties.

In an *enoteca* (wine bar) or pizzeria, it's not inappropriate to order one dish. An enoteca menu is often limited to a selection of cheeses, cured meats, salads, and desserts; if there's a kitchen, you may also find soups, pasta, meat, and fish. Most pizzerias don't offer just pizza, but also a variety of antipasti, salads, and simple pasta dishes, as well as dolce. Pizza at a caffè is to be avoided—it's usually frozen and reheated in a microwave oven.

Lunch is usually served from 12:30 to 2, and dinner 7:30 to 9:30 or 10. Enoteche are open in the morning and late afternoon for a snack at the counter. Most pizzerias open at 7:30 pm and close around midnight or 1 am, or later in summer and on weekends. Most bars and caffès are open 7 am to 8 or 9 pm; a few stay open until midnight or so.

Unless otherwise noted, the restaurants listed in this guide are open daily for lunch and dinner.

PAYING

Major credit cards are widely accepted in Italian eating establishments, though cash is usually the preferred, and sometimes the only means of payment—especially in small towns and rural areas. (More restaurants take Visa and MasterCard rather than American Express.) When you've finished your meal and are ready to go, ask for the check (*il conto*); unless it's well past closing time, no waiter will put a bill on your table until you've requested it.

Prices for goods and services in Italy include tax. The price of fish dishes is often given by weight (before cooking), so the price you see on the menu is for 100 grams of fish, not for the whole dish. (An average fish portion is about 350 grams.) Tuscan *bistecca fiorentina* is also often priced by weight (€4 for 100 grams or €40 for one kilogram [2.2 pounds]).

Most restaurants charge a separate "cover" charge per person, usually listed on the menu as *pane e coperto* (or just *coperto*); this charge is not for the service. It should be a modest charge (€1–€2.50 per person), except at the most expensive restaurants. A charge for service (*servizio*) may be included either as part of the menu prices or the total bill; if it is, tipping is unnecessary. It is customary to leave a small tip (€1–€5) in appreciation of good service when the service charge is not included in the bill. Tips are always given in cash. At some places in Florence, if you pay by credit card the restaurant will automatically slap a 15% tip onto your bill, which means you should leave absolutely nothing on the table.

When you leave a dining establishment, take your meal bill or receipt with you; although not a common experience, the Italian finance (tax) police can approach you within 100 yards of the establishment at which you've eaten and ask for a receipt. If you don't have one, they can fine you and will fine the business owner for not providing the receipt. The measure is intended to prevent tax evasion; it's not necessary to show receipts when leaving Italy.

⇨ *For guidelines on tipping, see Tipping below.*

RESERVATIONS AND DRESS

Reservations are always a good idea in restaurants and trattorie, especially on weekends and holidays. We mention them only when they're essential or not accepted. Book as far ahead as you can, and reconfirm as soon as you arrive in town. (Large parties should always call ahead to check the reservations policy; and should leave a 10% tip on the table if servizio is not included.)

Unless they're eating outdoors at a seaside resort and are perfectly tanned, Italian men never wear shorts or running shoes in a restaurant—no matter how humble—or in an enoteca. If you see people in shorts, you can be 100% sure that they are foreigners. The same "rules" apply to women's casual shorts, running shoes, plastic sandals, and clogs.

We mention dress only when men are required to wear a jacket and tie.

WINES, BEER, AND SPIRITS

The grape has been cultivated in Italy since the time of the Etruscans, and Italians justifiably take pride in their local vintages. Though almost every region produces good-quality wine, Tuscany is one of the most renowned areas. Wine in Italy is considerably less expensive than almost anywhere else, so it's often affordable to order a bottle of wine at a restaurant rather than to stick with the house wine (which, nevertheless, is probably quite good). Many bars have their own *aperitivo della casa* (house aperitif); Italians are imaginative with their mixed drinks, so you may want to try one.

You may purchase beer, wine, and spirits in any bar, grocery store, or enoteca, any day of the week. Italian and German beers are readily available, but they can be more expensive than wine.

There's no minimum drinking age in Italy. Italian children begin drinking wine mixed with water at mealtimes when they are teens (or thereabouts). Italians are seldom seen drunk in public, and public drinking, except in a bar or eating establishment, isn't considered acceptable behavior. Bars usually close by 9 pm; hotel and restaurant bars stay open until midnight. Brewpubs and discos serve until about 2 am.

ELECTRICITY

The electrical current in Italy is 220 volts, 50 cycles alternating current (AC); wall outlets take Continental-type plugs, with two round prongs.

Consider making a small investment in a universal adapter, which has several types of plugs in one lightweight, compact unit. Most laptops and mobile phone chargers are dual voltage (i.e., they operate equally well on 110 and 220 volts), and so require only an adapter. These days the same is true of small appliances such as hair dryers. Always check labels and manufacturer instructions to be sure. Don't use 110-volt outlets marked "for shavers only" for high-wattage appliances such as hair-dryers.

EMERGENCIES

No matter where you are in Italy, dial 113 for all emergencies, or find somebody (your concierge, a passerby) who will call for you, as not all 113 operators speak English; the Italian word to use to draw people's attention in an emergency is *aiuto* (help; pronounced "ah-YOU-toh"). *Pronto soccorso* means first aid and the emergency room of a hospital, and when said to an operator, it will get you an *ambulanza* (ambulance). If you just need a doctor, you should ask for *un medico*; most hotels can refer you to a local doctor. Don't forget to ask the doctor for *una ricevuta* (an invoice) to show your insurance company in order to get a reimbursement. Other useful Italian words to use in an emergency are *al fuoco* (fire; pronounced "ahl fuh-WOE-co") and *al ladro* (follow the thief; pronounced "ahl LAH-droh").

Italy has a national police force (*carabinieri*) as well as local police (*polizia*). Both are armed and have the power to arrest and investigate crimes. Always report the loss of your passport to either the carabinieri or the police, as well as to your embassy. Local traffic officers are known as *vigili* (though their official name is *polizia municipale*)—they are responsible for, among other things, giving out parking tickets and clamping cars, so before you even consider parking the (illegal) Italian way, make sure you are at least able to spot their white (in summer) or black uniforms. Many are women. Should you find yourself involved in a minor car accident in town, you should contact the vigili. Many police stations have English-speaking staff to deal with travelers' problems. When reporting a crime, you'll be asked to fill out and sign a report form (*una denuncia*); keep a copy for your insurance company.

A countrywide toll-free number (112) is used to call the carabinieri in case of emergency.

United States Embassies U.S. Consulate
✉ *Via Lungarno Vespucci 38* ☎ *055/266951.*
U.S. Embassy ✉ *Via Vittorio Veneto 121, Rome* ☎ *06/46741* ⊕ *www.usembassy.gov.*

General Emergency Contacts
Carabinieri ☎ *112.* **Emergencies** ☎ *113.*

▌ HEALTH

The most common types of illnesses are caused by contaminated food and water. In Italy tap water is safe to drink, and eating out in Italy is perfectly safe. As in any part of the world, avoid fresh vegetables and fruits that you haven't washed or peeled yourself. If you have problems, mild cases of traveler's diarrhea may respond to Imodium (known generically as loperamide) or Pepto-Bismol. Be sure to drink plenty of fluids; if you can't keep fluids down, seek medical help immediately.

▌ HOURS OF OPERATION

Business hours vary from region to region in Italy. In larger cities, such as Florence, Pisa, Lucca, Siena, and Perugia, stores and other businesses will generally be open 10–7. Many stores close 1–3:30 for a midday break, especially in small towns. More than half of the stores close Sunday and national holidays. Many businesses stay closed Monday morning but open in the afternoon. In August, many stores, restaurants, and other businesses shut down for two to four weeks for the traditional summer holiday.

HOLIDAYS

National holidays include New Year's Day; Epiphany (January 6); Easter Sunday and Monday; Liberation Day (April 25); Labor Day or May Day (May 1); Assumption of Mary, also known as Ferragosto (August 15); All Saints' Day (November 1); Immaculate Conception (December 8); and Christmas Day and Boxing Day (December 25 and 26).

The feast days of patron saints are observed locally. Many businesses and shops may be closed in Florence on June 24 (St. John the Baptist).

▌ MAIL

Allow from 7 to 10 days for mail to get to the United States. Receiving mail in Italy, especially packages, can sometimes take longer than you'd think: like weeks.

Most post offices are open Monday–Saturday 9–12:30; central post offices are open weekdays 9–6:30, Saturday 9–12:30. On the last day of the month, post offices close at midday. You can buy stamps at tobacco shops as well as post offices.

An expensive express delivery, *Postacelere* (for larger letters and packages), guarantees one-day delivery to most places in Italy and three- to five-day delivery abroad.

Mail sent to the United States costs €1.20 for up to 20 grams, and continues to escalate as envelopes get heavier.

Other package services to check are Quick Pack Europe, for delivery within Europe; and EMS Express Mail Service, a global three- to five-day service for letters and packages that can be less expensive than Postacelere.

Two-day mail is generally available during the week in all major cities and at popular resorts via UPS and Federal Express. Service is reliable; a Federal Express letter to the United States costs about €35. If your hotel can't assist you, try an Internet café, many of which also offer two-day mail services using major carriers—though keep in mind, you'll pay more for this service.

SHIPPING PACKAGES

You can ship parcels via air or surface. Air takes about two weeks, and surface anywhere up to three months to most countries. If you have purchased antiques, ceramics, or other objects, ask if the vendor will do the shipping for you; in most cases, this is a possibility. If so, ask whether the article will be insured against breakage. When shipping a package out of Italy, it is virtually impossible to find an overnight delivery option—the fastest delivery time is 48 to 72 hours.

▌ MONEY

As in most countries, prices vary from region to region and are a bit lower in the countryside than in cities. Umbria and the Marches offer good value for money. Admission to the Galleria degli Uffizi is €11 (surcharges for reservations and special exhibits may increase the ticket price). A movie ticket is €7.50. A daily English-language newspaper is €2.50. A taxi ride (1 km [1 mile]) costs around €9.

Prices throughout this guide are given for adults, in euros. Substantially reduced fees are sometimes available for children, students, and senior citizens from the EU; citizens of non-EU countries rarely get discounts, but be sure to inquire before you purchase your tickets because this situation is constantly changing.

▥TIP➔ Banks never have every foreign currency on hand, and it may take as long as a week to order. If you're planning to exchange funds before leaving home, don't wait until the last minute.

ATMS AND BANKS

Your own bank may charge a fee for using ATMs abroad or charge for the cost of conversion from euros to dollars. Nevertheless, you'll usually get a better rate of exchange at an ATM than you will at a currency-exchange office or even when changing money inside a bank with a teller. Extracting funds as you need them is also a safer option than carrying around a large amount of cash.

▥TIP➔ PIN numbers with more than four digits are not recognized at ATMs in many countries. If yours has five or more, remember to change it before you leave. PIN numbers beginning with a 0 (zero) tend to be rejected in Italy.

Fairly common in banks in large and small towns, as well as in airports and train stations, ATMs are the easiest way to get euros in Italy. All major banks are members of Cirrus and/or Plus. You won't find an ATM (*bancomat* in Italian) in hotels or grocery stores, however. Before you leave home, memorize your PIN in numbers, not letters, because ATM keypads in Italy frequently don't show letters. Check with your bank to confirm that you have an international PIN (*codice segreto*), to find out your maximum daily withdrawal allowance, and to learn what the bank fee is for withdrawing money.

CREDIT CARDS

In Italy, Visa and MasterCard are preferred over American Express, but in tourist areas American Express is usually accepted. Although increasingly common, credit cards aren't accepted at all establishments, and some places require a minimum expenditure. If you want to pay with a card in a small hotel, store, or restaurant, it's a good idea to make your intentions known early on. ▥TIP➔ Notify your credit-card companies of your travel plans before you leave home; the recent fraud-prevention programs frequently suspend a cardholder's credit when foreign activity is detected on the card.

CURRENCY AND EXCHANGE

The euro is the main unit of currency in Italy, as well as in 16 other European countries. Under the euro system, there are eight coins: 1, 2, 5, 10, 20, and 50 *centesimi* (cents, at 100 centesimi to the euro), and 1 and 2 euros. There are seven notes: 5, 10, 20, 50, 100, 200, and 500 euros.

At press time, the exchange rate is about 73 European cents to US$1.

■TIP➔ Even if a currency-exchange booth has a sign promising no commission, rest assured that there's some kind of huge, hidden fee. (Oh . . . that's right. The sign didn't say no fee). And as for rates, you're almost always better off getting foreign currency at an ATM or exchanging money at a bank.

EXCHANGE RATES
Google does currency conversion. Just type in the amount you want to convert and an explanation of how you want it converted (e.g., "14 Swiss francs in dollars"), and then voilà. Oanda.com also allows you to print out a handy table with the current day's conversion rates. XE.com is another good currency conversion website.

Conversion sites **Google** ⊕ *www.google. com.* **Oanda.com** ⊕ *www.oanda.com.* **XE.com** ⊕ *www.xe.com.*

▋PACKING

If you're traveling between Easter and October, it's always good to pack with layering in mind: it can be very cool in the morning, and then heat up during the course of the day. Murderously hot weather, especially in June, July, and August, calls for breathable fabrics. If you visit in October and November, pack rain gear, as it seems that all the rain that didn't happen in summer happens then. Winters in most parts of Tuscany and Umbria are not particularly cold, but there are exceptions. Pack your fleece.

You can get aspirin and the like over the counter, though it's best to bring it and other possible necessities with you. It's always wise to travel with tissues, as very often public toilets are not equipped with basic necessities. If you rent a car, be particularly vigilant when making a bathroom or food break: don't leave unattended luggage in the front or back seat of the car—thieves recognize rental cars, and often target them for smash-and-grabs.

▋PASSPORTS AND VISAS

You must have a valid passport for travel to Italy. U.S. citizens who plan to travel or live in Italy or the EU for longer than 90 days must acquire a valid visa from the Italian consulate serving their state before leaving the United States. Plan ahead, because the process of obtaining a visa will take at least 30 days and the Italian government does not accept visa applications submitted by visa expediters. ■TIP➔ Before your trip, make two copies of your passport's data page (one for someone at home and another for you to carry separately). Or scan the page and email it to someone at home and/ or yourself.

U.S. Passport Information U.S. Department of State ☎ *877/487–2778* ⊕ *travel.state.gov/ passport.*

U.S. Passport Expediters American Passport Express ☎ *800/455–5166* ⊕ *www.americanpassport.com.* **Passport Express** ☎ *800/362–8196, 401/272–4612* ⊕ *www.passportexpress.com.* **Travel Document Systems** ☎ *877/874–5100, 202/638– 3800* ⊕ *www.traveldocs.com.*

▋RESTROOMS

Standards of cleanliness and comfort vary greatly in Tuscany and Umbria. The type of toilet might be small and low with no seat or even a porcelain hole in the floor with places for your feet. In cities, restaurants, hotel common areas, department stores, and McDonald's tend to have the cleanest restrooms. Pubs and bars rank among the worst. Gas stations also have facilities; again, the cleanliness varies greatly. Carry tissues with you wherever you go, in case there's no paper.

Pay and attendant-supervised restrooms are available in large towns and cities. (You can get a map of the pay toilets in Florence at city tourist-information offices.) Expect to pay or tip €1. There are restrooms in most museums and all airports and train stations; in major train stations you'll also find well-kept pay toilets for €1; in Florence, it's €1 at the main train station at Santa Maria Novella. Churches, post offices, and public beaches don't have restrooms.

▌ SAFETY

Don't wear an exterior money belt or a waist pack, both of which peg you as a tourist. If you carry a bag or camera, be absolutely sure it has straps; you should sling it across your body bandolier-style and adjust the height to hip level or higher. Always be astutely aware of pickpockets, especially when on city buses, when making your way through train corridors, and in busy piazzas.

Women traveling alone in Tuscany and Umbria encounter few special problems. Younger women have to put up with male attention, but it's rarely dangerous. Ignoring whistling and questions is a good way to get rid of unwanted attention; a firm *no, vai via* ("no, go away") sometimes works, too.

▌▌▌TIP➔ Distribute your cash, credit cards, IDs, and other valuables between a deep front pocket, an inside jacket or vest pocket, and a hidden money pouch. Don't reach for the money pouch once you're in public.

Contact Transportation Security Administration (*TSA*) ⊕ *www.tsa.gov.*

▌ TAXES

An embarkation tax of €3.72 (between Italy and EU destinations) or €8.26 (international flights) will be included as part of your airline ticket cost.

When making a purchase, ask for a V.A.T. refund form and find out whether the merchant gives refunds—not all stores do, nor are they required to. Have the form stamped like any customs form by customs officials when you leave the country or, if you're visiting several European Union countries, when you leave the EU. After you're through passport control,

take the form to a refund-service counter for an on-the-spot refund (which is usually the quickest and easiest option), or mail it to the address on the form (or the envelope with it) after you arrive home. You receive the total refund stated on the form, but the processing time can be long, especially if you request a credit-card adjustment.

Global Refund is a Europe-wide service with 225,000 affiliated stores and more than 700 refund counters at major airports and border crossings. Its refund form, called a Tax Free Check, is the most common across the European continent. The service issues refunds in the form of cash, check, or credit-card adjustment.

V.A.T. Refunds Global Refund ☎ *866/706–6090* ⊕ *www.global-blue.com.*

▌ TIME

Italy is 6 hours ahead of New York (so when it's 1 pm in New York it's 7 pm in Florence). Like the rest of Europe, Italy uses the 24-hour (or "military") clock, which means that after 12 noon you continue counting forward: 13:00 is 1 pm, 23:30 is 11:30 pm.

Time Zones Timeanddate.com. This website can help you figure out the correct time anywhere in the world. ⊕ *www.timeanddate.com/worldclock.*

▌ TIPPING

The following guidelines apply in major cities; Italians tip—if they tip at all—in smaller amounts in smaller cities and towns. In restaurants in Tuscany and Umbria a service charge of 10% to 15% sometimes appears on your check. It's not necessary to tip in addition to this amount. If service is not included, leave a tip of €2 to not more than 10%. No one tips in bars in Florence.

Tip checkroom attendants 50 European cents per person and restroom attendants 50 European cents (more in expensive hotels and restaurants). Italians rarely tip taxi drivers, which is not to say that you shouldn't do it. A tip of 10%, depending on the length of the journey, is appreciated—but only if the driver is courteous and helps with your luggage. Railway and airport porters charge a fixed rate per bag. Tip an additional 5% if the porter is especially helpful. Give a barber €1–€1.50 and a hairdresser's assistant €1.50–€4 for a shampoo or cut, depending on the type of establishment.

On sightseeing tours, tip guides about €2 per person for a half-day group tour, more if they are very good. In museums and other sights where admission is free, a contribution (€1) is expected. Service-station attendants are tipped only for special services, for example, 50 European cents for checking your tires.

In hotels, give the *portiere* (concierge) about 10% of his bill for services, or €2.50–€5 if he has been generally helpful. For two people in a double room, leave the chambermaid about €1 per day, or about €7 a week, in a moderately priced hotel; tip a minimum of €1 for valet or room service. Double amounts in expensive hotels. In very expensive hotels, tip doormen €1 for calling a cab and €1 for carrying bags to the check-in desk, bellhops €2–€4 for carrying your bags to the room, and €2–€3 for room service.

▌ TOURS

GUIDED TOURS

Guided tours are a good option when you don't want to do it all yourself. You travel along with a group (sometimes large, sometimes small), stay in prebooked hotels, eat with your fellow travelers (the cost of meals is sometimes included, sometimes not), and follow a schedule. But not all guided tours are an if-it's-Tuesday-this-must-be-Belgium experience. A knowledgeable guide can take you places that you might never discover on your own. Tours aren't for everyone, but they can be just the thing for trips to places where

making travel arrangements is difficult or time-consuming. Whenever you book a guided tour, find out what's included and what isn't. A "land-only" tour includes all your travel (by bus, in most cases) in the destination, but not necessarily your flights to and from or even within it. Also, in most cases prices in tour brochures don't include fees and taxes. And remember that you'll be expected to tip your guide (in cash) at the end of the tour.

SPECIAL-INTEREST TOURS

ART
Abercrombie & Kent ☎ *800/554–7016* ⊕ *www.abercrombiekent.com.* **Context Travel** ☎ *888/467–1986* ⊕ *www.contexttravel.com.*

BIKING
Backroads ☎ *800/462–2848* ⊕ *www.backroads.com.* **Butterfield & Robinson** ☎ *866/551–9090* ⊕ *www.butterfield.com.* **Ciclismo Classico** ☎ *800/866–7314* ⊕ *www.ciclismoclassico.com.*

CULINARY
Divina Cucina ⊕ *www.divinacucina.com.* **Epiculinary** ☎ *888/380–9010* ⊕ *www.epiculinary.com.* **Taste Florence** ⊕ *www.tasteflorence.com.* **Toscana Saporita** ⊕ *www.toscanasaporita.com.* **Tuscan Women Cook** ☎ *815/717–7295* ⊕ *www.tuscanwomencook.com.*

CULTURE
Context Travel ⊕ *www.contexttravel.com.* **Italian Connection** ☎ *800/462–7911* ⊕ *www.italian-connection.com.* **Travcoa** ☎ *800/002–2005* ⊕ *www.travcoa.com.*

HIKING
Backroads ☎ *800/462–2848* ⊕ *www.backroads.com.* **Country Walkers** ☎ *800/464–9255* ⊕ *www.cwadventures.com.*

SHOPPING
Take My Mother Please ☎ *323/737–2200* ⊕ *www.takemymotherplease.com.*

WINE
Food & Wine Trails ☎ *800/367–5348* ⊕ *www.foodandwinetrails.com.*

▌TRIP INSURANCE

Comprehensive trip insurance is valuable if you're booking a very expensive or complicated trip (particularly to an isolated region) or if you're booking far in advance. Comprehensive policies typically cover trip-cancellation and interruption, letting you cancel or cut your trip short because of illness or, in some cases, acts of terrorism in your destination. Such policies might also cover evacuation and medical care. Some also cover you for trip delays because of bad weather or mechanical problems as well as for lost or delayed luggage.

Another type of coverage to consider is financial default—that is, when your trip is disrupted because a tour operator, airline, or cruise line goes out of business. Generally you must buy this when you book your trip or shortly thereafter, and it's available to you only if your operator isn't on a list of excluded companies.

Always read the fine print of your policy to make sure that you're covered for the risks that most concern you. Compare several policies to be sure you're getting the best price and range of coverage available.

Insurance Comparison Info Insure My Trip
☎ 800/487-4722 ⊕ www.insuremytrip.com.
Square Mouth ☎ 800/240-0369
⊕ www.squaremouth.com.

Comprehensive Insurers
Allianz ☎ 800/284-8300
⊕ www.allianztravelinsurance.com.
CSA Travel Protection ☎ 877/243-4135
⊕ www.csatravelprotection.com. **Travel Guard**
☎ 800/826-4919 ⊕ www.travelguard.com.
Travel Insured International ☎ 800/243-3174 ⊕ www.travelinsured.com. **Travelex Insurance** ☎ 800/228-9792 ⊕ www.travelex-insurance.com.

INDEX

PHOTO CREDITS

Front cover: Masterfile [Description: Replica of "David" by Michelangelo in the Piazza del Signoria, Florence]. 1, SIME s. a.s/ eStock Photo. 2, PCL/Alamy. 5, Jon Arnold Images/ Alamy. 8-9, SIME s. a.s/ eStock Photo. 10, Paul D. Van Hoy II/ age fotostock. 11 (left), Joe Viesti/ viestiphoto. com. 11 (right), Christine Webb/ Alamy. 12, Robert Harding Picture Library Ltd/ Alamy. 13, Angelo Cavalli/ age fotostock. 14, Ken Ross/ viestiphot.com. 15 (left), David Noton Photography/ Alamy. 15 (right), f1 online/ Alamy. 16 (top), Giulio Andreini/ age fotostock. 16 (bottom), Orientaly/ Shutterstock. 18 (left), Gijs van Ouwerkerk/ Shutterstock. 18 (top center), Anja Peternelj/ Shutterstock. 18 (top right), Knud Nielsen/Shutterstock. 18 (bottom right), Paul Merrett/ Shutterstock. 19 (left), Danilo Ascione/ Shutterstock. 19 (top center), Norma Joseph/ Alamy. 19 (top right), Ivonne Wierink/Shutterstock. 19 (bottom right), John Henshall/ Alamy. 20, Jeremy R. Smith Sr./Shutterstock. 21 (left), Chie Ushio. 21 (right), Danilo Donadoni/ age fotostock. 22, Javier Larrea/ age fotostock. 23, Stefano Cellai/ age fotostock. 24, Public Domain. 25 (left), Marco Scataglini/ age fotostock. 25 (right), Stefano Cellai/ age fotostock. 26, Nico Tondini/age fotostock. 28, Giulio Andreini/ age fotostock. 29 (left and right), Classic Vision/ age fotostock. 29 (center), SuperStock/ age fotostock. 30 (left), Chie Ushio. 30 (right), Planet Art. 31 (top), Classic Vision/ age fotostock. 31 (center), SuperStock/ age fotostock. 31 (bottom left), Paola Ghirotti/ Fototeca ENIT. 31 (bottom right), Corbis. 32 (left), Fototeca ENIT. 32 (center), SuperStock/ age fotostock. 32 (right), Bruno Morandi/ age fotostock. 33 (left), SuperStock/ age fotostock. 33 (center), Sandro Vannini/ viestiphoto. com. 33 (right), PTE/ age fotostock. 34 (all), Planet Art. Chapter 2: Florence: 35, Stefano Cellai/ age fotostock. 36 (top), Walter Bibikow/ viestiphoto. com. 36 (bottom), Photodisc. 37, Sergio Pitamitz/ age fotostock. 38, CuboImages srl/ Alamy. 39 (top), Paolo Gallo/ Alamy. 39 (bottom), Sue Wilson/ Alamy. 50, Wojtek Buss/ age fotostock. 52-53, Wojtek Buss/ age fotostock. 54 (all), Public Domain. 55 (top), eye35. com/ Alamy. 55 (inset), Alfi o Giannotti/ viestiphoto. com. 55 (bottom), Rough Guides/Alamy. 56 (top left), Mary Evans Picture Library/ Alamy. 56 (top right), Library of Congress Prints and Photographs Division. 56 (bottom), Bruno Morandi/ age fotostock. 68-69, Stefano Cellai/ age fotostock. 79 (left, top right, and bottom right), CuboImages srl/ Alamy. 79 (center right), Tibor Bognar. 80, Public Domain. 81, Ken Welsh/ Alamy. 111, Dave Pattison/ Alamy. 117, Peter Horree/ Alamy. Chapter 3: Pisa, Lucca & Northwest Tuscany: 127, Stefano Cellai/ age fotostock. 128 (top), AAD Worldwide Travel Images/ Alamy. 128 (bottom), Stefano Cellai/ age fotostock. 129 (top), Julius Honnor. 129 (bottom), Jack Sullivan/ Alamy. 142, Photodisc. 152, Bruno Morandi/ age fotostock. 160-61, Dutton Colin/SIME s. a.s/ eStock Photo. 168, Danilo Donadoni/ age fotostock. 176, Matz Sjöberg/ age fotostock. 179, Walter Bibikow/ viestiphoto.com. 180 (top left), Peter Phipp/ age fotostock. 180 (top center), Walter Bibikow/ viestiphoto. com. 180 (top right), Loren Irving/ age fotostock. 180 (bottom), Carson Ganci/ age fotostock. 181 (left), Angelo Cavalli/ age fotostock. 181 (center), Cornelia Doerr/ age fotostock. 181 (right), Bruno Morandi/ age fotostock. 183 (top), Siepmann/ age fotostock. 183 (bottom), Rechitan Sorin/Shutterstock. 184, Corbis. Chapter 4: Chianti, Siena & Central Tuscany: 187, Atlantide S.N.C./age fotostock. 188 (top), eye35. com/ Alamy. 188 (bottom), Walter Bibikow/ age fotostock. 189 (top), Danilo Donadoni/ age fotostock. 189 (bottom), Gapys Krzysztof/ Alamy. 191, Hemis/Alamy. 199 (left), Black Rooster Consortium. 199 (top right), Cephas Picture Library/ Alamy. 199 (center right), Adriano Bacchella/ viestiphoto. com. 199 (bottom right) and 200 (right), Cephas Picture Library/ Alamy. 201 (top left), Chuck Pefl ey/ Alamy. 201 (top right), Jon Arnold Images/ Alamy. 202 (top), CuboImages srl/ Alamy. 202 (center), Cephas Picture Library/ Alamy. 202 (bottom), Black Rooster Consortium. 204 (left), Steve Dunwell/ age fotostock. 204 (top right), IML Image Group Ltd/Alamy. 204 (bottom right), stradavinonobile.it. 211, Guven Guner/ Alamy. 216, fotostudiodonati/ age fotostock. 220, Javier Larrea/ age fotostock. 220 (inset), Photodisc. 222 (top), Vittorio Sciosia/viestiphoto. com. 222 (center), Vittorio Sciosia/ viestiphoto. com. 222 (bottom), Bruno Morandi/age fotostock. 227, CuboImages srl/ Alamy. 238, Photodisc. 245, Danilo Donadoni/ age fotostock. Chapter 5: Arezzo, Cortona & Eastern Tuscany: 247, Wojtek Buss/ age fotostock. 248 (top), San Rostro/ age fotostock. 248 (bottom left), Bruno Morandi/ age fotostock. 248 (bottom right) and 249 (top), Doco Dalfi ano/ age fotostock. 249 (bottom), Nick Higham/ Alamy. 256-57, San Rostro/ age fotostock. 262, LOOK Die Bildagentur der Fotografen GmbH/ Alamy. Chapter 6: Southern Tuscany: 267, Julian Nieman/ Alamy. 268, Christine Webb/ Alamy. 269 (left), Peter Packer/ Alamy. 269 (right), Nico Tondini/ age fotostock. 277, Walter Bibikow/ viestiphoto. com. 280, eye35. com/ Alamy. 287, Ernst Wrba/ Alamy. 288 (top left), CuboImages srl/ Alamy. 288 (bottom left), Peter Horree/ Alamy. 288 (right), Peter Adams Photography/ Alamy. 289 (left), CuboImages srl/ Alamy. 289 (center), Fabio Muzzi/ age fotostock. 289 (right) and 290 (top), Nico Tondini/ age fotostock. 290 (bottom), Mathias Braux. 291 (top and bottom), CuboImages srl/ Alamy. 292 (top), Foodfolio/ Alamy. 292 (bottom left), Nico Tondini/ age fotostock. 292 (bottom center), CuboImages srl/ Alamy. 292 (bottom right), Nico Tondini/ age fotostock. 304, Cornelia Doerr/ age fotostock. 313, Nico Tondini/ age fotostock. Chapter

7: Umbria & the Marches: 315, Atlantide S.N.C./age fotostock. 316, magicinfoto/Shutterstock. 317, sano7/Shutterstock. 318, B&Y Photography/Alamy. 319 (top), MEHMET OZCAN/iStockphoto. 319 (bottom), Doco Dalfi ano/age fotostock. 331, Atlantide S. N.C./age fotostock. 332, Picture Finders/ age fotostock. 333 (all), Fototeca ENIT. 334, Atlantide S.N.C./age fotostock. Back cover (from left to right): WDG Photo/Shutterstock; Igor Plotnikov/Shutterstock; Angelo Ferraris/Shutterstock. Spine: Nickolay Vinokurov/Shutterstock.

NOTES

NOTES

NOTES

ABOUT OUR WRITERS

After completing his master's degree in art history, Peter Blackman settled permanently in Italy in 1986. Since then he's worked as a biking and walking tour guide, managing to see more of Italy than most of his Italian friends. When he's not leading a trip, you'll find Peter at home in Chianti, listening to opera and planning his next journey. He updated our Central Tuscany, Eastern Tuscany, and Southern Tuscany chapters.

Florence resident Patricia Rucidlo holds master's degrees in Italian Renaissance history and art history. When she's not extolling the virtues of a Pontormo masterpiece or angrily defending the Medici, she's leading wine tours in Chianti and catering private dinner parties. For this edition she updated our Experience, Florence, Northwest Tuscany, and Travel Smart chapters.

Jonathan Willcocks, a Brit by birth with a degree from the Sorbonne, has been teaching courses in language, literature, and translation at the university in Perugia since the early 1990s. He updated our Umbria chapter.